BY JAMES HENRY BREASTED

THE DAWN OF CONSCIENCE

THE DEVELOPMENT OF RELIGION AND
THOUGHT IN ANCIENT EGYPT

A HISTORY OF EGYPT

A HISTORY OF THE ANCIENT EGYPTIANS

CHARLES SCRIBNER'S SONS

A HISTORY OF EGYPT

THE COLONNADED HALL OF THE TEMPLE OF ESNEH.

The temple is of the Græco-Roman age, but this colonnade is a fine example of the later rich and ornate plant-columns, which owe their origin to the earlier architects of the Saitic age.

A HISTORY OF EGYPT

FROM THE EARLIEST TIMES TO THE PERSIAN CONQUEST

BY

JAMES HENRY BREASTED, Ph.D.

PROFESSOR OF EGYPTOLOGY AND ORIENTAL HISTORY IN THE UNIVERSITY OF
CHICAGO; DIRECTOR OF HASKELL ORIENTAL MUSEUM; CORRESPONDING
MEMBER OF THE ROYAL ACADEMY OF SCIENCES OF BERLIN

WITH TWO HUNDRED ILLUSTRATIONS AND MAPS

SECOND EDITION, FULLY REVISED

NEW YORK
CHARLES SCRIBNER'S SONS

TO

MY MOTHER

PREFACE

THE ever increasing number of those who visit the Nile Valley with every recurring winter should alone form, it would seem, a sufficiently numerous public to call for the production of a modern history of Egypt. Besides these fortunate travellers, however, there is another growing circle of those who are beginning to realize the significance of the early East in the history of man. As the Nile poured its life-giving waters into the broad bosom of the Mediterranean, so from the civilization of the wonderful people who so early emerged from barbarism on the Nile shores, there emanated and found their way to southern Europe rich and diversified influences of culture to which we of the western world are still indebted. Had the Euphrates flowed into the Mediterranean likewise, our debt to Babylon would have been correspondingly as great as that which we owe the Nile Valley. It is to Egypt that we must look as the dominant power in the Mediterranean basin, whether by force of arms or by sheer weight of superior civilization throughout the earliest career of man in southern Europe, and for long after the archaic age had been superseded by higher culture. To us who are in civilization the children of early Europe, it is of vital interest to raise the curtain and peer beyond into the ages which bequeathed our forefathers so precious a legacy. Finally,

there is a third and possibly the most numerous class
of those who desire an acquaintance with the history of
Egypt, viz., the students of the Old Testament. All of
these readers have been remembered in the composition
of this book.

The plan adopted in the production of this history
is one which will in some measure also condition its
use. The sources from which our knowledge of the early
career of the Nile Valley peoples is drawn are of the
meagerest extent, and most inadequate in character.
They will be found further discussed herein (pp. 23 f.),
and in the author's *Ancient Records of Egypt*, Vol. I,
pp. 3–22. As used at the present day, in the historical
workshop of the scholar, they are accessible chiefly in
published form. These publications were in the vast
majority of cases edited before the attainment of such
epigraphic accuracy and care as are now deemed indispensable in the production of such work.[1] To copy
an inscription of any kind with accuracy is not easy.
So close and fine an observer of material documents as
Ruskin could copy a short Latin inscription with surprising inaccuracy. In his incomparable *Mornings in
Florence* he reproduces the brief inscription on the marble
slab covering the tomb which he so admired in the
church of Santa Croce; and in his copy of these eight
short lines, which I compared with the original, he mis-
spells one word, and omits two entire words ("*et magister*")
of the mediæval Latin. This experience of the great
art critic is not infrequently that of the schooled and
careful paleographer as well. The best known of the

---

[1] The remainder of this paragraph is taken from the author's *Ancient
Records of Egypt*, Vol. I, §§ 27–8.

Politarch inscriptions appeared in eight different publications, each of which diverges in some more or less important respect from all the rest, before a correct copy was obtained. The Greek and Latin inscriptions on the bronze crab from the base of the New York Obelisk were long incorrectly read, and the mistake in the date led Mommsen to a false theory of the early Roman prefects of Egypt. In the early days of Egyptology, when a reading knowledge of hieroglyphic was still necessarily elementary, it required a copyist of exceptional ability to produce a copy upon which much reliance can be placed at the present day. Had the science of Egyptology rapidly outgrown this early insufficiency, all would now be well; but such methods have continued down to the present day, and although many exhaustively accurate publications of hieroglyphic documents now appear with every year, it is nevertheless true that the large majority of standard Egyptian documents accessible in publications exhibit a degree of incompleteness and inaccuracy not, in the author's judgment, to be found in any other branch of epigraphic science.

Under these circumstances the author's first obligation has been to go behind the publications to the original monument itself in every possible instance. This task has consumed years and demanded protracted sojourn among the great collections of Europe. In this work a related enterprise has been of the greatest assistance. A mission to the museums of Europe to collect their Egyptian monuments for a Commission of the four Royal Academies of Germany (Berlin, Leipzig, Goettingen, and Munich), in order to make these documents available for a great Egyptian Dictionary endowed by the German Emperor, enabled the author to copy from the originals practically all the historical monuments of Egypt in Europe. For those still in Egypt, the author has been able to employ his own copies of many, especially at Thebes and Amarna, where he copied all the historical inscriptions in the tombs there; and in the museum at Gizeh (now Cairo). Of monuments in Egypt not included in the author's copies, squeezes were in most instances found in the enormous collection made by Lepsius and now in the Berlin Museum. For others the author was given access to the extensive collations made for the Dictionary above referred to; now and then a colleague furnished the necessary collation; and where all other sources failed, I was able in all important cases to secure large-scale photographs of the originals. The final remainder of monuments for which the author was dependent upon the publications alone is very small, and in most cases the publication was one made on modern methods, and almost as good as the original itself. In general, therefore, it may be fairly claimed that this account of the historical career of the Egyptians rests upon the surviving original records themselves.

The immense progress in our knowledge of the language achieved during the last twenty years cannot be said to have been applied as yet to the comprehensive study of the historical documents as a whole. Hence, in order to utilize historically the materials thus collected, it was essential, in the light of our improved philological equipment, to begin the study of the documents *ab ovo*, irrespective of earlier studies and results, and it was in almost all cases only after such unbiased study that any older translation or account of a document was consulted. The combined results of the revised copies from the originals and the new grammatical study of the documents have been embodied in a series of translations of the historical documents, arranged in chronological order, beginning with the earliest surviving records and continuing to the final loss of Egyptian national independence at the conquest by the Persians in 525 B.C. Supplied with historical introductions and explanatory notes, the original documents, otherwise scattered through hundreds on hundreds of inaccessible publications, are thus accessible in English to the reader who desires to know upon what documentary evidence a particular assertion of fact rests. The numerals I, II, III, and IV in the foot-notes in this history refer to the volumes of these translations,[1] and the Arabic numerals following the four Romans designate the numbered paragraphs into which the translations are divided, unless the "p.," indicating "page," is inserted between.

It is hoped that, by this means of keeping all technical discussion of sources in the four volumes of translated documents, the author has succeeded in unburdening this history of the workshop *débris*, which would otherwise often encumber it; while at the same time the advantage of close contact with the sources for every fact adduced is not sacrificed. For the average reader, a running fire of foot-note references to technical and out-of-the-way publications, known only to the inner

---

[1] See *Ancient Records of Egypt: The Historical Documents*, by James Henry Breasted, University of Chicago Press, Chicago, 1905. Volume I, *The First to the Seventeenth Dynasties.* Volume II, *The Eighteenth Dynasty.* Volume III, *The Nineteenth Dynasty.* Volume IV, *The Twentieth to the Twenty-sixth Dynasties.* Volume V, *Indices*

circle of initiates in the science of Egyptology, would mean absolutely nothing. On the other hand, the other extreme, of divorcing the statements in this book from all connection with the sources from which they are drawn, is, in the author's opinion, almost as bad; even though but a vanishing proportion of its readers ever should turn to verify the references adduced. To that small number such references are invaluable, for the author recalls with what difficulty in his student days he was able to trace the currently accepted facts of the science to the original sources from which they had come. If these studies shall be considered to have made any contribution to modern knowledge in this field, it will be in the reëxamination of the originals, the collection and focussing of all related materials with each document, and the assembly and translation of these materials complete in convenient form for reference. Any new results in this volume are due to this process and method.

On the other hand, in the immense field of *material* documents as contrasted with *written* documents, this work has made no attempt at a reëxamination of the vast sources available. Egyptian archæology is in its infancy, and but few of the fundamental studies and researches already completed in classical archæology have been made in this province. Now and again the written documents have thrown new and unexpected light in this direction which I have not failed to utilize. The man with the enviable combination of archæological and philological capacity would find a rich field to cultivate, in working for the production of an Egyptological Overbeck. Again in the realm of religion the mere quantity alone of the materials made any attempt at an exhaustive reëxamination of the documents impossible. The study of Egyptian religion has but begun, and decades will pass before even the preliminary special studies shall have been completed, which shall enable the student to go forward for a general survey and symmetrical reconstruction of the phenomena in one comprehensive presentation, which shall be in some measure final. Only the Amarna period and the solar faith have been made the object of the author's special attention. All the documents on the unparalleled religious revolution of Ikhnaton, and all the known hymns to the Sun, throughout Egyptian history, were collected and examined—in the case of the former from the originals. For Egyptian religion as a whole, however, the author would acknowledge deep obligation to Erman's admirable *Handbuch*, an obligation often indicated in the foot-notes, and elsewhere frequently evident to the technical reader. Although over twenty years old, Erman's *Aegypten* is still the standard *vade mecum* on Egyptian life. It has often been of invaluable service in the production of this work. To Eduard Meyer's exhaustive and final *Chronologie* I am, of course, indebted, especially in the earlier period. I would also gratefully acknowledge the clarifying influence of his incisive treatment of the Saitic age in his *Geschichte des alten Aegyptens*. To the colossal labors of Maspero and Wiedemann I have been indebted, especially in the bibliography, as indicated in the Preface to my *Ancient Records*, but I would gratefully indicate the obligation here also. Like all who work in Egyptian history, I also owe a debt to Winckler's invaluable version of the Amarna Letters.

For the illustrative materials, besides the published

plates, frequently severally indicated, and his own
photographs, the author would express his thanks to
many friends and colleagues to whom he is indebted for
photographs, drawings, or restorations. He is particularly indebted to his friend Schaefer, of Berlin; also to
Borchardt, Steindorff, Petrie, Zahn, Messerschmidt,
Rev. W. MacGregor of Tamworth, and Dr. Caroline
Ransom, for the unqualified use of photographs and
reconstructions. To Messrs. Underwood & Underwood
for permission to use a number of their superb stereographs of Egyptian monuments *in situ*, I desire to express
particular obligation. At the same time, may I add for
the benefit of those to whom a journey through the Nile
Valley is an impossibility, that the system of travel
represented in these beautiful stereographs makes possible
to every one a voyage up the Nile which falls little short
of the actual experience itself. Finally, I am not a little
indebted to the great kindness of Mr. John Ward, of
Lenoxvale, Belfast, for a magnificent series of photographs
made specially for him, of recent excavations at Karnak,
from which I was privileged to select a number, like the
avenue of rams (Fig. 129).

To Herr Karl Baedeker, of Leipzig. I owe the privilege
of inserting two maps (Nos. 6 and 11) from his un-
equalled guide-book of Egypt, deservedly the inseparable
companion of all tourists on the Nile. To the authorities
of the European museums at Berlin, London (British
Museum, University College, Petrie Collections), Paris
(Louvre, Bibliothèque Nationale, Musée Guimet), Vienna
(Hofmuseum), Leyden, Munich, Rome (Vatican and
Capitoline), Florence, Bologna, Naples, Turin, Pisa,
Geneva, Lyons, Liverpool, and some others, I would here

express deep appreciation of the courtesies and privileges uniformly extended to me during the prosecution of this work among them. I am indebted to Mr. R. S. Padan and Miss Imogen Hart for assistance in proofreading. My wife has constantly rendered me indispensable clerical aid, and never-failing assistance in reading of proof.

It is a great pleasure here also gratefully to recognize the coöperation and unfailing readiness of the publishers to do all in their power to make the typographical and illustrative side of the work all that it should be. Of this the appearance of the finished volume is ample evidence.

JAMES HENRY BREASTED.

WILLIAMS BAY, WISCONSIN,
    September 1, 1905.

CONTENTS

BOOK ONE

INTRODUCTION

CHAPTER   PAGE

 I. THE LAND 3

 II. PRELIMINARY SURVEY, CHRONOLOGY AND DOCU-
    MENTARY SOURCES 13

 III. EARLIEST EGYPT 25

BOOK TWO

THE OLD KINGDOM

 IV. EARLY RELIGION 53

 V. THE OLD KINGDOM: GOVERNMENT AND SOCIETY,
    INDUSTRY AND ART 74

 VI. THE PYRAMID BUILDERS 111

 VII. THE SIXTH DYNASTY: THE DECLINE OF THE OLD
    KINGDOM 131

BOOK THREE

THE MIDDLE KINGDOM: THE FEUDAL AGE

 VIII. THE DECLINE OF THE NORTH AND THE RISE OF
    THEBES 147

 IX. THE MIDDLE KINGDOM, THE FEUDAL AGE: STATE,
    SOCIETY AND RELIGION 157

 X. THE TWELFTH DYNASTY 177

BOOK FOUR

THE HYKSOS: THE RISE OF THE EMPIRE

CHAPTER   PAGE

XI. THE FALL OF THE MIDDLE KINGDOM: THE HYKSOS . 211

XII. THE EXPULSION OF THE HYKSOS AND THE TRIUMPH OF THEBES 223

BOOK FIVE

THE EMPIRE: FIRST PERIOD

XIII. THE NEW STATE: SOCIETY AND RELIGION . . 233

XIV. THE CONSOLIDATION OF THE KINGDOM: THE RISE OF THE EMPIRE 253

XV. THE FEUD OF THE THUTMOSIDS AND THE REIGN OF HATSHEPSUT 266

XVI. THE CONSOLIDATION OF THE EMPIRE: THUTMOSE III 284

XVII. THE EMPIRE 322

XVIII. THE RELIGIOUS REVOLUTION OF IKHNATON . . 355

XIX. THE FALL OF IKHNATON AND THE DISSOLUTION OF THE EMPIRE 379

BOOK SIX

THE EMPIRE: SECOND PERIOD

XX. THE TRIUMPH OF AMON AND THE REORGANIZATION OF THE EMPIRE 399

XXI. THE WARS OF RAMSES II 423

XXII. THE EMPIRE OF RAMSES II 442

XXIII. THE FINAL DECLINE OF THE EMPIRE: MERNEPTAH AND RAMSES III 464

BOOK SEVEN

THE DECADENCE

CHAPTER   PAGE

XXIV. The Fall of the Empire 505

XXV. Priests and Mercenaries: The Supremacy of the Libyans 522

XXVI. The Ethiopian Supremacy and the Triumph of Assyria 537

BOOK EIGHT

THE RESTORATION AND THE END

XXVII. The Restoration 565

XXVIII. The Final Struggles: Babylon and Persia . 582

Chronological Table of Kings 597

Index 603

EXPLANATION OF FOOT-NOTES AND ABBREVIATIONS

The Roman numerals I, II, III, IV followed by Arabics refer to the volumes and paragraphs of the author's *Ancient Records of Egypt*. See Preface, p. xi.

BT = Brugsch, *Thesaurus*.

Rec. = *Recueil de Travaux*, edited by Maspero.

RIH = de Rougé, *Inscriptions hiéroglyphiques*.

All other abbreviations are sufficiently full to be intelligible without further explanation.

ILLUSTRATIONS

The Colonnaded Hall of the Temple of Esneh. *Frontispiece*

FIG.   PAGE

1.—One of the Channels of the First Cataract . . 6

2.—The Inundation Seen from the Road to the Pyramids of Gizeh 6

3.—Looking Across the Nile to the Western Cliffs near Thebes 10

4.—The Huts and Palm Groves of Karnak, Thebes . 10

5.—The Nile Valley, Viewed Across the Modern Town of Edfu 14

6.—A Triple Shadûf 18

7.—The Cliffs of the Nile Cañon 18

8.—The Earliest Known Painting 27

9.—Flint Knife of the Predynastic Age . . . 29

10.—Predynastic Pottery with Incised Decoration . . 30

11.—Predynastic Pottery with Painted Designs of Boats, Animals, Men and Women 30

12.—A Predynastic Grave 34

13.—Gold Bar Bearing Menes' Name 34

14.—Alabaster Vessels of the First Dynasty . . 34

15.—Chair Legs, Carved Ivory, Early Dynasties . . 34

16.—Copper Vessels, First Dynasty 34

17.—Four Bracelets on Lady's Arm, First Dynasty . 36

18.—The King Breaks Ground for a New Canal, First Dynasty 36

FIG.   PAGE

19.—MAGNIFICENT CARVED CEREMONIAL PALETTE OF SLATE   36

20.—PORTRAIT HEAD OF KING KHASEKHEM: FROM TWO
       DIFFERENT ANGLES 38

21.—STATUE OF KING KHASEKHEM: HEAD IN FIG. 20 . . 38

22.—BRICK-LINED WOODEN FLOORED TOMB CHAMBER OF
       KING ENEZIB 38

23.—BRICK TOMB OF KING USEPHAIS 42

24.—SEALED JARS OF FOOD AND DRINK 42

25.—EARLIEST STONE STRUCTURE IN THE WORLD . . 42

26.—IVORY TABLET OF KING USEPHAIS 42

27.—EBONY TABLET OF MENES, FIRST DYNASTY, ABYDOS,
       3400 B.C. 43

28.—KING SEMERKHET (FIRST DYNASTY) SMITES THE
       BEDUIN OF SINAI 43

29.—THE PALERMO STONE 46

30.—THE CELESTIAL COW 55

31.—THE GODDESS OF THE HEAVENS 55

32.—THE CELESTIAL BARQUE OF THE SUN-GOD . . . 57

33.—RESTORATION OF A GROUP OF OLD KINGDOM "MAST-
       ABAS," OR MASONRY TOMBS 57

34.—GROUND PLAN OF A "MASTABA" OR MASONRY TOMB . 68

35.—RESTORATION OF THE PYRAMIDS OF ABUSIR AND CON-
       NECTED BUILDINGS 72

36.—COLLECTION OF TAXES BY TREASURY OFFICIALS . . 79

37.—VILLA AND GARDEN OF AN EGYPTIAN NOBLE OF THE
       OLD KINGDOM 90

38.—A NOBLE OF THE OLD KINGDOM HUNTING WILD FOWL
       WITH THE THROW-STICK FROM A SKIFF OF REEDS IN
       THE PAPYRUS MARSHES 91

39.—AGRICULTURE IN THE OLD KINGDOM 92

FIG.   PAGE

40.—A HERD IN THE OLD KINGDOM, FORDING A CANAL . 93

41.—METALWORKERS' WORKSHOP IN THE OLD KINGDOM . 94

42.—SHIPBUILDING IN THE OLD KINGDOM 95

43.—WORKMEN DRILLING OUT STONE VESSELS, OLD KING-
DOM 96

44.—PAPYRUS HARVEST IN THE OLD KINGDOM . . . 97

45.—TWO COLUMNS FROM AN OLD KINGDOM LEGAL DOCU-
MENT 98

46.—SCENES AT AN OLD KINGDOM MARKET 98

47.—THIRD DYNASTY ARCH 100

48.—DIORITE STATUE OF KHEPHREN 100

49.—LIMESTONE STATUE OF RANOFER 100

50.—LIMESTONE STATUE OF HEMSET 102

51.—HEAD OF THE WOODEN STATUE OF THE SHEKH EL-
BELED 102

52.—LIMESTONE STATUE OF AN OLD KINGDOM SCRIBE . 102

53.—LIFE-SIZE STATUE OF PEPI I, WITH FIGURE OF HIS SON;
BOTH OF BEATEN COPPER 104

54.—HEAD OF THE COPPER STATUE OF PEPI I, SHOWING
EYES OF INLAID ROCK CRYSTAL 104

55.—PAINTING OF GEESE FROM AN OLD KINGDOM TOMB
AT MEDÛM 104

56.—RELIEFS FROM THE INTERIOR OF AN OLD KINGDOM
MASTABA CHAPEL, DEPICTING HERDS AND FLOCKS. 106

57.—DECORATIVE HEAD OF LION, IN GRANITE . . . 106

58.—GOLDEN HAWK OF HIERACONPOLIS 106

59.—WOODEN PANEL OF HESIRE 106

60.—FIFTH DYNASTY COLUMNS. CLUSTER OF PAPYRUS STEMS
AND PALM CAPITAL 106

FIG.   PAGE

61.—ELEVATION OF PART OF THE COLONNADE SURROUNDING
THE COURT OF THE PYRAMID TEMPLE OF NUSERRE,
FIFTH DYNASTY 108

62.—BRICK MASTABA OF ZOSER'S REIGN AT BET KHALLÂF . 110

63.—THE "TERRACED PYRAMID" OF ZOSER AT SAKKARA . 110

64.—PYRAMID ATTRIBUTED TO SNEFRU AT MEDÛM . . . 110

65.—ROCK INSCRIPTIONS OF AMENEMHET III, IN WADI
MAGHARA, SINAI, INCLUDING SNEFRU AMONG THE
LOCAL GODS 114

66.—CASING BLOCKS AT THE BASE OF THE GREAT PYRAMID.
JOINTS OTHERWISE UNDISCERNABLE INDICATED BY
CHARCOAL LINES 114

67.—THE GREAT PYRAMID OF KHUFU (CHEOPS) AT GIZEH . 116

68.—THE PYRAMIDS OF GIZEH 118

69.—A GRANITE HALL IN THE GREAT MONUMENTAL GATE
OF KHAFRE 118

70.—THE GREAT SPHINX OF GIZEH 122

71.—RESTORATION OF THE SUN-TEMPLE OF NUSERRE AT
ABUSIR 124

72.—RELIEF SCENES FROM THE SUN-TEMPLE OF NUSERRE AT
ABUSIR 125

73.—RUINED PYRAMID OF UNIS (FIFTH DYNASTY) AT SAK-
KARA 128

74.—ISLAND OF ELEPHANTINE, THE HOME OF THE LORDS OF
THE SOUTHERN FRONTIER 128

75.—STATUE OF AN OLD EMPIRE DWARF 140

76.—TOMB OF HARKHUF AT ASSUAN 142

77.—HEAD OF KING MERNERE 142

78.—WESTERN CLIFFS OF SIUT 142

79.—OFFICES OF THE NOMARCH KNUMHOTEP AT BENIHASAN 150

FIG.   PAGE

80.—A Colossus of Alabaster about Twenty-two Feet
High Transported on a Sledge by One Hundred
and Seventy-two Men in Four Double Lines at
the Ropes 159

81.—A Middle Kingdom Coffin and Mortuary Furniture 170

82.—Mortuary Boat of Sesostris III 170

83.—Restoration of the Fortress of Semneh and Kummeh 185

84.—The Nubian Nile from the Ruined Moslem Stronghold on the Heights of Ibrim 186

85.—Ruins of the Middle Kingdom Mining Settlement at
Sarbut el-Khadem, Sinai 186

86.—View Across the Birket el-Kurûn in the Northwestern Fayum 192

87.—Obelisk of Sesostris I at Heliopolis . . . 192

88.—Wooden Statue of Prince Ewibre 192

89.—Head of Amenemhet III, from a Sphinx found at
Tanis 196

90.—Bust of a Statue of Amenemhet III . . . 196

91.—Brick Pyramid of Sesostris II, at Illahun . . 196

92.—Section of the Burial Chamber in the Pyramid of
Hawara 199

93.—Looking down the Axis of the Temple at Tanis . 202

94.—Capstone of the Pyramid of Amenemhet III, at
Dashur 202

95.—Three of the Ten Statues of Amenemhet I, Found
at His Pyramid of Lisht 202

96.—The Harper Singing to the Banqueters . . . 208

97.—Diadem of a Twelfth Dynasty Princess Found in
Her Tomb at Dashur 208

98.—Diadem of a Twelfth Dynasty Princess, Found in
Her Tomb at Dashur 208

FIG.   PAGE

99.—EXCAVATION OF STATUE OF NEFERKHERE–SEBEKHO-
    TEP, ON ISLAND OF ARKO, ABOVE THIRD CATARACT . 216

100.—BODY OF ONE OF THE SEKENENRES, SHOWING WOUND IN
    SKULL 216

101.—FRAGMENT OF A SITTING COLOSSUS OF KHIAN, IN GRAN-
    ITE 216

102.—WALLED CITY OF EL KAB, SEEN THROUGH A TOMB DOOR
    IN THE EASTERN CLIFFS FLANKING THE TOWN . 226

103.—BRONZE WEAPONS OF AHMOSE I 226

104.—A BODY OF SPEARMEN OF THE EMPIRE 234

105.—A CHARIOT OF THE EMPIRE 234

106.—"USHEBTI" OR RESPONDENT STATUETTES . . . 250

107.—HEART SCARAB OF THE "FIRST OF THE SACRED WOMEN
    OF AMON, ISIMKHEB" 250

108.—PART OF THE VALLEY OF THE KINGS' TOMBS, THEBES . 250

109.—GROUND PLAN OF THE TOMB OF SETI I . . . 251

110.—ENTRANCE GALLERY OF THE TOMB OF RAMSES V, THEBES 260

111.—SITTING STATUE OF SENMUT, THE FAVOURITE OF HAT-
    SHEPSUT 260

112.—SCENES FROM THE GREAT SERIES OF RELIEFS IN THE DER
    EL BAHRI TEMPLE AT THEBES 275

113.—NORTHERN COLONNADES ON THE MIDDLE TERRACE OF
    HATSHEPSUT'S TERRACED TEMPLE OF DER EL BAHRI,
    THEBES 280

114.—OBELISKS OF HATSHEPSUT AT KARNAK 280

115.—VIEW ACROSS THE AMON-OASIS, OR SIWA . . . 294

116.—OBELISK OF THUTMOSE III 294

117.—LISTS OF TOWNS IN ASIA TAKEN BY THUTMOSE III . 294

118.—A PHARAOH OF THE EMPIRE RECEIVING ASIATIC ENVOYS
    BEARING TRIBUTE 300

FIG.   PAGE

119.—ASIATIC PRISONERS IN EGYPT UNDER THE EMPIRE . 308

120.—HEAD OF THUTMOSE III 326

121.—HEAD OF AMENHOTEP II, SON OF THUTMOSE III . . 326

122.—HEAD OF THUTMOSE IV, SON OF AMENHOTEP II . 326

123.—AMARNA LETTER, NO. 296 326

124.—COSTUMES OF THE EMPIRE 340

125.—THE PERIPTERAL CELLA-TEMPLE 341

126.—PERSPECTIVE AND SECTION OF A TYPICAL PYLON TEMPLE
OF THE EMPIRE 342

127.—FRAGMENT OF CARVED STONE VASE FOUND IN CRETE . 342

128.—AMENHOTEP III'S COURT OF CLUSTERED PAPYRUS BUD
COLUMNS 342

129.—AVENUE OF RAM-SPHINXES BEFORE THE GREAT KARNAK
TEMPLE 346

130.—COLUMNS OF THE NAVE OF AMENHOTEP III'S UNFIN-
ISHED HALL 350

131.—COLOSSAL GRITSTONE STATUES OF AMENHOTEP III (MEM-
NON COLOSSI) 354

132.—PART OF A FUNERAL PROCESSION OF A HIGH PRIEST OF
MEMPHIS 358

133.—LION FROM AMENHOTEP III'S TEMPLE AT SOLEB . . 362

134.—A STOOL OF THE EMPIRE 362

135.—FRONT OF THE STATE CHARIOT OF THUTMOSE IV . . 362

136.—ROYAL PORTRAIT OF THE EMPIRE 366

137.—PORTRAIT OF AMENHOTEP, SON OF HAPI . . . 366

138.—DUCKS SWIMMING AMONG LOTUS FLOWERS . . . 366

139.—IKHNATON AND HIS QUEEN DECORATE THE PRIEST EYE
AND HIS WIFE 368

140.—GREAT BOUNDARY STELA OF AMARNA 370

141.—IKHNATON RECEIVING FLOWERS FROM HIS QUEEN . . 370

FIG.   PAGE

142.—LIMESTONE TORSO OF IKHNATON'S DAUGHTER . . 376

143.—HEAD OF IKHNATON 376

144.—MARSH LIFE 376

145.—HITTITE SOLDIER ARMED WITH AN AXE . . . 382

146.—HITTITE KING BEARING SPEAR AND SCEPTER . . 382

147.—EGYPTIAN OFFICIAL RECEIVING SEMITIC IMMIGRANTS . 382

148.—HARMHAB AS AN OFFICIAL REWARDED WITH GOLD BY
      THE KING 386

149.—SOUTHERN PYLONS OF HARMHAB AT KARNAK . . 390

150.—HARMHAB AS A PEASANT IN THE HEREAFTER . . 390

151.—BUST OF KHONSU 390

152.—BATTLE RELIEFS OF SETI I AT KARNAK . . . 396

153.—SETI I OFFERING AN IMAGE OF TRUTH TO OSIRIS . . 402

154.—SETI I AS A YOUTH OFFERING THE IMAGE OF TRUTH . 406

155.—CATTLE INSPECTION 412

156.—SWAMP HUNTING IN A REED BOAT 418

157.—SECTION OF ONE OF SETI I'S RELIEFS AT KARNAK . 419

158.—HEAD OF SETI I 424

159.—STELÆ OF RAMSES II AND ESARHADDON IN PHŒNICIA . 424

160.—SCENE FROM THE RELIEFS OF THE BATTLE OF KADESH . 434

161.—FRAGMENTS OF THOUSAND-TON COLOSSUS OF RAMSES II 442

162.—STORE CHAMBERS AT PITHOM 442

163.—HEAVY-ARMED SHERDEN OF RAMSES II'S MERCENARY
      BODYGUARD 448

164.—RESTORATION OF THE GREAT HALL AT KARNAK . . 448

165.—NAVE OF THE GREAT HALL OF KARNAK . . . 448

166.—THE RAMESSEUM, MORTUARY TEMPLE OF RAMSES II . 450

167.—THE CLIFF TEMPLE OF ABU SIMBEL 450

FIG.   PAGE

168.—BLACK GRANITE STATUE OF RAMSES II 450

169.—BATTLE SCENE FROM THE GREAT SERIES OF RELIEFS OF
    RAMSES II ON THE WALLS OF THE RAMESSEUM . . 452

170.—HEAD OF RAMSES II 464

171.—VICTORIOUS HYMN OF MERNEPTAH 464

172.—PELESET OR PHILISTINE PRISONERS OF RAMSES III . 464

173.—NAVAL VICTORY OF RAMSES III OVER NORTHERN MEDI-
    TERRANEAN PEOPLES 480

174.—RAMSES III'S MEDINET HABU TEMPLE 492

175.—RAMSES III'S MEDINET HABU TEMPLE 492

176.—RAMSES III HUNTING THE WILD BULL 492

177.—THE HIGH PRIEST OF AMON AMENHOTEP DECORATED BY
    RAMSES IX 510

178.—SCRIBE'S NOTES ON COFFIN OF SETI I 510

179.—THE DER EL BAHRI HIDING-PLACE 510

180.—"THE FIELD OF ABRAM" 536

181.—SENJIRLI STELA OF ESARHADDON 536

182.—SERAPEUM STELA OF PSAMTIK I 536

183.—GENERAL VIEW OF KARNAK FROM THE SOUTH . . 560

184.—ALABASTER STATUE OF AMENARDIS, SISTER OF PIANKHI 576

185.—BRONZ IBEX FROM THE PROW OF A SHIP . . . 590

186.—PORTRAIT HEAD OF THE SAITE AGE 590

MAPS

M   PAGE

1. —The Town of Illahûn, Showing the Crowded Quarters of the Poor 87

2. —The Fourth Dynasty Cemetery at Gizeh . . . 122

3. —The Fayum 192

4. —The Carmel Ridge, Showing Megiddo 286

5. —The Modern Tell-Nebi-Mindoh, Ancient Kadesh . 300

6. —Thebes 348

7. —The Asiatic Empire of Egypt 384

8. —The Vicinity of Kadesh 426

9. —The Battle of Kadesh 428

10. —The Battle of Kadesh 430

11. —Plan of the Karnak Temples 444

12. —Egypt and the Ancient World 476

13. —General Map of Egypt and Nubia . *At end of Volume*

BOOK I

INTRODUCTION

A HISTORY OF EGYPT

CHAPTER I

THE LAND

THE roots of modern civilization are planted deeply in
the highly elaborate life of those nations which rose into
power over six thousand years ago, in the basin of the eastern
Mediterranean, and the adjacent regions on the east of it.
Had the Euphrates finally found its way into the Mediterranean, toward which, indeed, it seems to have started, both
the early civilizations, to which we refer, might then have
been included in the Mediterranean basin.   As it is, the scene
of early oriental history does not fall entirely within that
basin, but must be designated as the eastern Mediterranean
region.   It lies in the midst of the vast desert plateau, which,
beginning at the Atlantic, extends eastward across the entire
northern end of Africa, and continuing beyond the depression of the Red Sea, passes northeastward, with some interruptions, far into the heart of Asia.   Approaching it, the
one from the south and the other from the north, two great
river valleys traverse this desert; in Asia, the Tigro-
Euphrates valley; in Africa that of the Nile.   It is in these
two valleys that the career of man may be traced from
the rise of European civilization back to a remoter age than
anywhere else on earth; and it is from these two cradles of
the human race that the influences which emanated from
their highly developed but differing cultures, can now be
more and more clearly traced as we discern them converging
upon the early civilization of Asia Minor and southern
Europe.

3

The Nile, which created the valley home of the early
Egyptians, rises three degrees south of the equator, and
flowing into the Mediterranean at over thirty one and a half
degrees north latitude, it attains a length of some four thousand miles, and vies with the greatest rivers of the world in
length, if not in volume.   In its upper course the river,
emerging from the lakes of equatorial Africa, is known as the
White Nile.   Just south of north latitude sixteen at Khartum, about thirteen hundred and fifty miles from the sea,
it receives from the east an affluent known as the Blue Nile,
which is a considerable mountain torrent, rising in the lofty
highlands of Abyssinia.   One hundred and forty miles
below the union of the two Niles the stream is joined by its
only other tributary, the Atbara, which is a freshet not
unlike the Blue Nile.   It is at Khartum, or just below it,
that the river enters the table land of Nubian sandstone,
underlying the Great Sahara.   Here it winds on its tortuous
course between the desert hills (Fig. 84), where it returns
upon itself, often flowing due south, until after it has finally
pushed through to the north, its course describes a vast S.

In six different places throughout this region the current
has hitherto failed to erode a perfect channel through the
stubborn stone, and these extended interruptions, where the
rocks are piled in scattered and irregular masses in the
stream, are known as the cataracts of the Nile; although
there is no great and sudden fall such as that of our cataract
at Niagara (Fig. 1).   These rocks interfere with navigation
most seriously in the region of the first, second and fourth
cataracts; otherwise the river is navigable almost throughout
its entire course.   At Elephantine it passes the granite barrier which there thrusts up its rough shoulder, forming the
first cataract, and thence emerges upon an unobstructed
course to the sea.

It is the valley below the first cataract which constituted
Egypt proper.   The reason for the change which here gives
the river a free course is the disappearance of the sandstone,
sixty eight miles below the cataract, at Edfu, where the num-

mulitic limestone which forms the northern desert plateau, offers the stream an easier task in the erosion of its bed. It has thus produced a vast cañon or trench (Figs. 3 and 7), cut across the eastern end of the Sahara to the northern sea. From cliff to cliff, the valley varies in width, from ten or twelve, to some thirty one miles. The floor of the cañon is covered with black, alluvial deposits, through which the river winds northward. It cuts a deep channel through the alluvium, flowing with a speed of about three miles an hour; in width it only twice attains a maximum of eleven hundred yards. On the west the Bahr Yusuf, a second, minor channel some two hundred miles long, leaves the main stream near Siut and flows into the Fayum. In antiquity it flowed thence into a canal known as the "North," which passed northward west of Memphis and reached the sea by the site of later Alexandria.[1] A little over a hundred miles from the sea the main stream enters the broad triangle, with apex at the south, which the Greeks so graphically called the "Delta." This is of course a bay of prehistoric ages, which has been gradually filled up by the river. The stream once divided at this point and reached the sea through seven mouths, but in modern times there are but two main branches, straggling through the Delta and piercing the coast-line on either side of the middle. The western branch is called the Rosetta mouth; the eastern that of Damiette.

The deposits which have formed the Delta, are very deep, and have slowly risen over the sites of the many ancient cities which once flourished there. The old swamps which must once have rendered the regions of the northern Delta a vast morass, have been gradually filled up, and the fringe of marshes pushed further out. They undoubtedly occupied in antiquity a much larger proportion of the Delta than they do now. In the valley above the depth of the soil varies from thirty three to thirty eight feet, and sometimes reaches a maximum of ten miles in width. The cultivable area thus formed, between the cataract and the sea, is less than ten

[1] IV, 224, l. 8, note.

thousand square miles in extent, being roughly equal to the area of the state of Maryland, or about ten per cent less than that of Belgium. The cliffs on either hand are usually but a few hundred feet in height, but here and there they rise into almost mountains of a thousand feet (Fig. 3). They are of course flanked by the deserts through which the Nile has cut its way. On the west the Libyan Desert or the Great Sahara rolls in illimitable, desolate hills of sand, gravel and rock, from six hundred and fifty to a thousand feet above the Nile. Its otherwise waterless expanse is broken only by an irregular line of oases, or watered depressions, roughly parallel with the river, and doubtless owing their springs and wells to infiltration of the Nile waters. The largest of these depressions is situated so close to the valley that the rock wall which once separated them has broken down, producing the fertile Fayum, watered by the Bahr Yusuf. Otherwise the western desert held no economic resources for the use of the early Nile-dwellers. The eastern or Arabian Desert is somewhat less inhospitable, and capable of yielding a scanty subsistence to wandering tribes of Ababdeh. A range of granite mountains parallel with the coast of the Red Sea contains gold-bearing quartz veins, and here and there other gold-producing mountains lie between the Nile and the Red Sea. Deposits of alabaster and extensive masses of various fine, hard igneous rocks led to the exploitation of quarries here also, while the Red Sea harbours could of course be reached only by traversing this desert, through which established routes thither were early traced. Further north similar mineral resources led to an acquaintance with the peninsula of Sinai and its desert regions, at a very remote date.

The situation afforded by this narrow valley was one of unusual isolation; on either hand vast desert wastes, on the north the harbourless coast-line of the Delta, and on the south the rocky barriers of successive cataracts, preventing fusion with the peoples of inner Africa. It was chiefly at the two northern corners of the Delta, that outside influences and

FIG. 1.—ONE OF THE CHANNELS OF THE FIRST CATARACT.

Looking northward from the Island of Philæ; ruins on Philæ in the foreground.

FIG. 2.—THE INUNDATION SEEN FROM THE ROAD TO THE PYRAMIDS OF GIZEH.

The road is on the right; in the distance the desert plateau on which the pyramids stand. Before them the village
of Kafr

foreign elements, which were always sifting into the Nile valley, gained access to the country. Through the eastern corner it was the prehistoric Semitic population of neighbouring Asia, who forced their way in across the dangerous intervening deserts; while the Libyan races, of possibly European origin, found entrance at the western corner. The products of the south also, in spite of the cataracts, filtered in ever increasing volume into the regions of the lower river and the lower end of the first cataract became a trading post, ever after known as "Suan" (Assuan) or "market," where the negro traders of the south met those of Egypt. The upper Nile thus gradually became a regular avenue of commerce with the Sudan. The natural boundaries of Egypt, however, always presented sufficiently effective barriers to would-be invaders, to enable the natives slowly to assimilate the new comers, without being displaced.

It will be evident that the remarkable shape of the country must powerfully influence its political development. Except in the Delta it was but a narrow line, some seven hundred and fifty miles long. Straggling its slender length along the river, and sprawling out into the Delta, it totally lacked the compactness necessary to stable political organization. A given locality has neighbours on only two sides, north and south, and these their shortest boundaries; local feeling was strong, local differences were persistent, and a man of the Delta could hardly understand the speech of a man of the first cataract region. It was only the ease of communication afforded by the river which in any degree neutralized the effect of the country's remarkable length.

The wealth of commerce which the river served to carry, it was equally instrumental in producing. While the climate of the country is not rainless, yet the rare showers of the south, often separated by intervals of years, and even the more frequent rains of the Delta, are totally insufficient to maintain the processes of agriculture. The marvellous productivity of the Egyptian soil is due to the annual inundation of the river, which is caused by the melting of the snows,

and by the spring rains at the sources of the Blue Nile.
Freighted with the rich loam of the Abyssinian highlands,
the rushing waters of the spring freshet hurry down the
Nubian valley, and a slight rise is discernible at the first
cataract in the early part of June. The flood swells rapidly
and steadily, and although the increase is usually interrupted for nearly a month from the end of September on,
it is usually resumed again, and the maximum level continues until the end of October or into November. The
waters in the region of the first cataract are then nearly fifty
feet higher than at low water; while at Cairo the rise is
about half that at the cataract. A vast and elaborate system
of irrigation canals and reservoirs first receives the flood,
which is then allowed to escape into the fields as needed.
Here it rests long enough to deposit its burden of rich, black
earth from the upper reaches of the Blue Nile. At such
times the appearance of the country is picturesque in the
extreme, the glistening surface of the waters being dotted
here and there by the vivid green of the waving palm groves,
which mark the villages, now accessible only along the dykes
belonging to the irrigation system (Fig. 2). Thus year by
year, the soil which would otherwise become impoverished
in the elements necessary to the production of such prodigious harvests, is invariably replenished with fresh resources.

As the river sinks below the level of the fields again, it is
necessary to raise the water from the canals by artificial
means, in order to carry on the constant irrigation of the
growing crops in the outlying fields, which are too high to
be longer refreshed by absorption from the river (Fig. 6).[1]
Thus a genial and generous, but exacting soil, demanded
for its cultivation the development of a high degree of skill

[1] The device used (called a " shadûf ") resembles the well-sweep of our
grandfathers. Fig. 6 shows the leathern bucket suspended from one end of the
sweep, while at the other end a huge lump of dried mud serves as a counter-
poise. When the water is very low, as many as three or even four such
" shadûfs " are necessary to raise the water from level to level until that of
the field is reached. A single crop requires the lifting of 1,600 to 2,000 tons
of water per acre in a hundred days.

in the manipulation of the life-giving waters, and at a very early day the men of the Nile valley had attained a surprising command of the complicated problems involved in the proper utilization of the river. If Egypt became the mother of the mechanical arts, the river will have been one of the chief natural forces to which this fact was due. With such natural assets as these, an ever replenished soil, and almost unfailing waters for its refreshment, the wealth of Egypt could not but be chiefly agricultural, a fact to which we shall often recur. Such opulent fertility of course supported a large population—in Roman times some seven million souls[1]—while in our own day it maintains over nine million, a density of population far surpassing that to be found anywhere in Europe. The other natural resources of the valley we shall be better able to trace as we follow their exploitation in the course of the historical development.

In climate Egypt is a veritable paradise, drawing to its shores at the present day an ever increasing number of winter guests. The air of Egypt is essentially that of the deserts within which it lies, and such is its purity and dryness, that even an excessive degree of heat occasions but slight discomfort, owing to the fact that the moisture of the body is dried up almost as fast as it is exhaled. The mean temperature of the Delta in winter is 56° Fahrenheit, and in the valley above it is ten degrees higher. In summer the mean in the Delta is 83°; and although the summer temperature in the valley is sometimes as high as 122°, the air is far from the oppressiveness accompanying the same degree of heat in other lands. The nights even in summer are always cool, and the vast expanses of vegetation appreciably reduce the temperature. In winter just before dawn the extreme cold is surprising, as contrasted with the genial warmth of midday at the same season. To the absence of rain we have already adverted. The rare showers of upper Egypt occur only when cyclonic disturbances in the southern Mediterranean or northern Sahara force undischarged

[1] Diodorus I, 31.

clouds into the Nile valley from the west; from the east they can not reach the valley, owing to the high mountain ridge along the Red Sea, which forces them upward and discharges them. The lower Delta, however, falls within the zone of the northern rainy season. In spite of the wide extent of marshy ground, left stagnating by the inundation, the dry airs of the desert, blowing constantly across the valley, quickly dry the soil, and there is never any malarial infection in Upper Egypt. Even in the vast morass of the Delta, malaria is practically unknown. Thus, lying just outside of the tropics, Egypt enjoyed a mild climate of unsurpassed salubrity, devoid of the harshness of a northern winter, but at the same time sufficiently cool to escape those enervating influences inherent in tropical conditions.

The prospect of this contracted valley spread out before the Nile dweller, was in antiquity, as it is to-day, somewhat monotonous. The level Nile bottoms, the gift of the river, clad in rich green, shut in on either hand by the yellow cliffs, are unrelieved by any elevations or by any forests, save the occasional groves of graceful palms, which fringe the river banks or shade the villages of sombre mud huts (Fig. 4), with now and then a sycamore, a tamarisk or an acacia. A network of irrigation canals traverses the country in every direction like a vast arterial system. The sands of the desolate wastes which lie behind the cañon walls, drift in athwart the cliffs, and often invade the green fields so that one may stand with one foot in the verdure of the valley, and the other in the desert sand. Thus sharply defined was the Egyptian's world: a deep and narrow valley of unparalleled fertility, winding between lifeless deserts, furnishing a remarkable environment, not to be found elsewhere in all the world. Such surroundings reacted powerfully upon the mind and thought of the Egyptian, conditioning and determining his idea of the world and his notion of the mysterious powers which ruled it. The river, the dominant feature of his valley, determined his notion of direction: his words for north and south were "down-stream" and "up-stream";

FIG. 3.—LOOKING ACROSS THE NILE TO THE WESTERN CLIFFS NEAR THEBES.

The low shores mark the level of the alluvium extending back to the cliffs.

FIG. 4.—THE HUTS AND PALM GROVES OF KARNAK, THEBES.

Seen from the roof of the temple of Khonsu. In the foreground is the gate or propylon of Euergetes I (Ptolemy III, 247–222 B.C.). Leading up to it is the avenue of sphinxes made by Amenhotep III, connecting Karnak and Luxor.

and when he broke through the barriers which separated him from Asia, and reached the Euphrates, he called it "that inverted water which goes down stream in going up stream" (southward).[1] For him the world consisted of the "Black Land" and the "Red Land," the black soil of the Nile valley and the reddish surface of the desert; or again of the "plain" and the "highlands," meaning the level Nile "bottoms" and the high desert plateau. "Highlander" was synonymous with foreigner, to "go up" was to leave the valley, while to "descend" was the customary term for returning home from abroad. The illimitable solitudes of the desert, which thrust itself thus insistently upon his vision and his whole economy of life, and formed his horizon toward both suns, tinctured with sombreness his views of the great gods who ruled such a world.

Such was in brief the scene in which developed the people of the Nile, whose culture dominated the basin of the eastern Mediterranean in the age when Europe was emerging into the secondary stages of civilization, and coming into intimate contact with the culture of the early east. Nowhere on earth have the witnesses of a great, but now extinct civilization, been so plentifully preserved as along the banks of the Nile. Even in the Delta, where the storms of war beat more fiercely than in the valley above, and where the slow accumulations from the yearly flood have gradually entombed them, the splendid cities of the Pharaohs have left great stretches, cumbered with enormous blocks of granite, limestone and sandstone, shattered obelisks, and massive pylon bases, to proclaim the wealth and power of forgotten ages; while an ever growing multitude of modern visitors are drawn to the upper valley by the colossal ruins that greet the wondering traveller almost at every bend in the stream. Nowhere else in the ancient world were such massive stone buildings erected, and nowhere else has a dry atmosphere, coupled with an almost complete absence of rain, permitted the sur-- vival of such a wealth of the best and highest in the life of

[1] II, 72.

an ancient people, in so far as that life found expression in material form. In the plenitude of its splendour, much of it thus survived into the classic age of European civilization, and hence it was, that as Egypt was gradually overpowered and absorbed by the western world, the currents of life from west and east commingled here, as they have never done elsewhere. Both in the Nile valley and beyond it, the west thus felt the full impact of Egyptian civilization for many centuries, and gained from it all that its manifold culture had to contribute. The career which made Egypt so rich a heritage of alien peoples, and a legacy so valuable to all later ages, we shall endeavour to trace in the ensuing chapters.

CHAPTER II

PRELIMINARY SURVEY, CHRONOLOGY AND DOCUMENTARY SOURCES

A RAPID survey of the purely external features which serve to demark the great epochs in the career of the Nile valley people, will enable us the more intelligently to study those epochs in detail, as we meet them in the course of our progress. In such a survey, we sweep our eyes down a period of four thousand years of human history, from a time when the only civilization known in the basin of the Mediterranean is slowly dawning among a primitive people on the shores of the Nile. We can cast but a brief glance at the outward events which characterized each great period, especially noting how foreign peoples are gradually drawn within the circle of Egyptian intercourse from age to age, and reciprocal influences ensue; until in the thirteenth century B. C. the peoples of southern Europe, long discernible in their material civilization, emerge in the written documents of Egypt for the first time in history. It was then that the fortunes of the Pharaohs began to decline, and as the civilization and power, first of the East and then of classic Europe, slowly developed, Egypt was finally submerged in the great world of Mediterranean powers, first dominated by Persia, and then by Greece and Rome.

The career of the races which peopled the Nile valley falls into a series of more or less clearly marked epochs, each of which is rooted deeply in that which preceded it, and itself contains the germs of that which is to follow. A more or less arbitrary and artificial but convenient sub-division of these epochs, beginning with the historic age, is furnished by the so-called dynasties of Manetho. This native historian of Egypt, a priest of Sebennytos, who flourished under Ptolemy I (305–285 B. C.), wrote a history of his country in the Greek language. The work has perished, and we only know it in an epitome by Julius Africanus and Eusebius, and extracts by Josephus. The value of the work was slight, as it was built up on folk-tales and popular traditions of the early kings. Manetho divided the long succession of Pharaohs as known to him, into thirty royal houses or dynasties, and although we know that many of his divisions are arbitrary, and that there was many a dynastic change where he indicates none, yet his dynasties divide the kings into convenient groups, which have so long been employed in modern study of Egyptian history, that it is now impossible to dispense with them.

After an archaic age of primitive civilization, and a period of small and local kingdoms, the various centres of civilization on the Nile gradually coalesced into two kingdoms: one comprising the valley down to the Delta; and the other made up of the Delta itself. In the Delta, civilization rapidly advanced, and the calendar year of 365 days was introduced in 4241 B. C., the earliest fixed date in the history of the world as known to us.[1] A long development, as the "Two Lands," which left their imprint forever after, on the civilization of later centuries, preceded a united Egypt, which emerged upon our historic horizon at the consolidation of the two kingdoms into one nation under Menes about 3400 B. C. His accession marks the beginning of the dynasties, and the preceding, earliest period may be conveniently designated as the predynastic age. In the excavations of the last ten years, the predynastic civilization has been gradually revealed in material documents exhibiting the various stages in the slow evolution which at last produced the dynastic culture.

A uniform government of the whole country was the secret of over four centuries of prosperity under the descendants of Menes at Thinis, near Abydos, close to the great bend of

[1] I, 44–45.

Fig. 5.—THE NILE VALLEY, VIEWED ACROSS THE MODERN TOWN OF EDFU.

Beyond the town the river winds through the "bottoms," behind which rise the eastern cliffs.

the Nile below Thebes, and probably also at or near later Memphis. The remarkable development of these four centuries in material civilization led to the splendour and power of the first great epoch of Egyptian history, the Old Kingdom. The seat of government was at Memphis, where four royal houses, the Third, Fourth, Fifth and Sixth Dynasties, ruled in succession for five hundred years (2980–2475 B. C.). Art and mechanics reached a level of unprecedented excellence never later surpassed, while government and administration had never before been so highly developed. Foreign enterprise passed far beyond the limits of the kingdom; the mines of Sinai, already operated in the First Dynasty, were vigourously exploited; trade in Egyptian bottoms reached the coast of Phœnicia and the Islands of the North, while in the south, the Pharaoh's fleets penetrated to the Somali coast on the Red Sea; and in Nubia his envoys were strong enough to exercise a loose sovereignty over the lower country, and by tireless expeditions to keep open the trade routes leading to the Sudan. In the Sixth Dynasty (2625–2475 B. C.) the local governors of the central administration, who had already gained hereditary hold upon their offices in the Fifth Dynasty (2750–2625 B. C.), were able to assert themselves as landed barons and princes, no longer mere functionaries of the crown. They thus prepared the way for an age of feudalism.

The growing power of the new landed nobility finally caused the fall of the Pharaonic house, and after the close of the Sixth Dynasty, about 2400 B. C., the supremacy of Memphis waned. In the internal confusion which followed, we can discern nothing of Manetho's ephemeral Seventh and Eighth Dynasties at Memphis, which lasted not more than thirty years; but with the Ninth and Tenth Dynasties the nobles of Heracleopolis gained the throne, which was occupied by eighteen successive kings of the line. It is now that Thebes first appears as the seat of a powerful family of princes, by whom the Heracleopolitans and the power of the North are gradually overcome till the South triumphs.

The exact lapse of time from the fall of the Old Kingdom to the triumph of the South is at present indeterminable, but it may be estimated roughly at two hundred and seventy five to three hundred years,[1] with a margin of uncertainty of possibly a century either way.

With the restoration of a united Egypt under the Theban princes of the Eleventh Dynasty about 2160 B. C., the issue of the tendencies already discernible at the close of the Old Kingdom is clearly visible. Throughout the land the local princes and barons are firmly seated in their domains, and with these hereditary feudatories the Pharaoh must now reckon. The system was not fully developed until the advent of a second Theban family, the Twelfth Dynasty, the founder of which, Amenemhet I, probably usurped the throne. For over two hundred years (2000–1788 B. C.) this powerful line of kings ruled a feudal state. This feudal age is the classic period of Egyptian history. Literature flourished, the orthography of the language was for the first time regulated, poetry had already reached a highly artistic structure, the earliest known literature of entertainment was produced, sculpture and architecture were rich and prolific, and the industrial arts surpassed all previous attainments. The internal resources of the country were elaborately developed, especially by close attention to the Nile and the inundation. Enormous hydraulic works reclaimed large tracts of cultivable domain in the Fayum, in the vicinity of which the kings of the Twelfth Dynasty, the Amenemhets and the Sesostrises, lived. Abroad the exploitation of the mines in Sinai was now carried on by the constant labour of permanent colonies there, with temples, fortifications and reservoirs for the water supply. A plundering campaign was carried into Syria, trade and intercourse with its Semitic tribes were constant, and an interchange of commodities with the early Mycenæan centres of civilization in the northern Mediterranean is evident. Traffic with Punt and the southern coasts of the Red Sea continued, while in Nubia the country between

[1] I. 53.

the first and second cataracts, loosely controlled in the Sixth Dynasty, was now conquered and held tributary by the Pharaoh, so that the gold mines on the east of it were a constant resource of his treasury.

The fall of the Twelfth Dynasty in 1788 B. C. was followed by a second period of disorganization and obscurity, as the feudatories struggled for the crown. Now and then an aggressive and able ruler gained the ascendency for a brief reign, and under one of these the subjugation of Upper Nubia was carried forward to a point above the third cataract; but his conquest perished with him. After possibly a century of such internal conflict, the country was entered and appropriated by a line of rulers from Asia, who had seemingly already gained a wide dominion there. These foreign usurpers, now known as the Hyksos, after Manetho's designation of them, maintained themselves for perhaps a century. Their residence was at Avaris in the eastern Delta, and at least during the later part of their supremacy, the Egyptian nobles of the South succeeded in gaining more or less independence. Finally the head of a Theban family boldly proclaimed himself king, and in the course of some years these Theban princes succeeded in expelling the Hyksos from the country, and driving them back from the Asiatic frontier into Syria.

It was under the Hyksos and in the struggle with them that the conservatism of millennia was broken up in the Nile valley. The Egyptians learned aggressive war for the first time, and introduced a well organized military system, including chariotry, which the importation of the horse by the Hyksos now enabled them to do. Egypt was transformed into a military empire. In the struggle with the Hyksos and with each other, the old feudal families perished, or were absorbed among the partisans of the dominant Theban family, from which the imperial line sprang. The great Pharaohs of the Eighteenth Dynasty thus became emperors, conquering and ruling from northern Syria and the upper Euphrates, to the fourth cataract of the Nile on

2

the south. Amid unprecedented wealth and splendour, they ruled their vast dominions, which they gradually welded together into a compact empire, the first known in the early world. Thebes grew into a great metropolis, the earliest monumental city. Extensive trade relations with the East and the Mediterranean world developed; Mycenæan products were common in Egypt, and Egyptian influences are clearly discernible in Mycenæan art. For two hundred and thirty years (1580–1350 B. C.) the Empire flourished, but was wrecked at last by a combination of adverse influences both within and without. A religious revolution by the young and gifted king Ikhnaton, caused an internal convulsion such as the country had never before experienced; while the empire in the north gradually disintegrated under the aggressions of the Hittites, who pushed in from Asia Minor. At the same time in both the northern and southern Asiatic dominions of the Pharaoh, an overflow of Beduin immigration, among which were undoubtedly some of the tribes which later coalesced with the Israelites, aggravated the danger, and together with the persistent advance of the Hittites, finally resulted in the complete dissolution of the Asiatic empire of Egypt, down to the very frontier of the northeastern Delta. Meanwhile the internal disorders had caused the fall of the Eighteenth Dynasty, an event which terminated the First Period of the Empire (1350 B. C.).

Harmhab, one of the able commanders under the fallen dynasty, survived the crisis and finally seized the throne. Under his vigourous rule the disorganized nation was gradually restored to order, and his successors of the Nineteenth Dynasty (1350–1205 B. C.) were able to begin the recovery of the lost empire in Asia. But the Hittites were too firmly entrenched in Syria to yield to the Egyptian onset. The assaults of Seti I, and half a generation of persistent campaigning under Ramses II, failed to push the northern frontier of the Empire far beyond the limits of Palestine. Here it remained and Syria was never permanently recovered. Semitic influences now powerfully affected Egypt.

Fig. 6.—A TRIPLE SHADÛF.

A device for raising the Nile water in order to irrigate the fields (see p. 8)
(Stereograph copyright Underwood & Underwood, N. Y.)

Fig. 7.—THE CLIFFS OF THE NILE CAÑON.

Looking down the valley from a point west of Thebes. (Stereograph
copyright Underwood & Underwood, N. Y.)

At this juncture the peoples of southern Europe emerge for the first time upon the arena of oriental history and together with Libyan hordes, threaten to overwhelm the Delta from the west. They were nevertheless beaten back by Merneptah. After another period of internal confusion and usurpation, during which the Nineteenth Dynasty fell (1205 B. C.), Ramses III, whose father, Setnakht founded the Twentieth Dynasty (1200–1090 B. C.), was able to maintain the Empire at the same limits, against the invasions of restless northern tribes, who crushed the Hittite power; and also against repeated immigrations of the Libyans. With his death (1167 B. C.) the empire, with the exception of Nubia which was still held, rapidly fell to pieces. Thus, about the middle of the twelfth century B. C. the Second Period of the imperial age closed with the total dissolution of the Asiatic dominions.

Under a series of weak Ramessids, the country rapidly declined and fell a prey first to the powerful high priests of Amon, who were obliged almost immediately to yield to stronger Ramessid rivals in the Delta at Tanis, forming the Twenty First Dynasty (1090–945 B. C.). By the middle of the tenth century B. C. the mercenaries, who had formed the armies of the second imperial period, had founded powerful families in the Delta cities, and among these the Libyans were now supreme. Sheshonk I, a Libyan mercenary commander, gained the throne as the founder of the Twenty Second Dynasty in 945 B. C. and the country enjoyed transient prosperity, while Sheshonk even attempted the recovery of Palestine. But the family was unable to control the turbulent mercenary commanders, now established as dynasties in the larger Delta towns, and the country gradually relapsed into a series of military principalities in constant warfare with each other. Through the entire Libyan period of the Twenty Second, Twenty Third and Twenty Fourth Dynasties (945–712 B. C.) the unhappy nation groaned under such misrule, constantly suffering economic deterioration.

Nubia had now detached itself and a dynasty of kings, probably of Theban origin had arisen at Napata, below the fourth cataract. These Egyptian rulers of the new Nubian kingdom now invaded Egypt, and although residing at Napata, maintained their sovereignty in Egypt with varying fortune for two generations (722–663 B. C.). But they were unable to suppress and exterminate the local dynasts, who ruled on, while acknowledging the suzerainty of the Nubian overlord. It was in the midst of these conflicts between the Nubian dynasty and the mercenary lords of Lower Egypt, that the Assyrians finally entered the Delta, subdued the country and placed it under tribute (670–662 B. C.). At this juncture Psamtik I, an able dynast of Sais, in the western Delta, finally succeeded in overthrowing his rivals, expelled the Ninevite garrisons, and as the Nubians had already been forced out of the country by the Assyrians, he was able to found a powerful dynasty, and usher in the Restoration. His accession fell in 663 B. C., and the entire period of nearly five hundred years from the final dissolution of the Empire about 1150 to the dawn of the Restoration in 663 B. C., may be conveniently designated the Decadence. After 1100 B. C. the Decadence may be conveniently divided into the Tanite-Amonite Period (1090–945 B. C.), the Libyan Period (945–712 B. C.), the Ethiopian Period (722–663 B. C.), and the Assyrian Period, which is contemporary with the last years of the Ethiopian Period.

Of the Restoration, like all those epochs in which the seat of power was in the Delta, where almost all monuments have perished, we learn very little from native sources; and all too little also from Herodotus and later Greek visitors in the Nile valley. It was outwardly an age of power and splendour, in which the native party endeavoured to restore the old glories of the classic age before the Empire; while the kings depending upon Greek mercenaries, were modern politicians, employing the methods of the new Greek world, mingling in the world-politics of their age, and showing little sympathy with the archaizing tendency. But their combinations failed to save Egypt from the ambition of Persia, and its history under native dynasties, with unimportant exceptions, was concluded with the conquest of the country by Cambyses in 525 B. C.

Such, in mechanical review, were the purely external events which marked the successive epochs of Egypt's history as an independent nation. With their dates, these epochs may be summarized thus:

Introduction of the Calendar, 4241 B. C.

Predynastic Age, before 3400 B. C.

The Accession of Menes, 3400 B. C.

The first Two Dynasties, 3400–2980 B. C.

The Old Kingdom: Dynasties Three to Six, 2980–2475 B. C.

Eighteen Heracleopolitans, 2445–2160 B. C.

The Middle Kingdom: Dynasties Eleven and Twelve, 2160–1788 B. C.

Internal Conflicts of the Feudatories, $\left.\right\}$ 1788–1580 B. C.
The Hyksos,

The Empire: First Period, The Eighteenth Dynasty, 1580–1350 B. C.

The Empire: Second Period, The Nineteenth and part of the Twentieth Dynasty, 1350–1150 B. C.

The Decadence $\left\{\begin{array}{l}\text{Last Two Generations of Twentieth Dynasty, about 1150 to 1090 B. C.}\\ \text{Tanite-Amonite Period, Twenty First Dynasty, 1090–945 B. C.}\\ \text{Libyan Period, Dynasties Twenty Two to Twenty Four, 945–712 B. C.}\\ \text{Ethiopian Period, 722–663 B. C. (Twenty Fifth Dynasty, 712–663 B. C.).}\\ \text{Assyrian Supremacy, 670–662 B. C.}\end{array}\right.$

The Restoration, Saite Period, Twenty Sixth Dynasty, 663–525 B. C.

Persian Conquest, 525 B. C.

The reader will find at the end of the volume a tuller table of reigns. The chronology of the above table is

obtained by two independent processes: first by "dead reckoning," and second by astronomical calculations based on the
Egyptian calendar. By "dead reckoning" we mean simply
the addition of the known minimum length of all the kings'
reigns, and from the total thus obtained, the simple computation (backward from a fixed starting point) of the date
of the beginning of the series of reigns so added. Employing all the latest dates from recent discoveries, it is mathe-
matically certain that from the accession of the Eighteenth
Dynasty to the conquest of the Persians in 525 B. C. the
successive Pharaohs reigned at least 1052 years in all.[1]   The
Eighteenth Dynasty therefore began not later than 1577 B.
C.   Astronomical calculations based on the date of the rising
of Sirius, and of the occurrence of new moons, both in terms
of the shifting Egyptian calendar, place the date of the
accession of the Eighteenth Dynasty with fair precision in
1580 B. C.[2]   For the periods earlier than the Eighteenth
Dynasty, we can no longer employ the method of dead reckoning alone, because of the scantiness of the contemporary
documents.   Fortunately another date of the rising of
Sirius, fixes the advent of the Twelfth Dynasty at 2000 B.
C., with a margin of uncertainty of not more than a year
or two either way. From this date the beginning of the
Eleventh Dynasty is again only a matter of "dead reckoning." The uncertainty as to the duration of the Heracleopolitan supremacy makes the length of the period between
the Old and Middle Kingdoms very uncertain.   If we give the
eighteen Heracleopolitans sixteen years each, which, under
orderly conditions, is a fair average in the orient, they will
have ruled 288 years.[3]   In estimating their duration at 285
years, we may err possibly as much as a century either way.
The computation of the length of the Old Kingdom is based
on contemporary monuments and early lists, in which the
margin of error is probably not more than a generation or
two either way, but the uncertain length of the Heracleopolitan rule affects all dates back of that age, and a shift

[1] I, 47-51.   [2] I, 38-46.   [3] I, 53.

of a century either way in the years B. C. is not impossible. The ancient annals of the Palermo Stone establish the length of the first two dynasties at roughly 420 years,[1] and the date of the accession of Menes and the union of Egypt as 3400 B. C.; but we carry back with us, from the Heracleopolitan age, the same wide margin of uncertainty as in the Old Kingdom. The reader will have observed that this system of chronology is based upon the contemporary monuments and lists dating not later than 1200 B. C. The extremely high dates for the beginning of the dynasties current in some histories are inherited from an older generation of Egyptologists; and are based upon the chronology of Manetho, a late, careless and uncritical compilation, which can be proven wrong from the contemporary monuments in the vast majority of cases, where such monuments have survived. Its dynastic totals are so absurdly high throughout, that they are not worthy of a moment's credence, being often nearly or quite double the maximum drawn from contemporary monuments, and they will not stand the slightest careful criticism. Their accuracy is now maintained only by a small and constantly decreasing number of modern scholars.

Like our chronology our knowledge of the early history of Egypt must be gleaned from the contemporary native monuments.[2] Monumental sources even when full and complete are at best but insufficient records, affording data for only the meagrest outlines of great achievements and important epochs. While the material civilization of the country found adequate expression in magnificent works of the artist, craftsman and engineer, the inner life of the nation, or even the purely external events of moment could find record only incidentally. Such documents are sharply differentiated from the materials with which the historian of European nations deals, except of course in his study of the earliest ages. Extensive correspondence between statesmen, journals and diaries, state documents and reports—such mate-

---

[1] I, 84–85.   [2] I, 1–37.

rials as these are almost wholly wanting in monumental records. Imagine writing a history of Greece from the few Greek inscriptions surviving. Moreover, we possess no history of Egypt of sufficiently early date by a native Egyptian; the compilation of puerile folk-tales by Manetho, in the third century B. C. is hardly worthy of the name history. But an annalist of the remote ages with which we are to deal, could have had little conception of what would be important for future ages to know, even if he had undertaken a full chronicle of historical events. Scanty annals were indeed kept from the earliest times, but these have entirely perished with the exception of two fragments, the now famous Palermo Stone,[1] which once bore the annals of the earliest dynasties from the beginning down into the Fifth Dynasty; and some extracts from the records of Thutmose III's campaigns in Syria. Of the other monuments of incidental character, but the merest fraction has survived. Under these circumstances we shall probably never be able to offer more than a sketch of the civilization of the Old and Middle Kingdoms, with a hazy outline of the general drift of events. Under the Empire the available documents, both in quality and quantity for the first time approach the minimum, which in European history would be regarded as adequate to a moderately full presentation of the career of the nation. Scores of important questions, however, still remain unanswered, in whatever direction we turn. Nevertheless a rough frame-work of the governmental organization, the constitution of society, the most important achievements of the emperors, and to a limited extent the spirit of the age, may be discerned and sketched in the main outlines, even though it is only here and there that the sources enable us to fill in the detail. In the Decadence and the Restoration, however, the same paucity of documents, so painfully apparent in the older periods, again leaves the historian with a long series of hypotheses and probabilities. For the reserve with which the author has constantly treated such periods, he begs the reader to hold the scanty sources responsible.

[1] See Fig. 29 and I, 76--167.

CHAPTER III

EARLIEST EGYPT

On the now bare and windswept desert plateau, through which the Nile has hollowed its channel, there once dwelt a race of men. Plenteous rains, now no longer known there, rendered it a fertile and productive region. The geological changes which have since made the country almost rainless, denuded it of vegetation and soil, and made it for the most part uninhabitable, took place many thousands of years before the beginning of the Egyptian civilization, which we are to study; but the prehistoric race, who before these changes, peopled the plateau, left behind them as the sole memorial of their existence vast numbers of rude flint implements, now lying scattered about upon the surface of the present desert exposed by the denudation. These men of the paleolithic age were the first inhabitants of whom we have any knowledge in Egypt. They can not be connected in any way with the historic or prehistoric civilization of the Egyptians, and they fall exclusively within the province of the geologist and anthropologist.

The forefathers of the people with whom we shall have to deal were related to the Libyans or north Africans on the one hand, and on the other to the peoples of eastern Africa, now known as the Galla, Somali, Bega and other tribes. An invasion of the Nile valley by Semitic nomads of Asia, stamped its essential character unmistakably upon the language of the African people there. The earliest strata of the Egyptian language accessible to us, betray clearly this composite origin. While still coloured by its African antecedents, the language is in structure Semitic. It is moreover a completed product as observable in our earliest preserved examples of it; but the fusion of the Libyans and

25

east Africans with the Nile valley peoples continued far into historic times, and in the case of the Libyans may be traced in ancient historical documents for three thousand years or more. The Semitic immigration from Asia, examples of which are also observable in the historic age, occurred in an epoch that lies far below our remotest historical horizon. We shall never be able to determine when, nor with certainty through what channels it took place, although the most probable route is that along which we may observe a similar influx from the deserts of Arabia in historic times, the isthmus of Suez, by which the Mohammedan invasion entered the country. While the Semitic language which they brought with them, left its indelible impress upon the old Nile valley people, the nomadic life of the desert which the invaders left behind them, evidently was not so persistent, and the religion of Egypt, that element of life which always receives the stamp of its environment, shows no trace of desert life. The affinities observable in the language are confirmed in case of the Libyans, by the surviving products of archaic civilization in the Nile valley, such as some of the early pottery, which closely resembles that still made by the Libyan Kabyles. Again the representations of the early Puntites, or Somali people, on the Egyptian monuments, show striking resemblances to the Egyptians themselves. The examination of the bodies exhumed from archaic burials in the Nile valley, which we had hoped might bring further evidence for the settlement of the problem, has, however, produced such diversity of opinion among the physical anthropologists, as to render it impossible for the historian to obtain decisive results from their researches. The conclusion once maintained by some historians, that the Egyptian was of African negro origin, is now refuted; and evidently indicated that at most he may have been slightly tinctured with negro blood, in addition to the other ethnic elements already mentioned.

As found in the earliest burials to-day, the predynastic Egyptians were a dark-haired people, already possessed of

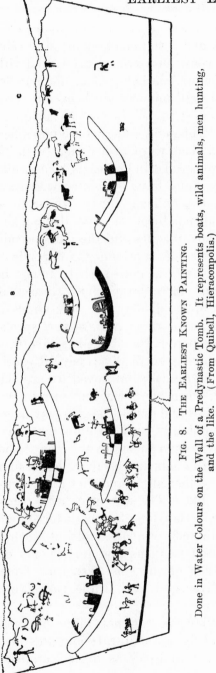

FIG. 8. THE EARLIEST KNOWN PAINTING. Done in Water Colours on the Wall of a Predynastic Tomb. It represents boats, wild animals, men hunting, and the like. (From Quibell, Hieraconpolis.)

the rudiments of civilization. The men wore a skin over the shoulders, sometimes skin drawers, and again only a short white linen kilt; while the women were clothed in long garments of some textile, probably linen, reaching from the shoulders to the ankles. Statuettes of both sexes without clothing whatever are, however, very common. Sandals were not unknown. They occasionally tattooed their bodies, and they also wrought ornaments such as rings, bracelets and pendants of stone, ivory and bone; with beads of flint, quartz, carnelian, agate and the like. The women dressed their hair with ornamented ivory combs and pins. For the eye- and face-paint necessary for the toilet, they had palettes of carved slate on which the green colour was ground. They were able to build dwellings of wattle, sometimes smeared with mud, and probably later of sun-dried brick.   In the furnishing of these houses they displayed considerable mechanical skill, and a rudimentary artistic taste. They ate with ivory spoons, sometimes even richly carved with figures of animals in the round, marching along the handle. Although the wheel was at first unknown to them, they produced fine pottery of the most varied forms in vast quantities.   The museums of Europe and America are now filled with their polished red and black ware, or a variety with incised geometrical designs, sometimes in basket patterns, while another style of great importance to us is painted with rude representations of boats, men, animals, birds, fish or trees (Fig. 11).   While they made no objects of glass, they understood the art of glazing beads, plaques and the like.   Crude statuettes in wood, ivory, or stone, represent the beginnings of that plastic art, which was to achieve such triumphs in the early dynastic age; and three large stone statues of Min, found by Petrie at Coptos, display the rude strength of the predynastic civilization of which we are now speaking.   The art of the prolific potter was obliged to give way slowly to the artificer in stone, who finally produced excellent stone vessels, which he gradually improved toward the end of predynastic period, when his bowls and jars in the hardest stones, like the diorites and porphyries, display magnificent work.   The most cunningly wrought flints that have ever been found among any people belong to this age.   The makers were ultimately able to affix carved ivory hafts, and with equal skill they put together stone and flint axes, flint-headed fish-spears and the like.   The war mace with pear-shaped head, as found also in Babylonia, is characteristic of the age.   Side by side with such weapons and implements they also produced and used weapons and implements of copper.   It is indeed the age of the slow transition from stone to copper.   Gold, silver and lead, while rare, were in use.

In the fruitful Nile valley we can not think of such a people as other than chiefly agricultural; and the fact that they emerge into historical times as agriculturalists,

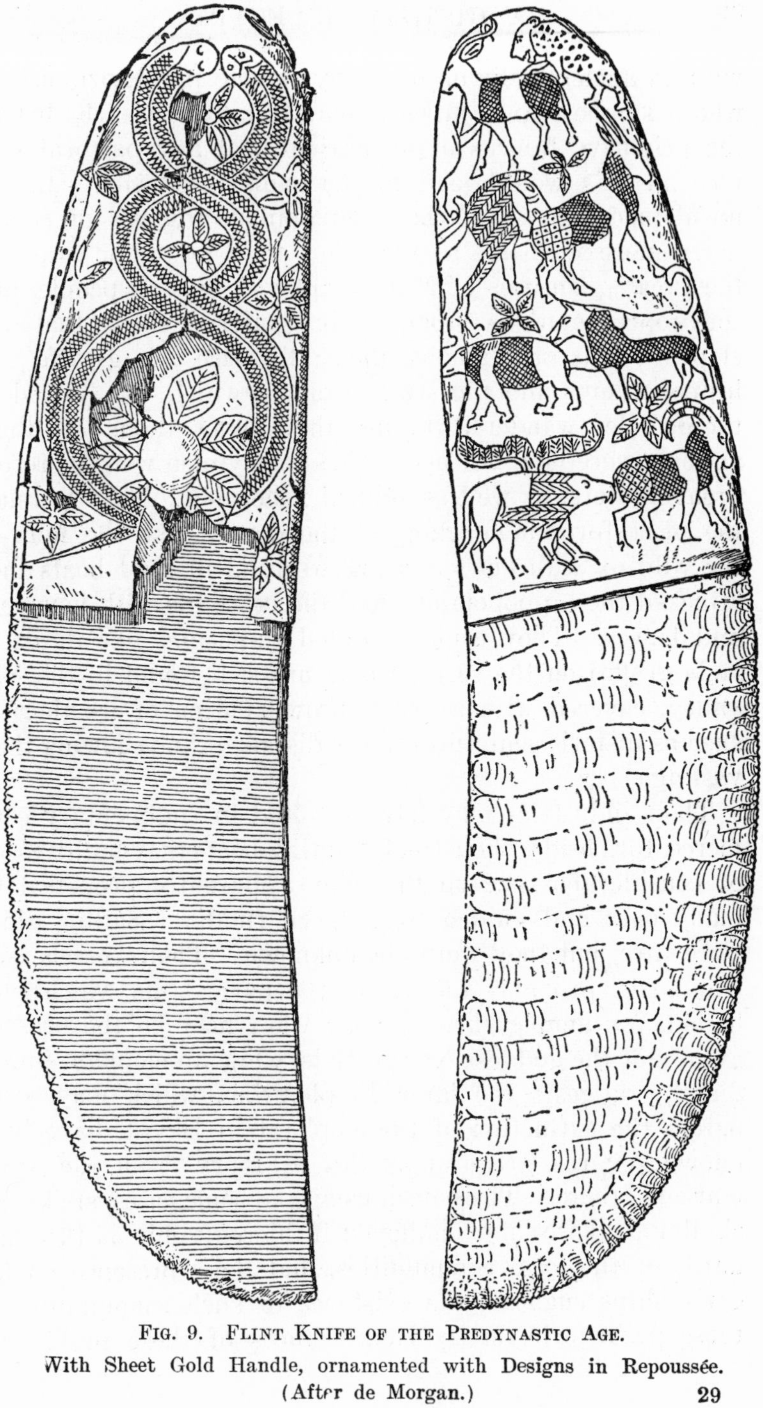

FIG. 9. FLINT KNIFE OF THE PREDYNASTIC AGE.
With Sheet Gold Handle, ornamented with Designs in Repoussée.
(After de Morgan.)

with an ancient religion of vastly remote prehistoric origin, whose symbols and outward manifestations clearly betray the primitive fancies of an agricultural and pastoral people—all this would lead to the same conclusion. In the unsubdued jungles of the Nile, animal life was of course much more plentiful at that time than now; for example, the great quantities of ivory employed by this people, and the representations upon their pottery, show that the elephant was still among them; likewise the giraffe, the hippopotamus and the strange okapi, which was deified as the god Set, wandered through the jungles, though all these animals were later extinct. These early men were therefore great hunters, as well as skillful fishermen. They pursued the most formidable game of the desert, like the lion, or the wild ox with bows and arrows; and in light boats they attacked the hippopotamus and the crocodile with harpoons and lances. They commemorated these and like deeds in rude graffiti on the rocks, which are still found in the Nile valley, covered with a heavy brown patina of weathering, such as historic sculptures never display; thus showing their vast age.

Their industries may have resulted in rudimentary commerce, for besides their small hunting-boats they built vessels of considerable size on the Nile, apparently propelled by many oars and guided by a large rudder. Sailing ships were rare, but they were not unknown. Their vessels bore standards, probably indicating the place from which each hailed, for among them appear what may be the crossed arrows of the goddess Neit of Sais, while an elephant immediately suggests the later Elephantine, which may, even before the extinction of the elephant in Egypt, have been known for the great quantities of ivory from the south marketed there. These ensigns are, in some cases, strikingly similar to those later employed in hieroglyphic as the standards of the local communities, and their presence on the early ships suggests the existence of such communities in those prehistoric days. Hence traces of these prehistoric

FIG. 10.—PREDYNASTIC POTTERY WITH INCISED DECORATION.

(Photograph by Petrie.)

FIG. 11.—PREDYNASTIC POTTERY WITH PAINTED DESIGNS OF BOATS, ANIMALS, MEN AND WOMEN.

(From de Morgan, *Origines*, I, pl. X.)

petty states should perhaps be recognized in the said administrative or feudal divisions of the country in historic times, the nomes, as the Greeks called them, to which we shall often have occasion to refer. If this be true, there were probably some twenty such states distributed along the river in Upper Egypt. However this may be, these people were already at a stage of civilization where considerable towns appear and city-states, as in Babylon, must have developed, each with its chief or dynast, its local god, worshipped in a crude sanctuary; and its market to which the tributary, outlying country was attracted. The long process by which such communities grew up can be only surmised from the analogy of similar developments elsewhere, but the small kingdoms and city-states, out of which the nation was ultimately consolidated, do not fall within the historic age, as in Babylon.

The gradual fusion which finally merged these petty states into two kingdoms: one in the Delta, and the other comprising the states of the valley above, is likewise a process of which we shall never know the course. Of its heroes and its conquerors, its wars and conquests, not an echo will ever reach us; nor is there the slightest indication of the length of time consumed by this process. It will hardly have been concluded, however, before 4000 B. C. Our knowledge of the two kingdoms which emerged at the end of this long prehistoric age, is but slightly more satisfactory. The Delta was, throughout the historic age, open to inroads of the Libyans who dwelt upon the west of it; and the constant influx of people from this source gave the western Delta a distinctly Libyan character which it preserved even down to the time of Herodotus. At the earliest moment when the monuments enable us to discern the conditions in the Delta, the Pharaoh is contending with the Libyan invaders, and the earlier kingdom of the North will therefore have been strongly Libyan, if indeed it did not owe its origin to this source. The temple at Sais, in the western Delta, the chief centre of Libyan influence in Egypt, bore the name "House of the King of Lower Egypt" (the Delta), and the emblem of Neit, its chief goddess was tattooed by the Libyans upon their arms. It may possibly therefore have been an early residence of a Libyan king of the Delta. Reliefs recently discovered in Sahure's pyramid-temple at Abusir show four Libyan chiefs wearing on their brows the royal uræus serpent of the Pharaohs, to whom it therefore descended from some such early Libyan king of the Delta. As its coat of arms or symbol the Northern Kingdom employed a tuft of papyrus plant, which grew so plentifully in its marshes as to be distinctive of it. The king himself was designated by a bee, and wore upon his head a red crown, both in colour and shape peculiar to his kingdom. All of these symbols are very common in later hieroglyphic. Red was the distinctive colour of the northern kingdom and its treasury was called the "Red House."

Unfortunately the Delta is so deeply overlaid with deposits of Nile mud, that the material remains of its earliest civilization are buried forever from our reach. That civilization was probably earlier and more advanced than that of the valley above. Already in the forty third century B. C. the men of the Delta had discovered the year of three hundred and sixty five days and they introduced a calendar year of this length beginning on the day when Sirius rose at sunrise, as determined in the latitude of the southern Delta, where these earliest astronomers lived, in 4241 B. C. It is the civilization of the Delta, therefore, which furnishes us with the earliest fixed date in the history of the world. The invention and introduction of this calendar is surprising evidence of the advanced culture of the age and locality to which it belongs. No nation of antiquity, from the earliest times through classic European history, was able to devise a calendar which should evade the inconvenience resulting from the fact that the lunar month and the solar year are incommensurable quantities, the lunar months being inconstant and also not evenly dividing the solar year. This earliest known calendar, with an amazingly practical insight into the needs to be subserved by a calendar, abandoned the lunar month altogether and substituted for it a conventional month of thirty days. Its devisers were thus the first people to perceive that a calendar must be an artificial device, entirely divorced from nature save in the acceptance of the day and the year. They therefore divided the year into twelve of these thirty day months, and a sacred period of five feast-days, intercalated at the end of the year. The year began on that day when Sirius first appeared on the eastern horizon at sunrise, which in our calendar was on the nineteenth of July.[1] But as this calendar year was in reality about a quarter of a day shorter than the solar year, it therefore gained a full day every four years, thus slowly revolving on the astronomical year, passing entirely around it once in fourteen hundred and sixty years, only to begin the revolution again. An astronomical event like the heliacal rising of Sirius, when dated in terms of the Egyptian calendar, may therefore be computed and dated within four years in terms of our reckoning, that is, in years B. C. This remarkable calendar, already in use at this remote age, is the one introduced into Rome by Julius Cæsar, as the most convenient calendar then known, and by the Romans it was bequeathed to us. It has thus been in use uninterruptedly over six thousand years. We owe it to the men of the Delta kingdom, who lived in the forty third century B. C.; and we should notice that it left their hands in much more convenient form, with its twelve thirty-day months, than after it had suffered irregular alteration in this respect at the hands of the Romans.

The kingdom of Upper Egypt was more distinctively Egyptian than that of the Delta. It had its capital at Nekheb, modern El Kab, and its standard or symbol was a lily plant, while another southern plant served as the ensign of the king, who was further distinguished by a tall white crown, white being the colour of the Southern Kingdom. Its treasury was therefore known as the "White House." There was a royal residence across the river from Nekheb, called Nekhen, the later Hieraconpolis, while corresponding

3   [1] Julian.

to it in the northern kingdom was a suburb of Buto, called
Pe.   Each capital had its patroness or protecting goddess:
Buto, the serpent-goddess, in the North; and in the South
the vulture-goddess, Nekhbet.   But at both capitals the
hawk-god Horus was worshipped as the distinctive patron
deity of both kings.   The people of the time believed in a
life hereafter, subject to wants of the same nature as those
of the present life.   Their cemeteries are widely distributed
along the margin of the desert in Upper Egypt, and of late
years thousands of interments have been excavated.   The
tomb is usually a flat bottomed oval or rectangular pit, in
which the body, doubled into the "contracted" or "embry-
onic" posture, lies on its
side (Fig. 12).   In the
earliest burials it is wrap-
ped in a skin, but later
also in woven fabric;
there is no trace of em-
balmment.   Beneath the
body is frequently a mat
of plaited rushes; it often
has in the hand or at the
breast a slate palette for
grinding face-paint, the
green malachite for which
lies near in a small bag.
The body is besides ac-
companied by other arti-
cles of toilet or of adorn-

FIG. 12.   A PREDYNASTIC GRAVE.

ment and is surrounded by jars of pottery or stone containing ash or organic matter, the remains of food, drink
and ointment for the deceased in the hereafter.   Not only
were the toilet and other bodily wants of the deceased thus
provided for, but he was also given his flint weapons or
bone tipped harpoons that he might replenish his larder
from the chase.   Clay models of objects which he might
need were also given him, especially boats.   The pits are

FIG. 13.—GOLD BAR BEARING MENE'S NAME.
(3400 B.C.)

Earliest known inscribed piece of jewelry.   Haskell
Museum.

FIG. 14.—ALABASTER VESSELS.

First Dynasty.   (Petrie, *Royal Tombs*.)

FIG. 15.—CHAIR LEGS, CARVED IVORY.

Early Dynasties.   Berlin Museum.

FIG. 16.—COPPER VESSELS.

First Dynasty.   (Petrie, *Royal Tombs*.)

sometimes roughly roofed over with branches, covered with
a heap of desert sand and gravel, forming rudimentary
tombs, and later they came to be lined with crude, sun-
dried brick. Sometimes a huge, roughly hemispherical bowl
of pottery was inverted over the body as it lay in the pit.
These burials furnish the sole contemporary material for
our study of the predynastic age. The gods of the hereafter were appealed to in prayers and magical formulæ,
which eventually took conventional and traditional form in
writing. A thousand years later in the dynastic age fragments of these mortuary texts are found in use in the pyramids of the Fifth and Sixth Dynasties. Pepi I, a king of
the Sixth Dynasty, in his rebuilding of the Denderah temple,
claimed to be reproducing a plan of a sanctuary of the predynastic kings on that spot. Temples of some sort they
therefore evidently had.

While they thus early possessed all the rudiments of
material culture, the people of this age developed a system
of writing also. The computations necessary for the discovery and use of the calendar show a use of writing in the
last centuries of the fifth millennium B. C. It is shown also
by the fact that nearly a thousand years later the scribes of
the Fifth Dynasty were able to copy a long list of the kings
of the North, and perhaps those of the South also (Fig. 29);
while the mortuary texts to which we have referred will not
have survived a thousand years without having been committed to writing in the same way. The hieroglyphs for the
Northern Kingdom, for its king, and for its treasury can not
have arisen at one stroke with the first king of the dynastic
age; but must have been in use long before the rise of the
First Dynasty; while the presence of a cursive linear hand
at the beginning of the dynasties is conclusive evidence that
the system was not then a recent innovation.

Of the deeds of these remote kings of the North and South,
who passed away before three thousand four hundred B. C.
we know nothing. Their tombs have never been discovered,
a fact which accounts for the lack of any written monuments

among the contemporary documents, all of which come from
tombs of the poorer classes, such as contain no writing even
in the dynastic age.　Seven names of the kings of the Delta,
like Seka, Khayu, or Thesh, alone of all the line have survived; but of the southern kingdom not even a royal name
has descended to us, unless it be that of the Scorpion, which,
occurring on some few remains of this early age, has been
conjectured to be that of one of the powerful chieftains of the
South.[1]　The scribes of the Fifth Dynasty who drew up this
list of kings, some eight hundred years after the line had
passed away, seem to have known only the royal names, and
were unable to, or at least did not record, any of their
achievements.[2]　As a class these kings of the North and
South were known to their posterity as the "worshippers of
Horus"; and as ages passed they became half mythic figures,
gradually to be endowed with semi-divine attributes, until
they were regarded as the demi-gods who succeeded the
divine dynasties, the great gods who had ruled Egypt in the
beginning.　Their original character as deceased kings, as
known to the earlier dynasties, led to their being considered
especially as a line of the divine Dead, who had ruled over
the land before the accession of human kings; and in the historical work of Manetho they appear simply as "the Dead."
Thus their real historical character was finally completely
sublimated, then to merge into unsubstantial myth, and the
ancient kings of the North and the South were worshipped
in the capitals where they had once ruled.

The next step in the long and slow evolution of national
unity was the union of the North and South.　The tradition
which was still current in the days of the Greeks in Egypt, to
the effect that the two kingdoms were united by a king
named Menes, is fully confirmed by the evidence of the early
monuments.　The figure of Menes, but a few years since
as vague and elusive as those of the "worshippers of Horus,"
who preceded him, has now been clothed with unmistakable

---

[1] Another possibly on the Palermo Stone and in the tomb of Methen; see
I, 166.　　　　　　　　　　[2] I, 90.

FIG. 17.—FOUR BRACELETS ON LADY'S ARM.

First Dynasty. Found at Abydos by Petrie. Cairo
Museum. (See p. 50.)

FIG. 18.—THE KING BREAKS GROUND FOR
A NEW CANAL.

Early Dynasties. (From Quibell, *Hieraconpolis*, I, 26c, 4.)

FIG. 19.—MAGNIFICENT CARVED CEREMONIAL PALETTE OF SLATE.

Dedicated by King Narmer (First Dynasty) in the temple of Hieraconpolis. See pp. 40 and 47.
(Quibell, *Hieraconpolis*, I, 29.)

reality, and he at last steps forth into history to head the long line of Pharaohs, who have yet to pass us in review. It must have been a skilful warrior and a vigourous administrator, who thus gathered the resources of the Southern Kingdom so well in hand that he was able to invade and conquer the Delta, and thus merge the two kingdoms into one nation, completing the long process of centralization which had been going on for many centuries. His native city was Thinis, an obscure place in the vicinity of Abydos, which was not near enough to the centre of his new kingdom to serve as his residence, and we can easily credit the narrative of Herodotus that he built a great dam, diverting the course of the Nile above the site of Memphis that he might gain room there for a city. This stronghold, perhaps not yet called Memphis, was probably known as the "White Wall," in reference of course to the White Kingdom, whose power it represented. If we may believe the tradition of Herodotus' time, it was from this place, situated so favourably on the border between the two kingdoms, that Menes probably governed the new nation which he had created. He carried his arms also southward against northern Nubia,[1] which then extended below the first cataract as far northward as the nome of Edfu. According to the tradition of Manetho, he was blessed with a long reign, and the memory of his great achievement was imperishable, as we have seen. He was buried in Upper Egypt, either at Abydos near his native Thinis, or some distance above it near the modern village of Negadeh, where a large brick tomb, probably his, still survives. In it and similar tombs of his successors at Abydos, written monuments of his reign have been found, and the reader may see in the accompanying illustration, even a piece of his royal adornments, bearing his name, which this ancient founder of the Egyptian state wore upon his person (Fig. 13).

The kings of this remote protodynastic age are no longer merely a series of names as but a few years since they still

[1] Newberry-Garstang, History, 20 (from unpublished evidence?).

were. As a *group* at least, we know much of their life and
its surroundings; although we shall never be able to discern
them as possessed of distinguishable personality. They
blend together without distinction as children of their age.
The outward insignia which all alike employed were now
accommodated to the united kingdom. The king's favourite
title was "Horus," by which he identified himself as the
successor of the great god, who had once ruled over the
kingdom. Everywhere, on royal documents, seals and the
like, appeared the Horus-hawk as the symbol of royalty. He
was mounted upon a rectangle representing the facade of a
building, probably the king's palace, within which was
written the king's official name. The other or personal
name of the ruler was preceded by the bee of the North
and the plant of the southern king, to indicate that he had
now absorbed both titles; while with these two symbols
there often appeared also Nekhbet, the vulture-goddess of
El Kab, the southern capital, side by side with Buto, the
serpent-goddess of the northern capital. On the sculptures
of the time, the protecting vulture hovers with outspread
wings over the head of the king, but as he felt himself
still as primarily king of Upper Egypt, it was not until
later that he wore the serpent of the North, the sacred
uræus upon his forehead. Similarly Set sometimes appears
with Horus, preceding the king's personal name, the two
gods thus representing the North and the South, dividing
the land between them in accordance with the myth which
we shall later have occasion to discuss. The monarch wore
the crown of either kingdom, and he is often spoken of as
the "double lord." Thus his dominion over a united Egypt
was constantly proclaimed. We see the king on ceremonious
occasions appearing in some state, preceded by four stan-
dard-bearers and accompanied by his chancellor, personal
attendants, or a scribe, and two fan-bearers. He wore the
white crown of Upper or the red crown of Lower Egypt, or
even a curious combination of the crowns of both kingdoms,
and a simple garment suspended by a strap over one

FIG. 20.—PORTRAIT HEAD OF KING
KHASEKHEM; FROM TWO DIF-
FERENT ANGLES.

Early Dynasties (Quibell, *Hierac.*, I, 39).

FIG. 21.—STATUE OF KING KHASEKHEM.
HEAD IN FIG. 20.

Early Dynasties (ibid.).   See translation, p. 47.

FIG. 22.—BRICK-LINED WOODEN FLOORED TOMB CHAMBER OF KING
ENEZIB. ·

(First Dynasty, Abydos.   From Petrie, *Royal Tombs*, I, 66. 1.)

shoulder, to which a lion's tail was appended behind. So dressed and so attended he conducted triumphant celebrations of his victories, or led the ceremonies at the opening of canals (Fig. 18), or the inauguration of public works. On the thirtieth anniversary of his appointment by his father as crown-prince to the heirship of the kingdom, the king celebrated a great jubilee called the "Feast of Sed," a word meaning "tail," and perhaps commemorating his assumption of the royal lion's tail at his appointment thirty years before. He was a mighty hunter, and recorded with pride an achievement like the slaying of a hippopotamus. His weapons were costly and elaborate as we shall see. His several palaces each bore a name, and the royal estate possessed gardens and vineyards, the latter being also named and carefully administered by officials who were responsible for the income therefrom. The furniture of such a palace, even in this remote age was magnificent and of fine artistic quality. Among it were vessels exquisitely wrought in some eighteen or twenty different varieties of stone, especially alabaster (Fig. 14); even in such refractory material as diorite, superb bowls were ground to translucent thinness, and jars of rock crystal were carved with matchless precision to represent natural objects. The pottery, on the other hand, perhaps because of the perfection of the stone vessels, is inferior to that of the predynastic age. The less substantial furniture has for the most part perished, but chests of ebony inlaid with ivory and stools with legs of ivory magnificently carved to represent bull's legs (Fig. 15), have survived in fragments. Glaze was now more thoroughly mastered than before, and incrustation with glazed plaques and ivory tablets was practiced. The coppersmith furnished the palace with finely wrought bowls, ewers and other vessels of copper (Fig. 16); while he materially aided in the perfection of stone vase-making by the production of excellent copper tools. The goldsmith combined with a high degree of technical skill also exquisite taste, and produced for the king's person and for the ladies of the royal household magnificent regalia in gold and precious stones (Figs. 13, 17),[1] involving the most delicate soldering of the metal, a process accomplished with a skill of which even a modern workman would not be ashamed.   While the products of the industrial craftsman had thus risen to a point of excellence, such that they claim a place as works of art, we find that the rude carvings and drawings of the predynastic people have now developed into reliefs and statues which clearly betray the professional artist.   The kings dedicated in the temples, especially in that of Horus at Hieraconpolis, ceremonial slate palettes, maces and vessels, bearing reliefs which display a sure and practiced hand (Fig. 19).[2]   The human and animal figures are done with surprising freedom and vigour, proclaiming an art long since conscious of itself and centuries removed from the naive efforts of a primitive people. By the time of the Third Dynasty the conventions of civilized life had laid a heavy hand upon this art; and although finish and power of faithful delineation had reached a level far surpassing that of the Hieraconpolis slates, the old freedom had disappeared.   In the astonishing statues of king Khasekhem at Hieraconpolis (Figs. 20–21), the rigid canons which ruled the art of the Old Kingdom are already clearly discernible.

The wreck of all this splendour, amid which these antique kings lived, has been rescued by Petrie with the most conscientious and arduous devotion, from their tombs at Abydos. These tombs are the result of a natural evolution from the pits in which the predynastic people buried their dead.   The

[1] The bracelets of Fig. 17 are of amethyst and turquoise mounted in gold. The uppermost has a rosette of gold, of exquisite workmanship.   The purpose of the gold bar (Fig. 13) is unknown.

[2] Fig. 19 shows both sides of the greatest of these palettes.   In the top row (left) the king, followed by his sandal bearer and preceded by four standard bearers and his vizier, inspects the decapitated bodies of his fallen enemies.   The middle row contains two fantastic animals of uncertain meaning, and in the bottom row, the king as a bull, breaches a walled city, and tramples down his enemy.   The other side (right) shows the king smiting a fallen foe, while as a Horus hawk he also leads captive the sign of the North, bearing a head with the rope in its mouth.   At the bottom are fallen foes.

pit has now been elaborated and enlarged and has become rectangular. It is brick lined and also frequently has a second lining of wood; while the surrounding jars of food and drink have developed into a series of small chambers surrounding the central room or pit, in which doubtless the body lay, although the tombs had been so often plundered and wasted that no body has ever been found in them (Figs. 22–25). The whole was roofed with heavy timbers and planking, probably surmounted by a heap of sand, and on the east front were set up two tall narrow stelæ bearing the king's name. Access to the central chamber was had by a brick stairway descending through one side (Fig. 23). The king's toilet furniture, a rich equipment of bowls, jars and vessels, metal vases and ewers, his personal ornaments, and all that was necessary for the maintenance of royal state in the hereafter were deposited with his body in this tomb; while the smaller surrounding chambers were filled with a liberal supply of food and wine in enormous pottery jars, sealed with huge cones of Nile mud mixed with straw, and impressed while soft with the name of the king, or of the estate or vineyard from which they came. The revenue in food and wine from certain of the king's estates was diverted and established as permanent income of the tomb to maintain for all time the table supply of the deceased king and of his household and adherents, whose tombs to the number of one or two hundred were grouped about his own. Thus he was surrounded in death by those who had been his companions in life; his women, his body-guard, and even the dwarf, whose dances had diverted his idle hours, all sleep beside their lord that he may continue in the hereafter the state with which he had been environed on earth. Thus early began the elaborate arrangements of the Egyptian upper classes for the proper maintenance of the deceased in the life hereafter.

This desire to create a permanent abiding place for the royal dead exerted a powerful influence in the development of the art of building. Already in the First Dynasty we find a granite floor in one of the royal tombs, that of Usephais, and toward the end of the Second Dynasty the surrounding brick chambers of king Khasekhemui's tomb enclose a chamber built of hewn limestone, the earliest stone masonry structure known in the history of man (Fig. 25). His predecessor, probably his father, had already built a stone temple which he recorded as a matter of note,[1] and Khasekhemui himself built a temple at Hieraconpolis, of which a granite doorpost has survived.

Such works of the skilled artificer and builder (for a number of royal architects were already attached to the court) indicate a well-ordered and highly organized state; but of its character little can be discerned from the scanty materials at our command. The king's chief assistant and minister in government seems to have been a chancellor, whom we have seen attending him on state occasions. The officials whom we later find as nobles with judicial functions, attached to the two royal residences of the North and South, Pe and Nekhen, already existed under these earliest dynasties, indicating an organized administration of judicial and juridical affairs. There was a body of fiscal officials, whose seals we find upon payments of naturalia to the royal tombs, impressed upon the clay jar-sealings; while a fragment of a scribe's accounts evidently belonging to such an administration, was found in the Abydos royal tombs. The endowment of these tombs with a regularly paid income clearly indicates an orderly and effective fiscal organization, of which several offices, like the "provision office," are mentioned on the seals. This department of the state was but a union of the two treasuries of the old kingdoms of the North and South, the "Red House" and the "White House"; hence we find among the seals in the royal tombs the "Vineyard of the Red House of the King's Estate." Evidently the union of the two kingdoms consisted only in the person of the king. The "Red House," however, soon disappeared, the double administration became one of termi-

[1] I, 134.

FIG. 23.—BRICK TOMB OF KING USEPHAIS.

First Dynasty, Abydos. (From Petrie, *Royal Tombs*, II, 56, 5.)

FIG. 24.—SEALED JARS OF FOOD AND DRINK.

Tomb of Merneit, First Dynasty, Abydos. (From Petrie, *Royal Tombs*, I, 38, 7.)

FIG. 25.—EARLIEST STONE STRUCTURE IN THE WORLD.

Limestone chamber, Tomb of King Khasekhemui, Second Dynasty, Abydos. (From Petrie, *Royal Tombs*, II, 57, 5.)

FIG. 26.—IVORY TABLET OF KING USEPHAIS.

(First Dynasty.) Smiting an "Easterner." MacGregor Collection.

FIG. 27. EBONY TABLET OF MENES, FIRST DYNASTY, ABYDOS, 3400 B. C.

One of the earliest known examples of hieroglyphics.   Top row: At the left the royal hawk of Menes; on the right a chapel with the symbols of the goddess Neit in the court, over which is a boat.   Second row: At the left the king holds a vessel marked "Electrum" (silver-gold alloy), and offers a libation "4 times"; on the right a bull is caught in an enclosure before a shrine bearing a phoenix.   Third row: The Nile with boats, towns, and islands.   Fourth row: Unintelligible archaic hieroglyphs.

FIG. 28. KING SEMERKHET. (FIRST DYNASTY.)   SMITES THE BEDUIN OF SINAI.

Relief on the rocks of the Wadi Maghara, Sinai, the earliest monument there, and the earliest known large sculpture. (From Weill, Sinai.)

(43)

nology and theory only, and the "White House" of the
southern kingdom survived throughout Egyptian history as
the sole treasury of the united kingdom. This history of
the early treasury is instructive as showing that the amalgamation of the administrative machinery of the two kingdoms
was a slow process which Menes was unable to complete.
In all probability the land all belonged to the estate of the
king, by whom it was entrusted to a noble class. There were
large estates conducted by these nobles, as in the period
which immediately followed; but on what terms they were
held we can not now determine. The people, with the possible exception of a free class of artificers and tradesmen,
will have been slaves on these estates. They lived also in
cities protected by heavy walls of sun-dried brick, and under
the command of a local governor. The chief cities of the
time were the two capitals, El Kab and Buto, with their
royal suburbs of Nekhen or Hieraconpolis, and Pe; the
"White Wall," the predecessor of Memphis; Thinis, the
native city of the first two dynasties; the neighbouring
Abydos; Heliopolis, Heracleopolis and Sais; while a number
of less importance appear in the Third Dynasty.

Every two years a "numbering" of the royal possessions
was made throughout the land by the officials of the treasury, and these "numberings" served as a partial basis for
the chronological reckoning. The years of a king's reign
were called, "Year of the First Numbering," "Year after
the First Numbering," "Year of the Second Numbering"
and so on. An earlier method was to name the year after
some important event which occurred in it, thus: "Year of
Smiting the Troglodytes," a method found also in early
Babylonia. But as the "numberings" finally became annual, they formed a more convenient basis for designating the
year, as habit seemed to have deterred the scribes from numbering the years themselves. Side by side with this official
year, there was doubtless a civil year which followed the seasons, and the lunar months continued to be the basis of temple payments and of many business transactions, although

it is not probable that a lunar year had ever existed. Such a system of government and administration as this of course could not operate without a method of writing, which we find in use both in elaborate hieroglyphics (Fig. 27) and in the rapid cursive hand of the accounting scribe. It already possessed not only phonetic signs representing a whole syllable or group of consonants but also the *alphabetic* signs, each of which stood for one consonant; true alphabetic *letters* having thus been discovered in Egypt two thousand five hundred years before their use by any other people. Had the Egyptian been less a creature of habit, he might have discarded his syllabic signs 3,500 years before Christ, and have written with an alphabet of twenty four letters. In the documents of these early dynasties the writing is in such an archaic form that many of the scanty fragments which we possess from this age are as yet unintelligible to us. Yet it was the medium of recording medical and religious texts, to which in later times a peculiar sanctity and effectiveness were attributed. The chief events of each year were also recorded in a few lines under its name, and a series of annals covering every year of a king's reign and showing to a day how long he reigned, was thus produced. A small fragment only of these annals has escaped destruction, the now famous Palermo Stone,[1] so called because it is at present in the museum of Palermo (Fig. 29).[2]

Already a state form of religion was developing, and it is this form alone of which we know anything; the religion of the people having left little or no trace. Even in the later dynasties we shall find little to say of the folk-religion, which was rarely a matter of permanent record. The royal temple of Menes's time was still a simple structure, being little more than a shrine or chapel of wood, with walls of

[1] I, 76–167.

[2] The front of the fragment is shown in Fig. 29. After the first row, each rectangle contains a year, and in the space over each row, was written the name of the king to whom the row of years belonged. The front contained the predynastic kings (top row) and dynasties one to three; the rest extending into the Fifth Dynasty was on the back.

plaited wattle (Fig. 27). There was an enclosed court before
it, containing a symbol or emblem of the god mounted on a
standard; and in front of the enclosure was a pair of poles,
perhaps the forerunners of the pair of stone obelisks which in
historic times were erected at the entrance of a temple. By
the second half of the Second Dynasty, however, stone temples were built,[1] as we have seen. The kings frequently
record in their annals[2] the draughting of a temple plan, or
their superintendence of the ceremonious inauguration of
the work when the ground was measured and broken. The
great gods were those familiar in later times, whom we shall
yet have occasion briefly to discuss; we notice particularly
Osiris and Set, Horus and Anubis, Thoth, Sokar, Min, and
Apis a form of Ptah; while among the goddesses, Hathor
and Neit are very prominent. Several of these, like Horus,
were evidently the patron gods of prehistoric kingdoms, preceding the kingdoms of the North and South, and thus going
back to a very distant age. Horus, as under the predynastic
kings, was the greatest god of the united kingdom, and occupied the position later held by Re. His temple at Hieraconpolis was especially favoured, and an old feast in his
honour, called the "Worship of Horus," celebrated every two
years, is regularly recorded in the royal annals (Fig. 29).[2]
The kings therefore continued without interruption the traditions of the "Worshippers of Horus," as the successors of
whom they regarded themselves. As long as the royal succession continued in the Thinite family the worship of Horus
was carefully observed; but with the ascendancy of the
Third Dynasty, a Memphite family, it gradually gave way
and was neglected. The priestly office was maintained of
course as in the Old Kingdom by laymen, who were divided,
as later, into four orders or phyles.

The more than four hundred years during which the first
two dynasties ruled must have been a period of constant
and vigourous growth. Of the seven kings of Menes's line,
who followed him during the first two centuries of that devel-

[1] I, 134.   [2] I, 91–167

FIG. 29.—THE PALERMO STONE.

Fragment of a copy of the annals of the earliest kings, from predynastic times to the middle of the Fifth Dynasty. when the copy was made.   See pp. 35, 36, 109.

opment, we can identify only two with certainty: Miebis and Usephais; but we have contemporary monuments from twelve of the eighteen kings who ruled during this period. The first difficulty which confronted them was the reconciliation of the Northern Kingdom and its complete fusion with the larger nation. We have seen how, in administration, the two kingdoms remained distinct, and hinted that the union was a merely personal bond. The kings on ascending the throne celebrated a feast called "Union of the Two Lands,"[1] by which the first year of each king's reign was characterized and named. This union, thus shown to be so fresh in their minds, could not at first be made effectual. The North rebelled again and again. King Narmer, who probably lived near the beginning of the dynastic age, was obliged to punish the rebellious Libyan nomes in the western Delta. He took captives to the number of "one hundred and twenty thousand," which deed must have involved the deportation of a whole district, whence he also plundered no less than "one million four hundred and twenty thousand small, and four hundred thousand large cattle." In the temple at Hieraconpolis he left a magnificent slate palette (Fig. 19) accompanied by a ceremonial mace-head, both of which bear scenes commemorating his victory. Later king Neterimu smote the northern cities of Shemre and "House of the North."[2] As late as the Third Dynasty a war with the North gave king Khasekhem occasion to name a year of his reign the "Year of Fighting and Smiting the North," a war in which he took captive "forty seven thousand two hundred and nine rebels." He likewise commemorated his victory in the temple of Horus at Hieraconpolis, dedicating there a great alabaster vase[3] bearing his name and that of the triumphant year, besides two remarkable statues[4] (Figs. 20–21) of himself, inscribed with the number of the captives. The later mythology attributed a lasting reconciliation of the two kingdoms to Osiris.[5]

[1] I, 140.   [2] I, 124.   [3] Hierac. I, pl. XXXVI–VIII.
[4] Ibid., pl. XXXIX–XLI.   [5] Louvre Stela C. 2.

While the severe methods employed against the North must have seriously crippled its economic prosperity, that of the nation as a whole probably continued to increase. The kings were constantly laying out new estates and building new palaces, temples and strongholds. Public works, like the opening of irrigation canals (Fig. 18) or the wall of Menes above Memphis, show their solicitude for the economic resources of the kingdom, as well as a skill in engineering and a high conception of government such as we can not but greatly admire in an age so remote. They were able also to undertake the earliest enterprises of which we know in foreign lands. King Semerkhet, early in the dynastic age, and probably during the First Dynasty, carried on mining operations in the copper regions of the Sinaitic peninsula, in the Wadi Maghâra. His expedition was exposed to the depredations of the wild tribes of Beduin, who already in this remote age, peopled those districts; and he recorded his punishment of them in a relief upon the rocks of the Wadi (Fig. 28).[1] Usephais, of the First Dynasty, must have conducted similar operations there; for he has left a memorial of his victory over the same tribes in a scene carved upon an ivory tablet, showing him striking down a native whom he has forced to the knees (Fig. 26). It is accompanied by the inscription: "First occurrence of smiting the Easterners." This designation of the event as the "*first* occurrence" would indicate that it was a customary thing for the kings of the time to chastise these barbarians, and that therefore he was expecting a "*second* occurrence," as a matter of course. A "smiting of the Troglodytes," the same people, recorded on the Palermo Stone[2] in the First Dynasty, doubtless falls in the reign of king Miebis. Indeed there are indications that the kings of this time maintained foreign relations with far remoter peoples. In their tombs have been found fragments of a peculiar, non-Egyptian pottery, closely resembling the

[1] Weill, Rev. Arch., 1903, II, p. 231; and Recueil des Inscr. Égypt. du Sinai, p. 96.   [2] I., 104.

ornamented Ægean ware produced by the island peoples
of the northern Mediterranean in pre-Mycenæan times. If
this pottery was placed in these tombs at the time of the
original burials, there were commercial relations between
Egypt and the northern Mediterranean peoples in the fourth
millennium before Christ. Besides the aggressive foreign
policy in the east, and this foreign connection in the north,
we find that an occasional campaign was necessary to
restrain the Libyans on the west. In the temple at Hieraconpolis Narmer left an ivory cylinder[1] commemorating his
victory over them, an event which is doubtless to be connected with the same king's chastisement of the Libyan
nomes in the western Delta, to which we have already
adverted. In the south at the first cataract, where, as late
as the Sixth Dynasty, the Troglodyte tribes of the neighbouring eastern desert made it dangerous to operate the quarries there, king Usephais of the First Dynasty was able to
maintain an expedition for the purpose of securing granite
to pave one of the chambers of his tomb at Abydos.

Thus this strong Thinite line gradually built up a vigourous nation of rich and prolific culture and consolidated its
power within and without. Scanty as are its surviving monuments, we see now gradually taking form the great state
which is soon to emerge as the Old Kingdom. These earliest
Pharaohs were buried, as we have seen, at Abydos or in the
vicinity, where nine of their tombs are known. A thousand
years after they had passed away, these tombs of the
founders of the kingdom were neglected and forgotten, and
as early as the twentieth century before Christ that of king
Zer was mistaken for the tomb of Osiris.[2] When found in
modern times it was buried under a mountain of potsherds,
the remains of votive offerings left there by centuries of
Osiris-worshippers. Its rightful occupants had long been
torn from their resting places, and their limbs, heavy with
gold and precious stones, had been wrenched from the
sockets to be carried away by greedy violators of the dead.

[1] Hierac. I, pl. XV, No. 7.   [2] I, 662.

4

It was on some such occasion that one of these thieves
secreted in a hole in the wall of the tomb the desiccated arm
of Zer's queen, still bearing under the close wrappings its
splendid regalia (Fig. 17). Perhaps slain in some brawl,
the robber, fortunately for us, never returned to recover his
plunder, and it was found there and brought to Petrie intact
by his well trained workmen in 1902.

BOOK II

THE OLD KINGDOM

CHAPTER IV

EARLY RELIGION

THERE is no force in the life of ancient man, the influence of which so pervades all his activities as does that of the religious faculty. Its fancies explain for him the world about him, its fears are his hourly master, its hopes his constant Mentor, its feasts are his calendar, and its outward usages are to a large extent the education and the motive toward the gradual evolution of art, literature and science. As among all other early peoples, it was in his surroundings that the Egyptian saw his gods. The trees and springs, the stones and hill-tops, the birds and beasts were creatures like himself, or possessed of strange and uncanny powers of which he was not master. Among this host of spirits animating everything around him, some were his friends, ready to be propitiated and to lend him their aid and protection; while others with craft and cunning lowered about his pathway, awaiting an opportunity to strike him with disease and pestilence, and there was no misfortune in the course of nature but found explanation in his mind as coming from one of these evil beings about him. Such spirits as these were local, each known only to the dwellers in a given locality, and the efforts to serve and propitiate them were of the humblest and most primitive character. Of such worship we know little or nothing in the Old Kingdom, but during the Empire we shall be able to gain fleeting glimpses into this naive and long forgotten world. But the Egyptian peopled not merely the local circle about him with such spirits; the sky above him and earth beneath his feet were equally before him for explanation. Long ages of confinement to his elongated valley, with its monotonous, even if sometimes grand scenery, had imposed a limited range upon his imagination; neither had he the qualities of mind which could be stirred by the world of nature to such exquisite fancies as those with which the natural beauties of Hellas inspired the imagination of the Greeks. In the remote ages of that earliest civilization, which we have briefly surveyed in the preceding chapter, the shepherds and plowmen of the Nile valley saw in the heavens a vast cow, which stood athwart the vault, with head in the west, the earth lying between fore and hind feet, while the belly of the animal, studded with stars, was the arch of heaven. The people of another locality however, fancied they could discern a colossal female figure standing with feet in the east and bending over the earth, till she supported herself upon her arms in the far west. To others the sky was a sea, supported high above the earth, with a pillar at each of its four corners. As these fancies gained more than local credence and came into contact with each other, they mingled in inextricable confusion. The sun was born every morning as a calf or as a child according to the explanation of the heavens as a cow or a woman, and he sailed across the sky in a celestial barque, to arrive in the west and descend as an old man tottering into the grave. Again the lofty flight of the hawk, which seemed a very comrade of the sun, led them to believe that the sun himself must be such a hawk, taking his daily flight across the heavens, and the sun-disk, with the outspread wings of the hawk, became the commonest symbol of their religion.

The earth, or as they knew it, their elongated valley, was to their primitive fancy, a man lying prone, upon whose back the vegetation grew, the beasts moved and man lived. If the sky was a sea upon which the sun and the heavenly lights sailed westward every day, there must then be a waterway by which they could return; so there was beneath the earth another Nile, flowing through a long dark passage with successive caverns, through which the celestial barque took its way at night, to appear again in the east at early morn-

FIG. 30.   THE CELESTIAL COW.

Various genii support her limbs, while in the middle, Shu, the god of the atmosphere upholds her.   Along her belly which forms the heavens, and bears the stars, moves the celestial barque of the sun-god, who wears the sun-disk on his head.

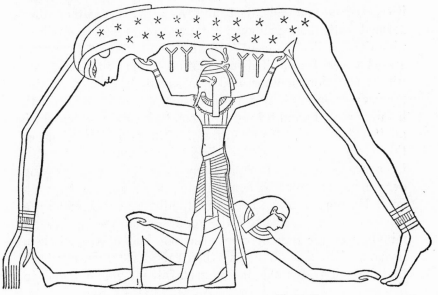

FIG. 31.   THE GODDESS OF THE HEAVENS.

Her body is studded with stars, Shu, the god of the air, supports her, while prone beneath her is the earth-god, Keb.

ing. This subterranean stream was connected with the Nile
at the first cataract, and thence issued from two caverns,
the waters of their life-giving river. It will be seen that
for the people among whom this myth arose, the world
ended at the first cataract; all that they knew beyond
was a vast sea. This was also connected with the Nile
in the south, and the river returned to it in the north,
for this sea, which they called the "Great Circle"[1] surrounded their earth. It is the idea inherited by the Greeks,
who called the sea Okeanos, or Ocean. In the beginning
only this ocean existed, upon which there then appeared
an egg, or as some said a flower, out of which issued the
sun-god. From himself he begat four children, Shu and
Tefnut, Keb and Nut. All these, with their father, lay
upon the ocean of chaos, when Shu and Tefnut, who represent the atmosphere, thrust themselves between Keb and
Nut. They planted their feet upon Keb and raised Nut on
high, so that Keb became the earth and Nut the heavens.
Keb and Nut were the father and mother of the four divinities, Osiris and Isis, Set and Nephthys; together they
formed with their primeval father the sun-god, a circle of
nine deities, the "ennead" of which each temple later possessed a local form. This correlation of the primitive divinities as father, mother and son, strongly influenced the
theology of later times until each temple possessed an artificially created triad, of purely secondary origin, upon which
an "ennead" was then built up. Other local versions of
this story of the world's origin also circulated. One of
them represents Re as ruling the earth for a time as king
over men, who plotted against him, so that he sent a goddess, Hathor, to slay them, but finally repented and by a
ruse succeeded in diverting the goddess from the total exter-
mination of the human race, after she had destroyed them
in part. The cow of the sky then raised Re upon her back
that he might forsake the ungrateful earth and dwell in
heaven.

[1] II, 661.

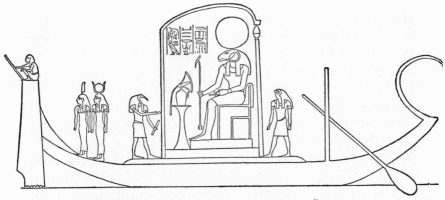

FIG. 32. THE CELESTIAL BARQUE OF THE SUN-GOD.

The ram-headed god, wearing the sun-disk is enthroned in a chapel; the ibis-headed Thoth, his vizier, stands in the royal presence and addresses him like an earthly king.

FIG. 33. RESTORATION OF A GROUP OF OLD KINGDOM "MASTABAS," OR MASONRY TOMBS. (After Perrot-Chipiez.)

The door of the chapel is visible in front, and on the roof may be seen the top of the shaft which descends through the superstructure to the subterranean sepulchre chamber containing the mummy.

Besides these gods of the earth, the air and the heavens, there were also those who had as their domain the nether world, the gloomy passage, along which the subterranean stream carried the sun from west to east. Here, according to a very early belief, dwelt the dead, whose king was Osiris. He had succeeded the sun-god as king on earth, aided in his government by his faithful sister-wife, Isis. A benefactor of men, and beloved as a righteous ruler, he was nevertheless craftily misled and slain by his brother Set. When, after great tribulation, Isis had gained possession of her lord's body, she was assisted in preparing it for burial by one of the old gods of the nether world, Anubis, the jackal-god, who thereafter became the god of embalmment. So powerful were the charms now uttered by Isis over the body of her dead husband that it was reanimated, and regained the use of its limbs; and although it was impos-sible for the departed god to resume his earthly life, he passed down in triumph as a living king, to become lord of the nether world. Isis later gave birth to a son, Horus, whom she secretly reared among the marshy fastnesses of the Delta as the avenger of his father. Grown to manhood, the youth pursued Set and in the ensuing awful battle, which raged from end to end of the land, both were fear-fully mutilated. But Set was defeated, and Horus tri-umphantly assumed the earthly throne of his father. There-upon Set entered the tribunal of the gods, and charged that the birth of Horus was not without stain, and that his claim to the throne was not valid. Defended by Thoth, the god of letters, Horus was vindicated and declared "true in speech," or "triumphant." According to another version it was Osiris himself who was thus vindicated.

Not all the gods who appear in these tales and fancies became more than mythological figures. Many of them con-tinued merely in this role, without temple or form of wor-ship; they had but a folk-lore or finally a theological exist-ence. Others became the great gods of Egypt. In a land where a clear sky prevailed and rain was rarely seen, the incessant splendour of the sun was an insistent fact, which gave him the highest place in the thought and daily life of the people. His worship was almost universal, but the chief centre of his cult was at On, the Delta city, which the Greeks called Heliopolis. Here he was known as Re, which was the solar orb itself; or as Atum, the name of the decrepit sun, as an old man tottering down the west; again his name Khepri, written with a beetle in hieroglyphic, designated him in the youthful vigour of his rising. He had two barques with which he sailed across the heavens, one for the morning and the other for the afternoon, and when in this barque he entered the nether world to return to the east he brought light and joy to its disembodied denizens. The symbol of his presence in the temple at Heliopolis was an obelisk, while at Edfu, on the upper river, which was also an old centre of his worship, he appeared as a hawk, under the name Horus.

The Moon as the measurer of time furnished the god of reckoning, of letters, and of wisdom, whose chief centre was at Shmûn, or Hermopolis, as the Greeks who identified him with Hermes, called the place. He was identified with the ibis. The Sky, whom we have seen as Nut, was worshipped throughout the land, although Nut herself continued to play only a mythological role. The sky-goddess became the type of woman and of woman's love and joy. At the ancient shrine of Dendereh she was the cow-goddess, Hathor; at Sais she was the joyous Neit; at Bubastis, in the form of a cat, she appeared as Bast; while at Memphis her genial aspects disappeared and she became a lionness, the goddess of storm and terror. The myth of Osiris, so human in its incidents and all its characteristics, rapidly induced the wide propagation of his worship, and although Isis still remained chiefly a figure in the myth, she became the type of wife and mother, upon which the people loved to dwell. Horus also, although he really belonged originally to the sun-myth and had nothing to do with Osiris, was for the people the embodiment of the qualities of a good son, and in him they constantly saw the ultimate triumph of the just cause. The immense influence of the Osiris-worship on the life of Egypt we shall have occasion to notice further in discussing mortuary beliefs. The original home of Osiris was at Dedu, called by the Greeks Busiris, in the Delta; but Abydos, in Upper Egypt, early gained a reputation of peculiar sanctity, because the head of Osiris was buried there. He always appeared as a closely swathed figure, enthroned as a Pharaoh or merely a curious pillar, a fetish surviving from his prehistoric worship. Into the circle of nature-divinities it is impossible to bring Ptah of Memphis, who was one of the early and great gods of Egypt. He was the patron of the artisan, the artificer and artist, and his High Priest was always the chief artist of the court. Such were the chief gods of Egypt, although many another important deity presided in this or that temple, whom it would be impossible for us to notice here, even with a word.

The external manifestations and the symbols with which the Egyptian clothed these gods are of the simplest character and they show the primitive simplicity of the age in which these deities arose. They bear a staff like a Beduin native of to-day, or the goddesses wield a reed-stem; their diadems are of woven reeds or a pair of ostrich feathers, or the horns of a sheep. In such an age, the people frequently saw the manifestations of their gods in the numerous animals with which they were surrounded, and the veneration of these sacred beasts survived into an age of high civilization, when we should have expected it to disappear. But the animal-worship, which we usually associate with ancient Egypt, as a cult, is a late product, brought forward in the decline of the nation at the close of its history. In the periods with which we shall have to deal, it was unknown; the hawk, for example, was the sacred animal of the sun-god, and as such a living hawk might have a place in the temple, where he was fed and kindly treated, as any such pet might be; but he was not worshipped, nor was he the object of an elaborate ritual as later.[1]

[1] Erman, Handbuch, p. 25.

In their elongated valley the local beliefs of the earliest Egyptians could not but differ greatly among themselves, and although for example there were many centres of sun-worship, each city possessing a sun-temple regarded the sun as its particular god, to the exclusion of all the rest; just as many a town of Italy at the present day would not for a moment identify its particular Madonna with the virgin of any other town. As commercial and administrative intercourse were increased by political union, these mutually contradictory and incompatible beliefs could not longer remain local. They fused into a complex of tangled myth, of which we have already offered some examples and shall yet see more. Neither did the theologizing priesthoods ever reduce this mass of belief into a coherent system; it remained as accident and circumstance brought it together, a chaos of contradictions. Another result of national life was, that as soon as a city gained political supremacy its gods rose with it to the dominant place among the innumerable gods of the land.

The temples in which the earliest Egyptian worshipped we have already had occasion to notice. He conceived the place as the dwelling of his god, and hence its arrangement probably conformed with that of a private house of the predynastic Egyptian. We have seen how the gradual evolution of a nation has left the prehistoric temple of woven wattle far behind, putting in its place at last a structure of stone in which doubtless the main features of the primitive arrangement survived. It was still the house of the god, although the Egyptian himself may have long since forgotten its origin. Behind a forecourt open to the sky rose a colonnaded hall, beyond which was a series of small chambers containing the furniture and implements for the temple services. Of the architecture and decoration of the building we shall later have occasion to speak further (pp. 106 f.). The centre of the chambers in the rear was occupied by a small room, the holy of holies, in which stood a shrine hewn from one block of granite. It contained the image of the god, a small figure of wood from one and a half to six feet high, elaborately adorned and splendid with gold, silver and costly stones. The service of the divinity who dwelt here consisted simply in furnishing him with those things which formed the necessities and luxuries of an Egyptian of wealth and rank at that time: plentiful food and drink, fine clothing, music and the dance. The source of these offerings was the income from an endowment of lands established by the throne, as well as various contributions from the royal revenues in grain, wine, oil, honey and the like.[1] These contributions to the comfort and happiness of the lord of the temple, while probably originally offered without ceremony, gradually became the occasion of an elaborate ritual which was essentially alike in all temples. Outside in the forecourt was the great altar, where the people gathered on feast days, when they were permitted to share the generous food offerings, which ordinarily were eaten by the priests and servants of the temple, after they had been presented to the god. These feasts, besides those marking times and seasons, were frequently commemorations of some important event in the story or myth of the god, and on such occasions the priests brought forth the image in a portable shrine, having the form of a small Nile boat.

The earliest priesthood was but an incident in the duties of the local noble, who was the head of the priests in the community; but the exalted position of the Pharaoh as the nation developed, made him the sole official servant of the gods, and there arose at the beginning of the nation's history a state form of religion, in which the Pharaoh played the supreme role. In theory, therefore, it was he alone who worshipped the gods; in fact, however, he was of necessity represented in each of the many temples of the land by a high priest, by whom all offerings were presented "for the sake of the life, prosperity and health" of the Pharaoh. Some of these high priesthoods were of very ancient origin: particularly that of Heliopolis, whose incumbent was called

[1] I, 153–167; 213.

"Great Seer"; while he of Ptah at Memphis was called "Great Chief of Artificers." Both positions demanded two incumbents at once and were usually held by men of high rank. The incumbents of the other high priesthoods of later origin all bore the simple title of "overseer or chief of priests." It was the duty of this man not merely to conduct the service and ritual of the sanctuary, but also to administer its endowment of lands, from the income of which it lived, while in time of war he might even command the temple contingent. He was assisted by a body of priests, whose sacerdotal service was with few exceptions merely incidental to their worldly occupations. They were laymen, who from time to time served for a stated period in the temple; thus in spite of the fiction of the Pharaoh as the sole worshipper of the god, the laymen were represented in its service. In the same way the women of the time were commonly priestesses of Neit or Hathor; their service consisted in nothing more than dancing and jingling a sistrum before the god on festive occasions. The state fiction had therefore not quite suppressed the participation of the individual in the service of the temple. In harmony with the conception of the temple as the god's dwelling the most frequent title of the priest was "servant of the god."

Parallel with this development of a state religion, with its elaborate equipment of temple, endowment, priesthood and ritual, the evolution of the provision for the dead had kept even pace. In no land, ancient or modern, has there ever been such attention to the equipment of the dead for their eternal sojourn in the hereafter. The beliefs which finally led the Egyptian to the devotion of so much of his wealth and time, his skill and energy to the erection and equipment of the "eternal house" are the oldest conceptions of a real life hereafter of which we know. He believed that the body was animated by a vital force, which he pictured as a counterpart of the body, which came into the world with it, passed through life in its company, and accompanied it into the next world. This he called a "ka," and it is often spoken of in modern treatises as a "double," though this designation describes the form of the ka as represented on the monuments, rather than its real nature. Besides the ka every person possessed also a soul, which he conceived in the form of a bird flitting about among the trees; though it might assume the outward semblance of a flower, the lotus, a serpent, a crocodile sojourning in the river, or of many other things. Even further elements of personality seemed to them present, like the shadow possessed by every one, but the relations of all these to each other were very vague and confused in the mind of the Egyptian; just as the average Christian of a generation ago, who accepted the doctrine of body, soul and spirit, would have been unable to give any lucid explanation of their interrelations. Like the varying explanations of the heavens and the world there were many once probably local notions of the place to which the dead journeyed; but these beliefs, although mutually irreconcilable, continued to enjoy general acceptance, and no one was troubled by their incompatibility, even if it ever occurred to them. There was a world of the dead in the west, where the sun-god descended into his grave every night, so that "westerners" was for the Egyptian a term for the departed; and wherever possible the cemetery was located on the margin of the western desert. There was also the nether world where the departed lived awaiting the return of the solar barque every evening, that they might bathe in the radiance of the sun-god, and seizing the bow-rope of his craft draw him with rejoicing through the long caverns of their dark abode. In the splendour of the nightly heavens the Nile-dweller also saw the host of those who had preceded him; thither they had flown as birds, rising above all foes of the air, and received by Re as the companions of his celestial barque, they now swept across the sky as eternal stars. Still more commonly the Egyptian told of a field in the northeast of the heavens, which he called the "field of food," or the "field of Yaru," the lentil field, where the grain grew taller than any ever seen on the banks of the Nile, and the departed dwelt in security and plenty. Besides the bounty of the soil he received too, from the earthly offerings presented in the temple of his god: bread and beer and fine linen. It was not every one who succeeded in reaching this field of the blessed; for it was surrounded by water. Sometimes the departed might induce the hawk or the ibis to bear him across on their pinions; again friendly spirits, the four sons of Horus, brought him a craft upon which he might float over; sometimes the sungod bore him across in his barque; but by far the majority depended upon the services of a ferryman called ''Turnface'' or ''Look-behind,'' because his face was ever turned to the rear in poling his craft. He will not receive all into his boat, but only him of whom it was said, ''there is no evil which he has done,'' or ''the just who hath no boat,'' or him who is ''righteous before heaven and earth and before the isle,''[1] where lies the happy field to which they go. These are the earliest traces in the history of man of an ethical test at the close of life, making the life hereafter dependent upon the character of the life lived on earth. It was at this time, however, chiefly ceremonial rather than moral purity which secured the waiting soul passage across the waters. Yet a noble of the Fifth Dynasty desires it known that he has never defrauded ancient tombs, and says in his mastaba, ''I have made this tomb as a just possession, and never have I taken a thing belonging to any person. . . . Never have I done aught of violence toward any person.''[2] Another, perhaps a private citizen, says, ''Never was I beaten in the presence of any official since my birth; never did I take the property of any man by violence; I was doer of that which pleased all men.''[3] Nor was it always negative virtues which they claimed; a noble of Upper Egypt at the close of the Fifth Dynasty says, ''I gave bread to the hungry of the Cerastes-Mountain (the district he governed);

---

[1] Pyramid of Pepi I, 400; Mernere 570, Erman, Zeitschrift für Aegyptische Sprache, XXXI, 76–77.

[2] I, 252.   [3] I, 279.

I clothed him who was naked therein. . . . I never oppressed
one in possession of his property, so that he complained of
me because of it to the god of my city; never was there
one fearing because of one stronger than he, so that he complained because of it to the god."[1]

Into these early beliefs, with which Osiris originally had
nothing to do, the myth which told of his death and departure into the nether world, now entered, to become the
dominating element in Egyptian mortuary belief. He had
become the "first of those in the west" and "king of the
glorified"; every soul that suffered the fate of Osiris might
also experience his restoration to life; might indeed become
an Osiris. So they said: "As Osiris lives, so shall he also
live; as Osiris died not, so shall he also not die; as Osiris
perished not, so shall he also not perish."[2] As the limbs
of Osiris were again imbued with life, so shall the gods
raise him up and put him among the gods. "The door of
heaven is open to thee, and the great bolts are drawn back
for thee. Thou findest Re standing there; he takes thee by
the hand and leads thee into the holy place of heaven, and
sets thee upon the throne of Osiris, upon this thy brazen
throne, that thou mayest reign over the glorified. . . .The
servants of the god stand behind thee and the nobles of
the god stand before thee and cry, 'Come thou god! Come
thou god! Come thou possessor of the Osiris throne!' Isis
speaks with thee, and Nephthys salutes thee. The glorified
come to thee and bow down, that they may kiss the earth
at thy feet. So art thou protected and equipped as a god,
endowed with the form of Osiris, upon the throne of the
'First of the Westerners.' Thou doest what he did among
the glorified and imperishable. . . . Thou makest thy house
to flourish after thee, and protectest thy children from sorrow."[3] Believing thus that all might share the goodly destiny of Osiris, or even become Osiris himself, they contemplated death without dismay, for they said of the dead,

[1] I, 281.　　　　　　　　　　　　　[2] Pyramids, Chap. 15.
[3] Erman, Handbuch, pp. 96–99.

"They depart not as those who are dead, but they depart as those who are living."[1]   Here there entered, as a salutary influence also the incident of the triumphant vindication of Osiris when accused; for there is a hint of a similar justification for *all*, which, as we shall yet see, was the most fruitful germ in Egyptian religion.   The myth of Osiris thus introduced an ultimately powerful ethical element, which, while not altogether lacking before, needed the personal factor supplied by the Osiris myth to give it vital force.   Thus several nobles of the Fifth and Sixth Dynasties threaten those who in the future would appropriate their tombs, that "judgment shall be had with them for it by the great god";[2] and another says that he never slandered others, for "I desired that it might be well with me in the great god's presence."[3]

These views are chiefly found in the oldest mortuary literature of Egypt which we possess, a series of texts supposed to be effective in securing for the deceased the enjoyment of a happy life, and especially the blessed future enjoyed by Osiris. They were engraved upon the passages of the Fifth and Sixth Dynasty pyramids, where they have been preserved in large numbers, and it is largely from them that the above sketch of the early Egyptian's notions of the hereafter has been taken.[4]   From the place in which they are found, they are usually called the "Pyramid Texts." Many of these texts grew up in the predynastic age and some have therefore been altered to accommodate them to the Osiris faith, with which they originally had no connection—a process which has of course resulted in inextricable confusion of originally differing mortuary beliefs.

So insistent a belief or set of beliefs in a life beyond the grave necessarily brought with it a mass of mortuary usages with which in the earliest period of Egypt's career we have already gained some acquaintance.   It is evident that however persistently the Egyptian transferred the life of the departed to some distant region, far from the tomb where

[1] Ibid.
[3] I, 331.
[2] I, 253, 330, 338, 357.
[4] See Erman, Handbuch.

the body lay, he was never able to detach the future life entirely from the body. It is evident that he could conceive of no survival of the dead without it. Gradually he had developed a more and more pretentious and a safer repository for his dead, until, as we have seen, it had become a vast and massive structure of stone. In all the world no such colossal tombs as the pyramids are to be found; while the tombs of the nobles grouped about have in the Old Kingdom become immense masonry structures, which but a few centuries before, a king would have been proud to own. Such a tomb as that of Pepi I's vizier in the Sixth Dynasty contained no less than thirty one rooms. The superstructure of such

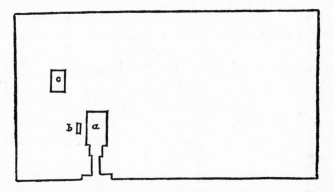

FIG. 34. GROUND PLAN OF A "MASTABA" OR MASONRY TOMB.

a is the chapel; *b* is the "surdab" (cellar), the secret chamber containing the portrait statue; *c* is the shaft leading down to the subterranean chamber containing the mummy. For the elevation see Fig. 33.

a tomb was a massive rectangular oblong of masonry, the sides of which slanted inward at an angle of roughly seventy five degrees. It was, with the exception of its room or rooms, solid throughout, reminding the modern natives of the "mastaba," the terrace, area or bench on which they squat before their houses and shops. Such a tomb is therefore commonly termed a "mastaba." The simplest of such mastabas has no rooms within, and only a false door in the east side, by which the dead, dwelling in the west, that is, behind this door, might enter again the world of the living.

This false door was finally elaborated into a kind of chapel-chamber in the mass of the masonry, the false door now being placed in the west wall of the chamber. The inner walls of this chapel bore scenes carved in relief, depicting the servants and slaves of the deceased at their daily tasks on his estate (Figs. 44, 56); they plowed and sowed and reaped; they pastured the herds and slaughtered them for the table, they wrought stone vessels or they built Nile boats —in fact they were shown in field and workshop producing all those things which were necessary for their lord's welfare in the hereafter, while here and there his towering figure appeared superintending and inspecting their labours as he had done before he "departed into the West." It is these scenes which are the source of our knowledge of the life and customs of the time. Far below the massive mastaba was a burial chamber in the native rock reached by a shaft which passed down through the superstructure of masonry. On the day of burial the body, now duly embalmed, was subjected to elaborate ceremonies embodying occurrences in the history of Osiris. It was especially necessary by potent charms to open the mouth and ears of the deceased that he might speak and hear in the hereafter. The mummy was then lowered down the shaft and laid as of old upon its left side in a fine rectangular cedar coffin, which again was deposited in a massive sarcophagus of granite or limestone. Food and drink were left with it, besides some few toilet articles, a magic wand and a number of amulets for protection against the enemies of the dead, especially serpents. The number of serpent-charms in the Pyramid Texts, intended to render these foes harmless, is very large. The deep shaft leading to the burial chamber was then filled to the top with sand and gravel, and the friends of the dead now left him to the life in the hereafter, which we have pictured.

Yet their duty toward their departed friend had not yet lapsed. In a tiny chamber beside the chapel they masoned up a portrait statue of the deceased, sometimes cutting small channels, which connected the two rooms, the chapel and

the statue-chamber, or "serdab," as the modern natives
call it. As the statue was an exact reproduction of the
deceased's body, his ka might therefore attach itself to this
counterfeit, and through the connecting channels enjoy the
food and drink placed for it in the chapel. The offerings to
the dead, originally only a small loaf in a bowl, placed by
a son, or wife, or brother on a reed mat at the grave, have
now become as elaborate as the daily cuisine once enjoyed
by the lord of the tomb before he forsook his earthly house.
But this labour of love, or sometimes of fear, has now
devolved upon a large personnel, attached to the tomb, some
of whom, as its priests, constantly maintained its ritual.
Very specific contracts[1] were made with these persons,
requiting them for their services with a fixed income drawn
from endowments legally established and recorded for this
purpose by the noble himself, in anticipation of his death.
The tomb of Prince Nekure, son of king Khafre of the
Fourth Dynasty, was endowed with the revenues from
twelve towns.[2] A palace-steward in Userkaf's time appointed eight mortuary priests for the service of his tomb;[3]
and a nomarch of Upper Egypt endowed his tomb with
income from eleven villages and settlements.[4] The income
of a mortuary priest in such a tomb was in one instance
sufficient to enable him to endow the tomb of his daughter
in the same way.[5] Such endowments and the service thus
maintained were intended to be permanent, but in the course
of a few generations the accumulated burden was intolerable, and ancestors of a century before, with rare exceptions, were necessarily neglected in order to maintain those
whose claims were stronger and more recent. Or, as in the
temples the offerings after having been presented to the
gods were employed in the maintenance of the people
attached to the temple, so now a favourite noble of the king
might be rewarded by the diversion to his tomb of a certain
portion of the plentiful income which had already been pre-

[1] I, 200–209, 231–5.   [2] I, 191.
[3] I, 226–7.   [4] I, 379.
[5] Erman, Handbuch, p. 123.

sented at the tomb of some royal ancestor or other relative
of the king's house.[1] It had now become so customary for
the king to assist his favourite lords and nobles in this way[2]
that we find a frequent mortuary prayer beginning "An
offering which the king gives," and as long as the number
of those whose tombs were thus maintained was limited to
the noble and official circle around the king, such royal
largesses to the dead were quite possible. But in later
times, when the mortuary practices of the noble class had
spread to the masses, they also employed the same prayer,
although it is impossible that the royal bounty could have
been so extended. Thus this prayer is to-day the most frequent formula to be found on the Egyptian monuments,
occurring thousands of times on the tombs or tomb-stones
of people who had no prospect of enjoying such royal distinction; and in the same tomb it is always repeated over
and over again. In the same way the king also assisted his
favourites in the *erection* of their tombs, and the noble often
records with pride that the king presented him with the
false door, or the sarcophagus, or detailed a body of royal
artificers to assist in the construction of his tomb.[3]

If the tomb of the noble had now become an endowed
institution, we have seen that that of the king was already
such in the First Dynasty. In the Third Dynasty, at least,
the Pharaoh was not satisfied with *one* tomb, but in his
double capacity as king of the Two Lands he erected *two*,
just as the palace was double for the same reason. We find
the monarch's tomb now far surpassing that of the noble
in its extent and magnificence. The mortuary service of
the Pharaoh's lords might be conducted in the chapel in
the east side of the mastaba; but that of the Pharaoh himself
required a separate building, a splendid mortuary temple
on the east side of the pyramid. A richly endowed priesthood was here employed to maintain its ritual and to fur-

[1] I, 173, l. 5, 241.
[2] I, 204, 207, 209, 213–227, 242–249, 274–7, 370.
[3] I, 210–212, 237–40, 242–9, 274–7, 308.

FIG. 35. RESTORATION OF THE PYRAMIDS OF ABUSIR AND CONNECTED BUILD-
INGS. (After Borchardt.)

Close to each pyramid on the hither side is the pyramid-temple. From
two of these, covered masonry causeways lead down to the edge of the desert
plateau, where each terminates in a monumental gate of massive masonry
(see Fig. 69). Before the gate is a landing platform with steps leading
down to the water, where boats may land during the inundation.

nish the food, drink and clothing of the departed king. Its
large personnel demanded many outbuildings, and the whole
group of pyramid, temple and accessories was surrounded
by a wall. All this was on the edge of the plateau overlooking the valley, in which, below the pyramid, there now grew
up a walled town. Leading up from the town to the pyramid
enclosure was a massive causeway of stone which terminated
at the lower or townward end in a large and stately structure of granite or limestone sometimes with floors of alabaster, the whole forming a superb portal, a worthy entrance
to so impressive a tomb (Figs. 35, 69). Through this portal
passed the white-robed procession on feast days, moving from
the town up the long white causeway to the temple, above

which rose the mighty mass of the pyramid. The populace in the city below probably never gained access to the pyramid-enclosure. Over the town wall, through the waving green of the palms, they saw the gleaming white pyramid, where lay the god who had once ruled over them; while beside it rose slowly year by year another mountain of stone, gradually assuming pyramid form, and there, would some time rest his divine son, of whose splendour they had now and then on feast days caught a fleeting glimpse. While the proper burial of the Pharaoh and his nobles had now become a matter seriously affecting the economic conditions of the state, such elaborate mortuary equipment was still confined to a small class, and the common people continued to lay away their dead without any attempt at embalmment in the pit of their prehistoric ancestors on the margin of the western desert.

CHAPTER V

THE OLD KINGDOM: GOVERNMENT AND SOCIETY, INDUSTRY AND ART

THE origins of the kingship and of the customs which made it so peculiar in ancient Egypt, as the reader has already observed, are rooted in a past so remote that we can discern but faint traces of the evolution of the office. With the consolidation under Menes it was already an institution of great age, and over four centuries of development which then followed, had at the dawn of the Old Kingdom already brought to the office a prestige and an exalted power, demanding the deepest reverence of the subject whether high or low. Indeed the king was now officially a god, and one of the most frequent titles was the "Good God"; such was the respect due him that there was reluctance to refer to him by name. The courtier might designate him impersonally as "one," and "to let one know" becomes the official phrase for "report to the king." His government and ultimately the monarch personally were called the "Great House," in Egyptian Per-o, a term which has descended to us through the Hebrews as "Pharaoh." There was also a number of other circumlocutions, which the fastidious courtier might employ in referring to his divine lord. When he died he was received into the circle of the gods, to be worshipped like them ever after in the temple before the vast pyramid in which he slept.

Court customs had gradually developed into an elaborate official etiquette, for the punctilious observance of which, already in this distant age, a host of gorgeous marshals and court chamberlains were in constant attendance at the palace. There had thus grown up a palace life, not unlike that of

74

modern times in the East, a life into which we gain obscure glimpses in the numerous titles borne by the court lords of the time. With ostentatious pride they arrayed these titles on the walls of their tombs, mingled with sounding predicates indicating their high duties and exalted privileges in the circle surrounding the king. There were many ranks, and the privileges of each, with all possible niceties of precedence, were strictly observed and enforced by the court marshals at all state levees and royal audiences. Every need of the royal person was represented by some palace lord, whose duty it was to supply it, and who bore a corresponding title, like the court physician or the leader of the court music. Although the royal toilet was comparatively simple, yet a small army of wig-makers, sandal-makers, perfumers, launderers, bleachers and guardians of the royal wardrobe, filled the king's chambers. They record their titles upon their tomb-stones with visible satisfaction. Thus to take an example at random, one of them calls himself "Overseer of the cosmetic box . . . doing in the matter of cosmetic art to the satisfaction of his lord; overseer of the cosmetic pencil, sandal-bearer of the king, doing in the matter of the king's sandals to the satisfaction of his lord."[1] The king's favourite wife became the official queen, whose eldest son usually received the appointment as crown prince to succeed his father. But as at all oriental courts, there was also a royal harem with numerous inmates. Many sons usually surrounded the monarch, and the vast revenues of the palace were liberally distributed among them. A son of king Khafre in the Fourth Dynasty left an estate of fourteen towns, besides a town house and two estates at the royal residence, the pyramid city. Besides these, the endowment of his tomb comprised twelve towns more.[2] But these princes assisted in their father's government, and did not live a life of indolence and luxury. We shall find them occupying some of the most arduous posts in the service of the state.

[1] Cairo stela, 1787.   [2] I, 190-9.

However exalted may have been the official position of the Pharaoh as the sublime god at the head of the state, he nevertheless maintained close personal relations with the more prominent nobles of the realm. As a prince he had been educated with a group of youths from the families of these nobles, and together they had been instructed in such manly arts as swimming.[1] The friendships and the intimacies thus formed in youth must have been a powerful influence in the later life of the monarch. We see the Pharaoh giving his daughter in marriage to one of these youths with whom he had been educated,[2] and the severe decorum of the court was violated in behalf of this favourite, who was not permitted on formal occasions to kiss the dust before the Pharaoh, but enjoyed the unprecedented privilege of kissing the royal foot.[3] On the part of his intimates such ceremonial was purely a matter of official etiquette; in private the monarch did not hesitate to recline familiarly in complete relaxation beside one of his favourites, while the attending slaves anointed them both.[4] The daughter of such a noble might become the official queen and mother of the next king.[5] We see the king inspecting a public building with his chief architect, the vizier. As he admires the work and praises his faithful minister, he notices that the latter does not hear the words of royal favour. The king's exclamation alarms the waiting courtiers, the stricken minister is quickly carried to the palace itself, where the Pharaoh hastily summons the priests and chief physicians. He sends to the library for a case of medical rolls, but all is in vain. The physicians declare his condition hopeless. The king is smitten with sorrow and retires to his chamber to pray to Re. He then makes all arrangements for the deceased noble's burial, ordering an ebony coffin, and having the body anointed in his own presence. The eldest son of the dead was then empowered to build the tomb, the king furnishing and endowing it.[6]

[1] I, 256.   [2] I, 254 ff.   [3] I, 260.
[4] I, 270.   [5] I, 344.   [6] I, 242-9.

It is evident that the most powerful lords of the kingdom were thus bound to the person of the Pharaoh by close personal ties of blood and friendship. These relations were carefully fostered by the monarch, and in the Fourth and early Fifth Dynasty, there are aspects of this ancient state in which its inner circle at least reminds one of a great family, so that, as we have observed, the king assisted all its members in the building and equipment of their tombs, and showed the greatest solicitude for their welfare, both here and in the hereafter.

At the head of government there was theoretically none to question the Pharaoh's power. In actual fact he was as subject to the demands of policy toward this or that class, powerful family, clique or individual, or toward the harem, as are his successors in the oriental despotisms of the present day. These forces, which more or less modified his daily acts, we can follow at this distant day only as we see the state slowly moulded in its larger outlines by the impact of generation after generation of such influences from the Pharaoh's environment. In spite of the luxury evident in the organization of his court, the Pharaoh did not live the life of a luxurious despot, such as we frequently find among the Mamlukes of Moslem Egypt. In the Fourth Dynasty at least, he had as prince already seen arduous service in the superintendence of quarrying and mining operations, or he had served his father as vizier or prime minister, gaining invaluable experience in government before his succession to the throne. He was thus an educated and enlightened monarch, able to read and write, and not infrequently taking his pen in hand personally to indite a letter of thanks and appreciation to some deserving officer in his government.[1] He constantly received his ministers and engineers to discuss the needs of the country, especially in the conservation of the water supply and the development of the system of irrigation. His chief architect sent in plans for laying out the royal estates, and we see the monarch discussing with

[1] I, 268-270, 271.

him the excavation of a lake two thousand feet long in one
of them.[1] He read many a weary roll of state papers, or
turned from these to dictate dispatches to his commanders
in Sinai, Nubia and Punt, along the southern Red Sea. The
briefs of litigating heirs reached his hands and were probably not always a matter of mere routine to be read by secretaries. When such business of the royal offices had been
settled the monarch rode out in his palanquin, accompanied
by his vizier and attendants, to inspect his buildings and
public works, and his hand was everywhere felt in all the
important affairs of the nation.

The location of the royal residence was largely determined
by the pyramid which the king was building. As we have
remarked, the palace and the town formed by the court and
all that was attached to it, probably lay in the valley below
the margin of the western desert-plateau, on which the pyramid rose. From dynasty to dynasty, or sometimes from
reign to reign, it followed the pyramid, the light construction of the palaces and villas not interfering seriously with
such mobility. After the Third Dynasty the residence was
always in the vicinity of later Memphis. The palace itself
was double, or at least it possessed two gates in its front,
corresponding to the two ancient kingdoms, of which it was
now the seat of government. Each door or gate had a
name indicating to which kingdom it belonged; thus Snefru
named the two gates of his palace "Exalted is the White
Crown of Snefru upon the Southern Gate," and "Exalted
is the Red Crown of Snefru upon the Northern Gate."[2]
Throughout Egyptian history the facade of the palace was
called the "double front," and in writing the word "palace"
the scribe frequently placed the sign of *two* houses after it.
The royal office was also termed the "double cabinet,"
although it is not likely that there were two such bureaus,
one for the South and one for the North; the division probably went no further than the purely external symbolism of
the two palace gates. The same was doubtless true of the

[1] Ibid.   [2] I, 148.

central administration as a whole. We thus hear of a "double granary" and a "double white house" as departments of the treasury. These doubtless no longer corresponded to existing double organizations; they have become a fiction surviving from the first two dynasties; but such double names were always retained in the later terminology of the government. Adjoining the palace was a huge court, connected with which were the "halls" or offices of the central government. The entire complex of palace and adjoining offices was known as the "Great House," which was

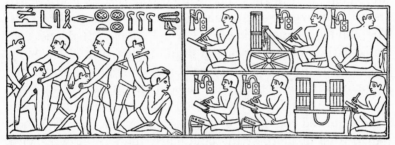

FIG. 36. COLLECTION OF TAXES BY TREASURY OFFICIALS.

On the right the scribes and fiscal officers keep record, while deputies with staves bring in the taxpayers. Over these are the words: " Seizing the town-rulers for a reckoning."

thus the centre of administration as well as the dwelling of the royal household. Here was focussed the entire system of government, which ramified throughout the country.

For purposes of local government, Upper Egypt was divided into some twenty administrative districts, and later we find as many more in the Delta. These "nomes" were presumably the early principalities, from which the local princes who ruled them in prehistoric days, had long disappeared. At the head of such a district or nome there was in the Fourth and Fifth Dynasties an official appointed by the crown, and known as "First under the King." Besides his administrative function as "local governor" of the nome, he also served in a judicial capacity, and therefore bore also the title of "judge." In Upper Egypt these "local governors" were also sometimes styled "magnates of the

Southern Ten," as if there were a group among them enjoying higher rank and forming a college or council of ten.
While we are not so well informed regarding the government
of the North, the system there was evidently very similar,
although there were perhaps fewer local governors. Within
the nome which he administered the "local governor" had
under his control a miniature state, an administrative unit
with all the organs of government: a treasury, a court of
justice, a land-office, a service for the conservation of the
dykes and canals, a body of militia, a magazine for their
equipment; and in these offices a host of scribes and recorders, with an ever growing mass of archives and local records.
The chief administrative bond which coordinated and centralized these nomes was the organization of the treasury,
by the operation of which there annually converged upon the
magazines of the central government the grain, cattle, poultry and industrial products, which in an age without coinage,
were collected as taxes by the local governors. The local
registration of land, or the land-office, the irrigation service,
the judicial administration, and other administrative functions were also centralized at the Great House; but it was
the treasury which formed the most tangible bond between
the palace and the nomes. Over the entire fiscal administration there was a "Chief Treasurer," residing of course
at the court. In a state in which buildings and extensive
public works demanded so much attention, the labour of
obtaining such enormous quantities of materials from the
mines and quarries required the oversight of two important
treasury officials, whom we would call assistant treasurers.
These the Egyptian styled "Treasurers of the God," meaning of the king. They were the men who superintended the
quarrying and transportation of the stone for the temples
and the massive pyramids of the Old Kingdom; besides
leading many an expedition into Sinai to exploit the mines
there.

As the reader may have already inferred, the judicial
functions of the local governors were merely incidental to

their administrative labours. There was therefore no clearly defined class of professional judges, but the administrative officials were learned in the law and assumed judicial duties. Like the treasury, the judicial administration also converged in one person, for the local judges were organized into six courts and these in turn were under a chief justice of the whole realm. Many of the judges bore the additional predicate "attached to Nekhen" (Hieraconpolis), an ancient title descended from the days when Nekhen was the royal residence of the Southern Kingdom. There was a body of highly elaborated law, which has unfortunately perished entirely. The local governors boast of their fairness and justice in deciding cases, often stating in their tombs: "Never did I judge two brothers in such a way that a son was deprived of his paternal possession."[1] The system of submitting all cases to the court in the form of written briefs, a method so praised by Diodorus,[2] seems to have existed already in this remote age, and the Berlin Museum possesses such a legal document pertaining to litigation between an heir and an executor.[3] It is the oldest document of the kind in existence. Special cases of private nature were "heard" by the chief justice and a judge "attached to Nekhen,"[4] while in a case of treason in the harem, the accused queen was tried before a court of two judges "attached to Nekhen," especially appointed by the crown for that purpose, the chief justice not being one of them.[5] It is a remarkable testimony to the Pharaoh's high sense of justice, and to the surprisingly judicial temper of the time, that in this distant age such a suspected conspirator in the royal harem was not immediately put to death without more ado. Summary execution, without any attempt legally to establish the guilt of the accused, would not have been considered unjustifiable in times not a century removed from our own in the same land. Under certain circumstances, not yet clear to us, appeal might be made directly to the

---

[1] I, 331, 357.　　　　　　　　　　　　[2] Book I, 75-76.
[3] Pap. des Kgl. Mus., 82-3.　　[4] I, 307.　　[5] I, 310.

king, and briefs in the case submitted to him. Such a brief is the document from the Old Kingdom now in Berlin, above noticed (Fig. 45).

The immediate head of the entire organization of government was the Pharaoh's prime minister, or as he is more commonly called in the east, the vizier. At the same time he also regularly served as chief justice; he was thus the most powerful man in the kingdom, next to the monarch himself, and for that reason the office was held by the crown prince in the Fourth Dynasty. His "hall" or office served as the archives of the government, and he was the chief archivist of the state. The state records were called "king's writings."[1] Here all lands were registered, and all local archives centralized and coordinated; here wills were recorded, and when executed the resulting new titles were issued.[2] The will of a king's son in the Fourth Dynasty has been preserved practically complete,[3] and another from the beginning of the Fifth Dynasty,[4] both having been cut in hieroglyphs on the stone wall of the tomb-chapel, where they could defy the lapse of nearly five thousand years, while the papyrus archives of the vizier perished thousands of years ago. Several other similar mortuary enactments have also survived.[5] All lands presented by the Pharaoh were conveyed by royal decree, recorded in the "king's writings" at the vizier's offices.[6]

All administration like the palace was in theory at least twofold: a fiction surviving from the predynastic times, before the union of the two kingdoms. We thus hear of a "double granary" in the treasury, or a "double cabinet," the office of the king. And these terms, which perhaps correspond to existing realities in some cases, were retained in the later terminology of the government, long after such division into two departments had ceased to exist. Over the vast army of scribes and officials of all possible ranks

[1] I, 268 ff.; 273.   [2] I, 175 ll. 14–16.
[3] I, 190–199.   [4] I, 213–217.
[5] I, 231 ff. and others throughout Fifth and Sixth Dynasty records.
[6] I, 173.

from high to low, who transacted the business of the Great House, the vizier was supreme. When we add, that besides some minor offices, he was also often the Pharaoh's chief architect, or as the Egyptian said, "Chief of all Works of the King," we shall understand that this great minister was the busiest man in the kingdom. All powerful as he was, the people appealed to him in his judicial capacity, as to one who could right every wrong, and the office was traditionally the most popular in the long list of the Pharaoh's servants. It was probably this office which was held by the great wise man, Imhotep, under king Zoser, and the wisdom of two other viziers of the Third Dynasty, Kegemne and Ptah-hotep, committed to writing, survived for many centuries after the Old Kingdom was a memory. Such was the reverence with which the incumbents of this exalted office were regarded, that the words, "Life, Prosperity, Health," which properly followed only the name of the king or a royal prince, were sometimes added to that of the vizier.

Such was the organization of this remarkable state, as we are able to discern it during the first two or three centuries of the Old Kingdom. In the thirtieth century before Christ it had reached an elaborate development of state functions under local officials, such as was not found in Europe until far down in the history of the Roman Empire. It was, to sum up briefly, a closely centralized body of local officials, each a centre for all the organs of the local government, which in each nome were thus focussed in the local governor before converging upon the palace. A Pharaoh of power, force and ability, and loyal governors in the nomes, meant a strong state; but let the Pharaoh betray signs of weakness and the governors might gain an independence which would threaten the dissolution of the whole. It was the maintenance of the nomes each as a separate unit of government, and the interposition of the governor at its head between the Pharaoh and the nome, which rendered the system dangerous. These little states within the state, each frequently having its own governor, might too easily become independent centres of political power. How this process actually took place we shall be able to observe as we follow the career of the Old Kingdom in the next chapter. Such a process was rendered the more easy because the government did not maintain any uniform or compact military organization. Each nome possessed its militia, commanded by the civil officials, who were not necessarily trained soldiers; there was thus no class of exclusively military officers. The temple estates likewise maintained a body of such troops. They were for the most part employed in mining and quarrying expeditions, supplying the hosts necessary for the transportation of the enormous blocks often demanded by the architects. In such work they were under the command of the "treasurer of the God." In case of serious war, as there was no standing army, this militia from all the nomes and temple estates, besides auxiliaries levied among the Nubian tribes, were brought together as quickly as possible and the command of the motley host, without any permanent organization, was entrusted by the monarch to some able official. As the local governors commanded the militia of the nomes, they held the sources of the Pharaoh's dubious military strength in their own hands.

The land which was thus administered must to a large extent have belonged to the crown. Under the oversight of the local governors' subordinates it was worked and made profitable by slaves or serfs, who formed the bulk of the population. They belonged to the ground and were bequeathed with it.[1] We have no means of determining how large this population was, although, as we have before stated, it had reached the sum of seven million by Roman times.[2] The descendants of the numerous progeny of older kings, with possible remnants of the prehistoric landed nobility, had created also a class of land-holding nobles, whose great estates must have formed a not inconsiderable fraction of the available lands of the kingdom. Such lords did not necessarily enter upon an official career or partici-

[1] I. 171.   [2] Diodorus I, 31.

pate in the administration. But the nobles and the peasant serfs, as the highest and the lowest, were not the only classes of society. There was a free middle class, in whose hands the arts and industries had reached such a high degree of excellence; but of these people we know almost nothing. They did not build imperishable tombs, such as have furnished us with all that we know of the nobles of the time; and they transacted their business with documents written on papyrus, which have all perished, in spite of the enormous mass of such materials which must have once existed. Later conditions would indicate that there undoubtedly was a class of industrial merchants in the Old Kingdom who produced and sold their own wares. That there were free landholders not belonging to the ranks of the nobles is also highly probable.

The social unit was as in later human history, the family. A man possessed but one legal wife, who was the mother of his heirs. She was in every respect his equal, was always treated with the greatest consideration, and participated in the pleasures of her husband and her children; the affectionate relations existing between a noble and his wife are constantly and noticeably depicted on the monuments of the time. Such relations had often existed from the earliest childhood of the pair; for it was customary in all ranks of society for a youth to marry his sister. Besides the legitimate wife, the head of his household, the man of wealth possessed also a harem, the inmates of which maintained no legal claim upon their lord. The harem was already at this early day a recognized institution in the East, and nothing immoral was thought of in connection with it. The children of the time show the greatest respect for their parents, and it was the duty of every son to maintain the tomb of his father. The respect and affection of one's parents and family were highly valued, and we often find in the tombs the statement, " I was one beloved of his father, praised of his mother, whom his brothers and sisters loved. "[1] As among many other peoples,

[1] I, 357.

the natural line of inheritance was through the eldest daughter, though a will might disregard this. The closest ties of blood were through the mother, and a man's natural protector, even in preference to his own father, was the father of his mother. The debt of a son to the mother who bore and nourished him, cherished and cared for him while he was being educated, is dwelt upon with emphasis by the wise men of the time. While there was probably a loose form of marriage which might be easily dissolved, a form presumably due to the instability of fortune among the slaves and the poorer class, yet immorality was strongly condemned by the best sentiment. The wise man warns the youth, " Beware of a woman from abroad, who is not known in her city. Look not upon her when she comes, and know her not. She is like the vortex of deep waters, whose whirling is unfathomable. The woman, whose husband is far away, she writes to thee every day. If there is no witness with her she arises and spreads her net. O deadly crime, if one hearkens!"[1] To all youths marriage and the foundation of a household are recommended as the only wise course. Yet there is no doubt that side by side with these wholesome ideals of the wise and virtuous, there also existed wide-spread and gross immorality.

The outward conditions of the lower class were not such as would incline toward moral living. In the towns their low mud-brick, thatch-roofed houses were crowded into groups and masses, so huddled together that the walls were often contiguous. A rough stool, a rude box or two, and a few crude pottery jars constituted the furniture of such a hovel. The barracks of the workmen were an immense succession of small mud-brick chambers under one roof, with open passages between long lines of such rooms. Whole quarters for the royal levies of workmen were erected on this plan, in the pyramid-towns, and near the pyramids. On the great estates, the life of the poor was freer, less congested and promiscuous, and undoubtedly more stable and wholesome.

[1] Pap. de Boulaq I, 16, 13 ff.; Erman, Aegypten, 223.

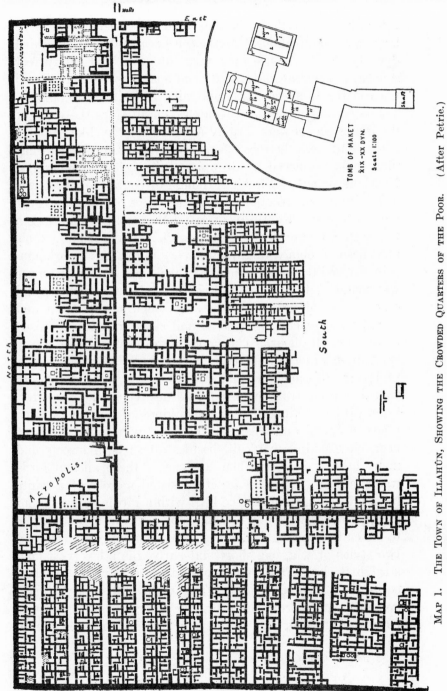

MAP 1. THE TOWN OF ILLAHÛN, SHOWING THE CROWDED QUARTERS OF THE POOR. (After Petrie.)

The houses of the rich, the noble and official class were large and commodious. Methen, a great noble of the third dynasty, built a house over three hundred and thirty feet square.[1] The materials were wood and sun-dried brick, and the construction was light and airy as suited the climate. There were many latticed windows, on all sides the walls of the living rooms were largely a mere skeleton, like those of many Japanese houses. Against winds and sandstorms, they could be closed by dropping gaily coloured hangings. Even the palace of the king, though of course fortified, was of this light construction; hence the cities of ancient Egypt have disappeared entirely or left but mounds containing a few scanty fragments of ruined walls. Beds, chairs, stools and chests of ebony, inlaid with ivory in the finest workmanship, formed the chief articles of furniture. Little or no use was made of tables, but the rich vessels of alabaster, and other costly stones, of copper, or sometimes of gold and silver, were placed upon bases and standards which raised them from the floor. The floors were covered with heavy rugs, upon which guests, especially ladies, frequently sat, in preference to the chairs and stools. The food was rich and varied; we find that even the dead desired in the hereafter, " ten different kinds of meat, five kinds of poultry, sixteen kinds of bread and cakes, six kinds of wine, four kinds of beer, eleven kinds of fruit, besides all sorts of sweets and many other things."[2] The costume of these ancient lords was simple in the extreme; it consisted merely of a white linen kilt, secured above the hips with a girdle or band, and hanging often hardly to the knees, or again in another style, to the calf of the leg. The head was commonly shaven, and two styles of wig, one short and curly, the other with long straight locks parted in the middle, were worn on all state occasions. A broad collar, often inlaid with costly stones, generally hung from the neck, but otherwise the body was bare from the waist up. With long staff in hand, the gentle-

[1] I, 173.
[2] Dümichen Grabpalast, 18–26; Erman, Aegypten, 265.

man of the day was ready to receive his visitors, or to make a tour of inspection about his estate. His lady and her daughters all appeared in costumes even more simple. They were clothed in a thin, close-fitting, sleeveless, white linen garment hanging from the breast to the ankles, and supported by two bands passing over the shoulders. The skirt, as a modern modiste would say " lacked fullness," and there was barely freedom to walk. A long wig, a collar and necklace, and a pair of bracelets completed the lady's costume. Neither she nor her lord was fond of sandals; although they now and then wore them. While the adults thus dispensed with all unnecessary clothing, as we should expect in such a climate, the children were allowed to run about without any clothing whatever. The peasant wore merely a breech-clout, which he frequently cast off when at work in the fields; his wife was clad in the same long close-fitting garment worn by the wife of the noble; but she too when engaged in heavy work, such as winnowing grain, cast aside all clothing.

The Egyptian was passionately fond of nature and of out-door life. The house of the noble was always surrounded by a garden, in which he loved to plant figs and palms and sycamores, laying out vineyards and arbours, and excavating before the house a pool, lined with masonry coping, and filled with fish. A large body of servants and slaves were in attendance, both in house and garden; a chief steward had charge of the entire house and estate, while an upper gardener directed the slaves in the care and culture of the garden. This was the noble's paradise; here he spent his leisure hours with his family and friends, playing at draughts, listening to the music of harp, pipe and lute, watching his women in the slow and stately dance of the time, while his children sported about among the trees, splashed in the pool, or played with ball, doll or jumping-jack. Again in a light boat of papyrus reeds, accompanied by his wife and sometimes by one of his children, the noble delighted to float about in the shade of the tall rushes, in the inundated marshes and swamps. The myriad life that teemed and swarmed all

FIG. 37.　VILLA AND GARDEN OF AN EGYPTIAN NOBLE OF THE OLD KINGDOM.
(After Perrot and Chipiez.)

about his frail craft gave him the keenest pleasure. While
the lady plucked water-lilies and lotus flowers, and the lad
could try his skill at catching hoopoe birds, my lord launched
his boomerang among the flocks of wild fowl that fairly
darkened the sky above him, finding his sport in the use of
the difficult weapon, which for this reason, he preferred to
the more effective and less difficult bow.　Or again he seized
his double-pointed fish-spear, and tried his skill in the stream,
endeavouring if possible to transfix two fish at once, one on

each of the two prongs. Sometimes an aggressive hippopotamus, or a troublesome crocodile demanded the long harpoon with rope attached, and the fishers and hunters of the marshes were summoned to assist in dispatching the dangerous brute. Not infrequently the noble undertook the more arduous sport of the desert, where he might bring down the huge wild ox with his long bow; capture alive numbers of antelopes, gazelles, oryxes, ibexes, wild oxen, wild

Fig. 38. A Noble of the Old Kingdom Hunting Wild Fowl with the Throw-stick from a Skiff of Reeds in the Papyrus Marshes.

asses, ostriches and hares; or catch fleeting glimpses of the strange beasts, with which his fancy peopled the wilderness: the gryphon, a quadruped with head and wings of a bird, or the Sag, a lioness with the head of a hawk, and a tail which terminated in a lotus flower! In this lighter side of the Egyptian's life, his love of nature, his wholesome and sunny view of life, his never failing cheerfulness in spite of his constant and elaborate preparation for death, we find a pervading characteristic of his nature, which is so evident

in his art, as to raise it far above the sombre heaviness that
pervades the contemporary art of Asia.

Some five centuries of uniform government, with centralized control of the inundation, in the vast system of dykes
and irrigation canals, had brought the productivity of the
nation to the highest level; for the economic foundation of
this civilization in the Old Kingdom, as in all other periods
of Egyptian history, was agriculture. It was the enormous

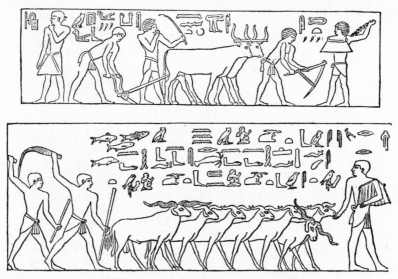

FIG. 39.   AGRICULTURE IN THE OLD KINGDOM.

Above: are plowing, breaking clods, and sowing; below: the sheep are being
driven across the sown fields in order to trample in the seed. As the leading
shepherd wades through the marshy field he sings to the sheep: " The shepherd
is in the water among the fish; he talks with the nar-fish, he passes the time
of day with the west-fish. . . ." The song is written over his flock.

harvests of wheat and barley gathered by the Egyptian
from the inexhaustible soil of his valley, which made possible the social and political structure which we have been
sketching. Besides grain, the extensive vineyards and wide
fields of succulent vegetables, which formed a part of every
estate, greatly augmented the agricultural resources of the
land. Large herds of cattle, sheep, goats, droves of donkeys
(for the horse was unknown), and vast quantities of poultry,

wild fowl, the large game of the desert already noticed and innumerable Nile fish, added not inconsiderably to the produce of the field, in contributing to the wealth and prosperity which the land was now enjoying. It was thus in field and pasture that the millions of the kingdom toiled to produce the annual wealth by which its economic processes continued. Other sources of wealth also occupied large numbers of workmen. There were granite quarries at the first cataract, sandstone was quarried at Silsileh, the finer and harder stones chiefly at Hammamat between Coptos and the Red Sea. Alabaster at Hatnub behind Amarna, and limestone at many places, particularly at Ayan or Troia opposite Mem-

FIG. 40. A HERD IN THE OLD KINGDOM, FORDING A CANAL.

phis. They brought from the first cataract granite blocks twenty or thirty feet long and fifty or sixty tons in weight. They drilled the toughest of stone, like diorite, with tubular drills of copper, and the massive lids of granite sarcophagi were sawn with long copper saws which, like the drills, were reinforced by sand or emery. Miners and quarrymen were employed in large numbers during the expeditions to Sinai, for the purpose of procuring copper, the green and blue malachite used in fine inlays, the turquoise and lapis-lazuli. The source of iron, which was already used for tools to a limited extent, is uncertain. Bronze was not yet in use. The smiths furnished tools of copper and iron: bolts, nails, hinges and mountings of all sorts for artisans of all classes;

they also wrought fine copper vessels for the tables of the rich, besides splendid copper weapons. They achieved marvels also in the realm of plastic art, as we have yet to see. Silver came from abroad, probably from Cilicia in Asia Minor; it was therefore even more rare and valuable than gold. The quartz-veins of the granite mountains along the Red Sea were rich in gold, and it was taken out in the Wadi Foakhir, on the Coptos road. It was likewise mined largely by foreigners and obtained in trade from Nubia, in the eastern deserts of which it was also found. Of the jewelry worn by the Pharaoh and his nobles, in the Old Kingdom, almost

FIG. 41. METALWORKERS' WORKSHOP IN THE OLD KINGDOM.

Above: at the left, weighing of precious metals and malachite; in the middle, the furnace with men at blow-pipes; at the right, casting and hammering. Below: putting together necklaces and costly ornaments. Note the dwarves employed on this work.

nothing has survived, but the reliefs in the tomb-chapels often depict the gold-smith at his work, and his descendants in the Middle Kingdom have left works which show that the taste and cunning of the first dynasty had developed without cessation in the Old Kingdom.

For the other important industries the Nile valley furnished nearly all materials indispensable to their development. In spite of the ease with which good building stone was procured, enormous quantities of sun-dried bricks were turned out by the brick-yards, as they still are at the present

day, and, as we have seen, the masons erected whole quarters
for the poor, villas of the rich, magazines, store-houses, forts
and city walls of these cheap and convenient materials. In
the forestless valley the chief trees were the date palm, the
sycamore, tamarisk and acacia, none of which furnished
good timber. Wood was therefore scarce and expensive, but
the carpenters, joiners and cabinet makers flourished nevertheless, and those in the employ of the palace or on the
estates of the nobles wrought wonders in the cedar, imported
from Syria, and the ebony and ivory which came in from
the south. In every town and on every large estate shipbuilding was constant. There were many different styles of
craft from the heavy cargo-boat for grain and cattle, to the

FIG. 42. SHIPBUILDING IN THE OLD KINGDOM.

gorgeous many-oared "dahabiyeh," of the noble, with its
huge sail. We shall find these shipwrights building the
earliest known sea-going vessels, on the shores of the Red
Sea.

While the artistic craftsman in stone still produced magnificent vessels, vases, jars, bowls and platters in alabaster,
diorite, porphyry and other costly stones, yet his work was
gradually giving way to the potter, whose rich blue- and
green-glazed fayence vessels could not but win their way.
He produced also vast quantities of large coarse jars for
the storage of oils, wines, meats and other foods in the
magazines of the nobles and the government; while the use
of smaller vessels among the millions of the lower classes

made the manufacture of pottery one of the chief industries of the country. The pottery of the time is without decoration, and is hardly a work of art. Glass was still chiefly employed as glaze and had not yet been developed as an independent material. In a land of pastures and herds, the production of leather was of course understood. The tanners had thoroughly mastered the art of curing the hides, and produced fine soft skins, which they dyed in all colours, covering stools and chairs, beds and cushions, and furnishing gay canopies and baldachins. Flax was plentifully cultivated, and the Pharaoh's harvest of flax was under the control of a noble of rank.[1] The women of the

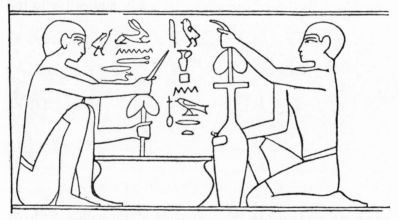

FIG. 43. WORKMEN DRILLING OUT STONE VESSELS.

One says, "This is a very beautiful vessel"; his comrade replies, "It is indeed." Their conversation is recorded before them.

serfs on the great estates were the spinners and weavers. Even the coarser varieties for general use show good quality, but surviving specimens of the *royal* linens are of such exquisite fineness that the ordinary eye requires a glass to distinguish them from silk, and the limbs of the wearer could be discerned through the fabric. Other vegetable fibres furnished by the marshes supported a large industry in coarser textiles. Among these, the papyrus was the most useful.

[1] I, 172, l. 5.

Broad, light skiffs were made of it by binding together long bundles of these reeds; rope was twisted from them, as also from palm-fibre; sandals were plaited, and mats woven of them; but above all, when split into thin strips, it was possible to join them into sheets of tough paper. That the writing of Egypt spread to Phœnicia and furnished the classic world with an alphabet, is in a measure due to this convenient writing material, as well as to the method of writing upon it with ink. While a royal dispatch in cuneiform on clay often weighed eight or ten pounds, and could not be carried on the person of the messenger, a papyrus-roll of fifty times the surface afforded by the clay tablet might

FIG. 44.   PAPYRUS HARVEST IN THE OLD KINGDOM.

On the left the stalks are plucked by two men; next two more bind them in bundles, and four men then carry the bundles away.

be conveniently carried about in the bosom, employed in business, or used as a book. That its importation into Phœnicia was already in progress in the twelfth century B. C.[1] is therefore quite intelligible. The manufacture of papyrus-paper had already grown into a large and flourishing industry in the Old Kingdom.

The Nile was alive with boats, barges, and craft of all descriptions, bearing the products of these industries, and of field and pasture, to the treasury of the Pharaoh, or to the markets where they were disposed of. Here barter was the common means of exchange: a crude pot for a fish, a bundle of onions for a fan; a wooden box for a jar of ointment (Fig. 46). In some transactions, however, presumably those involving larger values, gold and copper in rings of a fixed weight, circulated as money, and stone weights were

[1] IV, 582; see below p. 517.

7

already marked with their equivalence in such rings. This ring-money is the oldest currency known. Silver was rare and more valuable than gold. Business had already reached a high degree of development; books and accounts were kept; orders and receipts were given; wills and deeds were made; and written contracts covering long periods of time were entered upon. Every noble had his corps of clerks and secretaries and the exchange of letters and official documents with his colleagues was incessant. Under the scanty remnants of the sun-dried brick houses on the island of Elephantine, inhabited by the nobles of the southern border in the twenty sixth century B. C., the modern peasants recently found the remnants of the household papers and business documents which were once filed in the great man's office. But the ignorant finders so mutilated the precious records that only fragments have now survived (Fig. 45). The letters, records of legal proceedings, and memoranda, still recognizable among them, are now being published by the Berlin Museum, where the papyri are preserved.

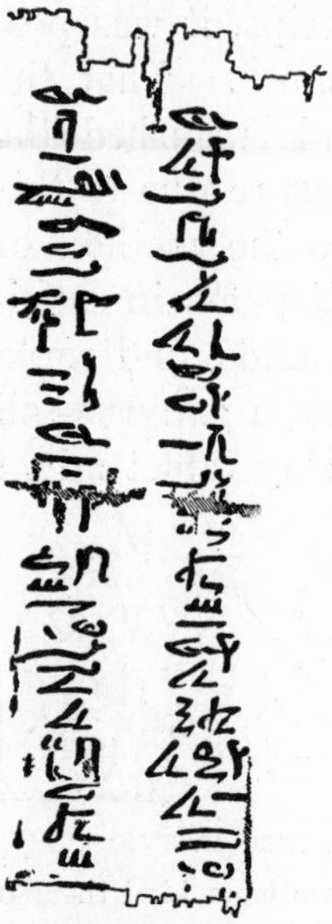

FIG. 45. TWO COLUMNS FROM AN OLD KINGDOM LEGAL DOCUMENT.

Written in Hieratic on Papyrus. See p. 81. (Original in Berlin.)

Under such circumstances, an education in the learning of the time was indispensable to an official career. Connected with the treasury, for whose multifold records so many skilled scribes were necessary, there were schools where lads received the education and the training which fitted them for the scribal offices. Learning possessed but one aspect for the Egyptian, namely: its practical usefulness. An ideal pleasure in the search for truth, the pursuit of science for its own sake, were unknown to him. The learned equipment was an advantage which lifted a youth

Fig. 46.—SCENES AT AN OLD KINGDOM MARKET.

(After Lepsius. *Denkmaeler*.)

above all other classes in the opinion of the scribe, and for that reason, the boy must be early put into the school and diligently kept to his tasks. While precept was incessantly in the lad's ears, the master did not stop with this; his principle was, "A boy's ears are on his back, and he hearkens when he is beaten."[1] The content of the instruction, besides innumerable moral precepts, many of them most wholesome and rational, was chiefly the method of writing. The elaborate hieroglyphic with its numerous animal and human figures, such as the reader has doubtless often seen on the monuments in our museums, or in works on Egypt, was too slow and labourious a method of writing for the needs of everyday business. The attempt to write these figures rapidly with ink upon papyrus had gradually resulted in reducing each sign to a mere outline, much rounded off and abbreviated. This cursive business hand, which we call "hieratic," had already begun under the earliest dynasties, and by the rise of the Old Kingdom, it had developed into a graceful and rapid system of writing, which showed no nearer resemblance to the hieroglyphic than does our own hand-writing to our print. The introduction of this system into the administration of government and the transaction of every day business, produced profound changes in government and society, and created for all time the class distinction between the illiterate and the learned, which is still a problem of modern society. It was the acquirement of this method of writing which enabled the lad to enter upon the coveted official career as a scribe or overseer of a magazine, or steward of an estate. Hence the master put before the boy model-letters, proverbs, and literary compositions, which he labouriously copied into his roll, the copy-book of this ancient school-boy. A large quantity of these copy-books from the Empire, some fifteen hundred years after the fall of the Old Kingdom, has been found; and many a composition which would otherwise have been lost, has thus survived, in the uncertain hand of a pupil in the scribal schools.

[1] Pap. Anast. 3.3 = Ibid. 5, 8.

They can easily be identified by the corrections of the master on the margin. When he could write well, the lad was placed in charge of some official, in whose office he assisted, gradually learning the routine and the duties of the scribe's life, until he was himself competent to assume some office at the bottom of the ladder.

Education thus consisted solely of the practically useful equipment for an official career. Knowledge of nature and of the external world as a whole was sought only as necessity prompted such search. As we have already intimated, it never occurred to the Egyptian to enter upon the search for truth for its own sake. Under these circumstances, the science of the time, if we may speak of it as such at all, was such a knowledge of natural conditions as enabled the active men of this age to accomplish those practical tasks with which they were daily confronted. They had much practical acquaintance with astronomy, developed out of that knowledge which had enabled their ancestors to introduce a rational calendar nearly thirteen centuries before the rise of the Old Kingdom. They had already mapped the heavens, identified the more prominent fixed stars, and developed a system of observation with instruments sufficiently accurate to determine the positions of stars for practical purposes; but they had produced no theory of the heavenly bodies as a whole, nor would it ever have occurred to the Egyptian that such an attempt was useful or worth the trouble. In mathematics all the ordinary arithmetical processes were demanded in the daily transactions of business and government, and had long since come into common use among the scribes. Fractions, however, caused difficulty. The scribes could operate only with those having *one* as the numerator, and all other fractions were of necessity resolved into a series of several, each with *one* as the numerator. The only exception was two thirds, which they had learned to use without so resolving it. Elementary algebraic problems were also solved without difficulty. In geometry they were able to master the simpler problems, though the area of a trape-

FIG. 47.—THIRD DYNASTY ARCH.　　FIG. 48.—DIORITE STATUE OF KHEPHREN.　　FIG. 49.—LIMESTONE STATUE OF RANOFER.

From a Tomb at Bet Khallâf, found by Garstang.　　(Cairo Museum.)　　(Cairo Museum.)

zoid caused some difficulties and errors, while the area of
the circle had been determined with close accuracy. The
necessity of determining the content of a pile of grain had
led to a roughly approximate result in the computation of
the content of the hemisphere, and a circular granary to
that of the cylinder. But no theoretical problems were discussed, and the whole science attempted only those problems
which were continually met in daily life. The laying out
of a ground-plan like the square base of the Great Pyramid
could be accomplished with amazing accuracy, and the
orientation displays a nicety that almost rivals the results of
modern instruments. A highly developed knowledge of mechanics was thus at the command of the architect and craftsman. The arch was employed in masonry and can be dated
as far back as the thirtieth century B. C., the oldest dated
arches known (Fig. 47). In the application of power to the
movement of great monuments, only the simplest devices
were employed; the pulley was unknown and probably the
roller also. Medicine was already in possession of much
empirical wisdom, displaying close and accurate observation; the calling of the physician already existed and the
court physician of the Pharaoh was a man of rank and influence. His recipes were many of them rational and useful;
others were naively fanciful, like the prescription of a decoc-
tion of the hair of a black calf to prevent gray hair. They
had already been collected and recorded in papyrus rolls,[1]
and the recipes of this age were famous for their virtue in
later times. Some of them finally crossed with the Greeks
to Europe, where they are still in use among the peasantry
of the present day. That which precluded any progress
toward real science was the belief in magic, which later
began to dominate all the practice of the physician. There
was no great distinction between the physician and the
magician. All remedies were administered with more or
less reliance upon magical charms; and in many cases the
magical "hocus pocus" of the physician was thought to be

[1] I, 246.

of itself more effective than any remedy that could be administered. Disease was due to hostile spirits, and against these only magic could avail.

Art flourished as nowhere else in the ancient world. Here again the Egyptian's attitude of mind was not wholly that which characterized the art of the later Greek world. Art as the pursuit and the production exclusively of the ideally beautiful, was unknown to him. He loved beauty as found in nature, his spirit demanded such beauty in his home and surroundings. The lotus blossomed on the handle of his spoon, and his wine sparkled in the deep blue calyx of the same flower; the muscular limb of the ox in carved ivory upheld the couch upon which he slept, the ceiling over his head was a starry heaven resting upon palm trunks, each crowned with its graceful tuft of drooping foliage; or papyrus-stems rose from the floor to support the azure roof upon their swaying blossoms; doves and butterflies flitted across his in-door sky; his floors were frescoed with the opulent green of rich marsh-grasses, with fish gliding among their roots, where the wild ox tossed his head at the birds twittering on the swaying grass-tops, as they strove in vain to drive away the stealthy weasel creeping up to plunder their nests. Everywhere the objects of every day life in the homes of the rich showed unconscious beauty of line and fine balance of proportion, while the beauty of nature and of out-of-door life which spoke to the beholder in the decoration on every hand, lent a certain distinction even to the most commonplace objects. The Egyptian thus sought to beautify and to make beautiful all objects of utility, but all such objects served some practical use. He was not inclined to make a beautiful thing solely for its beauty. In sculpture, therefore, the practical dominated. The splendid statues of the Old Kingdom were not made to be erected in the market place, but solely to be masoned up in the mastaba-tomb, that they might be of practical advantage to the deceased in the hereafter, as we have seen in the preceding chapter. It was this motive chiefly to which the marvellous

FIG. 50.—LIMESTONE STATUE OF HEMSET.

(Louvre; after Capart, *Recueil des Monuments.*)

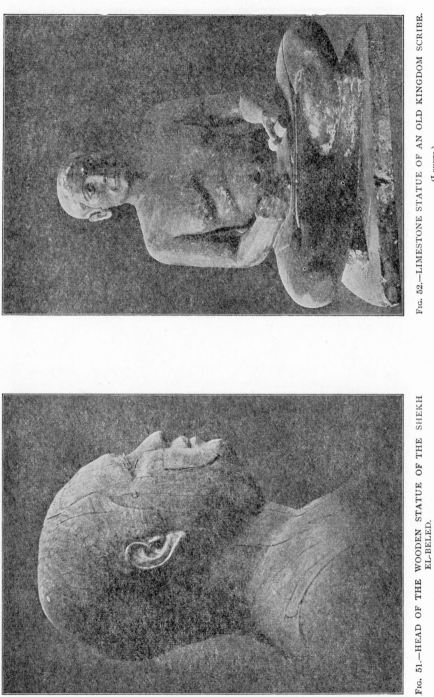

Fig. 52.—LIMESTONE STATUE OF AN OLD KINGDOM SCRIBE.

(Louvre.)

Fig. 51.—HEAD OF THE WOODEN STATUE OF THE SHEKH EL-BELED.

(Cairo Museum.)

development of portrait sculpture in the Old Kingdom was due.

The sculptor might either model his subject with faithful delineation, an intimate, personal style; or again depict him as a conventional type, a formal, typical style. Both styles, representing the same man, though strikingly different, may appear in the same tomb. Every device was adopted to increase the resemblance to life. The whole statue was colored in the natural hues, the eyes were inlaid in rock-crystal, and the vivacity with which these Memphite sculptures were instinct, has never been surpassed. The finest of the sitting statues is the well-known portrait of Khafre (Fig. 48), the builder of the second pyramid of Gizeh. The sculptor has skilfully met the limitations imposed upon him by the intensely hard and refractory material (diorite), and while obliged, therefore, to treat the subject summarily, has slightly emphasized salient features, lest the work should lack pronounced character. The unknown master, who must take his place among the world's great sculptors, while contending with technical difficulties which no modern sculptor attempts, has here given a real king imperishable form, and shown us with incomparable skill the divine and impassive calm with which the men of the time had endued their sovereign. In softer material, the sculptor gained a freer hand, of which one of the best examples is the sitting figure of Hemset in the Louvre (Fig. 50). It is surprisingly vivacious, in spite of the summarization of the body, an insufficiency which is characteristic of all Old Kingdom sculpture in the round. It is the head which appeals to the artist as the most individual element in his model, and on the head therefore he exhausts all his skill. These forms of kings and nobles show little variety in attitude; indeed there is but one other posture in which a person of rank could be depicted. Perhaps the best example of it is the figure of the priest Ranofer, a speaking likeness of the proud noble of the time (Fig. 49). While the character of the subject does not appeal to us, nevertheless one of the most remarkable portraits of the Old Kingdom is the sleek, well-

fed, self-satisfied old overseer, whose wooden statue, like all
those that we have thus far noticed, is in the Cairo Museum
(Fig. 51). As every one now knows, he has been dubbed
the "Shekh el-beled" or "Sheik of the village," because the
natives who excavated the figure, discovered in the face such
a striking resemblance to the sheik of their village, that they
all cried out with one accord, "Shekh el-beled!" In depicting the servants, who were to accompany the deceased noble
into the hereafter, the sculptor was freed from the most
tyrannical of the conventions which governed the posture of
the noble himself. With great life-likeness he has wrought
the miniatures of the household servants, as they continue in
the tomb the work which they had been accustomed to do
for their lord in his home. Even the noble's secretary must
accompany him into the next world, and such is the vivacity
with which the sculptor has fashioned the famous "Louvre
scribe" (Fig. 52), that as one looks into the shrewd, hard-
featured countenance, it would hardly be a surprise if the
reed pen should begin to move nimbly across the papyrus-
roll upon his knees, as he resumes the dictation of his master,
interrupted now these five thousand years. Superb animal
forms, like the granite lion's-head from the sun-temple of
Nuserre (Fig. 57) were also wrought in the hardest stone.

It had never been supposed that the artists of this remote
age would attempt so ambitious a task as the production of
a life-size statue in metal; but the sculptors and copper-
smiths of the court of Pepi I, in celebration of the king's
first jubilee, accomplished even this (Figs. 53–54). Over a
wooden core they wrought the face and figure of the king,
in beaten copper, inserting eyes of obsidian and white limestone. In spite of the ruinous state in which it now is, in
spite of fracture and oxidation, the head is still one of the
strongest portraits which have survived from antiquity.
The gold-smith also invaded the realm of plastic art. In
the "gold-house" as his workshop was called, he turned
sculptor, and produced for the temples such cultus-statues
of the gods as the magnificent figure of the sacred hawk of

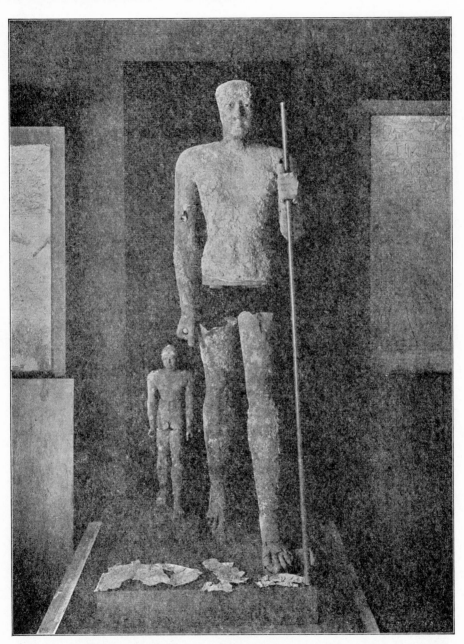

FIG. 53.—LIFE-SIZE STATUE OF PEPI I, WITH FIGURE OF HIS SON; BOTH OF BEATEN COPPER.

(Cairo Museum.)

FIG. 54.—HEAD OF THE COPPER STATUE OF PEPI I,
SHOWING EYES OF INLAID ROCK CRYSTAL.

(Cairo Museum.)

FIG. 55.—PAINTING OF GEESE FROM AN OLD KINGDOM TOMB AT MEDÛM.

(The panel has been cut in the middle; the two geese eating should face each other.   Cairo Museum.)

Hieraconpolis (Fig. 58), of which Quibell found the head in the temple at that place. The body of beaten copper had perished; but the head, crowned with a circlet and surmounted by two tall feather-plumes, the whole wrought in beaten gold, was practically intact. The head is of one piece of metal, and the eyes are the two polished ends of a single rod of obsidian, which passes through the head from eye to eye.

In relief, now greatly in demand for temple decoration, and the chapel of the mastaba-tomb, the Egyptian was confronted by the problem of foreshortening and perspective. He must put objects having roundness and thickness, upon a flat surface. How this should be done had been determined for him before the beginning of the Old Kingdom. A conventional style had already been established before the third dynasty, and that style was now sacred and inviolable tradition. While a certain freedom of development survived, that style in its fundamentals persisted throughout the history of Egyptian art, even after the artist had learned to perceive its shortcomings. The age which produced it had not learned to maintain one point of view in the drawing of any given scene or object; two different points of view were combined in the same figure: in drawing a man a front view of the eyes and shoulders was regularly placed upon a profile of the trunk and legs. This unconscious incongruity was afterward also extended to temporal relations, and successive instants of time were combined in the same scene. Accepting these limitations, the reliefs of the Old Kingdom, which are really slightly modelled drawings, are often sculptures of rare beauty (Fig. 56). It is from the scenes which the Memphite sculptor placed on the walls of the mastaba-chapels that we learn all that we know of the life and customs of the Old Kingdom. The exquisite modelling, of which such a sculptor was capable, is perhaps best exhibited in the wooden doors of Hesire (Fig. 59). All such reliefs were coloured, so that when completed, we may call them raised and modelled paintings; at least they do not fall within the domain of plastic art, as do Greek reliefs. Painting was also practiced independently, and the familiar line of geese from a tomb at Medum (Fig. 55) well illustrates the strength and freedom with which the Memphite of the time could depict the animal forms with which he was familiar. The characteristic poise of the head, the slow walk, the sudden droop of the neck as the head falls to seize the worm, all these are the work of a strong and confident draughtsman, long schooled in his art.

The sculpture of the Old Kingdom may be characterized as a natural and unconscious realism, exercised with a technical ability of the highest order. In the practice of this art, the sculptor of the Old Kingdom compares favourably even with modern artists. He was the only artist in the early orient who could put the human body into stone, and living in a society such that he was daily familiarized with the nude form, he treated it with sincerity and frankness. I cannot forbear quoting the words of an unprejudiced classical archæologist, M. Charles Perrot, who says of the Memphite sculptors of the Old Kingdom, "It must be acknowledged that they produced works which are not to be surpassed in their way by the greatest portraits of modern Europe."[1] The sculpture of the Old Kingdom, however, was superficial; it was not interpretative, did not embody ideas in stone, and shows little contemplation of the emotions and forces of life. It is characteristic of the age that we must speak of this Memphite art as a whole. We know none of its greatest masters, and only the names of an artist or two during the whole period of Egyptian history.

It is only very recently that we have been able to discern the fundamentals of Old Kingdom architecture. Too little has been preserved of the house and palace of the time to permit of safe generalizations upon the light and airy style of architecture which they represent. It is only the massive stone structures of this age which have been preserved. Besides the mastabas and pyramids, which we have already

[1] Perrot and Chipiez, History of Art, II, p. 194.

FIG. 56.—RELIEFS FROM THE INTERIOR OF AN OLD KINGDOM MASTABA CHAPEL, DEPICTING HERDS AND FLOCKS. (Berlin Museum)

FIG. 57.—DECORATIVE HEAD OF LION, IN GRANITE. (Cairo Museum.)

FIG. 58.—GOLDEN HAWK OF HIERACONPOLIS. (Cairo Museum.)

FIG. 59.—WOODEN PANEL OF HESIRE. (Cairo Museum.)

FIG. 60.—FIFTH DYNASTY COLUMNS. CLUSTER OF PAPYRUS STEMS (left) AND PALM CAPITAL (right). Berlin Museum.

briefly noticed, the temple is the great architectural achievement of the Old Kingdom. Its arrangement has been touched upon in the preceding chapter. The architect employed only straight lines, these being perpendiculars and horizontals, very boldly and felicitously combined. The arch, although known, was not employed as a member in architecture. In order to carry the roof across the void, either the simplest of stone piers, a square pillar of a single block of granite was employed, or an already elaborate and beautiful monolithic column of granite supported the architrave. These columns, the earliest known in the history of architecture, must have been employed before the Old Kingdom, for they are fully developed in the Fifth Dynasty. They represent a palm-tree (Fig. 60), the capital being the crown of foliage; or they are conceived as a bundle of papyrus stalks, bearing the architrave upon the cluster of buds at the top, which form the capital (Figs. 60, 61). The proportions are faultless, and surrounded with such exquisite colonnades as these, flanked by brightly coloured reliefs, the courts of the Old Kingdom temples belong to the noblest architectural conceptions bequeathed to us by antiquity. Egypt thus became the source of columned architecture. While the Babylonian builders displayed notable skill in giving varied architectural effect to great masses, they were limited to this, and the colonnade was unknown to them; whereas the Egyptian already at the close of the fourth millennium before Christ had solved the fundamental problem of great architecture, developing with the most refined artistic sense and the greatest mechanical skill the treatment of voids, and thus originating the colonnade.

The age was dealing with material things and developing material resources, and in such an age literature has little opportunity; it was indeed hardly born as yet. The sages of the court, the wise old viziers, Kegemne, Imhotep, and Ptahhotep, had put into proverbs the wholesome wisdom of life, which a long career had taught them, and these were probably already circulating in written form, although the

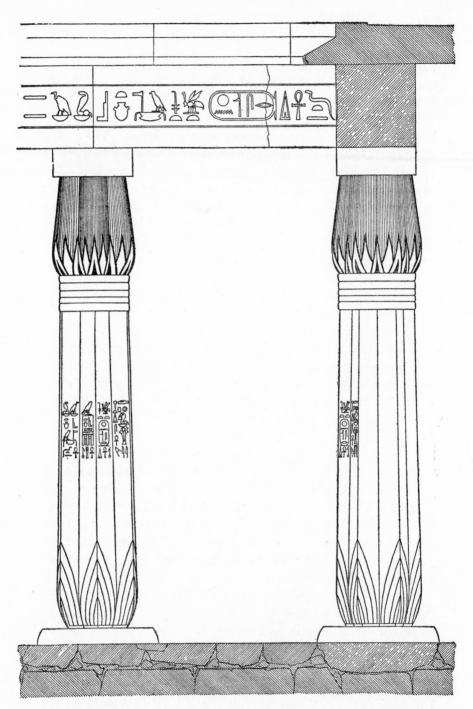

Fig. 61.   Elevation of Part of the Colonnade Surrounding the Court of
the Pyramid Temple of Nuserre (Fifth Dynasty).   (After Borchardt.)

oldest manuscript of such lore which we possess, dates from the Middle Kingdom. The priestly scribes of the Fifth Dynasty compiled the annals of the oldest kings, from the bare names of the kings, who ruled the two prehistoric kingdoms, to the Fifth Dynasty itself; but it was a bald catalogue of events, achievements and temple donations, without literary form. It is the oldest surviving fragment of royal annals. As the desire to perpetuate the story of a distinguished life increased, the nobles began to record in their tombs simple narratives characterized by a primitive directness, in long successions of simple sentences, each showing the same construction, but lacking expressed connectives.[1] Events and honours common to the lives of the leading nobles were related by them all in the identical words, so that conventional phrases had already gained place in literature not unlike the inviolable canons of their graphic art. There is no individuality. The mortuary texts in the pyramids display sometimes a rude force, and an almost savage fire. They contain scattered fragments of the old myths but whether these had then enjoyed more than an oral existence we do not know. Mutilated religious poems, exhibiting in form the beginnings of parallelism, are imbedded in this literature, and are doubtless examples of the oldest poetry of earliest Egypt. All this literature, both in form and content, betrays its origin among men of the early world. Folk songs, the offspring of the toiling peasant's flitting fancy, or of the personal devotion of the household servant, were common then as now, and in two of them which have survived, we hear the shepherd talking with the sheep,[2] or the bearers of the sedan-chair assuring their lord in song that the vehicle is lighter to them when he occupies it, than when it is empty.[3] Music also was cultivated; and there was a director of the royal music at the court. The instruments were a small harp, on which the performer played sitting, and two kinds of flute, a larger and a smaller. Instrumental music was

---

[1] I, 292–4, 306–315, 319–324.   [2] See infra, Fig. 39.

[3] Zeitschrift 38, 65; Davies, Der el-Gebrâwi, II, pl. VIII.

always accompanied by the voice, reversing modern custom, and the full orchestra consisted of two harps and two flutes, a large and a small one. Of the character and nature of the music played or to what extent the scale was understood, we can say nothing.

Such, in so far as we have been able to condense our present knowledge, was the active and aggressive age which unfolds before us, as the kings of the Thinite dynasties give way to those of Memphis. It now remains for us to trace the career of this, the most ancient state, whose constitution is still discernible.

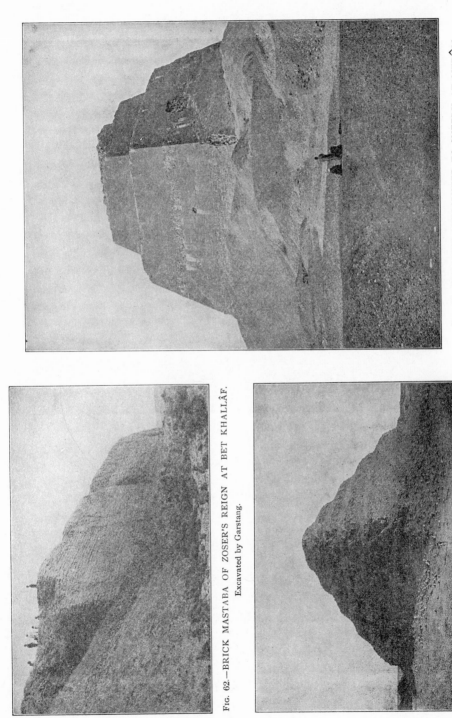

FIG. 64.—PYRAMID ATTRIBUTED TO SNEFRU AT MEDÛM.

FIG. 62.—BRICK MASTABA OF ZOSER'S REIGN AT BET KHALLÂF.
Excavated by Garstang.

FIG. 63.—THE "TERRACED PYRAMID" OF ZOSER AT SAKKARA.

CHAPTER VI

THE PYRAMID BUILDERS

A.t the close of the so-called Second Dynasty, early in the thirtieth century B. C., the Thinites were finally dislodged from the position of power which they had maintained so well for over four centuries, according to Manetho, and a Memphite family, whose home was the "White Wall" gained the ascendancy. But there is evidence that the sharp dynastic division recorded by Manetho never took place, and this final supremacy of Memphis may have been nothing more than a gradual transition thither by the Thinites themselves. In any case the great queen, Nemathap, the wife of King Khasekhemui, who was probably the last king of the Second Dynasty, was evidently the mother of Zoser, with whose accession the predominance of Memphis becomes apparent. During this Memphite supremacy, the development which the Thinites had pushed so vigourously, was skilfully and ably fostered. For over five hundred years the kingdom continued to flourish, but of these five centuries only the last two have left us even scanty literary remains, and we are obliged to draw our meagre knowledge of its first three centuries almost entirely from material documents, the monuments which it has left us. In some degree such a task is like attempting to reconstruct a history of Athens in the age of Pericles, based entirely upon the temples, sculptures, vases, and other material remains surviving from his time. While the rich intellectual, literary, and political life which was then unfolding in Athens involved a mental endowment and a condition of state and society which Egypt, even at her best, never knew, yet it must not be forgotten that, tremendous as is the impression which we receive from the monuments of the Old Kingdom, they are but the skeleton, upon which we might put flesh, and endue the whole with life, if but the chief literary monuments of the time had survived. It is a difficult task to see behind these Titanic achievements, the busy world of commerce, industry, administration, society, art, and literature out of which they grew. Of half a millennium of political change, of overthrow and usurpation, of growth and decay of institutions, of local governors, helpless under the strong grasp of the Pharaoh, or shaking off the restraint of a weak monarch, and developing into independent barons, so powerful at last as to bring in the final dissolution of the state;—of all this we gain but fleeting and occasional glimpses, where more must be guessed than can be known.

The first prominent figure in the Old Kingdom is that of Zoser, with whom as we have said the Third Dynasty arose. It was evidently his forceful government which firmly established Memphite supremacy. He continued the exploitation of the copper mines in Sinai, while in the south he extended the frontier. If we may credit a late tradition of the priests, the turbulent tribes of northern Nubia, who for centuries after Zoser's reign continued to make the region of the first cataract unsafe, were so controlled by him that he could grant to Khnum, the god of the cataract at least nominal possession of both sides of the river from Elephantine at the lower end of the cataract up to Takompso, some seventy five or eighty miles above it. As this tradition was put forward by the priests of Isis in Ptolemaic times as legal support of certain of their claims, it is not improbable that it contains a germ of fact.[1]

The success of Zoser's efforts was perhaps in part due to the counsel of the great wise man, Imhotep, who was one of his chief advisers. In priestly wisdom, in magic, in the formulation of wise proverbs, in medicine and architecture, this remarkable figure of Zoser's reign left so notable a reputation that his name was never forgotten. He was the

[1] Sethe, Untersuchungen, II, 22–26.

patron spirit of the later scribes, to whom they regularly poured out a libation from the water jar of their writing-outfit before beginning their work.[1] The people sang of his proverbs centuries later, and two thousand five hundred years after his death he had become a god of medicine, in whom the Greeks who called him Imouthes, recognized their own Asklepios.[2] A temple was erected to him near the Serapeum at Memphis, and at the present day every museum possesses a bronze statuette or two of this apotheosized wise man, the proverb-maker, physician and architect of Zoser. The priests who conducted the rebuilding of the temple of Edfu under the Ptolemies, claimed to be reproducing the structure formerly erected there after plans of Imhotep; and it may therefore well be that Zoser was the builder of a temple there. Manetho records the tradition that stone building was first introduced by Zoser, whom he calls Tosorthros, and although, as we have seen, stone structures of earlier date are now known, yet the great reputation as a builder ascribed to Zoser's counsellor Imhotep is no accident, and it is evident that Zoser's reign marked the beginning of extensive build-ing in stone. Until his reign the royal tombs were built of sun-dried bricks, only containing in one instance a granite floor and in another a chamber of limestone. This brick tomb was greatly improved by Zoser, in whose time there was built at Bet Khallâf, near Abydos, a massive brick mas-taba (Fig. 62), through one end of which a stairway de-scended, and passing into the gravel beneath the superstruc-ture, merged into a descending passage, which terminated in a series of mortuary chambers.[3] The passage was closed in five places by heavy portcullis stones. This was the first of the two royal tombs now usually erected (see p. 71). In all probability Zoser himself never used this tomb, built so near those of his ancestors; but assisted by Imhotep under-took the construction of a mausoleum on a more ambitious

[1] Schaefer, Zeitschrift, 1898, 147–8; Gardiner, ibid., 40, 146.
[2] Sethe, Untersuchungen, II.
[3] Garstang, Mahasna and Bet Khallâf, London, 1902.

8

plan than any of his ancestors had ever attempted. In the desert behind Memphis he laid out a tomb (Fig. 63), very much like that at Bet Khallâf, but the mastaba was now built of stone; it was nearly thirty eight feet high, some two hundred and twenty seven feet wide, and an uncertain amount longer from north to south. As his reign continued he enlarged it upon the ground, and increased its height also by building five rectangular additions superimposed upon its top, each smaller than its predecessor. The result was a terraced structure, one hundred and ninety five feet high, in six stages, the whole roughly resembling a pyramid. It is often called the "terraced pyramid," and does indeed constitute the transitional form between the flat-topped rectangular superstructure or mastaba first built by Zoser at Bet Khallâf and the pyramid of his successors, which immediately followed. It is the first large structure of stone known in history.

The wealth and power which enabled Zoser to erect so imposing and costly a tomb were continued by the other kings of the dynasty, whose order and history it is as yet impossible to reconstruct. We now know that we should attribute to them the two great stone pyramids of Dashur. These vast and splendid monuments, the earliest pyramids, are a striking testimony to the prosperity and power of this Third Dynasty. Such colossal structures make a powerful appeal to the imagination, but we cannot picture to ourselves save in the vaguest terms the course of events that produced them. They leave a host of questions unanswered. At the close of the dynasty, the nation was enjoying wide prosperity under the vigourous and far-seeing Snefru. He built vessels nearly one hundred and seventy feet long, for traffic and administration upon the river;[1] he continued the development of the copper mines in Sinai, where he defeated the native tribes and left a record of his triumph.[2] He placed Egyptian interests in the peninsula upon such a permanent basis that he was later looked upon as the founder and establisher of Egyptian supremacy there;

[1] I, 146–7.   [2] I, 168–9.

FIG. 65.—ROCK INSCRIPTIONS OF AMENEMHET III, IN WADI MAGHARA, SINAI, INCLUDING SNEFRU AMONG THE LOCAL GODS.

(Ordnance Survey Photo.)

FIG. 66.—CASING BLOCKS AT THE BASE OF THE GREAT PYRAMID. JOINTS OTHERWISE UNDISCERNIBLE INDICATED BY CHARCOAL LINES.

(Photograph by L. D. Covington.)

one of the mines was named after him;[1] a thousand years
later it is his achievements in this region, with which the
later kings compared their own, boasting that nothing like
it had been done there "since the days of Snefru";[2] and
together with the local divinities, Hathor and Soped, his
protection was invoked as a patron god of the region by the
venturesome officials who risked their lives for the Pharaoh
there[3] (Fig. 65). He regulated the eastern frontier, and it
is not unlikely that we should attribute to him the erection
of the fortresses at the Bitter Lakes in the Isthmus of Suez,
which existed already in the Fifth Dynasty. Roads and
stations in the eastern Delta still bore his name fifteen hundred years after his death.[4] In the west it is not improbable that he already controlled one of the northern oases.[5]
More than all this, he opened up commerce with the north
and sent a fleet of forty vessels to the Phœnician coast to
procure cedar logs from the slopes of Lebanon.[6] Following
the example of Zoser, he was equally aggressive in the south,
where he conducted a campaign against northern Nubia,
bringing back seven thousand prisoners, and two hundred
thousand large and small cattle.[7]

Snefru, powerful and prosperous, as "Lord of the Two
Lands," also erected two tombs. The earlier is situated at
Medûm, between Memphis and the Fayum. It was begun,
like that of Zoser, as a mastaba of limestone, with the tomb
chamber beneath it. Following Zoser, the builder enlarged
it seven times to a terraced structure, the steps in which
were then filled out in one smooth slope from top to bottom
at a different angle, thus producing the first pyramid (Fig.
64). Snefru's other pyramid, far larger and more imposing, now dominates the group at Dashur. It was the greatest building thus far attempted by the Pharaohs and is an
impressive witness to the rapid progress made by the
Third Dynasty in the arts. A newly found inscription

---

[1] LD, II, 137 g. [2] I, 731. [3] I, 722.
[4] I, 165, 5; 312, l. 21.
[5] I, 174, l. 9. [6] I, 146. [7] I, 146.

shows that Snefru's mortuary endowments here were still respected three hundred years later.

With Snefru the rising tide of prosperity and power has reached the high level which made the subsequent splendour of the Old Kingdom possible. With him there had also grown up the rich and powerful noble and official class, whose life we have already sketched,—a class who are no longer content with the simple brick tombs of their ancestors at Abydos and vicinity. Their splendid mastabas of hewn limestone are still grouped as formerly about the tomb of the king whom they served. It is the surviving remains in these imposing cities of the dead, dominated by the towering mass of the pyramid which has enabled us to gain a picture of the life of the great kingdom, the threshold of which we have now crossed. Behind us lies the long slow development which contained the promise of all that is before us; but that development also we were obliged to trace in the tomb of the early Egyptians, as we have followed him from the sand-heap that covered his primitive ancestor to the colossal pyramid of the Pharaoh.

The passing of the great family of which Snefru was the most prominent representative, did not, as far as we can now see, effect any serious change in the history of the nation. Indeed Khufu, the great founder of the so-called Fourth Dynasty, may possibly have been a scion of the Third. He had in his harem at least a lady who had also been a favourite of Snefru. But it is evident that Khufu was not a Memphite. He came from a town of middle Egypt near modern Beni Hasan, which was afterward, for this reason, called "Menat-Khufu," "Nurse of Khufu"; and his name in its full form, "Khnum-khufu," which means "Khnum protects me," is a further hint of his origin, containing as it does the name of Khnum, the ram-headed god of Menat-Khufu. Likewise, after his death, one of his mortuary priests was also priest of Khnum of Menat-Khufu.[1] We have no means of knowing how the noble of a provincial town succeeded in

[1] Mariette, Les Mastabas B 1 = Rougé, Inscriptions Hiérogl., 78.

FIG. 67.—THE GREAT PYRAMID OF KHUFU (CHEOPS) AT GIZEH.

Seen from the northwest; the Nile valley in the background.

supplanting the powerful Snefru and becoming the founder
of a new line.   We only see him looming grandly from the
obscure array of Pharaohs of his time, his greatness proclaimed by the noble tomb which he erected at Gizeh, opposite modern Cairo.   It has now become the chief project of
the state to furnish a vast, impenetrable and indestructible
resting place for the body of the king, who concentrated upon
this enterprise the greatest resources of wealth, skill and
labour at his command.   How strong and effective must have
been the organization of Khufu's government we appreciate
in some measure when we learn that his pyramid contains
some two million three hundred thousand blocks, each weighing on the average two and a half tons.[1]   The mere organization of labour involved in the quarrying, transportation and
proper assembly of this vast mass of material is a task which
in itself must have severely taxed the public offices.   Herodotus relates a tradition current in his time that the pyramid
had demanded the labour of a hundred thousand men during
twenty years, and Petrie has shown that these numbers are
quite credible.   The maintenance of this city of a hundred
thousand labourers, who were non-producing and a constant
burden on the state, the adjustment of the labour in the quarries so as to ensure an uninterrupted accession of material
around the base of the pyramid, will have entailed the development of a small state in itself.   The blocks were taken
out of the quarries on the east side of the river south of
Cairo, and at high water, when the flats were flooded, they
were floated across the valley to the base of the pyramid hill.
Here an enormous stone ramp or causeway had been erected,
a labour of ten years if we may believe Herodotus, and up this
incline the stones were dragged to the plateau on which the
pyramid stands.   Not merely was this work quantitatively
so formidable but in quality also it is the most remarkable
material enterprise known to us in this early world, for the
most ponderous masonry in the pyramid amazes the modern
beholder by its fineness.   It was but five centuries since the

[1] Petrie, Gizeh.

crude granite floor of the tomb of Usephais at Abydos was laid, and perhaps not more than a century since the earliest stone structure now known, the limestone chamber in the tomb of Khasekhemui at the same place was erected. The pyramid is or was about four hundred and eighty one feet high, and its square base measured some seven hundred and fifty five feet on a side, but the average error is "less than a ten thousandth of the side in equality, in squareness and in level";[1] although a rise of ground on the site of the monument prevented direct measurements from corner to corner. Some of the masonry finish is so fine that blocks weighing tons are set together with seams of considerable length, showing a joint of one ten thousandth of an inch, and involving edges and surfaces "equal to optician's work of the present day, but on a scale of acres instead of feet or yards of material."[2] The entire monument is of limestone, except the main sepulchral chamber and the construction chambers above it, where the workmanship distinctly deteriorates. The latter part, that is the upper portion, was evidently built with greater haste than the lower sections. The passages were skilfully closed at successive places by plug-blocks and portcullisses of granite; while the exterior, clothed with an exquisitely fitted casing of limestone (Fig. 66), which has since been quarried away, nowhere betrayed the place of entrance, located in the eighteenth course of masonry above the base near the centre of the north face. It must have been a courageous monarch who from the beginning planned this the greatest mass of masonry ever put together by human hands, and there are evidences in the pyramid of at least two changes of plan. Like all the pyramidoid monuments which precede it, it was therefore probably projected on a smaller scale, but before the work had proceeded too far to prevent, by complication of the interior passages, the plan was enlarged to the present enormous base, covering an area of thirteen acres. Three small pyramids, built for members of Khufu's family, stand in a line close by on the

[1] Petrie, History of Egypt, I, p. 40. [2] Ibid.

FIG. 68.—THE PYRAMIDS OF GIZEH.

From the desert on the southwest: Khufu (right); Khafre (middle); Menkure (left).

FIG. 69.—A GRANITE HALL IN THE GREAT MONUMENTAL GATE OF KHAFRE.

The entrance of the causeway (see Fig. 37) leading up to Khafre's (the second) Pyramid at Gizeh (see p. 120).

east. The pyramid was surrounded by a wide pavement of limestone, and on the east front was the temple for the mortuary service of Khufu, of which all but portions of a splendid basalt pavement has disappeared. The remains of the causeway leading up from the plain to the temple still rise in sombre ruin, disclosing only the rough core masonry, across which the modern village of Kafr is now built. Further south is a section of the wall which surrounded the town on the plain below, probably the place of Khufu's residence, and perhaps the residence of the dynasty. In leaving the tomb of Khufu our admiration for the monument, whether stirred by its vast dimensions or by the fineness of its masonry should not obscure its real and final significance; for the great pyramid is the earliest and most impressive witness surviving from the ancient world to the final emergence of organized society from prehistoric chaos and local conflict, thus coming for the first time completely under the power of a far-reaching and comprehensive centralization effected by one controlling mind.

Khufu's name has been found from Desuk in the northwestern and Bubastis in the eastern Delta, to Hieraconpolis in the south, but we know almost nothing of his other achievements. He continued operations in the peninsula of Sinai;[1] perhaps opened for the first time, and in any case kept workmen in the alabaster quarry of Hatnub; and Ptolemaic tradition also made him the builder of a Hathor temple at Dendera.[2] It will be evident that all the resources of the nation were completely at his disposal and under his control; his eldest son, as was customary in the Fourth Dynasty, was vizier and chief judge; while the two "treasurers of the God," who were in charge of the work in the quarries, were undoubtedly also sons of the king, as we have seen. The most powerful offices were kept within the circle of the royal house, and thus a great state was swayed at the monarch's slightest wish, and for many years held to its chief task, the creation of his tomb. An obscure king, Dedefre or

[1] I, 176.   [2] Dümichen Dendera, p. 15.

Radedef, whose connection with the family is entirely uncertain, seems to have succeeded Khufu. His modest pyramid has been found at Aburoâsh, on the north of Gizeh, but Dedefre himself remains with us only a name, and it is possible that he belongs near the close of the dynasty.

It is uncertain whether his successor, Khafre, was his son or not. But the new king's name, which means "His Shining is Re," like that of Dedefre, would indicate the political influence of the priests of Re at Heliopolis. He built a pyramid (Figs. 68, 70) beside that of Khufu, but it is somewhat smaller and distinctly inferior in workmanship. It was given a sumptuous appearance by making the lowermost section of casing of granite from the first cataract. Scanty remains of the pyramid-temple on the east side are still in place, from which the usual causeway leads down to the margin of the plateau and terminates in a splendid granite building (Fig. 69), which served as the gateway to the causeway and the pyramid enclosure above. Its interior surfaces are all of polished red granite and translucent alabaster. In a well in one hall of the building seven statues of Khafre were found by Mariette. We have had occasion to examine the best of these in the preceding chapter.[1] This splendid entrance stands beside the Great Sphinx, and is still usually termed the "temple of the sphinx," with which it had, however, nothing to do. Whether the sphinx itself is the work of Khafre is not yet determined. In Egypt the sphinx is an oft recurring portrait of the king, the lion's body symbolizing the Pharaoh's power. The Great Sphinx is therefore the portrait of a Pharaoh, and an obscure reference to Khafre in an inscription between its forepaws dated fourteen hundred years later in the reign of Thutmose IV,[2] perhaps shows that in those times he was considered to have had something to do with it. Beyond these buildings we know nothing of Khafre's deeds, but these show clearly that the great state which Khufu had done so much to create was still firmly controlled by the Pharaoh.

[1] Fig. 48 and p. 103.　　　　　　　　　　　　　　　　[2] II, 815.

Under Khafre's successor, Menkure, however, if the size of the royal pyramid is an adequate basis for judgment, the power of the royal house was no longer so absolute. Moreover, the vast pyramids which his two predecessors had erected may have so depleted the resources of the state that Menkure was not able to extort more from an exhausted nation. The third pyramid of Gizeh which we owe to him, is less than half as high as those of Khufu and Khafre; its ruined temple recently excavated by Reisner, unfinished at his death, was faced with sun-dried brick, instead of sumptuous granite, by his successor. Of his immediate successors, we possess contemporary monuments only from the reign of Shepseskaf. Although we have a record that he selected the site for his pyramid in his first year,[1] he was unable to erect a monument sufficiently large and durable to survive, and we do not even know where it was located; while of the achievements of this whole group of kings at the close of the Fourth Dynasty, including several interlopers, who may now have assumed the throne for a brief time, we know nothing whatever.

The century and a half during which the Fourth Dynasty maintained its power was a period of unprecedented splendour in the history of the Nile valley people, and as we have seen, the monuments of the time were on a scale of grandeur which was never later eclipsed. It reached its climacteric point in Khufu, and after probably a slight decline in the reign of Khafre, Menkure was no longer able to command the closely centralized power which the family had so successfully maintained up to that time. It passed away, leaving the group of nine pyramids at Gizeh as an imperishable witness of its greatness and power. They were counted in classic times among the seven wonders of the world, and they are to-day the only surviving wonder of the seven. The cause of the fall of the Fourth Dynasty, while not clear in the details, is in the main outlines tolerably certain. The priests of Re at Heliopolis, whose influence is also evident

[1] I, 151.

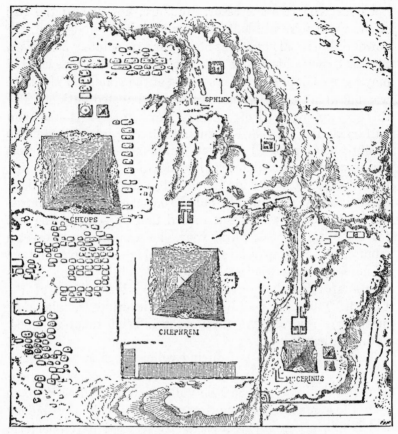

MAP 2.   THE FOURTH DYNASTY CEMETERY AT GIZEH.

in the names of the kings following Khufu, had succeeded in organizing their political influence, becoming a clique of sufficient power to overthrow the old line. The state theology had always represented the king as the successor of the sun-god and he had borne the title "Horus," a sun-god, from the beginning; but the priests of Heliopolis now demanded that he be the bodily son of Re, who henceforth would appear on earth to become the father of the Pharaoh. A folk-tale of which we have a copy[1] some nine hundred years later than the fall of the Fourth Dynasty, relates how

[1] Papyrus Westcar.

Fig. 70.—THE GREAT SPHINX OF GIZEH.

In the background the Pyramids of Khafre (Chephren right) and Menkure (Mycerinus left).

Khufu was enjoying an idle hour with his sons, while they narrated wonders wrought by the great wise men of old. When thereupon prince Harzozef told the king that there still lived a magician able to do marvels of the same kind, the Pharaoh sent the prince to fetch the wise man. The latter, after he had offered some examples of his remarkable powers, reluctantly told the king in response to questions, that the three children soon to be born by the wife of a certain priest of Re were begotten of Re himself, and that they should all become kings of Egypt. Seeing the king's sadness at this information the wise man assured him that there was no reason for his melancholy, saying, "Thy son, his son, and then one of them," meaning "Thy son shall reign; then thy grandson, and after that one of these three children." The conclusion of the tale is lost, but it undoubtedly went on to tell how the three children finally became Pharaohs, for it narrates with many picturesque details and remarkable prodigies how the children were born wearing all the insignia of royalty. The names given these children by the disguised divinities who assisted at their birth were: Userkaf, Sahure and Kakai, the names of the first three kings of the Fifth Dynasty. Although the popular tradition knew of only two kings of the Fourth Dynasty after Khufu, having never heard of Dedefre, Shepseskaf and others whose reigns had left no great pyramids, it nevertheless preserved the essential contention of the priests of Re and in kernel at least the real origin of the Fifth Dynasty. In this folk-tale we have the popular form of what is now the state fiction: every Pharaoh is the bodily son of the sun-god, a belief which was thereafter maintained throughout the history of Egypt[1]

The kings of the Fifth Dynasty, who continued to reside in the vicinity of Memphis, began to rule about 2750 B. C. They show plain traces of the origin ascribed to them by the popular tradition; the official name which they assume at the coronation must invariably contain the name of Re, a custom which the Heliopolitan priests had not been able

[1] II, 187–212.

strictly to enforce in the Fourth Dynasty. Before this name must now be placed a new title, "Son of Re." Besides the old "Horus" title and a new title representing Horus trampling upon the symbol of Set, this new designation "Son of Re" was the fifth title peculiar to the Pharaohs, later producing the complete Pharaonic titulary as it remained throughout their history. Their adherence to the cult of Re as the state religion par excellence found immediate and practical

FIG. 71.   RESTORATION OF THE SUN-TEMPLE OF NUSERRE AT ABUSIR.
(After Borchardt.)

expression in the most splendid form. By the royal residence near later Memphis each king erected a magnificent temple to the sun, each bearing a name like "Favourite place of Re," or "Satisfaction of Re." These sanctuaries are all of the same essential plan: a large fore-court with cultus chambers on each side, and a huge altar; while in the rear, rising from a mastaba-like base was a tall obelisk (Fig. 71). This was the symbol of the god, standing exposed to the sky, and there

was therefore no holy of holies.   There are reasons for supposing that the obelisk and connected portions of the building were but an enlargement of the holy of holies in the
temple at Heliopolis.   The interior of the walls was covered
with sculptured representations of the production of life,
with scenes from the river, swamps and marshes, the fields
and the desert, and ceremonies from the state cult (Fig. 72);
while the outside of the temple bore reliefs depicting the
warlike achievements of the Pharaoh.   On either side of

Fig. 72.   Relief Scenes from the Sun-Temple of Nuserre at Abusir.
In the upper right hand corner, the anointing of the Pharaoh's foot.

the sanctuary on a brick foundation were set up two ships
representing the two celestial barques of the sun-god, as he
sailed the heavens morning and evening.   The sanctuary
was richly endowed[1] and its service was maintained by a
corps of priests of five different ranks, besides an "overseer" who had charge of the temple property.   As the line
of kings grew, and with it the number of temples increased,

[1] I, 159, 8.

the priesthood of the old temple assumed functions likewise in the new one. We can follow these temples one for each king at least into the reign of Isesi, the eighth monarch of the line.[1] Enjoying wealth and distinction such as had been possessed by no official god of earlier times, Re gained a position of influence which he never again lost. Through him the forms of the Egyptian state began to pass over into the world of the gods, and the myths from now on were dominated and strongly coloured by him, if indeed some of them did not owe their origin to the exalted place which Re now occupied. In the sun-myth he became king of Upper and Lower Egypt and, like a Pharaoh, he had ruled Egypt with Thoth as his vizier.

The change in the royal line is also evident in the organization of the government. The eldest son of the king is no longer the most powerful officer in the state, but the position which he held in the Fourth Dynasty as vizier and chief judge is now the prerogative of another family, with whom it remains hereditary. Each incumbent, through five generations, bore the name Ptahhotep. It would almost seem as if the priests of Ptah and the priests of Heliopolis had made common cause, dividing the power between them, so that the high priest of Re became Pharaoh, and the followers of Ptah received the viziership. In any case the Pharaoh was now obliged to reckon with a family of his lords as successive viziers. This hereditary succession, so striking in the highest office of the central government, was now common in the nomes, and the local governors were each gaining stronger and stronger foothold in his nome as the generations passed, and son succeeded father in the same nome. That the new dynasty was obliged to consider the nobles who had assisted in its rise to power, is also to be discerned in the appointment by Userkaf, the first of the line, of his palace steward to the governorship of a district in middle Egypt called the "New Towns,"[2] to which office he added the income of two priesthoods in the vicinity, which had been

[1] Borchardt, Festschr. f. Ebers, p. 13.   [2] I, 213 ff.

established by Menkure, and probably previously held by a favourite of the Fourth Dynasty. But the endowment established by the Fourth Dynasty was respected.

While Userkaf, as the founder of the new dynasty, may have had enough to do to make secure the succession of his line, he has left his name[1] on the rocks at the first cataract, the earliest of the long series of rock-inscriptions there, which from now on will furnish us many hints of the career of the Pharaohs in the south. Sahure, who followed Userkaf, continued the development of Egypt as the earliest known naval power in history. He dispatched a fleet against the Phœnician coast, and a relief just discovered in his pyramid temple at Abusir, shows four of the ships with Phœnician captives among the Egyptian sailors. This is the earliest surviving representation of sea-going ships (c. 2750 B. C.), and the oldest known picture of Semitic Syrians. Another fleet was sent by Sahure to still remoter waters, on a voyage to Punt, as the Egyptian called the Somali coast at the south end of the Red Sea, and along the south side of the gulf of Aden. From this region, which like the whole east, he termed the "God's-Land," he obtained the fragrant gums and resins so much desired for the incense and ointments indispensable in the life of the oriental. Voyages to this country may have been made as early as the First Dynasty, for at that time the Pharaohs already used myrrh in considerable quantities, although this may have been obtained in trade with the intermediate tribes who brought it overland, down the Blue Nile, the Atbara and the Upper Nile. In the Fourth Dynasty a son of Khufu had possessed a Puntite slave,[3] but Sahure was the first Pharaoh whose records[4] show direct communication with the country of Punt for this purpose. His expedition brought back 80,000 measures of myrrh, probably 6,000 weight of electrum (gold-silver alloy), besides 2,600 staves of some costly wood, presumably ebony. We find his officials[5] at the first

[1] Mariette, Mon. div., 54 e.   [2] I, 161, 7; 236.
[3] LD, II, 23, Erman, Aegypten, 670. [4] I, 161, 8.
[5] De Morgan, Catalogue de Monuments, I, 88.

cataract also, one of whom left the earliest of the long series of inscriptions on the rocks, doubtless an indication of expeditions into Nubia.

We can only discern enough of the next four reigns to gain faint impressions of a powerful and cultured state, conserving all its internal wealth and reaching out to distant regions around it for the materials which its own natural resources do not furnish. Toward the end of the dynasty, in the second half of the twenty seventh century B. C., Isesi opened the quarries of the Wadi Hammamat in the eastern desert three days' journey from the Nile. These quarries had perhaps already furnished the materials for the numerous breccia vases of the earlier kings, but Isesi was the first of the Pharaohs to leave his name[1] there. As the Nile at this point approaches most closely to the Red Sea in all its upper course, caravans leaving Coptos and passing by the Hammamat quarries, could reach the sea in five days. It was therefore the most convenient route to Punt; it was probably along this route that the expedition of Sahure, already mentioned, had passed, while Isesi, who now also sent his "treasurer of the God," Burded, in command of an expedition[2] thither, must also have used it. His successor, Unis, must have been active in the south, for we find his name at the frontier of the first cataract, followed by the epithet "lord of countries."[3]

There is now further evidence that the overshadowing greatness of the Pharaohs as felt and acknowledged by the official class was in some measure paling. To none of the earlier victorious records left by the Pharaohs in Sinai had the officials who led these expeditions presumed to affix their names, or in any way to indicate their connection with the enterprise. In relief after relief upon the rocks we see the Pharaoh smiting his enemies, as if he had suddenly appeared there, like the god they believed he was; and there is not the slightest hint that each expedition was in reality led

[1] LD, II, 115 1.   [2] I, 351, 353.
[3] Petrie, Season, XII, No. 312.

FIG. 73.—RUINED PYRAMID OF UNIS (FIFTH DYNASTY) AT SAKKARA.

Earliest pyramid containing religious inscriptions.

FIG. 74.—ISLAND OF ELEPHANTINE, THE HOME OF THE LORDS OF THE SOUTHERN FRONTIER.

Their tombs are in the cliffs on the farther shore.

by some noble functionary of the government. Under Isesi, however, the self consciousness of the official can no longer be completely repressed, and for the first time we find under the usual triumphant relief a single line[1] stating that the expedition was carried out under the command of a certain officer. It is but a hint of the rising power of the officials, who from now on never fail to make themselves increasingly prominent in all records of the royal achievements. It is a power with which the Pharaoh will find more and more difficulty in dealing as time passes. There is perhaps another evidence that the Fifth Dynasty kings no longer possessed the unlimited power enjoyed by their predecessors of the Fourth Dynasty. Their limestone pyramids ranged along the desert margin south of Gizeh, at Abusir and Sakkara, are small,—less than half as high as the great pyramid, and the core is of such poor construction, being largely loose blocks, or even rubble and sand, that they are now in complete ruin, each pyramid being a low mound with little semblance of the pyramid form. The centralized power of the earlier Pharaohs was thus visibly weakening, and it was indeed in every way desirable that there should be a reaction against the totally abnormal absorption by the Pharaoh's tomb of such an enormous proportion of the national wealth. The transitional period of the Fifth Dynasty, lasting probably a century and a quarter, during which nine kings reigned was therefore one of significant political development, and in material civilization one of distinct progress. Art and industry flourished as before, and great works of Egyptian sculpture were produced; while in literature king Isesi's vizier and chief judge composed his proverbial wisdom, which we have already discussed. The state religion received a form worthy of so great a nation, the temples throughout the land enjoyed constant attention, and the larger sanctuaries were given endowments[2] commensurate with the more elaborate daily offerings on the king's behalf. It is this period which has preserved our first religious liter-

[1] I, 264, 266.   [2] I, 154–167.

9

ature of any extent, as well as our earliest lengthy example of the Egyptian language. In the pyramid of Unis (Fig. 73), the last king of the dynasty, is recorded the collection of mortuary ritualistic utterances, the so-called Pyramid Texts which we have before discussed. As most of them belong to a still earlier age and some of them originated in predynastic times, they represent a much earlier form of language and belief than those of the generation to which the pyramid of Unis belongs.

CHAPTER VII

THE SIXTH DYNASTY: THE DECLINE OF THE OLD KINGDOM

In the fullest of the royal lists, the Turin Papyrus, there is no indication that the line of Menes was interrupted until the close of the reign of Unis. That a new dynasty arose at this point there can be no doubt. As the reader has already perceived, the movement which brought in this new dynasty was due to a struggle of the local governors for a larger degree of power and liberty. The establishment of the Fifth Dynasty by the influence of the Heliopolitan party had given them the opportunity they desired. They gained hereditary hold upon their offices, and the kings of that family had never been able to regain the complete control over them maintained by the Fourth Dynasty. Gradually the local governors had then shaken off the restraint of the Pharaoh; and when about 2625 B. C., after the reign of Unis, they succeeded in overthrowing the Fifth Dynasty, they became landed barons, each firmly entrenched in his nome, or city, and maintaining an hereditary claim upon it. The old title of "local governor" disappeared as a matter of course, and the men who had once borne it now called themselves "great chief" or "great lord" of this or that nome. They continued the local government as before, but as princes with a large degree of independence, not as officials of the central government. We have here the first example traceable in history of the dissolution of a centralized state by a process of aggrandizement on the part of local officials of the crown, like that which resolved the Carlovingian empire into duchies, landgraviates or petty principalities. The new lords were not able to render their tenure unconditionally hereditary, but here the Pharaoh still maintained a powerful hold upon them; for at the death of a noble his position, his fief and his title must be conferred upon the inheriting son by the gracious favour of the monarch. These nomarchs or "great lords" are loyal adherents of the Pharaoh, executing his commissions in distant regions, and displaying the greatest zeal in his cause; but they are no longer his officials merely; nor are they so attached to the court and person of the monarch as to build their tombs around his pyramid. They now have sufficient independence and local attachment to locate their tombs near their homes. We find them excavated in the cliffs at Elephantine, Kasr-Sayyâd, Shekh-Sa'îd and Zâwiyet el-Mêtîn, or built of masonry at Abydos. They devote much attention to the development and prosperity of their great domains, and one of them even tells how he brought in emigrants from neighbouring nomes to settle in the feebler towns and infuse new blood into the less productive districts of his own nome.[1]

The chief administrative bond which united the nomes to the central government of the Pharaoh will have been the treasury as before; but the Pharaoh found it necessary to exert general control over the great group of fiefs, which now comprised his kingdom, and already toward the end of the Fifth Dynasty he had therefore appointed over the whole of the valley above the Delta a "governor of the South," through whom he was able constantly to exert governmental pressure upon the southern nobles; there seems to have been no corresponding "governor of the North," and we may infer that the lords of the North were less aggressive. Moreover the kings still feel themselves to be kings of the South governing the North.

The seat of government, the chief royal residence, as before in the vicinity of Memphis, was still called the "White Wall," but after the obscure reign of Teti II, the first king of the new dynasty, the pyramid-city of his successor, the powerful Pepi I, was so close to the "White Wall" that

[1] I, 281.

the name of his pyramid, "Men-nofer," corrupted by the Greeks to Memphis, rapidly became the name of the city and "White Wall" survived only as an archaic and poetic designation of the place. The administration of the residence had become a matter of sufficient importance to demand the attention of the vizier himself. He henceforth assumed its immediate control, receiving the title "governor of the pyramid-city" or "governor of the city" merely, for it now became customary to speak of the residence as the "city." Notwithstanding thorough-going changes, the new dynasty continued the official cult maintained by their predecessors. Re remained supreme and the old foundations were respected.

In spite of the independence of the new nobles, it is evident that Pepi I possessed the necessary force to hold them well in hand. His monuments, large and small, are found throughout Egypt. Now began also the biographies of the officials of the time, affording us a picture of the busy life of the self-satisfied magnates of that distant age; while to these we may fortunately add also their records at the mines and in the quarries. Loyalty now demands no more than a relief showing the king as he worships his gods or smites his enemies; and this done the vanity of the commander of the expedition and his fellows may be gratified in a record of their deeds or adventures, which becomes longer and longer as time passes. Pepi I sent his chief architect and the two "treasurers of the God," besides the master builder of his pyramid, and a body of artisans, to the quarries at Hammamat to procure the necessary fine stone for his pyramid, and they left in the quarry, besides two royal reliefs, three other inscriptions, giving a full list of their names and titles.[1] At the alabaster quarry of Hatnub the governor of the South, who was also "great lord of the Hare-nome," recorded his execution of a commission there for Pepi I;[2] while a military commander perpetuates his achievement of a similar commission for the same king in the Wadi

[1] I, 295-301.   [2] 1, 304-5.

Maghara in Sinai.[1] The pride of office among the official class is undiminished. So many titles have now become purely honourary,—high sounding predicates worn by nobles, who performed none of the duties once devolving upon the incumbents, that the actual administrators of many offices added the word "real" after such titles. We have a very interesting and instructive example of this official class under the new regime, in Uni, a faithful adherent of the royal house, who has fortunately left us his biography. Under king Teti II he had begun his career at the bottom as an obscure under-custodian in the royal domains.[2] Pepi I now appointed him as a judge, at the same time giving him rank at the royal court, and an income as a priest of the pyramid-temple.[3] He was soon promoted to a superior cus- todianship of the royal domains, and in this capacity he had so gained the royal favour that when a conspiracy against the king arose in the harem he was nominated with one col- league to prosecute the case.[4] Pepi I thus strove to single out men of force and ability with whom he might organize a strong government, closely attached to his fortunes and to those of his house. In the heart of the southern country he set up among the nobles the "great lord of the Hare-nome," and made him governor of the South; while he married as his official queens the two sisters of the nomarch of Thinis, both bearing the same name, Enekhnes-Merire, and they became the mothers of the two kings who followed him.[5]

The foreign policy of Pepi I was more vigourous than that of any Pharaoh of earlier times. In Nubia he gained such control over the negro tribes that they were obliged to con- tribute quotas to his army in case of war, and when such war was in the north, where safety permitted, these negro levies were freely employed. The Beduin tribes of the north, having become too bold in their raiding of the eastern Delta, or having troubled his mining expeditions in Sinai, Pepi commissioned Uni to collect such an army among the negroes, supplemented by levies throughout Egypt. The king over-

[1] I, 302–3.   [2] I, 294.   [3] I, 307.   [4] I, 310.   [5] I, 344–9.

looked many men of much higher rank, and placing Uni in command of this army, sent him against the Beduin.[1]   He of course scattered them without difficulty, and having devastated their country, returned home.   On four more such punitive expeditions Pepi I sent him against the tribes of this country; and a final show of hostility on their part at last called him further north than the region on the east of the Delta.   Embarking his force, he carried them in troopships along the coast of southern Palestine, and punished the Beduin as far north as the highlands of Palestine.[2]   This marks the northernmost advance of the Pharaohs of the Old Kingdom, and is in accordance with the discovery of a Sixth Dynasty scarab at Gezer below Jerusalem, in strata below those dated in the Middle Kingdom.   The naive account of these wars left by Uni in his biography is one of the most characteristic evidences of the totally unwarlike spirit of the early Egyptian.

Having thus firmly established his family at the head of the state, the fact that Pepi I's death, after a reign of probably twenty years, left his son, Mernere, to administer the kingdom as a mere youth, seems not in the least to have shaken its fortunes.   Mernere immediately appointed Uni, the old servant of his house, as governor of the South,[3] under whose trusty guidance all went well.   The powerful nobles of the southern frontier were also zealous in their support of the young king.   They were a family of bold and adventurous barons, living on the island of Elephantine (Fig. 74) just below the first cataract.   The valley at the cataract was now called the "Door of the South" and its defense against the turbulent tribes of northern Nubia was placed in their hands, so that the head of the family bore the title "Keeper of the Door of the South."   They made the place so safe that when the king dispatched Uni to the granite quarries at the head of the cataract to procure the sarcophagus and the finer fittings for his pyramid, the noble was able to accomplish his errand with "only one warship," an unprecedented feat.[4]

[1] I, 311–313.   [2] I, 314–315.   [3] I, 320.   [4] I, 322.

The enterprising young monarch then commissioned Uni to establish unbroken connection by water with the granite quarries by opening a succession of five canals through the intervening granite barriers of the cataract; and the faithful noble completed this difficult task, besides the building of seven boats, launched and laden with great blocks of granite for the royal pyramid in only one year.[1]

The north was too difficult of access, too distinctly separated by natural limits from the valley of the Nile for the Pharaohs of this distant age to attempt more in Asia than the defense of their frontier and the protection of their mining enterprises in Sinai. The only barrier between them and the south, however, was the cataract region. Mernere had now made the first cataract passable for Nile boats at high water, and a closer control, if not the conquest of northern Nubia was quite feasible. It was not of itself a country which the agricultural Egyptian could utilize. The strip of cultivable soil between the Nile and the desert on either hand was in Nubia so scanty, even in places disappearing altogether, that its agricultural value was slight. But the high ridges and valleys in the desert on the east contained rich veins of gold-bearing quartz, and iron ore[2] was plentiful also, although no workings of it have been found there. The country was furthermore the only gateway to the regions of the south, with which constant trade was now maintained. Besides gold, the Sudan sent down the river ostrich feathers, ebony logs, panther skins and ivory; while along the same route, from Punt and the countries further east, came myrrh, fragrant gums and resins and aromatic woods. It was therefore an absolute necessity that the Pharaoh should command this route. We know little of the negro and negroid tribes who inhabited the cataract region at this time. Immediately south of the Egyptian frontier dwelt the tribes of Wawat, extending well toward the second cataract, above which the entire region of the upper cataracts

[1] I, 324.

[2] Rössing, Geschichte der Metalle., pp. 81, 83 sq.

was known as Kush, although the name does not commonly occur on the monuments until the Middle Kingdom. In the upper half of the huge "S" formed by the course of the Nile between the junction of the two Niles and the second cataract, was included the territory of the powerful Mazoi, who afterward appeared as auxiliaries in the Egyptian army in such numbers that the Egyptian word for soldier ultimately became "Matoi," a late (Coptic) form of Mazoi. Probably on the west of the Mazoi was the land of Yam, and between Yam and Mazoi on the south and Wawat on the north were distributed several tribes, of whom Irthet and Sethut were the most important. The last two, together with Wawat, were sometimes united under one chief.[1] All these tribes were still in the barbarous stage. They dwelt in squalid settlements of mud huts along the river, or beside wells in the valleys running up country from the Nile; and besides the flocks and herds which they maintained, they also lived upon the scanty produce of their small grain-fields.

Doubtless utilizing his new canal, Mernere now devoted special attention to the exploitation of these regions. His power was so respected by the chiefs of Wawat, Irthet, Mazoi and Yam that they furnished the timber for the heavy cargo-boats built by Uni for the granite blocks which he took out at the first cataract.[2] In his fifth year Mernere did what no Pharaoh before him had ever done, in so far as we are informed. He appeared at the first cataract in person to receive the homage of the southern chiefs, and left upon the rocks a record of the event,—a relief[3] depicting the Pharaoh leaning upon his staff, while the Nubian chiefs bow down in his presence. The unprecedented nature of the event is intimated in the accompanying inscription: "The coming of the king himself, appearing behind the hill-country [of the cataract], that he might see that which is in the hill-country, while the chiefs of Mazoi, Irthet and Wawat did obeisance and gave great praise."[4]

Mernere now utilized the services of the Elephantine

_____

[1] I, 336.   [2] I, 324.   [3] I, 316–318.   [4] Ibid.

nobles in tightening his hold upon the southern chiefs.
Harkhuf, who was then lord of Elephantine, was also appointed governor of the South,[1] perhaps as the successor of
Uni, who was now too old for active service, or had meantime
possibly died; although the title had now become an honourable epithet or title of honour worn by more than one deserving noble at this time. It was upon Harkhuf and his relatives,
a family of daring and adventurous nobles, that the Pharaoh
now depended as leaders of the arduous and dangerous expeditions which should intimidate the barbarians on his frontiers and maintain his prestige and his trade connections in
the distant regions of the south. These men are the earliest
known explorers of inner Africa and the southern Red Sea.
At least two of the family perished in executing the
Pharaoh's hazardous commissions in these far off lands, a
significant hint of the hardships and perils to which they
were all exposed. Besides their princely titulary as lords
of Elephantine they all bore the title "caravan-conductor,
who brings the products of the countries to his lord," which
they proudly display upon their tombs, excavated high in
the front of the cliffs facing modern Assuan, where they still
look down upon the island of Elephantine, the one time home
of the ancient lords who occupy them.[2] Here Harkhuf has
recorded how Mernere dispatched him on three successive
expeditions to distant Yam.[3] On the first, as he was still
young, he was therefore accompanied by his father Iri. He
was gone seven months. On the second journey he was
allowed to go alone and returned in safety in eight months.
His third expedition was more adventurous and correspondingly more successful. Arriving in Yam, he found its chief
engaged in a war with the southernmost settlements of the
Temehu, tribes related to the Libyans, on the west of Yam.
Harkhuf immediately went after him and had no difficulty
in reducing him to subjection. The tribute and the products
of the south obtained in trade during his stay were loaded
upon three hundred asses, and with a heavy escort furnished

[1] I, 332.   [2] Fig. 74.   [3] I, 333–6. See also Fig. 76.

by the chief of Yam, Harkhuf set out for the north. The chief of Irthet, Sethu and Wawat, awed by the large force of Egyptians, and the escort of Yamites accompanying Harkhuf, made no effort to plunder his richly laden train, but brought him an offering of cattle and gave him guides. He reached the cataract with his valuable cargo in safety, and was met there by a messenger of the Pharaoh, with a Nile boat full of delicacies and provisions from the court, dispatched by the king for the refreshment of the now weary and exhausted noble.

These operations for the winning of the extreme south were interrupted by the untimely death of Mernere. He was buried behind Memphis in the granite sarcophagus procured for him by Uni, in the pyramid for which Uni had likewise laboured so faithfully, and here his body survived (Fig. 77), in spite of vandals and tomb-robbers, until its removal to the museum at Gizeh in 1881. As Mernere reigned only four years and died early in his fifth year without issue, the succession devolved upon his half-brother, who, although only a child, ascended the throne as Pepi II. His accession and successful rule speak highly for the stability of the family, and the faithfulness of the influential nobles attached to it. Pepi II was the son of Enekhnes-Merire, the second sister of the Thinite nomarch, whom Pepi I first had taken as his queen. Her brother Zau, Pepi II's uncle, who was now nomarch of Thinis, was appointed by the child-king as vizier, chief judge and governor of the residence city.[1] He thus had charge of the state during his royal nephew's minority, and as far as we can now discern, the government proceeded without the slightest disturbance.

Pepi II, or in the beginning, of course, his ministers, immediately resumed the designs of the royal house in the south. In the young king's second year, Harkhuf was for the fourth time dispatched to Yam, whence he returned bringing a rich pack train and a dwarf (Figs. 41, 75) from one of the pigmy tribes of inner Africa. These uncouth, bandy-legged

[1] I, 344-9.

creatures were highly prized by the noble class in Egypt; they were not unlike the merry genius Bes in appearance, and they executed dances in which the Egyptians took the greatest delight. The land from which they came was connected by the Nile-dwellers with the mysterious region of the west, the sojourn of the dead, which they called the "land of spirits," and the dwarfs from this sacred land were especially desired for the dances with which the king's leisure hours were diverted. The child-king was so delighted on receiving news of Harkhuf's arrival at the frontier with one of these pigmies that he wrote the fortunate noble a long letter of instructions, cautioning him to have it closely watched lest any harm should come to it, or it should fall into the Nile; and promising Harkhuf a greater reward than king Isesi had given to his "treasurer of the God," Burded, when he brought home a dwarf from Punt. Harkhuf was so proud of this letter that he had it engraved on the front of his tomb (Fig. 76), as an evidence of the great favour which he enjoyed with the royal house.[1]

FIG. 75.   STATUE OF AN OLD EMPIRE DWARF.   (From Maspero's Archaeology.)

Not all of these hardy lords of Elephantine, who adventured their lives in the tropical fastnesses of inner Africa in the twenty sixth century before Christ were as fortunate as Harkhuf. One of them, a governor of the South, named Sebni, suddenly received news of the death of his father,

[1] I, 350–354.

prince Mekhu, while on an expedition south of Wawat. Sebni quickly mustered the troops of his domain, and with a train of a hundred asses marched rapidly southward, punished the tribe to whom Mekhu's death was presumably due, rescued the body of his father, and loading it upon an ass, returned to the frontier. He had before dispatched a messenger to inform the Pharaoh of the facts, sending a tusk of ivory five feet long, and adding that the best one in his cargo was *ten* feet long. On reaching the cataract he found that this messenger had returned, bearing a gracious letter from the Pharaoh, who had also sent a whole company of royal embalmers, undertakers, mourners and mortuary priests, with a liberal supply of fine linen, spices, oils and rich perfumes, that they might immediately embalm the body of the deceased noble and proceed to the interment. Sebni then went to Memphis to pay his respects to the Pharaoh and deliver the rich cargo which his father had collected in the south. He was shown every mark of royal favour for his pious deed in rescuing his father's body. Splendid gifts and the "gold of praise" were showered upon him, and later an official communication from the vizier conveyed to him a parcel of land.[1]

A loose sovereignty was now extended over the Nubian tribes, and Pepinakht, one of the Elephantine lords, was placed in control with the title "governor of foreign countries."[2] In this capacity Pepi II sent him against Wawat and Irthet, whence he returned after great slaughter among the rebels, with numerous captives and children of the chiefs as hostages.[3] A second campaign there was still more successful, as he captured the two chiefs of these countries themselves, besides their two commanders and plentiful spoil from their herds.[4] Expeditions were pushed far into the upper cataract region, which is once called Kush in the Elephantine tombs,[5] and, in general, the preliminary work was done which made possible the complete conquest of lower Nubia in the Middle Kingdom. Indeed that conquest would

[1] I, 362–74.   [2] I, 356.   [3] I. 358.   [4] I, 359.   [5] I, 361.

now have been begun had not internal causes produced the fall of the Sixth Dynasty.

The responsibility for the development of Egyptian commerce with the land of Punt and the region of the southern Red Sea also fell upon the lords of Elephantine. Evidently they had charge of the whole south from the Red Sea to the Nile. Not less dangerous than their exploits in Nubia were the adventures of the Elephantine commanders who were sent to Punt. There was no water way connecting the Nile with the Red Sea, and these leaders were obliged to build their ships at the eastern terminus of the Coptos caravan route from the Nile, on the shore of the sea in one of the harbours like Kosêr or Leucos Limên. Sailing vessels were much improved in the Sixth Dynasty by the mounting of the ancient steering oar on a kind of rudder post and the attachment of a tiller. While so engaged, Enenkhet, Pepi II's naval commander, was fallen upon by the Beduin, who slew him and his entire command. Pepinakht was immediately dispatched by the Pharaoh to rescue the body of the unfortunate noble. He accomplished his dangerous errand successfully, and having punished the Beduin, he returned in safety.[1] In spite of these risks, the communication with Punt was now active and frequent. A subordinate official of the Elephantine family boasts in his lord's tomb that he accompanied him to Punt no less than probably eleven times and returned in safety.[2] It will be seen that the usually accepted seclusion of the Old Kingdom can no longer be maintained. Far from allowing himself to be isolated by the deserts which enveloped his land on east and west, or the cataract which had once formed his southern boundary, the Pharaoh was now maintaining an active and flourishing commerce with the south; while the royal fleets brought cedar from the heights of Lebanon on the north. Under these circumstances direct commercial intercourse with the distant island civilization which preceded the Mycenæan culture in

[1] I, 360.   [2] I, 361.

FIG. 76.—TOMB OF HARKHUF AT ASSUAN.

The end of the letter of p. 140 is discernible on the right edge. (From stereograph copyright by Underwood & Underwood, N. Y.)

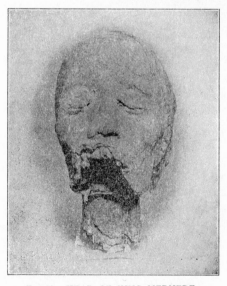

FIG. 77.—HEAD OF KING MERNERE.

(Cairo Museum.)

FIG. 78.—WESTERN CLIFFS OF SIUT.

Containing tombs of Ninth and Tenth Dynasty Nomarchs. (From stereograph copyright by Underwood & Underwood, N. Y.)

the north would have been nothing remarkable, and archæological evidence now shows that it existed.

Pepi II, having ascended the throne as a mere child, doubtless born just before his father's death, enjoyed the longest reign yet recorded in history. The tradition of Manetho states that he was six years old when he began to reign, and that he continued until the hundredth year, doubtless meaning of his life. The list preserved by Eratosthenes avers that he reigned a full century. The Turin Papyrus of kings supports the first tradition, giving him over ninety years, and there is no reason to doubt its truth. His was thus the longest reign in history. Several brief reigns followed, among them possibly that of the queen Nitocris, to whose name were attached the absurdest legends. Two kings, Iti and Imhotep, whose officials visited Hammamat to secure the stone for their pyramids and statues,[1] may possibly belong in this time, though they may equally well have ruled at the close of the Fifth Dynasty; but after the death of Pepi II all is uncertain, and impenetrable obscurity veils the last days of the Sixth Dynasty. When it had ruled something over one hundred and fifty years the power of the landed barons became a centrifugal force, which the Pharaohs could no longer withstand, and the dissolution of the state resulted. The nomes gained their independence, the Old Kingdom fell to pieces, and for a time was thus resolved into the petty principalities of prehistoric times. Nearly a thousand years of unparalleled development since the rise of a united state, thus ended, in the twenty fifth century B. C., in political conditions like those which had prevailed in the beginning.

It had been a thousand years of inexhaustible fertility when the youthful strength of a people of boundless energy had for the first time found the organized form in which it could best express itself. In every direction we see the products of a national freshness and vigour which are never spent; the union of the country under a single guiding hand which had quelled internal dissensions and directed the combined energies of a great people toward harmonious effort,

[1] I, 386–390.

had brought untold blessing. The Pharaohs to whom the unparalleled grandeur of this age was due not only gained a place among the gods in their own time, but two thousand years later, at the close of Egypt's history as an independent nation, in the Twenty Sixth Dynasty, we still find the priests who were appointed to maintain their worship. And at the end of her career, when the nation had lost all that youthful elasticity and creative energy which so abounded in the Old Kingdom, the sole effort of her priests and wise men was to restore the unsullied religion, life and government which in their fond imagination had existed in the Old Kingdom, as they looked wistfully back upon it across the millennia. To us it has left the imposing line of temples, tombs and pyramids, stretching for many miles along the margin of the western desert, the most eloquent witnesses to the fine intelligence and titanic energies of the men who made the Old Kingdom what it was; not alone achieving these wonders of mechanics and internal organization, but building the earliest known sea-going ships and exploring unknown waters, or pushing their commercial enterprises far up the Nile into inner Africa. In plastic art they had reached the highest achievement; in architecture their tireless genius had created the column and originated the colonnade; in government they had elaborated an enlightened and highly developed state, with a large body of law; in religion they were already dimly conscious of a judgment in the hereafter, and they were thus the first men whose ethical intuitions made happiness in the future life dependent upon character. Everywhere their unspent energies unfolded in a rich and manifold culture which left the world such a priceless heritage as no nation had yet bequeathed it. It now remains to be seen, as we stand at the close of this remarkable age, whether the conflict of local with centralized authority shall exhaust the elemental strength of this ancient people; or whether such a reconciliation can be effected as will again produce harmony and union, permitting the continuance of the marvellous development of which we have witnessed the first fruits.

BOOK III

THE MIDDLE KINGDOM

THE FEUDAL AGE

CHAPTER VIII

THE DECLINE OF THE NORTH AND THE RISE OF THEBES.

THE internal struggle which caused the fall of the Old Kingdom developed at last into a convulsion, in which the destructive forces were for a time completely triumphant. Exactly when and by whom the ruin was wrought is not now determinable, but the magnificent mortuary works of the greatest of the Old Kingdom monarchs fell victims to a carnival of destruction in which many of them were annihilated. The temples were not merely pillaged and violated, but their finest works of art were subjected to systematic and determined vandalism, which shattered the splendid granite and diorite statues of the kings into bits, or hurled them into the well in the monumental gate of the pyramid-causeway. Thus the foes of the old regime wreaked vengeance upon those who had represented and upheld it. The nation was totally disorganized. From the scanty notes of Manetho it would appear that an oligarchy, possibly representing an attempt of the nobles to set up their joint rule, assumed control for a brief time at Memphis. Manetho calls them the Seventh Dynasty. He follows them with an Eighth Dynasty of Memphite kings, who are but the lingering shadow of ancient Memphite power. Their names as preserved in the Abydos list show that they regarded the Sixth Dynasty as their ancestors; but none of their pyramids has ever been found, nor have we been able to date any tombs of the local nobility in this dark age. In the mines and quarries of Sinai and Hammamat, where records of every prosperous line of kings proclaim their power, not a trace of these ephemeral Pharaohs can be found. It was a period

147

of such weakness and disorganization that neither king nor noble was able to erect monumental works which might have survived to tell us something of the time. How long this unhappy condition may have continued it is now quite impossible to determine. In the alabaster quarries at Hatnub quantities of inscriptions nevertheless record work there by the lords of the Hare-nome, thus indicating the gathering power of the noble houses who disregard the king and date events in years of their own rule. One of these dynasts even records with pride his repulse of the king's power, saying: "I rescued my city in the day of violence from the terrors of the royal house."[1] A generation after the fall of the Sixth Dynasty a family of Heracleopolitan nomarchs wrested the crown from the weak Memphites of the Eighth Dynasty, who may have lingered on, claiming royal honours for nearly another century.

Some degree of order was finally restored by the triumph of the nomarchs of Heracleopolis. This city, just south of the Fayum, had been the seat of a temple and cult of Horus from the earliest dynastic times, and the princes of the town now succeeded in placing one of their number on the throne. Akhthoes, who, according to Manetho, was the founder of the new dynasty, must have taken grim vengeance on his enemies, for all that Manetho knows of him is that he was the most violent of all the kings of the time, and that, having been seized with madness, he was slain by a crocodile. The new house is known to Manetho as the Ninth and Tenth Dynasties, but its kings were still too feeble to leave any enduring monuments; neither have any records contemporary with the family survived except during the last three generations when the powerful nomarchs of Siut were able to excavate cliff-tombs (Fig. 78) in which they fortunately left records[2] of the active and successful career of their family. They offer us a hint of what the state of the country had been when the Heracleopolitan princes restored order, for the nobles of Siut say of their own domains: "Every official

[1] I, 690. [2] I, 391–414.

was at his post, there was no one fighting, nor any shooting an arrow. The child was not smitten beside his mother, nor the citizen beside his wife. There was no evil-doer . . . nor any one doing violence against his house."[1] "When night came, he who slept on the road gave me praise, for he was like a man in his house; the fear of my soldier was his protection.'"[2]

These Siut nomarchs enjoyed the most intimate relations with the royal house at Heracleopolis; we first find the king attending the burial of the head of their noble house; and while the daughter of the deceased prince ruled in Siut, her son, Kheti, then a lad, was placed with the children of the royal household to be educated.[3] When old enough, he relieved his mother of the regency, and if we may judge of the entire country from the administration of this Siut noble, the land must have enjoyed prosperity and plenty. He dug canals, reduced taxation, reaped rich harvests, and maintained large herds; while he had always in readiness a body of troops and a fleet. Such was the wealth and power of these Siut nobles that they soon became a buffer state on the south of inestimable value to the house of Heracleopolis, and Kheti was made military "commander of Middle Egypt."[4]

Meantime among the nobles of the South a similar powerful family of nomarchs was slowly rising into notice. Some four hundred and forty miles above Memphis, and less than one hundred and forty miles below the first cataract, along the stretch of Nile about forty miles above the great bend, where the river approaches most closely to the Red Sea before turning abruptly away from it, the scanty margin between river and cliffs expands into a broad and fruitful plain in the midst of which now lie the mightiest ruins of ancient civilization to be found anywhere in the world. They are the wreck of Thebes, the world's first great monumental city. At this time it was an obscure provincial town and the neighbouring Hermonthis was the seat of a

[1] I, 404. [2] I, 395, l. 10. [3] I, 413. [4] I, 410.

family of nomarchs, the Intefs and Mentuhoteps. Toward the close of the Heracleopolitan supremacy, Thebes had gained the leading place in the South, and its nomarch, Intef, was "keeper of the Door of the South."[1] The South stood together and in time of scarcity we see the nomes aiding each other with grain and provisions.[2] Intef was soon able to organize the whole South in rebellion, mustering his forces from the cataract northward at least as far as Thebes. He and his successors finally wrenched the southern confederation from the control of Heracleopolis, and organized an independent kingdom, with Thebes at its head. This Intef was ever after recognized as the ancestor of the Theban line, and the monarchs of the Middle Kingdom set up his statue in the temple at Thebes among those of their royal predecessors who were worshipped there.[3]

At this juncture, the unshaken fidelity of the Siut princes was the salvation of the house of Heracleopolis; for Tefibi of Siut, perhaps a son of the nomarch Kheti, whom we first found there, now placed his army in the field against the aggression of Thebes. He marched southward to stem an invasion of the southerners, and meeting them on the west shore of the river, drove them back, recovering lost territory as far south as "the fortress of the Port of the South," probably Abydos.[4] A second army which was advancing to meet him on the east shore was likewise defeated; the ships of a southern fleet were forced ashore, their commander driven into the river and the ships apparently captured by Tefibi.[5] His son Kheti was now appointed as "military commander of the whole land," and "great lord of Middle Egypt."[6] He continued loyal support of his sovereign, Merikere of Heracleopolis, and was the veritable "king-maker" of that now tottering house. He suppressed an insurrection on the southern frontier, and brought the king southward, apparently to witness the submission of the rebellious districts. Returning northward with the king, Kheti narrates with

[1] I, 420.   [2] I, 457–9.   [3] I, 419.
[4] I, 396.   [5] Ibid.   [6] I, 398, 403, 1, 23.

pride how his (Kheti's) enormous fleet stretched for miles up the river as he passed his home. At Heracleopolis, where they landed in triumph, Kheti says,[1] "the city came, rejoicing over her lord . . . women mingled with men, old men and children." Thus in the tomb inscriptions (Fig. 78) of these Siut lords we gain a fleeting glimpse of the Heracleopolitan kings, just as they are about to disappear finally from the scene.

Meanwhile the fortunes of Thebes have been constantly rising. Intef, the nomarch, had been succeeded (whether immediately or not is uncertain) by another Intef, who was the first of the Thebans to assume royal honours and titles, thus becoming Intef I, the first king of the dynasty. He pressed the Heracleopolitans vigourously, pushed his frontier northward, and captured Abydos and the entire Thinite nome. He made its northern boundary the "Door of the North,"[2] that is, the northern frontier of his kingdom, as Elephantine at the first cataract was the "Door of the South." His "Door of the North" was in all probability Tefibi of Siut's "fortress of the Port of the South."[3] His long reign of over fifty years ended, he was followed by his son, Intef II, of whom we know little beyond the fact of his succession.[4] It was now that the accession of a line of Mentuhoteps, probably a collateral branch of the Theban family, established the universal supremacy of Thebes. Mentuhotep II evidently brought the war with the North to a triumphant close. He boasted with impunity of his victories over his countrymen and on the walls of his temple at Gebelên he depicted himself striking down Egyptian and foreigner together, while the accompanying inscription designates the scene as the "binding of the chiefs of the Two Lands, capturing the South and Northland, the foreign countries and the two regions [Egypt], the Nine Bows [foreigners], and the Two Lands" [Egypt].[5] About the middle of the twenty second century B. C., therefore, the Heracleopolitan power,

[1] I, 401.　　　　　　　　　　　　　　　　　[2] I, 422, 423 D, l. 4.

[3] See above, p. 150.　　　　[4] I, 423 G.　　　　[5] I, 423 H.

never very vigourous, completely collapsed, the supremacy passed from the North to the South, and thus, perhaps nearly three centuries after the fall of the Sixth Dynasty and the close of the Old Kingdom, Egypt was reunited under a strong and vigourous line of princes, capable of curbing in a measure the powerful and refractory lords, who are now firmly entrenched in the nomes all over the land. Nothing is certainly known of the family relations of this new Theban house. The kingship presumably passed from father to son, but there are clear evidences of rival claims to the sceptre, nor is the order of the kings entirely certain.

Royal expeditions abroad, long interrupted, were now resumed. Nibtowere-Mentuhotep III's vizier, Amenemhet left a series of very interesting inscriptions in the Hammamat quarries, telling of his twenty five days' sojourn there for the purpose of procuring the blocks for the king's sarcophagus and lid, with an expedition of ten thousand men, the largest thus far known in the history of Egypt. Min, the god of the region, granted them the greatest marvels in furthering their work; a gazelle ran before the workmen and dropped her young upon the very block which they were able to use for the sarcophagus-lid; and later a rain-storm filled the neighbouring well to the brim. The work was thus speedily completed, and Amenemhet boasts "My soldiers returned without loss; not a man perished, not a troop was missing, not an ass died, not a workman was enfeebled."[1] The men for these expeditions were drawn from all parts of the kingdom; it is thus evident that the last three Mentuhoteps controlled the whole country, and that they had restored the power and prestige of the Pharaoh's office. Its relation to the local lords and nomarchs we shall soon be able to discern more clearly, as the Theban family known as the Twelfth Dynasty presently emerges into view.

The forces of expansion, latent for several centuries, now found opportunity in Nubia again, as in the Sixth Dy-

[1] I, 434–453.

nasty, before the fall of the Old Kingdom. Nibhepetre-
Mentuhotep IV was so fully in control of the country
that he could resume the designs of the Sixth Dynasty
for the conquest of Nubia, and dispatched his treasurer
Kheti with a fleet into Wawat[1] in his forty-first year.
Building enterprises, so long interrupted, were again undertaken, and on the western plain of Thebes Mentuhotep IV
erected a small terraced temple under the cliffs, which afterward served as the model for queen Hatshepsut's beautiful
sanctuary beside it at Dêr el-Bahri. Its ruins, recently discovered, constitute the oldest building at Thebes. It was
evidently of mortuary character, and the reliefs on the walls
depicted foreign peoples bringing tribute to the Pharaoh.
Mentuhotep IV's long reign of at least forty six years gave
him ample opportunity to solidify and organize his power,
and he was regarded in after centuries as the great founder
and establisher of Theban supremacy. His successor, Mentuhotep V, was also able to continue the long interrupted
foreign enterprises of the Old Kingdom Pharaohs. He
united the responsibility for all commerce with the southern
countries in the hands of a powerful official, already existent in the Sixth Dynasty, under the old title "keeper of the
Door of the South." Mentuhotep V's chief treasurer,
Henu, who bore this important office, was dispatched to the
Red Sea by the Hammamat road with a following of three
thousand men. Such was the efficiency of his organization
that each man received two jars of water and twenty small
biscuit-like loaves daily, involving the issuance of six thousand jars of water and sixty thousand such loaves by the
commissary every day[2] during the desert march and the stay
in the quarries of Hammamat. Everything possible was
done to make the desert route thither safe and passable.
Henu dug fifteen wells and cisterns,[3] and settlements of colo-
nists were afterward established at the watering stations.[4]
Arriving at the Red Sea end of the route, Henu built a ship
which he dispatched to Punt, while he himself returned by

[1] I. 426.   [2] I, 430.   [3] I, 431.   [4] I, 456.

way of Hammamat, where he secured and brought back with him fine blocks for the statues in the royal temples.[1] Mentuhotep V ruled at least eight years.[2]

After this succession of five Mentuhoteps, we find that the Eleventh Dynasty was then displaced by a new and vigourous Theban family with an Amenemhet at its head. We have already seen one powerful Amenemhet at Thebes as the vizier of Mentuhotep III. This new Amenemhet was able to supplant the last son of the Eleventh Dynasty, and assume the throne as first king of the Twelfth Dynasty. It is very probable also that the new king had royal blood in his veins; in any case his family always regarded the nomarch Intef as their ancestor; they paid him honour and placed his statue in the Karnak temple of Thebes.[3] After a rule of a little over one hundred and sixty years[4] the Eleventh Dynasty was thus brought to a close about 2000 B. C. They left few monuments; their modest pyramids of sun-dried brick on the western plain of Thebes were in a perfect state of preservation a thousand years later,[5] but they barely survived into modern times and their vanishing remains were excavated by Mariette. Nevertheless they laid the foundations of Theban power and prepared the way for the vigourous development which now followed under their successors.

It was not without hostilities that Amenemhet gained his exalted station. We hear of a campaign on the Nile with a fleet of twenty ships of cedar,[6] followed by the expulsion of some unknown enemy from Egypt. Victorious in these conflicts, Amenemhet was confronted by a situation of the greatest difficulty. Everywhere the local nobles, the nomarchs whose gradual rise we witnessed in the Old Kingdom, were now ruling their great domains like independent sovereigns. They looked back upon a long line of ancestry reaching into the generations of their fathers, whose power had caused the fall of the Old Kingdom; and we find them repairing

---

[1] I, 432–433.   [2] I, 418.   [3] I, 419.
    I. 418.   [5] IV, 514.   [6] I, 465.

the fallen tombs of these founders of their houses.[1] While
the Eleventh Dynasty kings had evidently curbed these ambitious lords to some extent, Amenemhet was obliged to go
about the country and lay a strong hand upon them one
after another. Here and there some aggressive nomarch
had seized the territory and towns of a neighbour, thus gaining dangerous power and wealth. It was necessary for the
safety of the crown in such cases to restore the balance of
power. "He established the southern landmark, perpetuating the northern like the heavens; he divided the great
river along its middle; its eastern side of the 'Horizon of
Horus' was as far as the eastern highland; at the coming
of his majesty to cast out evil shining like Atum himself;
when he restored that which he found ruined; that which a
city had taken from its neighbour; while he caused city to
know its boundary with city, establishing their landmarks
like the heavens, distinguishing their waters according to
that which was in the writings, investigating according to
that which was of old, because he so greatly loved justice."[2]
Thus the nomarch of the Oryx-nome relates how Amenemhet
proceeded at the installation of his grandfather as nomarch
there.

To suppress the landed nobles entirely and to reëstablish
the bureaucratic state of the Old Kingdom, with its local governors, was however quite impossible. The development
which had become so evident in the Fifth Dynasty had now
reached its logical issue; Amenemhet could only accept the
situation and deal with it as best he might. He had achieved
the conquest of the country and its reorganization only by
skilfully employing in his cause those noble families whom
he could win by favour and fair promises. With these he must
now reckon, and we see him rewarding Khnumhotep, one
of his partisans, with the gift of the Oryx-nome, the boundaries of a part of which he established as we have already
learned from the above record in a famous tomb[3] of the
family at Benihasan. The utmost that Amenemhet could

---

[1] I, 688-9. [2] I, 625. [3] I, 619-639.

accomplish, therefore, was the appointment in the nomes of nobles favourably inclined toward his house. The state which the unprecedented vigour and skill of this great states-man finally succeeded in thus erecting, again furnished Egypt with the stable organization, which enabled her about 2000 B. C. to enter upon her second great period of produc-tive development, the Middle Kingdom.

CHAPTER IX

THE MIDDLE KINGDOM OR THE FEUDAL AGE: STATE, SOCIETY AND RELIGION.

It had been but natural that the kings of the Eleventh Dynasty should reside at Thebes, where the founders of the family had lived during the long war for the conquest of the North. But Amenemhet was evidently unable to continue this tradition. It is easy to imagine reasons why he concluded that his presence was necessary to maintain his position among the Northern nomarchs, who may still have felt leanings toward the fallen house of Heracleopolis. Moreover all the kings of Egypt since the passing of the Thinites a thousand years before had lived there, except the Eleventh Dynasty which he had supplanted. The location which he selected was on the west side of the river some miles south of Memphis. The exact spot cannot now be identified, but it was probably near the place now called Lisht, where the ruined pyramid of Amenemhet has been discovered. The name given to the residence city was significant of its purpose; Amenemhet named it Ithtowe, which means "Captor of the Two Lands." In hieroglyphic the name is always written enclosed within a square fortress with battlemented walls; from this stronghold Amenemhet swayed the destinies of a state which required all the skill and political sagacity of a line of unusually strong rulers in order to maintain the prestige of the royal house.

The nation was made up of an aggregation of small states or petty princedoms, the heads of which owed the Pharaoh their loyalty, but they were not his officials or his servants. Some of these local nobles were "great lords" or nomarchs, ruling a whole nome; others were only "counts" of a smaller

157

domain with its fortified town. It was thus a feudal state not essentially different from that of later Europe which Amenemhet had organized. It was a state which could exist only as long as there was a strong man like himself in the palace at Ithtowe; and the slightest evidence of weakness meant its rapid dissolution. We are dependent for our knowledge of these barons upon their surviving tombs and mortuary monuments. All such remains in the Delta have perished, so that we can speak with certainty only of the conditions in the South, and even here it is only in Middle Egypt that we are adequately informed.

The noble families of the provincial aristocracy, as we have seen, could in some cases look back upon a line of ancestry reaching into the Old Kingdom, four or five centuries earlier;[1] they had thus gained a strong foothold in their bar-

FIG. 79.   OFFICES OF THE NOMARCH KHNUMHOTEP AT BENIHASAN.

On the left is the chief treasurer before whom gold and silver are being weighed; in the middle is the steward of the estate, who records the amount of grain brought in and deposited in the granary on the right.

onies and domains. We recall also that under the weak Pharaohs of the decadence following the Old Kingdom they had ruled as almost independent dynasts, dating events in years of their own rule and no longer in those of the reign of the Pharaoh, whom in some cases they had defied and even successfully resisted.[2] The nomarch had indeed become a miniature Pharaoh in his little realm, and such he continued to be under the Twelfth Dynasty. On a less sumptuous scale his residence was surrounded by a personnel not unlike that of the Pharaonic court and harem; while his government demanded a chief treasurer, a court of justice,

[1] I, 688-9.   [2] I, 690.

with offices (Fig. 79), scribes and functionaries, and all the essential machinery of government which we find at the royal residence. The nomarch by means of this organization himself collected the revenues of his domain, was high priest or head of the sacerdotal organization, and commanded the militia of his realm which was permanently organized. His power was considerable; the nomarch of the Oryx-nome led four hundred of his own troops into Nubia and six hundred through the desert to the gold mines on the Coptos road.[1] The nomarch at Coptos was able to send an

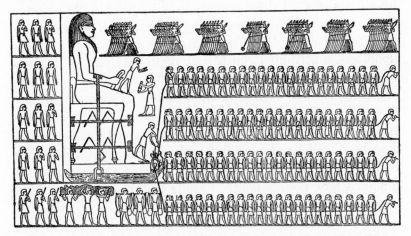

FIG. 80. A Colossus of Alabaster about Twenty-two Feet High Transported on a Sledge by 172 Men in Four Double Lines at the Ropes. (From a Middle Kingdom Tomb at El Bersheh.)

expedition of his own to the Hammamat quarries which brought back two blocks seventeen feet long, and a second expedition which returned with a block twenty feet six inches long drawn by nearly two hundred men along the desert road over fifty miles to the Nile.[2] The people of the nomarch of the Hare-nome dragged from the quarry of Hatnub ten miles to the river a huge block of alabaster weighing over sixty tons and large enough for a statue of the nomarch some twenty two feet high. Such lords were able to build temples [4] and

[1] I, 520-521.

[2] I, p. 225, note c.

[3] I, 694-706.

[4] I, 403; 637, and note a.

erect public buildings in their principal towns.[1] They taught
the crafts and encouraged industries and their immediate
interest and direct personal oversight resulted in a period of
unprecedented economic development.[2] One of the Siut
nomarchs of the Heracleopolitan domination furnishes a hint
of what was to follow, saying: "I was rich in grain. When
the land was in need I maintained the city with kha and
heket [grain-measures], I allowed the citizen to fetch for
himself grain; and his wife, the widow and her son. I
remitted all imposts [unpaid arrears] which I found counted
by my fathers. I filled the pastures with cattle, every man
had many breeds, the cows brought forth twofold, the folds
were full of calves."[3] A new irrigation canal which he made
doubtless contributed much to the productivity of his domains.[4] Faithful officials of the nomarch show the same
solicitude for the welfare of the community over which they
were placed; thus an assistant treasurer in the Theban nome
residing at Gebelen in the Eleventh Dynasty tells us: "I
sustained Gebelen during unfruitful years, there being four
hundred men in distress. But I took not the daughter of
a man, I took not his field. I made ten herds of goats, with
people in charge of each herd; I made two herds of cattle
and a herd of asses. I raised all kinds of small cattle. I
made thirty ships, then thirty more ships, and I brought
grain for Esneh and Tuphium, after Gebelen was sustained.
The nome of Thebes went up stream [to Gebelen for sup-
plies]. Never did Gebelen send up-stream or down-stream
to another district [for supplies]."[5] The nomarch thus
devoted himself to the interests of his people, and was concerned to leave to posterity a reputation as a merciful and
beneficent ruler. All the above records are taken from tomb-
inscriptions, records designed to perpetuate such a memory
among the people. Still more positive in the same direction is a passage in the biography of Ameni, nomarch of the
Oryx-nome, as inscribed in his tomb at Benihasan: "There

[1] I, 637.   [2] I, 638.   [3] I, 408.   [4] I, 407.   [5] I, 459.

was no citizen's daughter whom I misused, there was no widow whom I oppressed, there was no peasant whom I repulsed, there was no herdsman whom I repelled, there was no overseer of serf-labourers, whose people I took for [unpaid] imposts, there was none wretched in my community, there was none hungry in my time. When years of famine came I ploughed all the fields of the Oryx-nome, as far as its southern and northern boundary, preserving its people alive, and furnishing its food, so that there was none hungry therein. I gave to the widow as to her who had a husband; I did not exalt the great above the small in all I gave. Then came great Niles, rich in grain and all things, but I did not collect the arrears of the field.''[1] After making all due allowance for the natural desire of the nomarch to record the most favourable aspects of his government, it is evident that the paternal character of his local and personal rule, in a community of limited numbers, with which he was acquainted by almost daily contact, had proved an untold blessing to the country and population at large.

The domains over which the nomarch thus ruled were not all his unqualified possessions. His wealth consisted of lands and revenues of two classes: the "paternal estate," received from his ancestors and entailed in his line; and the "count's estate,''[2] over which the dead hand had no control; it was conveyed as a fief by the Pharaoh anew at the nomarch's death. It was this fact which to some extent enabled the Pharaoh to control the feudatories and to secure the appointment of partisans of his house throughout the country. Nevertheless he could not ignore the natural line of succession, which was through the eldest daughter; and as we have observed at Siut, she might even rule the domain after the death of her father until her son was old enough to assume its government.[3] The magnificent tombs of the lords of the Oryx-nome at Benihasan reveal very clearly the influence of these customs in the fortunes of this family. At the triumph of Amenemhet I, as we have seen, he appointed one of his partisans, a certain Khnumhotep, as count of Menet-Khufu, chief city of the "Horizon of Horus," an appanage of the Oryx-nome, to which Khnumhotep also soon succeeded as nomarch. As a special favour of Sesostris I, after Amenemhet I's death, Khnumhotep's two sons inherited their father's fiefs, Nakht being appointed count of Menet-Khufu, and Ameni, of whose beneficent rule we have just read, receiving the Oryx-nome. Their sister Beket married a powerful official at the court, the vizier and governor of the residence-city, Nehri, who was nomarch of the neighbouring Hare-nome; and the son of this union, a second Khnumhotep, thereupon by succession through his mother, was appointed to succeed his uncle Nakht as count of Menet-Khufu. Observing the value in the Pharaoh's eyes of being the son of a nomarch's daughter, this second Khnumhotep himself married Kheti, the eldest daughter of his neighbour on the north, the nomarch of the Jackal-nome. Thus the eldest son of Khnumhotep the second had a claim through his mother upon the Jackal-nome, to which in due course the Pharaoh appointed him; while the second son of the marriage, after honours at court, received his father's fief of Menet-Khufu.[1] The history of this line through four generations thus shows that the Pharaoh could not overlook the claims of the heir of a powerful family, and the deference which he showed them evidently limited the control which he might exert over a less formidable dynasty of nobles.

To what extent these lords felt the restraint of the royal hand in their government and administration it is not now possible to determine. A royal commissioner, whose duty it was to look to the interests of the Pharaoh, seems to have resided in the nome, and there were "overseers of the crown-possessions" (probably under him) in charge of the royal herds in each nome;[2] but the nomarch himself was the medium through whom all revenues from the nome were conveyed to the treasury. "All the imposts of the king's house passed through my hand," says Ameni of the Oryx-nome.

[1] I, 619 ff.   [2] I, 522.

The treasury was the organ of the central government, which gave administrative cohesion to the otherwise loose aggregation of nomarchies. It had its income paying property in all the nomes. Some of this property, as we have observed, seems to have been administered by government overseers, while to a large extent it was entrusted to the noble, probably as part of the "count's estate." The "gang-overseers of the crown possessions of the Oryx-nome" gave to Ameni three thousand bulls, of which he rendered an annual account to the Pharaoh, saying, "I was praised on account of it in the palace [of the Pharaoh]. I carried all their dues to the king's house; there were no arrears against me in any office of his."[1] Thuthotep, the nomarch of the Hare-nome, depicted with great pride in his tomb at El Bersheh "great numbers of his cattle from the king and his cattle of the [paternal] estate in the districts of the Hare-nome."[2] We have no means of even conjecturing the amount or proportion of property held by the crown in the nomes and "count's estates," but it is evident that the claims of these powerful feudatories must have seriously curtailed the traditional revenues of the Pharaoh. He no longer had the resources of the country at his unconditional disposal as in the Old Kingdom, even though it was officially only by the king's grace that his lords held their fiefs. Other resources of the treasury were, however, now available, and if not entirely new, were henceforth more energetically exploited. Besides his internal revenues, including the tribute of the nomes and the Residence, the Pharaoh received a regular income from the gold-mines of Nubia, and those on the Coptos road to the Red Sea. The traffic with Punt and the southern coasts of the Red Sea seems to have been the exclusive prerogative of the crown, and must have brought in a considerable return; while the mines and quarries of Sinai, and perhaps also the quarries of Hammamat, had also been developed as a regular source of profit. The conquest of Nubia, and now and then a plundering expedition into Syria-

[1] I. 522.   [2] I, 522, note a.

Palestine, also furnished not unwelcome contributions to the treasury.

The central office of the treasury was still the "White House," which through its sub-departments of the granary, the herds, the "double gold-house," the "double silver-house," and other produce of the country, collected into the central magazines and stock-yards the annual revenues due the Pharaoh. Whole fleets of transports[1] upon the river were necessary for the conveyance of the great quantities of commodities involved. The head of the "White House" was as before, the chief treasurer, with his assistant, the "treasurer of the God," and the vigourous administration of the time is evident in the frequent records of these active officials, showing that notwithstanding their rank, they often personally superintended the king's interests in Sinai, Hammamat, or on the shores of the Red Sea at the terminus of the Coptos road. It is evident that the treasury had become a more highly developed organ since the Old Kingdom. The army of subordinates, stewards, overseers and scribes filling the offices under the heads of sub-departments was obviously larger than before. They began to display an array of titles, of which many successive ranks, heretofore unknown, were being gradually differentiated. Among these appear more prominently than heretofore the engineers and skilled artisans who were exploiting the mines and quarries under the administrative officials. Such conditions made possible the rise of an official middle class.

Justice, as in the Old Kingdom, was still dispensed by the administrative officials; thus a treasurer of the god boasts that he was one "knowing the law, discreet in exercising it."[2] The six "Great Houses" or courts of justice, with the vizier at their head, sat in Ithtowe.[3] There was besides a "House of Thirty," which evidently possessed judicial functions, and was also presided over by the vizier, but its relation to the six "Great Houses" is not clear. There was

---

[1] Tombstone of a commander of one of these fleets, Cairo, No. 20,143.

[2] I, 618.

[3] Sharpe, Eg. Inscr. I. 100.

now more than one "Southern Ten," and "Magnates of the Southern Tens" were frequently entrusted with various executive and administrative commissions by the king. As we shall see, they had the census and tax records in charge; but their connection with the judicial administration cannot be determined with clearness. Magistrates with the sole title of "judge," whose tomb-stones are occasionally found, may have been well-to-do middle class citizens who assumed judicial functions within a restricted local jurisdiction. The law which they administered, while it has not survived, had certainly attained a high development, and was capable of the finest distinctions. A nomarch at Siut makes a contract between himself as count, and himself as high priest in the temple of his city, showing the closest differentiation of the rights which he possessed in these two different capacities.[1]

The scanty records of the time throw but little light upon the other organs of government, like the administration of lands, the system of irrigation and the like. For the purpose of carrying on public works, as well as for taxation and census records, the country was divided into two administrative districts of the South and the North, and the "Magnates of the Southern Tens" served in both districts, showing that they were not confined to the South alone. The office of the governor of the South had disappeared, and already before the close of the Old Kingdom the title had become merely an honourable predicate, if used at all. An elaborate system of registration was in force. Every head of a family was enrolled as soon as he had established an independent household, with all the members belonging to it, including serfs and slaves. His oath to the correctness of the registration-list was taken by a "Magnate of the Southern Tens" in the land-office, one of the bureaus of the vizier's department, where all this registration was filed. These enrollments probably occurred at fixed intervals of some years and there are some indications that the period may

[1] I, 568 ff.

have been fifteen years.[1] The office of the vizier was thus the central archives of the government as before, and all records of the land-administration with census and tax registration were filed in his bureaus. Thus he calls himself one "confirming the boundary records, separating a landowner from his neighbour."[2] As formerly, he was also head of the judicial administration, presiding over the six "Great Houses" and the "House of Thirty"; and when he also held the office of chief treasurer, as did the powerful vizier Mentuhotep under Sesostris I, the account which he could give of himself on his tomb-stone read like the declaration of a king's powers.[3] That he might prove dangerous to the crown was evident in the history of Amenemhet I's probable rise from the viziership. His high office brought with it the rank of prince and count and in some instances he ruled a nome.

It was now more necessary than ever that the machinery of government should be in the hands of men of unquestioned loyalty. Young men were brought up in the circle of the king's house that they might grow up in attachment to it. Thus Sesostris III wrote entrusting a commission to his chief treasurer, Ikhernofret: "My majesty sendeth thee, my heart being certain of thy doing everything according to the desire of my majesty; since thou hast been brought up in the teaching of my majesty; thou hast been in the training of my majesty and the sole teaching of my palace."[4] Even then the closest surveillance was constantly necessary to ensure the king's safety and prevent the ambitious noble in the Pharaoh's service from gaining dangerous power. We shall discover the officials of Amenemhet I abusing his confidence and attempting his life; in far off Nubia Mentuhotep, Sesostris I's commander there, like Cornelius Gallus under Augustus, made himself so prominent upon the triumphal monuments of the king that his figure had to be erased, and in all likelihood the noble himself was dismissed in disgrace.[5] Discreet conduct toward the Pharaoh was the

---

[1] Kahun Papyri, pl. IX–X, pp. 19–29.
[2] I, 531.   [3] I, 530–534.   [4] I, 665.   [5] I, 514.

condition of a career, and the wise praise him who knows how to be silent in the king's service.[1] Sehetepibre, a magnate of Amenemhet III's court, left upon his tomb-stone an exhortation to his children that they serve the king with faithfulness, saying among many other things: "Fight for his name, purify yourselves by his oath, and ye shall be free from trouble. The beloved of the king shall be blessed; but there is no tomb for one hostile to his majesty; and his body shall be thrown to the waters."[2]

Under such conditions the Pharaoh could not but surround himself with the necessary power to enforce his will when obliged to do so. A class of military "attendants" or literally "followers of his majesty" therefore arose. They were professional soldiers, the first of whom we have any knowledge in ancient Egypt. In companies of a hundred men each they garrisoned the palace and the strongholds of the royal house from Nubia to the Asiatic frontier. How numerous they may have been, it is now impossible to determine. They formed at least the nucleus of a standing army, although it is evident that they were not as yet in sufficient numbers to be dignified by this term. Whence they were drawn is also uncertain, but their commanders at least were of higher birth than the middle class. We shall find them as the most prominent force in all the Pharaoh's wars, especially in Nubia, and also in charge of royal expeditions to the mines, quarries and Red Sea ports. Nevertheless the great mass of the army employed by the Pharaoh at this time was composed of the free born citizens of the middle class, forming the militia or the permanent force of the nomarch, who at the king's summons placed himself at their head and led them in the wars of his liege-lord. The army in time of war was therefore made up of contingents furnished and commanded by the feudatories. In peace they were also frequently drawn upon to furnish the intelligent power applied to the transportation of great monuments or employed in the execution of public works. All free citizens,

[1] I, 532.   [2] I, 748.

whether priests or not, were organized and enrolled in "generations," a term designating the different classes of youth, which were to become successively liable to draught for military or public service. As in the Old Kingdom, war continues to be little more than a series of loosely organized predatory expeditions, the records of which clearly display the still unwarlike character of the Egyptian.

The detachment of the nobles from the court since the Sixth Dynasty had resulted in the rise of a provincial society, of which we gain glimpses especially at Elephantine, Bersheh, Benihasan and Siut, where the tombs of the nomarchs are still preserved, and at Abydos, where all other classes now desired to be buried or to erect a memorial stone. The life of the nobles therefore no longer centred in the court, and the aristocracy of the time, being scattered throughout the country, took on local forms. The nomarch, with his large family circle, his social pleasures, his hunting and his sports, is an interesting and picturesque figure of the country nobleman, with whom we would gladly tarry if space permitted. Characteristic of this age is the prominence of the middle class. To some extent this prominence is due to the fact that a tomb, a tomb-stone and mortuary equipment have become a necessity also for a large proportion of this class, who felt no such necessity and left no such memorial of their existence in the Old Kingdom. In the cemetery at Abydos, among nearly eight hundred men of the time buried there, one in four bore no title either of office or of rank.[1] They sometimes designate themselves as "citizens of the town,"[2] but ordinarily the name stands alone on the tomb-stone, with no hint of the owner's station. Some of these men were tradesmen, some land-owners, others artisans and artificers; but among them were men of wealth and luxury. In the Art Institute at Chicago there is a fine coffin belonging to such an untitled citizen which he had made of costly cedar imported from Lebanon. To such we should undoubtedly add those who occasionally prefix to their names

[1] Catalogue Cairo, Nos. 20,001–20,780.   [2] Ibid. passim.

an indication of their calling, like "master sandal-maker," "gold-smith" or "copper-smith," without other designation of their station in life.   Of the people bearing titles of office on these Middle Kingdom tomb-stones of Abydos, the vast majority were small office-holders, displaying no title of rank and undoubtedly belonging to this same middle class. The government service now offered a career to the youth of this station in life; the assistant treasurer, who, as the reader will recall, was so solicitous for the maintenance of the Theban nome in time of famine,[1] expressly refers to himself as a "citizen."   The inheritance by the son of his father's calling, already not uncommon in the Old Kingdom, was now general.   The tomb-stones of the time exhort the passers-by, as they would that their children should inherit their offices, to pray for the deceased.   Such a custom must necessarily lead to the formation of an official middle class. Their ability to read and write also raised them above those of their own station who were illiterate.   A father bringing his son to be educated as a scribe at the court-school exhorts him to industry, and taking up calling after calling, shows that every handicraft abounds in difficulties and hardships; while that of the scribe alone brings honour, ease and wealth.[2] Although the state of the arts shows clearly that the craftsmen of the time were often men of the finest ability, whose station in life could not have been undesirable, the scribal and official middle class thus looked down upon them, and exalted the calling of the scribe above all others.   From this time on we shall find the scribe constantly glorying in his knowledge and his station.   While the monuments of the Old Kingdom revealed to us only the life of the titled nobility at the court and the serfs on their estates, in the Middle Kingdom we thus discern a prosperous and often well-to-do middle class in the provinces, sometimes owning their own slaves and lands and bringing their offerings of first fruits to the temple of the town as did the nomarch himself.[3]   The nomarch showed great concern for the welfare of this class

[1] See above, p. 160.   [2] Pap. Sallier II.   [3] I, 536.

and the reader will recall his gifts of grain to them in time of famine. One of them has left a short record of his prosperity on his tomb-stone, saying: "I was one having goodly gardens and tall sycamores; I built a wide house in my city, and I excavated a tomb in my cemetery-cliff. I made a canal for my city and I ferried [people] over it in my boat. I was one ready [for service], leading my peasants until the coming of the day when it was well with me [day of death], when I gave it [his wealth] to my son by will."[1] At the bottom of the social scale were the unnamed serfs, the "peasants" of the inscription just read, the toiling millions who produced the agricultural wealth of the land,—the despised class whose labour nevertheless formed the basis of the economic life of the nation. In the nomes they were also taught handicrafts and we see them depicted in the tombs at Benihasan and elsewhere engaged in the production of all sorts of handiwork. Whether their output was solely for the use of the nomarch's estates or also on a large scale for traffic in the markets with the middle class throughout the country, is entirely uncertain.

In no element of their life are there clearer evidences of change and development than in the religion of the Middle Kingdom Egyptians. Here again we are in a new age. The official supremacy of Re, so marked since the rise of the Fifth Dynasty, had continued through the internal conflicts which followed at the fall of the Old Kingdom and at the rise of the Twelfth Dynasty his triumph was complete. The other priesthoods, desirous of securing for their own, perhaps purely local deity, a share of the sun-god's glory, gradually discovered that their god was but a form and name of Re; and some of them went so far that their theologizing found practical expression in the god's name. Thus, for example, the priests of Sobk, a crocodile god, who had no connection with the sun-god in the beginning, now called him Sobk-Re. In like manner, Amon, hitherto an obscure local god of Thebes, who had attained some prominence by

[1] Florence, Stela 1774, from my own photograph.

FIG. 81.—A MIDDLE KINGDOM COFFIN AND MORTUARY FURNITURE.

Including boats, servants preparing food and beer, and a house (in the middle). Berlin Museum.

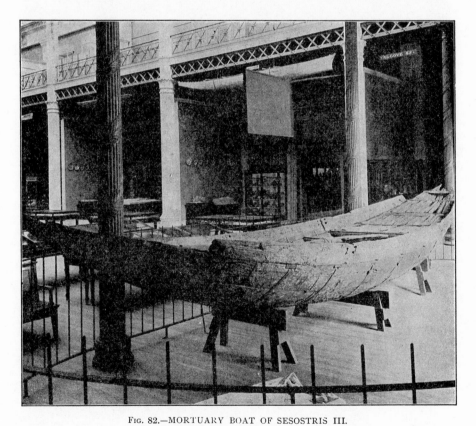

FIG. 82.—MORTUARY BOAT OF SESOSTRIS III.

From his pyramid at Dashur. It is 30 feet long, 8 feet wide, 4 feet deep, of cedar of Lebanon. (Field Columbian Museum, Chicago.)

the political rise of the city, was from now on a solar god, and was commonly called by his priests Amon-Re. There were in this movement the beginnings of a tendency toward a pantheistic solar monotheism, which we shall yet trace to its remarkable culmination.

While the temples had probably somewhat increased in size, the official cult was not materially altered, and there was still no large class of priests. Sesostris II's temple of Anubis at Kahun by the Fayum had over it only a noble with the office of "overseer of the temple," assisted by a "chief lector," with nine subordinates. Only the "overseer of the temple'" and the "lector" were constantly in service at the sanctuary, the nine subordinates being laymen, who served the temple only one month in the year, giving place each month to a new nine, to whom they turned over the temple property each time. Besides these, the menial duties of the sanctuary demanded six door-keepers and two servants.[1]

The triumph of Osiris was not less sweeping than that of Re, although for totally different reasons. The supremacy of Re was largely due to his political prominence, added to the prestige which the sun-god had always enjoyed in the Nile valley; while that of Osiris had no connection with the state, but was a purely popular victory. That his priests contributed to his triumph by persistent propaganda is nevertheless probable, but their field of operations will have been among the people. At Abydos the Osiris-myth was wrought into a series of dramatical presentations in which the chief incidents of the god's life, death and final triumph were annually enacted before the people by the priests. Indeed in the presentation of some portions of it the people were permitted to participate; and the whole was unquestionably as impressive in the eyes of the multitude as were the miracle and passion plays of the Christian age. We find upon their tomb-stones not uncommonly the prayer that in the future

[1] Borchardt, Zeitschrift für Aegyptische Sprache, 1900, 94.
[2] I, 662, 669.

they may be able to come forth from the tomb and view these festal presentations. Among the incidents enacted was the procession bearing the god's body to his tomb for burial. It was but natural that this custom should finally result in identifying as the original tomb of Osiris the place on the desert behind Abydos, which in this scene served as the tomb. Thus the tomb of king Zer of the First Dynasty, who had ruled over a thousand years before, was in the Middle Kingdom already regarded as that of Osiris.[1] As veneration for the spot increased, it became a veritable holy sepulchre, and Abydos gained a sanctity possessed by no other place in Egypt. All this wrought powerfully upon the people; they came in pilgrimage to the place and the ancient tomb of Zer was buried deep beneath a mountain of jars containing the votive offerings which they brought. If possible the Egyptian was now buried at Abydos within the wall which enclosed the god's temple until the tombs began to encroach upon the temple area, and the priests found it necessary to erect a wall around them, cutting them off from further absorption of the sacred enclosure. From the vizier himself down to the humblest cobbler, we find them crowding this most sacred cemetery of Egypt. Where burial at Abydos was impossible, however, as in the case of the nomarch, the dead of the noble class were at least carried thither after embalmment to associate with the great god and participate for a time in his ceremonies; after which they were then carried back to be interred at home. But the masses to whom even this was impossible erected memorial tablets there for themselves and their relatives, calling upon the god in prayer and praise to remember them in the hereafter. Royal officials and emissaries of the government, whose business brought them to the city, failed not to improve the opportunity to erect such a tablet, and the date and character of their commissions which they sometimes add, furnish us with invaluable historical facts, of which we should otherwise never have gained any knowledge.[2]

[1] Ibid.   [2] E. g. I, 671–2.

As the destiny of the dead became more and more closely identified with that of Osiris, the judgment which he had been obliged to undergo was supposed to await also all who departed to his realms. Strangely enough it is Osiris himself who presides over the ordeal to which every arrival in the nether world was now supposed to be subjected. He had already been known as a judge in the Old Kingdom, but it was not until the Middle Kingdom that this idea was clearly developed and took firm hold upon the mortuary beliefs of the time. Before Osiris, enthroned with forty two assistant judges, hideous demons, each representing one of the nomes into which Egypt was divided, the deceased was led into the judgment-hall. Here he addressed his judges, and to each one of the forty two assistants he pleaded not guilty to a certain sin, while his heart was weighed in the balances over against a feather, the symbol of truth, in order to test the truth of his plea. The forty two sins, of which he says he was not guilty, are those which are condemned as well by the modern conscience of the world. They may be summed up as murder, stealing, especially robbing minors, lying, deceit, false witness and slander, reviling, eaves-dropping, sexual impurity, adultery, and trespass against the gods or the dead as in blasphemy or stealing of mortuary offerings. It will be seen that the ethical standard was high; moreover in this judgment the Egyptian introduced for the first time in the history of man the fully developed idea that the future destiny of the dead must be dependent entirely upon the ethical quality of the earthly life, the idea of future accountability,—of which we found the first traces in the Old Kingdom. The whole conception is notable; for a thousand years or more after this no such idea was known among other peoples, and in Babylonia and Israel good and bad alike descended together at death into gloomy Sheol, where no distinction was made between them. Those who failed to sustain the ordeal before Osiris successfully were condemned to hunger and thirst, lying in the darkness of the tomb, from which they might not come

forth to view the sun. There were also frightful execu-
tioners, one of which, a hideous combination of crocodile,
lion and hippopotamus, was present at the judgment, and
to her the guilty were delivered to be torn in pieces. In
harmony with the triumph of the notion of judgment, it is
noticeable in the Middle Kingdom that the desire to enjoy
at least the reputation of a benevolent and blameless life
was more general than before. We now more often read
upon the tomb-stones such words as we noticed in the Old
Kingdom, "I gave bread to the hungry, water to the thirsty,
clothing to the naked and a ferry-boat to the boatless"; or
"I was father to the orphan, husband to the widow, and a
shelter to the shelterless." We have already referred to
the benevolence of the feudal lords of the time.

The blessed dead, who successfully sustained the judgment
each received the predicate "true of speech," a term which
was interpreted as meaning "triumphant," and from now
on so employed. Every deceased person, when spoken of
by the living, received this predicate; it was always written
after the names of the dead, and finally also after those of
the living in anticipation of their happy destiny. The prevailing notions regarding the future life had not been clarified by the universal sway of Osiris. On the contrary, all
the old beliefs were now intermingled in inextricable confusion, only worse confounded by the effort to accommodate
them to the Osiris faith, with which in the beginning they
had had nothing to do. The favourite idea is still that the
departed sojourn in the field of Yaru, enjoying peace and
plenty, to which they contribute by cultivating the fruitful
plains of the isle, which bring forth grain twelve feet high.
At the same time they may dwell in the tomb or tarry in its
vicinity; they may mount the heavens to be the comrades
of Re; they may descend to the realm of Osiris in the nether
world; or they may consort with the noble dead who once
ruled Egypt at Abydos.

In one important respect the beliefs of the Egyptian
regarding his future state have suffered a striking change.

He is now beset with innumerable dangers in the next world, against which he must be forewarned and forearmed. Besides the serpents common in the Pyramid Texts, the most uncanny foes await him. There is the crocodile, who may rob the deceased of all his potent charms, the foes of the air, who may withdraw breath from his nostrils; water may burst into flame as he would drink; he may be deprived of his mortuary food and drink, and be forced to devour the refuse of his own body; he may be robbed of his throne and place; his body may fall into decay; his foes may rob him of his mouth, his heart, or even of his head; and should they take his name away, his whole identity would be lost or annihilated. None of these apprehensions existed in the Pyramid Texts, which have since fallen into disuse; but, we repeat, the deceased must now be forewarned and forearmed against all these dangers, and hence a mass of magical formularies has arisen since the Old Kingdom by the proper utterance of which the dead may overcome all these foes and live in triumph and security. These charms are accompanied by others enabling the dead to assume any form that he wishes, to go forth from the tomb at will, or to return and rejoin the body. The judgment also is depicted in detail with all that the deceased must be prepared to say on that occasion. All this was written for the use of the deceased on the inside of his coffin, and although no canonical selection of these texts yet existed, they formed the nucleus of what afterward became the Book of the Dead, or, as the Egyptian later called it, ''The Chapters of Going Forth by Day,'' in reference to their great function of enabling the dead to leave the tomb. It will be seen that in this class of literature there was offered to an unscrupulous priesthood an opportunity for gain, of which in later centuries they did not fail to take advantage. Already they attempted what might not inappropriately be termed a ''guide-book'' of the hereafter, a geography of the other world, with a map of the two ways along which the dead might journey. This ''Book of the Two Ways'' was probably composed **for** no other purpose than for gain; and the tendency of which it is an evidence will meet us in future centuries as the most baleful influence of Egyptian life and religion.

In the material equipment of the dead, the mastaba, while it has not entirely disappeared, has largely been displaced by the excavated cliff-tomb, already found so practical and convenient by the nobles of Upper Egypt in the Old Kingdom. The kings, however, continue to build pyramids as we shall see. The furniture supposed to accompany the dead in the tomb is now frequently painted on the inside of his coffin. Besides this an elaborate equipment (Fig. 81) was placed beside the coffin, including a model boat with all its crew, in order that the deceased might have no difficulty in crossing the waters to the happy isles. By the pyramid of Sesostris III in the sands of the desert there were even buried five large Nile boats (Fig. 82), intended to carry the king and his house across these waters. In addition to the statue of the noble in his tomb, the king now rewarded deserving servants of the state by the gift of another portrait statue, bearing a dedication in the noble's honour, which was set up in one of the larger temples, where it shared in the offerings, which, after they had been presented to the god, were distributed for other use; and what was even more desired, it enabled the deceased noble to participate in all the feasts celebrated in the temple, as he had been wont to do in life.

CHAPTER X

THE TWELFTH DYNASTY.

WE have seen that under the vigourous and skilful leadership of Amenemhet I the rights and privileges attained by the powerful landed nobles were for the first time properly adjusted and subjected to the centralized authority of the kingship, thus enabling the country, after a long interval, again to enjoy the inestimable advantages accruing from a uniform control of the nation's affairs. This difficult and delicate task doubtless consumed a large part of Amenemhet I's reign, but when it was once thoroughly accomplished, his house was able to rule the country for over two centuries. It is probable that at no other time in the history of Egypt did the land enjoy such widespread and bountiful prosperity as now ensued. Amenemhet himself says of it:

I was one who cultivated grain and loved the harvest-god;
The Nile greeted me in every valley;
None was hungry in my years, none thirsted then;
Men dwelt in peace, through that which I wrought, conversing
     of me.[1]

In the midst of all this, when Amenemhet fancied that he had firmly established himself and his line upon the throne of the land which owed him so much, a foul conspiracy to assassinate him was conceived among the official members of his household. It would seem that it even went so far as the final attack upon the king's person in the night, and that he only escaped with his life after a combat with his assailants in his bed-chamber. However this may be, the palace halls rang with the clash of arms, and the king's life

[1] I, 483.

was in danger.[1] In 1980 B. C., probably no long time after this incident, and doubtless influenced by it, Amenemhet appointed his son Sesostris, the first of the name, to share the throne as coregent with him. The prince brought to his high office a new fund of energy, and as the internal affairs of the country were finally made more and more stable, he was able to devote his attention to the winning of the extreme South, an enterprise which had been interrupted by the rise of the feudal barons and the fall of the Sixth Dynasty. In spite of the achievements of that dynasty in the South, the country below the first cataract as far north as Edfu was still reckoned as belonging to Nubia and still bore the name Tapedet, "Bow-Land,"[2] usually applied to Nubia. In the twenty ninth year of the old king the Egyptian forces penetrated Wawat to Korusko, the termination of the desert route cutting off the great westward bend of the Nile, and captured prisoners among the Mazoi in the country beyond.[3] We can hardly doubt that the young Sesostris was the leader of this expedition. Work was also resumed in the quarries of Hammamat,[4] while in the North "the Troglodytes, the Asiatics and Sand-dwellers" on the east of the Delta were punished. This eastern frontier was strengthened at the eastern terminus of the Wadi Tumilat by a fortification, perhaps that already in existence under the Old Kingdom Pharaohs; and a garrison, with its sentinels constantly upon the watch towers, was stationed there.[6] Thus in North and South alike an aggressive policy was maintained, the frontiers made safe and the foreign connections of the kingdom carefully regarded.

As the old king felt his end approaching, he delivered to his son brief instructions[7] embodying the ripe wisdom which he had accumulated during his long career. The reader may clearly discern in these utterances the bitterness with which the attempt upon his life by his own immediate circle had imbued the aged Amenemhet. He says to his son:

[1] I, 479–480.   [2] I, 500, l. 4.   [3] I, 472–3, 483.   [4] I, 466–8.
[5] I, 469–71; 483, l. 3.   [6] I, 493, ll. 17–19.   [7] I, 474–483.

Hearken to that which I say to thee,
That thou mayest be king of the earth,
That thou mayest be ruler of the lands,
That thou mayest increase good.
Harden thyself against all subordinates.
The people give heed to him who terrorizes them;
Approach them not alone.
Fill not thy heart with a brother,
Know not a friend,
Nor make for thyself intimates,
Wherein there is no end.
When thou sleepest, guard for thyself thine own heart;
For a man has no people,
In the day of evil.
I gave to the beggar,
I nourished the orphan;
I admitted the insignificant,
As well as him who was of great account.
But he who ate my food made insurrection;
He to whom I gave my hand, aroused fear therein.[1]

The story of ingratitude which was finally capable of a murderous assault upon him, then follows, in order to enforce the embittered counsel of the old king. It was probably not long after this that Sesostris was dispatched at the head of an army to chastise the Libyans on the western frontier. During the absence of the prince on this campaign in 1970 B. C., Amenemhet died, after a reign of thirty years. Swift messengers were dispatched to inform Sesostris of his father's demise. Without letting the army know what had happened he quickly left the camp that night and hastened to the Residence at Ithtowe, where he assumed the throne before any pretender among the sons of the harem could forestall him.[2] The whole proceeding is characteristic of the history of every royal line from the earliest times in the orient. Similarly, the news of the old king's death, accidentally overheard in the royal tent of Sesostris, threw a certain Sinuhe, one of the nobles there, into a state of abject terror,

---

[1] I, 478–9. [2] I, 491.

such that he immediately concealed himself, and watching
his opportunity fled into Asia, where he remained for many
years. Whether he had been guilty of some act which in-
curred the displeasure of the prince coregent, or whether
he had some indirect claim upon the throne which became
valid at Amenemhet's death, is uncertain; but his precipi-
tate flight from Egypt is another striking evidence of the
dangerous forces which were liberated by the death of a
Pharaoh.[1]

The achievements of the house of Amenemhet outside of
the limits of Egypt: in Nubia, Hammamat and Sinai, have
left more adequate records in these regions than their beneficent and prosperous rule in Egypt itself; and the progress
of the dynasty, at least in inscribed records, can be more
clearly traced abroad than at home. It will therefore be
easier to follow the foreign enterprises of the dynasty before
we dwell upon their achievements at home. Profiting by his
ten years' experience as coregent with his father, Sesostris
I was able to maintain with undimmed splendour the prestige of his house. He proved himself quite capable of continuing the great enterprises which he had inherited. The
conquest of Nubia was pushed as before; the feudatories
were called upon to muster their quotas, and Ameni, later
nomarch of the Oryx-nome, relates in his Benihasan tomb
that his father, who had been appointed nomarch by Amenemhet I, was now too old to undertake such a campaign,
and that he himself, therefore, as his father's representative placed himself at the head of the troops of the Oryx-
nome, and penetrated Kush under the leadership of his liege,
Sesostris I. The war was thus carried above the second cataract into the great region known as Kush, which now
becomes common in the monumental records, although the
name occurs but once upon the monuments of the Old Kingdom.[2] We know nothing of the course of the campaign,
but it did not involve serious fighting, for Ameni boasts
that he returned without the loss of a man.[3] The nomarch

[1] I, 486 ff.   I, 361.   [3] I, 519.

of Elephantine, as in the Sixth Dynasty, also played a prominent part in the war and it was perhaps upon this expedition that an elephant was captured, to which he refers in his tomb at Assuan.[1] The campaign is notable as the first in a foreign country ever led by the Pharaoh personally, in so far as we know. The date of the expedition is unknown, but it was doubtless earlier than that which occurred eight years after the death of the king's father, for Sesostris I then no longer regarded it as necessary to lead the conquest of the South in person. He therefore dispatched Mentuhotep, one of his commanders, on a further campaign in Kush. Mentuhotep left a large stela[2] at Wadi Halfa, just below the second cataract, recording his triumph and giving us the first list of conquered foreign districts and towns which we possess. Unfortunately we know so little of Nubian geography in this distant age that only one of the ten districts enumerated can be located. It was called Shet, and lay above the second cataract some thirty or forty miles south of Wadi Halfa, near modern Kummeh. It is thus probable that Mentuhotep's stela was erected close to, if not in the region which he conquered. To this stela we have already referred as the one on which Mentuhotep made himself so prominent that his figure was erased and that of a god placed over it. All appearances would indicate that the successful commander was deposed and disgraced. The country was now sufficiently subjugated, so that the chiefs could be forced to work the mines on the east, in the Wadi Alâki and vicinity, and Ameni of the Oryx-nome was dispatched to Nubia at the head of four hundred troops of his nome to bring back the output of gold. The king improved the occasion to send with Ameni the young crownprince, who afterward became Amenemhet II, in order that he might familiarize himself with the region where he should one day be called upon to continue the process of subjugation and of incorporation into the Pharaoh's kingdom.[3]

Similarly the gold country on the east of Coptos was now

[1] I, p. 247, note b.   [2] I, 510–514.   [3] I, 520.

exploited, and the faithful Ameni was entrusted with the mission of convoying the vizier, who had been sent thither, to convey the precious metal safely to the Nile valley. This he successfully accomplished with a force of six hundred men, mustered from the Oryx-nome.[1] The development of Egypt's foreign interests was evidently closely watched by Sesostris I, and it is under him that we first hear of intercourse with the oases. While the Pharaoh was not yet able to take possession of them, it is evident that he was in communication with their towns. Ikudidi, a steward of Sesostris I, was dispatched by him to the great oasis of El Khargeh on the west of Abydos, whence the caravans started thither. His visit in the city of the holy sepulchre of Osiris was an opportunity improved by Ikudidi, as by so many of his colleagues; and he erected a memorial stela there, praying for the favour of the god. His incidental reference on this monument to the occasion of his visit at Abydos is our sole source of information regarding his expedition to the oasis.[2]

It was doubtless the realization of the evident advantage which he had enjoyed by the association with his father as coregent that induced Sesostris I to appoint his own son in the same way. When he died in 1935 B. C., after a reign of thirty five years, his son, Amenemhet II had already been coregent for three years,[3] and assumed the sole authority without difficulty. This policy was also continued by Amenemhet II and his son Sesostris II had also ruled three years[4] in conjunction with his father before the latter's death. For fifty years under these two kings in succession the nation enjoyed unabated prosperity. The mines of Sinai were reopened,[5] and the traffic with Punt, resumed by Amenemhet II, was continued under his son.[6] The road across the desert from Coptos, five days to the Red Sea, had already been supplied with wells and stations by the Theban

---

[1] I, 521. [2] I, 524-8. [3] I, 460.
[4] Ibid. [5] I, 602. [6] I, 604-6, 618.

kings of the Eleventh Dynasty.[1] The route was north of the Hammamat road and terminated in a small harbour at the mouth of the modern Wadi Gasûs, some miles north of the later harbour of Kosêr, the Leucos Limên of the Ptolemies. Two of the commanders who sailed from this port (Wadi Gasûs) left inscriptions[2] there to commemorate their safe return. The distant shores of Punt gradually became more familiar to Egyptian folk and a popular tale narrates the marvellous adventures of a shipwrecked seaman in these waters. The Nubian gold-mines continued to be a source of wealth to the royal house, and Egyptian interests in Nubia were protected by fortresses in Wawat, garrisoned and subject to periodical inspection.[3] With the death of Sesostris II in 1887 B. C., all was ripe for the complete and thorough conquest of the two hundred miles of Nile valley that lie between the first and second cataracts.

Sesostris III was possibly the only one of his house who had not enjoyed a period of joint power with his father in preparation for the duties of his high office. Nevertheless he proved himself worthy of the great line from which he sprang. Immediately on his accession he took the preliminary steps toward the completion of the great task in Nubia. The most important of these measures was the establishment of unbroken connection by water with the country above the first cataract. It was over six hundred years since the excavation of the canal through the cataract by Uni in the Sixth Dynasty, and meantime it may have been demolished by the action of the powerful current. In any case, we hear nothing more of it. At the most difficult point in the granite barrier the engineers of Sesostris III cut a channel through the rock some two hundred and sixty feet long, nearly thirty four feet wide and nearly twenty six feet deep.[4] It was named "Beautiful-are-the-Ways-of-Khekure" (the throne name of Sesostris III), and many a war-galley of the Pharaoh must have been drawn up through it during

[1] See above, p. 153.   [2] I, 604–6, 617–18.   [3] I, 616.   [4] I, 642–4.

the early campaigns of this king, of which we unfortunately
have no records. In the eighth year it was found to be
choked up and had to be cleared for the expedition then
passing up river.[1] The subjugation of the country had
then made such progress that Sesostris III was in that year
able to select a favourable strategic position as his frontier
at modern Kummeh and Semneh, which are opposite each
other on the banks of the river just above the second cataract. This point he formally declared to be the southern
boundary of his kingdom. He erected on each side of the
river a stela marking the boundary-line, and one of these
two important landmarks has survived; it bears the following significant inscription: "Southern boundary made in
the year eight, under the majesty of the king of Upper and
Lower Egypt, Sesostris III, who is given life for ever and
ever:—in order to prevent that any negro should cross it
by water or by land, with a ship, or any herds of the
negroes; except a negro who shall cross it to do trading . . .
or with a commission. All kind treatment shall be accorded
them, but without allowing a ship of the negroes to pass
by Heh [Semneh] going down stream, forever."[2] It was
of course impossible to maintain the frontier in this way
without a constant display of force. Sesostris III had therefore erected a strong fortress on each side of the river at
this point. The stronger and larger of the two, at Semneh,
on the west side, was called "Mighty is Khekure" (Sesostris III),[3] and within its fortified enclosure he built a temple
to Dedwen, a native god of Nubia. These two strongholds
(Fig. 83) still survive, and although in a state of ruin, they
show remarkable skill in the selection of the site and
unexpected knowledge of the art of constructing effective
defenses.

Four years later disturbances among the turbulent Nubian
tribes south of the frontier again called the king into Nubia.
Although Egypt did not claim sovereignty in Kush, the
country above the second cataract, it was nevertheless nec-

[1] I, 645–7.   [2] I, 652.   [3] I, 752.

essary for the Pharaoh to protect the trade-routes leading through it to his new frontier, from the extreme south—routes, along which the products of the Sudan were now constantly passing into Egypt. It will be noticed that the declaration of the boundary permitted the passage of any negro who came to trade, or bore a matter of business from some southern chief. From now on it was more often south of his frontier that the Pharaoh was obliged to appear in force,

FIG. 83. RESTORATION OF THE FORTRESSES OF SEMNEH AND KUMMEH.
(After Perrot and Chipiez.)

than in the country between the first two cataracts. Moreover, there was rich plunder to be had on these campaigns over the border, so that the maintenance of the southern trade routes was not without its compensations. Sesostris III was able to send his chief treasurer, Ikhernofret, to restore the cultus image of Osiris at Abydos with gold captured in Kush;[1] it continued to be more plentiful and therefore less valuable than silver. The letter written by the

[1] I, 665.

king to the treasurer on this occasion we have already read in the preceding chapter.[1]

The Kushite tribes including the barbarians on the east of the Nile valley, must have made an unusual raid over the border just before the sixteenth year, for in that year Sesostris III undertook an extensive campaign against them, in which he devastated their country, burnt their harvests and carried off their cattle. He then renewed his declaration of the southern boundary at Semneh, erecting a stela[2] in the temple there bearing his second proclamation of the place of the frontier, and exhorting his descendants to maintain it where he had established it. He also erected on the boundary a statue[3] of himself as if to awe the natives of the region by his very presence. At the same time he strengthened the frontier defenses by a fortress at Wadi Halfa, probably due to him, and another at Matuga, twelve miles further south, in which his name was found. He erected also another stronghold on the island of Uronarti, just below Semneh. Here he placed a duplicate of the second proclamation.[4] He called this new fort "Repulse of the Troglodytes,"[5] and an annual feast bearing the same name was established in the temple of Semneh, where it was maintained with a regular calendar of offerings. This feast was still celebrated and its calendar of offerings renewed under the Empire.[6] Three years later a campaign, which may have been only a journey of inspection, was led into Kush by the king himself, and as far as we know this was his last expedition thither.[7] He seems to have led all his wars there in person; his vigourous policy so thoroughly established the supremacy of the Pharaoh in the newly won possessions that the Empire regarded him as the real conqueror of the region, and he was worshipped already in the Eighteenth Dynasty as the god of the land.[8] Thus the gradual progress of the Pharaohs southward, which had begun in prehistoric times at El Kab (Nekhen) and had

---

[1] See above, p. 166.   [2] I, 653–660.   [3] I, 660.   [4] I, 654.
[5] Ibid.   [6] II, 167 ff.   [7] I, 692.   [8] II, 167 ff.

FIG. 84.—THE NUBIAN NILE FROM THE RUINED MOSLEM
STRONGHOLD ON THE HEIGHTS OF IBRIM.

(Stereograph copyright by Underwood & Underwood, N. Y.)

FIG. 85.—RUINS OF THE MIDDLE KINGDOM MINING SETTLEMENT AT SARBUT
EL-KHADEM, SINAI.

(Ordnance Survey photograph.)

absorbed the first cataract by the beginning of the Sixth Dynasty, had now reached the second cataract, and had added two hundred miles of the Nile valley to the kingdom. While this conquest had been already begun in the Sixth Dynasty, it was the kings of the Twelfth Dynasty who made it an accomplished fact.

It is under the aggressive Sesostris III also that we hear of the first invasion of Syria by the Pharaohs. Sebek-khu, one of his military attendants, at that time commandant of the residence city, who had also served in Nubia, mentions on his memorial stone[1] at Abydos that he accompanied the king on a campaign into a region called Sekmem in Retenu (Syria). The Asiatics were defeated in battle, and Sebek-khu took a prisoner. He narrates with visible pride how the king rewarded him: "He gave me a staff of electrum into my hand, a bow, and a dagger wrought with electrum, together with his [the prisoner's] weapons." Here is a trace of the military enthusiasm, which two centuries and a half later achieved the conquest of the Pharaoh's empire in the same region. Unfortunately we do not know the location of Sekmem in Syria, but it is evident that in some degree the Pharaohs of the Middle Kingdom were preparing the way for the conquest in Asia, as those of the Sixth Dynasty had done in Nubia. Already in Sesostris I's time regular messengers[2] to and from the Pharaonic court were traversing Syria and Palestine: Egyptians and the Egyptian tongue were not uncommon there, and the dread of the Pharaoh's name was already felt. At Gezer, between Jerusalem and the sea, the stela of an Egyptian official of this age has recently been found[3] within the precincts of the "high place" in the "fourth city" from the bottom of the Gezer "tell." Khnumhotep of Menet-Khufu depicts in his well known Benihasan tomb the arrival of thirty seven Semitic tribesmen, who evidently came to trade with the nomarch, offering him the fragrant cosmetics so much used

[1] I, 676–687.   [2] I, 496, l. 94.   [3] PEFQS 1903, 37, 125.

by the Egyptians.[1] Their leader was a "ruler of the hill-country, Absha," a name well known in Hebrew as Abshai.[2] The unfortunate noble, Sinuhe, who fled to Syria at the death of Amenemhet I, found not far over the border a friendly sheik, who had been in Egypt, further north he found Egyptians abiding.[3] While a fortress existed at the Delta frontier to keep out the marauding Beduin,[4] there can be no doubt that it was no more a hindrance to legitimate trade and intercourse than was the blockade against the negroes maintained by Sesostris III at the second cataract. This Suez region and likewise the Gulf of Suez were already connected with the eastern arm of the Nile by canal, the earliest known connection between the Mediterranean and the Red Sea. Fragmentary but massive remains of the temple buildings erected by this dynasty in the cities of the northeastern Delta, like Tanis and Nebesheh, show their activity in this region. The needs of the Semitic tribes of neighbouring Asia were already those of highly civilized peoples and gave ample occasion for trade. The tribesmen in the Benihasan tomb wear garments of finely patterned, woven, woolen stuff and sandals of leather, carry metal weapons and use a richly wrought lyre. Already the red pottery produced by the Hittite peoples in Cappadocia, of Asia Minor, was possibly finding its way to the Semites of southern Palestine. Doubtless the commerce along this route, through Palestine, over Carmel and northward to the trade-routes leading down the Euphrates to Babylon, while not yet heavy, was already long existent. Commerce with southern Europe had also begun. The peoples of the Ægean, whose civilization was now rapidly developing into that of the Mycenæan age, were not unknown in Egypt at this time. They were called Haunebu, and a treasurer of the Eleventh Dynasty, whose duty was the maintenance of safe frontier ports, boasts of himself as one "who quells the Haunebu."[5] This shows that their intercourse with Egypt was not always

[1] I, p. 281, note d.   [2] II Sam., 10: 10.   [3] I, 493, l. 26, 494.
[4] I, 493, ll. 16–19.   [5] I, 428.

peaceful. A scribe of the time likewise boasts that his pen
included the Haunebu also in his records. Their pottery has
been found at Kahun in burials of this age, and the Ægean
decorative art of the time, especially in its use of spirals, is
influenced by that of Egypt. Europe thus emerges more
clearly upon the horizon of the Nile people during the Middle
Kingdom.

While Sesostris III's campaign into Syria was evidently
no more than a plundering expedition, as far from achieving
the conquest of the country as were the expeditions of the
Sixth Dynasty into Nubia, nevertheless it must have added
much to the reputation of his house. As the first Pharaoh
who had personally led a campaign in a foreign land, the
Nubian wars of Sesostris I had brought undying prestige
to the name, a prestige which had been greatly increased
by the achievements of Sesostris III. To the name Sesostris, therefore, tradition attached the first foreign conquests
of the Pharaohs. Around this name clustered forever after
the stories of war and conquest related by the people. In
Greek times Sesostris had long since become but a legendary
figure which cannot be identified with any particular king.
That some of the deeds of Rameses II were possibly also
interwoven into the Greek legend of Sesostris is not the
slightest reason for identifying Sesostris with that Nineteenth Dynasty king; nor, we repeat, will the preposterous
deeds narrated of the legendary Sesostris permit of his iden-
tification with any particular historical king.

For thirty eight years Sesostris III continued his vigourous rule of a kingdom which now embraced a thousand
miles of Nile valley. He had even succeeded in suppressing the feudal nobles; and their tombs, as at Beni-Hasan
and Bersheh, now disappear. As old age drew on, he
appointed his son as coregent, and an account of the
appointment was recorded on the walls of the temple at
Arsinoe in the Fayum. At Sesostris III's death in 1849

B. C., this coregent son Amenemhet, the third of the name, seems to have assumed the throne without difficulty.

A number of peaceful enterprises for the prosperity of the country and the increase of the royal revenues were successfully undertaken by Amenemhet III. While operations in the mines of Sinai had been resumed as early as the reign of Sesostris I, the foreign projects of the dynasty had elsewhere quite surpassed their achievements here. It remained for Amenemhet III to develop the equipment of the stations in the peninsula, so that they might become more permanent than the mere camp of an expedition while working the mines for a few months. These expeditions suffered great hardships and an official of the time describes the difficulties which beset him when some unlucky chance had decreed that he should arrive there in summer. He says that "although it was not the season for going to this Mine-Land," he went without flinching, and in spite of the fact that "the highlands are hot in summer and the mountains brand the skin," he encouraged his workmen who complained of "this evil summer season," and having accomplished the work brought back more than had been required of him. He left a stela [1] there telling of his experience and encouraging those of his posterity who might find themselves in a similar predicament. Under such conditions permanent wells and cisterns, barracks for the workmen, houses for the directing officials, and fortifications against the marauding Beduin were indispensable. While some of these things may have been already furnished by his predecessors, Amenemhet III made the station at Sarbut el-Khadem a well equipped colony for the exploitation of the mineral wealth of the mountains. He excavated a large cistern in the rocks and opened it with festival celebrations in his forty fourth year. [2] A temple for the local Hathor was erected, and we find an official of the treasury journeying thither with offerings by water, a fact which shows that the Gulf of Suez was commonly utilized to avoid the wearisome desert journey. [3] The mines

[1] I, 733-740.   [2] I, 725-727.   [3] I, 717-718; similar offerings I, 738.

were placed each under charge of a foreman, after whom it was named, and at periodic visits of the treasury officials a fixed amount of ore was expected from each mine.[1] The occasional raids of the neighbouring Beduin were doubtless of little consequence in view of the troops still controlled by the "treasurer of the god," who could easily disperse the plundering bands that might venture too close to the colony. Here Egyptians died and were buried in the burning valley with all the equipment customary at home, and the ruins still surviving (Fig. 85) show that what had before been but an intermittent and occasional effort had now become a perma-nent and uninterrupted industry, contributing a fixed annual amount to the royal treasury.

It is doubtless true that the circumstances in which these kings of the feudal period found themselves forced them to seek new sources of wealth outside of the country; but at the same time, as we have before intimated, they raised the productive capacity of the land to an unprecedented level. Unfortunately, the annals or records of these achievements have not survived. It was particularly Amenemhet III of whom we have evidence of attention to the irrigation system. His officials in the fortress of Semneh at the second cataract had instructions to record the height of the Nile on the rocks there, which thus in a few years became a nilometer, recording the maximum level of the high water from year to year. These records,[2] still preserved upon the rocks, are from twenty five to thirty feet higher than the Nile rises at the present day. Such observations, communicated without delay to the officials of lower Egypt in the vizier's office, enabled them to estimate the crops of the coming season, and the rate of taxation was fixed accordingly.

In Lower Egypt a plan was also devised for extending the time during which the waters of the inundation could be made available by an enormous scheme of irrigation, which was carried out with brilliant success. A glance at the

[1] I, 731.

[2] LD II, 139; Lepsius, Sitzungsber. der Berliner Akad. 1844, 374 ff.

map (No. 13) will show the reader an opening in the western highlands of the Nile valley some sixty five miles above the southern apex of the Delta. This gap in the western hills leads into the great depression of the Libyan desert known as the Fayum, a basin which does not differ from those of the western oases, and is indeed an extensive oasis close to the Nile valley, with which it is connected by the gap already

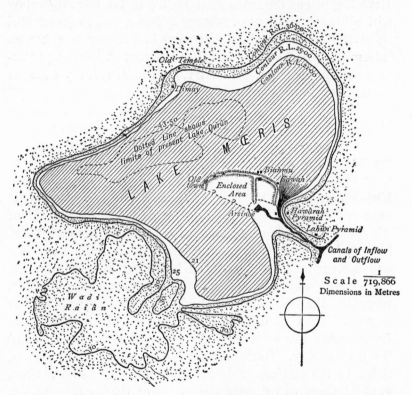

MAP 3. THE FAYUM. (After Maj. R. H. Brown, R.E.)

mentioned. Shaped like a huge maple-leaf, of which the stem, pointing nearly eastward, represents the connection with the Nile valley, it is generally speaking about forty miles across each way. Its lower tracts in the northwest, occupied to-day by the lake called Birket el-Kurun (Fig. 86), are very much depressed, the surface of the lake at

FIG. 86.—VIEW ACROSS THE BIRKET EL-KURÛN IN THE NORTHWESTERN FAYUM.

FIG. 87.—OBELISK OF SESOSTRIS I AT
HELIOPOLIS.

(Stereograph copyright by Underwood & Underwood, N. Y.)

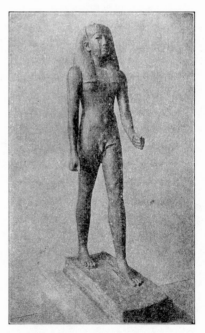

FIG. 88.—WOODEN STATUE OF PRINCE
EWIBRE.   (Cairo Museum.)

present being over one hundred and forty feet below sea-level. In prehistoric times the high Nile had filled the entire Fayum basin, producing a considerable lake. The kings of the Twelfth Dynasty conceived the plan of controlling the inflow and outflow for the benefit of the irrigation system then in force. At the same time they undertook vast retention walls inside the Fayum at the point where the waters entered, in order to reclaim some of the area of the Fayum for cultivation. The earlier kings of the Twelfth Dynasty began this process of reclamation, but it was especially Amenemhet III who so extended this vast wall that it was at last probably about twenty seven miles long, thus reclaiming a final total of twenty seven thousand acres.[1] These enormous works at the point where the lake was most commonly visited gave the impression that the whole body of water was an artificial product, excavated, as Strabo says, by king "Lamares," in which we recognize with certainty the throne name of Amenemhet III. This then was the famous lake Moeris of the classic geographers and travellers. Strabo, the most careful ancient observer of the lake, supports the vaguer description of Herodotus, and states that during the time of high Nile, the waters replenished the lake through the canal which still flows through the gap; but that when the river fell again, they were allowed to escape through the same canal, and employed in irrigation. Strabo saw the regulators for controlling the inflow and the outflow as well. The attention given the Fayum by Amenemhet III would indicate that this system of control was at least as old as the works near the entrance of the famous lake which gave him the reputation of having excavated it. Modern calculations have shown that enough water could have been accumulated to double the volume of the river below the Fayum during the hundred days of low Nile from the first of April on.[2]

The rich and flourishing province recovered from the lake was doubtless royal domain, and there are evidences that it

[1] Maj. R. H. Brown, R.E. The Fayûm and Lake Moeris, London, 1892.
[2] Ibid.

was a favourite place of abode with the kings of the latter part
of the Twelfth Dynasty. A prosperous town, known to the
Greeks as Crocodilopolis, or Arsinoe, with its temple to Sobk,
the crocodile-god, had already arisen in the new province,
and an obelisk of Sesostris I lies at Ebgig far out in the
heart of the reclaimed land. Two colossal statues of Amenemhet III, or at least of the king reputed to be the maker
of the lake in Herodotus's time, stood just outside the great
wall in the midst of the waters. In the gap, on the north
bank of the inflowing canal, was a vast building, some eight
hundred by a thousand feet, which formed a kind of religious and administrative centre for the whole country. It
contained a set of halls for each nome where its gods were
enshrined and worshipped, and the councils of its government gathered from time to time. It would seem from the
remarks of Strabo that each set of halls was thus the office
of the central government pertaining to the administration
of the respective nome, and the whole building was therefore the Pharaoh's seat of government for the entire country. It was still standing in Strabo's time, when it had
already long been known as the Labyrinth, one of the
wonders of Egypt, famous among travellers and historians
of the Græco-Roman world, who compared its intricate complex of halls and passages with the Cretan Labyrinth of
Greek tradition. It is the only building of this remote age,
not exclusively a temple, known to have survived so long;
and Strabo's description of its construction accounts for its
durability, for he says: "It is a marvellous fact that each
of the ceilings of the chambers consists of a single stone, and
also that the passages are covered in the same way with
single slabs of extraordinary size, neither wood nor other
building material having been employed." The town which
had grown up around this remarkable building was seen
by Strabo; but both have now completely disappeared.
Sesostris II had also founded a town just outside the gap
called Hotep-Sesostris, "Sesostris is Contented," and he
later built his pyramid beside it. Under these circum-

stances the Fayum had become the most prominent centre of the royal and governmental life of this age; and its great god Sobk was rivalling Amon in the regard of the dynasty, whose last representative bore the name Sobk-nefru-Re, which contains that of the god. The name of the god also appeared in a whole series of Sobk-hoteps of the next dynasty.

For nearly half a century the beneficent rule of Amenemhet III maintained peace and prosperity throughout his flourishing kingdom. The people sang of him:

"He makes the Two Lands verdant more than a great Nile.
He hath filled the Two Lands with strength.
He is life, cooling the nostrils;
. . . .
The treasures which he gives are food for those who are in his
    following;
He feeds those who tread his path.
The king is food and his mouth is increase."[1]

Business was on a sound basis, values were determined in terms of weight in copper, and it was customary to append to the mention of an article the words "of x deben [of copper]," a deben being 1404 grains.[2] Throughout the land the evidences of this prosperity under Amenemhet III and his predecessors still survive in the traces of their extensive building enterprises, although these have so suffered from the rebuilding under the Empire that they are but a tithe of what was once to be seen. Moreover the vandalism of the Nineteenth Dynasty, especially under Ramses II, obliterated priceless records of the Middle Kingdom by the most reckless appropriation of its monuments as building material. Probably all the more important towns of the country had received modest temples at the hands of the Old Kingdom Pharaohs, but these have left almost no trace, and we can gain no comprehensive picture of what the Twelfth Dynasty may have found throughout the country when they

---

[1] I, 747.   [2] I, 785.

began their own works. At Thebes, their home, which was only an obscure village in the Old Kingdom, they found but a modest chapel, which they replaced with a more pretentious temple of Amon, already begun by Amenemhet I.[1] It was continued or enlarged by Sesostris I, who also built a dwelling and refectory for the priests of the temple[2] beside the sacred lake, a building which was still standing eight hundred years later.[3] Amenemhet III erected the great brick wall around the ancient capital of El Kab (Nekheb),[4] which still stands, as the only city wall of such age now surviving in a condition so nearly intact (Fig. 102). The ancient temple at Edfu was not forgotten; while at Abydos the wide popularity and deep veneration of Osiris demanded a new temple, which was surrounded with an enclosure, within which for some time the rich and noble were permitted to erect their tombs.[5] The vicinity of the Fayum, as well as its own traditional sanctity, secured also for the temple of Harsaphes at Heracleopolis enlargement and a rich equipment.[6] Of the Fayum itself we have already spoken. Memphis and its ancient god Ptah were doubtless not neglected, but chance has left little evidence of the activity of the Middle Kingdom there. The vicinity of Ithtowe and the other royal residences of the time may have detracted somewhat from its prominence. The supreme god of the state, the ancestor and at the same time immediate father of the Pharaohs, was of necessity honoured with rich contributions from the beginning. Sesostris I held a council at which he announced to the court his intention of rebuilding the temple of Re at Heliopolis as soon as the plans could be prepared. According to immemorial custom, he himself led the ceremonies when the ground plan was staked out and the foundations of the building were begun. The dedicatory inscription, in which he recorded the history of the building, perished long ago, but a scribe's practice copy of it, as it stood in the court of the temple some five hundred years

---

[1] I, 484.   [2] IV, 488-9.   [3] Ibid.

[4] I, 741-2.   [5] I, 534, note b.   [6] I, 674-5.

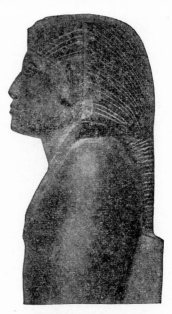

FIG. 89.—HEAD OF AMENEMHET III, FROM A
SPHINX FOUND AT TANIS.

FIG. 90.—BUST OF A STATUE OF
AMENEMHET III.

(St. Petersburg Museum.)

FIG. 91.—BRICK PYRAMID OF SESOSTRIS II, AT ILLAHUN.

after its erection, still survives in a leather roll in the Berlin Museum.[1] In exaggerated metaphor Sesostris I boasts of the imperishability of his name, as enshrined in the massive monument, saying:

"My beauty shall be remembered in his house,
My name is the pyramidion, and my name is the lake."[2]

The splendid temples of Heliopolis and the great city which surrounded them have all vanished, and with them the sacred lake to which Sesostris refers, but by a curious chance the only surviving monument on the ancient site is one of his obelisks (Fig. 87), still surmounted by the pyramidion, which, as the king boasted, has indeed perpetuated his name. The Delta blossomed under these enlightened rulers, refreshed as it was by the waters of the Fayum lake which their foresight stored up for summer use. All the Delta cities of all ages, as we have so often mentioned, have perished, and but little survives to testify to the activity of these kings there, but in the eastern part, especially at Tanis and Bubastis (Fig. 93), massive remains still show the interest which the Twelfth Dynasty manifested in the Delta cities. Fragmentary remains of temples built by the monarchs of this line have been found at many of the chief towns from the first cataract to the northwestern Delta. Besides the great works of the kings, it should not be forgotten that the wealthier and more powerful of the nomarchs also erected temples[3] and considerable buildings for purposes of government.[4] Chapels for their mortuary service were built in the towns,[5] and had the various structures due to these great lords survived, there is no doubt that they would have added materially to our impressions of the solidity and splendour with which the economic life of the nation was developing on every hand.

Such impressions are also strengthened by the tombs of the time, which are indeed the only buildings which have survived from the feudal age; and even these are in a sad

[1] I, 498–506. [2] I, 503. [3] I, 637, note a. [4] I, 637. [5] I, 706.

state of ruin. We have already referred to the survival of
the mastaba form of tomb, but it was now fast disappearing
and the nobles were hewing out their burial chambers and
the shafts descending to them in the cliffs of the valley.
The chapel-hall connected with such burials, with its scenes
from the life and activity of the departed noble, are our
chief source for the history and life of the feudal age. The
colonnade which sometimes formed the front of such a tomb
was not without architectural merit. The pyramids of the
Twelfth Dynasty kings are eloquent testimony to the fact
that the construction of the royal tomb was no longer the
chief office of the state. More wholesome views of the function of the kingship have now gained the ascendancy and
the resources of the nation are no longer absorbed in the
pyramid as in the Old Kingdom. In the Eleventh Dynasty
the Theban kings had already returned to the original material of the royal tomb and built their unpretentious pyramids
of brick. Amenemhet I followed their example in the erection of his pyramid at Lisht; the core was of brick masonry
and the monument was then protected by casing masonry
of limestone[1] (Fig. 94). The custom was continued by all
the kings of the dynasty with one exception. Their pyramids are scattered from the mouth of the Fayum northward
to Dashur, just south of Memphis. Sesostris I preferred to
lie at Lisht beside his illustrious father; Amenemhet II was
the first to go northward to Dashur, and his son, Sesostris
II, selected his new town, Hotep-Sesostris, now Illahun, at
the mouth of the Fayum, as the site of his pyramid (Fig.
91). Sesostris III returned to Dashur, where he located his
pyramid on the north of that of Amenemhet II, while Amenemhet III (Fig. 94) lies on the south side of Amenemhet II's
pyramid. The pyramid of Hawara, in the Fayum beside the
Labyrinth, formerly supposed to be that of Amenemhet III,
is not certainly identified, and may possibly belong to Amenemhet IV, the only king of the dynasty whose pyramid is

[1] Mém. sur les Fouilles de Licht, par J. E. Gautier et G. Jéquier, Cairo,
1902.

not located with certainty. All these pyramids show the
most complicated and ingenious arrangements of entrance
and passages in order to baffle the tomb-robbers. That of
Hawara is the most notable in this respect. It was some:
thing over one hundred and ninety feet high and the base
was nearly three hundred and thirty four feet square
The entrance is in the middle of the western half of

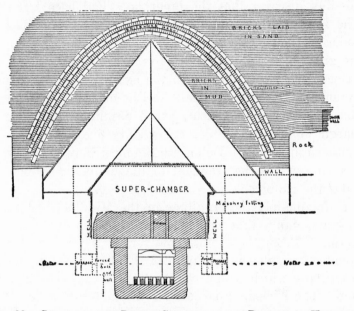

FIG. 92. SECTION OF THE BURIAL CHAMBER IN THE PYRAMID OF HAWARA.
(After Petrie.)

the south side and descending into the rock beneath the
pyramid it turns four times until it approaches the burial
chamber from the north side. Three amazing trapdoor-
blocks of enormous size and weight were intended to withstand the attacks of robbers, while numerous cunning and
misleading devices were inserted to puzzle the marauders.
The sepulchre chamber is twenty two feet long, eight feet
wide and six feet high, but is nevertheless cut from a single
block of intensely hard quartzite, weighing 110 tons. It had
no door and the only means of access was through a roofing

block weighing some forty five tons.[1] Nevertheless it was
entered and robbed in antiquity, doubtless with the connivance of later officials, or even of the later kings themselves.
The corruption of the officials in charge of the erection of
the building is evident in the fact that of the three trapdoor-
blocks they only closed the outer one, knowing full well
that with this one closed no member of the royal family could
possibly discover that the inner ones had been left open.
'The failure of these magnificent structures to protect the
bodies of their builders must have had something to do with
the gradual discontinuance of pyramid building which now
ensued.   Henceforward, with the exception of a few small
pyramids at Thebes, we shall meet no more of these remarkable tombs, which, stretching in a desultory line along the
margin of the western desert for sixty five miles above the
southern apex of the Delta, are the most impressive surviving witnesses to the grandeur of the civilization which preceded the Empire.

Unfortunately the buildings of the Middle Kingdom are
so fragmentary that we can gain little idea of their architecture.   From the tombs, however, it is evident that the
architectural elements employed did not differ materially
from those which we have already found in the Old Kingdom.   The Theban Pharaohs of the Eleventh Dynasty introduced a new type in the remarkable terraced temple of
Der el-Bahri, which served as a model to the great architects
of the Empire. The few traces of the Labyrinth which enabled
Petrie to determine the extent of its ground-plan, and the
description furnished by Strabo, are sufficient to establish
little more than the massiveness of its style.   The domestic
architecture has also completely perished. From the plan
of the town which Petrie found by the pyramid of Sesostris
II at Illahun (Map 1) we gain only an impression of the contracted quarters in which the workmen of the time were
obliged to live, but of the houses of the rich, in which there

[1] Petrie, Kahun, Gurob and Hawara, pp. 13–17.

was opportunity for architectural effect, we have very little knowledge.

Art had made a certain kind of progress since the Old Kingdom. Sculpture had become much more ambitious and attempted works of the most impressive size. The statues of Amenemhet III, which overlooked Lake Moeris, were probably forty or fifty feet high, and we have already referred to the alabaster colossus of Thuthotep, the nomarch of the Hare-nome, which was some twenty two feet high. These colossi, furthermore, were now produced in greater numbers than ever before. Ten such portraits of Amenemhet I (Fig. 95) were found at his pyramid at Lisht, and Sihathor, an assistant treasurer of Amenemhet II, records with great pride how he was entrusted with the oversight of the work on the sixteen statues of the king for his pyramid at Dashur.[1] Fragments of such colossi in massive granite are scattered over the ruins of Tanis (Fig. 93) and Bubastis, and we recall that Sesostris III erected his statue on the southern Nubian border.[2] Under such circumstances the royal sculptors could not but betray to some extent the mechanical and imitative spirit in which they worked. Their figures rarely possess the striking vivacity and the strong individuality which are so characteristic of the Old Kingdom sculpture. The long dominant canons are also showing their effect in suppressing the individuality of the sculptor's work and manner. We find a king searching the ancient rolls to ascertain the form of a god, that he might "fashion him as he was formerly, when they made the statues in their council, in order to establish their monuments upon earth";[3] from which it is evident that the gods were supposed to have held a council in the beginning, at which they determined for all time exactly the form and appearance of each. With the form of the king and his nobles the same inviolable tradition ruled, and the art of the Middle Kingdom no longer possessed the freshness and vigour necessary to accept these conventions and at the same time to triumph completely over

[1] I, 601.   [2] I, 660.   [3] I, 756.

them as did the sculptors of the Old Kingdom. Nevertheless, there is now and then a portrait of surprising strength and individuality, like the superb statue of Amenemhet III (Fig. 90) in St. Petersburg, the head of the same king as a sphinx at Tanis (Fig. 89), or the colossal head of Sesostris III recently unearthed at Karnak. Such heads are masterpieces of Egyptian art, embodying those qualities of superhuman strength and imperturbable calm, of which the Egyptian sculptor was so completely master. The flesh-forms have been so summarized in the exquisitely hard medium that something of the eternal immobility of the stone itself has been wrought into the features of the great king. Such work contrasts sharply with the soft and effeminate beauty of the wooden figure of prince Ewibre (Fig. 88). The chapels in the cliff-tombs of the nomarchs were elaborately decorated with paintings depicting the life of the deceased and the industries on his great estates. It cannot be said that these paintings, excellent as many of them unquestionably are, show any progress over those of the Old Kingdom, while as flat relief they are for the most part distinctly inferior to the earlier work.

The close and familiar oversight of the nomarch lent a distinct impetus to the arts and crafts,[1] and the provinces developed large numbers of skilled craftsmen throughout the country. Naturally the artisans of the court were unsurpassed. We discern in their work the result of the development which had been going on since the days of the earliest dynasties. The magnificent jewelry (Figs. 97-8) of the princesses of the royal house displays both technical skill and refined taste, quite surpassing our anticipations. Had the tomb robbers of the Dashur necropolis not overlooked these burials we should never have rated the capacities of the Middle Kingdom so high. Little ever produced by the later gold-smiths of Europe can surpass either in beauty or in workmanship these regal ornaments worn by

[1] I, 638.

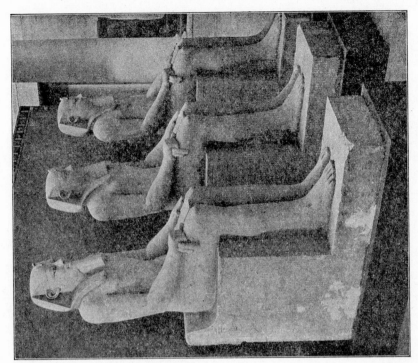

Fig. 95.—THREE OF THE TEN LIMESTONE STATUES OF AMENEMHET I. FOUND AT HIS PYRAMID OF LISHT. (Cairo Museum.)

Fig. 93.—LOOKING DOWN THE AXIS OF THE TEMPLE AT TANIS. (Petrie, *Tanis*, I.)

Fig. 94.—CAPSTONE OF THE PYRAMID OF AMENEMHET III, AT DASHUR.

the daughters of the house of Amenemhet nearly two thousand years before Christ.

Literature also left worthy monuments to witness the rich and varied life of this great age. We have seen how the art of writing was fostered by the administrative necessities of the state. A system of uniform orthography, hitherto lacking, was now developed and followed by skilled scribes with consistency. A series of model letters[1] studied by the school-boys of the twentieth century B. C. has survived, and they show with what pains composition was studied. The language of this age and its literary products were in later times regarded as classic, and in spite of its excessive artificialities, the judgment of modern study confirms that of the Empire. Although it unquestionably existed earlier, it is in Egypt and in this period that we first find a literature of entertainment. The unfortunate noble, Sinuhe, who fled into Syria on the death of Amenemhet I, returned to Egypt in his old age, and the story of his flight, of his life and adventures in Asia became a favourite tale,[2] which attained such popularity that it was even written on sherds and flags of stone to be placed in the tomb for the entertainment of the dead in the hereafter. A prototype of Sindebad the Sailor, who was shipwrecked in southern waters on the voyage to Punt, returned with a tale of marvellous adventures on the island of the serpent queen where he was rescued, and loaded with wealth and favours, was sent safely back to his native land.[3] The life of the court and the nobles found reflection among the people in folk-tales, narrating the great events in the dynastic transitions and a tale of the rise of the Fifth Dynasty was now in common circulation, although our surviving copy[4] was written a century or two after the fall of the Twelfth Dynasty. The most skilled literati of the time delighted to employ the popular tale as a

[1] Kahun Papyri, pp. 67–70.   [2] I, 486–497.
[3] Unpublished papyrus in St. Petersburg; see Golénischeff, Abh. 16e Berliner Orientalistenkongresses.
[4] Papyrus Westcar, Berlin, P. 3033.

medium for the exercise of their skill in the artificial style now regarded as the aim of all composition. A story commonly known at the present day as the Tale of the Eloquent Peasant was composed solely in order to place in the mouth of a marvellous peasant a series of speeches in which he pleads his case against an official who had wronged him, with such eloquence that he is at last brought into the presence of the Pharaoh himself, that the monarch may enjoy the beauty of the honeyed rhetoric which flows from his lips. Unfortunately much of these speeches consists of figures of speech so far fetched, and poetic verbiage so obscure, that our modern knowledge of the language has not yet made them very intelligible.[1] We have already had occasion to notice the instruction left by the aged Amenemhet I for his son, which was very popular and has survived in no less than seven fragmentary copies.[2] The instruction concerning a wise and wholesome manner of life, which was so prized by the Egyptians, is represented by a number of compositions of this age, like the advice of the father to his son on the value of the ability to write;[3] or the wisdom of the viziers of the Old Kingdom; although there is no reason why the Wisdom of Ptahhotep and Kegemne,[4] preserved in a papyrus of the Middle Kingdom, should not be authentic compositions of these old wise men. A remarkable philosophizing treatise represents a man weary of life involved in a long dialogue with his reluctant soul as he vainly attempts to persuade it that they should end life together and hope for better things beyond this world.[5] A strange and obscure composition of the time represents a Sibylline prophet named Ipuwer, standing in the presence of the king and delivering grim prophecies of coming ruin, in which the social and political organization shall be overthrown, the poor shall become rich and the rich shall suffer need, foreign enemies shall enter and the established order of things shall be completely overturned. After predicting frightful calam-

---

[1] Berlin Papyrus 3023 and 3025. [2] I, 474 ff.
[3] Pap. Sallier II. [4] Pap. Prisse. [5] Berlin Papyrus 3024.

ities involving all classes, the prophet announces a saviour who shall restore the land: "He shall bring cooling to the flame. Men shall say, 'he is the shepherd of all the people; there is no evil in his heart. If his flocks go astray he will spend the day to search them. The thought of men shall be aflame; would that he might achieve their rescue . . . ' Verily he shall smite evil when he raises his arm against it. . . . Where is he this day? Doth he sleep among you?"[1] In this strange "Messianic" oracle the prophet proclaims the coming of the good king, who, like the David of the Hebrew prophets, shall save his people. The motive of the composition may be a skilful encomium of the reigning family, by representing the prophet as depicting the anarchy which had preceded in the dark age before their rise, and proclaiming their advent to save the people from destruction. Specimens of this remarkable class of literature, of which this is the earliest example, may be traced as late as the early Christian centuries, and we cannot resist the conclusion that it furnished the Hebrew prophets with the form and to a surprising extent also with the content of Messianic prophecy. It remained for the Hebrew to give this old form a higher ethical and religious significance.

So many of the compositions of the Egyptian scribe are couched in poetic language that it is difficult to distinguish between poetry and prose. All of the works thus far discussed are to a large extent poetry; but even among the common people there were compositions which are distinctively poems: the song of the threshers as they drove their cattle to and fro upon the threshing-floor, a few simple lines breathing the simple and wholesome industry of the people; or the lay of the harper (Fig. 96) as he sings to the banqueters in the halls of the rich,—a song burdened with premonitions of the coming darkness and admonishing to unbridled enjoyment of the present ere the evil day come:

[1] Leyden Papyrus I, 344; see Lange, Sitzungsber. der Berliner Akad.; XXVII, 601–610.

How happy is this good prince!
This goodly destiny is fulfilled:
The body perishes, passing away,
While others abide, since the time of the ancestors.
The gods who were aforetime rest in their pyramids;
Likewise the noble and the wise, entombed in their pyramids.
As for those who built houses,—their place is no more;
Behold what hath become of them.
I have heard the words of Imhotep and Harzozef,
Whose utterances are of much reputation;
Yet how are the places thereof?
Their walls are in ruin,
Their places are no more,—
As if they had never been.
None cometh from thence,
That he might tell us of their state;
That he might restore our hearts,
Until we too depart to the place,
Whither they have gone.
Encourage thy heart to forget it,
And let the heart dwell upon that which is profitable for thee.
Follow thy desire while thou livest,
Lay myrrh upon thy head,
Clothe thee in fine linen,
Imbued with luxurious perfumes,
The genuine things of the gods.
Increase yet more thy delights,
Let not thy heart be weary,
Follow thy desire and thy pleasure,
And mould thine affairs on earth,
After the mandates of thy heart,
Till that day of lamentation cometh to thee,
When the stilled heart hears not their mourning;
For lamentation recalls no man from the tomb.
Celebrate the glad day!
Rest not therein!
For lo, none taketh his goods with him,
Yea, no man returneth again, that is gone thither.

The earliest known example of poetry exhibiting rigid strophic structure and all the conscious artificialities of literary art, is a remarkable hymn to Sesostris III written during that king's life time. Of the six strophes, the one following may serve to illustrate its character and structure:

Twice great is the king of his city, above a million arms: as for other rulers of men, they are but common folk.

Twice great is the king of his city: he is as it were a dyke, damming the stream in its water flood.

Twice great is the king of his city: he is as it were a cool lodge, letting every man repose unto full daylight.

Twice great is the king of his city: he is as it were a bulwark, with walls built of sharp stones of Kesem.

Twice great is the king of his city: he is as it were a place of refuge, excluding the marauder.

Twice great is the king of his city: he is as it were an asylum, shielding the terrified from his foe.

Twice great is the king of his city: he is as it were a shade, the cool vegetation of the flood in the season of harvest.

Twice great is the king of his city: he is as it were a corner warm and dry in time of winter.

Twice great is the king of his city: he is as it were a rock barring the blast in time of tempest.

Twice great is the king of his city: he is as it were Sekhmet to foes who tread upon his boundary.

The dramatic presentation of the life and death of Osiris at Abydos undoubtedly demanded much dialogue and recitation, which must at least have assumed permanent form and have been committed to writing. Unfortunately this, the earliest known drama, has perished. It is characteristic of this early world that in neither the art or the literature, of which we have a considerable mass from the Middle Kingdom, can we discern any individuals to whom these great works should be attributed. Among all the literary productions which we have enumerated, it is only of the wisdom, the "instruction," that we know the authors. Of the literature of the age we may say that it now displays a wealth of imagery and a fine mastery of *form* which five hundred years earlier, at the close of the Old Kingdom, was but just emerging. The *content* of the surviving works does not display evidence of constructive ability in the larger sense, involving both form and content; it lacks general coherence. It is possible, however, that the Osirian drama, which offered greater constructive opportunity, might have altered this verdict if it had survived.

It was thus over a nation in the fullness of its powers, rich and productive in every avenue of life, that Amenemhet III ruled; and his reign crowned the classic age which had dawned with the advent of his family. He seems to have maintained his vigourous grasp of affairs to the end, for he completed the reservoir at Sarbut el-Khadem in Sinai and the great wall of El Kab in the forty fourth year of his reign. But when he passed away in 1801 B. C. the strength of the line was waning. This was possibly due to the fact that the prince whom he had selected as his successor and appointed as coregent did not survive the old king himself. In any case he seems to have interred in a tomb beside his pyramid a young and handsome prince who already bore the royal cartouche, with the throne-name Ewibre (Fig. 88). But it should be remarked that the form of the name is quite unlike those of the Twelfth Dynasty, and there is a king Ewibre of the Thirteenth or Fourteenth Dynasty in the Turin list. A fourth Amenemhet, after a short coregency with the old king, succeeded at the death of Amenemhet III, but his brief reign of a little over nine years has left few monuments, and the decline of the house, to whom the nation owed two centuries of imperishable splendour, was evident. Amenemhet IV left no son, for he was succeeded by the princess Sebek-nefru-Re, the Skemiophris of Manetho. After struggling on for nearly four years she too, the last of her line, disappeared. The family had ruled Egypt two hundred and thirteen years, one month and some days.

Fig. 97.—DIADEM OF A TWELFTH DYNASTY PRINCESS, FOUND IN HER TOMB AT DASHUR. (Cairo Museum.)

Fig. 98.—DIADEM OF A TWELFTH DYNASTY PRINCESS, FOUND IN HER TOMB AT DASHUR. (Cairo Museum.)

Fig. 96.—THE HARPER SINGING TO THE BANQUETERS.

See pp. 205-6. (Leyden Museum.)

BOOK IV

THE HYKSOS:

THE RISE OF THE EMPIRE

CHAPTER XI

THE FALL OF THE MIDDLE KINGDOM. THE HYKSOS.

THE transition of authority to another dynasty (the Thirteenth) had seemingly taken place without disturbing the tranquil prosperity of the land. In any case the new house immediately gained full control, and the first king, Sekhemre-Khutowe, ruled from the Delta[1] to the southern frontier at the second cataract, where, for the first four years of his reign, the annual records of the Nile levels regularly appear.[2] The fortresses there were garrisoned under a commandant as before[3] and the tax and census lists were being compiled in the North as usual.[4] But the reign was a short one. The Pharaohs who followed regarded themselves as successors of the Twelfth Dynasty and assumed the names of its greatest rulers; but this brought them none of its strength and prestige. The succession may have lasted during four reigns, when it was suddenly interrupted, and the list of Turin records as fifth king after the Twelfth Dynasty one Yufni, a name which does not display the royal form, showing that at this point the usurper, that ceaseless menace to the throne in the orient, had again triumphed.

Rapid dissolution followed, as the provincial lords rose against each other and strove for the throne. Pretender after pretender struggled for supremacy; now and again one more able than his rivals would gain a brief advantage and wear his ephemeral honours, only to be quickly supplanted by another. Private individuals contended with the rest and occasionally won the coveted goal, only to be overthrown by a successful rival. Two Sebekemsafs, probably belong-

[1] I, 751.　　　　[2] I, 751–2.　　　　[3] I, 752.
[4] Kahun Papyri, pl. IX, l. 1; p. 86.

211

ing at about this time, left their modest pyramids at Thebes, for the pyramid of one of them was examined by the Ramessid commissioners and found robbed.[1] The bodies of the king and his queen, Nubkhas, which had laid undisturbed for at least five hundred years, were dragged out of the coffins, and in a remarkable confession the thieves were forced by the commissioners to tell how they had despoiled the royal remains of their ornaments and amulets of gold and costly stones.[2] It is thus certain that at least one group of these obscure kings resided at Thebes and must have been of Theban origin. At one time a usurper named Neferhotep succeeded in overthrowing one of the many Sebekhoteps of the time, and established stable government. He made no secret of his origin, and on the monuments added the names of his untitled parents without scruple.[3] On a stela at Abydos he left a remarkable record of his zeal for the temple of Osiris there[4] and another determining certain limits of the necropolis. He reigned eleven years when he was succeeded by his son, Sihathor, who shortly[5] gave way to his father's brother, Neferkhere-Sebekhotep. This Sebekhotep was the greatest king of this dark age. He did not however advance the Middle Kingdom frontier southward to the Island of Argo, above the Third Cataract, as heretofore supposed. His statue on Argo is but life-size, not a colossus, and was certainly transported thither by some late Nubian king from some point in Egypt. It was but a brief restoration, and the monuments which had survived bear no records to inform us of its character.

The darkness which followed is only the more obscure by contrast. Foreign adventurers took advantage of the opportunity, and one of the pretenders who achieved a brief success may have been a Nubian. In any case he placed the word Nehsi, "Negro," in his royal cartouche. Another, whose second royal name was Mermeshu, "Commander of the Army," was evidently a military aspirant to the throne. The country was broken up into petty king-

---

[1] IV, 517.   [2] IV, 538.   [3] I, 573.
[4] I. 753-772.   [5] Turin Pap. Frag. No. 80; Petrie, Scarabs, No. 309.

doms, of which Thebes was evidently the largest in the
South. Nubkheprure-Intef, one of a group of three Intefs
who ruled there, frankly discloses the conditions in a decree[1] deposing an official at Coptos who had proved a traitor.
In this document Intef curses any other king or ruler in
Egypt who may show the culprit mercy, naively declaring
that no such king or ruler shall become Pharaoh of the
whole country. These Intefs were buried at Thebes, where
the pyramids of two of them, still standing toward the close
of the Twentieth Dynasty, were inspected by the Ramessid
commissioners, who found that one of them had been tun-
nelled into by tomb-robbers.[2] But very few of the long list
of kings in the royal list of Turin can be found mentioned
upon contemporary monuments. Here and there a fragment of masonry, a statue, or sometimes only a scarab bearing a royal name, furnishes contemporary testimony of the
reign of this or that one among them. There was neither
power, nor wealth, nor time for the erection of permanent
monuments; king still followed king with unprecedented
rapidity, and for most of them our only source of knowledge is therefore the bare name in the Turin list, the dis-
ordered fragments of which have not even preserved for us
the order of these ephemeral rulers except as we find
groups upon one fragment. The order of the fragments
themselves remains uncertain, so that the succession of
the above most important groups is also questionable.
Where preserved at all the length of the reign is usually
but a year, or occasionally two or three years, while in
two cases we find after a king's name but three days. Without any dynastic division which can be discerned, we find
here the remains of at least one hundred and eighteen
names of kings, whose ceaseless struggles to gain or to
hold the throne of the Pharaohs, make up the obscure
history of this dark century and a half since the fall
of the Twelfth Dynasty. Evidently some of these kings
ruled contemporaneously, but even so, such a period of con-

[1] I, 773–780.   [2] IV, 514 f.

stant struggle and usurpation is almost equalled during the days of the Moslem viceroys of Egypt, when, under the dynasty of the Abbasids, which lasted one hundred and eighteen years (750–868 A. D.), seventy seven viceroys held the throne of Egypt. In European history it is paralleled by the series of military Emperors after Commodus, when in about ninety years probably eighty emperors succeed each other.[1] Manetho, who knew nothing of this confused age, disposed of its host of kings in two lines, as a Thirteenth Dynasty in Thebes, and a Fourteenth from Xois, a city of the Delta.

Economically the condition of the country must have rapidly degenerated. The lack of a uniform administration of the irrigation system, which the nation owed to the kingship as an institution, and the generally unstable conditions, unavoidably checked the agricultural and industrial productivity of the land; while oppressive taxation and the tyranny of warring factions in need of funds sapped the energies and undermined the prosperity which had been so ably conserved by the house of Amenemhet for two centuries. While we possess no monuments which tell us of this ruin, their very absence is evidence of it, and the analogy of similar periods in Moslem Egypt, particularly under the Mamlukes, makes certain the unhappy condition of the nation during this period.

Without centralized resources or organization the hapless nation was an easy prey to foreign aggression. About 1675 B. C., before the end of the Thirteenth Dynasty, there poured into the Delta from Asia a possibly Semitic invasion such as that, which in prehistoric times, had stamped the language with its unmistakable form; and again in our own era, under the influence of Islam, overwhelmed the land. These invaders, now generally called the Hyksos, after the designation applied to them by Josephus (quoting Manetho), themselves left so few monuments in Egypt that even their nationality is still the subject of much difference of opinion;

[1] Meyer. Aeg. Chron, p. 62.

while the length and character of their supremacy, for the same reason, are equally obscure matters. The documentary materials bearing on them are so meagre and limited in extent that the reader may easily survey them and judge the question for himself, even if this chapter is thereby in danger of relapsing into a "laboratory note-book." The late tradition regarding the Hyksos, recorded by Manetho and preserved to us in the essay of Josephus against Apion, is but the substance of a folk-tale like that narrating the fall of the Fourth Dynasty,[1] or many other such tales from which their knowledge of Egypt's past was chiefly drawn by the Greeks. The more ancient and practically contemporary evidence should therefore be questioned first. Two generations after the Hyksos had been expelled from the country the great queen Hatshepsut thus narrated her restoration of the damage which they had wrought:

I have restored that which was ruins,
I have raised up that which was unfinished,
Since the Asiatics were in the midst of Avaris of the Northland
⌊Delta⌋,
And the barbarians were in the midst of them [the people of the
Northland],
Overthrowing that which had been made,
While they ruled in ignorance of Re.[2]

The still earlier evidence of a soldier in the Egyptian army that expelled the Hyksos shows that a siege of Avaris was necessary to drive them from the country;[3] and further that the pursuit of them was continued into southern Palestine[4] and ultimately into Phœnicia or Cœlesyria.[5] Some four hundred years after their expulsion a folk-tale,[6] narrating the cause of the final war against them, was circulating among the people. It gives an interesting account of them:

"Now it came to pass that the land of Egypt was the possession of the polluted, no lord being king at the time when it happened; but king Sekenenre, he was ruler of the South-

---

[1] Infra, pp. 122–3. [2] II, 303. [3] II, 8–10, 12.
[4] II, 13. [5] II, 20. [6] Pap. Sallier I.

ern City [Thebes] . . . King Apophis was in Avaris, and the whole land was tributary to him; the [Southland] bearing their impost, and the Northland likewise bearing every good thing of the Delta. Now king Apophis made Sutekh his lord, serving no other god, who was in the whole land, save Sutekh. He built the temple in beautiful and everlasting work . . ."[1]

From these earlier documents it is evident that the Hyksos were an Asiatic people who ruled Egypt from their stronghold of Avaris in the Delta. The later tradition as quoted from Manetho by Josephus in the main corroborates the above more trustworthy evidence, and is as follows:[2]

"There was a king of ours whose name was Timaios, in whose reign it came to pass, I know not why, that God was displeased with us, and there came unexpectedly men of ignoble birth out of the eastern parts, who had boldness enough to make an expedition into our country, and easily subdued it by force without a battle. And when they had got our rulers under their power, they afterward savagely burnt down our cities and demolished the temples of the gods, and used all the inhabitants in a most hostile manner, for they slew some and led the children and wives of others into slavery. At length they made one of themselves king, whose name was Salatis, and he lived at Memphis and made both Upper and Lower Egypt pay tribute, and left garrisons in places that were most suitable for them. And he made the eastern part especially strong, as he foresaw that the Assyrians, who had then the greatest power, would covet their kingdom and invade them. And as he found in the Saite [read Sethroite] nome a city very fit for his purpose (which lay east of the arm of the Nile near Bubastis, and with regard to a certain theological notion was called Avaris), he rebuilt it and made it very strong by the walls he built around it and by a numerous garrison of two hundred and forty thousand armed men, whom he put into it to keep it. There Salatis went every summer, partly to gather

[1] Pap. Sallier I, I, ll. 1–3.   [2] Contra Apion I, 14.

Fig. 101.—FRAGMENT OF A SITTING COLOSSUS OF KHIAN, IN GRANITE. Found at Bubastis.

Fig. 99.—EXCAVATION OF STATUE OF NEFERKHERE-SEBEK-HOTEP, ON ISLAND OF ARKO ABOVE THE THIRD CATARACT, BY UNIVERSITY OF CHICAGO EXPEDITION IN 1907.
Statue visible at the right

Fig. 100.—BODY OF ONE OF THE SEKENENRES, SHOWING WOUND IN SKULL. (Cairo Museum.)

in his corn and pay his soldiers their wages, and partly to train his armed men and so to awe foreigners.''

If we eliminate the absurd reference to the Assyrians and the preposterous number of the garrison at Avaris, the tale may be credited as in general a probable narrative. The further account of the Hyksos in the same essay shows clearly that the late tradition was at a loss to identify the Hyksos as to nationality and origin. Still quoting from Manetho, Josephus says: ''All this nation was styled Hyksos, that is, Shepherd Kings; for the first syllable 'hyk' in the sacred dialect denotes a king, and 'sos' signifies a shepherd, but this is only according to the vulgar tongue; and of these was compounded the term Hyksos. Some say they were Arabians.'' According to his epitomizers, Manetho also called them Phœnicians. Turning to the designations of Asiatic rulers as preserved on the Middle Kingdom and Hyksos monuments, there is no such term to be found as ''ruler of shepherds,'' and Manetho wisely adds that the word ''sos'' only means shepherd in the late vulgar dialect. There is no such word known in the older language of the monuments. ''Hyk'' (Egyptian Hk'), however, is a common word for ruler, as Manetho says, and Khian, one of the Hyksos kings, often gives himself this title upon his monuments, followed by a word for ''countries,'' which by slight and very common phonetic changes might become ''sos''; so that ''Hyksos'' is a not improbable Greek spelling for the Egyptian title ''Ruler of Countries.''

Looking further at the scanty monuments left by the Hyksos themselves, we discover a few vague but nevertheless significant hints as to the character of these strange invaders, whom tradition called Arabians and Phœnicians; and contemporary monuments designated as ''Asiatics,'' ''barbarians,'' and ''rulers of countries.'' An Apophis, one of their kings, fashioned an altar, now at Cairo, and engraved upon it the dedication: ''He [Apophis] made it as his monument for his father Sutekh, lord of Avaris, when he [Sutekh]

set all lands under his [the king's] feet."[1]   General as is
the statement it would appear that this Apophis ruled over
more than the land of Egypt.   More significant are the monuments of Khian, the most remarkable of this line of kings.
They have been found from Gebelen in southern Egypt to
the northern Delta; but they do not stop here.   Under a
Mycenæan wall in the palace of Cnossos in Crete an alabaster vase-lid bearing his name was discovered by Mr. Evans;[2]
while a granite lion with his cartouche upon the breast,
found many years ago at Bagdad, is now in the British
Museum.   One of his royal names was "Encompasser [liter-
ally 'embracer'] of the Lands," and we recall that his constant title upon his scarabs and cylinders is "ruler of countries."   Scarabs of the Hyksos rulers have been turned up
by the excavations in southern Palestine.   Meagre as these
data are, one cannot contemplate them without seeing con-
jured up before him the vision of a vanished empire which
once stretched from the Euphrates to the first cataract of
the Nile, an empire of which all other evidence has perished,
for the reason that Avaris, the capital of its rulers, was in
the Delta, where, like so many other Delta cities, it suffered
a destruction so complete that we cannot even locate the spot
on which it once stood.   There was, moreover, every reason
why the victorious Egyptians should annihilate all evidence
of the supremacy of their hated conquerors.   In the light
of these developments it becomes evident why the invaders
did not set up their capital in the midst of the conquered
land, but remained in Avaris, on the extreme east of the
Delta, close to the borders of Asia.   It was that they might
rule not only Egypt, but also their Asiatic dominions.   Accepting the above probabilities, we can also understand how
the Hyksos could retire to Asia and withstand the Egyptian
onset for six years in southern Palestine, as we know from
contemporary evidence [3] they did.   It then becomes clear

[1] Mar. Mon. div., 38.
[2] Annual of British School at Athens, VII, 65, Fig. 21.
[3] II, 13.

also how they could retreat to Syria when beaten in southern Palestine; these movements were possible because they controlled Palestine and Syria.

If we ask ourselves regarding the nationality, origin and character of this mysterious Hyksos empire, we can hazard little in reply. Manetho's tradition that they were Arabians and Phœnicians may well be correct.[1] Such an overflow of southern Semitic emigration into Syria, as we know has since then taken place over and over again, may well have brought together these two elements; and a generation or two of successful warrior-leaders might weld them together into a rude state. We have already seen[2] that the Semitic tribes trading with Egypt in the Twelfth Dynasty were possessed of considerably more than the rudiments of civilization; while the wars of the Pharaohs in Syria immediately after the expulsion of the Hyksos show the presence of civilized and highly developed states there. Now, such an empire as we believe the Hyksos ruled could hardly have existed without leaving its traces among the peoples of Syria-Palestine for some generations after the beginning of the succeeding Egyptian supremacy in Asia. It would therefore be strange if we could not discern in the records of the subsequent Egyptian wars in Asia some evidence of the surviving wreck of the once great Hyksos empire which the Pharaohs demolished.

For two generations after the expulsion of the Hyksos we can gain little insight into the conditions in Syria. At this point the ceaseless campaigns of Thutmose III, as recorded in his Annals, enable us to discern which nation was then playing the leading role there. The great coalition of the kings of Palestine and Syria, with which Thutmose III was called upon to contend at the beginning of his wars, was led and dominated throughout by the powerful king of Kadesh on the Orontes. It required ten years of constant campaigning by Thutmose III to achieve the capture of the stubborn city and the subjugation of the kingdom of which it was

---

[1] But see Meyer, Aeg. Chron., pp. 95 ff.   [2] Infra, p. 188.

the head; but with power still unbroken it revolted, and Thutmose III's twenty years of warfare in Syria were only crowned with victory when he finally succeeded in again defeating Kadesh, after a dangerous and persistent struggle. The leadership of Kadesh from the beginning to the end of Thutmose III's campaigns is such as to convey the impression that many Syrian and Palestinian kinglets were its vassals. It is in this Syrian domination of the king of Kadesh that, in the author's opinion, we should recognize the last nucleus of the Hyksos empire, finally annihilated by the genius of Thutmose III. Hence it was that Thutmose III, the final destroyer of the Hyksos empire, became also the traditional hero who expelled the invaders from Egypt; and as Misphragmouthosis he thus appears in Manetho's story as the liberator of his country. That it was a Semitic empire we cannot doubt, in view of the Manethonian tradition and the subsequent conditions in Syria-Palestine. Moreover the scarabs of a Pharaoh who evidently belonged to the Hyksos time, give his name as Jacob-her or possibly Jacob-El, and it is not impossible that some chief of the Jacob-tribes of Israel for a time gained the leadership in this obscure age. Such an incident would account surprisingly well for the entrance of these tribes into Egypt, which on any hypothesis must have taken place at about this age; and in that case the Hebrews in Egypt will have been but a part of the Beduin allies of the Kadesh or Hyksos empire, whose presence there brought into the tradition the partially true belief that the Hyksos were shepherds, and led Manetho to his untenable etymology of the second part of the word. Likewise the naive assumption of Josephus, who identifies the Hyksos with the Hebrews, may thus contain a kernel of truth, however accidental. But such precarious combinations should not be made without a full realization of their hazardous character.

Of the reign of these remarkable conquerors in Egypt we know no more than of their contemporaries, the Egyptian dynasts of this age already discussed, who continued to rule in Thebes and probably throughout Upper Egypt. Both the account in Manetho and the folk-tale above quoted state that the Hyksos kings laid the whole country under tribute, and we have already observed that Hyksos monuments have been found as far south as Gebelen. The beginning of their rule may have been a gradual immigration without hostilities, as Manetho relates. It is perhaps in this epoch that we should place one of their kings, a certain Khenzer, who seems to have left the affairs of the country largely in the hands of his vizier, Enkhu, so that the latter administered and restored the temples.[1] As this vizier lived in the period of Neferhotep and the connected Sebekhoteps, it is possible that we should place the gradual rise of Hyksos power in Egypt just after that group of Pharaohs.

From the contemporary monuments we learn the names of three Apophises and of Khian (Fig. 101), besides possibly Khenzer and Jacob-her, whom we have already noted. Among the six names preserved from Manetho by Josephus we can recognize but two, an Apophis and Iannas, who is certainly the same as Khian of the contemporary monuments. The only contemporary date is that of the thirty third year of an Apophis, in the mathematical papyrus of the British Museum. The Manethonian tradition in which we find three dynasties of Shepherds or Hyksos (the Fifteenth to Seventeenth) is totally without support from the contemporary monuments in the matter of the duration of the Hyksos supremacy in Egypt. A hundred years is ample for the whole period. Even if it was actually much longer, this fact would not necessarily extend the length of the period from the fall of the Twelfth Dynasty to the end of the Hyksos rule; for it is evident that many of the numerous kings of this period, enumerated in the Turin Papyrus, may have ruled in the South as vassals of the Hyksos, like the Sekenenre, whom the folk-tale makes the Theban vassal of one of the Apophises.

What occasioned the unquestionable barbarities on the

[1] I, 781-787.

part of the conquerors, it is now impossible to discern; but it is evident that hostilities must have eventually broken out, causing the destruction of the temples, later restored by Hatshepsut. Their patron god Sutekh is of course the Egyptianized form of some Syrian Baal; Sutekh being an older form of the well known Egyptian Set. The Hyksos kings themselves must have been rapidly Egyptianized; they assumed the complete Pharaonic titulary, and they appropriated statues of their predecessors in the Delta cities, wrought, of course, in the conventional style peculiar to the Pharaohs (Fig. 101). Civilization did not essentially suffer; a mathematical treatise dated under one of the Apophises is preserved in the British Museum. We have already seen one of the Apophises building a temple in Avaris, and a fragment of a building inscription[1] of an Apophis at Bubastis says that he made "numerous flag-staves tipped with copper for this god," such flag-staves flying a tuft of gaily coloured pennants being used to adorn a temple front. The influence upon Egypt of such a foreign dominion, including both Syria-Palestine and the lower Nile valley, was epoch making, and had much to do with the fundamental transformation which began with the expulsion of these aliens. It brought the horse into the Nile valley and taught the Egyptians warfare on a large scale. Whatever they may have suffered, the Egyptians owed an incalculable debt to their conquerors

[1] Nav. Bubastis, I, pl. 35c.

CHAPTER XII

THE EXPULSION OF THE HYKSOS AND THE TRIUMPH
OF THEBES

I<small>T</small> must have been about 1600 B. C., nearly two hundred years after the fall of the Twelfth Dynasty, that the Sekenenre of the folk-tale[1] was ruling in Thebes under the suzerainty of a Hyksos Apophis in Avaris. This tale, as current four hundred years later in Ramessid days, is our only source for the events that immediately followed. After its account of the Hyksos, which the reader will recall as quoted above, there follows the brief description of a sacred feast, and later a council of Apophis and his wise men; but what took place at this council is quite uncertain. It concerned a plot or design against king Sekenenre, however, for the story then proceeds: "Now many days after this, king Apophis sent to the prince [king Sekenenre] of the Southern City [Thebes] the report which his scribes and wise men had communicated to him. Now when the messenger whom king Apophis had sent reached the prince of the Southern City, he was taken to the prince of the Southern City. Then said one to the messengers of king Apophis, 'What brings thee to the Southern City, and wherefore hast thou joined them that journey?' The messenger said to him, 'It is king Apophis who sends to thee, saying: "One [that is the messenger] has come [to thee] concerning the pool of the hippopotami, which is in the city [Thebes]. For they permit me no sleep, day and night the noise of them is in my ear."' Then the prince of the Southern City lamented a [long] time, and it came to pass that he could not return [answer] to the messenger of king Apophis."

[1] Infra, pp. 215–16.

The surviving fragments at this point would indicate that Sekenenre now sent gifts to Apophis and promised to do all that he demanded, after which, "[the messenger of king] Apophis betook himself away, to proceed to the place where his lord was. Then the prince of the Southern City caused to summon his great princes, likewise his officers and leaders . . . , and he recounted to them all the matters concerning which king Apophis had sent to him. Then they were with one accord silent for a long time, and could not answer him either good or bad. Then king Apophis sent to— —,"[1] but here the tantalizing bit of papyrus is torn off, and we shall never know the conclusion of the tale. However, what we have in it is the popular and traditional version of an incident, doubtless regarded as the occasion of the long war between the Theban princes and the Hyksos in Avaris. The preposterous *casus belli,* the complaint of Apophis in the Delta that he was disturbed by the noise of the Theban hippopotami is folk-history, a wave mark among the people, left by the tide which the Hyksos war set in motion. Manetho corroborates the general situation depicted in the tale; for he says that the kings of the Thebaid and other parts of Egypt made a great and long war upon the Hyksos in Avaris. His use of the plural "kings" immediately suggests the numerous local dynasts, whom we have met before, each contending with his neighbour and effectually preventing the country from presenting a united front to the northern foe. There were three Sekenenres. The mummy of the last of the three discovered in the great find at Der el-Bahri, and now at the Cairo museum, exhibits frightful wounds in the head (Fig. 100), so that he doubtless fell in battle, not improbably in the Hyksos war. They were followed by a king Kemose who probably continued the war. Their small pyramids of brick at Thebes have long since passed away, but they were still uninjured when inspected some four hundred and fifty years later by the Ramessid commissioners, whose investigation[2] of the necropolis we have referred to before.

[1] Pap. Sallier I, II, l. 1–III, l. 3.   [2] IV, 518–19.

It is evident that this Theban family were gradually thrusting themselves to the front with more and more successful aggressiveness, so that these three Sekenenres and Kemose form the latter part of Manetho's Seventeenth Dynasty. They were obliged to maintain themselves not merely against the Hyksos, but also against numerous rival dynasts, especially in the extreme South above El Kab, where, removed from the turmoil of northern war, and able to carry on a flourishing internal commerce, the local princes enjoyed great prosperity, while those of the North had doubtless in many instances perished. We shall later find these prosperous dynasts of the South holding out against the rising power of Thebes while the latter was slowly expelling the Hyksos.

Following Kemose's short reign, Ahmose I, possibly his son, the first king of Manetho's Eighteenth Dynasty, assumed the leadership of the Theban house, about 1580 B. C., and became the deliverer of Egypt from her foreign lords. Sekenenre III had already won the friendship of the powerful princes of El Kab (Fig. 102), and by rich gifts and plentiful honours Ahmose I retained the valuable support of these princes, against both the Hyksos and the obstinate local dynasts of the upper river, who constantly threatened his rear. Ahmose thus made El Kab a buffer, which protected him from the attacks of his Egyptian rivals south of that city. No document bearing on the course of the war with the Hyksos in its earlier stages has survived to us, nor have any of Ahmose's royal annals been preserved, but one of his El Kab allies, named Ahmose, son of Ebana (his mother's name), whose father, Baba, served under Sekenenre III, has fortunately left an account of his own military career on the walls of his tomb at El Kab. He thus narrates the story of his service under Ahmose of Thebes: "I spent my youth in the city of Nekheb [El Kab], my father being an officer of the king of Upper and Lower Egypt, Sekenenre, triumphant; Baba, son of Royenet, was his name. Then I served as an officer in his stead in the ship [called]

15

'The Offering,' in the time of king Ahmose I, triumphant, while I was a young man, not having taken a wife . . . Then after I set up a household I was transferred to the northern fleet because of my valour.'' He was thus taken from El Kab and given service against the Hyksos in the north. At first, although a naval officer, he was assigned to infantry service in attendance upon the king, for his biography proceeds: ''I followed the king on foot when he rode abroad in his chariot. One [meaning the king] besieged the city of Avaris; I showed valor on foot before his majesty; then I was appointed to the ship [called] 'Shining-in-Memphis.' One fought on the water in the canal Pazedku of Avaris. Then I fought hand to hand, I brought away a hand [cut off as a trophy]. It was reported to the royal herald. One gave to me the gold of valor [a decoration]. There was again fighting in this place; I again fought hand to hand there; I brought away a hand. One gave to me the gold of valor in the second place.''[1] The siege of Avaris was now interrupted by an uprising of one of the local dynasts above El Kab, which was regarded as so serious by the king that he himself went south to quell it, and took Ahmose, son of Ebana, with him. The latter thus briefly narrates the incident: ''One fought in this Egypt south of this city [El Kab]; I brought away a living captive, a man, I descended into the water; behold he was brought as a seizure upon the road of this city, [although] I crossed with him over the water. It was announced to the royal herald. Then one presented me with gold in double measure.''[2] Having sufficiently quelled his southern rivals, Ahmose resumed the siege of Avaris, for at this point our naval officer abruptly announces its capture: ''One captured Avaris; I took captive there one man and three women, total four heads. His majesty gave them to me for slaves.''[3] The city thus fell on the fourth assault after the arrival of Ahmose, son of Ebana, but it is quite uncertain how many such assaults had been made before his transference thither.

[1] II, 7–10.   [2] II, 11.   [3] II, 12.

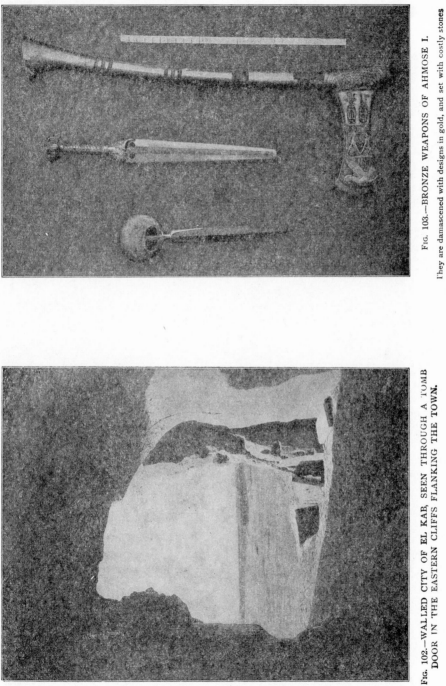

FIG. 103.—BRONZE WEAPONS OF AHMOSE I.

They are damascened with designs in gold, and set with costly stones
Cairo Museum.

FIG. 102.—WALLED CITY OF EL KAB, SEEN THROUGH A TOMB
DOOR IN THE EASTERN CLIFFS FLANKING THE TOWN.

for the siege had evidently lasted many years and had been interrupted by a rebellion in Upper Egypt. Our naval officer does not tell us who were the defenders of Avaris, but we do not need to be told in view of what we know from Manetho and the folk-tale; likewise as we follow his narrative a step farther he fails to inform us who were his foes in the next encounter; but it is clear that they can be no other than the Hyksos, fleeing into Asia after being driven from Avaris, following the fall of which, our biographer says: "One besieged Sharuhen for three years and his majesty took it. Then I took captive there two women and one hand. One gave to me the gold of bravery besides giving me the captives for slaves."[1] This is the earliest siege of such length known in history, and it is surprising evidence of the stubbornness of the Hyksos defense and the tenacity of king Ahmose in dislodging them from a stronghold in such dangerous proximity to the Egyptian frontier. For Sharuhen was probably in southern Judah,[2] whence the Hyksos might again easily invade the Delta. But Ahmose was not content with driving them out of Sharuhen. We find another member of the El Kab family, called Ahmose-Pen-Nekhbet, fighting under king Ahmose I in Zahi,[3] which is Phœnicia and Syria, and it is therefore evident that Ahmose pursued the Hyksos northward from Sharuhen, forcing them back to at least a safe distance from the Delta frontier. In the twenty second year of his reign he was still using in his building operations oxen which he had taken from the Asiatics,[4] so that this or another campaign of his in Asia must have continued to within a few years of that time. Returning to Egypt, now entirely free from all fear of its former lords, he gave his attention to the recovery of the Egyptian possessions in Nubia.

During the long period of disorganization following the Middle Kingdom, the Nubians had naturally taken advantage of their opportunity and fallen away. How far Ahmose penetrated it is impossible to determine, but he evidently met

[1] II, 13.   [2] Josh. 19: 6.   [3] II, 20.   [4] II, 26–27.

with no serious resistance in the recovery of the old territory between the first and second cataracts.[1] But his rule was not yet firmly established in Egypt itself, for he was no sooner well out of the country on the Nubian campaign than his inveterate rivals south of El Kab again arose against him. They were totally defeated in a battle on the Nile, and our old friend Ahmose, son of Ebana, was rewarded for his valour in the action with five slaves and five stat (nearly three and a half acres) of land in El Kab.[2] All the sailors engaged in the battle were treated with equal generosity. Even then Ahmose was obliged to quell one more rebellion before he was left in undisputed possession of the throne; for in closing the narrative of his service under this king, Ahmose, son of Ebana, says: "Then came that fallen one, whose name was Teti-en; he had gathered to himself rebels. His majesty slew him and his servants, annihilating them. There were given to me three heads [slaves] and five stat of land in my city."[3] We thus see how king Ahmose bound his supporters to his cause. He did not stop, however, with gold, slaves and land, but in some cases even granted the local princes, the descendants of the great feudal lords of the Middle Kingdom, high and royal titles like "first king's son," which, while conveying few or no prerogatives, satisfied the vanity of old and illustrious families, like that of El Kab, who deserved well at his hands. Similarly we find barons who were left in possession of their old titles, but evidently the estates of such magnates were taken out of their hands and administered by the central government, for they resided at Thebes and were buried there. Thus we find there the tombs of the lords of Thinis and of Aphroditopolis; a lord of the former city assisted Queen Hatshepsut in the transportation of her obelisks.[4]

There were but few of the local nobles who thus supported Ahmose and gained his favour; the larger number opposed both him and the Hyksos and perished in the struggle. Their more fortunate fellows, being now nothing more than

[1] II, 14.   [2] II, 15.   [3] II, 16.   [4] II, p. 138, note e.

court and administrative officials, the feudal lords thus practically disappeared.   The lands which formed their hereditary possessions were confiscated and passed to the crown,
where they permanently remained.   There was one notable
exception to the general confiscation; the house of El Kab,
to which the Theban dynasty owed so much, was allowed
to retain its lands, and two generations after the expulsion
of the Hyksos, the head of the house appears as lord, not
only of El Kab but also Esneh and all the intervening territory.   Besides this he was given administrative charge,
though not hereditary possession, of the lands of the south
from the vicinity of Thebes (Per-Hathor) to El Kab.   Yet
this exception serves but to accentuate more sharply the total
extinction of the landed nobility, who had formed the substance of the governmental organization under the Middle
Kingdom.   All Egypt was now the personal estate of the
Pharaoh, just as it was after the destruction of the Mamlukes
by Mohammed Ali early in the nineteenth century.   It is
this state of affairs which in Hebrew tradition was represented as the direct result of Joseph's sagacity.[1]

[1] Gen. 47: 19–20.

BOOK V

THE EMPIRE: FIRST PERIOD

CHAPTER XIII

THE NEW STATE: SOCIETY AND RELIGION

The task of building up a state, which now confronted Ahmose I, differed materially from the reorganization accomplished at the beginning of the Twelfth Dynasty by Amenemhet I. The latter dealt with social and political factors no longer new in his time, and manipulated to his own ends the old political units without destroying their identity, whereas Ahmose had now to begin with the erection of a fabric of government out of elements so completely divorced from the old forms as to have lost their identity, being now in a state of total flux. The course of events, which culminated in the expulsion of the Hyksos, determined for Ahmose the form which the new state was to assume. He was now at the head of a strong army, effectively organized and welded together by long campaigns and sieges protracted through years, during which he had been both general in the field and head of the state. The character of the government followed involuntarily out of these conditions. Egypt became a military state. It was quite natural that it should remain so, in spite of the usually unwarlike character of the Egyptian. The long war with the Hyksos had now educated him as a soldier, the large army of Ahmose had spent years in Asia and had even been for a longer or shorter period among the rich cities of Syria. Having thoroughly learned war and having perceived the enormous wealth to be gained by it in Asia, the whole land was roused and stirred with a lust of conquest, which was not quenched for several centuries. The wealth, the rewards and the promotion open to the professional soldier were a constant incentive to a military career, and the middle classes, otherwise so unwarlike, now entered the ranks with ardour. Among the survivors of the noble class, chiefly those who had attached themselves to the Theban house, the profession of arms became the most attractive of all careers, and in the biographies[1] which they have left in their tombs at Thebes they narrate with the greatest satisfaction the campaigns which they went through at the Pharaoh's side, and the honours which he bestowed upon them. Many a campaign, all record of which would have been irretrievably lost, has thus come to our knowledge through one of these military biographies, like that of Ahmose,[2] son of Ebana, from which we have quoted. The sons of the Pharaoh, who in the Old Kingdom held administrative offices, are now generals in the army.[3] For the next century and a half the story of the achievements of the army will be the story of Egypt, for the army is now the dominant force and the chief motive power in the new state. In organization it quite surpassed the militia of the old days, if for no other reason than that it was now a standing army. It was organized into two grand divisions, one in the Delta and the other in the upper country.[4] In Syria it had learned tactics and proper strategic disposition of forces, the earliest of which we know anything in history. We shall now find partition of an army into divisions, we shall hear of wings and centre, we shall even trace a flank movement and define battle lines. All this is fundamentally different from the disorganized plundering expeditions naively reported as wars by the monuments of the older periods (Fig. 104). Besides the old bow and spear, the troops henceforth carry also a war axe. They have learned archery fire by volleys and the dreaded archers of Egypt now gained a reputation which followed and made them feared even in classic times. But more than this, the Hyksos having brought the horse into Egypt, the Egyptian armies now for the first time possessed a large proportion of chariotry. Cavalry in the modern sense of the term was

---

[1] II, 1–16, 17–25, et passim. [2] Ibid.
[3] III, 350, 362. [4] III, 56.

FIG. 104.—A BODY OF SPEARMEN OF THE EMPIRE.

Part of the military escort of Hatshesput's expedition to Punt.   From the reliefs in her temple at Der el-Bahri, Thebes.

FIG. 105.—A CHARIOT OF THE EMPIRE.

It is of full size, made of wood, bronze and leather.   Museo Archaeologico, Florence.

not employed.   The deft craftsmen of Egypt soon mastered the art of chariot-making (Fig. 105), while the stables of the Pharaoh contained thousands of the best horses to be had in Asia.   In accordance with the spirit of the time, the Pharaoh was accompanied on all public appearances by a body-guard of élite troops and a group of his favourite military officers.

With such force at his back, he ruled in absolute power; there was none to offer a breath of opposition; there was not a whisper of that modern monitor of kings, public opinion, an inconvenience with which rulers in the orient are rarely obliged to reckon, even at the present day.   With a man of strong powers on the throne, all were at his feet, but let him betray a single evidence of weakness, and he was quickly made the puppet of court coteries and the victim of harem intrigues as of old.   At such a time, as has happened so often since in Egypt, an able minister might overthrow the dynasty and found one of his own.   But the man who expelled the Hyksos was thoroughly master of the situation. It is evidently in large measure to him that we owe the reconstruction of the state which was now emerging from the turmoils of two centuries of internal disorder and foreign invasion.

This new state is revealed to us more clearly than that of any other period of Egyptian history under native dynasties, and while we shall recognize many elements surviving from earlier times, we shall be able to discern much that is new in the great structure of government which was now rising under the hands of Ahmose I and his successors.   The supreme position occupied by the Pharaoh meant a very active participation in the affairs of government.   He was accustomed every morning to meet the vizier, still the main spring of the administration, to consult with him on all the interests of the country and all the current business which necessarily came under his eye.[1]   Immediately thereafter he held a conference with the chief treasurer.[2]   These two men headed

[1] iI, 678.   [2] Ibid.

the chief departments of government: the treasury and the judiciary. The Pharaoh's office, in which they made their daily reports to him, was the central organ of the whole government where all its lines converged. All other reports to government were likewise handed in here, and theoretically they all passed through the Pharaoh's hands. Even in the limited number of such documents preserved to us, we discern the vast array of detailed questions in practical administration which the busy monarch decided. The punishment of condemned criminals was determined by him,[1] the documents in the case being sent up to him for a decision while the victims awaited their fate in the dungeon. Besides frequent campaigns in Nubia and Asia, he visited[2] the quarries and mines in the desert or inspected[3] the desert routes, seeking suitable locations for wells and stations. Likewise the internal administration required frequent journeys to examine new buildings and check all sorts of official abuses.[4] The official cults in the great temples, too, demanded more and more of the monarch's time and attention as the rituals in the vast state temples increased in complexity with the development of the elaborate state religion. Under these circumstances the burden inevitably exceeded the powers of one man, even with the assistance of his vizier. From the earliest days of the Old Kingdom, as the reader will recall, there had been but one vizier. Early in the Eighteenth Dynasty, however, the business of government and the duties of the Pharaoh had so increased that he appointed two viziers, one residing at Thebes, for the administration of the South, from the cataract as far as the nome of Siut; while the other, who had charge of all the region north of the latter point, lived at Heliopolis.[5] This innovation probably took place after the transfer of the southern country between El Kab and the cataract from the jurisdiction of the Nubian province to that of the vizier.

For administrative purposes the country was divided into

---

[1] IV, 541.   [2] III, 170.   [3] IV, 464.
[4] III, 58.   [5] Inscription of Mes.

irregular districts, some of which consisted of the old and strong towns of feudal days, each with its surrounding villages; while others contained no such town centre, and were evidently arbitrary divisions established solely for governmental reasons.   There were at least twenty seven such administrative districts between Siut and the cataract,[1] and the country as a whole must have been divided into over twice that number.   The head of government in the old towns still bore the feudal title "count," but it now indicated solely administrative duties and might better be translated "mayor" or "governor."   Each of the smaller towns had a "town-ruler," but in the other districts there were only recorders and scribes, with one of their number at their head.[2]   As we shall see, these men were both the administrators, chiefly in a fiscal capacity, and the judicial officials within their jurisdictions.

The great object of government was to make the country economically strong and productive.   To secure this end, its lands, now chiefly owned by the crown, were worked by the king's serfs, controlled by his officials, or entrusted by him as permanent and indivisible fiefs to his favourite nobles, his partisans and relatives.   Divisible parcels might also be held by tenants of the untitled classes.   Both classes of holdings might be transferred by will or sale in much the same way as if the holder actually owned the land.[3]   Other royal property, like cattle and asses, was held by the people of both classes, subject, like the lands, to an annual assessment for its use.   For purposes of taxation all lands and other property of the crown, except that held by the temples, were recorded in the tax-registers of the White House, as the treasury was still called.   All "houses" or estates and the "numbers belonging thereto,"[4] were entered in these registers.   On the basis of these, taxes were assessed.   They were still collected in naturalia: cattle, grain, wine, oil, honey, textiles, and the like.   Besides the cattle-yards, the "granary"

[1] II, 716–745.   [2] II, 717.
[3] Inscription of Mes.   [4] II, 826, l. 31.

was the chief sub-department of the White House, and there were innumerable other magazines for the storage of its receipts. All the products which filled these repositories were termed "labour," the word employed in ancient Egypt as we use "taxes." If we may accept Hebrew tradition as transmitted in the story of Joseph, such taxes comprised one fifth of the produce of the land.[1] It was collected by the local officials, whom we have already noticed, and its reception in and payment from the various magazines demanded a host of scribes and subordinates, now more numerous than ever before in the history of the country. The chief treasurer at their head was under the authority of the vizier, to whom he made a report every morning, after which he received permission to open the offices and magazines for the day's business.[2] The collection of a second class of revenue, that paid by the local officials themselves as a tax upon their offices, was exclusively in the hands of the viziers. The southern vizier was responsible for all the officials of Upper Egypt in his jurisdiction from Elephantine to Siut;[3] and in view of this fact, the other vizier doubtless bore a similar responsibility in the North. This tax on the officials consisted chiefly of gold, silver, grain, cattle and linen; the mayor of the old city of El Kab, for example, paid some 5,600 grains of gold, 4,200 grains of silver, one ox and one "two-year old" into the vizier's office every year, while his subordinate paid 4,200 grains of silver, a bead necklace of gold, two oxen and two chests of linen. Unfortunately the list[4] from which these numbers are taken, recorded in the tomb of the vizier Rekhmire at Thebes, is too mutilated to permit the calculation of the exact total of this tax on all the officials under the jurisdiction of the southern vizer; but they paid him annually at least some 220,000 grains of gold, nine gold necklaces, over 16,000 grains of silver, some forty chests and other measures of linen, one hundred and six cattle of all ages and some grain; and these figures are short

[1] Gen. 47: 23-27.   [2] II, 679.
[3] II, 716-745.   [4] Ibid.

by probably at least twenty per cent. of the real total. As the king presumably received a similar amount from the northern vizier's collections, this tax on the officials formed a stately sum in the annual revenues. We can unfortunately form no estimate of the total of all revenues. Of the royal income from all sources in the Eighteenth Dynasty the southern vizier had general charge. The amount of all taxes to be levied and the distribution of the revenue when collected were determined in his office, where a constant balance sheet was kept. In order to control both income and outgo, a monthly fiscal report was made to him by all local officials, and thus the southern vizier was able to furnish the king from month to month with a full statement of prospective resources in the royal treasury.[1] The taxes were so dependent, as they still are, upon the height of the inundation and the consequent prospects for a plentiful or scanty harvest, that the level of the rising river was also reported to him.[2] He held also all the records of the temple estates, and in the case of Amon, whose chief sanctuary was in the city of which the vizier was governor, he naturally had charge of the rich temple fortune, even ranking the High Priest of Amon in the affairs of the god's estate.[3] As the income of the crown was, from now on, so largely augmented by foreign tribute, this was also received by the southern vizier and by him communicated to the king. The great vizier, Rekhmire depicts himself in the gorgeous reliefs in his tomb receiving both the taxes of the officials who appeared before him each year with their dues,[4] and the tribute of the Asiatic vassal-princes and Nubian chiefs.[5]

In the administration of justice the southern vizier played even a greater role than in the treasury. Here he was supreme. The old magnates of the Southern Tens, once possessed of important judicial functions, have sunk to a mere attendant council at the vizier's public audiences,[6] where they seem to have retained not even advisory functions. They

---

[1] II, 703. [2] II, 709. [3] II, 746–751.
[4] II, 716–745. [5] II, 760–761 [6] II, 712.

are never mentioned in the court records of the time, though
they still live in poetry and their old fame survived even
into Greek times. The vizier continues to bear his traditional title, "chief of the six great houses" or courts of justice, but these are never referred to in any of the surviving
legal documents and have evidently disappeared save in the
title of the vizier. As always heretofore the officers of administration are incidentally the dispensers of justice. They
constantly serve in a judicial capacity. Although there is
no class of judges with *exclusively* legal duties, every man
of important administrative rank is thoroughly versed in
the law and is ready at any moment to serve as judge. The
vizier is no exception. All petitioners for legal redress
applied first to him in his audience hall; if possible in person, but in any case in writing. For this purpose he held a
daily audience or "sitting" as the Egyptian called it.[1]
Every morning the people crowded into the "hall of the
vizier," where the ushers and bailiffs jostled them into line
that they might "be heard," in order of arrival, one after
another.[2] In cases concerning land located in Thebes he
was obliged by law to render a decision in three days, but
if the land lay in the "South or North" he required two
months.[3] This was while he was still the only vizier; when
the North received its own vizier such cases there were referred to him at Heliopolis.[4] All crimes in the capital city
were denounced and tried before him, and he maintained a
criminal docket of prisoners awaiting trial or punishment,
which strikingly suggests modern documents of the same
sort.[5] All this, and especially the land cases, demanded
rapid and convenient access to the archives of the land.
They were therefore all filed in his offices. No one might
make a will without filing it in the "vizier's hall."[6] Copies
of all nome archives, boundary records and all contracts were
deposited with him[7] or with his colleague in the North [8] Every

---

[1] II, 675, 714–715. [2] II, 715. [3] II, 686.
[4] Inscription of Mes. [5] II, 683. [6] II, 688.
[7] II, 703, [8] Inscription of Mes.

petitioner to the king was obliged to hand in his petition in writing at the same office.[1]

Besides the vizier's "hall," also called the "great council," there were local courts throughout the land, not primarily of a legal character, being, as we have already explained, merely the body of administrative officials in each district, who were corporately empowered to try cases with full competence. They were the "great men of the town," or the local "council," and acted as the local representatives of the "great council." In suits involving real estate titles, a commissioner of the "great council" was sent out to execute the decisions of the "great council" in coöperation with the nearest local "council." Or sometimes a hearing before the local "council" was necessary before the "great council" could render a decision.[2] The number of these local courts is entirely uncertain, but the most important two known were at Thebes and Memphis. At Thebes its composition varied from day to day; in cases of a delicate nature, where the members of the royal house were implicated, it was appointed by the vizier,[3] and in case of conspiracy against the ruler, the monarch himself commissioned them, though without partiality, and with instructions merely to determine who were the guilty, accompanied by power to execute the sentence.[4] All courts were largely made up of priests. It is difficult to discern the relation of these courts to the "hall of the vizier," but in at least one case, when satisfaction was not obtained at the vizier's hall, the petitioner recovered a stolen slave by suit before one of these courts.[5] They did not, however, always enjoy the best reputation among the people, who bewailed the hapless plight of "the one who stands alone before the court when he is a poor man and his opponent is rich, while the court oppresses him (saying), 'Silver and gold for the scribes! Clothing for the servants!' "[6] For of course the bribe of the rich was often stronger than the

[1] II, 691. [2] Gardiner, Inscription of Mes. [3] II, 705.
[4] IV, 423–4. [5] Spiegelberg, Studien. [6] Pap. Anast. II, 8, 6.

justice of the poor man's cause, as it frequently is at the present day. The law to which the poor appealed was undoubtedly just. The vizier was obliged to keep it constantly before him, contained in forty rolls which were laid out before his dais at all his public sessions where they were doubtless accessible to all.[1] Unfortunately the code which they contained has perished, but of its justice we can have no doubt, for the vizier was said to be a judge "judging justly, not showing partiality, sending two men [opponents] forth satisfied, judging the weak and the powerful,"[2] or again, "not preferring the great above the humble, rewarding the oppressed . . . , bringing the evil to him who committed it."[3] Even the king dealt according to law; Amenhotep III called himself in his titulary "establisher of law," and when before one of the courts which we have already described, the king boasts that "the law stood firm; I did not reverse judgment, but in view of the facts I was silent that I might cause jubilation and joy."[4] Even conspirators against the king's life were not summarily put to death, but, as we have seen, were handed over to a legally constituted court to be properly tried, and condemned only when found guilty. The punishments inflicted by Haremhab upon his corrupt officials who robbed the poor, were all according to "law."[5] The great body of this law was undoubtedly very old,[6] and some of it, like the old texts of the Book of the Dead, was ascribed to the gods; but Haremhab's new regulations were new law enacted by him.[6] Diodorus tells of five different kings before Persian times who enacted new laws, and in the Middle Kingdom even a nobleman relates having made laws, meaning, of course, that he had formulated them at the king's request.[7] The social, agricultural and industrial world of the Nile-dwellers under the Empire was therefore not at the mercy of arbitrary whim on the part of either king or court, but was governed by a large body of long respected law, embodying the principles of justice and humanity.

- II, 675, 712. [2] II, 713. [3] II, 715. [4] Spiegelberg, Studien.
[5] III, 51 ff. [6] See above, pp. 80–82. [7] III. 65. [8] I, 531.

The southern vizier was the motive power behind the organization and operation of this ancient state. We recall that he went in every morning and took council with the Pharaoh on the affairs of the country; and the only other check upon his untrammelled control of the state was a law constraining him to report the condition of his office to the chief treasurer. Every morning as he came forth from his interview with the king he found the chief treasurer standing by one of the flag-staves of the palace front, and there they exchanged reports.[1] The vizier then unsealed the doors of the court and of the offices of the royal estate so that the day's business might begin; and during the day all ingress and egress at these doors was reported to him, whether of persons or of property of any sort.[2] His office was the means of communication with the local authorities, who reported to him in writing on the first day of each season, that is, three times a year.[3] It is in his office that we discern with unmistakable clearness the complete centralization of all local government in all its functions. This supervision of the local administration required frequent journeys and there was therefore an official barge of the vizier on the river in which he passed from place to place. It was he who detailed the king's bodyguard for service as well as the garrison of the residence city;[4] general army orders proceeded from his office;[5] the forts of the South were under his control;[6] and the officials of the navy all reported to him.[7] He was thus minister of war for both army and navy, and in the Eighteenth Dynasty at least, "when the king was with the army," he conducted the administration at home.[8] He had legal control of the temples throughout the country, or, as the Egyptian put it, "he established laws in the temples of the gods of the South and the North,"[9] so that he was minister of ecclesiastical affairs. He had economic oversight of many important resources of the country; no timber could be cut without his permission, and the admin-

---

[1] II, 678-9.   [2] II, 676, 680.   [3] II, 687, 692, 708, 711.   [4] II, 693-4.
[5] II, 695.   [6] II, 702.   [7] II, 710.   [8] II, 710.   [9] II, 757.

istration of irrigation and water supply was also under his charge.[1] In order to establish the calendar for state business, the rising of Sirius was reported to him.[2] He exercised advisory functions in all the offices of the state;[3] so long as his office was undivided with a vizier of the North he was grand steward of all Egypt, and there was no prime function of the state which did not operate immediately or secondarily through his office, while all others were obliged to report to it or work more or less closely in connection with it. He was a veritable Joseph and it must have been this office which the Hebrew narrator had in mind as that to which Joseph was appointed. He was regarded by the people as their great protector and no higher praise could be proffered to Amon when addressed by a worshipper than to call him "the poor man's vizier who does not accept the bribe of the guilty."[4] His appointment was a matter of such importance that it was conducted by the king himself, and the instructions given him by the monarch on that occasion were not such as we should expect from the lips of an oriental conqueror three thousand five hundred years ago. They display a spirit of kindness and humanity and exhibit an appreciation of state craft surprising in an age so remote. The king tells the vizier that he shall conduct himself as one "not setting his face toward the princes and councillors, neither one making brethren of all the people";[5] again he says, "It is an abomination of the god to show partiality. This is the teaching: thou shalt do the like, shalt regard him who is known to thee like him who is unknown to thee, and him who is near . . . like him who is far. . . . Such an official shall flourish greatly in the place. . . . Be not enraged toward a man unjustly . . . but show forth the fear of thee; let one be afraid of thee, for a prince is a prince of whom one is afraid. Lo, the true dread of a prince is to do justice. . . . Be not known to the people and they shall not say, 'He is only a man.' "[6] Even the vizier's subordinates are

---

[1] II, 697–8.   [2] II, 709.   [3] II, 696.
[4] Pap. Anast. II, 6, 5–6.   [5] II, 666.   [6] II, 668–9.

to be men of justice, for the king admonishes the new vizier, "Lo, one shall say of the chief scribe of the vizier, 'A scribe of justice' shall one say of him."[1]   In a land where the bribery of the court still begins with the lowest subordinates before access is gained to the magistrates, such "justice" was necessary indeed.   The viziers of the Eighteenth Dynasty desired the reputation of hard working, conscientious officials, who took the greatest pride in the proper administration of the office.   Several of them have left a record of their installation, with a long list of the duties of the office, engraved and painted upon the walls of their Theban tombs, and it is from these that we have drawn our account of the vizier.[2]

Such was the government of the imperial age in Egypt. In society the disappearance of the landed nobility, and the administration of the local districts by a vast army of petty officials of the crown, opened the way more fully than in the Middle Kingdom for innumerable careers among the middle class.   These opportunities must have worked a gradual change in their condition.   Thus one official relates his obscure origin thus: "Ye shall talk of it, one to another, and the old men shall teach it to the youth.   I was one whose family was poor and whose town was small, but the Lord of the Two Lands [the king] recognized me; I was accounted great in his heart, the king in his role as sun-god in the splendour of his palace saw me.   He exalted me more than the [royal] companions, introducing me among the princes of the palace. . . . He appointed me to conduct works while I was a youth, he found me, I was made account of in his heart, I was introduced into the gold-house to fashion the figures and images of all the gods.'"[3]   Here he administered his office so well in overseeing the production of the costly images of gold that he was rewarded publicly with decorations of gold by the king and even gained place in the councils of the treasury.   Such possibilities of promotion

[1] II, 670.   [2] II, 665–761.
[3] Unpublished stela in Leyden (V, I), by courtesy of the curator.

and royal favour awaited success in local administration; for in some local office the career of this unknown official in the small town must have begun. There thus grew up a new official class, its lower ranks drawn from the old middle class, while on the other hand in its upper strata were the relatives and dependents of the old landed nobility, by whom the higher and more important local offices were administered. Here the official class gradually merged into the large circle of royal favourites who filled the great offices of the central government or commanded the Pharaoh's forces on his campaigns. As there was no longer a feudal nobility, the great government officials became the nobles of the Empire. The old middle class of merchants,[1] skilled craftsmen and artists also still survived and continued to replenish the lower ranks of the official class. Below these were the masses who worked the fields and estates, the serfs of the Pharaoh. They formed so large a portion of the inhabitants that the Hebrew scribe, evidently writing from the outside, knew only this class of society beside the priests.[2] These lower strata passed away and left little or no trace, but the official class was now able to erect tombs and mortuary stelæ in such surprising numbers that they furnish us a vast mass of materials for reconstructing the life and customs of the time. An official who took a census in the Eighteenth Dynasty divided the people into "soldiers, priests, royal serfs and all the craftsmen,"[3] and this classification is corroborated by all that we know of the time; although we must understand that all callings of the free middle class are here included among the "soldiers." The soldier in the standing army has therefore now also become a social class. The free middle class, liable to military service, are called "citizens of the army," a term already known in the Middle Kingdom,[4] but now very common; so that liability to military service becomes the significant designation of this class of society. Politically the soldier's influence grows with every reign and he soon becomes the

[1] III, 274.　　[2] Gen. 47: 21.　　[3] II, p. 165, note a.　　[4] I, 681.

involuntary reliance of the Pharaoh in the execution of numerous civil commissions where formerly the soldier was never employed. Side by side with him appears another new and powerful influence, the ancient institution of the priesthood. As a natural consequence of the great wealth of the temples under the Empire, the priesthood becomes a profession, no longer merely an incidental office held by a layman, as in the Old and Middle Kingdoms. As the priests increase in numbers they gain more and more political power; while the growing wealth of the temples demands for its proper administration a veritable army of temple officials of all sorts, who were unknown to the old days of simplicity. Probably one fourth of all the persons buried in the great and sacred cemetery of Abydos at this period were priests. Priestly communities had thus grown up. Heretofore the priests of the various sanctuaries had never been united by any official ties, but existed only in individual and entirely separated communities without interrelation. All these priestly bodies were now united in a great sacerdotal organization embracing the whole land. The head of the state temple at Thebes, the High Priest of Amon, was the supreme head of this greater body also and his power was thereby increased far beyond that of his older rivals at Heliopolis and Memphis. The members of the sacerdotal guild thus became a new class, so that priest, soldier and official now stood together as three great social classes, yet possessing common interests; their leaders were the Pharaoh's nobles, who replaced the old aristocracy; but their lower ranks were not to be distinguished from the free middle class, the tradesmen and craftsmen; while at the bottom, as the chief economic basis of all, were the peasant serfs.

The priests whom we now find so numerous as to have become a class of society, were the representatives of a richer and more elaborate state religion than Egypt had ever seen. The days of the old simplicity were forever past. The wealth gained by foreign conquest enabled the Pharaohs from now on to endow the temples with such riches as no sanctuary of the old days had ever possessed. The temples grew into vast and gorgeous palaces, each with its community of priests, and the high priest of such a community in the larger centres was a veritable sacerdotal prince, ultimately wielding considerable political power. The High Priest's wife at Thebes was called the chief concubine of the god, and his real consort was no less a person than the queen herself, who was therefore known as the "Divine Consort." In the gorgeous ritual which now prevailed, her part was to lead the singing of the women who were also still permitted to participate in the service in large numbers. She possessed also a fortune, which belonged to the temple endowment, and for this reason it was desirable that the queen should hold the office in order to retain this fortune in the royal house.

The triumph of a Theban family had brought with it the supremacy of Amon. He had not been the god of the residence in the Middle Kingdom, and although the rise of a Theban family had then given him some distinction, it was not until now that he became the great god of the state. His essential character and individuality had already been obliterated by the solar theology of the Middle Kingdom, when he had become Amon-Re, and with some attributes borrowed from his ithyphallic neighbour, Min of Coptos, he now rose to a unique and supreme position of unprecedented splendour. He was popular with the people, too, and as a Moslem says, "Inshallah," "If Allah will," so the Egyptian now added to all his promises "If Amon spare my life." They called him the "vizier of the poor," the people carried to him their wants and wishes, and their hopes for future prosperity were implicitly staked upon his favour. But the fusion of the old gods had not deprived Amon alone of his individuality, for in the general flux almost any god might possess the qualities and functions of the others, although the dominant position was still occupied by the sun-god.

The mortuary beliefs of the time are the outgrowth of tendencies already plainly observable in the Middle Kingdom. The magical formulæ by which the dead are to triumph in the hereafter become more and more numerous, so that it is no longer possible to record them on the inside of the coffin, but they must be written on papyrus and the roll placed in the tomb. As the selection of the most important of these texts came to be more and more uniform, the "Book of the Dead" began to take form. All was dominated by magic; by this all-powerful means the dead might effect all that he desired. The luxurious lords of the Empire no longer look forward with pleasure to the prospect of plowing, sowing and reaping in the happy fields of Yaru. They would escape such peasant labour, and a statuette (Fig 106) bearing the implements of labour in the field and inscribed with a potent charm is placed in the tomb, thereby ensuring to the deceased immunity from such toil, which will always be performed by this representative whenever the call to the fields is heard. Such "Ushebtis," or "respondents," as they were termed, were now placed in the necropolis by scores and hundreds. But this means of obtaining material good was now unfortunately transferred also to the ethical world, in order to secure exemption from the consequences of an evil life. A sacred beetle or scarabæus (Fig. 107) is cut from stone and inscribed with a charm, beginning with the significant words, "O my heart, rise not up against me as a witness." So powerful is this cunning invention when laid upon the breast of the mummy under the wrappings that when the guilty soul stands in the judgment-hall in the awful presence of Osiris, the accusing voice of the heart is silenced and the great god does not perceive the evil of which it would testify. Likewise the rolls of the Book of the Dead containing, besides all the other charms, also the scene of judgment, and especially the welcome verdict of acquittal, are now sold by the priestly scribes to anyone with the means to buy; and the fortunate purchaser's name is then inserted in the blanks left for this purpose throughout the document; thus securing for himself the certainty of such a verdict, before it was known whose name should be so inserted. The invention of these devices by the priests was undoubtedly as subversive of moral progress and the elevation of the popular religion as the sale of indulgences in Luther's time. The moral aspirations which had come into the religion of Egypt with the ethical influences so potent in the Osiris-myth, were now choked and poisoned by the assurance that, however vicious a man's life, exemption in the hereafter could be purchased at any time from the priests. The priestly literature on the hereafter, produced probably for no other purpose than for gain, continued to grow. We have a "Book of What is in the Nether World," describing the twelve caverns, or hours of the night through which the sun passed beneath the earth; and a "Book of the Portals," treating of the gates and strongholds between these caverns. Although these edifying compositions never gained the wide circulation enjoyed by the Book of the Dead, the former of the two was engraved in the tombs of the Nineteenth and Twentieth Dynasty kings at Thebes, showing that these grotesque creations of the perverted priestly imagination finally gained the credence of the highest circles.

The tomb of the noble consists as before of chambers hewn in the face of the cliff, and in accordance with the prevailing tendency it is now filled with imaginary scenes from the next world, with mortuary and religious texts, many of them of a magical character. At the same time the tomb has become more a personal monument to the deceased and the walls of the chapel bear many scenes from his life, especially from his official career, particularly as a record of the honours which he received from the king. Thus the cliffs opposite Thebes (Figs. 131, 166), honey-combed as they are with the tombs of the lords of the Empire, contain whole chapters of the life and history of the period, with which we shall now deal. In a solitary valley (Fig. 108) behind these cliffs, as we shall see, the kings now likewise excavate their tombs in the limestone walls and the pyramid is no longer employed. Vast galleries (Figs. 109, 110) are pierced

FIG. 106.—"USHEBTI" OR RESPONDENT
STATUETTES.

The substitute of the deceased when called upon for
menial labor in the hereafter. See p. 249. (Art
Institute, Chicago.)

FIG. 107.—HEART SCARAB OF THE "FIRST
OF THE SACRED WOMEN OF AMON,
ISIMKHEB." See p. 249. (Field Museum,
Chicago.)

FIG. 108.—PART OF THE VALLEY OF THE KINGS' TOMBS, THEBES.

The entrances of two tombs are discernible at the right of the center. See pp. 250–51; 279–80.

into the mountain, and passing from hall to hall, they terminate many hundreds of feet from the entrance in a large chamber, where the body of the king is laid in a huge stone sarcophagus. It is possible that the whole excavation is intended to represent the passages of the nether world along which the sun passes in his nightly journey. On the western plain of Thebes, the plain east of this valley, as on the east side of the pyramid, arose the splendid mortuary temples of the emperors, of which we shall later have occasion to say more. But these elaborate mortuary customs are now no longer confined to the Pharaoh and his nobles; the necessity for such equipment in preparation for the hereafter is now felt by all classes. The manufacture of such materials, resulting from the gradual extension of these customs, has become an industry; the embalmers, undertakers and manufacturers of coffins and tomb furniture occupy a quarter at Thebes, forming almost a guild by themselves, as they did in later Greek times. The middle class were now frequently able to excavate and decorate a tomb; but when too poor for this luxury, they rented a place for their dead in great common tombs maintained by the priests, and here the embalmed body was deposited in a chamber where the mummies were piled up like cord-wood, but nevertheless received the benefit of the ritual

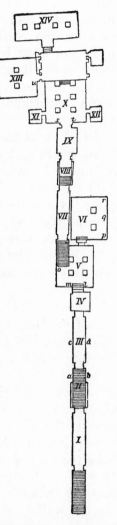

FIG. 109. Ground Plan of the Tomb of Seti I, excavated in the Valley of the Kings' Tombs at Thebes. The shaded portions are descending steps. I–IV and VII–IX are galleries, which descend as they advance. The other rooms are pillared halls. In hall X was the magnificent alabaster sarcophagus of the king, now in Sir John Soane's Museum in London.

maintained for all in common. The very poor still buried
in the sand and gravel on the desert margin as of old,
but even they looked with longing upon the luxury enjoyed
in the hereafter by the rich, and at the door of some luxurious tomb they buried a rude statuette of their dead,
bearing his name, in the pathetic hope that thus he might
gain a few crumbs from the bounty of the rich man's mortuary table.

Out of the chaos which the rule of foreign lords had produced, the new state and the new conditions slowly emerged
as Ahmose I gradually gained leisure from his arduous wars.
With the state religion, the foreign dynasty had shown no
sympathy and the temples lay wasted and deserted in many
places. We find Ahmose therefore in his twenty second
year opening new workings in the famous quarries of Ayan
or Troja, opposite Gizeh, from which the blocks for the Gizeh
pyramids were taken, in order to secure stone for the temples in Memphis, Thebes (Luxor) and probably elsewhere.[1]
For these works he still employed the oxen which he had
taken from the Syrians in his Asiatic wars. None of these
buildings of his, however, has survived. For the ritual of
the state temple at Karnak he furnished the sanctuary with
a magnificent service of rich cultus utensils in precious
metals, and he built a new temple-barge upon the river of
cedar exacted from the Lebanon princes.[2] His greatest work
remains the Eighteenth Dynasty itself, for whose brilliant
career his own achievements had laid so firm a foundation.
Notwithstanding his reign of at least twenty two years,
Ahmose must have died young (1557 B. C.) for his mother
was still living in the tenth year of his son and successor,
Amenhotep I.[3] By him[4] he was buried in the old Eleventh
Dynasty cemetery at the north end of the western Theban
plain in a masonry tomb, which has now long perished. The
jewelry of his mother (Fig. 103), stolen from her neighbouring tomb at a remote date, was found by Mariette concealed in the vicinity. The body of Ahmose I, as well as
this jewelry, are now preserved in the Museum at Cairo.

[1] II, 26–28, 33 ff.　　[2] II, 32.　　[3] II, 49–51.　　[4] Masp. Mom. roy., 534.

CHAPTER XIV

THE CONSOLIDATION OF THE KINGDOM; THE RISE
OF THE EMPIRE

The time was not yet ripe for the great achievements which awaited the monarchs of the new dynasty. The old dominion of the Middle Kingdom, from the second cataract to the sea, was still far from the consolidation necessary to retain it in administrative and industrial stability. Nubia had been long without a strong arm from the north and the southern rebels in Egypt had prevented Ahmose I from continuous exertion of force above the cataract. The Troglodytes, who later harassed the Romans on this same frontier, and who were never thoroughly subdued by them, now possessed a leader, and Ahmose's campaign against them had not been lasting in its effects. It was easy for these barbarians to retreat into the eastern desert as the Egyptians approached, and then return after the danger had passed. Amenhotep I, Ahmose's successor, was therefore obliged to invade Nubia in force and penetrated to the Middle Kingdom frontier at the second cataract,[1] where the temple of the Sesostrises and Amenemhets had long been in the hands of the barbarians, and was doubtless in ruin. The two Ahmoses of El Kab were with the king, and Ahmose, son of Ebana, reports that "his majesty captured that Troglodyte of Nubia in the midst of his soldiers."[2] With the loss of their leader, there was but one outcome for the action; both the Ahmoses captured prisoners, displayed great gallantry and were rewarded by the king.[3] Northern Nubia was now placed under the administration of the mayor or governor of the old city of Nekhen, which now became the northern

---

[1] II, 38–9. [2] II, 39. [3] II, 39, 41.

limit of a southern administrative district, including all the territory on the south of it, controlled by Egypt, at least as far as northern Nubia, or Wawat. From this time the new governor was able to go north with the tribute of the country regularly every year.[1]

Hardly had Amenhotep I won his victory at the second cataract, than another danger on the opposite frontier in the north recalled him thither. Ahmose, son of Ebana, boasts that he brought the king back to Egypt in his ship, probably from the second cataract, that is some two hundred miles, in two days.[2] The long period of weakness and disorganization accompanying the rule of the Hyksos had given the Libyans the opportunity, which they always improved, of pushing in and occupying the rich lands of the Delta. Though our only source does not mention any such invasion, it is evident that Amenhotep I's war with the Libyans at this particular time can be explained in no other way. Finding their aggressions too threatening to be longer ignored, the Pharaoh now drove them back and invaded their country. We know nothing of the battles that may have been fought, but Amose-Pen-Nekhbet of El Kab states that he slew three of the enemy and brought away their severed hands, for which he was of course rewarded by the king.[3] Having relieved his frontiers and secured Nubia, Amenhotep was at liberty to turn his arms toward Asia. Unfortunately we have no records of his Syrian war, but he possibly penetrated far to the north, even to the Euphrates. In any case he accomplished enough to enable his successor to boast of ruling as far as the Euphrates,[4] before the latter had himself undertaken any Asiatic conquests. Whether from this war or some other source he gained wealth for richly wrought buildings at Thebes, including a chapel on the western plain for his tomb[5] there, and a superb temple-gate at Karnak, later demolished by Thutmose III.[6] The architect who erected these buildings, all of which have per-

---

[1] II, 47–48. [2] II, 39, ll. 27–28. [3] II, 42, 22. [4] II, 73.
[5] IV, 513 and notes. [6] Bull. de l'Inst., 4me ser., No. 3, 164–5.

ished, narrates the king's death at Thebes, after a reign of at least ten years.[1]

Whether Amenhotep left a son entitled to the throne or not, we do not know. His successor, Thutmose I, was the son of a woman whose birth and family are of doubtful connection, and she was almost certainly not of royal blood. Her great son evidently owed his accession to the kingship to his marriage with a princess of the old line, named Ahmose, through whom he could assert a valid claim to the throne. On making good this claim, he lost no time in issuing a proclamation announcing throughout the kingdom that he had been crowned. This occurred about January, 1540 or 1535 B. C. The officials in Nubia regarded the proclamation of sufficient importance to engrave it on tablets which they set up at Wadi Halfa, Kubbân and perhaps elsewhere.[2] The official to whom this action was due had reason to make evident his adherence to the new king, for he had been appointed to a new and important office immediately on the king's accession. It was no longer possible for the mayor of Nekhen to administer Nubia and collect the tribute. The country demanded the sole attention of a responsible governor who was practically a viceroy. He was given the title "Governor of the south countries, king's-son of Kush," although he was not necessarily a member of the royal household or of royal birth. With great ceremony, in the presence of the Pharaoh, one of the treasury officials was wont to deliver to the incumbent the seal of his new office, saying: "This is the seal from the Pharaoh, who assigns to thee the territory from Nekhen to Napata."[3] The jurisdiction of the viceroy thus extended to the fourth cataract, and it was the region between this southern limit and the second cataract which was known as Kush. There was still no great or dominant kingdom in Kush, nor in lower Nubia, but the country was under the rule of powerful chiefs, each controlling a limited territory. It was impossible to suppress these native rulers at once and nearly two hundred years after this we

[1] II, 45-6.   [2] II, 54-60.   [3] II, 1020-25.

still find the chiefs of Kush and a chief of Wawat as far north as Ibrim.[1] Although possessing only a nominal au thority, it was but slowly that they were replaced by Egyptian administrative officers. Moreover, in Thutmose I's time the southern half of the new province was far from being sufficiently pacified. The appointment of Thure, the first viceroy, therefore brought him a serious task. The turbulent tribes from the hills above the Nile valley were constantly raiding the towns along the river[2] and making stable government and the orderly development of the country's natural resources impossible. Seeing that Thure was unable to stop this, the king went south early in his second year personally to oversee the task of more thorough subjugation. Arriving at the first cataract in February or March, he found the canal through the rapids obstructed with stone,[3] just as it had perhaps been since Hyksos days. Desirous of losing no time, and anxious to take advantage of the fast falling water, he did not stop to clear it, but forced the rapids with the aid of the admiral, Ahmose, son of Ebana, whose exploits we have followed so long. This officer now again distinguished himself "in the bad water in the passage of the ship by the bend," presumably in the cataract, and was again liberally rewarded by the king.[4] By early April Thutmose had reached Tangur, about seventy five miles above the second cataract.[5] Ahmose, son of Ebana, describes the battle, which probably took place somewhere on this advance, between the second and third cataracts. The king engaged in hand to hand combat with a Nubian chief; "his majesty cast the first lance, which remained in the body of that fallen one." The enemy were totally defeated and many prisoners were taken.[6] Of these, the other hero of El Kab, Ahmose-Pen-Nehkbet, captured no less than five.[7] The water was now so low that the advance was necessarily for the most part by land: but the king pressed on to the third cataract. He was the first Pharaoh to stand here at the northern gateway of the Dongola Prov-

[1] II, 1037. [2] II, 80. [3] II, 75. [4] II, 80. [5] II, p. 28, note b. [6] II, 80. [7] II, 84

ince, the great garden of the Upper Nile, through which there wound before him over two hundred miles of unbroken river. With the long advance now behind him, he erected here five triumphant stelæ commemorating the new conquest. On the Island of Tombos he erected a fortress, of which some remains still survive, and garrisoned it with troops from the army of conquest.[2] In August of the same year, five months after he had passed Tangur on the way up, he erected a tablet of victory[3] on Tombos, on which he boasts of ruling from the frontier at Tombos on the south, to the Euphrates on the north, a statement to which his own achievements in Asia did not yet entitle him. Returning slowly northward with the Nubian chief, whom he had slain, hanging head downward at the prow of his royal barge, he reached the first cataract again some seven months after he had erected the stela on Tombos.[4] We can only explain the slowness of his return by supposing that he devoted much time to the reorganization and thorough pacification of the country on his way. It was now April, and as the low water of that season was favourable to the enterprise, the king ordered the canal at the first cataract cleared. The viceroy, Thure, had charge of the work, and he has left three records[5] of its successful accomplishment inscribed on the rocks by the stream, two on the island of Sehel and one on the neighbouring shore. The king then sailed through the canal in triumph with the body of the Nubian chief still hanging head downward at the bow of his barge, where it remained till he landed at Thebes.

The subjugation of the Nubian province was now thoroughly done, and Thutmose was able to give his attention to a similar task at the other extremity of his realm, in Asia. Evidently the conquest of Amenhotep I, which had enabled Thutmose to claim the Euphrates as his northern boundary, had not been sufficient to ensure to the Pharaoh's treasury the regular tribute which he was now enjoying from Nubia, but the conditions in Syria-Palestine were very

[1] II, p. 28, note a.   [2] II, 72.   [3] II, 67-73.   [4] II, 74-77.   [5] Ibid.

17

favourable for a prolonged lease of power on the Pharaoh's part.

The geographical conformation of the country along the eastern end of the Mediterranean, which we may call Syria-Palestine, is not such as to permit the gradual amalgamation of small and petty states into one great nation, as that process took place in the valleys of the Nile and the Euphrates. From north to south, roughly parallel with the coast, the region is traversed by rugged mountain ranges, in two main ridges, known as the Lebanon and Anti-Lebanon in the north. In the south, the western ridge, with some interruptions, drops finally into the bare and forbidding hills of Judah, which merge then into the desert of Sinai south of Palestine. South of the plain of Esdraelon, or Jezreel, it throws off the ridge of Carmel, which drops, like a Gothic buttress, abruptly to the sea. The eastern ridge shifts somewhat further eastward in its southern course, interrupted here and there, and spreading on the east of the Dead Sea in the mountains of Moab, its southern flanks are likewise lost in the sandy plateau of northern Arabia. Between the two Lebanons, that is, in the northern half of the depression between the eastern and western ridges, is a fertile valley traversed by the river Orontes. This Orontes valley is the only extensive region in Syria-Palestine not cut up by the hills and mountains, where a strong kingdom might develop. The coast is completely isolated from the interior by the ridge of Lebanon, on whose western base a people might rise to wealth and power only by the exploitation of the resources of the sea; while in the south, Palestine with its harbourless coast and its large tracts of unproductive soil, hardly furnished the economic basis for the development of a strong nation. It is moreover badly cut up by the ridge of Carmel and the deep clove in which lie the Jordan and the Dead Sea. Along almost its entire eastern frontier, Syria-Palestine merges into the northern extension of the Arabian desert, save in the extreme north, where the valley of the Orontes and that of the Euphrates almost blend, just as they part, the one to seek the Mediterranean, while the other turns away toward Babylon and the Persian Gulf (Map 7).

The country was settled chiefly by Semites, probably the descendants of an early overflow of population from the deserts of Arabia, such as has occurred in historic times over and over again. In the north these were subsequently Aramæans, while in the south they may be designated as Canaanites. In general these peoples showed little genius for government, and were totally without any motives for consolidation. Divided by the physical conformation of the country, they were organized into numerous city-kingdoms, that is, petty principalities, consisting of a city, with the surrounding fields and outlying villages, all under the rule of a local dynast, who lived in the said city. Each city had not only its own kinglet, but also its own god, a local ba'al (Baal) or "lord," with whom was often associated a ba'lat or "lady," a goddess like her of Byblos. These miniature kingdoms were embroiled in frequent wars with one another, each dynast endeavouring to unseat his neighbour and absorb the latter's territory and revenues. Exceeding all the others in size was the kingdom of Kadesh, the surviving nucleus of Hyksos power. It had developed in the only place where the conditions permitted such an expansion, occupying a very advantageous position on the Orontes. It thus commanded the road northward through inner Syria, the route of commerce from Egypt and the south, which, following the Orontes, diverged thence to the Euphrates, to cross to Assyria or descend the Euphrates to Babylon. Being likewise at the northern end of both Lebanons, Kadesh commanded also the road from the interior seaward through the Eleutheros valley.[1] These advantages had enabled it to subjugate the smaller kingdoms and to organize them into a loose feudal state, in which we should, in the author's opinion, recognize the empire of the Hyksos, as already indicated.[2] We shall now discern it for two generations, struggling desperately to maintain its independence, and

[1] See Map 7 and the author's Battle of Kadesh.   [2] Pp. 219 ff.

only crushed at last by twenty years of warfare under Thutmose III.

While, with this exception, these kingdoms of the interior showed small aptitude for government, some of them nevertheless possessed a high degree of civilization in other directions. In the art of war especially they had during Hyksos supremacy taught the Egyptian much. They were masters of the art of metal-working, they wrought weapons of high quality, and the manufacture of chariots was a considerable industry. Metal vessels of varied designs were also produced. Their more strenuous climate demanded woolen clothing, so that they had mastered the art of dyeing and weaving wool, in which they produced textile fabrics of the finest quality and of rich and sumptuous design. These Semites were already inveterate traders, and an animated commerce was passing from town to town, where the market place was a busy scene of traffic as it is to-day. On the scanty foothold available on the western declivities of the Lebanon some of these Semites, crossing from the interior, had early gained a footing on the coast, to become the Phœnicians of historic times. They rapidly subdued the sea, and from being mere fishermen, they soon developed into hardy mariners. Bearing the products of their industries, their galleys were now penetrating beyond the harbours of Cyprus, where they exploited the rich copper mines, and creeping along the coast of Asia Minor they gained Rhodes and the islands of the Ægean. In every favourable harbour they established their colonies, along the southern litoral of Asia Minor, throughout the Ægean, and here and there on the mainland of Greece. Their manufactories multiplied in these colonies, and everywhere throughout the regions which they reached, their wares were prominent in the markets. As their wealth increased, every harbour along the Phœnician coast was the seat of a rich and flourishing city, among which Tyre, Sidon, Byblos, Arvad and Simyra were the greatest, each being the seat of a powerful dynasty. Thus it was that in the Homeric poems the Phœnician merchant and his wares were pro-

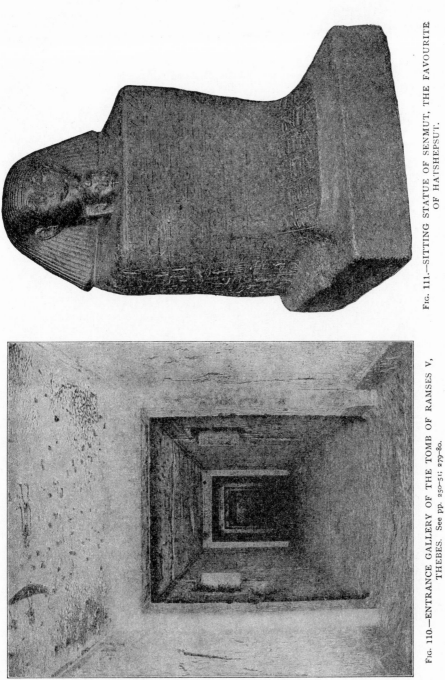

Fig. 110.—ENTRANCE GALLERY OF THE TOMB OF RAMSES V,
THEBES. See pp. 250-51; 279-80.

Fig. 111.—SITTING STATUE OF SENMUT, THE FAVOURITE
OF HATSHEPSUT.

He holds the queen's infant daughter, Nefrure, between his knees. See
expungement of his name on right foot (Cf. p. 283). Berlin Museum.

verbial, for the commercial and maritime power enjoyed by the Phœnicians at the rise of the Egyptian Empire continued into Homeric times.

How far west these Phœnician mariners penetrated it is now difficult to determine, but it is not impossible that their Spanish and Carthaginian colonies already existed. The civilization which they found in the northern Mediterranean was that of the Mycenæan age, and these Phœnician avenues of commerce served as a link connecting Egypt and the Mycenæan civilization of the north. The people who appear with Mycenæan vessels as gifts and tribute for the Pharaoh in this age, are termed by the Egyptian monuments Keftyew, and so regular was the traffic of the Phœnician fleets with these people that the Phœnician craft plying on these voyages were known as "Keftyew ships."[1] It is impossible to locate the Keftyew with certainty, but they seem to have extended from the southern coast of Asia Minor as far west as Crete. All this northern region was known to the Egyptians as the "Isles of the Sea," for having no acquaintance with the interior of Asia Minor, they supposed it to be but island coasts, like those of the Ægean. In northern Syria, on the upper reaches of the Euphrates, the world, as conceived by the Egyptian, ended in marshes in which the Euphrates had its rise, and these again were encircled by the "Great Circle,"[2] the ocean, which was the end of all.

In this Semitic world of Syria-Palestine, now dominated by Egypt, she was to learn much; nevertheless throughout this region the influence of Egyptian art and industry was supreme. Much more highly organized than the neighbouring peoples of Asia, the mighty kingdom on the Nile had from time immemorial been regarded with awe and respect, while its more mature civilization, by its very presence on the threshold of hither Asia, was a powerful influence upon the politically feeble states there. There was little or no native art among these peoples of the western Semitic world, but they were skilful imitators, ready to absorb and adapt

[1] II, 492.   [2] II, 661.

to their uses all that might further their industries and their commerce.. The products which their fleets marketed throughout the eastern Mediterranean were therefore tinctured through and through with Egyptian elements, while the native Egyptian wares which they carried to Europe and the Ægean introduced there the unalloyed art of the Nile valley. In these Phœnician galleys the civilization of the Orient was being gradually disseminated through southern Europe and the west. Babylonian influences, while not so noticeable in the art of Syria-Palestine, were nevertheless powerfully present there. Since the days of the brief empire of Sargon of Agade, about the middle of the third thousand years B. C., Babylon had gained in the west a commercial supremacy, which had gradually introduced there the cuneiform system of writing. It was readily adaptable to the Semitic dialects prevalent in Syria-Palestine and gained a footing by a process similar to that which, during the commercial dominance of Phœnicia, brought the Phœnician alphabet to Greece. It was even adopted also by the Hittites, who were not Semites, and likewise by another non-Semitic nation in this region, the kingdom of Mitanni. Thus Syria-Palestine became common ground, where the forces of civilization from the Nile and the Euphrates mingled at first in peaceful rivaly, but ultimately to meet upon the battlefield. The historical significance of this region is found in the inevitable struggle for its possession between the kingdom of the Nile on the one hand and those of the Tigro-Euphrates valley and hither Asia on the other. It was in the midst of this struggle that Hebrew national history fell, and in its relentless course the Hebrew monarchies perished.

Other non-Semitic peoples were also beginning to appear on Egypt's northern horizon. A group of warriors of Iran, now appearing for the first time in history, had by 1500 B. C. pushed westward to the upper Euphrates. At the rise of the Egyptian Empire therefore, these Iranians were already settled in the country east of the Euphrates, within the huge bend where the river turns away from the Mediterranean, and there established the kingdom of Mitanni. It was the earliest and westernmost outpost of the Aryan race as yet disclosed to us. The source from which they had come must have been the original home of that Aryan race behind the northeastern mountains at the sources of the Oxus and Jaxartes rivers. The influence and language of Mitanni extended westward to Tunip in the Orontes valley and eastward to Nineveh. They formed a powerful and cultivated state, which, planted thus on the road leading westward from Babylon along the Euphrates, effectively cut off the latter from her profitable western trade, and doubtless had much to do with the decline in which Babylon, under her foreign Kassite dynasty, now found herself. Assyria was as yet but a new and insignificant city-kingdom, whose coming struggle with Babylon only rendered the Pharaohs less liable to interference from the east, in the realization of their plans of conquest in Asia. Everything thus conspired to favour the permanence of Egyptian power there.

Under these conditions Thutmose I prepared to quell the perpetual revolt in Syria and bring it into such complete subjection as he had achieved in Nubia. None of his records of the campaign has survived, but the two Ahmoses of El Kab were still serving with the army of conquest and in their biographies they refer briefly to this war also. Kadesh must have been cowed for the time by Amenhotep I, for, in so far as we know, Thutmose met with no resistance from her, which the two Ahmoses considered worthy of mention. Thus, without serious opposition, the Pharaoh reached Naharin, or the land of the "rivers," as the name signifies, which was the designation of the country from the Orontes to the Euphrates and beyond, merging into Asia Minor. Here the revolt was naturally the most serious as it was farthest removed from the Pharaoh's vengeance. The battle resulted in a great slaughter of the Asiatics, followed by the capture of large numbers of prisoners. "Meanwhile," says Ahmose, son of Ebana, "I was at the head of our troops and his majesty beheld my bravery. I brought off a chariot, its horses and him who was upon it as a living prisoner, and I took them to his majesty. One presented me with gold in double measure."[1] His namesake of El Kab, who was younger and more vigourous, was even more successful, for he captured no less than twenty one hands severed from the dead, besides a horse and a chariot.[2] These two men are typical examples of the followers of the Pharaoh at this time. And it is evident that the king understood how to make their own prosperity dependent upon the success of his arms. Unfortunately for our knowledge of Thutmose I's further campaigns, if there were any, the first of these biographies and of course also the warlike career which it narrates, closes with this campaign, though the younger man campaigned with Thutmose II and lived on in favour and prosperity till the reign of Thutmose III.

Somewhere along the Euphrates at its nearest approach to the Mediterranean, Thutmose now erected a stone boundary-tablet, marking the northern and at this point the eastern limit of his Syrian possessions.[3] He had made good the boast so proudly recorded, possibly only a year before, on the tablet marking the other extreme frontier of his empire at the third cataract of the Nile. Henceforth he was even less measured in his claims; for he later boasted to the priests of Abydos, "I made the boundary of Egypt as far as the circuit of the sun,"[4] which, in view of the limited and vague knowledge of the world possessed by the Egyptians of that day, was almost true.

Two Pharaohs had now seen the Euphrates, the Syrian dynasts were fully impressed with the power of Egypt, and their tribute, together with that of the Beduin and other inhabitants of Palestine, began to flow regularly into the Egyptian treasury.[5] Thus Thutmose I was able to begin the restoration of the temples so neglected since the time of the Hyksos. The modest old temple of the Middle Kingdom

[1] II, 81.　　[2] II, 85.　　[3] II, 478.　　[4] II, 98.　　[5] II, 101.

monarchs at Thebes was no longer in keeping with the Pharaoh's increasing wealth and pomp. His chief architect, Ineni, was therefore commissioned to erect two massive pylons, or towered gateways, in front of the old Amontemple, and between these a covered hall, with the roof supported upon large cedar columns, brought of course, like the splendid silver-gold-tipped flag staves of cedar at the temple front, from the new possessions in the Lebanon. The huge door was likewise of Asiatic bronze, with the image of the god upon it, inlaid with gold.[1] He likewise restored the revered temple of Osiris at Abydos, equipping it with rich ceremonial implements and furniture of silver and gold, with magnificent images of the gods, such as it had doubtless lost in Hyksos days.[2] Admonished by his advancing years he also endowed it with an income for the offering of mortuary oblations to himself, giving the priests instructions regarding the preservation of his name and memory.[3]

[1] II, 103-4.   [2] II, 92-96.   [3] II, 97.

CHAPTER XV

As Thutmose I approached the thirtieth anniversary of
his accession to the heirship of the throne, which was also
the thirtieth anniversary of his coronation, he dispatched
his faithful architect, Ineni, to the granite quarries of the
first cataract to procure two obelisks with which to celebrate
the coming Hebsed-festival, or thirty years' jubilee. In a
barge over two hundred feet long and one third as wide
Ineni floated the great shafts down the river to Thebes, and
erected them before the pylons of the Karnak temple, which
he had likewise constructed for the king.[1] He inscribed one
of them, which stands to this day before the temple door,
with the king's names and titles,[2] but before he had begun
the inscription upon the other unexpected changes inter-
fered, so that it never bore the name of Thutmose I. He
was now an old man[3] and the claim to the throne which he
had thus far successfully maintained, was probably weakened by the death of his queen, Ahmose, through whom alone
he had any valid title to the crown. She was the descendant
and representative of the old Theban princes who had fought
and expelled the Hyksos, and there was a strong party who
regarded the blood of this line as alone entitled to royal
honours. She had borne Thutmose I four children, two sons
and two daughters; but both sons and one of the daughters
had died in youth or childhood. The surviving daughter,
Makere-Hatshepsut, was thus the only child of the old line,
and so strong was the party of legitimacy, that they had
forced the king, years before, at about the middle of his

[1] II, 105.　　　[2] II, 86-8.　　　[3] II, 64, l. 11.

reign, to proclaim her his successor, in spite of the disinclination general throughout Egyptian history to submit to the rule of a queen. Among other children, Thutmose I had also two sons by other queens: one, who afterward became Thutmose II, was the son of a princess Mutnofret; while the other, later Thutmose III, had been born to the king by an obscure concubine named Isis. The close of Thutmose I's reign is involved in deep obscurity, and the following reconstruction is not without its difficulties.[2] The traces left by family dissensions on temple walls are not likely to be sufficiently decisive to enable us to follow the complicated struggle with certainty three thousand five hundred years later. In the period of confusion at the close of Thutmose I's reign probably fall the beginning of Thutmose III's reign and all of the reign of Thutmose II. When the light finally breaks Thutmose III is on the throne for a long reign, the beginning of which had been interrupted for a short time by the ephemeral rule of Thutmose II. Thus, although Thutmose III's reign really began before that of Thutmose II, seven eighths of it falls after Thutmose II's death, and the numbering of the two kings is most convenient as it is. Involved in the obscure struggle, with touches of romance and dramatic incidents interspersed, are the fortunes of the beautiful and gifted princess of the old line, Hatshepsut, the daughter of Thutmose I. Possibly after the death of her brothers she had been married to her half brother, the concubine's son, whom we must call Thutmose III. As he was a young prince of no prospects, having, through neither his father nor his mother, any claim to the succession, he had been placed in the Karnak temple as a priest with the rank of prophet. Ere long he had won the priesthood to his support, for, on the death of the old queen, Ahmose, Thutmose III had the same right to the throne which his father had once asserted, that is, by inheritance through his wife. To this legal right the priesthood of Amon, who supported him, agreed to add that of divine sanction. Whether

---

[1] II, 307.   [2] II, 128–130.

by previous peaceful understanding with Thutmose I, or as a hostile revolution totally unexpected on his part, the succession of Thutmose III was suddenly effected by a highly dramatic coup d'état in the temple of Amon. On a feast day, as the image of the god was borne, amid the acclamations of the multitude, from the holy place into the court of the temple, the priest, Thutmose III, was stationed with his colleagues in the northern colonnade in Thutmose I's hall of the temple. The priests bore the god around both sides of the colonnade, as if he were looking for some one, and he finally stopped before the young prince, who prostrated himself upon the pavement. But the god raised him up, and as an indication of his will, had him placed immediately in the "Station of the King," which was the ceremonial spot where only the king might stand in the celebration of the temple ritual. Thutmose I, who had but a moment before been burning incense to the god, and presenting him with a great oblation, was thus superseded by the will of the same god, clearly indicated in public.[1] Thutmose III's five-fold name and titulary were immediately published, and on the third of May, in the year 1501, B. C., he suddenly stepped from the duties of an obscure prophet of Amon into the palace of the Pharaohs. Years afterward, on the occasion of inaugurating some of his new halls in the Karnak temple of Amon, he repeated this incident to his assembled court, and added that instead of going to Heliopolis to receive there the acknowledgment of the sun-god as king of Egypt, he was taken up into the heavens where he saw the sun-god in all his most glorious splendour, and was duly crowned and given his royal names by the god himself. This account of unparalleled honour from the gods he then had engraved upon a wall of the temple, that all might know of it for all time.[2]

Thutmose I was evidently not regarded as a source of serious danger, for he was permitted to live on. Thutmose III early shook off the party of legitimacy. When he had

---

[1] II, 131–136, 138–148.   [2] Ibid.

been ruling for thirteen months he restored the ancient brick temple of his ancestor, Sesostris III, at Semneh, by the second cataract, putting in its place a temple of fine Nubian sandstone, in which he carefully reërected the old boundary stela of the Middle Kingdom[1] and reënacted the decree of Sesostris endowing the offerings in the temple with a permanent income.   Here he makes no reference to any coregency of Hatshepsut, his queen, in the royal titulary preceding the dedication.   Indeed he allowed her no more honourable title than "great or chief royal wife."   But the party of legitimacy was not to be so easily put off.   The nomination of Hatshepsut to the succession some fifteen years before, and, what was still more important, her descent from the old Theban family of the Sekenenres and the Ahmoses, were things taken seriously by the nobles of this party.   As a result of their efforts Thutmose III was forced to acknowledge the coregency of his queen and actually to give her a share in the government.   Before long her partisans had become so strong that the king was seriously hampered, and eventually even thrust into the background.   Hatshepsut thus became king, an enormity with which the state fiction of the Pharaoh's origin could not be harmonized.   She was called "the female Horus!"   The word "majesty" was put into a feminine form (as in Egyptian it agrees with the sex of the ruler) and the conventions of the court were all warped and distorted to suit the rule of a woman.

Hatshepsut immediately undertook independent works and royal monuments, especially a magnificent temple for her own mortuary service, which she erected in a bay of the cliffs on the west side of the river at Thebes.   It is the temple now known as that of Der el-Bahri; we shall have occasion to refer to it more fully as we proceed.   Whether the priestly party of Thutmose III and the party of legitimacy so weakened themselves in the struggle with each other as to fall easy victims of a third party, or whether some other varying wind of fortune favoured the party of Thutmose II, we can-

[1] II, 167–176.

not now discern.   In any case, when Thutmose III and his
aggressive queen had ruled about five years, Thutmose II,
allying himself with the old dethroned king, Thutmose I,
succeeded in thrusting aside Thutmose III and Hatshepsut
and seizing the crown.   Then Thutmose I and II, father and
son, began a bitter persecution of the memory of Hatshepsut,
cutting out her name on the monuments and placing both
their own over it wherever they could find it.

News of the enmities within the royal house had probably
now reached Nubia, and on the very day of Thutmose II's
accession, the report of a serious outbreak there was handed
to him.   It was of course impossible to leave the court and
the capital to the intrigues of his enemies at the moment
when he had barely grasped the sceptre.   He was therefore
obliged to dispatch an army under the command of a subordinate, who, however, immediately advanced to the third cataract, where the cattle of the Egyptians settled in the country
had been in grave danger.   According to instructions the
Egyptian commander not merely defeated the enemy, but
slew all their males whom he could find.   They captured a
child of the rebellious Nubian chief and some other natives,
who were carried to Thebes as hostages and paraded in the
presence of the enthroned Pharaoh.[1]   After this chasten-
ing Nubia again relapsed into quiet; but in the north the
new Pharaoh was obliged to march against the Asiatic
revolters as far as Niy, on the Euphrates.[2]   On the way out,
or possibly on the return, he was obliged to conduct a punitive expedition in southern Palestine against the marauding
Beduin.   He was accompanied by Ahmose-Pen-Nekhbet of
El Kab, who captured so many prisoners that he did not
count them.[3]   This was the last campaign of the old warrior,
who, like his relative and townsman, Ahmose, son of Ebana,
then retired to an honoured old age at El Kab.   The imposing
temple of Hatshepsut, now standing gaunt and unfinished,
abandoned by the workmen, was used by Thutmose II on
his return from the north for recording a memorial of his

[1] II, 119–122.   [2] II, 125.   [3] II, 123–4.

Asiatic campaign. On one of the vacant walls he depicted his reception of tribute from the vanquished, the words "horses" and "elephants" being still legible in the accompanying inscription.[1] At this juncture it is probable that the death of the aged Thutmose I so weakened the position of the feeble and diseased[2] Thutmose II that he made common cause with Thutmose III, then apparently living in retirement, but of course secretly seeking to reënstate himself. In any case we find them together for a brief coregency,[3] which was terminated by the death of Thutmose II, after a reign of not more than three years at most.

Thutmose III thus held the throne again, but he was not able to maintain himself alone against the partisans of Hatshepsut, and was forced to a compromise, by which the queen was recognized as coregent. Matters did not stop here; her party was so powerful, that, although they were unable to dispose of Thutmose III entirely, he was again relegated to the background, while the queen played the leading rôle in the state. Both she and Thutmose III numbered the years of their joint reign from the first accession of Thutmose III, as if it had never been interrupted by the short reign of Thutmose II. The queen now entered upon an aggressive career as the first great woman in history of whom we are informed. Her father's architect, Ineni, thus defines the position of the two: after a brief reference to Thutmose III as "the ruler upon the throne of him who begat him," he says: "His sister, the Divine Consort, Hatshepsut, adjusted the affairs of the Two Lands by reason of her designs; Egypt was made to labour with bowed head for her, the excellent seed of the god, who came forth from him. The bow-cable of the South, the mooring-stake of the southerners, the excellent stern-cable of the Northland is she; the mistress of command, whose plans are excellent, who satisfies the Two Regions when she speaks." Thus, in perhaps the first occurrence of the ship of state, Ineni likens

---

[1] II, 125.   [2] Masp. Mom. roy., 547.   [3] II, 593–5.

her, in vivid oriental imagery, to the mooring cables of a Nile boat.[1]

This characterization is confirmed by the deeds of the queen. Her partisans had now installed themselves in the most powerful offices. Closest to the queen's person stood one Senmut (Fig. 111), who deeply ingratiated himself in her favour. He had been the tutor of Thutmose III as a child,[2] and he was now entrusted with the education of the queen's little daughter Nefrure (Fig. 111), who had passed her infancy in charge of the ancient Ahmose-Pen-Nekhbet of El Kab, now no longer capable of any more serious commission.[3] Senmut was then placed in control of the young girl's fortune as her steward.[4] He had a brother named Senmen,[5] who likewise supported Hatshepsut's cause. The most powerful of her coterie was Hapuseneb,[6] who was both vizier and High Priest of Amon. He was also head of the newly organized priesthood of the whole land;[7] he thus united in his person all the power of the administrative government with that of the strong priestly party, which was now enlisted in Hatshepsut's favour. With such new forces Hatshepsut's party was now operating. The aged Ineni was succeeded as "overseer of the gold and silver treasury" by a noble named Thutiy,[8] while one Nehsi[9] was chief treasurer and colleague of Hapuseneb. The whole machinery of the state was thus in the hands of these partisans of the queen. It is needless to say that the fortunes, and probably the lives of these men were identified with the success and the dominance of Hatshepsut; they therefore took good care that her position should be maintained. In every way they were at great pains to show that the queen had been destined for the throne by the gods from the beginning. In her temple at Der el-Bahri, where work was now actively resumed, they had sculptured on the walls a long series of reliefs[10] showing the birth of the queen. Here all the details of the old state fiction that the sovereign

---

[1] II, 341.   [2] Karnak statue.   [3] II, 344.   [4] II, 363 ff.   [5] II, 348.
[6] II, 388 ff.   [7] II, 388.   [8] II, 369 ff.   [9] II, 290.   [10] II, 187 ff.

should be the bodily son of the sun-god were elaborately depicted. Thutmose I's queen, Ahmose, is shown in converse with Amon (the successor of the sun-god Re in Theban theology), who tells her as he leaves, "Hatshepsut shall be the name of this my daughter [to be born]. . . . She shall exercise the excellent kingship in this whole land."[1] The reliefs thus show how she was designed by the divine will from the first to rule Egypt, and hence they proceed to picture her birth, accompanied by all the prodigies, which both the conventions of the court and the credulity of the folk associated with the advent of the sun-god's heir.[2] The artist who did the work followed the current tradition so closely that the new-born child appears as a *boy*, showing how the introduction of a woman into the situation was wrenching the inherited forms. To such scenes they added others, showing her coronation by the gods, and then the acknowledgment of her as queen by Thutmose I before the assembled court on New Year's day.[3] The accompanying narrative of these events they copied from the old Twelfth Dynasty records of Amenemhet III's similar appointment by his father, Sesostris III. As a discreet reminder to any who might be inclined to oppose the queen's rule, these inscriptions were so framed by the queen's party that they represent Thutmose I as saying to the court, "Ye shall proclaim her word, ye shall be united at her command. He who shall do her homage shall live, he who shall speak evil in blasphemy of her majesty shall die."[4] On the pylon, which Thutmose I built as a southern approach to the Karnak temple, he was even depicted before the Theban gods praying for a prosperous reign for his daughter.[5] With such devices as these it was sought to overcome the prejudice against a queen upon the throne of the Pharaohs.

Hatshepsut's first enterprise was, as we have intimated, to continue the building of her magnificent temple against the western cliffs at Thebes where her father and brother had inserted their names over hers. The building was in

[1] II, 198.   [2] II, 187 ff.   [3] II, 215.   [4] II, 237, ll. 15–16.   [5] II, 243 ff.

18

design quite unlike the great temples of the age. It was modelled after the little terraced temple of Mentuhotep II in a neighbouring bay of the cliffs. In a series of three terraces it rose from the plain to the level of an elevated court, flanked by the massive yellow cliffs, into which the holy of holies was cut. In front of the terraces were ranged fine colonnades, which, when seen from a distance, to this day exhibit such an exquisite sense of proportion and of proper grouping, as to quite disprove the common assertion that the Greeks were the first to understand the art of adjusting external colonnades, and that the Egyptian understood only the employment of the column in interiors (Fig. 113). The architect of the temple was Senmut, the queen's favourite,[1] while Ineni's successor, Thutiy,[2] wrought the bronze doors, chased with figures in electrum, and other metal work. The queen found especial pleasure in the design of the temple. She saw in it a paradise of Amon and conceived its terraces as the "myrrh-terraces" of Punt, the original home of the gods. She refers in one of her inscriptions to the fact that Amon had desired her "to establish for him a Punt in his house."[3] To carry out the design fully it was further necessary to plant the terraces with the myrrh trees from Punt. Her ancestors had often sent expeditions thither, but none of these parties had ever been equipped to bring back the trees; and indeed for a long time, as far back as any one could remember, even the myrrh necessary for the incense in the temple service had been passed from hand to hand by overland traffic until it reached Egypt.[4] Foreign traffic had suffered severely during the long reign of the Hyksos. But one day as the queen stood before the shrine of the god, "a command was heard from the great throne, an oracle of the god himself, that the ways to Punt should be searched out, that the highways to the myrrh-terraces should be penetrated."[5] For, so says the god, "It is a glorious region of God's-Land, it is indeed my place of delight; I have made it for myself in order to divert my

II, 351, ll. 6–7. [2] II, 375. [3] II, 295. [4] II, 287. [5] II, 285, l. 5.

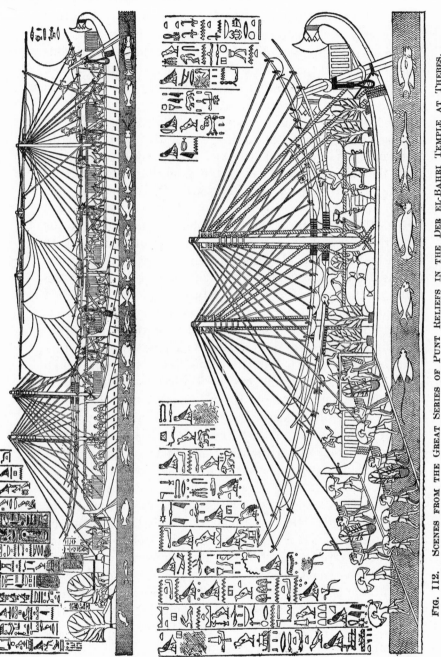

FIG. 112.   SCENES FROM THE GREAT SERIES OF PUNT RELIEFS IN THE DER EL-BAHRI TEMPLE AT THEBES.
Here Queen Hatshepsut depicts her Expedition to the Land of Punt (pp. 276 ff.).   The Upper Row shows the Departure of
the Fleet; in the Lower Row the Vessels are being loaded and the Myrrh-trees carried on board.

heart.''[1]   The queen adds, ''it was done according to all that the majesty of this god commanded.''[2]

The organization and dispatch of the expedition were naturally entrusted by the queen to the chief treasurer, Nehsi, in whose coffers the wealth brought back by the expedition were to be stored.[3]   With propitiatory offerings to the divinities of the air to ensure a fair wind, the five vessels of the fleet set sail early in the ninth year of the queen's reign.[4] The route was down the Nile and through a canal leading from the eastern Delta through the Wadi Tumilat, and connecting the Nile with the Red Sea.   This canal, as the reader will recall (see p. 188), was already in regular use in the Middle Kingdom.   Besides plentiful merchandise for barter, the fleet bore a great stone statue of the queen, to be erected in Punt.   If still surviving there, it is the most remote statue ever erected by an Egyptian ruler.   They arrived in Punt in safety; the Egyptian commander pitched his tent on the shore, where he was received with friendliness by Perehu, the chief of Punt, followed by his absurdly corpulent wife and three children.[5]   It was so long since any Egyptians had been seen in Punt that the Egyptians represented the Puntites as crying out, ''Why have ye come hither unto this land, which the people [of Egypt] know not?   Did ye descend upon the roads of heaven, or did ye sail upon the waters, upon the sea of God's-Land?''[6]   The Puntite chief having been won with gifts, a stirring traffic is soon in progress,[7] the ships are drawn up to the beach, the gang-planks run out, and the loading goes rapidly forward, until the vessels are laden ''very heavily with marvels of the country of Punt; all goodly fragrant woods of God's-Land, heaps of myrrh-resin, of fresh myrrh-trees, with ebony and pure ivory, with green gold of Emu, with cinnamon-wood, with incense, eye-cosmetic, with baboons, monkeys, dogs, with skins of the southern panther, with natives and their children.   Never was the like of this brought for any king who

[1] II, 288.   [2] II, 285, 1. 6.   [3] II, 290.   [4] II, 252–3. 292
[5] II, 254.   [6] II, 257.   [7] II, 259.

has been since the beginning.''[1]   After a fair voyage, without mishap, and with no transfer of cargo as far as our
sources inform us, the fleet finally moored again at the docks
of Thebes.[2]   Probably the Thebans had never before been
diverted by such a sight as now greeted them, when the
motley array of Puntites and the strange products of their
far-off country passed through the streets to the queen's
palace, where the Egyptian commander presented them to
her majesty.   After inspecting the results of her great expedition, the queen immediately presented a portion of them
to Amon, together with the impost of Nubia, with which
Punt was always classed.   She offered to the god thirty one
living myrrh-trees, electrum, eye-cosmetic, throw-sticks of
the Puntites, ebony, ivory shells, a live southern panther,
which had been especially caught for her majesty, many panther skins and 3,300 small cattle.[3]   Huge piles of myrrh of
twice a man's stature were now measured in grain-measures
under the oversight of the queen's favourite, Thutiy, and
large rings of commercial gold were weighed in tall balances
ten feet high.[4]   Then, after formally announcing to Amon
the success of the expedition which his oracle had called
forth,[5] Hatshepsut summoned the court, giving to her favourites, Senmut, and the chief treasurer, Nehsi, who had dispatched the expedition, places of honour at her feet, while
she told the nobles the result of her great venture.[6]   She
reminded them of Amon's oracle commanding her ''to establish for him Punt in his house, to plant the trees of God's-
Land beside his temple in his garden, according as he commanded.''   She proudly continues, ''It was done. . . . I
have made for him a Punt in his garden, just as he commanded me. . . . It is large enough for him to walk abroad
in it.''[7]   Thus the splendid temple was made a terraced
myrrh-garden for the god, though the energetic queen was
obliged to send to the end of the known world to do it for
him.   She had all the incidents of the remarkable expedition

[1] II, 265.   [2] II, 266.   [3] II, 270–272.   [4] II, 273–282.
[5] II, 283–8.   [6] II, 289–295.   [7] II, 295.

recorded in relief[1] on the wall once appropriated by Thutmose II for the record of his Asiatic campaign,[2] where they
still form one of the great beauties of her temple. All her
chief favourites found place among the scenes. Senmut was
even allowed to depict himself on one of the walls praying to
Hathor for the queen, an unparalleled honour.[3]

This unique temple was in its function the culmination of
a new development in the arrangement and architecture of
the royal tomb and its chapel or temple. Perhaps because
they had other uses for their resources, perhaps because they
recognized the futility of so vast a tomb, which yet failed
to preserve from violation the body of the builder, the
Pharaoh, as we have seen, had gradually abandoned the construction of a pyramid. With its mortuary chapel on the
east front, it had survived probably into the reign of Ahmose
I, but it had been gradually declining in size and importance,
while the shaft and chambers under it and the chapel before
it remained relatively large. Amenhotep I was the last to
follow the old traditions; he pierced a passage two hundred
feet long into the western cliffs of Thebes, terminating in a
mortuary chamber for the reception of the royal body.[4]
Before the cliff, at the entrance to the passage, he built a
modest mortuary chapel, surmounted by a pyramidal roof, to
which we have already adverted.[5] Probably for purposes
of safety Thutmose I then took the radical step of separating
the tomb from the mortuary chapel before it. The latter
was still left upon the plain at the foot of the cliffs, but the
sepulchre chamber, with the passage leading to it (Figs.
109–10) was hewn into the rocky wall of a wild and desolate
valley (Fig. 108), lying behind the western cliffs, some two
miles in a direct line from the river, and accessible only by
a long detour northward, involving nearly twice that distance. It is evident that the exact spot where the king's
body was entombed was intended to be kept secret, that all
possibility of robbing the royal burial might be precluded.

---

[1] See p. 275; II, 246–295.   [2] Infra, pp. 270–71.   [3] II, 345.
[4] IV, 513 and notes.   [5] P. 254.

Thutmose I's architect, Ineni, says that he superintended "the excavation of the cliff-tomb of his majesty alone, no one seeing and no one hearing."[1]   The new arrangement was such that the sepulchre was still behind the chapel or temple, which thus continued to be on the east of the tomb as before, although the two were now separated by the intervening cliffs.   The valley, now known as the "Valley of the Kings' Tombs" rapidly filled with the vast excavations of Thutmose I's successors.   It continued to be the cemetery of the Eighteenth, Nineteenth and Twentieth Dynasties, and over forty tombs of the Theban kings were excavated there. Forty one now accessible form one of the wonders which attract the modern Nile-tourists to Thebes, and Strabo speaks of forty which were worthy to be visited in his time. Hatshepsut's terraced sanctuary was therefore her mortuary temple, dedicated also to her father.   As the tombs multiplied in the valley behind, there rose upon the plain before it temple after temple endowed for the mortuary service of the departed gods, the emperors who had once ruled Egypt. They were besides also sacred to Amon as the state god; but they bore euphemistic names significant of their mortuary function.   Thus, for example, the temple of Thutmose III was called "Gift of Life."[2]   Hatshepsut's architect, Hapuseneb, who was also her vizier, likewise excavated her tomb[3] in the desolate valley.   In its eastern wall, immediately behind the terraced temple, the passage descended at a sharp decline for many hundred feet, and terminated in several chambers, one of which contained a sarcophagus both for herself and her father, Thutmose I.   But the family feud was probably responsible for his construction of his own tomb, on a modest scale, as we have seen, and he doubtless never used the sarcophagus made for him by his daughter.   Both sarcophagi, however had been robbed in antiquity and contained no remains when recently discovered.

The aggressive queen's attention to the arts of peace, her active devotion to the development of the resources of her

[1] II, 106   [2] II, 552.   [3] II, 389.

empire, soon began to bring in returns.   Besides the vast
income of the crown from internal sources, Hatshepsut was
also receiving tribute from her wide empire, extending from
the third cataract of the Nile to the Euphrates.   As she herself
claimed, ''My southern boundary is as far as Punt . . . ;
my eastern boundary is as far as the marshes of Asia, and
the Asiatics are in my grasp; my western boundary is as
far as the mountain of Manu [the sun-set] . . . my fame is
among the Sand-dwellers [Beduin] altogether.   The myrrh
of Punt has been brought to me . . . , all the luxurious marvels of this country were brought to my palace in one collection. . . . They have brought to me the choicest products
. . . of cedar, of juniper and of meru-wood; . . . all the
goodly sweet woods of God's-Land.   I brought the tribute
of Tehenu [Libya], consisting of ivory and seven hundred
tusks which were there, numerous panther skins of five
cubits along the back and four cubits wide.''[1]   Evidently
no serious trouble in Asia had as yet resulted from the fact
that there was no longer a warrior upon the throne of the
Pharaohs.   This energetic woman therefore began to employ
her new wealth in the restoration of the old temples, which,
although two generations had elapsed, had not even yet
recovered from the neglect which they had suffered under
the Hyksos.[2]   She recorded her good work upon a rock
temple of Pakht at Beni Hasan, saying, ''I have restored
that which was ruins, I have raised up that which was unfinished since the Asiatics were in the midst of Avaris of the
Northland, and the barbarians in the midst of them, overthrowing that which had been made while they ruled in
ignorance of Re.''[3]

It was now seven or eight years since she and Thutmose
III had regained the throne and fifteen years since they had
first seized it.   Thutmose III had never been appointed heir
to the succession, but his queen had enjoyed that honour, and
it was now nearing the thirtieth anniversary of her appointment, when she might celebrate her jubilee.   She must there-

[1] II, 321.   II, 296 ff.   [3] II, 303.

Fig. 113.—NORTHERN COLONNADES ON THE MIDDLE TERRACE OF HAT-SHEPSUT'S TERRACED TEMPLE OF DER EL-BAHRI, THEBES.

Fig. 114.—OBELISKS OF HATSHEPSUT AT KARNAK.

The standing shaft is ninety-seven and one-half feet high.

fore make preparation for the erection of the obelisks, which were the customary memorial of such jubilees. Of this, the queen herself tells us: "I sat in the palace, I remembered him who fashioned me, my heart led me to make for him two obelisks of electrum, whose points mingled with heaven."[1] Her inevitable favourite, Senmut, was therefore called in and instructed to proceeed to the granite quarries at the first cataract to secure the two gigantic shafts for the obelisks. He levied the necessary forced labour and began work early in February of the queen's fifteenth year. By early August, exactly seven months later, he had freed the huge blocks from the quarry,[2] was able to employ the high water then rapidly approaching to float them, and towed them to Thebes before the inundation had again fallen. The queen then chose an extraordinary location for her obelisks, namely, the very colonnaded hall of the Karnak temple erected by her father, where her husband Thutmose III had been named king by oracle of Amon; although this necessitated the removal of all her father's cedar columns in the south half of the hall and four of those in the north half, besides, of course, unroofing the hall, and demolishing the south wall, where the obelisks were introduced. They were richly overlaid with electrum, the work on which was done for the queen by Thutiy.[3] She avers that she measured out the precious metal by the peck, like sacks of grain,[4] and she is supported in this extraordinary statement by Thutiy, who states that by royal command he piled up in the festival hall of the palace no less than nearly twelve bushels of electrum.[5] The queen boasts of their beauty, "their summits being of electrum of the best of every country, which are seen on both sides of the river. Their rays flood the Two Lands when the sun rises between them as he dawns in the horizon of heaven."[6] They towered so high (Fig. 114) above the dismantled hall of Thutmose I that the queen recorded a long

---

[1] II, 317, ll. 6–7.   [2] II, 318.   [3] II, 376, l. 28.

[4] II, 319, l. 3.   [5] II, 377, l. 36–38.   [6] II, 315.

oath, swearing by all the gods that they were each of one block.[1] They were indeed the tallest shafts ever erected in Egypt up to that time, being ninety seven and a half feet high and weighing nearly three hundred and fifty tons each. One of them still stands, an object of constant admiration to the modern visitor at Thebes (Fig. 114). Hatshepsut at the same time erected two more large obelisks at Karnak, though they have now perished.[2] It is possible that she also set up two more, at her terraced temple, making six in all; for she has recorded there the transportation of two great shafts on the river, depicting the achievement in a relief,[3] which shows the obelisks end to end on a huge barge, towed by thirty galleys, with a total of some nine hundred and sixty oarsmen. But this scene may refer to the first two obelisks as they were brought down the river by Senmut.

Besides her obelisks, erected in her sixteenth year, we learn of another enterprise of Hatshepsut in the same year from a relief in the Wadi Maghara[4] in Sinai, whither the tireless queen had sent a mining expedition, resuming the work there which had been interrupted by the Hyksos invasion. This work in Sinai continued in her name until the twentieth year of her reign.[5] Some time between this date and the close of the year twenty one, when we find Thutmose III ruling alone, the great queen must have died. If we have spent some space on her buildings and expeditions, it has been because she was a woman, in an age when warfare was impossible for her sex, and great achievements could only be hers in the arts and enterprises of peace. Great though she was, her rule was a distinct misfortune, falling, as it did, at a time when Egypt's power in Asia had not yet been seriously tested, and Syria was only too ready to revolt.

Thutmose III was not chivalrous in his treatment of her when she was gone. He had suffered too much. Burning to lead his forces into Asia, he had been assigned to such puerile functions as offering incense to Amon on the return

[1] II, 318.   [2] II, 304–336.   [3] II, 322 ff.   [4] II, 337.
[5] Petrie, Cat. of Egyptian Antiquities found in the Peninsula of Sinai, etc., p. 19.

of the queen's expedition to Punt; or his restless energies
had been allowed to expend themselves on building his mortuary temple of the western plain of Thebes.   Considering
the age in which he lived, we must not too much blame him
for his treatment of the departed queen.   Around her obelisks in her father's hall at Karnak he now had a masonry
sheathing built, covering her name and the record of her
erection of them on the base.   Everywhere he had her name
erased and in the terraced temple on all the walls both her
figure and her name have been hacked out.   Her partisans
doubtless all fled.   If not they must have met short shrift.
In the relief-scenes in the same temple, where Senmut and
Nehsi and Thutiy had been so proud to appear, their names
and their figures were ruthlessly chiselled away.   The queen
had given Senmut three statues in the Theban temples and
on all these his name was erased; in his tomb and on his mortuary stela his name vanished.   A statue of the vizier Hapuseneb was treated in the same way.[1]   Thutiy's tomb was
likewise visited and his name obliterated, the tomb of
Senmen, Senmut's brother, did not escape, and the name of a
colleague of theirs who was buried in the next tomb was so
effectually erased that we do not know who he was.   Even
distant Silsileh was visited at the king's orders that the
tomb of the queen's "chief steward" might be dealt with
in the same way.[2]   And these mutilated monuments stand to
this day, grim witnesses of the great king's vengeance.   But
in Hatshepsut's splendid temple her fame still lives, and the
masonry around her Karnak obelisk has fallen down, exposing the gigantic shaft to proclaim to the modern world the
greatness of Hatshepsut.

[1] II, p. 160, note f.   [2] II, 348.

CHAPTER XVI

THE CONSOLIDATION OF THE EMPIRE: THUTMOSE III.

In the year fifteen Hatshepsut and Thutmose III still controlled their Asiatic dependencies as far north as the Lebanon.[1] From that time until we find him marching into Asia, late in the year twenty two, we are not informed of what took place there; but the conditions which then confronted him and the course of his subsequent campaigns, make it evident how matters had gone with Egyptian supremacy during the interim. Not having seen an Egyptian army for many years, the Syrian dynasts grew continually more restless, and finding that their boldness called forth no response from the Pharaoh, the king of Kadesh, once probably the suzerain of all Syria-Palestine, had stirred all the city-kings of northern Palestine and Syria to accept his leadership in a great coalition, in which they at last felt themselves strong enough to begin open revolt. Kadesh thus assumed its head with a power in which we should evidently recognize the surviving prestige of her old time more extended and unchallenged suzerainty. "Behold from Yeraza [in northern Judea] to the marshes of the earth [upper Euphrates], they had begun to revolt against his majesty."[2] But southern Palestine was loth to take up arms against the Pharaoh. Sharuhen, which had suffered a six years' siege at the hands of Ahmose in Hyksos days, was too well aware of what to expect thoughtlessly to assume the offensive against Egypt. Hence the whole region of southern Palestine, which had witnessed that siege, was not differently minded, but a small minority probably desired to join the revolt. Hence civil war arose in Sharuhen, as well as in the south generally,

[1] II, 137, 162.   [2] II, 416.

as the allies sought to compel the southern dynasts to join the
uprising and send a quota to the army which they were raising.[1] Not only were "all the allied countries of Zahi,"[2] or
western Syria, in open rebellion against the Pharaoh, but it
is also evident that the great kingdom of Mitanni, on the east
of the Euphrates, had done all in her power to encourage the
rebellion and to support it when once in progress; for Thutmose III was ultimately obliged to invade Mitanni and
punish its king before he could maintain Egyptian supremacy in Naharin. It was natural that Mitanni, an aggressive
and active power, competing with the infant Assyria on
more than equal terms, should view with distrust the presence of a new and great empire on its western borders. The
Mitannian king had finally learned what to expect from
Egypt and he would naturally exert himself to the utmost
to rehabilitate the once great kingdom of Kadesh, as a buffer
between himself and Egypt. Against such formidable resources as these, then, Thutmose III was summoned to contend, and no Pharaoh before his time had ever undertaken so
great a task.

In what condition the long unused Egyptian army may
have been, or how long it took Thutmose to reorganize and pre-
pare it for service, we have no means of knowing. The armies
of the early orient, at least those of Egypt, were not large,
and it is not probable that any Pharaoh ever invaded Asia
with more than twenty five or thirty thousand men, while less
than twenty thousand is probably nearer the usual figure.[3]
Late in his twenty second year we find Thutmose with his
army ready to take the field. He marched from Tharu, the
last Egyptian city on the northeastern frontier, about the 19th
of April, 1479 B. C.[4] Nine days later, that is, on April 28th,
he reached Gaza, one hundred and sixty miles from Tharu.[5]
In the Egyptian calendar the day was the fourth of Pakhons,
his coronation day, just twenty two years since the oracle of
Amon had proclaimed him king in his father's colonnaded

---

[1] II, 416.   [2] II, 616   [3] See the author's Battle of Kaqesh, pp. 8–11.
[4] II, 409, 415.   [5] II, 409, 417.

temple hall at Karnak. It had been long indeed, but the
opportunity for which he had ceaselessly plotted and planned
and striven was at last his. He was not the man to waste
the day in a futile celebration, but having arrived in the

MAP 4. THE CARMEL RIDGE.

Showing Megiddo, Taanach, the Roads leading across the Ridge to Megiddo,
and Positions of the Two Armies at the Beginning of the Battle.

evening of the coronation anniversary, he was away for the
north again the very next morning.[1] Marching along the
Shephelah and through the sea-plain, he crossed the plain of
Sharon, turning inland as he did so, and camped on the
evening of May 10th at Yehem, a town of uncertain location,
some eighty or ninety miles from Gaza, on the southern slopes

[1] II, 418.

of the Carmel range.[1] Meantime the army of the Asiatic allies under the command of the king of Kadesh, had pushed southward as far as the territory of their adherents extended, and had occupied the strong fortress of Megiddo, in the plain of Jezreel, on the north slope of the Carmel ridge. This place, which here appears in history for the first time, was not only a powerful stronghold, but occupied an important strategic position, commanding the road from Egypt between the two Lebanons to the Euphrates, hence its prominent rôle in oriental history from this time on. Thutmose, of course, regarded all this country as his own, and hence afterward says: "The lands of the Fenkhu [Asiatics] . . . had begun to invade my boundary."[2]

Thus far he had been advancing through friendly towns, or at least through regions where no open disaffection prevailed; but as he neared Carmel it was necessary to move with caution. At Yehem he learned of the enemy's occupation of Megiddo, and he called a council of his officers to ascertain the most favourable route for crossing the ridge and reaching the plain of Esdraelon.[3] There were three roads practicable for an army leading from Yehem over the mountain; one which made a direct line by way of Aruna for the gates of Megiddo; and two involving a detour to either side, the first leading around southward by way of Taanach, about five miles southeast of Megiddo; and the other northward through Zefti, emerging on the northwest of Megiddo.[4] Thutmose characteristically favoured the direct route, but his officers urged that the other roads were more open, while the middle one was a narrow pass. "Will not horse come behind horse," they asked, "and man behind man likewise? Shall our advance-guard be fighting while our rear-guard is yet standing in Aruna?"[5] These objections showed a good military understanding of the dangers of the pass; but Thutmose swore a round oath that he would move against his enemies by the most direct route, and they might follow or not as they pleased.[6] Accordingly, making his

[1] II, 419. [2] II, 439. [3] II, 420.
[4] II, 421. See Map 4. [5] Ibid. [6] II, 422.

preparations very deliberately, he moved to Aruna on the thirteenth of May.[1] To prevent surprise and also to work upon the courage of his army, he personally took the head of the column, vowing that none should precede him, but that he would go "forth at the head of his army himself, showing the way by his own footsteps."[2] Aruna lay well up in the mountain ridge, accessible only by a stretch of narrow road; but he reached it in safety, and passed the night of the thirteenth there. At this point his army must have been distributed for a long distance along the road from Aruna back to Yehem; but on the morning of the fourteenth he pushed quickly forward again. He had not been long on the march when he came in touch with the enemy.[4] Had they been in force he must have suffered, in view of his long and straggling line of march, extended along the narrow mountain road. Fortunately the pass now widened and he was able to expand his advance in a spreading valley. Here, on the urgent advice of his officers, he held the enemy in check until his rear, which was still in Aruna, came up.[5] The enemy had not been in sufficient force to take advantage of his precarious position, and he now pushed on his advance again. It was just past midday when his forward column emerged from the pass upon the plain of Esdraelon, and by one o'clock Thutmose halted without opposition on the south of Megiddo, "on the bank of the brook Kina."[6] The Asiatics had thus lost an inestimable opportunity to destroy him in detail. They seem to have been too far toward the southeast to draw in quickly and concentrate against his thin line of march as it defiled from the mountains. It is impossible to determine their exact position, but when the skirmishing in the mountains took place their southern wing was at Taanach,[7] doubtless in the expectation that Thutmose would cross the mountain by the Taanach road. From Taanach their line could not have extended as far north as Megiddo, otherwise it would have been impossible for the Egyptians peacefully to emerge from the defile and debouch upon the

---

[1] II, 424–5.   [2] Ibid.   [3] II, 425.   [4] II, 426.   [5] II, 427.   [6] II, 428.   [7] II, 426.

slope south of Megiddo. Thutmose went into camp on the
plain by Megiddo, sending out orders to the entire army to
make ready for the battle on the morrow. Preparations for
the conflict then went quietly on, and the best of order and
spirit prevailed in the camp.[1] Late in the afternoon of the
same day (the fourteenth), or during the ensuing night,
Thutmose took advantage of the enemy's position on the east
and southeast of his own force to draw his line around the
west side of Megiddo and boldly threw out his left wing on
the northwest of the city.[2] He thus secured, in case of necessity, a safe and easy line of retreat westward along the Zefti
road, while at the same time his extreme left might cut off
the enemy from flight northward.

Early the next morning, the fifteenth of May, Thutmose
gave orders to form and move out in order of battle. In a
glittering chariot of electrum he took up his position with
the centre; his right or southern wing rested on a hill south
of the brook of Kina; while, as we have seen, his left was
northwest of Megiddo.[3] To protect their stronghold the
Asiatics now drew in between Thutmose's line and the city,
from which, of course, supplementary forces emerged. He
immediately attacked them, leading the onset himself "at
the head of his army."[4] "The king himself, he led the way
of his army, mighty at its head like a flame of fire, the king
who wrought with his sword. He went forth, none like him,
slaying the barbarians, smiting Retenu, bringing their
princes as living captives, their chariots wrought with gold,
bound to their horses."[5] The enemy gave way at the first
charge, "they fled headlong to Megiddo in fear, abandoning
their horses and their chariots of gold and silver, and the
people hauled them up, pulling them by their clothing into
this city; the people of this city having closed it against
them and lowered clothing to pull them up into this city.
Now if only the army of his majesty had not given their
heart to plundering the things of the enemy they would have

[1] II, 429.   [2] Proved by his position the next day.
[3] II, 430, l. 3.   [4] Ibid., l. 4.   [5] II, 413.

captured Megiddo at this moment, when the wretched vanquished king of Kadesh and the wretched vanquished king
of this city [Megiddo] were hauled up in haste to bring
them into this city."[1]   But the discipline of an oriental
army cannot to this day withstand a rich display of plunder;
much less could the host of Egypt in the fifteenth century
B. C. resist the spoil of the combined armies of Syria.
"Then were captured their horses, their chariots of gold and
silver were made spoil. . . . Their champions lay stretched
out like fishes on the ground. The victorious army of his
majesty went round counting the spoils, their portions. Behold there was captured the tent of that wretched vanquished
foe [the king of Kadesh] in which was his son. . . . The
whole army made jubilee, giving praise to Amon for the
victory which he had granted to his son. . . . They brought
in the booty which they had taken, consisting of hands [sev-
ered from the slain], living prisoners, of horses, chariots,
gold and silver."[2]   It is evident that in the disorganized
rout the camp of the king of Kadesh fell into the hands of
the Egyptians and they brought its rich and luxurious furniture to the Pharaoh.

But the stern Thutmose was not to be placated by these
tokens of victory; he saw only what had been lost. "Had ye
afterwards captured this city," said he to the troops, "behold
I would have given [a rich offering to] Re this day; because
every chief of every country that has revolted is within it;
and because it is the capture of a thousand cities, this capture
of Megiddo."[3]   Hereupon he gave orders for the instant
investment of the city; "they measured this city, surrounding it with an enclosure, walled about with green timber of
all their pleasant trees. His majesty himself was upon the
fortification east of the city, inspecting what was done."[4]
Thutmose boasts after his return to Egypt, saying, "Amon
gave to me all the allied countries of Zahi shut up in one
city. . . . I snared them in one city, I built around them with
a rampart of thick wall."[5]   They called this wall of invest-

[1] II, 430, 1. 5.   [2] II, 431.   [3] II, 432.   [4] II, 433.   [5] II, 616, 440.

ment: "Thutmose is the Surrounder of the Asiatics,"[1] according to the custom under the Empire of naming every royal building after the king. The closest vigilance was enjoined upon the troops that none might escape, and no one from within the city was allowed to approach the siege-lines unless with the purpose of surrendering. But, as we shall see, before Thutmose had succeeded in closely investing the place, the king of Kadesh had escaped northward, which was exactly what Thutmose had desired to prevent in swinging his left wing around the northwest angle of the city on the night before the battle. As the siege went on, the dynasts who were fortunate enough not to be shut up in the city hastened to make their peace with the incensed Pharaoh; "the Asiatics of all countries came with bowed head, doing obeisance to the fame of his majesty."[2] Of the course of the siege meanwhile and of the assaults of the Egyptians, we are not informed. The priestly scribe of our only source remarks, "Now all that his majesty did to this city, to that wretched foe and his wretched army was recorded on each day by its [the day's] name . . . recorded upon a roll of leather in the temple of Amon to this day."[3] But this precious roll, like the book of chronicles of the kings of Judah,[4] has perished, and our narrative suffers much from its loss. The season was far enough advanced so that the Egyptians foraged on the grain-fields of the plain of Esdraelon, while its herds furnished them the fat of the land. They were the first host, of whom we have knowledge, to ravage this fair plain, destined to be the battle ground of the east and west from Thutmose III to Napoleon. But within the walls all was different; proper provision for a siege had not been made, and famine finally wrought its customary havoc in the beleaguered town, which, after sustaining the siege for some weeks, at length surrendered. But the king of Kadesh was not among the prisoners. "These Asiatics who were in the wretched Megiddo . . . came forth to the fame of Thutmose III, who is given life, saying, 'Give us a chance,

---

[1] II, 433.   [2] II, 440.   [3] II, 433.   [4] I Kings 15: 23.

that we may present to thy majesty our impost.' "[1] Then they came, bringing that which belonged to them, to do obeisance to the fame of his majesty, to crave the breath of their nostrils, because of the greatness of his power."[2] "Then," says Thutmose, "my majesty commanded to give to them the breath of life,"[3] and it is evident that he treated them with the greatest leniency. The frightful destruction of whole cities, of which the Assyrian kings boasted when recounting their treatment of rebels, is nowhere found among the records of the Pharaohs. To compensate for the failure to capture the dangerous king of Kadesh himself, they secured his family as hostages; for Thutmose says, "Lo, my majesty carried off the wives of that vanquished one, together with his children, and the wives of the chiefs who were there, together with their children."[4]

Rich as had been the spoil on the battle-field, it was not to be compared with the wealth which awaited the Pharaoh in the captured city. Nine hundred and twenty four chariots, including those of the kings of Kadesh and Megiddo, two thousand two hundred and thirty eight horses, two hundred suits of armour, again including those of the same two kings, the gorgeous tent of the king of Kadesh, some two thousand large cattle and twenty two thousand five hundred small cattle, the magnificent household furniture of the king of Kadesh, and among it his royal sceptre, a silver statue, perhaps of his god, and an ebony statue of himself, wrought with gold and lapis-lazuli.[5] Immense quantities of gold and silver were also taken from the city, but they are combined with the spoil of other cities in Thutmose's account of the plunder, and we cannot determine how much came out of Megiddo alone. The cattle, of course, came from the country round about; otherwise the city would not have suffered from famine. Before they left, the army also harvested the fields of the plain of Esdraelon around Megiddo, and gathered over one hundred and thirteen thousand bushels, after the army had foraged on the fields during the siege.[6]

[1] II, 441. [2] II, 434. [3] II, 442. [4] II, 596. [5] II, 435. [6] II, 437.

Thutmose lost no time in marching as far northward as the hostile strongholds and the lateness of the season would permit. He reached the southern slopes of Lebanon, where the three cities of Yenoam, Nuges and Herenkeru formed a kind of Tripolis under the government of "that foe," who was possibly the king of Kadesh. They quickly succumbed, if their king had not already been among those to send in their submission, while Thutmose was still besieging Megiddo. In order to prevent another southward advance of the still unconquered king of Kadesh and to hold command of the important road northward between the Lebanons, Thutmose now built a fortress at this point, which he called "Thutmose-is-the-Binder-of-the-Barbarians,"[1] using the same rare word for "barbarian" which Hatshepsut applies to the Hyksos. He now began the reorganization of the conquered territory, supplanting the old revolting dynasts, of course, with others who might be expected to show loyalty to Egypt.[2] These new rulers were allowed to govern much as they pleased, if only they regularly and promptly sent in the yearly tribute to Egypt. In order to hold them to their obligations Thutmose carried off with him to Egypt their eldest sons, whom he placed in a special quarter or building called "Castle in Thebes."[3] Here they were educated and so treated as to engender feelings of friendliness toward Egypt; and whenever a king of one of the Syrian cities died "his majesty would cause his son to stand in his place."[4] Thutmose now controlled all Palestine as far north as the southern end of Lebanon, and further inland also Damascus.[5] In so far as they had rebelled, he stripped all the towns of their wealth, and returned to Egypt with some four hundred and twenty six pounds of gold and silver in commercial rings or wrought into magnificent vessels and other objects of art, besides untold quantities of less valuable property and the spoil of Megiddo already mentioned.[6]

Early in October Thutmose had reached Thebes, and we can be certain that it was such a return to the capital as no

[1] II, 548.   [2] II, 434.   [3] II, 402.   [4] II, 467.   [5] II, 402.   [6] II, 436.

Pharaoh before him had ever enjoyed. In less than six months, that is, within the limits of the dry season in Palestine, he had marched from Tharu, gained a sweeping victory at Megiddo, captured the city after a long and arduous investment, marched to the Lebanon and taken three cities there, built and garrisoned a permanent fort near them, begun reorganizing the government in northern Palestine, and completed the return journey to Thebes.[1] With what difficulties such an achievement was beset we may learn by a perusal of Napoleon's campaign from Egypt through the same country against Akko, which is almost exactly as far from Egypt as Megiddo. We may then understand why it was that Thutmose immediately celebrated three "Feasts of Victory" in his capital. They were each five days long and coincided with the first, second and fifth calendar feasts of Amon. The last was held in Thutmose's mortuary temple on the western plain of Thebes, which was now completed, and this may have been the first celebration held in it. These feasts were made permanent, endowed with an annual income of plentiful offerings.[2] At the feast of Opet, which was Amon's greatest annual feast and lasted eleven days, he presented to the god the three towns which he had captured in southern Lebanon,[3] besides a rich array of magnificent vessels of gold, silver and costly stones from the prodigious spoil of Retenu.[4] In order to furnish income to maintain the temple on the sumptuous plan thus projected, he gave Amon not only the said three towns, but also extensive lands in Upper and Lower Egypt, supplied them with plentiful herds and with hosts of peasant serfs taken from among his Asiatic prisoners.[5] Thus was established the foundation of that vast fortune of Amon, which now began to grow out of all proportion to the increased wealth of other temples. Hence the state-temple, the old sanctuary of his father at Karnak, was no longer adequate for the rich and elaborate state-cult; for even his father's great hall had been dismantled by Hatshepsut in order to insert her obelisks.

[1] II, 409, 549.　[2] II, 550–53.　[3] II, 557.　[4] II, 558, 543–47.　[5] II, 555, 596.

FIG. 115.—VIEW ACROSS THE AMON-OASIS, OR SIWA.
(From a photograph by Steindorff.)

FIG. 116.—OBELISK OF THUTMOSE III.
As it stood in Alexandria, before its removal to New York.

FIG. 117.—LISTS OF TOWNS IN ASIA
TAKEN BY THUTMOSE III.
On the walls of the Karnak temple (p. 306).

There it stood, with the obelisks preventing the replacement of over a third of the roof, the south half without roof or columns, and four cedar columns of Thutmose I, with two of sandstone which he had himself inserted, occupying the north half.[1] It was further disfigured by the masonry which Thutmose III had built around Hatshepsut's obelisks.[2] But it was the hall where he had been called to be king of Egypt by the oracle of Amon himself. Hatshepsut's partisan, Thutiy, had now been supplanted by another architect and chief of craftsmen named Menkheperre-seneb,[3] whose very name, "Thutmose III is Healthy," was indicative of his loyalty. He was called in and an attempt was made to restore the north half of the old hall, replacing the cedar columns by shafts of sandstone.[4] But the southern half was left untouched. In this make-shift hall the great feasts celebrating his victorious return from the first campaign were some of them held, but for others he naturally resorted to his mortuary temple of Amon, which, as we have seen, was now complete on the western plain. Judging from the small temple of Ptah by the great Karnak temple which Thutmose also rebuilt at his return from this campaign,[5] he probably showed like generosity to the two ancient sanctuaries at Heliopolis and Memphis, of which the former was still in a traditional sense the temple of the state god, for Re was now identified with Amon.

The great task of properly consolidating the empire was now fairly begun; but Egyptian power in Asia during the long military inactivity of Hatshepsut's reign had been so thoroughly shaken that Thutmose III was far from ready, as a result of the first campaign, to march immediately upon Kadesh, his most dangerous enemy. Moreover, he desired properly to organize and render perfectly secure the states already under the power of Egypt. In the year twenty four therefore he marched in a wide curve through the conquered territory of northern Palestine and southern Syria, while the dynasts came to pay their tribute and do him homage in

[1] II, 100.   [2] II, 306.   [3] II, 772.   [4] II, 600–602.   [5] II 609 ff.

"every place of his majesty's circuit where the tent was pitched."[1] The news of his great victory of the year before had by this time reached Assyria, now just rising on the eastern horizon, with her career as yet all before her. Her king naturally desired to be on good terms with the great empire of the west, and the gifts of costly stone, chiefly lapis-lazuli from Babylon, and the horses which he sent to Thut-mose, so that they reached him while on this campaign, were, of course, interpreted by the Egyptians as tribute.[2] In all probability no battles were fought on this expedition.

Returning to Thebes as before, in October, the king imme-diately planned for the enlargement of the Karnak temple, to suit the needs of the empire of which he dreamed. Moreover the slowly rising bed of the river had now raised the waters of the inundation until they invaded the temple area, and it had become necessary to elevate the temple pavement. The splendid gate of Amenhotep I was sacrificed to this necessity. By the latter part of February, at the feast of the new moon, which happened by a lucky chance to fall upon the day of the tenth feast of Amon, he was able personally to celebrate the foundation-ceremonies with the greatest splendour.[3] To render the act especially auspicious the god appeared and even himself participated in the stretching of the measuring cord as the foundation-plan was laid out.[4] As the west end, the real front of the temple, was marred by Hatshepsut's obelisks, rising from his father's dismantled hall, and he was unable or unwilling to build around his father's obelisks, which stood before the western entrance of the temple, Thutmose III laid out his imposing colonnaded halls at the other, or east end, of the temple, where they to-day form one of the great architectural beauties of Thebes. The greatest hall is nearly one hundred and forty feet long, and lies transversely across the axis of the temple. This hall was called "Menkheperre [Thutmose III] is Glorious in Monuments," a name which it still bore six hundred and fifty years later.[5] Behind it is the sanc-

---

[1] II, 447, l. 25.   [2] II, 446.   [3] II, 608.   [4] Ibid.   [5] II, p. 237, note f.

tuary or holy of holies, while grouped about it are some half
a hundred halls and chambers. Among these, on the south
side, was a hall for the mortuary service of his ancestors. In
the chamber to which this hall led he "commanded to record
the names of his fathers, to increase their offerings and to
fashion statues of all these their bodies."[1] These names
formed a great list on the walls, which still exists in the Bibliothèque Nationale at Paris. The statues of his fathers,
while many have perished, have recently been discovered in
a court south of the temple, where they had been concealed
for safety in time of war.

The third campaign, of the next year (twenty five) was
evidently spent like the first, in organizing the southern half
of the future Asiatic empire, the northern half being still
unsubdued. When he returned, his building at Karnak was
sufficiently far advanced to record upon the walls of one of
the chambers the plants and animals of Asia which he had
found on his march and brought home with him to beautify
the garden of the temple of Amon,[2] the sacred lake of which
he supplied with a masonry coping.

No records of the fourth campaign have survived, but the
course of his subsequent operations was such that it must
have been confined like the others to the territory already
regained. It had now become evident to Thutmose that he
could not march northward between the Lebanons and operate against Kadesh, while leaving his flank exposed to the
unsubdued Phoenician cities of the coast. It was likewise
impossible to strike Naharin and Mitanni without first destroying Kadesh, which dominated the Orontes valley. He
therefore planned a series of campaigns, directed first against
the northern coast, which he might then use as a base of operations against Kadesh; and this being once disposed of, he
could again push in from the coast against Mitanni and the
whole Naharin region. No modern strategist could have conceived a series of operations better suited to the conditions,
nor have gone about putting them into execution with more

[1] II, 604-5.   [2] II, 450-52.

indomitable energy than Thutmose now displayed. He therefore organized a fleet and placed in command of it a trusty officer named Nibamon, who had served with his father.[1] In the year twenty nine, on his fifth campaign, he moved for the first time against the northern coast cities, the wealthy commercial kingdoms of Phœnicia. He must have employed the new fleet and transported his army by sea, for he began operations in northern Phœnicia, which, with all southern Phœnicia and Kadesh still unconquered, he could not have reached by land. It is possible that he gained his first foothold by offering to Tyre special inducements to submit, for it is evident that some Pharaoh granted this city exceptional privileges, making it practically a free city.[2] It is easily conceivable that the rich harbour-town would readily embrace the opportunity to save her commerce from destruction and escape tribute, or at least a portion of the usual obligation in the future. The name of the first city which Thutmose took is unfortunately lost, but it was on the coast opposite Tunip, and must have been a place of considerable importance, for it brought him rich spoils; and there was in the town a temple of Amon,[3] erected by one of Thutmose III's predecessors (either Thutmose I or possibly Amenhotep I). The cities of the interior, seeing that this attack from the coast must be fatal to them if successful, had sent troops to assist in its defense. Thus Tunip[4] sent forces to strengthen the garrison of this unknown city, the fall of which would involve the ultimate capture of Tunip also. Thutmose now seized the fleet of the city,[5] and was able rapidly to move his army southward against the powerful city of Arvad. A short siege, compelling Thutmose to cut down the groves about the town, as at Megiddo, sufficed to bring the place to terms, and with its surrender[6] a vast quantity of the wealth of Phœnicia fell into the hands of the Egyptians. Besides this, it being now autumn, the gardens and groves "were filled with their fruit, their wines were found

---

[1] II, 779. [2] Amarna Letters, ed. Winckler, p. XXXIII; n. 2; 70 rev. 12 ff.
[3] II, 457-9. [4] II, 459. [5] II, 460. [6] II, 461.

left in their presses as water flows, their grain on the [hill-side] terraces . . . ; it was more plentiful than the sand of the shore. The army were overwhelmed with their por-tions."[1] Under these circumstances it was useless for Thut-mose to attempt to maintain discipline, and during the first days following the surrender, "behold the army of his majesty was drunk and anointed with oil every day as at a feast in Egypt."[2] The dynasts along the coast now came in with their tribute and offered submission.[3] Thutmose had thus gained a secure footing on the northern coast, easily accessible by water from Egypt, and forming an admirable base for operations inland as he had foreseen. He then re-turned to Egypt, possibly not for the first time, by water.[4]

All was now in readiness for the long planned advance upon Kadesh. It had taken five campaigns to gain the south and the coast; the sixth was at last directed against his long invulnerable enemy. In the year thirty the close of the spring rains found Thutmose disembarking his army from the fleet at Simyra,[5] by the mouth of the Eleutheros, up the valley of which he immediately marched upon Kadesh.[6] It was a convenient and easy road, and the shortest route from the sea to Kadesh to be found anywhere along the coast; indeed it was then, as it is now, the only practicable highway for a military advance inland across the mountains toward the region of Kadesh. The city lay on the west side of the Orontes river at the north end of the high valley between the two Leb-anons, the ridge of Anti-Lebanon dropping to the plain just south and east of the town (Maps 5, 7). A small tributary of the Orontes from the west joined the larger stream just below the city, so that it lay on a point of land between the two. A canal, still traceable and doubtless in existence in Thutmose's day, was cut across the tongue of land above the town, thus connecting the two streams and entirely sur-rounding the place by water. An inner moat encircling the high curtain-walls within the banks of the rivers reënforced the natural water-defences, so that, in spite of its location in

---

[1] Ibid.　[2] II, 462.　[3] Ibid.　[4] II, 460.　[5] II, 463.　[6] II, 464.

a perfectly level plain, it was a place of great strength, and probably the most formidable fortress in Syria. In its rela- tion to the surrounding country also the place was skilfully chosen as one of great strategic importance; for, as the reader recalls, it commanded the Orontes valley, and. as

MAP 5. THE MODERN TELL-NEBI-MINDOH, ANCIENT KADESH.
Showing the Mound of Ruins between the Orontes on the right and its Tributary on the left (after Koldewey).

Thutmose had found, it was impossible to advance northward without reckoning with it. It will be remembered, further- more, that it also dominated the only road inland from the coast for a long distance both north and south. This was the road up the Eleutheros valley, along which we have fol- lowed Thutmose.[1] The capture of such a place by siege was

[1] See the author's Battle of Kadesh, pp. 13–21, 49, and infra, pp. 258–59.

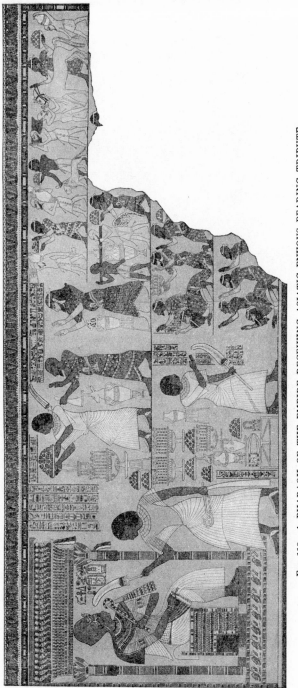

Fig. 118.—A PHARAOH OF THE EMPIRE RECEIVING ASIATIC ENVOYS BEARING TRIBUTE.

They are introduced by white-robed Egyptian officials. The Asiatics are distinguished by their gay robes and beards.　See pp. 307–08.

an achievement of no slight difficulty, and it is with peculiar regret that one reads in the narrative of the priestly scribe who excerpted Thutmose's annals, merely these words regarding it: "His majesty arrived at the city of Kadesh, overthrew it, cut down its groves, harvested its grain."[1] We can only discern from these laconic words that as at Megiddo Thutmose was obliged to fell the groves to build his siege-walls, and that the army lived on the forage from the surrounding grain fields during the investment, which must therefore have continued from early spring into harvest time. At least one assault was made, in which Amenemhab, one of Thutmose's commanders, whom we shall meet in later campaigns also, captured two of the patricians of the city. He was rewarded in the presence of the army with two orders or decorations for distinguished service: "a lion of the finest gold" and "two flies," besides rich ornaments.[2] The siege had now continued long enough to encourage the coast cities in the hope that Thutmose had suffered a reverse. In spite of the chastisement inflicted upon Arvad the year before, the opulent harbour town could not resist an attempt to rid itself of the annual obligation to Thutmose, which cost it so large a portion of its yearly gains. As soon as Kadesh fell and Thutmose was able to leave it, he quickly returned to Simyra, embarked his army on his waiting fleet and sailed to Arvad to inflict swift retribution.[3] Sailing for Egypt as the rainy season drew on, he took with him the sons of the north Syrian kings and dynasts, to be educated at Thebes,[4] as he had already done with the young princes of the south in former years.

The revolt of Arvad, while Thutmose was still besieging Kadesh, showed him that he must devote another campaign to the thorough subjugation of the coast before he could safely push inland beyond the valley of the Orontes on the long planned advance into Naharin. He therefore spent the summer of the year thirty one, the seventh campaign, in completely quenching any slumbering embers of revolt in

[1] II, 465.   [2] II, 585.   [3] II, 465.   [4] II, 467.

the coast cities. In spite of his display of force at Simyra,
Ullaza, a harbour-town near Simyra, had showed serious disaffection, owing to encouragement from the king of Tunip,
who sent his two sons to conduct the revolt. On the 27th
of April, Thutmose appeared in the harbour of the recreant
city;[1] he made short work of the place and captured the
king of Tunip's son.[2] The local dynasts came in as usual
with their submission and Thutmose collected about one
hundred and eighty five pounds of silver from them and the
captured city, besides great quantities of natural produce.[3]
He then sailed from harbour to harbour along the coast, displaying his force and thoroughly organizing the administration of the cities.[4] In particular he saw to it that every
harbour-town should be liberally supplied with provisions for
his coming campaign in Naharin. On his return to Egypt
he found envoys from the extreme south, probably eastern
Nubia, bringing to the Pharaoh their tribute,[5] showing that
he was maintaining an aggressive policy in the far south
while at the same time so active in the north.

The organization and the collection of resources necessary
for the great campaign now before him evidently occupied
Thutmose all the year following his return from this expedition; for it was not until the spring of the year thirty three
that he landed his forces in the harbour of Simyra,[6] on his
eighth campaign, and marched inland for the second time
along the Kadesh road. He turned northward and captured
the town of Ketne.[7] Continuing the march down the
Orontes, he fought a battle at the city of Senzar, which he
also took. In this action his general, Amenemhab, again
won distinction.[8] Thutmose probably crossed and forsook
the Orontes at this point; in any case, he now entered
Naharin and marched rapidly on. He soon met resistance
and fought a slight action in which Amenemhab captured
three prisoners.[9] But no serious force confronted him until
he had arrived at "The Height of Wan, on the west of

---

[1] II, 470. [2] Ibid. [3] II, 471. [4] II, 472. [5] II, 474-5
[6] II, 476. II, 598. [8] II, 584. [9] II, 581.

Aleppo," where a considerable battle was fought, in the course of which Amenemhab took thirteen prisoners, each bearing a bronze spear inlaid with gold.[1] This doubtless shows that the royal troops of the king of Aleppo were engaged. Aleppo itself must have fallen, for the Pharaoh could otherwise hardly have pushed on without delay, as he evidently did. "Behold his majesty went north, capturing the towns and laying waste the settlements of that foe of wretched Naharin,"[2] who was, of course, the king of Mitanni. Egyptian troops were again plundering the Euphrates valley, a license which they had not enjoyed since the days of their fathers under Thutmose I, some fifty years before.

As he advanced northward, Thutmose now turned slightly toward the Euphrates, in order to reach Carchemish. In the battle fought at that city it must have been his long unscathed foe, the king of Mitanni, whose army Thutmose scattered far and wide, "not one looked behind him, but they fled forsooth like a herd of mountain goats."[3] Amenemhab seems to have pushed the pursuit across the Euphrates to the east side, as he was obliged to cross it in bringing back to the king the prisoners whom he had taken.[4] This battle at last enabled Thutmose to do what he had been fighting ten years to attain, for he himself now crossed the Euphrates into Mitanni and set up his boundary tablet on the east side, an achievement of which none of his fathers could boast.[5] But without wintering in Naharin, it was impossible for Thutmose to advance further, and he was too wise a soldier to risk exposing to the inclement northern winter the seasoned veterans of so many campaigns, whom it would have taken him years to replace. He therefore returned unmolested to the west shore, where he found the tablet of his father, Thutmose I, and with the greatest satisfaction he set up another of his own alongside it.[6] It was now late in the season, his troops had already harvested the fields of the Euphrates valley,[7] and he was obliged to begin the return march. But one serious enter-

---

[1] II, 582.   [2] II, 479.   [3] Ibid.   [4] II, 583.
[5] II, 478, 481; 656, ll. 7–8.   [6] II, 478.   [7] II, 480.

prise still awaited him before he could return to the coast.
The city of Niy, further down the Euphrates, was still unconquered and all his work in Naharin might be undone were
this place left unscathed. Having set up his boundary tablets, therefore, he marched down the river and took Niy
without trouble so far as we know.[1] The object of the campaign having been accomplished and its arduous duties past,
Thutmose organized a great elephant hunt in the region of
Niy, where these animals have now been extinct for ages.
He and his party attacked the North Syrian herd of one
hundred and twenty animals. In the course of the hunt the
king came to close quarters with one great beast and was in
some danger when his general, Amenemhab rushed between
and cut off the animal's trunk; whereupon the infuriated
beast charged upon his hardy assailant, who escaped between
two rocks overhanging a neighbouring pool. For thus diverting the animal at the critical moment the faithful Amenemhab was of course liberally rewarded by the king.[2]

Meantime all the local princes and dynasts of Naharin
appeared at his camp and brought in their tribute as a token
of their submission.[3] Even far off Babylon was now anxious
to secure the goodwill of the Pharaoh, and its king sent him
gifts wrought of lapis-lazuli.[4] But what was still more important, the mighty people of the Kheta, whose domain stretched
far away into the unknown regions of Asia Minor, sent him
a rich gift. As he was on the march from Naharin to reach
the coast again their envoys met him, with eight massive commercial rings of silver, weighing nearly ninety eight pounds,
beside some unknown precious stone and costly wood.[5] Thus
the Kheta, probably the Biblical Hittites, enter for the first
time, as far as we know, into relations with the Egyptian Pharaohs. On Thutmose's arrival at the coast, he laid upon the
chiefs of the Lebanon the yearly obligation to keep the Phœnician harbours supplied with the necessary provision for his
campaigns.[6] From any point in this line of harbours, which
he could reach from Egypt by ship in a few days, he was

[1] II, 481.　[2] II, 588.　[3] II, 482.　[4] II, 484.　[5] II, 485.　[6] II, 483.

then able to strike inland without delay and bring delin-
quents to an immediate accounting. His sea power was such
that the king of Cyprus became practically a vassal of
Egypt, as later in Saitic times. Moreover, his fleet made
him so feared in the islands of the north that he was able to
exert a loose control over the eastern Mediterranean, westward an indefinite distance to the Ægean. Thus his general, Thutiy, includes "the isles in the midst of the sea" as
within his jurisdiction as governor of the north countries;
although his control will doubtless have consisted in little
more than the reception of the annual gifts which the island
dynasts thought it wise to send him.

His arrival at Thebes in October found awaiting him a
newly returned expedition which in the midst of his responsibilities in Asia he had found time to dispatch to Punt. His
emissaries brought back the usual rich and varied cargo of
ivory, ebony, panther-skins, gold and over two hundred and
twenty three bushels of myrrh, besides male and female
slaves and many cattle.[1] At some time during these wars
Thutmose is also found in possession of the entire oasis-
region on the west of Egypt (Fig. 115). The oases thus
became Pharaonic territory and were placed under the government of Intef, Thutmose III's herald,[2] who was a descendant of the old line of lords of Thinis-Abydos, whence the
Great Oasis was most easily reached (Map 13). The oasis
region remained an appanage of the lords of Thinis and
became famous for its fine wines.

The great object for which Thutmose had so long striven
was now achieved; he had followed his fathers to the Euphrates. The kings whom they had been able to defeat
singly and in succession, he had been obliged to meet united,
and against the combined military resources of Syria and
northern Palestine under their old time Hyksos suzerain of
Kadesh, he had forced his way through to the north. In
ten long years of scattered and often guerilla warfare he
had crushed them with blow on blow, until he had at last

[1] II, 486.   [2] II, 763.

20

planted his boundary stone beside that of his father on the frontier, won two generations before. He had even surpassed his father and crossed the Euphrates, an unprecedented feat in the annals of Egyptian conquest. He might pardonably permit himself some satisfaction in the contemplation of what he had accomplished. Nearly thirty three years had elapsed since the day when Amon called him to the throne. Already on his thirtieth anniversary his architect, Puemre, had erected the jubilee obelisks at Thebes;[1] but on his return from the great campaign the date for the customary second jubilee-celebration was approaching. A pair of enormous obelisks, which had been in preparation for the event, were erected at the Karnak temple and one of them bore the proud words, "Thutmose, who crossed the great 'Bend of Naharin' [the Euphrates] with might and with victory at the head of his army." The other obelisk of this pair has perished, but this one now stands in Constantinople.[2] Indeed all of the great king's obelisks in Egypt have either perished or been removed, so that not a single obelisk of his still stands in the land he ruled so mightily, while the modern world possesses a line of them reaching from Constantinople, through Rome and London to New York (Fig. 116). The last two, which commemorate his fourth jubilee-celebration now rise on opposite shores of the Atlantic, as they once stood on either side of the approach to the sun-temple at Heliopolis.[3]

With such monuments as these before them the people of Thebes soon forgot that he who erected them was once a humble priest in the very temple where his giant obelisks now rose. On its walls, moreover, they saw long annals of his victories in Asia, endless records of the plunder he had taken, with splendid reliefs picturing the rich portion which fell to Amon. A list (Fig. 117) of one hundred and nineteen towns which he captured on his first campaigns was three times displayed upon the pylons, while from his recent successes in the north the same walls bore a record of no less

[1] II, 382-4. [2] II, 629-31. [3] II, 632-6.

than two hundred and forty eight towns which had submitted to him.[1] However much they may have impressed the Thebans, these records are for us of priceless value. Unfortunately they are but excerpts from the state records, made by priests who wished to explain the source of the gifts received by the temple, and to show how Thutmose was repaying his debt to Amon for the many victories which the favouring god had vouchsafed him. Hence they are but meagre sources from which to reconstruct the campaigns of the first great strategist of whom we know anything in history. But the Thebans were not obliged to study the monuments of Karnak for witness to the greatness of their king. In the garden of Amon's temple, as we have seen, grew the strange plants of Syria-Palestine, while animals unknown to the hunter of the Nile valley wandered among trees equally unfamiliar. Envoys from the north and south were constantly appearing at the court. Phœnician galleys, such as the upper Nile had never seen before delighted the eyes of the curious crowd at the docks of Thebes; and from these landed whole cargoes of the finest stuffs of Phœnicia, gold and silver vessels of magnificent workmanship, from the cunning hand of the Tyrian artificer or the workshops of distant Asia Minor, Cyprus, Crete and the Ægean islands; exquisite furniture of carved ivory, delicately wrought ebony, chariots mounted with gold and electrum, and bronze implements of war; besides these, fine horses for the Pharaoh's stables and untold quantities of the best that the fields, gardens, vineyards, orchards and pastures of Asia produced. Under heavy guard emerged from these ships, too, the annual tribute of gold and silver in large commercial rings, some of which weighed as much as twelve pounds each, while others for purposes of daily trade were of but a few grains weight. Winding through the streets, crowded with the wondering Theban multitude, the strange tongued Asiatics in long procession bore their tribute to the Pharaoh's treasury. They were received by the vizier, Rekhmire, and when unusually

[1] II, 402-3.

rich tribute was presented, he conducted them into the
Pharaoh's presence, who, enthroned in splendour, reviewed
them and praised the vizier and his officials for their zeal
in his behalf. The Asiatics then delivered their tribute at
the office of the vizier, where all was duly entered on his
books, even to the last measure of grain. It was such scenes
as this that the vizier and treasury officials loved to perpetuate in gorgeous paintings on the walls of their tombs, where
they are still preserved at Thebes[1] (Fig. 118). The amount
of wealth which thus came into Egypt must have been enormous for those times, and on one occasion the treasury was
able to weigh out some eight thousand nine hundred and
forty three pounds of gold-silver alloy.[2] Nubia also, under
the Egyptian viceroy, was rendering with great regularity
her annual impost of gold, negro slaves, cattle, ebony, ivory
and grain; much of the gold in the above hoard must have
come from the Nubian mines. It was a great day, too, for
the Theban crowds when the Nubian barges landed their
motley cargo. Similar sights diverted the multitudes of the
once provincial Thebes when every year, toward the close
of September or the opening days of October, Thutmose's
war-galleys moored in the harbour of the town; but at this
time not merely the *wealth* of Asia was unloaded from the
ships; the Asiatics themselves, bound one to another in long
lines, were led down the gang planks to begin a life of slave-
labour for the Pharaoh (Fig. 119). They wore long matted
beards, an abomination to the Egyptians; their hair hung in
heavy black masses upon their shoulders, and they were
clad in gaily coloured woolen stuffs, such as the Egyptian,
spotless in his white linen robe, would never put on his body.
Their arms were pinioned behind them at the elbows or
crossed over their heads and lashed together; or, again, their
hands were thrust through odd pointed ovals of wood, which
served as hand-cuffs. The women carried their children
slung in a fold of the mantle over their shoulders. With
their strange speech and uncouth postures the poor wretches

[1] II, 760-1, 773. [2] II, 761.

FIG. 119.—ASIATIC PRISONERS IN EGYPT UNDER THE EMPIRE.

Recognizable by their long beards and heavy robes, they march in pairs, their hands in pairs in long, oval wooden manacles; between the pairs of prisoners are Egyptian guards also in pairs; at the rear a woman carrying her children. Continued at the right in Fig. 148. (Leyden Museum.)

were the subject of jibe and merriment on the part of the multitude; while the artists of the time could never forbear caricaturing them. Many of them found their way into the houses of the Pharaoh's favourites, and his generals were liberally rewarded with gifts of such slaves; but the larger number were immediately employed on the temple estates, the Pharaoh's domains, or in the construction of his great monuments and buildings,[1] especially the last, a custom which continued until Saladin built the citadel at Cairo with the labour of the knights whom he captured from the ranks of the crusaders. We shall later see how this captive labour transformed Thebes.

The return of the king every autumn, under such circumstances, with the next campaign but six months distant, began for him a winter, if not so arduous, at least as busily occupied as the campaigning season in Asia. At the time of the feast of Opet, that is in October, shortly after his return, Thutmose made a tour of inspection throughout Egypt, closely questioning the local authorities wherever he landed, for the purpose of suppressing corruption in the local administration by preventing all collusion between them and the officers of the central government in extortionate oppression of the people while collecting taxes.[2] On these journeys, too, he had opportunity of observing the progress on the noble temples which he was either erecting, restoring or adorning at over thirty different places of which we know, and many more which have perished. He revived the long neglected Delta and from there to the third cataract his buildings were rising, strung like gems, along the river. He built a new town with its temple at the mouth of the Fayum; while at Dendereh, Coptos, El Kab, Edfu, Kom Ombo, Elephantine and many other places his captives of war and his imperial revenues were producing the magnificent works which he and his architects planned. Returning to Thebes his interests were wide and his power was felt in every avenue of administration. Besides the attention con-

[1] II, 756-9.　　　　[2] III, 58.

tinually demanded by Nubian affairs, of which we shall
speak more fully later, he organized the other gold-country,
that on the Coptos road, placing it under a "governor of the
gold-country of Coptos."[1]   It is evident that every resource
of his empire was being thus exploited.   The increasing
wealth of the Amon temple demanded reorganization of its
management.   This the king personally accomplished, giving
the priests full instructions and careful regulations for the
conduct of the state temple and its growing fortune.[2]   As
the fruit of a moment's respite from the cares of state, he
even handed to his chief of artificers in the state and temple
workshops designs sketched by his own royal hand for vessels which he desired for the temple service.   Thutmose
himself thought sufficiently well of this accomplishment to
have it noted over a relief depicting these vessels on the
temple walls at Karnak, after they had been presented to
the god; while in the opinion of the official who received the
commission it was a fact so remarkable that he had the
execution of these vessels by his artificers shown in the
paintings on the walls of his tomb chapel.   Both these evidences of Thutmose's restless versatility still survive at
Thebes.[3]   The great state temple received another pylon on
the south and the whole mass of buildings, with the adjoining
grove and garden, was given unity by an enclosure wall, with
which Thutmose surrounded them.

His campaigning was now as thoroughly organized as the
administration at Thebes.   As soon as the spring rains in
Syria and Palestine had ceased, he regularly disembarked
his troops in some Phœnician or north Syrian harbour.   Here
his permanent officials had effected the collection of the necessary stores from the neighbouring dynasts, who were obli-
gated to furnish them.   His palace-herald, or marshal, Intef,
who was of the old princely line of Thinis, and still held his
title as "count of Thinis and lord of the entire oasis-
region,"[4] accompanied him on all his marches, and as Thutmose advanced inland Intef preceded him until the proximity

----

¹ II, 774.   ² II, 571.   ³ II, 545, 775.   ⁴ II, 763.

of the enemy prevented. Whenever he reached a town in which the king was expected to spend the night, he sought out the palace of the local dynast and prepared it for Thutmose's reception, "When my lord arrived in safety where I was, I had prepared it, I had equipped it with everything that is desired in a foreign country, made better than the palaces of Egypt, purified, cleansed, set apart, their mansions adorned, each chamber for its proper purpose. I made the king satisfied with that which I did."[1] One is reminded of the regular and detailed preparation of Napoleon's tent, which he always found awaiting him after his day's march, as he rode into the quarters each night. All the king's intercourse with the outside world, and the regulation of the simple court state maintained on the campaigns, was in Intef's hands. When the Syrian princes came in to offer their allegiance and pay their tribute, it was Intef also who had charge of the interview; he informed the vassals what they were expected to contribute and he counted the gold, silver and *naturalia* when they were paid in at the camp. When any of the Pharaoh's captains distinguished himself upon the battlefield, it was again Intef who reported it to the king, that the proper reward might be rendered to the fortunate hero.[2]

Had it been preserved, the life of these warriors of Thutmose would form a stirring chapter in the history of the early east. The career of his general, Amenemhab, who cut off the elephant's trunk and rescued the king, is but a hint of the life of the Pharaoh's followers in bivouac and on battlefield, crowded to the full with perilous adventure and hard-won distinction. We shall meet one more exploit of this same Amenemhab, but his is the only such career which has survived in authentic narrative. The fame of these tried veterans of Thutmose, of course, found its way among the common people and doubtless many a stirring adventure from the Syrian campaigns took form in folk-tales, told with eager interest in the market-places and the streets of

[1] II, 771.   [2] II, 763–771.

Thebes.   A lucky chance has rescued one of these tales written by some scribe on a page or two of papyrus.   It concerns
one Thutiy, a great general of Thutmose, and his clever capture of the city of Joppa by introducing his picked soldiers
into the town, concealed in panniers, borne by a train of
donkeys.[1]   The tale is probably the prototype of "Ali Baba
and the Forty Thieves."   But Thutiy was not a creation of
fancy; his tomb, though now unknown, must exist somewhere in Thebes, for it was plundered many years ago by
the natives, who took from it some of the rich gifts which
Thutmose gave him as a reward for his valour.   A splendid
golden dish, which found its way into the Louvre, bears the
words: "Given as a distinction from king Thutmose III to
the prince and priest who satisfies the king in every country,
and the isles in the midst of the sea, filling the treasury with
lapis-lazuli, silver and gold, the governor of countries, commander of the army, favourite of the king, the king's scribe,
Thutiy."[2]   A jewel of his in the Leyden museum calls him
"governor of the north countries,"[3] so that he must have
administered Thutmose's northern vassal-kingdoms.[4]

Had chance so decreed we might have known not only the
whole romance of Thutmose's personal adventures on the
field and those of his commanders, but also the entire course
of his campaigns, which we could have followed step by step;
for a record of every day's happenings throughout each
campaign was carefully kept by one Thaneni, a scribe
appointed for the purpose by Thutmose.   Thaneni tells us
of his duties with great pride, saying: "I followed king
Thutmose III; I beheld the victories of the king which he
won in every country. He brought the chiefs of Zahi [Syria]
as living prisoners to Egypt; he captured all their cities, he
cut down their groves. . . . I recorded the victories which
he won in every land, putting them into writing according

---

[1] II, 577.

[2] From my own copy of the original; see Birch, Mém. sur une patère Egypt-
ienne du Musée du Louvre, Paris, 1858; and Pierret, Salle hist. de la Gal.
Égypt., Paris, 1889, No. 358, p. 87.

[3] My own copy.   [4] See p. 322.

to the facts.'"[1] It is these records of Thaneni upon rolls of leather which are referred to in the account[2] of the first campaign during the siege of Megiddo. But the priceless rolls have perished and we have upon the wall at Karnak only the capricious extracts of a temple scribe, more anxious to set forth the spoil and Amon's share therein than to perpetuate the story of his king's great deeds. How much he has passed over, the biography of Amenemhab shows only too well; and thus all that we have of the wars of Egypt's greatest commander has filtered through the shrivelled soul of an ancient bureaucrat, who little dreamed how hungrily future ages would ponder his meagre excerpts.

The advancement of Egypt's Asiatic frontier to the Euphrates again was, in the light of past experience, not an achievement from which he might expect lasting results; nor was Thutmose III the man to drop the work he had begun as if it were complete with the campaign of the year thirty three. The spring of the thirty fourth year therefore found him again in Zahi on his ninth campaign.[3] Some disaffection, probably in the Lebanon region, obliged him to take three towns, one of which at least was in the district of Nuges, where he had erected a fortress at the close of the first campaign.[4] Considerable spoil was captured and the Syrian dynasts as usual hastened to pay their tribute and express their loyalty.[5] Meanwhile the magazines of the harbour-towns were replenished as formerly, but especially with ships for the fleet, and with masts and spars for naval repairs.[6] The tribute of the year was rendered notable by a present of one hundred and eight blocks of copper, weighing nearly four pounds apiece, beside some lead and costly stones from the king of Cyprus, who had not heretofore recognized the might of Thutmose in this manner.[7]

This year evidently saw the extension of his power in the south also; for he secured the son of the chief of Irem, the

---

[1] II, 392. [2] See above, p. 291. [3] II, 489. [4] II, 490.
[5] II, 491. [6] II, 492. [7] II, 493.

neighbour of Punt as a hostage;[1] and the combined tribute of Nubia amounted to over one hundred and thirty four pounds of gold alone, besides the usual ebony, ivory, grain, cattle and slaves.[2] The sway of Thutmose was absolute from above the third cataract to the Euphrates and his power was at its zenith when he learned of a general revolt in Naharin. It was now nearly two years since he had seen that region and in so short a time its princes had ceased to fear his power. They formed a coalition, with some prince at its head, possibly the king of Aleppo, whom Thutmose's Annals call "that wretched foe of Naharin."[3] The alliance was strong in numbers, for it included the far north, or "the ends of the earth,"[4] as the Egyptians called the distant regions of Asia where their knowledge of the country ceased. Thutmose's continual state of preparation enabled him to appear promptly on the plains of Naharin in the spring of the year thirty five. He engaged the allies in battle at a place called Araina,[5] which we are unable to locate with certainty, but it was probably somewhere in the lower Orontes valley. "Then his majesty prevailed against these barbarians. . . . They fled headlong, falling one over another before his majesty."[6] It is perhaps this battle which Amenemhab mentions as occurring in the land of Tikhsi.[7] If so, he fought before Thutmose, as the latter advanced against the enemy and both took booty from the field: the king several pieces of armour, and his general three prisoners, for which act he was again decorated by Thutmose. The troops, of course, found rich plunder on the field: horses, bronze armour and weapons, besides chariots richly wrought with gold and silver.[8] The alliance of the Naharin dynasts was completely shattered and its resources for future resistance destroyed or carried off by the victorious Egyptians. Far as were these Syrian princes from Egypt, they had learned the length and the might of the Pharaoh's arm, and it was seven years before they again revolted.

---

[1] II, 494.   [2] II, 494–5.   [3] II, 498.   [4] Ibid.
[5] Ibid.   [6] II, 499.   [7] II, 587.   [8] II, 500–501.

Thutmose's annals for the next two years are lost, and we know nothing of the objective of his eleventh and twelfth campaigns; but the year thirty eight found him in the southern Lebanon region on his thirteenth campaign, again chastising the region of Nuges,[1] which had felt his power for the first time fifteen years before on the first campaign. On this expedition he received not only another gift from the king of Cyprus, but also one from far off Arrapakhitis, later a province of Assyria.[2] The turbulent Beduin of southern Palestine forced him to march through their country the next year, and the inevitable Amenemhab captured three prisoners in an action in the Negeb.[3] He then spent the rest of this fourteenth campaign in Syria, where it became merely a tour of inspection; but in both years he kept the harbours supplied as before, ready for every emergency. The tribute seems to have come in regularly for the next two years (forty and forty one),[4] and again the king of "Kheta the great" sent gifts, which Thutmose as before records among the "tribute."[5]

The princes of Syria, sorely chastised as they had been, were nevertheless unwilling to relinquish finally their independence, and regard the suzerainty of Egypt as an inevitable and permanent condition of their rule. Incited by Kadesh, Thutmose's inveterate enemy, they again rose in a final united effort to shake off the Pharaoh's strong hand. All Naharin, especially the king of Tunip, and also some of the northern coast cities, had been induced to join the alliance. The great king was now an old man, probably over seventy years of age, but with his accustomed promptitude he appeared with his fleet off the north coast of Syria in the spring of the year forty two. It was his seventeenth and last campaign. Like his first, it was directed against his arch enemy, Kadesh. Instead of approaching the place from the south, as before, Thutmose determined to isolate her from her northern support and to capture Tunip first. He therefore landed at some point between the mouth of the Orontes and the Nahr

[1] II, 507. [2] II, 511–12. [3] II, 517, 580. [4] II, 520–527. [5] II, 525.

el-Kebîr and captured the coast city of Erkatu,[1] the exact location of which is not certain; but it must have been nearly opposite Tunip, against which he then marched. He was detained at Tunip until the harvest season, but he captured the place after a short resistance.[2] He then accomplished the march up the Orontes to Kadesh without mishap and wasted the towns of the region.[3] The king of Kadesh, knowing that his all was lost unless he could defeat Thutmose's army, made a desperate resistance. He engaged the Egyptians in battle before the city, and in the effort to make head against Thutmose's seasoned troops the Syrian king resorted to a stratagem. He sent forth a mare against the Egyptian chariotry, hoping thus to excite the stallions and produce confusion, or even a break in the Egyptian battle line, of which he might take advantage. But Amenemhab leaped from his chariot, sword in hand, pursued the mare on foot, ripped her up and cut off her tail, which he carried in triumph to the king.[4] Thutmose's siege-lines now closed in on the doomed city, and the first assault was ordered. For this purpose he selected all the élite of his army, in order to breach the walls. Amenemhab was placed in command. The dangerous feat was successfully accomplished, the flower of Thutmose's tried veterans poured in through the breach, Amenemhab at their head, and the strongest city of Syria was again at the Pharaoh's mercy.[5] The Naharin auxiliaries in the city fell into Thutmose's hands, and it was not even necessary for him to march into the north. In any case, at his advanced age he might have been pardoned for avoiding so arduous an expedition after a long campaign. It is also probable that the season was too far advanced for him to undertake so long a march before the cold of winter should set in. However, as the event proved, no further display of force in the north was necessary.

Never again as long as the old king lived did the Asiatic princes make any attempt to shake off his yoke. In seventeen campaigns, during a period of nineteen years, he had

---

[1] II, 529.　　　[2] II, 530.　　　[3] II, 531.　　　[4] II, 589.　　　[5] II, 590.

beaten them into submission, until there was no spirit for
resistance left among them. With the fall of Kadesh disappeared the last vestige of that Hyksos power which had once
subdued Egypt. Thutmose's name became a proverb in their
midst, and when, four generations later, his successors failed
to shield their faithful vassals in Naharin from the aggression
of the Kheta, the forsaken unfortunates remembered Thutmose's great name, and wrote pathetically to Egypt: ''Who
formerly could have plundered Tunip without being plundered by Manakhbiria (Thutmose III)?''[1] But even now,
at three score and ten or more, the indomitable old warrior
had the harbours equipped with the necessary supplies,[2] and
there is little doubt that if it had been necessary he would
have led his army into Syria again. For the last time in
Asia he received the envoys of the tribute-paying princes
in his tent,[3] and then returned to Egypt. There the Nubian
envoys brought him over five hundred and seventy eight
pounds of gold from Wawat alone.[4]

One would have thought that the old king might now enjoy
a well-earned repose for the few years that remained to him;
but having at last established the sovereignty of Egypt in
Asia on a permanent basis, he turned his attention to Nubia.
It is evident that Menkheperreseneb, the head of his gold and
silver treasury,[5] was now receiving thence six to eight hundred pounds of gold every year, for, as we now see, even
the incomplete data at our command show in his forty first
year nearly eight hundred pounds.[6] His viceroy, Nehi, had
now been administering Kush for twenty years[7] and had
placed the productivity of the country on a high plane; but
it was the desire of the great king to extend still further his
dominions in the south. In his last years his buildings show
that he was extremely active throughout the province; as
far as the third cataract we trace his temples at Kalabsheh,
Amâda, Wadi Halfa, Kummeh and Semneh, where he restored the temple of his great ancestor Sesostris III, and at

---

[1] Amarna Letters, ed. Winckler, 41, 6–8.   [2] II, 535.   [3] II, 533–4, 536–7.
[4] II, 539.   [5] II, 772 ff.   [6] II, 526–27.   [7] II, 651–2.

Soleb. We learn through the clearance of the canal at the first cataract, which he was obliged to effect in the fiftieth year,[1] that an expedition of his was then returning from a campaign against the Nubians. It is impossible to suppose that the aged Thutmose accompanied it. There must have been earlier expeditions also in the same region, for Thutmose was able to record in duplicate upon the pylons of his Karnak temple a list of one hundred and fifteen places which he conquered in Nubia and another containing some four hundred such names. The geography of Nubia is too little known to enable us to locate the territory represented, and it is uncertain exactly how far up the Nile his new frontier may have been, but it was doubtless well up toward the fourth cataract, where we find it under his son.

Twelve years more were vouchsafed the great king after he had returned from his last campaign in Asia. As he felt his strength failing he made coregent his son, Amenhotep II,[2] born to him by Hatshepsut-Meretre, a queen of whose origin we know nothing. About a year later, on the 17th of March, in the year 1447 B. C., when he was within five weeks of the end of his fifty fourth year upon the throne, he closed his eyes upon the scenes among which he had played so great a part.[3] He was buried in his tomb in the Valley of the Kings by his son, and his body still survives (Fig. 120). Before his death the priests of Amon had put into the mouth of their god a hymn of praise[4] to him, which, although a highly artificial composition, is not without effectiveness as literature; and shows at the same time not only how universal was his sway as the priests saw it, but also how deeply he had wrought upon the imagination of his contemporaries. After a long introduction in praise of Thutmose, Amon, his god, says to him:

I have come, giving thee to smite the princes of Zahi,
I have hurled them beneath thy feet among their highlands;
I have made them see thy majesty as lord of radiance,
So that thou hast shone in their faces like my image.

[1] II. 649–650.   [2] II, 184.   [3] II, 592.   [4] II, 655 ff.

I have come, giving thee to smite the Asiatics,
Thou hast made captive the heads of the Asiatics of Retenu;
I have made them see thy majesty equipped with thy adornment,
When thou hast taken the weapons of war in the chariot.

I have come, giving thee to smite the eastern land,
Thou hast trampled those who are in the districts of God's-Land;
I have made them see thy majesty as a circling star,
When it scatters its flame in fire and gives forth its dew.

I have come, giving thee to smite the western land,
Keftyew and Cyprus are in terror;
I have made them see thy majesty as a young bull,
Firm of heart, ready-horned and irresistible.

I have come, giving thee to smite those who are in their marshes,
The lands of Mitanni tremble under fear of thee;
I have made them see thy majesty as a crocodile,
Lord of fear in the water, inapproachable.

I have come, giving thee to smite those who are in their isles,
Those who are in the midst of the great sea hear thy roarings;
I have made them see thy majesty as an avenger,
Rising upon the back of his slain victim.

I have come, giving thee to smite the Libyans,
The isles of the Utentyew belong to the might of thy prowess;
I have made them see thy majesty as a fierce-eyed lion,
While thou makest them corpses in their valleys.

I have come, giving thee to smite the uttermost ends of the
        lands;
The circuit of the Great Curve (Okeanos) is enclosed in thy grasp;
I have made them see thy majesty as a soaring hawk,
Seizing that which he seeth, as much as he desires.

I have come, giving thee to smite those who are nigh thy border,
Thou hast smitten the Sand-Dwellers as living captives;
I have made them see thy majesty as a southern jackal,
Swift-footed, stealthy-going, who roves the Two Lands.

We have seen enough of Thutmose to know that this was
not all poetry, the adulation of a fawning priesthood. His
character stands forth with more of colour and individuality
than that of any king of early Egypt, except Ikhnaton. We
see the man of a tireless energy unknown in any Pharaoh
before or since; the man of versatility, designing exquisite

vases in a moment of leisure; the lynx-eyed administrator, who launched his armies upon Asia with one hand and with the other crushed the extortionate tax-gatherer. His vizier, Rekhmire, who stood closest to his person, says of him: "Lo, his majesty was one who knew what happened; there was nothing of which he was ignorant; he was Thoth [the god of knowledge] in everything; there was no matter which he did not carry out."[1] While he was proud to leave a record of his unparalleled achievements, Thutmose protests more than once his deep respect for the truth in so doing. "I have not uttered exaggeration," says he, "in order to boast of that which I did, saying, 'I have done something,' although my majesty had not done it. I have not done anything . . . against which contradiction might be uttered. I have done this for my father, Amon . . . because he knoweth heaven and he knoweth earth, he seeth the whole earth hourly."[2] Such protestations, mingled with reverence for his god as demanding the truth, are not infrequently on his lips.[3] His reign marks an epoch not only in Egypt but in the whole east as we know it in his age. Never before in history had a single brain wielded the resources of so great a nation and wrought them into such centralized, permanent and at the same time mobile efficiency, that for years they could be brought to bear with incessant impact upon another continent as a skilled artisan manipulates a hundred-ton forge hammer; although the figure is inadequate unless we remember that Thutmose forged his own hammer. The genius which rose from an obscure priestly office to accomplish this for the first time in history reminds us of an Alexander or a Napoleon. He built the first real empire, and is thus the first character possessed of universal aspects, the first world-hero. From the fastnesses of Asia Minor, the marshes of the upper Euphrates, the islands of the sea, the swamps of Babylonia, the distant shores of Libya, the oases of the Sahara, the terraces of the Somali coast and the upper cataracts of the Nile the princes of his time rendered their

[1] II, 664.   [2] II, 570.   [3] II, 452.

tribute to his greatness. He thus made not only a world-wide impression upon his age, but an impression of a new order. His commanding figure, towering like an embodiment of righteous penalty among the trivial plots and treacherous schemes of the petty Syrian dynasts, must have clarified the atmosphere of oriental politics as a strong wind drives away miasmic vapours. The inevitable chastisement of his strong arm was held in awed remembrance by the men of Naharin for three generations. His name was one to conjure with, and centuries after his empire had crumbled to pieces it was placed on amulets as a word of power. It should be a matter of gratification to us of the western world that one of this king's greatest monuments, his Heliopolitan obelisks,[1] now rises on our own shores as a memorial of the world's first empire-builder.

[1] Of this pair one is on the Thames embankment in London, and the other in Central Park, New York City. See p. 306.

CHAPTER XVII

THE EMPIRE

THE imperial age was now at its full noontide in the Nile valley. The old seclusiveness had totally disappeared, the wall of partition between Asia and Africa, already shaken by the Hyksos, was now broken down completely by the wars of Thutmose III. Traditional limits disappeared, the currents of life eddied no longer within the landmarks of tiny kingdoms, but pulsed from end to end of a great empire, embracing many kingdoms and tongues, from the upper Nile to the upper Euphrates. The wealth of Asiatic trade, circulating through the eastern end of the Mediterranean, which once flowed down the Euphrates to Babylon, was thus diverted to the Nile Delta, centuries earlier united by canal with the Red Sea. All the world traded in the Delta markets. Assyria was still in her infancy and Babylonia no longer possessed any political influence in the west. The Pharaoh looked forward to an indefinite lease of power throughout the vast empire which he had conquered.

Of his administration in Asia we know very little. The whole region was under the general control of a "governor of the north countries"; Thutmose III's general, Thutiy, being the first to hold that office.[1] To bridle the turbulent Asiatic dynasts it was necessary permanently to station troops throughout Syria-Palestine. Strongholds named after the Pharaoh were established and the troops placed in them as garrisons under deputies with power to act as the Pharaoh's representatives.[2] Thutmose III erected one such at the south end of Lebanon;[3] he resuscitated another founded by his predecessors at some city on the Phœnician coast,

---

[1] See p. 312. [2] Amarna Letters. [3] II. 548.

where we find a sanctuary of Amon,[1] the state god of Egypt, and there was probably such a temple in each of the garrison towns. Yet another stronghold at Ikathi,[2] in furthest Naharin, was doubtless his foundation. Remains of an Egyptian temple found by Renan at Byblos,[3] doubtless belong to this period. As we have seen, the city-kings were allowed to rule their little states with great freedom, as long as they paid the annual tribute with promptness and regularity. When such a ruler died his son, who had been educated at Thebes, was installed in the father's place. The Asiatic conquests were therefore rather a series of tributary kingdoms than provinces, which indeed represent a system of foreign government as yet in its infancy, or only roughly foreshadowed in the rule of the viceroy of Kush. How the local government of the city-kings was related to the administration of the "governor of the north countries" is entirely uncertain. His office was apparently largely a fiscal one, for Thutiy, Thutmose III's governor, adds to his name the phrase "filling the treasury with lapis-lazuli, silver and gold."[4] But it is evident that the dynasts collected their own taxes and rendered a part to the Pharaoh. We are unable to determine what portion of his income the Asiatic vassal was thus obliged to contribute; nor have we the slightest idea how large was the Pharaoh's total revenue from Asia.

As so often in similar empires of later age, when the great king died the tributary princes revolted. Thus when the news of Thutmose III's death reached Asia the opportunity was improved and the dynasts made every preparation to throw off the irksome obligation of the annual tribute. Amenhotep II had reigned as coregent but a year when his father died[5] and the storm broke. All Naharin, including the Mitanni princes, and probably also the northern coast cities, were combined or at least simultaneous in the uprising. With all his father's energy the young king prepared for the

---

[1] II, 457–8. [2] II, 787. [3] Rougé, Revue arch. n. s. VII, 1863, pp. 194 ff.
[4] See above, p. 312. [5] II, 184.

crisis and marched into Asia against the allies, who had collected a large army.[1] The south had evidently not ventured to rebel, but from northern Palestine on, the revolt was general. Leaving Egypt with his forces in April of his second year (1447 B. C.), Amenhotep was in touch with the enemy in northern Palestine early in May and immediately fought an action at Shemesh-Edom[2]against the princes of Lebanon. In this encounter he led his forces in person, as his father before him had so often done, and mingled freely in the hand-to-hand fray. With his own hand he took eighteen prisoners and sixteen horses.[3] The enemy was routed. By the twelfth of May he had crossed the Orontes for the last time in his northward advance, probably at Senzar and turned northeastward for the Euphrates.[4] He fought a skirmish with the Naharin advance just after crossing the river,[5] but pushed rapidly on and captured seven of the rebellious dynasts in the land of Tikhsi.[6] On the 26th of May, fourteen days after leaving the Orontes, he arrived at Niy, which opened its gates to him; and with the men and women of the town acclaiming him from the walls he entered the place in triumph.[7] Ten days later, on the fifth of June, he had rescued a garrison of his troops from the treachery of the revolting town of Ikathi[8] and punished its inhabitants. Whether the march to this town carried him northward from Niy, up the Euphrates or across it and into Mitanni, is uncertain; but the latter is the more probable, for his records say of him, "The chiefs of Mitanni come to him, their tribute upon their backs, to beseech his majesty that there may be given to them his sweet breath of life; a mighty occurrence, it has never been heard since the time of the gods. This country, which knew not Egypt, beseeches the Good God [the Pharaoh]."[9] As he reached his extreme advance, which thus probably surpassed his father's, he set up a boundary tablet,[10]as his father and grandfather had done. His return was a triumphal procession as he approached Memphis.

[1] II, 792, l. 4.   [2] II, 783.   [3] Ibid.   [4] II, 784.   [5] Ibid.
[6] II, 797.   [7] II, 786.   [8] II, 787.   [9] II, 804.   [10] II, 800, ll. 4–5.

The populace assembled in admiring crowds while his lines passed, driving with them over five hundred of the north Syrian lords, two hundred and forty of their women, two hundred and ten horses and three hundred chariots. His herald had in charge for the chief treasurer nearly sixteen hundred and sixty pounds of gold in the form of vases and vessels, besides nearly one hundred thousand pounds of copper.[1] Proceeding to Thebes, he took with him the seven kings of Tikhsi, who were hung head downward on the prow of his royal barge as he approached the city. He personally sacrificed them in the presence of Amon and hanged their bodies on the walls of Thebes, reserving one for a lesson to the Nubians as we shall see.[2] His unexpected energy had evidently crushed the revolt before it had been able to muster all its forces, and in so far as we know, the lesson was so effective that no further attempt was made against his suzerainty in Asia.

The young Pharaoh now directed his energies toward ensuring the security of the other extremity of his empire and establishing his southern frontier. On his arrival at Thebes he dispatched an expedition into Nubia, bearing the body of the seventh king of the land of Tikhsi, which was hung up on the wall of Napata, as a hint of what the Nubians might expect should they attempt revolt against their new sovereign. The operations of Thutmose III in upper Nubia now made it possible for Amenhotep to establish his frontier at the fourth cataract; it was guarded by Napata, just below the cataract, and the region of Karoy, in which the town lay, was from this time on known as the southern limit of Egyptian administration. To this point extended the jurisdiction of the "viceroy of Kush and governor of the south countries."[3] This carried the territory of Egypt around the great bend in the river to the region where the stream often flows southward. Here Amenhotep set up tablets marking his southern frontier,[4] and beyond these there was no more control of the rude Nubian tribes than was necessary to keep

[1] II, 790.   [2] II, 797.   [3] II, 1025.   [4] II, 800.

open the trade-routes from the south and prevent the barbarians from becoming so bold as to invade the province in plundering expeditions. About nine months after his return from the Asiatic campaign, the Nubian expedition erected two stelas, one at Amâda and the other at Elephantine, recording his completion of the temples begun by his father at these places.[1] He there tells us of the fate of the Tikhsi kings, and although the second campaign had not yet taken place, he refers to his Naharin war as his "first campaign," a significant prophecy of the life of conquest which he expected to lead. It was now regarded as a matter of course that Amon had pressed into the eager hand of every Pharaoh sceptre and sword alike. The work of Amenhotep's great father was so thoroughly done, however, that, as far as we know, he was not obliged to invade either Asia or Nubia again.

In Thebes he built his now vanished mortuary temple on the west side of the river, by that of his father, while in the Karnak temple he restored the long dismantled hall of Hatshepsut's obelisks, setting up again the columns which she had removed and richly adorning them with precious metal. He recorded the restoration on the wall which his father had built around the obelisks of Hatshepsut to hide their inscriptions forever from view.[2] Besides a small colonnaded structure at Karnak, he also built at Memphis and Heliopolis, restoring the neighbouring quarries of Troja; but all his works there have perished. We are able to discern little of him personally, but he seems to have been a worthy son of the great king. Physically he was a very powerful man and claims in his inscriptions that no man could draw his bow. The weapon was found in his tomb and bears the words after his name: "Smiter of the Troglodytes, overthrower of Kush, hacking up their cities . . . the great Wall of Egypt, protector of his soldiers."[3] It is this story which furnished Herodotus with the legend that Cambyses was unable to draw the bow of the king of Ethiopia. He cele-

---

[1] II, 791–8.   [2] II, 803–6.   [3] II, p. 310, note d.

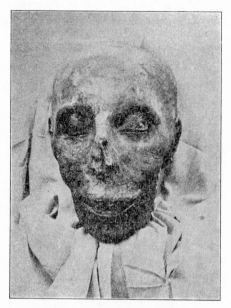

FIG. 120.—HEAD OF THUTMOSE III.

(From his mummy. Cairo Museum.)

FIG. 121.—HEAD OF AMENHOTEP II, SON OF
THUTMOSE III.

(From his mummy still in his tomb at Thebes.)

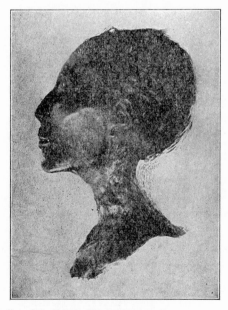

FIG. 122.—HEAD OF THUTMOSE IV, SON OF
AMENHOTEP II.

(From his mummy. Cairo Museum.)

FIG. 123.—AMARNA LETTER, NO. 296.

Containing list of the dowry of the Mitannian
King Dushratta's daughter, Tadukhipa.
(Berlin Museum.)

brated his jubilee on the thirtieth anniversary of his appointment as crown prince and erected an obelisk in Elephantine
in commemoration of the event. Dying about 1420 B. C., after
a reign of some twenty six years, he was interred like his ancestors in the valley of the kings' tombs, where his body rests
to this day (Fig. 121), though even now a prey to the clever
tomb-robbers of modern Thebes, who in November, 1901,
forced the tomb and cut through the wrappings of the
mummy in their search for royal treasure on the body of their
ancient ruler.[1] Their Theban ancestors in the same craft,
however, had three thousand years ago taken good care that
nothing should be left for their descendants.[2]

Amenhotep II was followed by his son, Thutmose IV. It
is possible that this prince was not at first designed to be
his father's successor, if we may believe a folk-tale which
was in circulation some centuries later. The story recounted
how, long before his father's death, a hunting expedition
once carried him to the desert near the pyramids of Gizeh,
where the Pharaohs of the Fourth Dynasty had already slept
over thirteen hundred years. He rested in the shadow of
the great Sphinx at noon time, and falling asleep, the sun-
god, with whom the Sphinx in his time was identified, appeared to him in a dream, beseeching him to clear his image
from the sand which already at that early day encumbered
it, and at the same time promising him the kingdom. The
prince made a vow to do as the great god desired. The god's
promise was fulfilled and the young king immediately upon
his accession hastened to redeem his vow. He cleared the
gigantic figure of the Sphinx and recorded the whole incident on a stela in the vicinity. A later version, made by the
priests of the palace, was engraved on a huge granite architrave taken from the neighbouring Osiris-temple and erected
against the breast of the Sphinx between the forelegs, where
it still stands.[3]

He was early called upon to maintain the empire in Asia.
We are, however, entirely ignorant of the course of his cam-

[1] IV, 507–8.   [2] Infra, pp. 510–11.   [3] II, 810–815.

paign there, which, like his father, he called his "first campaign."[1] It is evident, however, that he was obliged to
advance into the far north, eventually invading Naharin, so
that he was afterward able to record in the state temple at
Thebes the spoil, "which his majesty captured in Naharin
the wretched, on his first victorious campaign."[2] The immediate result of his appearance in Naharin was completely
to quiet all disaffection there as far as the vassal-princes
were concerned. He returned by way of Lebanon where he
forced the chiefs to furnish him with a cargo of cedar for
the sacred barge of Amon at Thebes.[3] Arriving at Thebes,
he settled a colony of the prisoners, possibly from the city
of Gezer in Palestine,[4] in the enclosure of his mortuary
temple, which he had erected by those of his ancestors on
the plain at Thebes. Perhaps the recognition of a common
enemy in the Kheta now produced a *rapprochement* between
the Pharaoh and Mitanni, for the latter was soon to suffer
from the aggressions of the king of Kheta. Thutmose evidently desired a friend in the north, for he sent to Artatama,
the Mitannian king, and desired his daughter in marriage.[5]
After some proper display of reluctance, Artatama consented,
and the Mitannian princess was sent to Egypt, where she
probably received an Egyptian name, Mutemuya, and became
the mother of the next king of Egypt, Amenhotep III. A
firm alliance with Mitanni was thus formed, which forbade
all thought of future conquest by the Pharaoh east of the
Euphrates. A friendly alliance was also cemented with
Babylonia.[6] Although it is probable that Thutmose found
it unnecessary to invade Asia again, he was called the "conqueror of Syria" by his nobles,[7] and the tribute of the Syrian
princes regularly appeared at the office of the vizier or the
treasurer.[8] In the spring of the year eight news of a serious
revolt in Nubia reached him.[9] After a triumphant voyage
up the river, having stopped to greet the gods in all the
larger temples, he passed the first cataract, and advancing

[1] II, 817.   [2] Ibid.   [3] II, 822, 838.
[4] II, 821.   [5] Amarna Letters, 21, 16–18.   [6] Amarna Letters, 1, l. 63.
[7] II, 822.   [8] II, 819–820.   [9] II, 826.

into Wawat, he seems to have found the enemy surprisingly near the northern boundary of Nubia. There was of course but one possible issue for the battle which followed, and great quantities of spoil fell into Thutmose's hands.[1] Again he settled the prisoners which he took as serfs of his mortuary temple.[2]

It is probable that Thutmose did not long survive the war in Nubia. He was therefore unable to beautify Thebes and adorn the state temple as his fathers had done. But the respect in which he held his grandfather, Thutmose III, led him to the completion of a notable work of the latter. For thirty five years the last obelisk planned by Thutmose III had been lying unfinished at the southern portal of the Karnak temple enclosure or temenos. His grandson now had it engraved in the old conqueror's name, recorded also upon it his own pious deed in continuing the work, and erected the colossal shaft, one hundred and five and a half feet high, the largest surviving obelisk, at the southern portal of the enclosure, where he had found it lying. It now stands before the Lateran in Rome. Not long after this gracious act, which may possibly have been in celebration of his own jubilee, Thutmose was gathered to his fathers (about 1411 B. C.) and was buried in the valley where they slept (Fig. 122).

The son who succeeded him was the third of the Amenhoteps and the last of the great emperors. He was but the great grandson of Thutmose III, but with him the high tide of Egyptian power was already slowly on the ebb, and he was not the man to stem the tide. An early evidence of the effeminate character, which he afterward showed, is noticeable in his relation with his queen. Already as crown prince, or at least early in his reign he married a remarkable woman, of uncertain origin, named Tiy. There is not a particle of evidence to prove her of foreign birth, as is so often claimed. In celebration of the marriage, Amenhotep issued a large number of scarabs, or sacred beetles, carved in stone and engraved with a record[3] of the event, in which the unti-

[1] II, 829.   [2] II, 824.   [3] II, 861-2.

tled parentage of his queen frankly follows her name in the very royal titulary itself, which declares her to be the queen-consort. But the record closes with the words: "She is the wife of a mighty king whose southern boundary is as far as Karoy and northern as far as Naharin";[1] as if to remind any who might reflect upon the humble origin of the queen of the exalted station which she now occupied. From the beginning the new queen exerted a powerful influence over Amenhotep, and he immediately inserted her name in the official caption placed at the head of royal documents. Her power continued throughout his reign and was the beginning of a remarkable era characterized by the prominence of the queens in state affairs and on public occasions, a peculiarity which we find only under Amenhotep III and his immediate successors. The significance of these events we shall later dwell upon.

In the administration of his great empire Amenhotep III began well. The Asiatics gave him no trouble at his accession, and he ruled in security and unparalleled splendour. Toward the close of his fourth year, however, trouble in Nubia called him south. Early in October he had improved the high water to pass the cataract with his fleet. His viceroy of Nubia, Mermose, had levied an army of Nubians in the region from the vicinity of Kubbân for seventy five miles up to Ibrim.[2] These, with the Pharaoh's Egyptians, were to be employed against the Nubians of the upper country, a striking evidence of the very Egyptianized character of lower Nubia. When they had reached Ibhet, which is at least above the second cataract, they found the enemy and engaged them in battle, probably on the anniversary of the king's coronation, the first day of his fifth year. They took seven hundred and forty prisoners and slew three hundred and twelve, as recorded on a tablet of victory which they set up at the second cataract.[3] The outlying villages and wells were visited by small parties and the inhabitants punished to prevent further recurrences of insubordination;[4] where-

[1] II, 862.   [2] II, 852.   [3] II, 853-4.   [4] II, 850.

upon Amenhotep marched southward for a month, taking captives and spoil as he went.[1] Arriving finally at the "height of Hua," a place of uncertain location, which, however, occurs in the lists, together with Punt, and must have been a long distance south, perhaps above the cataracts, he camped in the land of Uneshek on the south of Hua. This marked his extreme southern advance.[2] In the land of Karoy, with which the reader is now acquainted as the region about Napata, he collected great quantities of gold for his Theban buildings,[3] and at Kebehu-Hor, or "the Pool of Horus," he erected his tablet of victory,[4] but we are unable to locate the place with certainty. It was certainly not essentially in advance of the frontier of his father. This was the last great invasion of Nubia by the Pharaohs. It was constantly necessary to punish the outlying tribes for their incessant predatory incursions into the Nile valley; but the valley itself, as far as the fourth cataract, was completely subjugated, and as far as the second cataract largely Egyptianized, a process which now went steadily forward until the country up to the fourth cataract was effectually engrafted with Egyptian civilization. Egyptian temples had now sprung up at every larger town, and the Egyptian gods were worshipped therein; the Egyptian arts were learned by the Nubian craftsmen, and everywhere the rude barbarism of the upper Nile was receiving the stamp of Egyptian culture. Nevertheless the native chieftains, under the surveillance of the viceroy, were still permitted to retain their titles and honours, and doubtless continued to enjoy at least a nominal share in the government. We find them as far north as Ibrim,[5] which had marked the southern limit of Amenhotep III's levy of negro auxiliaries, and was therefore probably the extreme point to which local administration solely by Egyptian officials extended southward. The annual landing of the viceroy at Thebes, bringing the yearly tribute of all the Nubian lands, was now a long established custom.[6]

[1] II, 850, ll. 11   [2] II, 847-8.   [3] II, 889.
[4] II, 845.   [5] II, 1037.   [6] II, 1035-41.

In Asia Amenhotep enjoyed unchallenged supremacy; at the court of Babylon even, his suzerainty in Canaan, as they called Syria-Palestine, was acknowledged; and when the dynasts attempted to involve Kurigalzu, king of Babylon, in an alliance with them against the Pharaoh, he wrote them an unqualified refusal, stating that he was in alliance with the Pharaoh, and even threatened them with hostilities if they formed a hostile alliance against Egypt.[1] At least this is the Babylonian version of the affair and whether true or not, it shows Babylon's earnest desire to stand well with the Pharaoh. All the powers: Babylonia, Assyria, Mitanni and Alasa-Cyprus, were exerting every effort to gain the friendship of Egypt. A scene of world politics, such as is unknown before in history, now unfolds before us. From the Pharaoh's court as the centre radiate a host of lines of communication with all the great peoples of the age. The Tell el-Amarna letters (Fig. 123), perhaps the most interesting mass of documents surviving from the early east, have preserved to us this glimpse across the kingdoms of hither Asia as one might see them on a stage, each king playing his part before the great throne of the Pharaoh. The letters, some three hundred in number, are written on clay tablets in the Babylonian cuneiform, and were discovered in 1888 at the capital city of Amenhotep III's son, Ikhnaton, the place known in modern times as Tell el-Amarna, from which the correspondence takes its name. They date from the reign of Amenhotep III and that of his son and successor, Amenhotep IV, or Ikhnaton, being correspondence of a strictly official character between these Pharaohs on the one hand, and on the other the kings of Babylonia, Nineveh, Mitanni, Alasa (Cyprus) and the Pharaoh's vassal kings of Syria-Palestine. Five letters[2] survive from the correspondence of Amenhotep III with Kallimma-Sin (Kadashman-Bel), king of Babylonia, one from the Pharaoh and the others from Kallimma-Sin. The Babylonian king is constantly in need of gold and insistently importunates his

[1] Amarna Letters, 7   [2] Amarna Letters, 1-5

brother of Egypt to send him large quantities of the precious metal, which he says is as plentiful as dust in Egypt according to the reports of the Babylonian messengers. Considerable friction results from the dissatisfaction of Kallimma-Sin at the amounts with which Amenhotep favours him. He refers to the fact that Amenhotep had received from his father a daughter in marriage, and makes this relationship a reason for further gifts of gold. As the correspondence goes on another marriage is negotiated between a daughter of Amenhotep and Kallimma-Sin or his son. Similarly Amenhotep enjoys the most intimate connection with Shuttarna, the king of Mitanni, the son of Artatama, with whom his father, Thutmose IV, had enjoyed the most cordial relations. Indeed Amenhotep was perhaps the nephew of Shuttarna, from whom he now received a daughter, named Gilukhipa, in marriage. In celebration of this union Amenhotep issued a series of scarab-beetles of stone bearing an inscription commemorating the event, and stating that the princess brought with her a train of three hundred and seventeen ladies and attendants.[1] This occurred in Amenhotep's tenth year. On the death of Shuttarna the alliance was continued under his son, Dushratta, from whom Amenhotep later received, as a wife for his son and successor, a second Mitannian princess, Tadukhipa, the daughter of Dushratta. The correspondence between the two kings is very illuminating and may serve as an example of such communications. The following is a letter[2] of Dushratta to his Egyptian ally:

"To Nimmuria, the great king, the king of Egypt, my brother, my son-in-law, who loves me, and whom I love:— Dushratta, the great king, thy father-in-law, who loves thee, the king of Mitanni, thy brother. It is well with me. With thee may it be well, with thy house, my sister and thy other wives, thy sons, thy chariots, thy horses, thy chief men, thy land, and all thy possessions, may it be very well indeed. In the time of thy fathers, they were on very

[1] II, 866-7.   [2] Amarna Letters, 17.

friendly terms with my fathers, but thou hast increased [this friendship] still more and with my father thou hast been on very friendly terms indeed. Now, therefore, since thou and I are on mutually friendly terms, thou hast made it ten times closer than with my father. May the gods cause this friendship of ours to prosper. May Tishub [the god of Mitanni], the lord, and Amon eternally ordain it as it is now.''

"Inasmuch as my brother sent his messenger, Mani, saying: 'My brother, send me thy daughter for my wife, to be queen of Egypt,' I did not grieve the heart of my brother, and I continually ordered what was friendly. And as my brother wished, I presented her to Mani. And he beheld her and when he saw her, he rejoiced greatly; and when he brings her safely to my brother's land, then may Ishtar and Amon make her correspond to my brother's wish.''

"Gilia, my messenger, has brought to me my brother's message; when I heard it, it seeemed to me very good, and I was very glad indeed and said: 'So far as I am concerned, even if all the friendly relation which we have had with one another had ceased, nevertheless, on account of this message, we would forever continue friendly.' Now when I wrote my brother I said: 'So far as I am concerned, we will be very friendly indeed, and mutually well disposed'; and I said to my brother: 'Let my brother make [our friendship] ten times greater than with my father,' and I asked of my brother a great deal of gold, saying: 'More than to my father let my brother give me and send me. Thou sentest my father a great deal of gold: a namkhar of pure (?) gold, and a kiru of pure (?) gold, thou sentest him; but thou sentest me [only] a tablet of gold that is as if it were alloyed with copper. . . . So let my brother send gold in very great quantity, without measure, and let him send more gold to me than to my father. For in my brother's land gold is as common as dust . . . .''

In this vein the men who were now shaping the destinies of all hither Asia wrote to one another. In response to sim-

ilar entreaties, Amenhotep sent a gift of twenty talents of
gold to the king of Assyria,[1] and gained his friendship also.
The vassalship of the king of Alasa-Cyprus continued, and
he regularly sent the Pharaoh large quantities of copper,
save when on one occasion he excuses himself because his
country had been visited by a pestilence. So complete was
the understanding between Egypt and Cyprus that even the
extradition of the property of a citizen of Cyprus who had
died in Egypt was regarded by the two kings as a matter of
course, and a messenger was sent to Egypt to receive the
property and bring it back to Cyprus for delivery to the wife
and son of the deceased.[2] Desirous of holding the first
place with Egypt, the island king even ventures to advise the
Pharaoh against any alliance with Kheta or Babylonia, a
policy which we shall later find practiced by Babylonia
herself.

Thus courted and flattered, the object of diplomatic attention from all the great powers, Amenhotep found little occasion for anxiety regarding his Asiatic empire. The Syrian
vassals were now the grandsons of the men whom Thutmose
III had conquered; they had grown thoroughly habituated
to the Egyptian allegiance. The time was so far past when
they had enjoyed independence that they knew no other condition than that of vassals of Egypt. In an age of turbulence and aggression, where might was the only appeal, it
finally seemed to them the natural condition of things and it
was not without its advantages in rendering them free from
all apprehension of attack from without. An Egyptian education at the Pharaoh's capital had, moreover, made him
many a loyal servant among the children of the dynasts,
who had succeeded disloyal or lukewarm fathers in Syria.
They protest their fidelity to the Pharaoh on all occasions.
Thus the prince Akizzi of Katna writes to Amenhotep: "My
lord, here in this place I am thy servant. I am pursuing the
way of my lord, and from my lord I do not depart. Since
my fathers became thy servants this land has been thy land,

[1] Amarna Letters, 23, 30 ff.   [2] Amarna Letters, 25, 30 ff.

the city of Katna thy city, and I am my lord's. My lord, if the troops and chariots of my lord came, food, drink, cattle, sheep, honey and oil were brought for the king's troops and chariots."[1] Such letters were introduced by the most abject and self-abasing adulation; the writer says: "To my lord, the king, my gods, my sun: Abimilki, thy servant. Seven and seven times at the feet of my lord I fall. I am the dust under the sandals of my lord, the king. My lord is the sun which rises over the lands every day, etc.";[2] the vassals fall down before the Pharaoh not only seven times but also "on breast and back" (see Fig. 147). They are "the ground upon which thou treadest, the throne upon which thou sittest, the foot-stool of thy feet"; even "thy dog"; and one is pleased to call himself the groom of the Pharaoh's horse. They have all been installed by the Pharaoh's grace, and he sends oil to anoint them at accession to office. They inform the court at the first sign of disloyalty among their fellows and are even commissioned to proceed against rebellious princes. Throughout the land in the larger cities are garrisons of Egyptian troops, consisting of infantry and chariotry. But they are no longer solely native Egyptians, but to a large extent Nubians and Sherden, roving, predatory bands of sea-robbers, perhaps the ancestors of the historical Sardinians. From now on they took service in the Egyptian army in ever larger and larger numbers. These forces of the Pharaoh were maintained by the dynasts and one of their self-applied tests of loyalty in writing to the Pharaoh was, as we have seen above, their readiness and faithfulness in furnishing supplies. Syria thus enjoyed a stability of government which had never before been hers. The roads were safe from robbers, caravans were convoyed from vassal to vassal, and a word from the Pharaoh was sufficient to bring any of his subject-princes to his knees. The payment of tribute was as regular as the collection of taxes in Egypt itself. But in case of any delay a represensative of the Pharaoh, who was stationed in the various larger towns,

[1] Ibid., 138, 4–13.   [2] Ibid., 149, 1–7.

needed but to appear in the delinquent's vicinity to recall the unfulfilled obligation. Amenhotep himself was never obliged to carry on a war in Asia. On one occasion he appeared at Sidon, and one of his officials mentions prisoners taken by his majesty on the battlefield,[1] but this may refer to the Nubian campaign. It was deemed sufficient, as we shall later see, to send troops under the command of an efficient officer, who found no difficulty in coping with the situation for a generation after Amenhotep's accession. Thus one of the vassal princes later wrote to Amenhotep's son: "Verily, thy father did not march forth, nor inspect the lands of his vassal princes."[2]

Under such circumstances Amenhotep was at leisure to devote himself to those enterprises of peace which have occupied all emperors under similar conditions. Trade now developed as never before. The Nile, from the Delta to the cataracts, was alive with the freight of all the world, which flowed into it from the Red Sea fleets and from long caravans passing back and forth through the Isthmus of Suez, bearing the rich stuffs of Syria, the spices and aromatic woods of the East, the weapons and chased vessels of the Phœnicians, and a myriad of other things, which brought their Semitic names into the hieroglyphic and their use into the life of the Nile-dwellers. Parallel with the land traffic through the isthmus were the routes of commerce on the Mediterranean, thickly dotted with the richly laden galleys of Phœnicia, converging upon the Delta from all quarters and bringing to the markets of the Nile the decorated vessels or damascened bronzes from the Mycenæan industrial settlements of the Ægean. The products of Egyptian industry were likewise in use in the palace of the sea-kings of Cnossos, in Rhodes, and in Cyprus, where a number of Egyptian monuments of this age have been found. Scarabs and bits of glazed ware with the name of Amenhotep III or queen Tiy have also been discovered on the mainland of Greece at Mycenæ. The northern Mediterranean peoples were feeling the impact of Egyptian

[1] II, 916, 918.   ' Amarna Letters, 87, 62–64.

22

civilization now appearing in the north with more insistent force than ever before. In Crete Egyptian religious forms had been introduced, in one case under the personal leadership of an Egyptian priest (Fig. 127). Mycenæan artists were powerfully influenced by the incoming products of Egypt. Egyptian landscapes appear in their metal work, and the lithe animal forms in instantaneous postures which were caught by the pencil of the Theban artists were now common in Mycenæ. The superb decorated ceilings of Thebes likewise appear in the tombs of Mycenæ and Orchomenos. Even the pre-Greek writing of Crete shows traces of the influence of the hieroglyphics of the Nile. The men of the Mycenæan world, the Keftyew, who brought these things to their countrymen, were now a familiar sight upon the streets of Thebes, where the wares which they offered were also modifying the art of Egypt. The plentiful silver of the north now came in with the northern strangers in great quantities, and, although under the Hyksos the baser metal had been worth twice as much as gold, the latter now and permanently became the more valuable medium. The ratio was now about one and two thirds to one, and the value of silver steadily fell until Ptolemaic times (third century B. C. on), when the ratio was twelve to one.

Such trade required protection and regulation. Roving bands of Lycian pirates infested the coasts of the eastern Mediterranean; they boldly entered the harbours of Cyprus and plundered the towns, and even landed on the coast of the Delta.[1] Amenhotep was therefore obliged to develop a marine police which patroled the coast of the Delta and constantly held the mouths of the river closed against all but lawful comers. Custom houses were also maintained by these police officials at the same places, and all merchandise not consigned to the king was dutiable.[2] The income from this source must have been very large, but we have no means of estimating it. All the land-routes leading into the country were similarly policed, and foreigners who could not satis-

[1] Amarna Letters, 28.   [2] II, 916, ll. 33–4.   Amarna Letters, 29; 32; 33.

factorily explain their business were turned back, while legitimate trade was encouraged, protected and properly taxed.

The influx of slaves, chiefly of Semitic race, which had begun under Thutmose III, still continued, and the king's chief scribe distributed them throughout the land and enrolled them among the tax-paying serfs.[2] As this host of foreigners intermarried with the natives, the large infusion of strange blood began to make itself felt in a new and composite type of face, if we may trust the artists of the day. The incalculable wealth which had now been converging upon the coffers of the Pharaoh for over a century also began to exert a profound influence, which, as under like conditions, in later history, was far from wholesome. On New Year's Day the king presented his nobles with a profusion of costly gifts which would have amazed the Pharaohs of the pyramid-age. On one such occasion the chief treasurer carried in before the monarch "chariots of silver and gold, statues of ivory and ebony, necklaces of every costly stone, weapons of warfare, and work of all craftsmen." They included thirteen statues of the king, seven sphinx portraits of the monarch, eight superb necklaces, six hundred and eighty richly wrought shields and two hundred and thirty quivers of the same workmanship, three hundred and sixty bronze swords and one hundred and forty bronze daggers, both damascened with precious metal, thirty ebony staves tipped with silver and gold, two hundred and twenty ivory and ebony whips, seven elaborately wrought chests, many sunshades, chairs, vases and innumerable small objects.[3] In the old days the monarch rewarded a faithful noble with land, which, in order to pay a return, must be properly cultivated and administered, thus fostering simplicity and wholesome country virtues on a large domain; but the favourite now received convertible wealth, which required no administration to be utilized. The luxury and display of the metropolis supplanted the old rustic simplicity and

[1] II, 916, ll. 32–3.　　　[2] Ibid., ll. 31, 36.　　　[3] II, 801 ff.

sturdy elemental virtues. From the Pharaoh down to the humblest scribe this change was evident, if in nothing else than the externals of costume; for the simple linen kilt from the hips to the knees, which once satisfied all, not excluding the king, has now given way to an elaborate costume, with long plaited skirt, a rich tunic with full flowing sleeves; the unpretentious head-dress of the old time has been replaced by an elaborately curled wig hanging down upon the shoulders; while the once bare feet are shod in elegant sandals, with tapering toes curled up at the tips. A noble of the

FIG. 124.   COSTUMES OF THE EMPIRE.

landed class from the court of the Amenemhets or the Sesostrises, could he have walked the streets of Thebes in Amenhotep III's day, would almost have been at a loss to know in what country he had suddenly found himself; while his own antiquated costume, which had survived only among the priests, would have awakened equal astonishment among the fashionable Thebans of the day. He would not have felt less strange than a noble of Elizabeth's reign upon the streets of modern London. All about him he would have found elegant chateaus and luxurious villas, with charming gardens and summer-houses grouped about vast temples, such as the Nile-dweller had never seen before.

The wealth and the captive labour of Asia and Nubia were being rapidly transmuted into noble architecture, and at Thebes a new and fundamental chapter in the history of the world's architecture was being daily written. Amenhotep gave himself with appreciation and enthusiasm to such works, and placed at the disposal of his architects all the resources which they needed for an ampler practice of their art than had ever before been possible. There were among them men of the highest gifts, and one of them, who bore the same name as the king, gained such a wide reputation for his wisdom that his sayings circulated in Greek some twelve hundred years later among the "Proverbs of the Seven Wise Men"; and in Ptolemaic times he was finally worshipped as a god, and took his place among the innumerable deities of Egypt as "Amenhotep, son of Hapu."[1]

Under the fingers of such men as these the old and traditional elements of Egyptian building were imbued with new life and combined into new forms in which they took on a wondrous beauty unknown before. Besides this, the unprecedented resources of wealth and labour at the command of

FIG. 125. THE PERIPTERAL CELLA-TEMPLE.

Built by Amenhotep III on the Island of Elephantine. It was destroyed for building material by the Turkish governor of Assuan in 1822. (After the "Description" by Napoleon's Expedition.)

such an architect enabled him to deal with such vast dimensions that the element of size alone must have rendered his buildings in the highest degree impressive. But of the two forms of temple which now developed, the smaller is not less

[1] II, 911.

effective than the larger. It was a simple rectangular cella or holy of holies, thirty or forty feet long and fourteen feet high, with a door at each end, surrounded by a portico, the whole being raised upon a base of about half the height of the temple walls. With the door looking out between two graceful columns, and the façade happily set in the retreating vistas of the side colonnades, the whole is so exquisitely proportioned that the trained eye immediately recognizes the hand of a master who appreciated the full value of simple fundamental lines. Little wonder that the architects of Napoleon's expedition who brought it to the notice of the modern world were charmed with it, and thought that they had discovered in it the origin of the Greek peripteral temple; nor can there indeed be any doubt that the architecture of Greece was influenced by this form. The other and larger

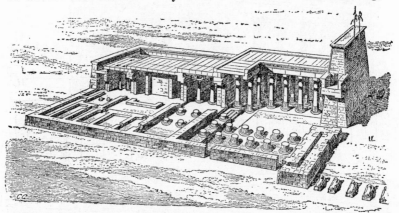

FIG. 126. PERSPECTIVE AND SECTION OF A TYPICAL PYLON TEMPLE OF THE EMPIRE.

The nearer half, with its Pylon-Tower, has been cut away to expose the arrangement of the interior. Compare with description on p. 343. (After Perrot-Chipiez.)

type of temple, which now found its highest development, differs strikingly from the one just discussed; and perhaps most fundamentally in the fact that its colonnades are all within and not visible from the outside. The holy of holies, as of old, is surrounded by a series of chambers, now larger

FIG. 127.—FRAGMENT OF CARVED STONE VASE FOUND IN CRETE.

In the middle of a festal procession an Egyptian priest, with upraised sistrum, leads singing Cretan youths. Eighteenth Century B.C.

FIG. 128.—AMENHOTEP III'S COURT OF CLUSTERED PAPYRUS BUD COLUMNS.

Luxor Temple.

than before, as rendered necessary by the rich and elaborate ritual which had arisen.   Before it is a large colonnaded hall, often called the hypostyle, while in front of this hall lies an extensive forecourt surrounded by a columned portico.   In front of this court rise two towers (together called a "pylon"), which form the façade of the temple.   Their walls incline inward, they are crowned by a hollow cornice and the great door of the temple opens between them.   While the masonry, which is of sandstone or limestone, does not usually contain large blocks, huge architraves, thirty or forty feet long and weighing one or two hundred tons, are not unknown.   Nearly all the surfaces except those on the columns are carved with reliefs, the outside showing the king in battle, while on the inside he appears in the worship of the gods, and all surfaces with slight exception were highly coloured.   Before the vast double doors of cedar of Lebanon mounted in bronze, rose, one on either side, a pair of obelisks, towering high above the pylon-towers, while colossal statues of the king, each hewn from a single block, were placed with backs to the pylon, on either side of the door.   In the use of these elements and this general arrangement of the parts, already common before Amenhotep's reign, his architects created a radically new type, destined to survive in frequent use to this day as one of the noblest forms of architecture.

At Luxor, the old southern suburb of Thebes, which had now grown into the city, there was a small temple to Amon, built by the kings of the Twelfth Dynasty.   Amenhotep had, probably early in his reign, pulled it down and built a new sanctuary with surrounding chambers and a hall before it, like that of Thutmose I at Karnak.   To this his architects had laid out in front a superb forecourt (Fig. 128), with the finest colonnades now surviving in Egypt.   Gaining confidence, they determined to erect in front of all this a new and more ambitious hall than had ever been attempted before, to be preceded in all probability by a still larger court.   The great hall was laid out with a row of gigantic columns on either side the central axis, quite surpassing in height any

pier ever before employed by the Egyptian (Fig. 130). Nor
were they less beautiful for their great size, being in every
respect masterpieces of exquisite proportion, with capitals
of the graceful, spreading papyrus-flower type (Fig. 130).
These columns were higher than those ranged on both sides
of the middle, thus producing a higher roof over a central
aisle or nave and a lower roof over the side aisles, the difference in level being filled with grated stone windows in a
clear-story. Thus were produced the fundamental elements
in basilica and cathedral architecture, which we owe to the
Theban architects of Amenhotep III. Unfortunately the
vast hall was unfinished at the death of the king, and his
son was too ardent an enemy of Amon to carry out the
work of his father. His later successors walled up the magnificent nave with drums from the columns of the side aisles
which were never set up, and the whole stands to-day a
mournful wreck of an unfinished work of art, the first
example of a type for which the world cannot be too grateful.

Amenhotep now proceeded to give the great buildings of
the city a unity which they had not before possessed. He
raised a massive pylon before the temple of Karnak, adorned
with unsurpassed richness; stelas of lapis-lazuli were set up
on either side and besides great quantities of gold and silver,
nearly twelve hundred pounds of malachite were employed
in the inlay work.[1] From the river an avenue led up to it
between two tall obelisks,[2] and before it his architect, Amenhotep, set up for him his portrait colossus, the largest thus
far erected, having been hewn from a single block of tough
gritstone sixty seven feet long, brought up the river from the
quarry near modern Cairo by an army of men.[3] The king
also built a temple to Mut, the goddess of Thebes, where his
ancestors had begun it, on the south of Karnak, and excavated a lake beside it. He then laid out a beautiful garden
in the interval of over a mile and a half, which separates
the Karnak from the Luxor temple and connected the great
temples by avenues of rams (Figs. 4; 129) carved in stone,

[1] II, 903.   [2] II, 903, 1. 57.   [3] II, 917.

each bearing a statue of the Pharaoh between the forepaws. The general effect must have been imposing in the extreme; the brilliant hues of the polychrome architecture, with columns and gates overwrought in gold and floors overlaid with silver, the whole dominated by towering obelisks clothed in glittering metal, rising high above the rich green of the nodding palms and tropical foliage which framed the mass,— all this must have produced an impression both of gorgeous detail and overwhelming grandeur, of which the sombre ruins of the same buildings, impressive as they are, offer little hint at the present day. As at Athens in the days of her glory, the state was fortunate in the possession of men of sensitive and creative mind, upon whose quick imagination her greatness had profoundly wrought, until they were able to embody her external manifestations in forms of beauty, dignity and splendour. Thebes was now rapidly becoming a worthy seat of empire, the first monumental city of antiquity. Nor did the western plain on the other side of the river, behind which the conquerors slept, suffer by comparison with the new glories of Karnak and Luxor. Along the foot of the rugged cliffs, from the modest chapel of Amenhotep I on the north, there stretched southward in an imposing line the mortuary temples of the emperors. At the south end of this line, but a little nearer the river, Amenhotep III now erected his own mortuary sanctuary, the largest temple of his reign. Two gigantic colossi of the king, nearly seventy feet high, each cut from one block and weighing over seven hundred tons, besides a pair of obelisks, stood before the pylon, which was approached from the river by an avenue of jackals sculptured in stone. Numerous other great statues of the Pharaoh were ranged about the colonnades of the court. A huge stela[1] of sandstone thirty feet high, inwrought with gold and encrusted with costly stones marked the ceremonial "Station of the King," where Amenhotep stood in performing the official duties of the ritual; another[2] over ten feet high bore a record of all his

---

[1] II, 904 ff.   [2] II, 878 ff.

works for Amon, while the walls and floors of the temple, overlaid with gold and silver, displayed the most prodigal magnificence. The fine taste and the technical skill required for such supplementary works of the craftsman were now developed to a point of classical excellence, beyond which Egyptian art never passed. In mere mass alone some of these works of industrial art were surprising, for the bronze hinges and other mountings of the vast cedar pylon-doors weighed together some tons, and required castings of unprecedented size; while the overlaying of such doors with sheets of bronze exquisitely damascened in precious metal with the figure of the god demanded a combination of æsthetic capacity with mastery of ponderous mechanics, which is not too common even at the present day.

Sculpture also flourished under such circumstances as never before. While there now developed an attention to details which required infinite patience and nicety, such arduous application did not hamper the fine feeling of which these Eighteenth Dynasty sculptors were capable; nor was the old method of a summary rendering of main lines forsaken. There appear in the works of this age (Figs. 136–7, 151) a refinement, a delicacy and a flexibility which were heretofore lacking, even in the best works, though perhaps the striking individuality of the Old Kingdom portraits was not so noticeable. These qualities were carried into work of such ample proportions that the sculptor's command of them under such circumstances is surprising, although not all of the colossal portrait statues are successful in these particulars. Especially in relief were the artists of this age masters. In the accompanying relief (Fig. 132), now in the Berlin Museum, study the abandoned grief of the two sons of the High Priest of Memphis as they follow their father's body to the tomb, and note how effectively the artist has contrasted with them the severe gravity and conventional decorum of the great ministers of state behind them, who themselves are again in striking contrast with a Beau Brummel of that day, who is affectatiously arranging the per-

FIG. 129.—AVENUE OF RAM-SPHINXES BEFORE THE GREAT KARNAK TEMPLE.

Leading from the temple entrance (behind the observer) to the Nile (further end). Photograph loaned by Mr. John Ward.

fumed curls of his elaborate wig. The man of whose work we
have here a mere fragment was a master of ripe and matured
culture, an observer of life, whose work exhibits alike the
pathos and the wistful questioning of human sorrow, recognizing both the necessity and the cruel indifference of official
conventionality, and seeing amid all the play of the vain
and ostentatious fashions of the hour. Here across thirty five
centuries there speaks to us a maturity in the contemplation
of life which finds a sympathetic response in every cultivated
observer. This fragmentary sketch not merely surpasses
anything to be found among any other early oriental people,
but belongs to a class of work totally lacking elsewhere in
this age. It is one of the earliest examples of sculpture
exhibiting that interpretation of life and appreciation of
individual traits (often supposed to have arisen first among
the sculptors of Greece), in which art finds its highest
expression.

Now, too, the Pharaoh's deeds of prowess inspired the
sculptors of the time to more elaborate compositions than
had ever before been approached. The battle scenes on the
noble chariot of Thutmose IV (Fig. 135) exhibit a complexity
in drawing unprecedented, and this tendency continues in
the Nineteenth Dynasty. While brute life does not afford
opportunity for such work as that just discussed, the perfection attained in the sculpture of animal forms by the
artists of this time marks again the highest level of achievement attained by Egyptian art, and Ruskin has even insisted
with his customary conviction that the two lions (Fig. 133)
of Amenhotep's reign, now in the British Museum, are the
finest embodiment of animal majesty which has survived to
us from any ancient people. While this may be an over
enthusiastic estimate of their value, it must not be forgotten
that these noble works were designed as the adornment of a
distant provincial sanctuary at Soleb in upper Nubia.[1] If
such work as this beautified the courts of a remote Nubian
temple, what may we not imagine were the sculptures in the

[1] II, 893, 896-7.

mortuary temple of the Pharaoh himself at Thebes? But this sumptuous building, probably the greatest work of art ever wrought in Egypt, has vanished utterly. Only the two weather-beaten colossi which guarded the entrance still look out across the plain (Fig. 131), one of them still bearing the scribblings in Greek of curious tourists in the times of the Roman Empire who came to hear the marvellous voice which issued from it every morning. A hundred paces behind lies prostrate and shattered in two the vast stela, once encrusted with gold and costly stones, marking the "Station of the King," and upon it one may still read the words of Amenhotep regarding the temple: "My majesty has done these things for millions of years, and I know that they will abide in the earth."[1] We shall later have occasion to observe how this regal temple fell a prey to the impiety of Amenhotep's degenerate descendants within two hundred years of his death. Of the painting of the time, the best examples were in the palaces, and these being of wood and sun-dried brick, have perished, but a fine perception, which enabled the artist in his representation of animals and birds to depict instantaneous postures is already observable, reaching its highest expression in the next reign. More elaborate drawings than any known in earlier times were, as we have seen, demanded by the Pharaoh in the representation of his battles, and the artist's powers of composition were taxed to the utmost. The battle scenes on the temples of this period have perished, but that they existed is certain, in view of such a composition as that on the chariot of Thutmose IV.

Adorned with such works as these, the western plain of Thebes was a majestic prospect as the observer advanced from the river, ascending Amenhotep's avenue of sculptured jackals. On the left, behind the temple and nearer the cliffs, appeared a palace of the king of woodern architecture in bright colours; very light and airy, the façade adorned with flagstaves bearing tufts of parti-coloured pennants, and having over the front entrance a gorgeous cushioned balcony

[1] II, 907.

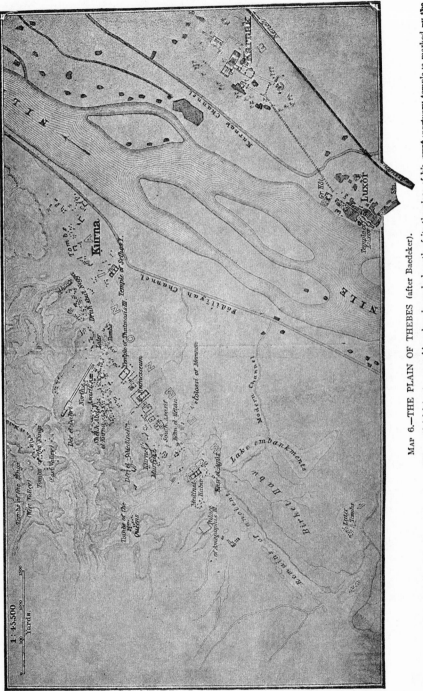

MAP 6.—THE PLAIN OF THEBES (after Baedeker).

The "Birḳet Habu" is the probable site of Amenhotep III's artificial lake (p. 349); his palace is marked north of it; the place of his great mortuary temple is marked by the two "Colossi of Memnon," which stood before it. See Fig. 131.

with graceful columns, in which the king showed himself to
his favourites on occasion (Fig.139). The art which adorned
such a palace was as exquisite in its refined æsthetics as in its
technical skill. Innumerable products of the industrial artist
which fill the museums of Europe indicate with what tem-
pered richness and delicate beauty such a royal chateau was
furnished and adorned. Magnificent vessels in gold and
silver with figures of men and animals, plants and flowers
rising from the rim, glittered on the king's table among
crystal goblets, glass vases, and gray porcelain vessels inlaid
with pale blue designs. The walls were covered with woven
tapestry of workmanship so fine and colour and design so
exquisite that skilled judges have declared it equal to the
best modern work. Besides painted pavements (Fig. 138)
depicting animal life, the walls also were adorned with fine
blue glazed tiles, the rich colour of which shone through elaborate designs in brilliant gold leaf, while glazed figures were
employed in encrusting larger surfaces. All this was done
with fine and intelligent consideration of the whole colour
scheme. In all the refined arts it is an age like that of Louis
XV, and the palace everywhere reflects the spirit of the age.

Here too Amenhotep laid out an exclusive quarter which
he gave to his queen, Tiy. He excavated a large lake in the
enclosure about a mile long and over a thousand feet wide,
and at the celebration of his coronation anniversary in his
twelfth year, he opened the sluices for filling it, and sailed
out upon it in the royal barge with his queen, in doubtless
just such a gorgeous festival "fantasia" as we find in the
"Arabian Nights" in the days of the inevitable Harûn
er-Rashîd. The music on such occasions was more elaborate
than ever before, for the art had make progress since the
days of the old simplicity. The harp was now a huge instru-
ment as tall as a man, and had some twenty strings; the lyre
had been introduced from Asia, and the full orchestra now
contained the harp, the lyre, the lute and the double pipes.
As a souvenir of the celebration another series of scarabs,
or beetle-amulets, was issued, inscribed with a brief narra-

tive of the event.[1]   Such festivals were now common in
Thebes and enriched the life of the fast growing metropolis
with a kaleidoscopic variety which may be only compared
with similar periods in Babylon or in Rome under the emperors.   The religious feasts of the seventh month were
celebrated with such opulent splendour that the month
quickly gained the epithet, "That of Amenhotep," a designation which clung to it until it became the usual name for
it in later ages, and in corrupt form it still survives among
the natives of modern Egypt, who employ it without the
faintest knowledge of the imperial ruler, their ancestor,
whose name is perpetuated in it.   In such an age literature
doubtless throve, but chance has unfortunately preserved to
us little of the literature of the Eighteenth Dynasty.   We
have heard a portion of the triumphant hymn to Thutmose
III and we shall read the remarkable sun-hymn of Ikhnaton;
but of narrative, song and legend, which must have flourished from the rise of the Empire, our surviving documents
date almost exclusively from the Nineteenth Dynasty.

Among the king's favourite diversions was the hunt, which
he practiced on an unprecedented scale.   When his scouts
brought him word that a herd of wild cattle had appeared
among the hills bordering the Delta, he would leave the
palace at Memphis in the evening, sail north all night and
reach the herd in the early morning.   A numerous body of
troops, with children from the villages, then surrounded the
herd and drove them into a large enclosure, a method also
employed in earlier times.   On one occasion his beaters
counted no less than one hundred and seventy wild cattle in
the enclosure.   Entering it in his chariot the king himself slew
fifty six of the savage beasts on the first day, to which number he added probably twenty more at a second onslaught,
which followed after four days' interval of rest.   Amenhotep
thought the achievement worthy of commemoration and
issued a series of scarabs bearing a record of the feat.[2]
When the chase-loving king had completed ten years of lion-

¹ II, 868–9.   ² II, 863–4.

Fig. 130.—COLUMNS OF THE NAVE OF AMENHOTEP III'S UNFINISHED HALL.

The side aisles and smaller columns should have been ranged on either side of this nave. The low wall on either side of the nave was erected by Ikhnaton's successors who were unable to complete the gigantic hall.

hunting he distributed to the nobles of the court a similar memorial of his prowess, which, after the usual royal titulary of himself and his queen, bore the words: "Statement of lions which his majesty brought down with his own arrows from the year one to the year ten: fierce lions, 102."[1] Some thirty or forty of these scarabs of the lion-hunt still survive.

It will be seen that in these things a new and modern tendency was coming to its own. The divine Pharaoh is constantly being exhibited in human relations, the affairs of the royal house are made public property, the name of the queen, not even a woman of royal birth, is constantly appearing at the head of official documents side by side with that of the Pharaoh. In constant intercourse with the nations of Asia he is gradually forced from his old superhuman state, suited only to the Nile, into less provincial and more modern relations with his neighbours of Babylon and Mitanni, who in their letters call him "brother." This lion-hunting, bull-baiting Pharaoh is far indeed from the godlike and unapproachable immobility of his divine ancestors. It was as if the emperor of China or the Dalailama of Thibet were all at once to make his personal doings known on a series of medals! To be sure, Amenhotep compromised with the traditions; he built a temple in Memphis,[2] where he was worshipped and enlarged the Nubian temple at Soleb also for his own worship[3] in conjunction with that of Amon. His queen likewise was goddess of the Nubian temple of Sedeinga. Amenhotep was thus still a god in Nubia, but in fact he had long since broken with this court and priestly fiction. Whether consciously or not he had assumed a modern standpoint, which must inevitably lead to sharp conflict with the almost irresistible inertia of tradition in an oriental country.

Meantime all went well; the lines of the coming internal struggle were not yet clearly drawn, and of the first signs of trouble from without he was unconscious. A veritable "Cæsar divus" he presided over the magnificence of Thebes. In the thirtieth year of his reign he celebrated the jubilee

---

[1] II, 865.   [2] II, p. 354, note a.   [3] II, 893 ff.

of his appointment as crown prince, which had coincided
with his accession. It was on this occasion probably that the
obelisks before the king's mortuary temple were erected.
To render the feast still more auspicious the chief treasurer,
in presenting to the king the enormous harvest returns from
Nubia to Naharin, was able to report a large increase, which
so pleased the king that the local officials of the treasury were
all received in audience and presented with rich rewards.[1]
The second jubilee, probably of the year thirty four, passed
without incident so far as we know; and in the year thirty
six, when the third jubilee was celebrated, the old monarch
was still able to grant the court an audience and receive
their congratulations.[2]

But ominous signs of trouble had meanwhile appeared on
the northern horizon. Mitanni had been invaded by the
Hittites (Kheta), but Dushratta, the Mitannian king, had
been able to repel them and sent to Amenhotep a chariot and
pair, besides two slaves, as a present from the booty which
the Hittites had left in his hands.[3] But the provinces of
Egypt had not been spared. Akizzi, the Pharaoh's vassal
king of Katna, wrote him that the Hittites had invaded his
territory in the Orontes valley, had carried off the image of
Amon-Re, bearing the name of Amenhotep, and had burned
the city as they went.[4] Nukhashshi, which lay still further
north, suffered a similar invasion, and its king, Hadadnirari,
wrote a despairing letter to Amenhotep with assurances of
loyalty and an appeal for support against the invaders.[5] All
this had not been done without the connivance of treacherous
vassals of the Pharaoh, who were themselves attempting the
conquest of territory on their own account. The afterward
notorious Aziru and his father, Abdashirta, were leaders in
the movement, entering Katna and Nukhashshi from the
south and plundering as they went. Others who had made
common cause with them threatened Ubi, the region of
Damascus. Akizzi of Katna and Rib-Addi of Byblos quickly

[1] II, 870–872.   [2] II, 873.   [3] Amarna Letters, 16, 30–37.
[4] Ibid., 138, Reverse, ll. 5, 18–31.   [5] Ibid., 37.

reported the defection of the Pharaoh's vassals; Akizzi wrote appealing for speedy aid: "O my lord, just as Damascus, in the land of Ubi, stretches out her hand to thy feet, so also Katna stretches out her hand to thy feet." The situation was far more critical than it appeared to the Pharaoh, for he had no means of recognizing the seriousness of the Hittite advance, and Akizzi assured him that the kings of Naharin were loyal, saying: "O my lord, even as I love my lord the king, so also do the king of Nukhashshi, the king of Niy, the king of Senzar and the king of Kinanat. For these kings are all servants of my lord the king." Amenhotep, therefore, instead of marching with his entire army immediately into north Syria, as Thutmose III would have done, sent troops only. These of course had no trouble in momentarily quelling the turbulent dynasts and putting a brief stop to their aggressions against the loyal vassals;[1] but they were quite unable to cope with the southern advance of the Hittites, who secured a footing in northern Naharin of the greatest value in their further plans for the conquest of Syria. Furthermore the king's long absence from Syria was telling upon Egyptian prestige there, and another threatening danger to his Asiatic possessions is stated to have begun from the day when the king had last left Sidon. An invasion of the Khabiri, desert Semites, such as had periodically inundated Syria and Palestine from time immemorial, was now taking place. It was of such proportions that it may fairly be called an immigration. Before Amenhotep III's death it had become threatening, and thus Ribaddi of Byblos later wrote to Amenhotep III's son: "Since thy father returned from Sidon, since that time the lands have fallen into the hands of the Khabiri."[2]

Under such ominous conditions as these the old Pharaoh, whom we may well call "Amenhotep the Magnificent," drew near his end. His brother of Mitanni, with whom he was still on terms of intimacy, probably knowing of his age and weakness, sent the image of Ishtar of Nineveh for the second

[1] Ibid., 83, 28–33, 94, 13–18.   [2] Ibid.. 69. 71–73.

23

time to Egypt, doubtless in the hope that the far-famed goddess might be able to exorcise the evil spirits which were causing Amenhotep's infirmity and restore the old king to health.[1] But all such means were of no avail, and about 1375 B. C., after nearly thirty six years upon the throne, "Amenhotep the Magnificent" passed away and was buried with the other emperors, his fathers, in the Valley of the Kings' Tombs.

[1] Ibid., 20.

FIG. 131.—COLOSSAL GRITSTONE STATUES OF AMENHOTEP III (MEMNON COLOSSI).

They stand on the western plain of Thebes and were once flanked by the great mortuary temple of Amenhotep III, which was destroyed by Merneptah. Behind them rise the western cliffs honey-combed with tombs.

CHAPTER XVIII

THE RELIGIOUS REVOLUTION OF IKHNATON

No nation ever stood in direr need of a strong and practical ruler than did Egypt at the death of Amenhotep III.
Yet she chanced to be ruled at this fatal crisis by a young
dreamer, who, in spite of unprecedented greatness in the
world of ideas, was not fitted to cope with a situation demanding an aggressive man of affairs and a skilled military
leader,—in fine such a man as Thutmose III. Amenhotep
IV, the young and inexperienced son of Amenhotep III and
the queen Tiy, was indeed strong and fearless in certain
directions, but he failed utterly to understand the practical
needs of his empire. He had inherited a difficult situation.
The conflict of new forces with tradition, was, as we have
seen, already felt by his father. The task before him was
such manipulation of these conflicting forces as might eventually give reasonable play to the new and modern tendency,
but at the same time to conserve enough of the old to prevent a catastrophe. It was a problem of practical statesmanship, but Amenhotep IV saw it chiefly in its ideal aspects.
His mother, Tiy, and his queen, Nofretete, perhaps a woman
of Asiatic birth, and a favourite priest, Eye, the husband
of his childhood nurse, formed his immediate circle. The
first two probably exercised a powerful influence over him,
and were given a prominent share in the government, at least
as far as its public manifestations were concerned, for in a
manner quite surpassing his father's similar tendency, he
constantly appeared in public with both his mother and his
wife. The lofty and impractical aims which he had in view
must have found a ready response 'n these his two most
influential counsellors. Thus, while Egypt was in sore need

of a vigourous and skilled administrator, the young king was in close counsel with a priest and two perhaps gifted women, who, however able, were not of the fibre to show the new Pharaoh what the empire really demanded. Instead of gathering the army so sadly needed in Naharin, Amenhotep IV immersed himself heart and soul in the thought of the time, and the philosophizing theology of the priests was of more importance to him than all the provinces of Asia. In such contemplations he gradually developed ideals and purposes which make him the most remarkable of all the Pharaohs, and the first *individual* in human history.

The profound influence of Egypt's imperial position had not been limited to the externals of life, to the manners and customs of the people, to the rich and prolific art, pregnant with new possibilities of beauty, but had extended likewise to the thought of the age. Such thought was chiefly theological and we must divest it of all the ideas which are connoted by the modern term "the thought of the age." Even before the conquests in Asia the priests had made great progress in the interpretation of the gods, and they had now reached a stage in which, like the later Greeks, they were importing semi-philosophical significance into the myths, such as these had of course not originally possessed. The interpretation of a god was naturally suggested by his place or function in the myth. Thus Ptah, the artificer-god of Memphis, furnished the priesthood there with a fruitful line of thought, moving in concrete channels, and thus guiding the thinker, in an age of intellectual beginnings, thinking in a language without terminology for such processes, even when they had once been followed out. Ptah had been from the remotest ages the god of the architect and craftsman, to whom he communicated plans and designs for architectural works and the products of the industrial arts. Contemplating this god, the Memphite priest, little used as his mind was to abstractions, found a tangible channel, moving along which he gradually gained a rational and with certain limitations a philosophical conception of the world. The workshop of the Memphite temple, where, under Ptah's guidance, were wrought the splendid statues, utensils and offerings for the temple, expands into a world, and Ptah, its lord, grows into the master-workman of the universal workshop. As he furnishes all designs to the architect and craftsman, so now he does the same for all men in all that they do; he becomes the supreme mind; he is mind and all things proceed from him. The world and all that is in it existed as thought in his mind; and his thoughts, like his plans for buildings and works of art, needed but to be expressed in spoken words to take concrete form as material realities. Gods and men alike proceeded from mind, and all that they do is but the mind of the god working in them. A priest of Ptah has expressed this in a short poem, a part of which vaguely and indefinitely shows how the minds of the time were explaining the world:

Ptah, the great, is the mind and tongue of the gods. . . .
Ptah, from whom proceeded the power
Of the mind,
And of the tongue.
That which comes forth from every mind,
And from every mouth:
Of all gods, of all people, of all cattle, of all reptiles,
That live, thinking and commanding
Everything that he (Ptah) wills.
.   .   .   .
It (the mind) is the one that bringeth forth every successful issue.
It is the tongue which repeats the thought of the mind:
It (the mind) was the fashioner of all gods. . . .
At a time when every divine word
Came into existence by the thought of the mind,
And the command of the tongue.[1]

Wherever we have used the word "mind" in this passage the Egyptian has "heart," which word served him for "mind" in exactly the same way as the Hebrews and many other peoples frequently employ it; much in the same man-

[1] See the author's account of this remarkable document, Zeitschrift für Aegyptische Sprache, XXXIX, 39 ff.

ner indeed as we ourselves often use it, with the difference that the Egyptian believed the heart and the bowels actually to be the seat of mind. Although such notions could have been entertained by very limited circles, they were not confined to the priests alone. Intef, the court herald of Thutmose III, states on his tombstone that he owed his success to the guidance of his "heart," to which he listened implicitly; and he adds that the people said: "Lo, it is an oracle of the god, which is in every body."[1] "Body" is here, as commonly, the word for abdomen or bowels, the seat of mind. The Egyptian had thus gained the idea of a single controlling intelligence, behind and above all sentient beings, including the gods. The efficient force by which this intelligence put his designs into execution was his spoken "word," and this primitive "logos" is undoubtedly the incipient germ of the later logos-doctrine which found its origin in Egypt. Early Greek philosophy may also have drawn upon it.

Similar ideas were now being propagated regarding all the greater gods of Egypt, but as long as the kingdom was confined to the Nile valley the activity of such a god was limited, in their thinking, to the confines of the Pharaoh's domain, and the world of which they thought meant no more. From of old the Pharaoh was the heir of the gods and ruled the two kingdoms of the upper and lower river which they had once ruled. Thus they had not in the myths extended their dominion beyond the river valley, and that valley originally extended only from the sea to the first cataract. But under the Empire all this is changed, the god goes where the Pharaoh's sword carries him; the advance of the Pharaoh's boundary-tablets in Nubia and Syria is the extension of the god's domain. The king is now called "The one who brings the world to him [the god], who placed him [the Pharaoh] on his throne."[2] For king and priest alike the world is only a great domain of the god. All the Pharaoh's wars are recorded upon the temple walls, and even in their mechanical arrangement his wars converge upon the temple door.[3] The

[1] II, 770. [2] II, 959, l. 3; 1000. [3] III, 80.

Fig. 132.—PART OF A FUNERAL PROCESSION OF A HIGH PRIEST OF MEMPHIS.

Eighteenth dynasty reliefs from his Memphite tomb. Below is a fragment of the group immediately behind the coffin (extreme right); above, the servants build funeral booths. See pp. 346-47. (Berlin Museum.)

theological theory of the state is simply that the king receives
the world that he may deliver it to the god, and he prays for
extended conquests that the dominion of the god may be
correspondingly extended.   Thus theological thinking is
brought into close and sensitive relationship with political
conditions; and theological theory must inevitably extend
the active government of the god to the limits of the domain
whence the king receives tribute.   It can be no accident that
the notion of a practically universal god arose in Egypt at the
moment when he was receiving universal tribute from the
world of that day.   Again the analogy of the Pharaoh's
power unquestionably operated powerfully with the Egyptian theologian at this time; for in the myth-making days the
gods were conceived as Pharaohs ruling the Nile valley,
because the myth-makers lived under Pharaohs who so ruled.
Living now under Pharaohs who ruled a world-empire, the
priest of the imperial age had before him in tangible form
a world-dominion and a world-concept, the prerequisite of
the notion of the world-god.   Conquered and organized and
governed, it had now been before him for two hundred years,
and out of the Pharaoh-ruled world he gradually began to
see the world-god.

We have thus far given this god no name.   Had you asked
the Memphite priests they would have said his name was
Ptah, the old god of Memphis; the priests of Amon at Thebes
would have claimed the honour for Amon, the state god, as
a matter of course, while the High Priest of Re at Heliopolis
would have pointed out the fact that the Pharaoh was the
son of Re and the heir to his kingdom, and hence Re must
be the supreme god of all the empire.   Obscure gods in the
local sanctuaries would have found similar champions in
their priesthoods because they were now identified with Re
and claimed his prerogatives.   But historically Re's claim
was undoubtedly the best.   Amon had never succeeded in
displacing him.   The introduction of official letters still, as
of old, commends the addressé to the favour of Re-Harakhte,
while in the popular tales of the time it is Re-Harakhte who

rules the world.   But none of the old divinities of Egypt
had been proclaimed the god of the empire, although in fact
the priesthood of Heliopolis had gained the coveted honour
for their revered sun-god, Re.   Already under Amenhotep
III an old name for the material sun, "Aton," had come into
prominent use, where the name of the sun-god might have
been expected.   Thus he called the royal barge on which
he sailed with Tiy on her beautiful lake, "Aton Gleams."[1]
A company of his body-guard bore the new god's name, and
there was probably a chapel dedicated to him at Heliopolis.
The sun-god, too, was now and again designated as "the sole
god" by Amenhotep III's contemporaries.

The already existent conflict with traditional tendencies
into which the Pharaoh had been forced, contained in itself
difficulties enough to tax the resources of any statesman
without the introduction of a departure involving the most
dangerous conflicts with the powerful priesthoods and touch-
ing religious tradition, the strongest conservative force of the
time.   It was just this rash step which the young king now
had no hesitation in taking.   Under the name of Aton, then,
Amenhotep IV introduced the worship of the supreme god,
but he made no attempt to conceal the identity of his new
deity with the old sun-god, Re.   Instructing his vizier in
the new faith, he said to him, "The words of Re are before
thee . . . my august father who taught me their essence.
. . . It was known in my heart, revealed to my face, I understood . . . "[2]   He thus attributes the new faith to Re as
its source, and claims to have been himself the channel of its
revelation. He immediately assumed the office of High Priest
of his new god with the same title, "Great Seer," as that of
the High Priest of Re at Heliopolis.[3]   But, however evident
the Heliopolitan origin of the new state religion might be,
it was not merely sun-worship; the word Aton was employed
in place of the old word for "god" (nuter),[4] and the god is
clearly distinguished from the material sun.   To the old sun-
god's name is appended the explanatory phrase " under his

[1] II, 869.   [2] II, 945.   [3] II, 934, l. 2.   [4] II, p. 407, note e.

name: 'Heat which is in the Sun [Aton],' " and he is likewise called "lord of the sun [Aton]." The king, therefore,
was deifying the vital heat which he found accompanying all
life. It plays in the new faith a similar important part,
which we find it assuming in the early cosmogonic philoso-
phies of the Greeks. Thence, as we might expect, the god
is stated to be everywhere active by means of his "rays,"
and his symbol is a disk in the heavens, darting earthward
numerous diverging rays which terminate in hands, each
grasping the symbol of life. In his age of the world it is
perfectly certain that the king could not have had the vaguest
notion of the physico-chemical aspects of his assumption
any more than had the early Greeks in dealing with a similar
thought; yet the fundamental idea is surprisingly true, and,
as we shall see, marvellously fruitful. The outward symbol
of his god thus broke sharply with tradition, but it was
capable of practical introduction in the many different
nations making up the empire and could be understood at a
glance by any intelligent foreigner, which was far from
the case with any of the traditional symbols of Egyptian
religion (Figs. 139–40).

The new god could not dispense with a temple like those
of the older deities whom he was ultimately to supersede.
Early in his reign Amenhotep IV sent an expedition to the
sandstone quarries of Silsileh to secure the necessary stone
and the chief nobles of his court were in charge of the works
at the quarry.[1] In the garden of Amon, which his father
had laid out between the temples of Karnak and Luxor,
Amenhotep located his new temple, which was a large and
stately building, adorned with polychrome reliefs. Thebes
was now called "City of the Brightness of Aton," and the
temple-quarter "Brightness of Aton the Great"; while the
sanctuary itself bore the name "Gem-Aton," a term of uncertain meaning.[2] Although the other gods were still tolerated
as of old,[3] it was nevertheless inevitable that the priesthood
of Amon should view with growing jealousy the brilliant rise

---

[1] II, 935.   [2] II, p. 388, note b.   [3] II, 937.

of a strange god in their midst, an artificial creation of which they knew nothing, save that much of the wealth formerly employed in the enrichment of Amon's sanctuary was now lavished on the intruder. One of Amenhotep III's High Priests of Amon had also been chief treasurer of the kingdom, and another, Ptahmose, was the grand vizier of the realm; while the same thing had occurred in the reign of Hatshepsut, when Hapuseneb had been both vizier and High Priest of Amon. Besides these powers, the High Priest of Amon was also the supreme head of the organization including all the priests of the nation. Indeed, the fact that such extensive political power was now wielded by the High Priests of Amon must have intensified the young king's desire to be freed from the sacerdotal thrall which he had inherited. His father had evidently made some attempt to shake off the priestly hand that lay so heavily on the sceptre, for he had succeeded Ptahmose by a vizier who was not High Priest of Amon. This new vizier, Ramose, was won by the young king's gifts,[1] and a servile court followed him, even superintending the quarry work for the new temple, as we have seen. The priesthood of Amon, however, was now a rich and powerful body. They had installed Thutmose III as king, and could they have supplanted with one of their own tools the young dreamer who now held the throne they would of course have done so at the first opportunity. But Amenhotep IV was the son of a line of rulers too strong and too illustrious to be thus set aside even by the most powerful priesthood in the land; moreover, he possessed unlimited personal force of character, and he was of course supported in his opposition of Amon by the older priesthoods of the north at Memphis and Heliopolis, long jealous of this interloper, the obscure Theban god, who had never been heard of in the north before the rise of the Middle Kingdom. A conflict to the bitter end, with the most disastrous results to the Amonite priesthood ensued. It rendered Thebes intolerable to the young king, and soon after he had finished

[1] II, 944–947.

FIG. 135.—FRONT OF THE STATE CHARIOT OF THUTMOSE IV.

Stucco surface carved with battle scenes in relief. From Mr. Theo. M. Davis's excavations at Thebes. (Cairo Museum.)

FIG. 133.—LION FROM AMENHOTEP III'S TEMPLE AT SOLEB.

Later removed by the Nubians to Napata. (British Museum.)

FIG. 134.—A STOOL OF THE EMPIRE.

Ebony inlaid with ivory. (British Museum.)

his new temple he resolved upon radical measures. He would break with the priesthoods and make Aton the sole god, not merely in his own thought, but in very fact; and Amon should fare no better than the rest of the time-honoured gods of his fathers. It was no "Götterdämmerung" which the king contemplated, but an immediate annihilation of the gods. As far as their external and material manifestations and equipment were concerned, this could be and was accomplished without delay. The priesthoods, including that of Amon, were dispossessed, the official temple-worship of the various gods throughout the land ceased, and their names were erased wherever they could be found upon the monuments. The persecution of Amon was especially severe. The cemetery of Thebes was visited and in the tombs of the ancestors the hated name of Amon was hammered out wherever it appeared upon the stone. The rows on rows of statues of the great nobles of the old and glorious days of the Empire, ranged along the walls of the Karnak temple, were not spared, but the god's name was invariably erased. Even the royal statues of his ancestors, including the king's father, were not respected; and, what was worse, as the name of that father, Amenhotep, contained the name of Amon, the young king was placed in the unpleasant predicament of being obliged to cut out his own father's name in order to prevent the name of Amon from appearing "writ large" on all the temples of Thebes. The splendid stela[1] erected by his father in his mortuary temple, recording all his great buildings for Amon, was mercilessly hacked and rendered illegible. Even the word "gods" was not permitted to appear on any of the old monuments and the walls of the temples at Thebes were painfully searched that wherever the compromising word appeared it might be blotted out.[2] And then there was the embarrassment of the king's own name, likewise Amenhotep, "Amon rests," which could not be spoken or placed on a monument. It was of necessity

[1] II, 878 ff.

[2] See Zeitschrift für Aegyptische Sprache, 40, 109–110 and II, p. 386, note b.

also banished and the king assumed in its place the name "Ikhnaton," which means "Spirit of Aton."

Thebes was now compromised by too many old associations to be a congenial place of residence for so radical a revolutionist. As he looked across the city he saw stretching along the western plain that imposing line of mortuary temples of his fathers which he had violated. They now stood silent and empty. The towering pylons and obelisks of Karnak and Luxor were not a welcome reminder of all that his fathers had contributed to the glory of Amon, and the unfinished hall of his father at Luxor, with the superb columns of the nave, still waiting for the roof, could hardly have stirred pleasant memories in the heart of the young reformer. A doubtless long contemplated plan was therefore undertaken. Aton, the god of the empire, should possess his own city in each of the three great divisions of the empire: Egypt, Asia and Nubia, and the god's Egyptian city should be made the royal residence. It must have been an enterprise requiring some time, but the three cities were duly founded. The Aton-city of Nubia was situated opposite modern Dulgo, at the foot of the Third Cataract, and was thus in the heart of the Egyptian province.[1] It was named "Gem-Aton" after the Aton-temple in Thebes. In Syria the Aton-city is unknown, but Ikhnaton will not have done less for Aton there than his fathers had done for Amon. In the sixth year, shortly after he had changed his name, the king was living in his own Aton-city in Egypt. He chose as its site a fine bay in the cliffs about one hundred and sixty miles above the Delta and nearly three hundred miles below Thebes. The cliffs, leaving the river in a semi-circle, retreat at this point some three miles from the stream and return to it again about five miles lower down. In the wide plain thus bounded on three sides by the cliffs and on the west by the river Ikhnaton founded his new residence and the holy city of Aton. He called it Akhetaton, "Hori-

---

[1] II, p. 388, note b; see also my "Monuments of Sudanese Nubia," Chicago, 1908, pp. 51–82.

zon of Aton,'' and it is known in modern times as Tell el-Amarna. In addition to the town, the territory around it was demarked as a domain belonging to the god, and included the plain on both sides of the river. In the cliffs on either side, fourteen large stelas (Fig. 140), one of them no less than twenty six feet in height, were cut into the rock, bearing inscriptions determining the limits of the entire sacred district around the city.[1] As thus laid out the district was about eight miles wide from north to south, and from twelve to over seventeen miles long from cliff to cliff. The king's oath regarding it is recorded on the extreme northern and southern stelas thus: ''His majesty raised his hand to heaven, to him who made him, even to Aton, saying, 'This is my testimony forever, and this is my witness forever, this landmark [stela]. . . . I have made Akhetaton for my father as a dwelling. . . . I have demarked Akhetaton on its south, on its north, on its west, on its east. I shall not pass beyond the southern landmark of Akhetaton toward the south, nor shall I pass beyond the northern landmark of Akhetaton toward the north. . . . He has made his circuit for his own, he has made his altar in its midst, whereon I make offering to him.' ''[2] Whether this statement that he would never pass beyond the boundary of the district, a vow which is found referring to all four cardinal points, is merely a legal phrase by which a property owner recognized that he had no rights beyond his just limit, the boundary of his property; or whether the king actually carried out this vow literally and remained the rest of his life in Akhetaton we cannot say. But the phrase is not found in any other boundary landmarks known to us. The region thus demarked was then legally conveyed to Aton by the king's own decree, saying: ''Now as for the area within the . . . landmarks from the eastern mountain [cliffs] to the western mountain of Akhetaton opposite, it belongs to my father, Aton, who is given life forever and ever: whether mountains or cliffs, or swamps . . . or uplands, or fields, or waters, or towns, or shores, or

---

[1] II, 949–972.   [2] II, 954.

people, or cattle, or trees, or anything which Aton, my father has made. . . . I have made it for Aton, my father, forever and ever."[1] And on another stela he says that they are to belong to the temple of Aton in Akhetaton forever and ever as offerings.[2] Besides this sacred domain the god was endowed with revenues from other lands in Egypt and Nubia,[3] and probably also in Syria. The city thus established was to be the real capital of the empire, for the king himself said: "The whole land shall come hither, for the beautiful seat of Akhetaton shall be another seat [capital], and I will give them audience whether they be north or south or west or east."[4] The royal architect, Bek, was sent to the first cataract to procure stone for the new temple,[5] or we should rather say temples, for no less than three were now built in the new city,[6] one for the queen mother, Tiy, and another for the princess Beketaton ("Maid-servant of Aton"), beside the state temple of the king himself.[7] Around the temples rose the palace of the king and the chateaus of his nobles, one of whom describes the city thus: "Akhetaton, great in loveliness, mistress of pleasant ceremonies, rich in possessions, the offerings of Re in her midst. At the sight of her beauty there is rejoicing. She is lovely and beautiful; when one sees her it is like a glimpse of heaven. Her number cannot be calculated. When the Aton rises in her he fills her with his rays and he embraces [with his rays] his beloved son, son of eternity, who came forth from Aton and offers the earth to him who placed him on his throne, causing the earth to belong to him who made him."[8]

On the day when the temple was ready to receive the first dues from its revenues the king proceeded thither in his chariot accompanied by his four daughters and a gorgeous retinue. They were received at the temple with shouts of "Welcome"; a rich oblation filled the high altar in the temple court, while the store-chambers around it were groaning with the wealth of the newly paid revenues.[9] The king

[1] II, 966.   [2] II, 972.   [3] II, 957.
[4] II. 955.   [5] II, 973 ff.   [6] II, 1016-18.
[7] Ibid.   [8] II. 1000.   [9] II. 982.

FIG. 136.—ROYAL PORTRAIT
OF THE EMPIRE. (Cairo
Museum.)

FIG. 137.—PORTRAIT OF AMENHOTEP, SON
OF HAPI. See p. 341. (Cairo Museum.)

FIG. 138.—DUCKS SWIMMING AMONG LOTUS FLOWERS.

Fragment of painting from the floor of Amenhotep III's palace in western Thebes. See pp. 348-49. (From
Tytus, *Preliminary Report.*)

himself participated in such ceremonies,[1] while the queen "sends the Aton to rest with a sweet voice, her two beautiful hands bearing the two sistrums."[2] But Ikhnaton no longer attempted to act as High Priest himself; one of his favourites, Merire ("Beloved of Re") was appointed by him to the office, coming one day for this purpose with his friends to the balcony of the palace, in which the king and queen appeared in state. The king then formally promoted Merire to the exalted office, saying: "Behold, I am appointing thee for myself to be 'Great Seer' [High Priest] of the Aton in the temple of Aton in Akhetaton. . . . I give to thee the office saying, 'Thou shalt eat the food of Pharaoh, thy lord, in the house of Aton.' "[3] Merire was so faithful in the administration of the temple that the king publicly rewarded him with "the gold," the customary distinction granted to zealous servitors of the Pharaoh. At the door of one of the temple buildings the king, queen and two daughters extend to the fortunate Merire the rewards of fidelity, and the king says to the attendants: "Hang gold at his neck before and behind, and gold on his legs; because of his hearing the teaching of Pharaoh concerning every saying in these beautiful seats which Pharaoh has made in the sanctuary in the Aton-temple in Akhetaton."[4] It thus appears that Merire had given heed to the king's teachings regarding the ritual of the temple, or, as he says, "every saying in these beautiful seats."

It becomes more and more evident that all that was devised and done in the new city and in the propagation of the Aton faith is directly due to the king and bears the stamp of his individuality. A king who did not hesitate to erase his own father's name on the monuments in order to annihilate Amon, the great foe of his revolutionary movement, was not one to stop half way, and the men about him must have been involuntarily carried on at his imperious will. But Ikhnaton understood enough of the old policy of the Pharaohs to know that he must hold his party by practical rewards, and

[1] 994, ll. 17-18.   [2] II, 995, ll. 21 f.   [3] II, 985.   [4] II, 987.

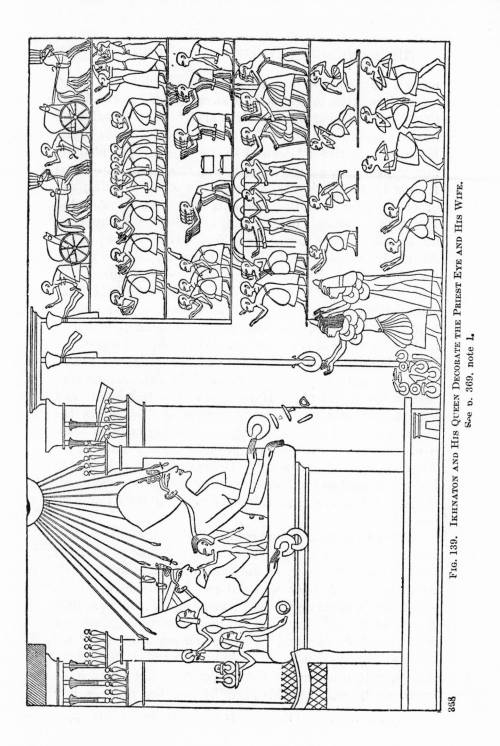

FIG. 139. IKHNATON AND HIS QUEEN DECORATE THE PRIEST EYE AND HIS WIFE.

See p. 369, note 1.

the leading partisans of his movement like Merire enjoyed
liberal bounty at his hands (Fig. 139).[1] Thus one of his
priests of Aton, and at the same time his master of the royal
horse, named Eye, who had by good fortune happened to
marry the nurse of the king, renders this very evident in
such statements as the following: "He doubles to me my
favours in silver and gold," or again, addressing the king,
"How prosperous is he who hears thy teaching of life! He
is satisfied with seeing thee without ceasing."[2]   The general
of the army, Mai, enjoyed similar bounty, boasting of it in
the same way: "He hath doubled to me my favours like
the numbers of the sand. I am the head of the officials, at
the head of the people; my lord has advanced me because
I have carried out his teaching, and I hear his word without
ceasing. My eyes behold thy beauty every day, O my lord,
wise like Aton, satisfied with truth. How prosperous is he
who hears thy teaching of life!"[3] Although there must have
been a nucleus of men who really appreciated the ideal
aspects of the king's teaching, it is thus evident that many
were chiefly influenced by "the loaves and the fishes."

Indeed there was one royal favour which must have been
welcome to them all without exception. This was the beautiful cliff-tomb which the king commanded his craftsmen to
hew out of the eastern cliffs for each one of his favourites.
For the old mortuary practices were not all suppressed by
Ikhnaton, and it was still necessary for a man to be buried
in the "eternal house," with its endowment for the support of the deceased in the hereafter.[4] But that eternal
house was no longer disfigured with hideous demons and
grotesque monsters which should confront the dead in the
future life; and the magic paraphernalia necessary to meet

[1] Description of Fig. 139: Leaning upon the cushioned balustrade of the
palace balcony with his queen and his infant daughters by his side, the king
throws down golden collars, vessels, rings and ornaments to his favourites.
The queen likewise throws two collars. The servants and suite of Eye dance
with joy or bow ceremoniously. Above (that is behind) are the waiting
chariots of Eye and his wife, while next to (below) these his scribes make
record of the event, carefully listing all the gifts.

[2] II, 994, ll. 16–17.　　　[3] II, 1002–3.　　　[4] II, 996.

24

and vanquish the dark powers of the nether world, which
filled the tombs of the old order at Thebes, were completely
banished. In thus suppressing these base and repulsive
devices, which the perverted imagination of a stupid priesthood had imposed upon an implicit people, the king's reform
was most salutary. The tomb now became a monument to
the deceased; the walls of its chapel bore fresh and natural
pictures from the life of the people in Akhetaton, particularly the incidents in the official career of the dead man, and
preferably his intercourse with the king. Thus the city of
Akhetaton is now better known to us from its cemetery than
from its ruins. Throughout these tombs the nobles take
delight in reiterating, both in relief and inscription, the intimate relation between Aton and the king. Over and over
again they show the king and the queen together standing
under the disk of Aton, whose rays, terminating in hands,
descend and embrace the king.[1] The vulture-goddess, Mut,
who, since the hoary age of the Thinites had appeared on
all the monuments extending her protecting wings over the
Pharaoh's head, had long since been banished. The nobles
constantly pray to the god for the king, saying that he
"came forth from thy rays,"[2] or "thou hast formed him
out of thine own rays";[3] and interspersed through their
prayers are numerous current phrases of the Aton faith,
which have now become conventional, replacing those of the
old orthodox religion, which it must have been very awkward
for them to cease using. Thus they demonstrated how
zealous they had been in accepting and appropriating the
king's new teaching. On state occasions, instead of the old
stock phrases, with innumerable references to the traditional
gods, every noble who would enjoy the king's favour was
evidently obliged to show his familiarity with the Aton faith
and the king's position in it by a liberal use of these allu-
sions. Even the Syrian vassals were wise enough to make
their dispatches pleasant reading by glossing them with
appropriate recognition of the supremacy of the sun-god.[4]

[1] II, 1012 and infra, Fig. 139, p. 368.   [2] II, 1000, l. 5; 991, l. 3.
[3] II, 1010, l. 3.   [4] Amarna Letters, 149, 6 ff., and often.

Fig. 140.—GREAT BOUNDARY STELA OF AMARNA.

The relief above shows Ikhnaton on each side, accompanied by his queen and daughters, worshiping the sun-disk, whose rays, terminating in hands, embrace them, and offer them the symbol of life.

Fig. 141.—IKHNATON RECEIVING FLOWERS FROM HIS QUEEN.

Brightly-colored relief in limestone. The conventional postures are abandoned, and the king leans lazily on his staff. (Berlin Museum.)

The source of such phrases was really the king himself, as we have before intimated, and something of the "teaching" whence they were taken, so often attributed to him, is preserved in the tombs[1] to which we have referred.

Either for the temple service or for personal devotions the king composed two hymns to Aton, both of which the nobles had engraved on the walls of their tomb chapels. Of all the monuments left by this unparalleled revolution, these hymns are by far the most remarkable; and from them we may gather an intimation of the doctrines which the speculative young Pharaoh had sacrificed so much to disseminate. They are regularly entitled: "Praise of Aton by king Ikhnaton and queen Nefernefruaton"; and the longer and finer of the two is worthy of being known in modern literature. The titles of the separate strophes are the addition of the present author, and in the translation no attempt has been made to do more than to furnish an accurate rendering. The one hundred and fourth Psalm of the Hebrews shows a notable similarity to our hymn both in the thought and the sequence, so that it seemed desirable to place the most noticeably parallel passages side by side.

THE SPLENDOUR OF ATON.

Thy dawning is beautiful in the horizon of heaven,
O living Aton, Beginning of life!
When thou risest in the eastern horizon of heaven,
Thou fillest every land with thy beauty;
For thou are beautiful, great, glittering, high over the earth;
Thy rays, they encompass the lands, even all thou hast made.
Thou art Re, and thou hast carried them all away captive;
Thou bindest them by thy love.
Though thou art afar, thy rays are on earth;
Though thou art on high, thy footprints are the day.

NIGHT.

When thou settest in the western horizon of heaven,
The world is in darkness like the dead.

Thou makest darkness and it is night,
Wherein all the beasts of the forest do creep forth.

[1] II, 977–1018.

They sleep in their chambers,
Their heads are wrapt up,
Their nostrils stopped, and none
  seeth the other.
Stolen are all their things, that
  are under their heads,
While they know it not.
Every lion cometh forth from his
  den,
All serpents, they sting.
Darkness reigns (?),
The world is in silence,
He that made them has gone to
  rest in his horizon.

The young lions roar after their
  prey;
They seek their meat from God.
     (Psalm 104, 20–21.)

Day and Man.

Bright is the earth,
When thou risest in the horizon,
When thou shinest as Aton by
  day.
The darkness is banished,
When thou sendest forth thy
  rays,
The Two Lands [Egypt] are in
  daily festivity,
Awake and standing upon their
  feet,
For thou hast raised them up.
Their limbs bathed, they take
  their clothing;
Their arms uplifted in adoration
  to thy dawning.
Then in all the world, they do
  their work.

The sun ariseth, they get them
  away,
And lay them down in their
  dens.
Man goeth forth unto his work,
And to his labour until the evening.
     (Psalm 104, 22–23.)

Day and the Animals and Plants.

All cattle rest upon their herbage,
All trees and plants flourish,
The birds flutter in their marshes,
Their wings uplifted in adoration to thee.
All the sheep dance upon their feet,

All winged things fly,
They live when thou hast shone upon them.

DAY AND THE WATERS.

The barques sail up-stream and down-stream alike.
Every highway is open because thou hast dawned.
The fish in the river leap up before thee,
And thy rays are in the midst of the great sea.

Yonder is the sea, great and wide,
Wherein are things creeping innumerable
Both small and great beasts.
There go the ships;
There is leviathan, whom thou hast formed to sport with him.
(Psalm 104, 25–26.)

CREATION OF MAN.

Thou art he who createst the man-child in woman,
Who makest seed in man,
Who giveth life to the son in the body of his mother,
Who soothest him that he may not weep,
A nurse [even] in the womb.
Who giveth breath to animate every one that he maketh.
When he cometh forth from the body,
. . . on the day of his birth,
Thou openest his mouth in speech,
Thou suppliest his necessities.

CREATION OF ANIMALS.

When the chicklet crieth in the egg-shell,
Thou givest him breath therein, to preserve him alive.
When thou hast perfected him
That he may pierce the egg,
He cometh forth from the egg,
To chirp with all his might;
He runneth about upon his two feet,
When he hath come forth therefrom.

THE WHOLE CREATION.

How manifold are all thy works!
They are hidden from before us,

O lord, how manifold are thy works!

O thou sole god, whose powers no other possesseth.[1]
Thou didst create the earth according to thy desire.
While thou wast alone:
Men, all cattle large and small,
All that are upon the earth,
That go about upon their feet;
All that are on high,
That fly with their wings.
The countries of Syria and Nubia,
The land of Egypt;
Thou settest every man in his place,
Thou suppliest their necessities.
Every one has his possessions,
And his days are reckoned.
Their tongues are divers in speech,
Their forms likewise and their skins,
For thou divider, hast divided the peoples.

In wisdom hast thou made them all;
The earth is full of thy creatures.

(Psalm 104. 24.)

WATERING THE EARTH.

Thou makest the Nile in the Nether World,
Thou bringest it at thy desire, to preserve the people alive.
O lord of them all, when feebleness is in them,
O lord of every house, who risest for them,
O sun of day, the fear of every distant land,
Thou makest [also] their life.
Thou hast set a Nile in heaven,
That it may fall for them,
Making floods upon the mountains, like the great sea;
And watering their fields among their towns.

How excellent are thy designs, O lord of eternity!
The Nile in heaven is for the strangers,

[1] The other hymns frequently say, "O thou sole god, beside whom there is no other."

And for the cattle of every land, that go upon their feet;
But the Nile, it cometh from the nether world for Egypt.

Thus thy rays nourish every garden,
When thou risest they live, and grow by thee.

THE SEASONS.

Thou makest the seasons, in order to create all thy works:
Winter bringing them coolness,
And the heat [of summer likewise].
Thou hast made the distant heaven to rise therein,
In order to behold all that thou didst make,
While thou wast alone,
Rising in thy form as living Aton,
Dawning, shining afar off and returning.

BEAUTY DUE TO LIGHT.

Thou makest the beauty of form, through thyself alone.
Cities, towns and settlements,
On highway or on river,
All eyes see thee before them,
For thou art Aton of the day over the earth.

REVELATION TO THE KING.

Thou art in my heart,
There is no other that knoweth thee,
Save thy son Ikhnaton.
Thou hast made him wise in thy designs
And in thy might.
The world is in thy hand,
Even as thou hast made them.
When thou hast risen, they live;
When thou settest, they die.
For thou art duration, beyond thy mere limbs,
By thee man liveth,
And their eyes look upon thy beauty,
Until thou settest.
All labour is laid aside,
When thou settest in the west;

When thou risest, they are made to grow
. . . . . . for the king.
Since thou didst establish the earth,
Thou hast raised them up for thy son,
Who came forth from thy limbs,
The king, living in truth,
The lord of the Two Lands Nefer-khepru-Re, Wan-Re,
The son of Re, living in truth, lord of diadems,
Ikhnaton, whose life is long;
[And for] the great royal wife, his beloved,
Mistress of the Two Lands, Nefer nefru aton, Nofretete,
Living and flourishing for ever and ever.

In this hymn the universalism of the empire finds full expression and the royal singer sweeps his eye from the far-off cataracts of the Nubian Nile to the remotest lands of Syria. These are not thoughts which we have been accustomed to attribute to the men of some fourteen hundred years before Christ. A new spirit has breathed upon the dry bones of traditionalism in Egypt, and he who reads these lines for the first time must be moved with involuntary admiration for the young king who in such an age found such thoughts in his heart. He grasped the idea of a world-dominator, as the creator of nature, in which the king saw revealed the creator's beneficent purpose for all his creatures, even the meanest; for the birds fluttering about in the lily-grown Nile-marshes to him seemed to be uplifting their wings in adoration of their creator; and even the fish in the stream leaped up in praise to God. It is his voice that summons the blossoms and nourishes the chicklet or commands the mighty deluge of the Nile. He called Aton, "the father and the mother of all that he had made," and he saw in some degree the goodness of that All-Father as did he who bade us consider the lilies. He based the universal sway of God upon his fatherly care of all men alike, irrespective of race or nationality, and to the proud and exclusive Egyptian he pointed to the all-embracing bounty of the common father of humanity, even placing Syria and Nubia

FIG. 142.—LIMESTONE TORSO OF IKH-
NATON'S DAUGHTER.

See p. 378.

FIG. 143.—HEAD OF IKHNATON.

Remarkable Limestone Bust recently acquired
by the Louvre.

FIG. 144.—MARSH LIFE.

Fragment of painted pavement from the palace of Ikhnaton at Amarna.
See p. 378. (From Petrie, *Amarna*.)

before Egypt in his enumeration. It is this aspect of Ikhnaton's mind which is especially remarkable; he is the first prophet of history. While to the traditional Pharaoh the state god was only the triumphant conqueror, who crushed all peoples and drove them tribute-laden before the Pharaoh's chariot, Ikhnaton saw in him the beneficent father of all men. It is the first time in history that a discerning eye has caught this great universal truth. Again his whole movement was but a return to nature, resulting from a spontaneous recognition of the goodness and the beauty evident in it, mingled also with a consciousness of the mystery in it all, which adds just the fitting element of mysticism in such a faith.

> How manifold are all thy works!
> They are hidden from before us,
> O thou sole god, whose powers no other possesseth.

While Ikhnaton thus recognized clearly the power, and to a surprising extent, the beneficence of God, there is not here a very spiritual conception of the deity nor any attribution to him of ethical qualities beyond those which Amon had long been supposed to possess. The king has not perceptibly risen from the beneficence to the righteousness in the character of God, nor to his demand for this in the character of men. Nevertheless, there is in his "teaching," as it is fragmentarily preserved in the hymns and tomb-inscriptions of his nobles, a constant emphasis upon "truth" such as is not found before nor since. The king always attaches to his name the phrase "living in truth," and that this phrase was not meaningless is evident in his daily life. To him it meant an acceptance of the daily facts of living in a simple and unconventional manner. For him what was was right and its propriety was evident by its very existence. Thus his family life was open and unconcealed before the people. He took the greatest delight in his children and appeared with them and the queen, their mother, on all possible occasions, as if he had been but the humblest scribe in the Aton-temple. He had himself depicted on the monuments while enjoying the most familiar and unaffected

intercourse with his family, and whenever he appeared in
the temple to offer sacrifice the queen and the daughters
she had borne him participated in the service. All that was
natural was to him true, and he never failed practically to
exemplify this belief, however radically he was obliged to
disregard tradition.

Such a principle unavoidably affected the art of the time
in which the king took great interest. Bek, his chief sculptor, appended to his title the words, "whom his majesty
himself taught." [1] Thus the artists of his court were taught
to make the chisel and the brush tell the story of what they
actually saw. The result was a simple and beautiful realism that saw more clearly than ever any art had seen before
(Figs. 119, 147–8). They caught the instantaneous postures
of animal life; the coursing hound, the fleeing game, the
wild bull leaping in the swamp (Fig. 144); for all these
belonged to the "truth," in which Ikhnaton lived. The
king's person was no exception to the law of the new art.
The monuments of Egypt bore what they had never borne
before, a Pharaoh not frozen in the conventional posture
demanded by the traditions of court propriety (Figs. 141,
143). The modelling of the human figure at this time was
so plastic that at the first glance one is sometimes in doubt
whether he has before him a product of the Greek age (Fig.
142). Even complex compositions of grouped figures in
the round were now first conceived. Fragments recently
discovered show that in the palace court at Akhetaton, a
group in stone depicted the king speeding his chariot at
the heels of the wounded lion. This was indeed a new
chapter in the history of art, even though now lost. It was
in some things an obscure chapter; for the strange treatment of the lower limbs by Ikhnaton's artists is a problem
which still remains unsolved and cannot be wholly accounted for by supposing a mal-formation of the king's
own limbs. It is one of those unhealthy symptoms which
are visible too in the body politic, and to these last we
must now turn if we would learn how fatal to the material
interests of the state this violent break with tradition
has been.

[1] II. 975.

CHAPTER XIX

THE FALL OF IKHNATON, AND THE DISSOLUTION OF THE EMPIRE

WHOLLY absorbed in the exalted religion to which he had given his life, stemming the tide of tradition that was daily as strong against him as at first, Ikhnaton was beset with too many enterprises and responsibilities of a totally different nature, to give much attention to the affairs of the empire abroad. Indeed, as we shall see, he probably did not realize the necessity of doing so until it was far too late. On his accession his sovereignty in Asia had immediately been recognized by the Hittites and the powers of the Euphrates valley. Dushratta of Mitanni wrote to the queen-mother, Tiy, requesting her influence with the new king for a continuance of the old friendship which he had enjoyed with Ikhnaton's father,[1] and to the young king he wrote a letter of condolence on his father, Amenhotep III's death, not forgetting to add the usual requests for plentiful gold.[2] Burraburyash of Babylon sent similar assurances of sympathy, but only the pass-port of his messenger, calling on the kings of Canaan to grant him speedy passage, has survived.[3] A son of Burraburyash later sojourned at Ikhnaton's court and married a daughter of the latter,[4] and her Babylonian father-in-law sent her a noble necklace of over a thousand gems. But such intercourse did not last long, as we shall see.

Meantime the power of the Hittites in northern Syria was constantly on the increase, as they were reinforced by the southern movement of their countrymen behind them. This remarkable race, who still form one of the greatest problems in the study of the early orient, were now emerging

[1] Amarna Letters, 22. [2] Ibid., 21. [3] Ibid., 14. [4] Ibid., 8, 41.

from the obscurity which had hitherto enveloped them. Their remains have been found from the western coast of Asia Minor eastward to the plains of Syria and the Euphrates, and southward as far as Hamath. They were a non-Semitic people, or rather peoples, of uncertain racial affinities, but evidently distinct from, and preceding, the Indo-Germanic influx after 1200 B. C. which brought in the Phrygians (see p. 478). As shown on the Egyptian monuments, they are beardless, with long hair hanging in two prominent locks before their ears and dropping to the shoulders; but their own native monuments often give them a heavy beard (Fig. 146). On the head they most often wore tall pointed caps like a sugar-loaf hat, but with little brim. As their climate demands, they wear heavy woollen clothing, usually in a long, close-fitting garment, depending from the shoulders and reaching to the knees or sometimes the ankles; while the feet are shod in high boots turned up at the toes. They possessed a crude, but by no means primitive, art which produced very creditable monuments in stone (Figs. 145–6) still scattered over the hills of Asia Minor. Their skill in the practical arts was considerable, and they produced a red figured pottery above mentioned which was disseminated in trade from the centre of its manufacture in Cappadocia to the Ægean on the west, and eastward through Syria and Palestine to Lachish and Gezer on the south. Already by 2000 B. C. we remember it had perhaps reached the latter place. They were masters of the art of writing, and the king had his personal scribe ever with him.[1] Their pictographic records are still in course of decipherment, and enough progress has not yet been made to enable the scholar to do more than recognize a word here and there. For correspondence they employed the Babylonian cuneiform and must therefore have maintained scribes and interpreters who were masters of Babylonian speech and writing. Large quantities of cuneiform tablets in the Hittite tongue have been found at Boghaz-köi (see below). In war they

[1] III, 337.

were formidable opponents. The infantry, among which foreign mercenaries were plentiful, bore bow and arrows, sword and spear and often an axe. They fought in close phalanx formation, very effective at close quarters; but their chief power consisted of chariotry. The chariot itself was more heavily built than in Egypt, as it bore three men, driver, bowman and shield-bearer, while the Egyptian dis- dispensed with the third man. One of the Hittite dynasts had consolidated a kingdom beyond the Amanus, which Thutmose III regularly called "Great Kheta," as prob- ably distinguished from the less important independent Hittite princes. His capital was a great fortified city called "Khatti" (identified in 1907), situated at modern Boghaz-köi, east of Angora and the Halys (Kisil-irmak) river in eastern Asia Minor. Active trade and inter- course between this kingdom and Egypt had been car- ried on from that time or began not long after.[1] This reached such proportions that the king of Cyprus was apprehensive lest too close relations between Egypt and the Hittite kingdom ("Great Kheta") might endanger his own position.[2] When Ikhnaton ascended the throne Seplel, the king of the Hittites, wrote him a letter of congratulation, and to all appearances had only the friendliest intentions toward Egypt.[3] For the first invasions of the most advanced Hittites, like that which Dushratta of Mitanni repulsed, he may indeed not have been responsible. Even after Ikhnaton's removal to Akhetaton, his new capital, a Hittite embassy appeared there with gifts and greetings.[4] But Ikhnaton must have regarded the old relations as no longer desirable, for the Hittite king asks him why he has ceased the correspondence[5] which his father had maintained. If he realized the situation, Ikhnaton had good reason indeed for abandoning the connection; for the Hittite empire now stood on the northern threshold of Syria, the most for- midable enemy which had ever confronted Egypt, and the greatest power in Asia. It is doubtful whether Ikhnaton

[1] Amarna Letters, 35.   [2] Ibid., 25, 49 f.
[3] Ibid., 35.   [4] II. 981.   [5] Amarna Letters, 35, 14 f.

could have withstood the masses of Asia Minor which were now shifting southward into Syria even if he had made a serious effort to do so; but no such effort was made. Immediately on his accession the disaffected dynasts who had been temporarily suppressed by his father resumed their operations against the faithful vassals of Egypt. One of the latter, in a later letter to Ikhnaton, exactly depicts the situation, saying: "Verily, thy father did not march forth, nor inspect the lands of the vassal-princes. . . . And when thou ascendedst the throne of thy father's house, Abd-ashirta's sons took the king's land for themselves. Creatures of the king of Mitanni are they, and of the king of Babylon, and of the king of the Hittites."[1] With the coöperation of the unfaithful Egyptian vassals Abd-ashirta and his son Aziru, who were at the head of an Amorite kingdom on the upper Orontes; together with Itakama, a Syrian prince, who had seized Kadesh as his kingdom, the Hittites took possession of Amki, the plain on the north side of the lower Orontes, between Antioch and the Amanus.[2] Three faithful vassal-kings of the vicinity marched to recover the Pharaoh's lost territory for him, but were met by Itakama at the head of Hittite troops and driven back. All three wrote immediately to the Pharaoh of the trouble and complained of Itakama.[3] Aziru of Amor had meantime advanced upon the Phœnician and north Syrian coast cities, which he captured as far as Ugarit at the mouth of the Orontes,[4] slaying their kings and appropriating their wealth.[5] Simyra and Byblos held out, however, and as the Hittites advanced into Nukhashshi, on the lower Orontes, Aziru coöperated with them and captured Niy, whose king he slew.[6] Tunip was now in such grave danger that her elders wrote the Pharaoh a pathetic letter beseeching his protection. "To the king of Egypt, my lord:—The inhabitants of Tunip thy servant. May it be well with thee, and at the feet of our lord we fall. My lord, Tunip, thy servant

[1] Ibid., 88. [2] Ibid., 119, 125. [3] Ibid., 131–133.
[4] Ibid., 123. [5] Ibid, 86; 119. [6] Ibid., 120.

Fig. 145. — HITTITE SOLDIER
ARMED WITH AN AXE.

Relief from Senjirli, North Syria.
(Berlin Museum.)

Fig. 146.—HITTITE KING BEARING SPEAR AND
SCEPTER.

Relief from Senjirli, North Syria. (Berlin Museum.)

Fig. 147.—EGYPTIAN OFFICIAL RECEIVING SEMITIC IMMIGRANTS.

See p. 388. Relief from the tomb of Harmhab, p. 408. (Leyden Museum.)

speaks, saying: 'Who formerly could have plundered Tunip without being plundered by Manakhbiria [Thutmose III]? The gods . . . of the king of Egypt, my lord, dwell in Tunip. May our lord ask his old men [if it be not so]. Now, however, we belong no more to our lord, the king of Egypt. . . . If his soldiers and chariots come too late, Aziru will make us like the city of Niy. If, however, we have to mourn, the king of Egypt will mourn over those things which Aziru has done, for he will turn his hand against our lord. And when Aziru enters Simyra, Aziru will do to us as he pleases, in the territory of our lord, the king, and on account of these things our lord will have to lament. And now, Tunip, thy city weeps, and her tears are flowing, and there is no help for us. For twenty years we have been sending to our lord, the king, the king of Egypt, but there has not come to us a word, no not one.' "[1] The fears of Tunip were soon realized, for Aziru now concentrated upon Simyra and quickly brought it to a state of extremity.

During all this, Rib-Addi, a faithful vassal of Byblos, where there was an Egyptian temple,[2] writes to the Pharoah in the most urgent appeals, stating what is going on, and asking for help to drive away Aziru's people from Simyra, knowing full well that if it falls his own city of Byblos is likewise doomed. But no help comes and the Syrian dynasts grow bolder. Zimrida of Sidon falls away and makes terms with Aziru,[3] and, desiring a share of the spoils for himself, moves against Tyre, whose king, Abi-milki, immediately writes to Egypt for aid.[4] The number of troops asked for by these vassals is absurdly small, and had it not been for the Hittite host, which was pressing south behind them, their operations might have caused Egypt very little anxiety. Aziru now captured the outer defences of Simyra and Rib-Addi continued to plead for assistance for his sister-city,[5] adding that he himself had suffered from the hostility of Amor for five years, beginning, as we have seen, under Amenhotep III. Several Egyptian deputies had been charged

[1] Ibid., 41. [2] See above, p. 323. [3] Ibid., 150. [4] Ibid., 151. [5] Ibid., 85.

MAP No. 7. THE ASIATIC EMPIRE OF EGYPT.

with the investigation of affairs at Simyra, but they did not succeed in doing anything, and the city finally fell. Aziru had no hesitation in slaying the Egyptian deputy resident in the place,[1] and having destroyed it, was now free to move against Byblos. Rib-Addi wrote in horror of these facts to the Pharaoh, stating that the Egyptian deputy, resident in Kumidi in northern Palestine, was now in danger.[2] But the wily Aziru so uses his friends at court that he escapes. He wrote to Tutu, one of Ikhnaton's court officials, who interceded for him,[3] and he speciously excuses himself to Khai, the Egyptian deputy in his vicinity.[4] With Machiavellian skill and cynicism he explains in letters to the Pharaoh that he is unable to come and give an account of himself at the Egyptian court, as he had been commanded to do, because the Hittites are in Nukhashshi, and he fears that Tunip will not be strong enough to resist them![5] What Tunip herself thought about his presence in Nukhashshi we have already seen. To the Pharaoh's demand that he immediately rebuild Simyra, which he had destroyed (as he claimed, to prevent it from falling into the hands of the Hittites), he replies that he is too hard pressed in defending the king's cities in Nukhashshi against the Hittites; but that he will do so within a year.[6] Ikhnaton is reassured by Aziru's promises to pay the same tribute as the cities which he has taken formerly paid.[7] Such acknowledgment of Egyptian suzerainty by the turbulent dynasts everywhere must have left in the Pharaoh a feeling of security which the situation by no means really justified. He therefore wrote Aziru granting him the year which he had asked for before he appeared at court, but Aziru contrived to evade Khani, the Egyptian bearer of the king's letter, which was thus brought back to Egypt without being delivered.[8] It shows the astonishing leniency of Ikhnaton in a manner which would indicate that he was opposed to measures of force, such as his fathers had employed. Aziru immediately wrote

[1] Ibid., 119; 120.   [2] Ibid., 94.   [3] Ibid., 44–5.   [4] Ibid., 46.
[5] Ibid., 45; 47.   [6] Ibid., 46. 26–34.   [7] Ibid. 49, 36–40.   [8] Ibid., 50.

to the king expressing his regret that an expedition against the Hittites in the north had deprived him of the pleasure of meeting the Pharaoh's envoy, in spite of the fact that he had made all haste homeward as soon as he had heard of his coming! The usual excuse for not rebuilding Simyra is offered.[1]

During all this time Rib-Addi is in sore straits in Byblos, and sends dispatch after dispatch to the Egyptian court, appealing for aid against Aziru. The claims of the hostile dynasts, however, are so skilfully made that the resident Egyptian deputies actually do not seem to know who are the faithful vassals and who the secretly rebellious. Thus Bikhuru, the Egyptian deputy in Galilee, not understanding the situation in Byblos, sent his Beduin mercenaries thither, where they slew all of Rib-Addi's Sherden garrison. The unhappy Rib-Addi was now at the mercy of his foes and he sent off two dispatches beseeching the Pharaoh to take notice of his pitiful plight;[2] while, to make matters worse, the city raised an insurrection against him[3] because of the wanton act of the Egyptian resident. He has now sustained the siege for three years, he is old and burdened with disease;[4] fleeing to Berût to secure help from the Egyptian deputy there, he returns to Byblos to find the city closed against him, his brother having seized the government in his absence and delivered his children to Aziru.[5] As Berût itself is soon attacked and falls, he forsakes it, again returns to Byblos and in some way regains control and holds the place for a while longer.[6] Although Aziru, his enemy, was obliged to appear at court and finally did so, no relief came for the despairing Rib-Addi. All the cities of the coast were held by his enemies and their ships commanded the sea, so that provisions and reinforcements could not reach him.[7] His wife and family urge him to abandon Egypt and join Aziru's party, but still he is faithful to the Pharaoh and asks for three hundred men to undertake the recovery of Berût, and thus gain a little room.[8] The Hittites are plundering

[1] Ibid., 51. [2] Ibid., 77; 100. [3] Ibid., 100. [4] Ibid., 71, 23.
[5] Ibid., 96. [6] Ibid., 65; 67. [7] Ibid., 104. [8] Ibid., 68.

FIG. 148.—HARMHAB AS AN OFFICIAL REWARDED WITH GOLD BY THE KING.

Relief from his tomb. The king is out of range on the right. Harmhab's servants hang golden collars about his neck, brought out by other menials on his left. From the left, led by Egyptian guards, approach Asiatic prisoners, whose presentation to the king by Harmhab is evidently the occasion of the honors he is receiving. See p. 399. Continued at the left in Fig. 119. (Leyden Museum.)

his territory and the Khabiri, or Beduin mercenaries of his enemy Aziru, swarm under his walls;[1] his dispatches to the court soon cease, his city of course fell, he was probably slain like the kings of the other coast cities, and in him the last vassal of Egypt in the north had perished.

Similar conditions prevailed in the south, where the advance of the Khabiri, the Aramæan Semites, may be compared with that of the Hittites in the north. Knots of their warriors are now appearing everywhere and taking service as mercenary troops under the dynasts. As we have seen, Aziru employed them against Rib-Addi at Byblos, but the other side, that is, the faithful vassals, engaged them also, so that the traitor, Itakama, wrote to the Pharaoh and accused his vassals of giving over the territory of Kadesh and Damascus to the Khabiri.[2] Under various adventurers the Khabiri are frequently the real masters, and Palestinian cities like Megiddo, Askalon and Gezer write to the Pharaoh for succour against them. The last named city, together with Askalon and Lachish, united against Abdkhiba, the Egyptian deputy in Jerusalem, already at this time an important stronghold of southern Palestine, and the faithful officer sends urgent dispatches to Ikhnaton explaining the danger and appealing for aid against the Khabiri and their leaders.[3] Under his very gates, at Ajalon, the caravans of the king were plundered.[4] "The king's whole land," wrote he, "which has begun hostilities with me, will be lost. Behold the territory of Shiri [Seir] as far as Ginti-Kirmil [Carmel],—its princes are wholly lost, and hostility prevails against me. . . . As long as ships were upon the sea, the strong arm of the king occupied Naharin and Kash, but now the Khabiri are occupying the king's cities. There remains not one prince to my lord, the king, every one is ruined. . . . Let the king take care of his land and . . . let him send troops. . . . For if no troops come in this year, the whole territory of my lord the king will perish. . . . If there are no troops in this year, let the king send his officer to fetch

[1] Ibid., 102; 104.　　[2] Ibid., 146.　　[3] Ibid., 179–185.　　[4] Ibid., 180, 55 f.

me and my brothers, that we may die with our lord, the king.''[1]　Abdkhiba was well acquainted with Ikhnaton's cuneiform scribe, and he adds to several of his dispatches a postscript addressed to his friend in which the urgent sincerity of the man is evident: "To the scribe of my lord, the king, Abdkhiba thy servant. Bring these words plainly before my lord the king: 'The whole land of my lord, the king, is going to ruin.' ''[2]　Fleeing in terror before the Khabiri, who burned the towns and laid waste the fields, many of the Palestinians forsook their towns and took to the hills, or sought refuge in Egypt, where the Egyptian officer in charge of some of them said of them: ''They have been destroyed and their town laid waste, and fire has been thrown [into their grain?]. . . . Their countries are starving, they live like goats of the mountain. . . . A few of the Asiatics, who knew not how they should live, have come [begging a home in the domain?] of Pharaoh, after the manner of your father's fathers since the beginning. . . . Now the Pharaoh gives them into your hand to protect their borders''[3] (Fig. 147). The task of those to whom the last words are addressed was hopeless indeed, for the general, Bikhuru, whom Ikhnaton sent to restore order and suppress the Khabiri was entirely unable to accomplish anything. As we have seen, he misunderstood the situation totally in Rib-Addi's case, and dispatched his Beduin auxiliaries against him. He advanced as far north as Kumidi, north of Galilee, but retreated as Rib-Addi had foreseen he would;[4] he was for a time in Jerusalem, but fell back to Gaza;[5] and in all probability was finally slain.[6] Both in Syria and Palestine the provinces of the Pharaoh had gradually passed entirely out of Egyptian control, and in the south a state of complete anarchy had resulted, in which the hopeless Egyptian party at last gave up any attempt to maintain the authority of the Pharaoh, and those who had not perished joined the enemy. The caravans of

---

[1] Amarna Letters, 181.　　　[2] Ibid., 179.　　　[3] III, 11.
[4] Amarna Letters, 94.　　　[5] Ibid., 182.　　　[6] Ibid., 97.

Burraburyash of Babylonia were plundered by the king of
Akko and a neighbouring confederate, and Burraburyash
wrote peremptorily demanding that the loss be made good
and the guilty punished, lest his trade with Egypt become a
constant prey of such marauding dynasts.[1] But what he
feared had come to pass, and the Egyptian Empire in Asia
was for the time at an end.

Ikhnaton's faithful vassals had showered dispatches upon
him, had sent special ambassadors, sons and brothers to represent to him the seriousness of the situation; but they had
either received no replies at all, or an Egyptian commander
with an entirely inadequate force was dispatched to make
futile and desultory attempts to deal with a situation which
demanded the Pharaoh himself and the whole available army
of Egypt. At Akhetaton, the new and beautiful capital, the
splendid temple of Aton resounded with hymns to the new
god of the Empire, while the Empire itself was no more.
The tribute of Ikhnaton's twelfth year was received at Akhetaton as usual, and the king, borne in his sedan-chair on the
shoulders of eighteen soldiers, went forth to receive it in
gorgeous state.[2] The habit of generations and a fast vanishing apprehension lest the Pharaoh might appear in Syria
with his army, still prompted a few sporadic letters from the
dynasts, assuring him of their loyalty, which perhaps continued in the mind of Ikhnaton the illusion that he was still
lord of Asia.

The storm which had broken over his Asiatic empire was
not more disastrous than that which threatened the fortunes
of his house in Egypt. But he was as steadfast as before
in the propagation of his new faith. At his command temples of Aton had now arisen all over the land. Besides the
Aton-sanctuary which he had at first built at Thebes, three
at least in Akhetaton and Gem-Aton in Nubia, he built others
at Heliopolis, Memphis, Hermopolis, Hermonthis and in the
Fayum.[3] He devoted himself to the elaboration of the

[1] Amarna Letters, 11. [2] II, 1014–15.
[3] II, 1017–18; see my remarks *Zeitschrift für Aegyptische Sprache*, 40, 110–
113.

temple ritual and the tendency to theologize somewhat dimmed the earlier freshness of the hymns to the god. His name was now changed and the qualifying phrase at the end of it was altered from "Heat which is in Aton" to "Fire which comes from Aton." Meantime the national convulsion which his revolution had precipitated was producing the most disastrous consequences throughout the land. The Aton-faith disregarded some of the most cherished beliefs of the people, especially those regarding the hereafter. Osiris, their old time protector and friend in the world of darkness, was taken from them and the magical paraphernalia which were to protect them from a thousand foes were gone. Some of them tried to put Aton into their old usages, but he was not a folk-god, who lived out in yonder tree or spring, and he was too far from their homely round of daily needs to touch their lives. The people could understand nothing of the refinements involved in the new faith. They only knew that the worship of the old gods had been interdicted and a strange deity of whom they had no knowledge and could gain none was forced upon them. Such a decree of the state could have had no more effect upon their practical worship in the end than did that of Theodosius when he banished the old gods of Egypt in favour of Christianity eighteen hundred years after Ikhnaton's revolution. For centuries after the death of Theodosius the old so-called pagan gods continued to be worshipped by the people in Upper Egypt; for in the course of such attempted changes in the customs and traditional faith of a whole people, the span of one man's life is insignificant indeed. The Aton-faith remained but the cherished theory of the idealist, Ikhnaton, and a little circle which formed his court; it never really became the religion of the people.

Added to the secret resentment and opposition of the people, we must consider also a far more dangerous force, the hatred of the old priesthoods, particularly that of Amon. At Thebes there were eight great temples of this god standing idle and forsaken; his vast fortune, embracing towns in

FIG. 149.—SOUTHERN PYLONS OF HARMHAB AT KARNAK.

Looking southwestward across the temple lake.

FIG. 150.—HARMHAB AS A PEASANT
IN THE HEREAFTER.

Relief from his tomb, showing later insertion
of the royal serpent on his forehead.
(Bologna Museum.)

FIG. 151.—BUST OF KHONSU.

End of the Eighteenth or early in the Nineteenth
Dynasty. (Cairo Museum.)

Syria and extensive lands in Egypt, had evidently been confiscated and probably diverted to Aton. There could not
but be, and, as the result shows, there was, during all of
Ikhnaton's reign a powerful priestly party which openly
or secretly did all in its power to undermine him. The
neglect and loss of the Asiatic empire must have turned
against the king many a strong man, and aroused indigna-
tion among those whose grandfathers had served under
Thutmose III. The memory of what had been done in those
glorious days must have been sufficiently strong to fire the
hearts of the military class and set them looking for a leader
who would recover what had been lost. Ikhnaton might
appoint one of his favourites to the command of the army,
as we have seen he did, but his ideal aims and his high
motives for peace would be as unpopular as they were unintelligible to his commanders. One such man, an officer
named Harmhab,[1] was now in the service of Ikhnaton and
enjoying the royal favour; he contrived not only to win the
support of the military class, but, as we shall later see,
he also gained the favour of the priests of Amon, who were
of course looking for some one who could bring them the
opportunity they coveted. At every point Ikhnaton had
offended against the cherished traditions of a whole people.
Thus both the people and the priestly and military classes
alike were fomenting plans to overthrow the hated dreamer
in the palace of the Pharaohs, of whose thoughts they understood so little. To increase his danger, fortune had decreed
him no son, and he was obliged to depend for support as
the years passed upon his son-in-law, a noble named Sakere,
who had married his eldest daughter, Meritaton, "Beloved
of Aton." Ikhnaton had probably never been physically
strong; his spare face, with the lines of an ascetic, shows
increasing traces of the cares which weighed so heavily upon
him. He finally nominated Sakere as his successor and
appointed him at the same time coregent. He survived but
a short time after this, and about 1358 B. C., having reigned

[1] III, 22 ff.

some seventeen years, he succumbed to the overwhelming forces that were against him. In a lonely valley some miles to the east of his city he was buried in a tomb which he had excavated in the rock for himself and family, and where his second daughter, Meketaton, already rested.

Thus disappeared the most remarkable figure in earlier oriental history. To his own nation he was afterward known as "the criminal of Akhetaton";[1] but for us, however much we may censure him for the loss of the empire, which he allowed to slip from his fingers; however much we may condemn the fanaticism with which he pursued his aim, even to the violation of his own father's name and monuments; there died with him such a spirit as the world had never seen before,—a brave soul, undauntedly facing the momentum of immemorial tradition, and thereby stepping out from the long line of conventional and colourless Pharaohs, that he might disseminate ideas far beyond and above the capacity of his age to understand. Among the Hebrews, seven or eight hundred years later, we look for such men; but the modern world has yet adequately to value or even acquaint itself with this man, who in an age so remote and under conditions so adverse, became the world's first idealist and the world's first *individual*.

Sakere was quite unequal to the task before him, and after an obscure and ephemeral reign at Akhetaton he disappeared, to be followed by Tutenkhaton ("Living image of Aton"), another son-in-law of Ikhnaton, who had married the king's third daughter, Enkhosnepaaton ("She lives by the Aton"). The priestly party of Amon was now constantly growing, and although Tutenkhaton still continued to reside at Akhetaton, it was not long before he was forced to a compromise in order to maintain himself. He forsook his father-in-law's city and transferred the court to Thebes, which had not seen a Pharaoh for twenty years. Akhetaton maintained a precarious existence for a time, supported by the manufactories of coloured glass and fayence, which had

[1] Inscription of Mes.

flourished there during the reign of Ikhnaton. These industries soon languished, the place was gradually forsaken,
until not a soul was left in its solitary streets. The roofs
of the houses fell in, the walls tottered and collapsed, the
temples fell a prey to the vengeance of the Theban party,
as we shall see, and the once beautiful city of Aton was
gradually transformed into a desolate ruin. To-day it is
known as Tell el-Amarna, and it still stands as its enemies,
time and the priests of Amon, left it. One may walk its
ancient streets, where the walls of the houses are still several feet high, and strive to recall to its forsaken dwellings
the life of the Aton-worshippers who once inhabited them.
Here in a low brick room, which had served as an archive-
chamber for Ikhnaton's foreign office, were found in 1885
some three hundred letters and dispatches in which we have
traced his intercourse and dealings with the kings and rulers
of Asia and the gradual disintegration of his empire there.
Here were the more than sixty dispatches of the unfortunate
Rib-Addi of Byblos. After the modern name of the place,
the whole correspondence is generally called the Tell
el-Amarna letters. All the other Aton-cities likewise perished utterly; but Gem-Aton in distant Nubia escaped.
Long afterward its Aton temple became a temple of "Amon,
Lord of Gem-Aton," and thus in far-off Nubia the ruins
of the earliest temple of monotheism still stand.[1]

On reaching Thebes, Tutenkhaton continued the worship
of Aton and made some enlargement or at least repairs of
the Aton-temple there; but he was obliged by the priests
of Amon to permit the resumption of Amon-worship. Indeed he was constrained to restore the old festal calendar
of Karnak and Luxor; he himself conducted the first "feast
of Opet," the greatest of all the festivals of Amon, and
restored the temples there.[2] Expediency also obliged him
to begin restoring the disfigured name of Amon, expunged
from the monuments by Ikhnaton, and his restorations are
found as far south as Soleb in Nubia.[3] He was then forced

[1] See reference, p. 364, note 1.
[2] Luxor reliefs, ibid., 34, 135.   [3] II, 896.

to another serious concession to the priests of Amon; he changed his name to Tutenkhamon. "Living image of Amon," showing that he was now completely in the hands of the priestly party.[1]

The empire which he ruled was still no mean one, extending as it did from the Delta of the Nile to the fourth cataract. The Nubian province under the viceroy was now thoroughly Egyptianized, and the native chiefs wore Egyptian clothing, assumed since Thutmose III's time.[2] The revolution in Egypt had not affected Nubia seriously, and it continued to pay its annual dues into the Pharaoh's treasury.[3] He also received tribute from the north which, as his viceroy of Kush, Huy claimed,[4] came from Syria. Although this is probably in some degree an exaggeration in view of our information from the Amarna letters; yet one of Ikhnaton's successors fought a battle in Asia, and this can hardly have been any other than Tutenkhaton.[5] He may thus have recovered sufficient power in Palestine to collect some tribute or at least some spoil, which fact may then have been interpreted to include Syria also. Tutenkhaton soon disappeared and was succeeded by another of the worthies of the Akhetaton court, Eye, who had married Ikhnaton's nurse, Tiy, and had excavated for himself a tomb at Akhetaton, from which came the great Aton-hymn which we have already read. He was sufficiently imbued with Ikhnaton's ideas to hold his own for a short time against the priests of Amon; and he built to some extent on the Aton-temple at Thebes. He abandoned his tomb at Akhetaton and excavated another in the Valley of the Kings' Tombs at Thebes. He soon had need of it, for ere long he too passed away and it would appear that one or two other ephemeral pretenders gained the ascendancy either now or before his accession. Anarchy ensued. Thebes was a prey of plundering bands, who forced their way into the royal tombs and as we now know robbed the tomb of Thutmose IV.[6] The prestige of the old Theban family which had been

[1] II, 1019.   [2] II, 1035.   [3] II, 1034 ff.
[4] II, 1027 ff.   [5] III, 20, ll. 2, 5 and 8.   [6] III, 32 A ff.

dominant for two hundred and fifty years; the family which two hundred and thirty years before had cast out the Hyksos and built the greatest empire the east had ever seen, was now totally eclipsed. The illustrious name which it had won was no longer a sufficient influence to enable its decadent descendants to hold the throne, and the Eighteenth Dynasty had thus slowly declined to its end about 1350 B. C. Manetho places Harmhab, the restorer, who now gained the throne, at the close of the Eighteenth Dynasty; but in so far as we know he was not of royal blood nor any kin of the now fallen house. He marks the restoration of Amon, the resumption of the old order and the beginning of a new epoch.

FIG. 152.—BATTLE RELIEFS OF SETI I AT KARNAK.

Below, on the left, Seti slays a Libyan chief; on the right, a battle with the Libyans. Above, the storming of Kadesh in Galilee (see p. 412). Behind the chariot, below, is a later insertion of the crown prince's figure, like that depicted in Fig. 157. p. 410.

BOOK VI

THE EMPIRE: SECOND PERIOD

CHAPTER XX

THE TRIUMPH OF AMON AND THE REORGANIZATION OF THE EMPIRE

WE have already noticed that in the service of Ikhnaton there had been an able organizer and skilful man of affairs quite after the manner of Thutmose III. Harmhab, as he was called, belonged to an old family once nomarchs of Alabastronpolis;[1] he had been entrusted with important missions and rewarded with the gold of distinguished service[2] (Fig. 148). He had in charge the fugitive Asiatics who fled from Palestine into Egypt before the Khabiri,[3] and he dispatched some of the officials who went out at that time to restore order there. Under Ikhnaton or his successors he had been sent on a commission to the south in connection with the tribute,[4] and in this as in all his other duties he showed himself a man of resourcefulness and ability. He had served with distinction on a campaign with one of Ikhnaton's successors in Asia, probably Tutenkhaton;[5] and during the precarious times incident to the rapid succession of weak kings following Ikhnaton's death he had skilfully maintained himself and gradually gained a position of power and influence. Finally becoming commander-in-chief of the army and chief councillor in the palace, he called himself "greatest of the great, mightiest of the mighty, great lord of the people, king's-messenger at the head of his army to the South and the North; chosen of the king, presider over the Two Lands, in order to carry on the administration of the Two Lands; general of generals of the Lord of the Two Lands."[6] Such titles no officer under the king had ever borne. Under what ruler he thus served is not certain,

[1] III, 27. [2] III, 5–9. [3] III, 10–12.
[4] III, 13. [5] III, 20. [6] Ibid.

but whoever he was such power in the hands of a subject
must necessarily have endangered his throne.   Harmhab
was now the real power of the throne; for the king "appointed him to be chief of the land, to administer the laws
of the Two Lands as hereditary prince of all this land. He
was alone without a rival. . . . The council bowed down
to him in obeisance at the front of the palace, the chiefs of
the Nine Bows [foreign peoples] came to him, South as
well as North; their hands were spread out in his presence,
they offered praise to him as to a god. All that was done was
done under his command. . . . When he came the fear of
him was great in the sight of the people; 'prosperity and
health' [the royal greeting] were craved for him; he was
greeted as 'Father of the Two Lands.' " [1]   This continued
for some years,[2] until 1350 B. C., when he was in effect king,
and the next step was but to receive the titles and insignia
of royalty.   He had the army behind him and he had won
the support of the priesthood of Amon at Thebes; it was
only necessary to proceed thither to be recognized as the
ruling Pharaoh; or as the piously veiled language of his
own record states it: "Now when many days had passed
by, while the eldest son of Horus [Harmhab] was chief
and hereditary prince in this whole land, behold the heart of
this august god, Horus, lord of Alabastronpolis, desired to
establish his son upon his eternal throne. . . . Horus proceeded with rejoicing to Thebes . . . and with his son in
his embrace, to Karnak, to introduce him before Amon, to
assign to him his office of king." [3]   He arrived just as the
Theban priests were celebrating the great feast of Opet, at
which the image of Amon at Karnak was carried to Luxor;[4]
and here Harmhab now appeared. As the priests of Amon
had once recognized Thutmose III as king, so now the
oracle of the god was not wanting in confirming their
choice. But the new Pharaoh must possess some legal
claim to the crown and this too was forthcoming; for after
the oracle of Amon had declared him the son of Re and

  [1] III, 25-26.   [2] III, 26, l. 9.   [3] III, 27.   [4] Ibid.

heir to the kingdom, Harmhab proceeded to the palace and
was joined in marriage to the princess Mutnezmet, the sister
of Ikhnaton's queen, Nefer nefru aton. Although she was
advanced in years, she was "Divine Consort," or high
priestess of Amon and a princess of the royal line, and that
was sufficient to make Harmhab's accession quite legal.[1]
The palace where this ceremony took place was in Luxor,
and as the image of Amon was carried back to Karnak the
priests bore it to the palace where Harmhab's accession
was again recognized by the god.[2] His royal titulary was
now published[3] and the new reign began.

The energy which had brought Harmhab his exalted office
was immediately evident in his administration of it. He was
untiring in restoring to the land the orderly organization
which it had once enjoyed. After remaining at least two
months at Thebes adjusting his affairs there and further
conciliating the priestly party by his attendance at the religious feasts,[4] he sailed for the north to continue this work.
"His majesty sailed down stream. . . . He organized this
land, he adjusted it according to the time of Re"[5] [as when
the sun-god was Pharaoh]. At the same time he did not
forget the temples, which had been closed so long under the
Aton regime. "He restored the temples from the pools of
the Delta marshes to Nubia. He shaped all their images in
number more than before, increasing the beauty in that
which he made. . . . He raised up their temples; he fashioned a hundred images with all their bodies correct and
with all splendid costly stones. He sought the precincts of
the gods which were in the districts in this land; he furnished them as they had been since the time of the first
beginning. He established for them daily offerings every
day. All the vessels of their temples were wrought of silver
and gold. He equipped them with priests and with ritual
priests and with the choicest of the army. He transferred
to them lands and cattle, supplied with all equipment."[6]
Among other works of this kind he set up a statue of him-

[1] III, 28.   [2] III, 30.   [3] III, 29.   [4] III, 23.   [5] III, 31.   [6] Ibid.

26

self and his queen in the temple of Horus of Alabastronpolis on which he frankly recorded the manner in which
he had gradually risen from the rank of a simple official
of the king to the throne of the Pharaohs.[1] Thus Amon
received again his old endowments and the incomes of all
the disinherited temples were restored. The people resumed
in public the worship of the innumerable gods which they
had practised in secret during the supremacy of Aton. The
sculptors of the king were sent throughout the land continuing the restoration begun by Tutenkhamon, reinserting
on the monuments defaced by Ikhnaton, the names of the
gods whom he had dishonoured and erased. Over and over
again appear in the temple of Amon at Karnak the records
of such restoration by command of Harmhab. All this
must have ensured to him the united support of the priestly
party throughout the land. At the same time, the worship
of Aton, while not forbidden, was in many places suppressed
by the destruction of his sanctuaries. At Thebes Harmhab
razed to the ground the temple of Aton and used the materials for building two pylons (Fig. 149), extending the
temple of Amon on the south; and the materials which he
left unused were employed in similar works by his successors. In the ruined pylons of Amon at Karnak to-day one
may pick out the blocks which formed the sanctuary of
Aton, still bearing the royal names of the despised Aton-
worshippers.[2] Harmhab also sent to Akhetaton and carried
away the materials of the Aton temple there which were
available for his buildings. Everywhere the name of the
hated Ikhnaton was treated as he had those of the gods.
At Akhetaton his tomb was wrecked and its reliefs chiselled
out; while the tombs of his nobles there were violated in the
same way. Every effort was made to annihilate all trace of
the reign of such a man; and when in legal procedure it was
necessary to cite documents or enactments from his reign he
was designated as "that criminal of Akhetaton."[3]

While thus uncompromising in his hostility to the

[1] III, 22–32.   [2] II, p. 383, notes a, b.   [3] Inscription of Mes.

FIG. 153.—SETI I OFFERING AN IMAGE OF TRUTH TO OSIRIS.

Relief from his temple at Abydos. See p. 417.

name and the movement of Ikhnaton, and while so determined in his restoration of the old order, Harmhab did not
fail to conciliate wherever possible. It is probable that one
of Ikhnaton's old favourites at Akhetaton, named Patonemhab, was appointed as High Priest of Heliopolis, over
whose influential priesthood, as the original source of the
Aton movement, it was necessary to place one of his partisans who would second the king in the destruction of
Ikhnaton's monuments there and the complete suppression
of his influence.[1] The triumph of Amon was complete; as
the royal favourites of Ikhnaton had once sung the good
fortune of the disciples of Aton, so now Harmhab's
courtiers recognized clearly the change in the wind of
fortune, and they sang: "How bountiful are the possessions
of him who knows the gifts of that god (Amon), the king
of gods. Wise is he who knows him, favoured is he who
serves him, there is protection for him who follows him."[2]
The priest of Amon, Neferhotep, who uttered these words,
was at the moment receiving the richest tokens of the king's
favour.[3] Such men exulted in the overthrow of Amon's
enemies: "Woe to him who assails thee! Thy city endures
but he who assails thee is overthrown. Fie upon him who
sins against thee in any land. . . . The sun of him who
knew thee not has set, but he who knows thee shines. The
sanctuary of him who assailed thee is overwhelmed in darkness, but the whole earth is in light.[4]

While the process of reorganizing the priesthoods was
but yielding to the revulsion which had followed Ikhnaton's
revolution, there were other directions in which the restoration of what Harmhab regarded as normal conditions was not
so easy. Gross laxity in the oversight of the local administration had characterized the reign of Ikhnaton and his successors; and those abuses which always arise under such conditions in the orient had grown to excess. Everywhere the
local officials, long secure from close inspection on the part of

---

[1] III, 22.   [2] III, 72.   [3] III, 71.
[4] Birch, Inscr. in the Hier., XXVI, see Erman, Handbuch.

the central government, had revelled in extortions, practised upon the long suffering masses until the fiscal and administrative system was honey-combed with bribery and corruption of all sorts. To ameliorate these conditions Harmhab first informed himself thoroughly as to the extent and character of the evils, and then in his private chamber he dictated to his personal scribe a remarkable series of special and highly particularized laws to suit every case of which he had learned.[1] These laws were comprised in at least nine paragraphs,[2] and they were all directed against the practice of extortion upon the poor by fiscal and administrative officials. The penalties were severe. A tax-collector found guilty of thus practising upon the poor man was sentenced to have his nose cut off, followed by banishment to Tharu, the desolate frontier city far out in the sands of the Arabian desert toward Asia.[3] The military age and the military empire suffered from the same abuses at the hands of irresponsible soldiery, which in the orient have always accompanied it, the common people and the poor being the greatest sufferers. The troops used in administration and stationed in the north and south were accustomed to steal the hides of the Pharaoh's loan-herds from the peasants responsible for them. "They went out from house to house beating and plundering without leaving a hide."[4] In every such demonstrable case the new law enacted that the peasant should not be held responsible for the hides by the Pharaoh's overseer of cattle. The guilty soldier was severely dealt with: "As for any citizen of the army concerning whom one shall hear, saying: 'He goeth about stealing hides'; beginning with this day the law shall be executed against him by beating him with a hundred blows, opening five wounds and taking away the hides which he took."[5] One of the greatest difficulties connected with the discovery of such local misgovernment was collusion with the local officials by inspecting officers sent out by the central government. The corrupt superiors, for a share in the plunder,

[1] III, 50.   [2] III, 45–47.   [3] III, 54.   [4] III, 56.   [5] Ibid.

would overlook the extortions which they had been sent on journeys of inspection to discover and prevent. This evil had been rooted out in the days of the aggressive Thutmose III, but it was now rampant again, and Harmhab apparently revived the methods of Thutmose III for controlling it.[1] For the collection of all the various produce of the land by the different departments of the treasury, laws were framed to prevent robbery and extortion on the part of the officials. In the introduction and application of the new laws Harmhab went personally from end to end of the kingdom.[2] At the same time he improved the opportunity to look for fitting men with whom he could lodge the responsibility for a proper administration of justice, in which direction there had also been great abuse since the Aton revolution. He gave special attention to the character of the two viziers whom he placed at the head of this judicial administration, the one in Thebes and the other in Heliopolis or Memphis. He calls them "perfect in speech, excellent in good qualities, knowing how to judge the heart, hearing the words of the palace, the laws of the judgment-hall. I have appointed them to judge the Two Lands. . . . I have set them in the two great cities of the South and North."[3] He warned them against the acceptance of a bribe: "Receive not the reward of another. . . . How shall those like you judge others while there is one among you committing a crime against justice?"[4] In order to discourage bribery among the local judges he took an unprecedented step. He remitted the tax of gold and silver levied upon all local officials for judicial duties, permitting them to retain the entire income of their offices,[5] in order that they might have no excuse for illegally enriching themselves. But he went still further; while organizing the local courts throughout the land [6] he passed a most stringent law against the acceptance of any bribe by a member of a local court or "council": "Now as for any official or any priest concerning whom it shall be heard, saying: 'He sits to execute judgment

among the council appointed for judgment and he commits
a crime against justice therein'; it shall be counted against
him as a capital crime. Behold my majesty has done this
to improve the laws of Egypt.''[1] In order to keep his
executive officials in close touch with himself, as well as to
lift them above all necessity of accepting any income from
a corrupt source, Harmhab had them provided for with
great liberality. They went out on inspection several times
a month, and on these occasions either just before their
departure or immediately after their return the king gave
them a sumptuous feast in the palace court, appearing himself upon the balcony, addressing each man by name and
throwing down gifts among them. They were also given
substantial portions of barley and spelt on these occasions,
and "there was not found one who had nothing."[2]

All these enactments were recorded by Harmhab on a
huge stela[3] some sixteen feet high and nearly ten feet wide,
which he set up before one of his Karnak pylons for which
he had taken materials from the Aton temple at Karnak,
as we have already mentioned. He added the remark:
"My majesty is legislating for Egypt to prosper the life of
her inhabitants,"[4] and he closed with the admonition,
"Hear ye these commands, which my majesty has made for
the first time, governing the whole land, when my majesty
remembered these cases of oppression which occur in the
presence of this land."[5] These sane and philanthropic reforms give Harmhab a high place in the history of humane
government; especially when we remember that even since
the occupation of the country by the English, within the
memory of almost every reader, the evils at which he struck
have been found exceedingly persistent and difficult to
root out.

With such serious tasks as these occupying him at home
and an inheritance of disorganization and anarchy abroad,
we shall not expect that Harmhab could have accomplished
much in foreign wars. He had had experience in Asia, and

[1] III, 64. [2] III, 66. [3] III, 45 ff. [4] III, 65. [5] III, 67.

Fɪɢ. 154.—SETI I AS A YOUTH OFFERING THE IMAGE OF TRUTH.

Relief in his tomb at Thebes. See plan, p. 251.

he knew what to expect there. Apparently he regarded the
foreign situation as hopeless, in view of all that was engag-
ing his full time and attention at home. A list of names
of foreign countries on the wall near his great code of laws
contains the conventional enumeration of conquests abroad,
which are probably not to be taken very seriously;[1] the name
of the Hittites appears among them, but later conditions show
that he could have accomplished no effective retrenchment
of their power in Syria. On the contrary, we should possibly place in his reign the treaty of alliance and friendship,
referred to by Ramses II some fifty years later, as having
existed before.[2] In the south there was no serious need of
aggressive action, although a revolt of the usual character
finally forced him to appear in Nubia and punish the tribes
there.[3] He was able also to send an expedition to Punt,
which returned with the now familiar wealth of that country.[4] If Harmhab had any ambition to leave a reputation
as a conqueror the times were against him. His accession
fell at a time when all his powers and all his great ability
were necessarily employed exclusively in reorganizing the
kingdom after the long period of unparalleled laxity which
preceded him. He performed his task with a strength and
skill not less than were required for great conquest abroad;
while at the same time he showed a spirit of humane solicitude for the amelioration of the conditions among the masses,
which has never been surpassed in Egypt, from his time until
the present day. Although a soldier, with all the qualities
which that calling implies in the early east, yet when he
became king he could truly say: "Behold, his majesty spent
the whole time seeking the welfare of Egypt."[5]

How long he reigned is uncertain, but in Ramses II's day
the reigns of Ikhnaton and the other Aton worshippers had
apparently been added to his reign, increasing it by twenty
five years or more, so that a lawsuit of Ramses II's time
refers to events of the fifty ninth year of Harmhab.[6] He

[1] III, 34.   [2] III, 377.   [3] III, 40 ff.
[4] III, 37 ff.   [5] III, 50.   [6] Inscription of Mes.

therefore probably reigned some thirty five years. While he was still serving the Pharaoh, in the days of his official career, he had built a tomb of the most superb and artistic workmanship at Memphis (Figs. 119, 147–8, 150). It was a characteristic of the man that he did not abandon this Memphite tomb and order one more splendid at Thebes in the Valley of the Kings' Tombs. He left untouched upon its walls all his old official titles as general, etc., which we have already quoted, merely placing alongside them his royal names and the Pharaonic titulary. Wherever his figure appeared among the reliefs in the tomb chapel, he caused the royal uræus serpent to be inserted on the forehead (Fig. 150), thus clearly distinguishing the figure as that of a king.[1] These insertions may still be traced at the present day.

The fruits of Harmhab's reorganization were destined to be enjoyed by his successors. Whether or not he succeeded in founding a dynasty we do not know. It is impossible to discover any certain connection between him and Ramses I, who now (1315 B. C.) succeeded him, but as Ramses I was already of advanced age on his accession, he must have had some legal title to the throne. Otherwise at such an age he would hardly have been able to make good his claims. He was too old to accomplish anything or to utilize the resources of the new nation which Harmhab had built up. He planned and began the vast colonnaded hall, the famous hypostyle of Karnak, afterward continued and completed by his successors. In his second year he found the new responsibility beyond his strength and he associated as co-regent with himself his son, Seti I,[2] then probably about thirty years old. Together with his son he may have organized a campaign in Nubia, for in any case in the same year he was able to add "slaves of the captivity of his majesty" to the endowment of the Nubian temple at Wadi Halfa.[3] The inscription recording this and other gifts to the said temple[4] is the only dated monument of Ramses I's reign,

[1] III, 1–21.   [2] III, 157.   [3] III, 78.   [4] III, 74 ff.

and as Seti's name is appended to it at the bottom, it is not impossible that the young coregent prince had carried on the campaign in Nubia himself and erected the tablet before he left. Six months after the dating of this tablet the old king was already dead (1313 B. C.), and Seti, as sole king of Egypt, succeeded him.[1]

During his short coregency of not more than a year, Seti I must have already laid all his plans and organized his army in readiness for an attempt to recover the lost empire in Asia. The desert road leading to Palestine from Tharu, the frontier fort of Egypt, whither Harmhab's noseless exiles were banished, was again put in condition. The fortified stations which protected the wells and cisterns distributed along it were rebuilt and repaired.[2] It was a march of ten days from Tharu through the desert to Gaza in southern Palestine,[3] and a plentiful supply of water was therefore absolutely essential throughout the march. It is probable that Egypt was still maintaining some degree of control in Palestine, but the conditions which we saw developing there during the reign of Ikhnaton had received no serious attention since then, with the possible exception of an ineffective campaign by one of Ikhnaton's successors. The information which Seti I now received as to the state of the country betrays a condition of affairs quite such as we should expect would have resulted from the tendency evident in the letters of Abdkhiba of Jerusalem to Ikhnaton.[4] They showed us the Beduin of the neighbouring desert pressing into Palestine and taking possession of the towns, whether in the service of the turbulent dynasts or on their own responsibility. We saw these letters corroborated by Egyptian monuments, portraying the panic-stricken Palestinians fleeing into Egypt before these foes. Seti I's messengers now bring him information of the very same character regarding the Beduin. They report: "Their tribal chiefs are in coalition and they are gaining a foothold in Palestine; they have taken to cursing and quarrelling, each

1 III, 157.   2 III, 84; 86.   3 II, 409.   4 See above, pp. 387-8.

of them slaying his neighbour, and they disregard the laws of the palace."[1]   It was among these desert invaders of Palestine that the movement of the Hebrews resulting in their settlement there took place. It was of little moment to the Pharaoh which particular tribe of Semites possessed the different regions of Palestine, if only they regularly paid their tribute to Egypt; but this was now no longer the case.

In his first year Seti was able to march out from Tharu and lead his expedition along the desert road, past the stations which he had restored.[2]   In the Negeb, or southern Palestinian country, he was met by the "Shasu" or "Shos," as the Egyptians called the Beduin of that region, and he scattered them far and wide.[3]   As he reached the frontier of Canaan, which was the name applied by the Egyptians to all western Palestine and Syria, he captured a walled town, which marked the northern limit of the struggle with the Beduin.[4]   Thence he pushed rapidly northward, capturing the towns of the plain of Megiddo (Jezreel), pushing eastward across the valley of the Jordan and erecting his tablet of victory in the Hauran,[5] and westward to the southern slopes of Lebanon, where he took the forest-girt city of Yenoam,[6] once the property of the temple of Amon, after its capture by Thutmose III, nearly one hundred and fifty years before. The neighbouring dynasts of the Lebanon immediately came to him and offered their allegiance. They had not seen a Pharaoh at the head of his army in Asia for over fifty years,—not since Amenhotep III had left Sidon;[7] and Seti immediately put them to the test by requiring a liberal contribution of cedar logs for the sacred barge of Amon which he was building at Thebes, as well as for the tall flag-staves which surmounted the temple pylons.[8]   These the subjects of the Lebanon felled in his presence, and Seti was able to send them to Egypt by water from the harbours which, like his great predecessor, Thutmose III, he was now

[1] III, 101, ll. 3-9.   [2] III, 83 f.   [3] III, 85 f.   [4] III, 87-8.
[5] III, 81.   [6] III, 89-90.   [7] See above. p. 353.   [8] III, 91-94.

subduing. It is remotely possible that he advanced as far north as Simyra and Ullaza,[1] and that the prince of Cyprus sent in his gifts as of old. However that may be, Tyre and Othu[2] submitted in any case and having thus secured the coast and restored the water route between Syria and Egypt for future operations, Seti returned to Egypt. The return of a victorious Pharaoh from conquest in Asia, so common in the days of the great conquerors, was now a spectacle which the grandees of the realm had not witnessed for two generations. The news of Seti's successes had preceded him, and the nobles of the administrative government hastened to the frontier to receive him. At Tharu, outside the gate of the frontier fortress beside the bridge over the fresh water canal, which, as the reader will recall (see p. 188), already connected the Nile with the bitter lakes of the Isthmus of Suez, they gathered in a rejoicing group, and as Seti's weary lines toiled up in the dust of the long desert march, with the Pharaoh at their head, driving before his chariot-horses the captive dynasts of Palestine and Syria, the nobles broke out in acclamation.[3] At Thebes there was another festive presentation of prisoners and spoil before Amon, such as had been common enough in the days of the empire, but which the Thebans had not witnessed for fifty years or more;[4] and in the course of the celebration the king sacrificed in the presence of the gods some of the prisoners whom he had taken.[5]

This campaign was quite sufficient to restore southern Palestine to the kingdom of the Pharaoh, and probably also most of northern Palestine. Before Seti could continue his operations in Asia, however, he was obliged to direct his forces against a threatening danger, which likewise at the beginning of the Eighteenth Dynasty had demanded the Pharaoh's attention and cost him a war. The Libyans west of the Nile mouths never failed to improve the opportunity of lax government in Egypt to push into the Delta and take possession of all the territory they could hold, and the exact

[1] III, 81; 92.   [2] III, 89.   [3] III, 98–103.   [4] III, 104–112.   [5] III, 113.

western border of the Delta was always more or less uncertain on their frontier. Seti spent his entire next year, the
second of his reign, in the Delta, as a series of court bills
for his table supplies shows;[1] and it is thus very probable
that he carried on his operations against the Libyans in that
year. He met them in battle at some unknown point in
the western Delta,[2] and according to the meagre accounts
which he has left us, was able to return in triumph to Thebes
with the usual prisoners and spoil to be presented in the
temple of Amon.[3] It is possible that this return to Thebes
did not take place immediately, but that he proceeded to
Asia after the overthrow of the Libyans, to continue the
restoration of Egyptian power in Syria which he had begun
so auspiciously the season before. In any case, we next find
him in Galilee, storming the walled city of Kadesh, which
must not be confused with Kadesh on the Orontes. Here
the Amorite kingdom, founded by Abdashirta and Aziru,
as we were able to follow it in the letters of Rib-Addi,[4]
formed a kind of buffer state, to which the Galilean Kadesh
belonged, lying between Palestine on the south and the
southern Hittite frontier in the Orontes valley on the north.
It was necessary for Seti to subdue this intermediate kingdom before he could come to blows with the Hittites lying
behind it. After harrying its territory and probably taking
Kadesh,[5] Seti pushed northward against the Hittites. Their
king, Seplel, who had entered into treaty relations with
Egypt toward the close of the Eighteenth Dynasty, was
now long dead; his son, Merasar, was ruling in his stead.[6]
Somewhere in the Orontes valley Seti came into contact
with them and the first battle between the Hittites and a
Pharaoh occurred. Of the character and magnitude of the
action we know nothing; we have only a battle relief showing
Seti in full career charging the enemy in his chariot.[7] It
is, however, not probable that he met the main army of the
Hittites; certain it is that he did not shake their power in

[1] III, 82, 2. [2] III, 120–132. [3] III, 133–9. [4] See above, pp. 383–7.
[5] III, 140–141. [6] III, 375. [7] III, 142–144.

FIG. 155.—CATTLE INSPECTION.

Painting from a Theban tomb of the Empire.　See p. 417.

Syria; Kadesh on the Orontes remained in their hands, and at most, Seti could not have accomplished more than to have driven back their extreme advance, thus preventing them from absorbing any more territory on the south or pushing southward into Palestine. He returned to Thebes for another triumph, driving his Hittite prisoners before him, and presenting them, with the spoil, to the god of the Empire, Amon of Karnak.[1]   The boundary which he had established in Asia roughly coincided inland with the northern limits of Palestine, and must have included also Tyre and the Phœnician coast south of the mouth of the Litâny. Though much increasing the territory of Egypt in Asia, it represented but a small third of what she had once conquered there.   Under these circumstances, it would have been quite natural for Seti to continue the war in Syria. For some reason, however, he did not, in so far as we know, ever appear with his forces in Asia again.   He possibly recognized the hopelessness of a struggle against the Hittites, who were now so firmly entrenched in Syria. The position of Egypt in Syria was indeed totally different from that of the Hittites, who were actually occupying the country, the warrior class at least residing there; whereas the Pharaohs had never attempted to colonize the country, but merely to hold it in vassalage, subject to the payment of yearly tribute.   Such a method of holding distant conquests was not likely to succeed at the threshold of the powerful Hittite kingdom, a nation unable to resist its own expansive force and overflowing constantly into Syria.   Had the Pharaoh succeeded in evicting them it would have required incessant war in northern Syria to have kept them within their old limits.   Seti may have perceived the changed conditions and understood that the methods which had built up the empire of Thutmose III could no longer apply with a power of the first rank already occupying Syria.   He therefore, either at this time or later, negotiated a treaty of peace with the Hittite king, Metella, who had succeeded his father, Merasar.[2]

[1] III, 145–152.   [2] III, 377.

Returning to Egypt, he devoted himself to the interests of peace, especially to the temples of the gods. The deface-ment of the monuments during the Aton revolution had been but partially repaired by Harmhab; Seti's father had reigned too briefly to accomplish anything in this direction, so that Seti himself found much to do in merely restoring the disfigured monuments of his ancestors, which he did with admirable piety. All the larger monuments of the Eigh-teenth Dynasty from the Nubian temple of Amâda on the south to Bubastis on the north, bear records of his restora-tion, with the words appended: "Restoration of the monu-ment, which Seti I made."[1] Throughout the great quarries of Egypt, Assuan, Silsileh, Gebelen, his workmen were dis-patched.[2] Captives of war were employed as of old, but where he utilized the labour of native Egyptians, Seti records with great pride the humane treatment and the gen-erous supplies accorded them. At Silsileh, whence the sand-stone was procured, every one of the thousand workmen employed there received daily nearly four pounds of bread, two bundles of vegetables and a roast of meat; while twice a month each man was given a clean linen garment.[3] At all the great sanctuaries of the old gods his buildings were now rising on a scale unprecedented in the palmiest days of the Empire,—a fact which shows that the income, even of the reduced empire of Seti I, reaching from the fourth cataract of the Nile to the sources of the Jordan, was still sufficient to support enterprises of imperial scope. In front of the pylon of Amenhotep III, forming the façade of the state temple at Karnak, Seti continued the vast colonnaded hall planned and begun by his father, and which surpassed in size even the enormous unfinished hypostyle of Amenhotep III at Luxor. The battle reliefs on the front of Amenhotep III's pylon were covered by Seti's masonry. He completed some of the columns of the northern aisles as well as the north wall, on the outside of which his sculptors engraved a colossal series of reliefs (Fig. 152) portraying his cam-

[1] III, 200.   [2] III, 201–210.   [3] III. 207.

paigns. Mounting from the base to the coping they cover the entire wall (over two hundred feet long), converging from each end upon a door in the middle, toward which the king is shown returning to Egypt, then presenting offerings, spoil and captives to Amon; and at last sacrificing the prisoners before the god, at the very door itself, as if the king were entering to perform the ceremony.[1] Similar works existed in the Eighteenth Dynasty temples, but they have all perished save the remnants of Amenhotep III's reliefs just referred to, and Seti's battle-reliefs therefore form the most imposing work of the kind now surviving in Egypt. The great hall which it was to adorn was never finished by him, and it was left to his successors to complete it. Like his fathers of the Eighteenth Dynasty, he erected a great mortuary temple on the western plain of Thebes. It was located at the northern end of the line of similar sanctuaries left by the earlier kings, and as Seti's father had died too soon to construct any such temple, it was also dedicated to him. This temple, now known as that of Kurna, was likewise left incomplete by Seti.[2] At Abydos he built a magnificent sanctuary dedicated to the great gods of the empire, the Osirian triad and himself, with a side chapel for the services of the old kings, especially of the First and Second Dynasties, whose tombs still lie in the desert behind the temple.[3] The list of their names which he engraved upon the walls still forms one of the most important sources for our chronological arrangement and assignment of the Pharaohs. Although this temple has lost the first and second pylons, it still remains perhaps the noblest monument of Egyptian art still surviving in the land. To its artistic value we shall revert again. A temple at Memphis, probably another at Heliopolis, with doubtless others in the Delta of which we know nothing; and in Nubia an enormous cliff-temple at Abu Simbel, left incomplete[4] and afterward finished by his son, Ramses II, completed the series of Seti's greater buildings.

[1] III, 80–156.   [2] III, 211–221.   [3] III, 225–243.   [4] III, 495.

These works drew heavily upon his treasury, and when
he reached the point of permanently endowing the mortuary service of the Abydos temple, he found it necessary
to seek additional sources of income. He therefore turned
his attention to the possible resources and found that the
supply of gold from the mountains of the Red Sea region
in the district of Gebel Zebâra was seriously restricted by
the difficulties which beset the route, especially in the matter
of water. The road from the Nile valley thither left the
river at a point a few miles above Edfu, and Seti visited
the place himself to discover what might be done to remedy
the difficulty. He found it necessary to go out into the
desert some two days journey to a point about thirty seven
miles from the river, where there was an old and probably
disused station known to the caravans of the Eighteenth
Dynasty.[1] Here, under his own superintendence, a well was
dug, yielding a plentiful supply of water.[2] Thereupon Seti
erected a small temple by the well and established a settlement at the place.[3] In all probability other stations further
out on the same route were erected. The thirsty caravaneers
sang his praise: "Ye gods dwelling in the well give ye to
him your duration; for he hath opened for us the way to
march in, when it was closed up before us. We proceed and
are saved; we arrive and are preserved alive. The difficult
way which is in our memories has become a good way."[4]
Then Seti established the income from the mines thus reached
as a permanent endowment for his temple at Abydos, and
called down terrifying curses on any posterity who should
violate his enactments.[5] Yet within a year after his death
they had ceased to be effective and had to be renewed by
his son.[6] In a similar effort to replenish his treasury from
gold mines further south in the Wadi Alâki, Seti dug a well
two hundred feet deep on the road leading southeast from
Kubbân in Nubia, but he failed to reach water, and the
attempt to increase the gold-supply from this region was
evidently unsuccessful.[7]

[1] III, 170.   [2] III, 171.   [3] III, 172–4.   [4] III, 195.
[5] III, 175–194.   [6] III, 263.   [7] III, 289.

The art developed in connection with Seti's buildings was hardly less strong, virile and beautiful than that prevailing during the Eighteenth Dynasty. The impulses which had come with Egypt's imperial position, while not as strong as under the great emperors, were nevertheless not entirely quenched. The conception of the great hall at Karnak, although not carried out with the refinement which we found in the Eighteenth Dynasty, as we shall see later on, was yet one of the noblest fruits of Egypt's power and wealth, and remains to-day, in spite of glaring faults, one of the most impressive surviving monuments of Egyptian architectural genius. In sculpture, Seti's battle-reliefs are the most ambitious attempt at elaborate composition left by the surviving school of the Eighteenth Dynasty, which they represent; while very effective as compositions, they are however defective in drawing. Nevertheless the figure of Seti with upraised spear, dispatching the Libyan chief, on this north wall at Karnak (Fig. 152), is one of the strongest and most vigourous examples of drawing to be found among the works of Egyptian artists; while as a composition it is almost equally good. The finest reliefs of the time, however, are to be found in Seti's temple at Abydos (Fig. 153), in which there is a rare combination of softness and refinement, with bold and sinuous lines and exquisite modelling. Hardly inferior to these are the reliefs in Seti's magnificent tomb (Fig. 154) at Thebes. The painting of the time also continues to show much of the power of the Amarna school of art. The Theban tombs have preserved exquisite examples like the inspection of the herds (Fig. 155) or the hunt in the marshes, the latter exhibiting a fine touch of animal savagery in the fierce abandon of a lithe cat as she tramples two wild birds beneath her feet and sinks her teeth at the same moment into a third victim (Fig. 156).

Beyond Seti's ninth year we know practically nothing of his reign. He seems to have spent his energies upon his extensive buildings, and among these he did not forget the excavation of the largest tomb yet made in the valley of

27

the kings at Thebes. It is of complicated construction and descends into the mountain through a series of galleries and extensive halls no less than four hundred and seventy feet in oblique depth (Fig. 109). As the thirtieth anniversary of his nomination as crown prince approached Seti began the preparation of the necessary obelisks; and about the same time his eldest son, whose name is unknown to us, was appointed to the succession as crown prince. Desirous of appearing to have shared in the achievements of his father, this prince had his figure inserted in the scene on the north wall of his father's Karnak hall, showing him in battle with the Libyans. As his figure is not original here, there was not room for it and part of an inscription had to be chiselled out in order to create the necessary space. The fraud is visible to this day, the colour by which it was once disguised having now vanished. Ramses, another son of Seti, born to him by one of his queens named Tuya, was, however, plotting to supplant his eldest brother, and during their father's last days Ramses laid his plans so effectively that he was ready for a successful coup at the old king's death. Some time before the approaching jubilee, while the obelisks for it were still unfinished, Seti died (about 1292 B. C.), having reigned over twenty years since his own father's death. He was laid to rest in a sumptuous sarcophagus of alabaster in the splendid tomb which he had excavated in the western valley. The body then deposited in the tomb, and preserved by happy accident, like many others of the Pharaohs whom we have seen, shows him to have been one of the stateliest figures that ever sat upon the throne of Egypt, in so far as we can judge at this time from the remains preserved to us (Fig. 158).

The plans of the young Ramses were immediately carried out. Whether his elder brother gained the throne long enough to have his figure inserted in his father's reliefs or whether his influence as crown prince had accomplished this, we cannot tell. In any case Ramses brushed him aside without a moment's hesitation and seized the throne. The

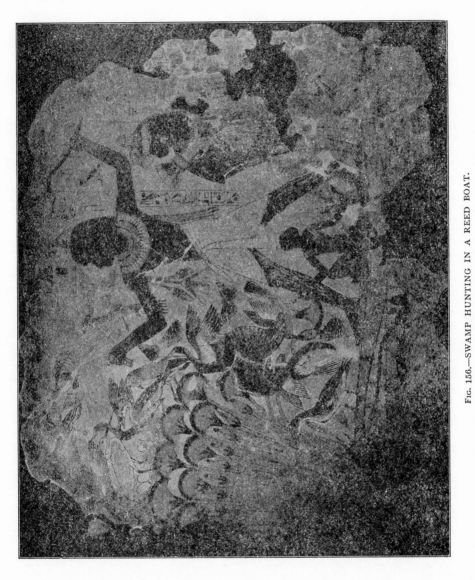

Fig. 156.—SWAMP HUNTING IN A REED BOAT.

Painting from a Theban tomb of the Empire. Before the hunter is the cat described on p. 417.

only public evidence of his brother's claims, his figure inserted by that of Seti in the battle with the Libyans (Fig. 152) was immediately erased with the inscriptions which stated his name and titles; while in their stead the artists of Ramses inserted the figure of their new lord, with the title "crown prince," which he had never borne (Fig. 157).

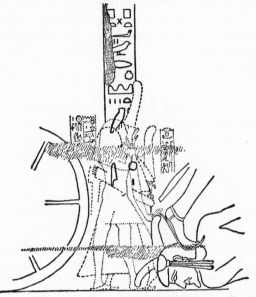

FIG. 157.   SECTION OF ONE OF SETI I'S RELIEFS AT KARNAK.

The *broken* lines are the figure of Seti's first born son, who had himself inserted here long after the completion of the reliefs, so that a column of the original inscription now continues down into the figure.   The *dotted* lines show the form of Ramses II, inserted by him over that of his elder brother whom he displaced and supplanted.

The colour which once carefully veiled all traces of these alterations has now long since disappeared, and the evidence of the bitter conflict of the two princes involving of course the harem and the officials of the court and a whole lost romance of court intrigue may still be traced by the trained eye on the north wall of the Karnak hypostyle. Such was the accession of the famous Pharaoh, Ramses II. But the usual court devices were immediately resorted to, that the manner of the Pharaoh's actual conquest of the throne might be forgotten. When Ramses addressed the court he alluded specifically to the day when his father had set him as a child before the nobles and published him as the heir to the kingdom.[1] The grandees knew too well the road to favour not to respond in fulsome eulogies expanding on the wonderful powers of the king in his childhood and narrating how he had even commanded the army at ten years of age.[2] The young monarch showed great vigour and high abilities, and if his unfortunate rival left a party to dispute his claims, no trace of their opposition is now discoverable.

Ramses lost no time however in making himself strong at Thebes, the seat of power. Thither he immediately hastened, probably from the Delta, and celebrated in the state temple the great annual Feast of Opet.[3] Having gained the priests of Amon he devoted himself with great zeal to pious works in memory of his father. For this purpose he sailed down the river from Thebes to Abydos,[4] which he had probably touched on his way up to Thebes. At Abydos he found has father's magnificent mortuary temple in a sad state; it was without roof, the drums of the columns and the blocks for the half raised walls lay scattered in the mire, and the whole monument, left thus unfinished by Seti, was fast going to destruction. Worse than this, the endowments which Seti had left for its support had been neglected, violated and misappropriated by the people left in charge of them,[5] in total disregard of the solemn adjurations and frightful curses recorded by their royal master, then less than a year dead. The tombs of the hoary kings of the First Dynasty, who had ruled over two thousand years before, were also found to be in need of attention.[6] Ramses summoned his court and announced to them his intention of completing and putting in repair all these works, but particularly the temple of his father.[7] He carried out his

[1] III, 267–8.   [2] III, 288, l. 17.   [3] III, 255–6, 260.   [4] III, 261.
[5] III, 263.   [6] III, 262.   [7] III, 264–5.

father's plans and completed the temple, at the same time renewing the landed endowments and reorganizing the administration of its property to which Ramses now added herds, the tribute of fowlers and fishermen, a trading ship on the Red Sea, a fleet of barges on the river, slaves and serfs, with priests and officials for the management of the temple-estate.[1]   All this, although recognized by the court as due to the most pious motives, was not wholly without advantage to the giver; for the conclusion of the enormous inscription[2] left by Ramses to record his good deeds in his father's temple, represents Ramses as thus securing the favour of his father, who, as the companion of the gods, intercedes with them in his son's behalf and thus ensures to Ramses the favour of the divine powers who grant him a long and powerful reign.[3]   This notion of the intercession of the dead with the gods on behalf of the living is found in one inscription as old as the Old Kingdom, occurs also in the Middle Kingdom and again, enunciated by Ramses in the mortuary temple of his father at Thebes which he likewise completed on finding it left unfinished by Seti.[4]

Perhaps the heavy draughts upon his treasury entailed by the mortuary endowments of his father now moved Ramses to look for new sources of income.   However this may be, we find him at Memphis in his third year consulting with his officials regarding the possibility of opening up the Wadi Alâki country in Nubia and developing there the mines which Seti I had unsuccessfully attempted to exploit.[5]   The viceroy of Kush, who was present, explained the difficulty to the king and related the fruitless attempt of his father to supply the route with water.   It was now so bad that when the caravaneers attempted the desert journey thither "it was only half of them that arrived there; for they died of thirst on the road, together with the asses which they drove before them."   They were obliged to take enough water for the round trip, as they could obtain none at the mines.   "Hence no gold was brought from this country for

[1] III, 274–7.   [2] III, 251–281.   [3] III, 279–281.
[4] III, 281, l. 103, note.   [5] III, 282–293.

lack of water.''[1] With subtle flattery the viceroy and court
advised another attempt to supply the route with water,[2]
and the result of the ensuing royal command to undertake
it was a letter from the viceroy of Kush announcing the
complete success of the enterprise and the discovery of a
copious spring of water at a depth of only twenty feet.[3]
At Kubbân, where the road leading to the mines left the
Nile-valley, Ramses had the viceroy erect a stela commemorating the achievement and bearing a record of the events
which we have sketched.[4] Such enterprises of internal exploitation were but preparatory in the plans of Ramses.
His ambition held him to greater purposes; and he contemplated nothing less than the recovery of the great Asiatic
empire, conquered by his predecessors of the Eighteenth
Dynasty.

[1] III, 286   [2] III, 288-9.   [3] III, 292.   [4] III, 282-295.

CHAPTER XXI

THE WARS OF RAMSES II

We have seen that the Nineteenth Dynasty had inherited a very dangerous situation in Syria. Ramses I had been too old and had reigned too briefly to accomplish anything there; Seti I, his son, had not been able to penetrate into the territory held by the Hittites, much less to sweep them back into Asia Minor and reclaim the old conquests of the Eighteenth Dynasty. When Ramses II ascended the throne the Hittites had remained in undisputed possession of these conquests for probably more than twenty years since the only attempt by Seti I to dislodge them. The long peace probably concluded with Seti gave their king, Metella, an opportunity, of which he made good use, to render their position in Syria impregnable. Advancing southward, up the valley of the Orontes, he had seized Kadesh, the centre of the Syrian power in the days of Thutmose III, which, we remember, had given him more trouble and held out with more tenacious resistance than any other kingdom in Syria. We have already seen the strategic importance of the location, an importance which was quickly grasped by the Hittite king, who made the place the bulwark of his southern frontier.

Ramses's plan for the war was like that of his great ancestor, Thutmose III: he purposed first to gain the coast, that he might use one of its harbours as a base, enjoying quick and easy communication with Egypt by water. Our sources tell us nothing of his operations on the first campaign, when this purpose was accomplished. We have only the mute evidence of a limestone stela (Fig. 159) cut into the face of the rocks overlooking the Dog River near Berût; it is so weathered that only the name of Ramses II and the date in

423

the "year four" can be read. It was in that year, therefore, that Ramses pushed northward along the coast of Phœnicia to this point.[1] Unfortunately for Ramses, this preparatory campaign, however necessary, gave the Hittite king, Metella, an opportunity to collect all his resources and to muster all available forces from every possible source. All the vassal kings of his great empire were compelled to contribute their levies to his army. We find among them the old enemies of Egypt in Syria: the kings of Naharin, Arvad, Carchemish, Kode, Kadesh, Nuges, Ekereth (Ugarit) and Aleppo. Besides these, Metella's subject kingdoms in Asia Minor, like Kezweden and Pedes, were drawn upon;[2] and not content with the army thus collected, he emptied his treasury to tempt the mercenaries of Asia Minor and the Mediterranean islands. Roving bands of Lycian sailors, such as had plundered the coasts of the Delta and of Cyprus in the Eighteenth Dynasty, besides Mysians, Cilicians, Dardanians, and levies of the unidentified Erwenet, took service in the Hittite ranks.[3] In this manner Metella collected an army more formidable than any which Egypt had ever hitherto been called upon to meet. In numbers it was large for those times, containing probably not less than twenty thousand men.

Ramses on his part had not been less active in securing mercenary support. From the remote days of the Old Kingdom Nubian levies had been plentifully sprinkled through the Egyptian armies; one of their tribes, the Mazoi, furnished gensdarmes-police for Ikhnaton's capital, and they were commonly found in similar service elsewhere in the Pharaoh's realm. Among the troops used to garrison Syria in the days of the Amarna letters sixty years before we find the "Sherden," or Sardinians, who there appear for the first time in history. These men were now taken into Ramses' army in considerable numbers, so that they constituted a recognized element in it, and the king levied "his infantry, his chariotry and the Sherden."[4] Ramses claims to have taken them as prisoners in one of his victories,[5] and

[1] III, 297. [2] III, 306. [3] Ibid. [4] III, 307. [5] Ibid.

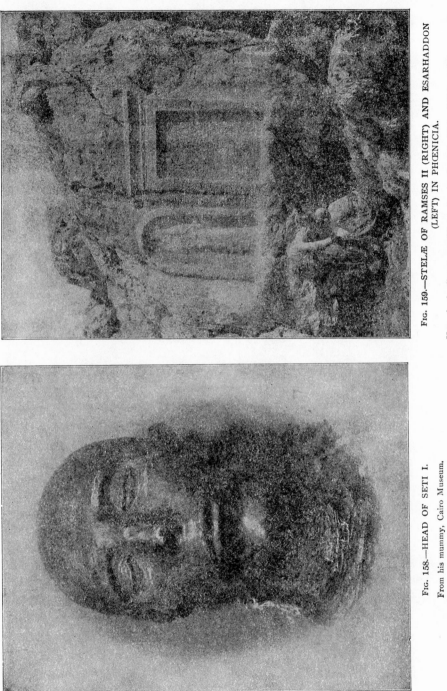

Fig. 158.—HEAD OF SETI I.

From his mummy, Cairo Museum.

Fig. 159.—STELÆ OF RAMSES II (RIGHT) AND ESARHADDON (LEFT) IN PHŒNICIA.

Hewn in the limestone cliffs at the mouth of the Nah rel-Kelb (Dog River) near Berût. See pp. 423 and 556.

doubtless some of them were therefore the remnants of
marauding bands, captured as they sailed in plundering
expeditions along the coasts of the western Delta.[1] He must
have commanded an army of not less than twenty thousand
men all told, although the proportion of mercenaries is unknown to us; nor is it known what proportion of his force
was chariotry, as compared with the infantry. He divided
these troops into four divisions, each named after one of
the great gods: Amon, Re, Ptah and Sutekh; and himself
took personal command of the division of Amon.[2]

About the end of April of his fifth year (1288 B. C.), when
the rains of Syria had ceased, Ramses marched out of Tharu,
on his northeastern frontier, at the head of these troops.
The division of Amon, with whom the Pharaoh was, formed
the advance, and the other divisions, Re, Ptah and Sutekh,
followed in the order mentioned. What route Ramses took
across Palestine it is now impossible to determine; but when
they reached the region of Lebanon they were on the sea-
road, along the coast of Phœnicia, which, as we have seen,
had been secured in the campaign of the year before. Here
Ramses had, at that time or before, founded a city, which
bore his name, and was evidently intended to serve as his
base for the campaign. Its location is uncertain, but it
may have been at or near the mouth of the Dog River, where
his stela of the previous year is located. Here he formed
the van of picked men and leaders of his force and turned
inland, perhaps up the valley of the Dog River, although
a much less precipitous road left the sea further south and
would have carried him up the Litâny. He then struck
into the valley of the Orontes, and marching down that river
northward during the last days of May, he camped on the
night of the twenty ninth day out from Tharu, on the last
and northernmost height of the elevated valley between the
northern ends of the two Lebanons, overlooking the vast
plain in which lay Kadesh, only a day's march distant, with

[1] III, 491.

[2] For the following account of the battle of Kadesh see the documents, III,
298–348; and my Battle of Kadesh, University of Chicago Press, 1904.

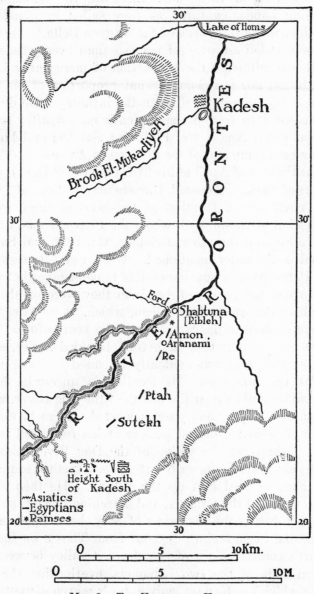

MAP 8.   THE VICINITY OF KADESH.

Showing the "Height south of Kadesh," where Ramses camped the night
before the battle, and his position early on the day of the battle.

its battlements probably visible on the northern horizon, toward which the Orontes wound its way across the plain.

The next morning Ramses broke camp early, and putting himself at the head of the division of Amon, he left the other divisions to follow after, while he set out down the last slope of the high valley to the ford of the Orontes at Shabtuna, later known to the Hebrews as Ribleh. Here the river left the precipitous, cañon-like valley in which it had hitherto flowed, and for the first time permitted a crossing to the west side on which Kadesh was, thus enabling an army approaching the city from the south to cut off a considerable bend in the river. Reaching the ford after a march of three hours at most and probably less, Ramses prepared for the crossing. Day after day his officers had reported to him their inability to find any trace of the enemy and had added their impression that he was still far in the north. At this juncture two Beduin of the region appeared and stated that they had deserted from the Hittite ranks, and that the Hittite king had retreated northward to the district of Aleppo, north of Tunip. In view of the failure of his scouting parties to find the enemy, Ramses readily believed this story, immediately crossed the river with the division of Amon and pushed rapidly on, while the divisions of Re, Ptah and Sutekh, marching in the order named, straggled far behind. Anxious to reach Kadesh and begin the siege that day, the Pharaoh even drew away from the division of Amon and with no van before him, accompanied only by his household troops, was rapidly nearing Kadesh as midday approached. Meantime Metella, the Hittite king, had drawn up his troops in battle-array on the northwest of Kadesh, and Ramses, without hint of danger was approaching the entire Hittite force, while the bulk of his army was scattered along the road some eight or ten miles in the rear, and the officers of Re and Ptah were relaxing in the shade of the neighbouring forests after the hot and dusty march. The crafty Metella, seeing that the story of his two Beduin, whom he had sent out for the very purpose of deceiving Ramses, had been implicitly accepted, fully appreciated how best to utilize the rare opportunity. He does not attack Ramses at once, but as the Pharaoh approaches the city the Hittite quickly transfers his entire army to the east side of the river, and while Ramses passes northward along the west side of Kadesh, Metella deftly dodges him, moving southward along the east side of the city, always keeping it between him and the Egyptians to prevent his troops from being seen. As he draws in on the east and southeast of the city he has secured a position on Ramses flank which is of itself enough, if properly utilized, to ensure him an overwhelming victory, even involving the destruction of Ramses and his army. The Egyptian forces were now roughly divided into two groups: near Kadesh were the two divisions of Amon and Re, while far southward the divisions of Ptah and Sutekh have not yet crossed at the ford of Shabtuna. The division of Sutekh was so far away that nothing more was heard of it and it took no part in the day's action. Ramses halted on the northwest of the city, not far from and perhaps on the very ground occupied by the Asiatic army a short time before.

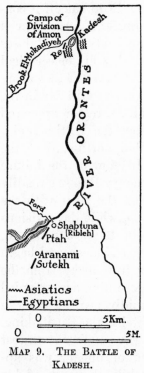

MAP 9. THE BATTLE OF KADESH.

Positions of the opposing forces at the time of the Asiatic attack.

Here he camped in the early afternoon, and the division of Amon, coming up shortly afterward, bivouacked around his tent. A barricade of shields was erected around the camp, and as the provision trains came up the oxen were unyoked and the two-wheeled carts were parked at one end of the enclosure. The weary troops were relaxing, feeding their horses and preparing their own meal, when two Asiatic spies were brought in by Ramses' scouts and taken to the royal tent. Brought before Ramses after a merciless beating, they confessed that Metella and his entire army were concealed behind the city. Thoroughly alarmed, the young Pharaoh hastily summoned his commanders and officials, chided them bitterly for their inability to inform him of the presence of the enemy, and commanded the vizier to bring up the division of Ptah with all speed. In all probability the frightened vizier himself undertook the dangerous commission, in the hope of retrieving his reputation. Ramses' dispatch to the division of Ptah alone, shows that he had no hope of bringing up the division of Sutekh, which was, as we have seen, straggling far in the rear above Shabtuna. At the same time it discloses his confidence that the division of Re, which had been but a few miles behind him at most, was within call at the gates of his camp. He therefore at this juncture little dreamed of the desperate situation into which he had been betrayed, nor of the catastrophe which at that very moment was overtaking the unfortunate division of Re. "Lo, while his majesty sat talking with his nobles," rebuking them for their negligence, "the Hittite king came, together with the numerous countries that were with him, they crossed the ford [of the Orontes] on the south of Kadesh," "they came forth from the south side of Kadesh, and they cut through the division of Re in its middle, while it was on the march, not knowing and not drawn up for battle." A modern military critic could hardly better describe, in a word, what had happened than do these brief words from the ancient account of the affair. The attacking force was entirely chariotry and Ramses' marching infantry was of course cut to pieces under the assault. The southern portion of this disorganized division must have entirely melted away, but the rest fled northward toward Ramses' camp in a wild rout, having lost many prisoners and strewing the way with their equipments. They

had at the first moment sent a messenger to inform Ramses
of the catastrophe, but in so far as we know, the first intimation received by the Pharaoh of the appalling disaster
which now faced him was the headlong flight of these fugitives of the annihilated division, among whom were two of
his own sons. They burst over the barricade into the aston-
ished camp with the Hittite chariotry in hot pursuit close

MAP 10. THE BATTLE OF
KADESH.

Showing Ramses II's di-
vided forces and his envelop-
ment by the enemy in the
second stage of the battle.

upon their heels. Ramses' heavy
infantry guard quickly dragged
these intruders from their chariots
and dispatched them; but behind
these was swiftly massing the whole
body of some twenty five hundred
Asiatic chariots. As they pressed
in upon the Egyptian position their
wings rapidly spread, swelled out
on either hand and enfolded the
camp. The division of Amon, weary
with the long and rapid march, in
total relaxation, without arms and
without officers, was struck as by an
avalanche when the fleeing remnants
of the division of Re swept through
the camp. They were inevitably involved in the rout and carried along
with it to the northward. The bulk
of Ramses' available force was
thus in flight, his southern divisions
were miles away and separated from
him by the whole mass of the
enemy's chariotry; the disaster was
complete.

Taken with but short shrift for preparation, the young
Pharaoh hesitated not a moment in attempting to cut his
way out and to reach his southern columns. With only his
household troops, his immediate followers and the officers,
who happened to be at his side, he mounted his waiting

chariot and boldy charged into the advance of the Hittite
pursuit as it poured into his camp on the west side. The
instant's respite thus gained he utilized to push out on the
west or south side of his camp a few paces and there, perceiving how heavily the enemy was massed before him,
immediately understood that further onset in that direction
was hopeless. Retiring into the camp again, he must have
noted how thin was the eastern wing of the surrounding
chariots along the river where there had not yet been time
for the enemy to strengthen their line. As a forlorn hope
he charged this line with an impetuosity that hurled the
Asiatics in his immediate front pell-mell into the river.
Metella, standing on the opposite shore amid a mass of
eight thousand infantry, saw several of his officers, his
personal scribe, his charioteer, the chief of his body-guard
and finally even his own royal brother go down before the
Pharaoh's furious onset. Among many rescued from
the water by their comrades on the opposite shore was the
half drowned king of Aleppo, who was with difficulty resuscitated by his troops. Again and again Ramses renewed the
charge, finally producing serious discomfiture in the enemy's
line at this point. At this juncture an incident common in
oriental warfare saved Ramses from total destruction. Had
the mass of the Hittite chariotry swept in upon his rear
from the west and south he must certainly have been lost.
But to his great good fortune his camp had fallen into the
hands of these troops and, dismounting from their chariots,
they had thrown discipline to the winds as they gave themselves up to the rich plunder. Thus engaged, they were
suddenly fallen upon by a body of Ramses' recruits who
may possibly have marched in from the coast to join his
army at Kadesh. At any rate, they did not belong to either
of the southern divisions. They completely surprised the
plundering Asiatics in the camp and slew them to a man.

The sudden offensive of Ramses along the river and the
unexpected onslaught of the "recruits" must have considerably dampened the ardour of the Hittite attack, giving the

Pharaoh an opportunity to recover himself. These newly arrived "recruits," together with the returning fugitives from the unharmed but scattered division of Amon, so augmented his power that there was now a prospect of his maintaining himself till the arrival of the division of Ptah. The stubborn defense which now followed forced the Hittite king to throw in his reserves of a thousand chariots. Six times the desperate Pharaoh charged into the replenished lines of the enemy, but for some reason Metella did not send against him the eight thousand foot which he had stationed on the east side of the river opposite Ramses' position; and the struggle remained a battle of chariotry as long as we can trace it. For three long hours, by prodigies of personal valour, the Pharaoh kept his scanty forces together, throwing many an anxious glance southward toward the road from Shabtuna, along which the division of Ptah was toiling in response to his message. Finally, as the long afternoon wore on and the sun was low in the west, the standards of Ptah glimmering through the dust and heat gladdened the eyes of the weary Pharaoh. Caught between the opposing lines, the Hittite chariotry was driven into the city, probably with considerable loss; but our sources do not permit us to follow these closing incidents of the battle. As evening drew on the enemy took refuge in the city and Ramses was saved. The prisoners taken were led before him while he reminded his followers that these captives had been brought off by himself almost single handed.

The records describe how the scattered Egyptian fugitives crept back and found the plain strewn with Asiatic dead, especially of the personal and official circle about the Hittite king. This was undoubtedly true; the Asiatics must have lost heavily in Ramses' camp, on the river north of the city and at the arrival of the division of Ptah; but Ramses' loss was certainly also very heavy, and in view of the disastrous surprise of the division of Re, probably much greater than that of his enemies. What made the issue a success for Ramses was his salvation from utter destruction, and that he eventually held possession of the field added little practical advantage.

One of the Egyptian accounts claims that Ramses renewed the action on the following day with such effect that Metella sent a letter craving peace, whereupon the request was granted by the Pharaoh who then returned in triumph to Egypt. The other sources make no reference to the second day's action and the events of the battle which we have just followed make it evident that Ramses would have been glad enough to secure a respite and lead his shattered forces back to Egypt. None of his records makes any claim that he captured Kadesh, as is so frequently stated in the current histories.

Once safely extricated from the perilous position into which his rashness had betrayed him, Ramses was very proud of his exploit at Kadesh. Throughout Egypt on his more important buildings he had over and over depicted what were to him and his fawning courtiers the most important incidents of the battle. On the temple walls at Abu Simbel, at Derr, at the Ramesseum, his mortuary temple at Thebes, at Luxor, at Karnak, at Abydos and probably on other buildings now perished his artists executed a vast series of vivacious reliefs depicting Ramses' camp, the arrival of his fugitive sons, the Pharaoh's furious charge down to the river and the arrival of the recruits who rescued the camp. Before Ramses the plain is strewn with dead, among whom the accompanying bits of explanatory inscription furnish the identity of the notable personages whom we mentioned above. On the opposite shore where their comrades draw the fugitives from the water a tall figure held head downward that he may disgorge the water which he has swallowed is accompanied by the words: "The wretched chief of Aleppo, turned upside down by his soldiers, after his majesty had hurled him into the water" (Fig. 160). These sculptures are better known to modern travellers in Egypt than any other like monuments in the country. They are twice accompanied by a report on the battle which reads like an official document. There early arose a poem on the battle, of which we shall later have more to say. The ever repeated refrain in all these records is the valiant stand of the young Pharaoh "while he was alone, having no army with him." These sources have enabled us to trace with certainty the maneuvres which led up to the battle of Kadesh, the first battle in history which can be so studied; and this fact must serve as our justification for treating it at such length. We see that already in the thirteenth century B. C. the commanders of the time understood the value of placing troops advantageously before battle. The immense superiority to

FIG. 160. SCENE FROM THE RELIEFS OF THE BATTLE OF KADESH.

The Asiatics fleeing across the Orontes, are drawn from the water by their comrades on the farther shore. The king of Aleppo is held head downward by his soldiers, that he may disgorge the water he has swallowed.

be gained by clever maneuvres masked from the enemy was clearly comprehended by the Hittite king when he executed the first flank movement of which we hear in the early orient; and the plains of Syria, already at that remote epoch, witnessed notable examples of that supposedly modern science, which was brought to such perfection by Napoleon,—the science of winning the victory before the battle.

Arrived in Thebes, Ramses enjoyed the usual triumph in the state temple, accompanied by four of his sons, as he offered to the gods the "captives from the northern countries, who came to overthrow his majesty, whom his majesty slew and whose subjects he brought as living captives to fill the storehouse of his father, Amon."[1] He assumed among his titles on his monuments the phrase, "Prostrator of the lands and countries while he was alone, having no other with him."[2] While he might satisfy his vanity with such conventional honours and take great satisfaction in the reputation for personal valour which the exploit at Kadesh undoubtedly brought him; yet when he came to weigh and seriously consider the situation which he had left in Syria he must have felt dark forebodings for the future of Egyptian power in Asia. The moral effect of his return to Egypt immediately after the battle without even laying siege to Kadesh, and having lost nearly a whole division of his army, even though he had shown a brilliant defense, could only be subversive of Egyptian influence among the dynasts of Syria and Palestine. Nor would the Hittites fail to make every possible use of the doubtful battle to undermine that influence and stir up revolt. Seti I had secured northern Palestine as Egyptian territory, and this region was so near the valley of the Orontes that the emissaries of the Hittites had little difficulty in exciting it to revolt. The rising spread southward to the very gates of Ramses' frontier forts in the northeastern Delta. We see him, therefore, far from increasing the conquests of his father, obliged to begin again at the very bottom to rebuild the Egyptian empire in Asia and recover by weary campaigns even the territory which his father had won. Our sources for this period are very scanty and the order of events is not wholly certain, but Ramses seems first to

[1] III, 351.   [2] Battle of Kadesh, p. 47.

have attacked the later Philistine city of Askalon and taken it by storm.[1] By his eighth year he had forced his way through to northern Palestine, and we then find him taking and plundering the cities of western Galilee, one after another.[2] Here he came in contact with the Hittite outposts, which had been pushed far southward since the day of Kadesh. He found a Hittite garrison in the strong town of Deper, which seems to be the Tabor of Hebrew history; but assisted by his sons he assaulted and took the place,[3] and the Hittite occupation of the region could have endured but a short time. It was perhaps at this time that he penetrated into the Hauran and the region east of the Sea of Galilee and left a stela there recording his visit.[4]

Having thus in three years recovered Palestine, Ramses was again at liberty to take up his ambitious designs in Asia at the point where he had begun them four years earlier. The vigour with which he now pushed his campaigns is quite evident in the results which he achieved, although we are entirely unable to follow their course. Advancing again down the valley of the Orontes, he must have finally succeeded in dislodging the Hittites. None of the scanty records of the time states this fact; but as he made conquests far north of Kadesh that place must certainly have fallen into his hands. In Naharin he conquered the country as far as Tunip, which he also reduced and placed a statue of himself there.[5] But these places had been too long exempt from tribute to the Pharaoh to take kindly to his yoke. Moreover, they were now occupied by Hittites, who possibly continued to reside there under the rule of Ramses. In any case, the Hittites soon stirred the region to revolt and Ramses found them in Tunip, when he again came north to recover them. In this it would seem that he was successful, and in storming Tunip he again met with some adventure involving his fighting without his coat-of-mail; but the record is unhappily too fragmentary to disclose the

[1] III. 355.　　[2] III. 356.　　[3] III. 357, 359-60.　　[4] III, 358.　　[5] III, 365.

exact nature of his exploit.[1] His lists credit him with having subdued Naharin, Lower Retenu (North Syria), Arvad,
the Keftyew and Ketne in the Orontes valley.[2] It is thus
evident that Ramses' ability and tenacity as a soldier had
now really endangered the Hittite empire in Syria, although
it is very uncertain whether he succeeded in holding these
northern conquests.

When he had been thus campaigning probably some
fifteen years an important event in the internal history of
the Hittite empire brought his wars in Asia to a sudden
and final end. Metella, the Hittite king, either died in
battle or at the hands of a rival, and his brother, Khetasar,
succeeded him upon the throne.[3] Khetasar, who may have
had quite enough to do at home to maintain himself without carrying on a dangerous war with Ramses for the
possession of northern Syria, proposed to the Pharaoh a
permanent peace and a treaty of alliance. In Ramses'
twenty first year (1272 B. C.) Khetasar's messengers bearing the treaty reached the Egyptian court, now in the
Delta, as we shall later see. The treaty which they bore
had of course been drafted in advance and accepted by
representatives of the two countries, for it was now in its
final form. It contained eighteen paragraphs inscribed
on a silver tablet, surmounted by a representation showing
engraved or inlaid figures of "Sutekh embracing the likeness of the great chief of Kheta"; and of a goddess similarly embracing the figure of Khetasar's queen, Putukhipa;
while beside these were the seals of Sutekh of Kheta, Re
of Ernen, as well as those of the two royal personages.
It is to be supposed that the Hittite king received a similar
copy of the document from Ramses. This earliest surviving
international treaty bore the title: "The treaty which the
great chief of Kheta, Khetasar, the valiant, the son of
Merasar, the great chief of Kheta, the valiant, the grandson of Seplel, the great chief of Kheta, the valiant, made,
upon a silver tablet for Usermare-Setepnere [Ramses II],

[1] III, 364-5.　　　[2] III, 366.　　　[3] III, 375, l. 10.

the great ruler of Egypt, the valiant, the son of Seti I, the great ruler of Egypt, the valiant; the grandson of Ramses I, the great ruler of Egypt, the valiant; the good treaty of peace and of brotherhood, setting peace between them forever."[1] It then proceeded to review the former relations between the two countries, passed then to a general definition of the present pact, and thus to its special stipulations. Of these the most important were: the renunciation by both rulers of all projects of conquest against the other, the reaffirmation of the former treaties existing between the two countries, a defensive alliance involving the assistance of each against the other's foes; coöperation in the chastisement of delinquent subjects, probably in Syria; and the extradition of political fugitives and immigrants. A codicil provides for the humane treatment of these last. A thousand gods and goddesses of the land of the Hittites, and the same number from the land of Egypt are called upon to witness the compact; some of the more important Hittite divinities being mentioned by the names of their cities. The remarkable document closes with a curse on the violators of the treaty and a blessing upon those who should keep it; or would logically so close save that the codicil already mentioned is here attached. Ramses immediately had two copies of the treaty engraved on the walls of his temples at Thebes, preceded by an account of the coming of the Hittite messengers, and followed by a description of the figures and other representations depicted on the silver tablet.[2] Recently a preliminary draught of the Hittite copy in cuneiform on a clay tablet, was found by Winckler at Boghaz-köi in Asia Minor.

It will be noticed that the treaty nowhere refers to the boundary recognized by both countries in Syria; and we can only suppose that it may have been contained in one of the earlier treaties reaffirmed by it. It is difficult to determine the exact location of this boundary. The cuneiform documents found by Winckler at Boghaz-köi since 1906 (see p.

[1] III, 373.   [2] III, 367–391.

381) show that the Hittite kings continued to control Amor
on the upper Orontes. It is not safe to affirm that he had
permanently advanced the boundary of his father's kingdom in Asia, save probably on the coast, where he carved
two more stelæ on the rocks near Berût, beside that of his
fourth year, with which we are already acquainted.[1] The
Hittite king is recognized in the treaty as on an equality
with the Pharaoh and receives the same conditions; but as
commonly in the orient the whole transaction was interpreted by Ramses on his monuments as a great triumph for
himself, and he now constantly designated himself as the
conqueror of the Hittites.[2] Once consummated, the peace
was kept, and although it involved the sacrifice of Ramses'
ambitions for conquest in Asia, the treaty must have been
entirely satisfactory to both the parties. Thirteen years
later (1259 B. C.) the Hittite king himself visited Egypt
to consummate the marriage of his eldest daughter as the
wife of Ramses. Bearing rich gifts in a brilliant procession, with his daughter at its head, Khetasar, accompanied
by the king of Kode, appeared in Ramses' palace,[3] and his
military escort mingled with the Egyptian troops whom
they had once fought upon the Syrian plains. The Hittite
princess was given an Egyptian name, Matnefrure, "Who
Sees the Beauty of Re," and assumed a prominent position
at court.

The visit of her father was depicted on the front of
Ramses' temple at Abusimbel, with accompanying narrative inscriptions,[4] and she was given a statue beside her
royal husband in Tanis.[5] Court poets celebrated the event
and pictured the Hittite king as sending to the king of Kode
and summoning him to join in the journey to Egypt that
they might do honour to the Pharaoh.[6] They averred that
Ptah revealed himself to Ramses as the divine agent in the
happy affair: "I have made the land of Kheta," said the
god to him, "into subjects of thy palace; I have put it

[1] See above, p. 423.   [2] III, 392.   [3] III, 410, 420, 424.
[4] III, 394–424.   [5] III, 416–417.   [6] III, 425–6.

into their hearts to present themselves with fearful steps before thee bearing their impost, which their chiefs have captured, all their possessions as tribute to the fame of his majesty. His eldest daughter is in front thereof to satisfy the heart of the Lord of the Two Lands.'"[1] The event made a popular impression also, and a folk-tale, which was not put into writing, so far as we know, until Greek times, began with the marriage and told how afterward, at the request of her father, an image of the Theban Khonsu was sent to the land of the princess, that the god's power might drive forth the evil spirits from her afflicted sister. The land of the Hittite princess is called Bekhten, probably meaning Bactria; and it is not improbable that some such occurrence took place during the intercourse between Khetasar and Ramses.[2] In any event the friendly relations between the two kingdoms continued without interruption, and it is even probable that Ramses received a second daughter of Khetasar in marriage.[3] Throughout Ramses' long reign the treaty remained unbroken and the peace continued at least into the reign of his successor, Merneptah.

Ramses' conflict with the Hittites, involving probably fifteen or sixteen years of severe campaigning in Asia, constitutes the basis of the claim to a high place as a soldier usually advanced in his behalf. His only battle which we can closely follow bears unmistakable testimony to his bravery, but does not exhibit him as a skilful commander. From the day of the peace compact with Khetasar, Ramses was never called upon to enter the field again. Perhaps as early as his second year he had quelled unimportant revolts in Nubia,[4] and these continued after the Hittite war,[5] but it is not known that any of these Nubian expeditions was ever conducted by him in person. A Libyan campaign is often vaguely referred to on his monuments, and it is probable that Sherden sea-rovers were involved with the Libyans in aggressions upon Ramses' western Delta

[1] III, 410.   [2] III, 429-447.   [3] III, 427-8.   [4] III, 478.   [5] III, 448-490.

frontier,[1] but we can gather nothing as to the character of this war.

With the Asiatic campaigns of Ramses II the military aggressiveness of Egypt which had been awakened under Ahmose I in the expulsion of the Hyksos was completely exhausted. Nor did it ever revive. It was with mercenary forces and under the influence of foreign blood in the royal family that sporadic attempts to recover Syria and Palestine were made in later times. Henceforward for a long time the Pharaoh's army is but a weapon of defense against foreign aggression; a weapon, however, which he was himself unable to control,—and before which the venerable line of Re was finally to disappear.

[1] III, 491.

CHAPTER XXII

THE EMPIRE OF RAMSES II

THE dominance of Egypt in Asiatic affairs had irresist-
ibly drawn the centre of power on the Nile from Thebes
to the Delta. Ikhnaton had rudely broken with the tradition of the Empire that the Pharaoh must reside at Thebes.
It is probable that Harmhab returned thither but we have
seen that after the rise of the Nineteenth Dynasty Seti I
was obliged to spend the early part of his reign in the north,
and we find him residing for months in the Delta.[1] Ramses
II's projects of conquest in Asia finally forced the entire
abandonment of Thebes as the royal residence. It remained
the religious capital of the state and at the greater feasts
in its temple calendar the Pharaoh was often present, but
his permanent residence was in the north. His constant
presence here resulted in a development of the cities of the
eastern Delta such as they had never before enjoyed. Tanis
became a great and flourishing city, with a splendid temple,
the work of Ramses' architects. High above its massive
pylons towered a monolithic granite colossus of Ramses,
over ninety feet in height, weighing nine hundred tons, and
visible across the level country of the surrounding Delta for
many miles.[2] The Wadi Tumilat, along which the canal
from the Nile eastward to the Bitter Lakes probably already
ran, forming a natural approach to Egypt from Asia, was
also the object of Ramses' careful attention, and he built
upon it, half way out to the Isthmus of Suez, a "store-city,"
which he called Pithom, or "House of Atum." At its western end he and Seti founded a city just north of Heliopolis,
now known as Tell el-Yehudîyeh. Somewhere in the eastern
Delta he founded a residence city, Per-Ramses, or "House

[1] III, 82, 2.   [2] Petrie, Tanis, I. 22–4.

442

FIG. 161.—FRAGMENTS OF THOUSAND-TON COLOSSUS OF RAMSES II.

From a sitting statue of elephantine granite erected before the second pylon of the Ramesseum.

FIG. 162.—STORE CHAMBERS AT PITHOM.

Part of a city affirmed by the Hebrew tradition to have been built by them. See pp. 446-47.
(Stereograph, copyright by Underwood & Underwood.)

of Ramses." Its location is not certain, although it has often been thought to be identical with Tanis; but it must have been close to the eastern frontier, for a poet of the time singing of its beauties refers to it as being between Egypt and Syria. It was also accessible to seafaring traffic. Per-Ramses became the seat of government and all records of state were deposited there; but the vizier resided at Heliopolis.[1] Ramses himself was one of the gods of the city. Through these cities and Ramses' other great enterprises in this region the central portion of the eastern Delta became known as "the land of Ramses," a name so completely identified with the region that Hebrew tradition read it back into the days of Joseph and his kindred, before any Ramses had ever sat on the throne. If the flourishing development now enjoyed by the Delta was an almost unavoidable accompaniment of Ramses' projects in Asia, his energetic spirit was not less felt throughout the kingdom, where no such motives operated. Of his buildings at Heliopolis nothing remains, and only the scantiest fragments of his temples at Memphis have survived.[2] We have already noticed his extensive building operations at Abydos, in the completion of his father's splendid temple there. With this he was not content, but erected also his own mortuary temple not far from that of Seti. At Thebes he spent enormous treasure and vast resources of labour in the completion of his father's mortuary temple, another beautiful sanctuary for his own mortuary service, known to all visitors at Thebes as the Ramesseum; a large court and pylon in enlargement of the Luxor temple; while, surpassing in size all buildings of the ancient or modern world, his architects completed the colossal colonnaded hall of the Karnak temple, already begun under the first Ramses, the Pharaoh's grandfather. Few of the great temples of Egypt have not some chamber, hall, colonnade or pylon which bears his name, in perpetuating which the king stopped at no desecration or destruction of the ancient monuments of the country. A

[1] Mes Inscription.   [2] III, 530–37.

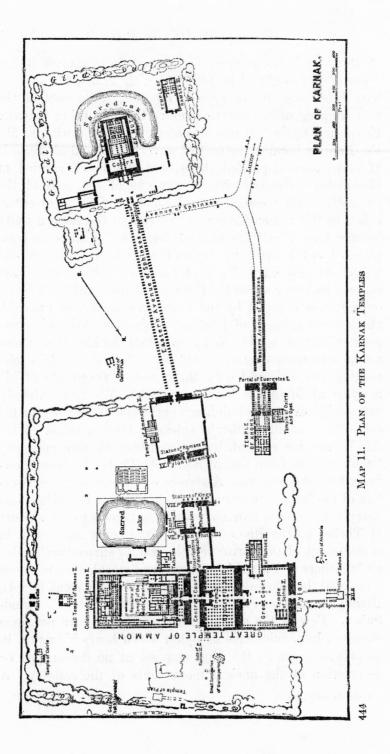

PLAN OF KARNAK.

MAP 11. PLAN OF THE KARNAK TEMPLES

building of king Teti of the Sixth Dynasty furnished material for Ramses's temple at Memphis;[1] he ransacked the
pyramid of Sesostris II at Illahun, tore up the pavement
around it and smashed its beautiful monuments to obtain
materials for his own neighbouring temple at Heracleopolis.[2]
In the Delta he was equally unscrupulous in the use of Middle
Kingdom monuments, while to make room for his enlargement of the Luxor temple he razed an exquisite granite
chapel of Thutmose III, reusing the materials, with the
name of Thutmose thereon turned inward.   Numberless
were the monuments of his ancestors on which he placed
his own name.   But in spite of these facts, his own legitimate building was on a scale quite surpassing in size and
extent anything that his ancestors had ever accomplished.
The buildings which he erected were filled with innumerable
supplementary monuments, especially colossal statues of
himself and obelisks.   The former are the greatest monolithic statues ever executed.   We have already referred to
the tallest of these in the temple at Tanis; there was another
granite monolith towering over the pylons of the Ramesseum at Thebes (Fig. 161) which, although not so high,
weighed about a thousand tons.   As the years passed and
he celebrated jubilee after jubilee the obelisks which he
erected in commemoration of these festivals rapidly rose
among his temples.   At Tanis alone he erected no less than
fourteen, all of which are now prostrate; three at least of
his obelisks are in Rome; and of the two which he erected
in Luxor, one is in Paris.[3]   Besides the wealth involved in
its erection, every such temple demanded a rich endowment.   After telling how his Abydos temple was built of
fine limestone, with granite door-posts and doors of copper
wrought with silver-gold alloy, Ramses says of its endowment that there were "established for him (the god) permanent daily offerings, at the beginnings of the seasons, all
feasts at their times. . . . He (Ramses) filled it with every-

[1] Annales, III, 29

[2] Petrie, Illahun, p. 4; Kahun, p 22; Naville, Ahnas, pp. 2, 9-11, pl. 1.

[3] III. 543-9.

thing, overflowing with food and provision, bulls, calves, oxen, geese, bread, wine, fruit. It was filled with peasant slaves, doubled in its fields, made numerous in its herds; the granaries were filled to overflowing, the grain-heaps approached heaven, . . . for the store-house of divine offerings, from the captivity of his victorious sword. His treasury was filled with every costly stone: silver, gold in blocks; the magazine was filled with everything from the tribute of all countries. He planted many gardens, set with every kind of tree, all sweet and fragrant woods, the plants of Punt.''[1] This was for the equipment of one temple only; similar endowment for all his numerous temples must have been a serious economic problem.

Notwithstanding the shift of the centre of gravity northward, the south was not neglected. In Nubia Ramses became the patron deity; no less than six new temples arose there, dedicated to the great gods of Egypt, Amon, Re, and Ptah; but in all of them Ramses was more or less prominently worshipped, and in one his queen, Nefretiri, was the presiding divinity. Of his Nubian sanctuaries, the great rock-temple at Abu Simbel is the finest and deservedly the goal of modern travellers in Egypt. Nubia became more and more Egyptianized, and between the first and second cataracts the country had received an indelible impression of Pharaonic civilization. Here the old native chiefs had practically disappeared, the administrative officials of the Pharaoh were in complete control, and there was even an Egyptian court of justice, with the viceroy as chief judge.[3]

Ramses' great building enterprises were not achieved without vast expense of resources, especially those of labour. While he was unable to draw upon Asia for captive labour as extensively as his great predecessors of the Eighteenth Dynasty, yet his building must have been largely accomplished by such means. There is probably little question of the correctness of the Hebrew tradition in attributing the oppression of some tribe of their ancestors to the builder of

[1] III, 526–7. [2] III. 492–504. [3] Erman, Life in Ancient Egypt, 504.

Pithom (Fig. 162) and Ramses; that a tribe of their forefathers should have fled the country to escape such labour
is quite in accord with what we know of the time. Intercourse with Palestine and Syria was now more intimate
than ever. A letter of a frontier official, dated in the reign
of Ramses II's successor, tells of passing a body of Edomite
Beduin through a fortress in the Wadi Tumilat, that they
might pasture their herds by the pools of Pithom as the
Hebrews had done in the days of Joseph.[1] In the rough
memoranda of a commandant's scribe, probably of the frontier fortress of Tharu, in the Isthmus of Suez, we find also
noted the people whom he had allowed to pass: messengers
with letters for the officers of the Palestinian garrisons, for
the king of Tyre, and for officers with the king (Merneptah)
then campaigning in Syria, besides officers bearing reports,
or hurrying out to Syria to join the Pharaoh.[2] Although
there was never a continuous fortification of any length
across the Isthmus of Suez, there was a line of strongholds,
of which Tharu was one and probably Ramses another,
stretching well across the zone along which Egypt might
be entered from Asia. This zone did not extend to the
southern half of the isthmus, but was confined to the territory between Lake Timsah and the Mediterranean, whence
the line of fortresses extended southward, passed the lake
and bent westward into the Wadi Tumilat. Hence Hebrew
tradition depicts the escape of the Israelites across the
southern half of the isthmus south of the line of defences,
which might have stopped them. The tide of commerce that
ebbed and flowed through the Isthmus of Suez was even
fuller than under the Eighteenth Dynasty, while on the Mediterranean the Egyptian galleys must have whitened the sea.

On the Pharaoh's table were rarities and delicacies from
Cyprus, the land of the Hittites and of the Amorites, Babylonia and Naharin. Elaborately wrought chariots, weapons,
whips and gold-mounted staves from the Palestinian and
Syrian towns filled his magazine, while his stalls boasted

[1] III, 636–38.   [2] III, 630–635.

fine horses of Babylon and cattle of the Hittite country.[1]
The appurtenances of a rich man's estate included a galley
plying between Egypt and the Syrian coast to bring to
the pampered Egyptian the luxuries of Asia;[2] and even
Seti I's mortuary temple at Abydos possessed its own sea-
going vessels, given by Ramses, to convey the temple offerings from the east.[3]   The houses of the rich were filled
with the most exquisite products of the Asiatic craftsman
and artist; and these works strongly influenced the art
of the time in Egypt.   The country swarmed with Semitic
and other Asiatic slaves, while Phœnician and other alien
merchants were so numerous that there was a foreign quar-

Fig. 163.   Heavy-armed Sherden of Ramses II's Mercenary Bodyguard.

ter in Memphis, with its temples of Baal and Astarte; and
these and other Semitic gods found a place in the Egyptian
pantheon.   The dialects of Palestine and vicinity, of which
Hebrew was one, lent many a Semitic word to the current
language of the day, as well as select terms with which the

[1] Pap. Anast., IV, 15, 2–17 = III, 8.   [2] Ibid., IV., 3, 10–11.   [3] III, 274.

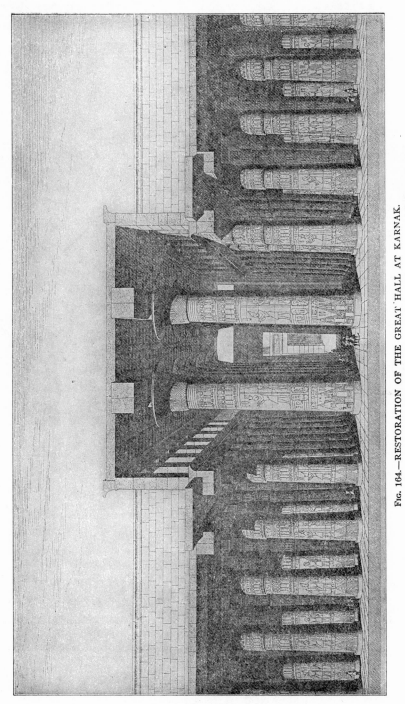

FIG. 164.—RESTORATION OF THE GREAT HALL AT KARNAK.

Nineteenth Dynasty Hypostyle in the state temple of Amon. See pp. 408, 417, 443, and 450-51   (After Perrot and Chipie)

FIG. 165.—NAVE OF THE GREAT HALL OF KARNAK.

Looking westward toward the Nile from behind the hall (see plan, p. 444). The cliffs behind the western plain
are seen through the main doorway.

learned scribes were fond of garnishing their writings. We find such words commonly in the Nineteenth Dynasty papyri four or five centuries before they appear in the Hebrew writings of the Old Testament. The royal family was not exempt from such influence; Ramses' favourite daughter was called "Bint-Anath," a Semitic name, which means "Daughter of Anath" (a Syrian goddess), and one of the royal steeds was named "Anath-herte," "Anath is Satisfied."

The effect of the vast influx of Asiatic life already apparent under the Eighteenth Dynasty was now profound, and many a foreigner of Semitic blood found favour and ultimately high station at the court or in the government. A Syrian named Ben-'Ozen was chief herald or marshal of Merneptah's court,[1] but he was never regent as sometimes stated. The commercial opportunities of the time brought wealth and power to such foreigners in Egypt; a Syrian sea-captain named Ben-Anath was able to secure a son of Ramses II as a husband for his daughter.[2] In the army great careers were open to such foreigners, although the rank and file of the Pharaoh's forces were replenished from western and southern peoples rather than from Asia. In a body of five thousand troops sent by Ramses to the Wadi Hammamat for service in the quarries there, not a single native Egyptian was to be found; over four thousand of them were Sherden and Libyans and the remainder were negroes, such as we have already seen in the Egyptian ranks as early as the Sixth Dynasty.[3] The dangerous tendencies inherent in such a system had already shown themselves and were soon felt by the royal house, although powerless to make head against them. The warlike spirit which had made Egypt the first world power had endured but a few generations, and a naturally peaceful people were returning to their accustomed peaceful life; while at the very moment

---

[1] Mar. Ab. II, 50; Cat. gen. d'Ab., No. 1136, p. 422; RIH, 32; BT, VI, 437.

[2] Ostracon, Louvre, Inv. 2262, Devér. Cat., p. 202; Rec. 16, 64.

[3] Battle of Kadesh, 9.

29

when this reversion to their old manner of living was taking place, the eastern Mediterranean and the Libyan tribes offered the Pharaoh an excellent class of mercenary soldiery which under such circumstances he could not fail to utilize.

While the wars in Asia had not recovered the empire of Thutmose III, all Palestine and possibly some of northern Syria continued to pay tribute to the Pharaoh, while on the south the boundary of the Empire was as before at Napata, below the fourth cataract. There were stately pageants when the magnificent Pharaoh, now in the prime of life, received the magnates of his empire, from the crown-prince down through all his exalted dignitaries to the mayors of the outlying towns, a brilliant procession, bringing him the tribute and impost of his realm from the southern limits of Nubia to the Hittite frontier in Syria.[1] The wealth thus gained still served high purposes. Art still flourished. Nothing better was ever produced by the Egyptian sculptor than the superb statue of the youthful Ramses (Fig. 168), which forms the chef d'œvre of the Turin Museum; and even the colossal statues like those of Abu Simbel (Fig. 167) are fine portraits. Granting that art was on the decline, there were still masters of relief who could put into stone the exquisite, even if cold, features of Bint-Anath, the Pharaoh's favourite daughter. How ever much the refinement of the Eighteenth Dynasty may be wanting in the great hall at Karnak (Figs. 164-5), it is nevertheless the most impressive building in Egypt, and at the last, as even Ruskin admits, size does tell. He who stands for the first time in the shadow of its overwhelming colonnades, that forest of mighty shafts, the largest ever erected by human hands,—crowned by the swelling capitals of the nave, on each one of which a hundred men may stand together,—he who observes the vast sweep of its aisles—roofed with hundred-ton architraves—and knows that its walls would contain the entire cathedral of Notre Dame and leave plenty

[1] III, 481-4.

FIG. 166.—THE RAMESSEUM, MORTUARY TEMPLE OF RAMSES II.

The western cliffs of the necropolis, pierced with many tomb doors, rise behind the temple.
See p. 451.

FIG. 167.—THE CLIFF TEMPLE OF ABU SIMBEL.

Looking southward across the front. See p. 451.

Fig. 168.—BLACK GRANITE STATUE OF RAMSES II.

See p. 450. (Turin Museum.)

of room to spare,—he who notes the colossal portal over
which once lay a lintel block over forty feet long and
weighing some hundred and fifty tons, will be filled with
respect for the age that produced this the largest columned
hall ever raised by man.   And if the discerning eye is rather
impressed by its size than by the beauty of its lines, it should
not be forgotten that the same architects produced Ramses'
mortuary temple, the Ramesseum (Fig. 166), a building
not inferior in refined beauty to the best works of the Eighteenth Dynasty.   In Nubia also, where the scanty margin
between the Nile and the cliffs was either insufficient or
could not be spared for temples of masonry, the rock-
hewn sanctuaries of Ramses form distinct contributions to
architecture.   No visitor to the temple of Abu Simbel (Fig.
167) will ever forget the solemn grandeur of this lonely
sanctuary looking out upon the river from the sombre cliffs.
But among the host of buildings which Ramses exacted from
his architects, there were unavoidably many which were
devoid of all life and freshness, or like his addition to the
Luxor temple, heavy, vulgar and of very slovenly workmanship.   All such buildings were emblazoned with gayly coloured reliefs depicting the valiant deeds of the Pharaoh in
his various wars, especially, as we have already noticed,
his desperate defence at the battle of Kadesh (Fig. 169).
This last was the most pretentious composition ever
attempted by the Egyptian draughtsman.   The winding
river, the moated city, the flying foe, the prudent king of
the Hittites surrounded by masses of his foot, discreetly
withholding his own person from the combat, in striking
contrast with the furious onset of the Pharaoh,—all this is
wrought out with skill, although obscured by unconscious-
ness of the proper relations of time and place, always characteristic of Egyptian as well as all other early oriental compositions.   Although the reliefs of the time thus show
marked progress in the art of composition, the innumerable
figures included in such a work individually receive too
little attention and are often badly drawn.   But no such

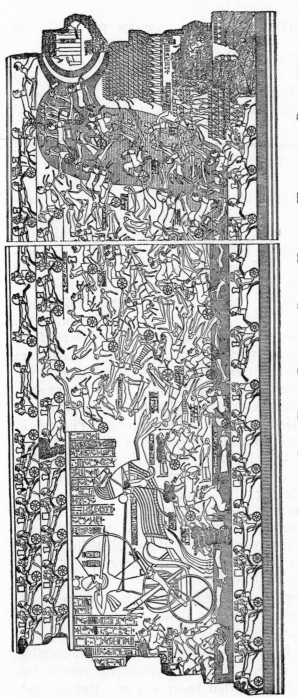

FIG. 169. BATTLE SCENE FROM THE GREAT KADESH RELIEFS OF RAMSES II ON THE WALLS OF THE RAMESSEUM.

It shows Ramses alone (though, of course, he should be accompanied by his household troops), surrounded by Asiatic chariotry (above and below). Before him are the fallen lords of the Hittite King's army, each accompanied by his name and titles (engraved beside him). The scene depicts the moment of the Pharaoh's charge, when he drove the eastern wing of the enemy into the river (Map 10). The fugitives swim across and are pulled out by their comrades on the other shore (see king of Aleppo, Fig. 160). On the right of the king of Aleppo, where the wall is broken, stands the Hittite King in his chariot, among a mass of 8,000 Asiatic foot. In the upper right hand corner is the doubly moated city of Kadesh.

452

ambitious compositions are elsewhere found in the oriental world for six hundred years or more.

This last incident was not only influential in graphic art; it also wrought powerfully upon the imagination of the court poets, one of whom produced a prose poem on the battle, which displays a good deal of literary skill, and is the nearest approach to the epic to be found in Egyptian literature. We are told how the foe covered the hills like grass-hoppers, the incidents that led up to the catastrophe are narrated with precision and clearness, and then as the Pharaoh finds himself alone in the midst of the foe the poet pictures him calling upon his father Amon for aid while the god in distant Thebes, hearing the cry of his son, answers and nerves his arm for the ordeal in a response which has all the fine and heroic spirit of the epic poem. The author's perception of dramatic contrasts is remarkable. He depicts the dismay of the royal charioteer that he may contrast it with Ramses' undaunted spirit and may put into the Pharaoh's mouth a fiery speech of encouragement. When it is all over and the crisis passed there is, among other incidents, a pleasing epic touch in Ramses' vow that the brave chariot-horses which bore him safely through the conflict shall always be fed by his own hand. A copy of this composition on papyrus was made by a scribe named Pentewere (Pentaur), who was misunderstood by early students of the document to be the author of the poem. The real author is unknown, although "Pentaur" still commonly enjoys the distinction. In manner this heroic poem strikes a new note; but it came at a period too late in the history of the nation to be the impulse toward a really great epic. The martial age and the creative spirit were passed in Egypt. In the tale, however, the Nineteenth Dynasty really showed great fertility, combined with a spontaneous naturalism, which quite swept away all trace of the artificialities of the Middle Kingdom. Already in the Middle Kingdom there had grown up collections of artless folk-tales woven often about a historical motive, and such tales, clothed in the simple language of the people, had early in the Eighteenth Dynasty gained sufficient literary respectability to be put into writing. While the Eighteenth Dynasty possessed such tales as these, yet by far the larger part of our surviving manuscripts of this class date from the Nineteenth Dynasty and later. It is now that we find the story of the conflict between the Hyksos king Apophis and Sekenere at Thebes a tale of which the lost conclusion doubtless contained a popular version of the expulsion of the Hyksos. The reader will recall its contribution to our scanty knowledge of the Hyksos.[1] The people now loved to dwell upon the exploits of Thutmose III's commanders, telling of Thutiy and his capture of Joppa by introducing his soldiers into the city in panniers loaded on donkeys, a tale which was perhaps the prototype of Ali Baba and the Forty Thieves. But the artless charm of the story of the doomed prince quite surpasses such historical tales. An only son, he is doomed by the Hathors at his birth to die by a crocodile, a serpent or a dog. Journeying to Syria, he succeeds in climbing a tower in which the king of Naharin had confined his daughter, that he among the young nobles of Syria whose strength of arm and steady nerve should enable him to swing himself aloft to the young girl's window might lead her away as his wife. But, as the prince had not divulged his real identity, having given himself out to be the son of an Egyptian officer, the king of Naharin refused to give him his daughter and afterward would have killed him. At this juncture the young girl saved her lover by avowing her firm intention of slaying herself if they slew him. The king then relented and the prince received his bride. Having escaped the crocodile and the serpent it is probable that he then fell a victim to his faithful dog which had followed him from Egypt, but the end of the story is wanting. It furnishes the earliest known example of that almost universal motive in which a youth must pass through some ordeal or competition in order to

---

[1] See above, pp. 215–16, 223–24.

win a wife; a motive which later found place in more pretentious compositions, even Greek drama, as in the tale of Œdipus and the Sphinx, immortalized in Sophocles' tragedy. A pastoral tale of idyllic simplicity represents two brothers as living together, the elder being married and a householder, while the younger dwells with him much after the manner of a son. There now befell the younger brother an adventure later appropriated for the Hebrew hero, Joseph. The wife of his elder brother tempted him and he, proving inflexible, the woman, to revenge herself, maligned him to her husband. The youth, warned by the cattle of his herd as he drove them to the stable, fled for his life, and the tale here merges into a series of half mythical incidents not so pleasing as the introductory chapter. The number of such tales must have been legion, and in Greek times they furnished all that many Greek writers, or even the priest Manetho knew of early Egyptian kings.

While much of such literature is poetic in content and spirit, it lacks poetic form. Such form, however, was not wanting, and among the songs of this period are some poems which might well find a place among a more pretentious literature.

There were love-songs also, which in a land where imagination was not strong possess qualities of genuine feeling which do not fail to appeal to us of the modern world. Religious poems, songs and hymns are now very numerous, and some of them display distinct literary character. We shall revert to them again in discussing the religion of this age. Numerous letters from scribes and officials of the time, exercises and practice letters composed by pupils of the scribal schools, bills, temple records and accounts,—all these serve to fill in the detail in a picture of unusual fullness and interest.

By far the larger portion of the surviving literature of the time is religious and in so far as it is the outgrowth of the state religion, the impression which it conveys is far from gratifying. Since the overthrow of Ikhnaton and the return to the conventions of the past, the state religion had lost all vitality, and in the hands of the orthodox priests no longer possessed the creative faculty. Yet the religion of the time was making a kind of progress, or at least it was moving in a certain direction and that very rapidly. The state, always closely connected with religion, was gradually being more and more regarded as chiefly a religious institution, designed to exalt and honour the gods through its head the Pharaoh. Among other indications of this tendency the names of the temples furnish a significant hint. Sanctuaries which formerly bore names like "Splendour of Splendours," "Splendid in Monuments," "Gift of Life," and the like, were now designated "Dwelling of Seti in the House of Amon," or "Dwelling of Ramses in the House of Ptah." This tendency, already observable in the Middle Kingdom, was now universal, and every temple was thus designated as the sanctuary of the ruling Pharaoh. That which had long been the sacerdotal theory and ideal of the state was now beginning to be practically realized: the Empire was to become the domain of the gods and the Pharaoh was to give himself up to the duties of a universal high-priesthood. The temple endowments, not being subject to taxes, now played an important economic role, and we have seen Seti I and Ramses in search of new sources of revenue as the demands of the priesthoods increased. The state was being gradually distorted to fulfill one function at the expense of all the rest, and its wealth and economic resources were thus being slowly engulfed, until its industrial processes should become but incidents in the maintenance of the gods. As the wealth and power of Amon in particular increased, his High Priest at Thebes became a more and more important political factor. We recall that he was head of the sacerdotal organization embracing all the priesthoods of the country; he thus controlled a most influential political faction. Hence it was that the High Priest of Amon under Merneptah (Ramses II's son and successor) and possibly already under Ramses himself was able to go further and to install his son as his own successor, thus firmly entrenching his family at the head of the most powerful hierarchy in Egypt.[1]   While such a family like a royal dynasty might suffer overthrow, the precedent was a dangerous one, and it ultimately resulted in the dethronement of the Pharaohs at the hands of the priests.   That event, however, was still some hundred and fifty years distant, and meantime the High Priest employed his power and influence with the Pharaoh in enforcing ever fresh demands upon his treasury, until before the close of the Nineteenth Dynasty Amon had even secured certain gold country in Nubia in his own right.   It was administered by the viceroy of Kush, who therefore assumed the additional title "Governor of the Gold Country of Amon."[2]   Thus there was gradually arising the sacerdotal state described by Diodorus, upon which the Egyptian priests of Greek times looked back as upon a golden age.   As the inward content of the prevailing religion had already long been determined by the dominant priesthood, so now its outward manifestations were being elaborated by them into a vast and inflexible system, and the popularity of every Pharaoh with the priesthood was determined by the degree of his aquiescence in its demands.

Though the state religion was made up of formalities, the Pharaohs were not without their own ethical standards, and these were not wholly a matter of appearances.   We have witnessed the efforts of Harmhab to enforce honesty in the dealings of the government with its subjects; we have noted Thutmose III's respect for truth.   In the dedicatory record of his mortuary temple at Thebes, Ramses III proclaims that he did not remove any old tombs to obtain the necessary room for the building;[3] and he also wishes it known that he gained his exalted station without depriving any one else of his throne.[4]   The barbarous disregard of the sanctity of the monuments of his ancestors by Ramses II however we have already noticed.   The things for which these

----

[1] III, 618.   [2] III, 640.   [3] IV, 4.   [4] IV, 188.

kings prayed were not character nor the blameless life. It is material things which they desire. Ramses IV prays to Osiris, "And thou shalt give to me health, life, long existence and a prolonged reign; endurance to my every member, sight to my eyes, hearing to my ears, pleasure to my heart daily. And thou shalt give to me to eat until I am satisfied, and thou shalt give to me to drink until I am drunk. And thou shalt establish my issue as kings forever and ever. And thou shalt grant me contentment every day, and thou shalt hear my voice in every saying, when I shall tell them to thee, and thou shalt give them to me with a loving heart. And thou shalt give to me high and plenteous Niles in order to supply thy divine offerings and to supply the divine offerings of all the gods and goddesses of South and North; in order to preserve alive the divine bulls, in order to preserve alive the people of all thy lands, their cattle and their groves, which thy hand has made. For thou art he who has made them all and thou canst not forsake them to carry out other designs with them; for that is not right."[1]

A higher type of personal religion was developing among the better class of the people than the sensual materialism which this royal prayer displays. A fine hymn to Amon, popular at this time, contains many of the old ideas prevalent in the Aton-faith, while other religious poems show that a personal relation is gradually growing up between the worshipper and his god, so that he sees in his god the friend and protector of men. Thus one says: "Amon-Re, I love thee and I have enfolded thee in my heart. . . . I follow not the care in my heart; what Amon says prospers."[2] Or again: "Amon lend thine ear to him who stands alone in the court of judgment,"[3] and when the court is won by rich bribes Amon becomes the vizier of the poor man.[4] Man feels also the sense of sin and cries out: "Punish me not for my many sins."[5] The proverbial wisdom of the time shows much of the same spirit. Whereas it formerly incul-

[1] IV, 470.
[2] Pap. Anast., II., 8, 6.
[3] Birch, Inscr. in the Hier. Char., pl. XXVI.
[4] Ibid., 6, 5-6.
[5] Erman, Handbuch.

cated only correct behaviour, it now exhorts to hate evil, and
to abhor what the god abhors.   Prayer should be the silent
aspiration of the heart and to Thoth the wise man prays,
"O thou sweet Well for the thirsty in the desert! It is
closed up for him who speaks, but it is open for him who
keeps silence. When he who keeps silence comes, lo he finds
the Well."[1] The poisonous power of the magical literature
now everywhere disseminated by the priests gradually
stifled these aspirations of the middle class, and these the
last symptoms of ethical and moral life in the religion of
Egypt slowly disappeared. It is at this time that we gain
our sole glimpse into the religious beliefs of the common
people. The appropriation of the temples by the state had
long ago driven them from their ancient shrines. The poor
man had no place amid such magnificance, nor could he
offer anything worthy the attention of a god of such splendour. The old modest cult of the great gods having long
since passed away, the poor man could only resort to the
host of minor genii or spirits of mirth and music, the demi-
gods, who, frequenting this or that local region, had interest
and inclination to assist the humble in their daily cares and
needs. Any object whatsoever might become the poor man's
god. A man writing from Thebes commends his friend to
Amon, Mut and Khonsu, the great divinities of that place,
but adds also, "to the great gate of Beki, to the eight apes
which are in the forecourt," and to two trees.[2] In the
Theban necropolis Amenhotep I and the queen Nefretiri
have become the favourite local divinities, and a man who
accidentally thrust his hand into a hole where lay a large
serpent, without being bitten, immediately erected a tablet
to tell the tale and express his gratitude to Amenhotep,
whose power alone had saved him.[3] Another had in some
way transgressed against a goddess who, according to popular belief, resided in a hill-top of the same necropolis, and
when at last the goddess released him from the power of
the disease with which she was afflicting him, he erected a

---

[1] Pap. Sallier, I, 8, 2 ff.   [2] Erman, Handbuch.   [3] Turin Stela.

similar memorial in her honour. In the same way the dead might afflict the living, and an officer who was tormented by his deceased wife wrote to her a letter of remonstrance and placed it in the hand of another dead person that it might be duly delivered to his wife in the hereafter. Besides the local gods, or demigods and the old kings, the foreign gods of Syria, brought in by the hosts of Asiatic slaves, appear also among those to whom the folk appeal; Baal, Kedesh, Astarte, Reshep, Anath and Sutekh are not uncommon names upon the votive tablets of the time, and Sutekh, a form of Set which had wandered into Syria from Egypt and had returned with the Hyksos, even became the favourite and patron of the royal city of Ramses II. Animal worship now also begins to appear both among the people and in official circles.

The young Pharaoh under whom these momentous transitions were slowly taking place was too plastic in dealing with them for us to discover the manner of man he was. For his records are almost all of sacerdotal origin, and in them all the priestly adulation of the time, with its endless reiteration of conventional flattery, prevails so largely, or we may say often so exclusively that we can discern little individuality through the mass of meaningless verbiage. His superb statue in Turin (Fig. 168) is proven by his surviving body to be a faithful portrait, showing us at least the outward man as he was. In person he was tall and handsome, with features of dreamy and almost effeminate beauty, in no wise suggestive of the manly traits which he certainly possessed. For the incident at Kadesh showed him unquestionably a man of fine courage with ability to rise to a supreme crisis; while the indomitable spirit evident there is again exhibited in the tenacity with which he pushed the war against the great Hittite empire and carried his conquests, even if not lasting, far into northern Syria. After his nearly fifteen years of campaigning, in which he more than redeemed the almost fatal blunder at Kadesh, he was quite ready to enjoy the well earned peace. He was inordinately vain and made far more ostentatious display of his wars on his monuments than was ever done by Thutmose III. He loved ease and pleasure and gave himself up without restraint to voluptuous enjoyments. He had an enormous harem, and as the years passed his children multiplied rapidly. He left over a hundred sons and at least half as many daughters, several of whom he himself married. He thus left a family so numerous that they became a Ramessid class of nobles whom we still find over four hundred years later bearing among their titles the name Ramses, not as a patronymic, but as the designation of a class or rank. Unable, perhaps, to find suitable wives of rank and wealth for his army of sons, one of them, as we have seen, received the daughter of a Syrian ship-captain. Ramses took great pride in his enormous family and often ordered his sculptors to depict his sons and daughters in long rows upon the walls of his temples. The sons of his youth accompanied him in his wars, and according to Diodorus one of them was in command of each of the divisions of his army.[1] His favourite among them was Khamwese, whom he made High Priest of Ptah at Memphis. But his affection included them all, and his favourite wives and daughters appear with noticeable frequency upon his monuments.

As Ramses reached the thirtieth year of his reign he celebrated his first jubilee, placing the ceremonies of the celebration in charge of his favourite son, Khamwese, the great magician and High Priest of Ptah, whose memory still lived in the folk-tales of Egypt a thousand years later. Twenty years more passed, during which Ramses celebrated a jubilee every one to three years, instituting no less than nine of these feasts, a far larger number than we are able to find in the reigns of any of his predecessors.[2] The obelisks erected on these occasions have already claimed our notice. With his name perpetuated in vast buildings distributed at all points along the Nile from the marshes

[1] Diod., I, 47; comp. Battle of Kadesh, p. 34.   [2] III, 543-560.

of the northern Delta to the fourth cataract, Ramses lived on in magnificence even surpassing that of Amenhotep III. His was the sunset glory of the venerable line which he represented. As the years passed the sons of his youth were taken from him and Khamwese was no longer there to conduct the celebration of the old king's jubilees. One by one they passed away until twelve were gone, and the thirteenth was the eldest and heir to the throne. Yet still the old king lived on. He had lost the vitality for aggressive rule. The Libyans and the maritime peoples allied with them, Lycians, Sardinians and the Ægean races whom he had once swept from his coasts or impressed into the service of his army now entered the western Delta with impunity. The Libyans pushed forward, gradually extending their settlements almost to the gates of Memphis and crossed the southern apex of the Delta under the very shadow of the walls of Heliopolis where the vizier lived. Senile decay rendered him deaf to alarms and complaints which would have brought instant retribution upon the invaders in the days of his vigourous youth. Amid the splendours of his magnificent residence in the eastern Delta the threatening conditions at its opposite extremity never roused him from the lethargy into which he had fallen. Finally, having ruled for sixty seven years, and being over ninety years of age, he passed away (1225 B. C.) none too soon for the redemption of his empire. We are able to look into the withered face of the hoary nonogenarian (Fig. 170), evidently little changed from what he was in those last days of splendour in the city of Ramses, and the resemblance to the face of the youth in the noble Turin statue is still very marked.

Probably no Pharaoh ever left a more profound impression upon his age. A quarter of a century later began a line of ten kings bearing his name. One of them prayed that he might be granted a reign of sixty seven years like that of his great ancestor,[1] and all of them with varying suc-

---

[1] IV, 471.

cess imitated his glory.   He had set his stamp upon them all for a hundred and fifty years, and it was impossible to be a Pharaoh without being a Ramses.   Had they possessed the aggressive vigour of the great Ramses' prime this influence might have been far less unwholesome, but in a time when Egypt and entirely lost its expansive force the influence of Ramses' memory served only to foster the sacerdotal tendencies which were now dominant in the state. It was thus the Ramses of the latter half of his reign, whose influence was most potent, and in a day when Egypt should have been girding her loins and husbanding her resources for a struggle involving her very existence, she was relinquishing her sword to mercenary strangers and lavishing her wealth upon temples already too richly endowed for the economic safety of the state.

CHAPTER XXIII

THE FINAL DECLINE OF THE EMPIRE: MERNEPTAH
AND RAMSES III

EGYPT was now on the defensive. This was the result of conditions both within and without. As we have seen, the nation had lost its expansive power and the impulse which resulted from the expulsion of the Hyksos three hundred and fifty years before was no longer felt. The exploits of Thutmose III's generals were still narrated, and garnished with legendary wonders they still circulated among the people. But the spirit which had stirred the heroes of the first Asiatic conquests had now vanished. While this was the condition within, without all was turbulence and unrest. The restless maritime peoples of the northern Mediterranean, creeping along the coasts, sought plunder or places for permanent settlement, and together with the Libyans on the one hand and the peoples of remoter Asia Minor on the other, they broke in wave on wave upon the borders of the Pharaoh's empire. Egypt was inevitably thrown on the defensive, her day of conquest and aggression was passed and for six hundred years no serious effort to extend her borders was made. For the next sixty years after the death of Ramses II we shall be able to watch the struggle of the Pharaohs merely to *preserve* the empire, which it had been the ambition of their great ancestors rather to *extend*. At this crisis in the affairs of the nation, after it had been under the rule of an aged man for twenty years and much needed the vigourous hand of a young and active monarch, the enfeebled Ramses was succeeded by his thirteenth son, Merneptah, now far advanced in years. Thus one old man succeeded another upon the throne. The result was what might have been expected. Nothing was

464

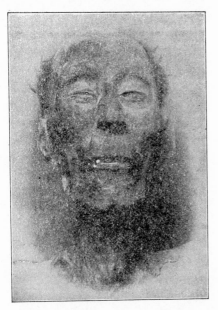

Fig. 170.—HEAD OF RAMSES II.

From his mummy. (Cairo Museum.)

Fig. 171.—VICTORIOUS HYMN
OF MERNEPTAH.

Containing the earliest-known reference to Israel. See pp. 465, 466,
470, and 471–72.

Fig. 172.—PELESET OR PHILISTINE PRISONERS OF RAMSES III.

Relief on the second pylon at Medinet Habu.

immediately done to check the bold incursions of the Libyans and their maritime allies on the west.   The death of
Ramses was not followed by any disturbance in the Asiatic
dominions in so far as we can see.   The northern border
in Syria was as far north as the upper Orontes valley, including at least part of the Amorite country in which Merneptah had a royal city bearing his name, probably inherited
from his father and renamed.   With the Hittite kingdom
he enjoyed undisturbed peace, doubtless under the terms
of the old treaty, negotiated by his father forty six years
before.   Indeed Merneptah sent shiploads of grain to the
Hittites to relieve them in time of famine; but he must have
been fully paid for the shipment, although one might infer
from his reference to it that it was a work of philanthropy.[1]
By the end of his second year, however, he had reason to
rue the good will shown his father's ancient enemy.   It will
be remembered that among the allies of the Hittites at the
battle of Kadesh there were already maritime peoples like
the Lycians and Dardanians.   In some way Merneptah
must have discovered that the Hittites were now involved
in the incursions of these peoples in the western Delta in
alliance with the Libyans.   Perhaps for the sake of further
conquest in Syria, they had given the Libyans and their
allies at least moral support and actively stirred rebellion
among the Pharaoh's Asiatic cities.   However this may be,
the year three (about 1223 B. C.) found widespread revolt
against him in Asia; Askalon at the very gates of Egypt,
the powerful city of Gezer at the lower end of the valley of
Ajalon, leading up from the sea-plain to Jerusalem; Yenoam, one of the Lebanon Tripolis given by Thutmose III
to Amon two hundred and sixty years before, the tribes
of Israel and all western Syria-Palestine as far as it was
controlled by the Pharaoh; all these rose against their
Egyptian overlord.   We have nothing but a song of triumph to tell us of the ensuing war; but it is evident that
Merneptah appeared in Asia in his third year,[2] and in

[1] III, 580, 1. 24.   [2] III, 629-35.

spite of his advanced years carried the campaign to a successful issue. It is probable, indeed, that even the Hittites did not escape his wrath, though we cannot suppose that the aged Merneptah could have done more than plunder a border town or two. The revolting cities were severely punished and all Palestine was again humiliated and brought completely under the yoke. Among the revolters who suffered were some of the tribes of Israel who had now secured a footing in Palestine, as we saw at the close of the Eighteenth and opening of the Nineteenth Dynasty. They were sufficiently amalgamated to be referred to as "Israel," and they here make their first appearance in history as a people. Gezer must have cost Merneptah some trouble and perhaps withstood a siege; in any case he thereafter styled himself in his titulary "Binder of Gezer,"[1] as if its subjugation were a notable achievement. Such a siege would explain why Merneptah was unable to move against the invaders of the western Delta until his fifth year, as the investment of such a stronghold as Gezer might have occupied him another year. When he returned the Egyptian domains in Asia had been saved, but it is not probable that he had advanced the inherited frontier.

Meantime the situation in the west was serious in the extreme; the hordes of Tehenu-Libyans were pushing further into the Delta from their settlements along the northern coast of Africa west of Egypt. It is possible that some of their advance settlers had even reached the canal of Heliopolis.[2] Little is known of the Libyans at this time. Immediately upon the Egyptian border seems to have been the territory of the Tehenu; further west came the tribes known to the Egyptians as Lebu or Rebu, the Libyans of the Greeks, by which name also the Egyptians designated these western peoples as a whole. On the extreme west, and extending far into then unknown regions, lived the Meshwesh, or Maxyes, of Herodotus. They were all doubtless the ancestors of the Berber tribes of North Africa. They

[1] III, 606.   [2] III, 576.

were far from being totally uncivilized barbarians, but were skilled in war, well armed and capable of serious enterprises against the Pharaoh. Just at this time they were rapidly consolidating, and under good leadership gave promise of becoming an aggressive and formidable state, with its frontier not ten days' march from the Pharaoh's residence in the eastern Delta. The whole western Delta was strongly tinctured with Libyan blood and Libyan families were now constantly crossing the western border of the Delta as far as the "great river" as the western or Canopic mouth of the Nile was called. Others had penetrated to the two northern oases which lie southwest of the Fayum. "They spend their time going about the land nghting to fill their bodies daily," says Merneptah's record, "they come to the land of Egypt to seek the necessities of their mouths."[1] Emboldened by their long immunity, the Libyans assumed an organized offensive, and what had been but a scattered immigration now became a compact invasion. Meryey, king of the Libyans, forced the Tehenu to join him and, supported by roving bands of maritime adventurers from the coast, he invaded Egypt. He brought his wife and his children with him,[2] as did also his allies[3] and the movement was clearly an immigration as well as an invasion. The allies were the now familiar Sherden or Sardinians; the Shekelesh, possibly the Sikeli natives of early Sicily; Ekwesh, perhaps Achæans, the Lycians, who had preyed on Egypt since the days of Amenhotep III; and the Teresh, doubtless the Tyrsenians or Etruscans.[4] It is with these wandering marauders that the peoples of Europe emerge for the first time upon the arena of history, although we have seen them in their material documents since the Middle Kingdom. This crossing to Africa by the northern Mediterranean peoples is but one of the many such ventures which in prehistoric ages brought over the white race whom we know as Libyans. Judging from the numbers who were afterward slain or captured, the Libyan king

[1] III, 580.   [2] III, 579.   [3] III, 595.   III, 579.

must have commanded at least some twenty thousand men or more.

Merneptah, at last aroused to the situation, was fortifying Heliopolis and Memphis,[1] when news of the danger reached him late in March of his fifth year. Instantly summoning his officials, he ordered them to muster the troops and have the army ready to move in fourteen days.[2] The aged king had a reassuring dream, in which Ptah appeared in gigantic stature beside him and extended him a sword, telling him to banish all fear.[3] By the middle of April the Egyptian force was in the western Delta, and on the evening of the same day came within striking distance of the enemy.[4] Near a place called Perire, the location of which, although not exactly certain, is to be placed somewhere on the main road leading westward out of the Delta into the Libyan country a few miles in from the frontier fort and station guarding the road at the point where it entered the Delta. In the vicinity of Perire,[5] among the opulent vineyards of the region there was a chateau of the Pharaoh and thence eastward extended the broad prospect of nodding grainfields where the rich Delta harvest was now fast ripening for the sickle. Upon such a prospect of smiling plenty the barbarian host looked down as they pushed past the western frontier forts. By the Pharaoh's Perire chateau, on the morning of April fifteenth, battle was joined. The contest lasted six hours when the Egyptian archers drove the allies from the field with immense loss. As is customary in modern times at this point in a battle, Merneptah now immediately threw in his horse in pursuit of the flying enemy, who were harried and decimated till they reached the "Mount of the Horns of the Earth," as the Egyptians called the edge of the plateau on the west of the Delta into which they escaped.[6] King Meryey had fled from the field as soon as he saw the action going against him. He made good his escape, but all his household fur-

---

[1] III, 576. [2] III, 581. [3] III, 582.
[4] III, 583. [5] III, 600. [6] III, 584, 600.

niture and his family fell into the hands of the Egyptians.[1]
The energetic pursuit resulted in a great slaughter and
many prisoners. No less than nine thousand of the invaders fell, of whom at least one third were among the
maritime allies of the Libyans; while probably as many
more were taken prisoner. Among the dead were six sons
of the Libyan king.[2] The booty was enormous; some nine
thousand copper swords and of weapons of all sorts and
similar equipment no less than over one hundred and twenty
thousand pieces. Besides these there were the fine weapons
and vessels in precious metal taken from the camp of the
Libyan king's household and chiefs, comprising over three
thousand pieces.[3] When the camp had been thoroughly
looted its leathern tents were fired and the whole went up
in smoke and flame.[4]

The army then returned in triumph to the royal residence
in the eastern Delta bearing laden upon asses the hands and
other trophies cut from the bodies of the slain.[5] The booty
and the trophies were brought beneath the palace balcony,
where the king inspected them and showed himself to the
rejoicing multitude.[6] He then assembled the nobles in the
great hall of the palace where he harangued them. What
was more important, there now came to him a letter from
the commandant of one of the fortresses on the frontier of
the western Delta, stating that the Libyan king had escaped
past the Egyptian cordon in the darkness of the night; and
adding information to the effect that the Libyans had repudiated and dethroned their discomfited king and chosen
another in his place who was hostile to him and would fight
him.[7] It was evident therefore that the aggressive party
in Libya had fallen and that no further trouble from that
quarter need be apprehended during the reign of Merneptah
at least.

In the rejoicing of the people which followed this great
deliverance, there is a note not only of exuberant triumph

[1] III, 584.　　[2] III, 588.　　[3] III, 589.　　[4] III, 589, 610.
[5] III, 587.　　[6] Ibid.　　[7] III, 586, 610.

but also of intense relief. The constant plundering at the
hands of Libyan hordes, which the people of the western
Delta had endured for nearly a generation was now ended.
Not only was a great national danger averted, but an intolerable situation was relieved. Little wonder that the people
sang: "Great joy has come in Egypt, rejoicing comes forth
from the towns of Tomeri [Egypt]. They talk of the victories which Merneptah has achieved among the Tehenu:
'How amiable is he, the victorious ruler! How magnified
is the king among the gods! How fortunate is he, the commanding lord! Sit happily down and talk or walk far out
upon the way for there is no fear in the heart of the people.
The strongholds are left to themselves, the wells are opened
again. The messengers skirt the battlements of the walls,
shaded from the sun, until their watchmen wake. The soldiers lie sleeping and the border-scouts are in the field [or
not] as they desire. The herds of the field are left as
cattle sent forth without herdman, crossing at will the fullness of the stream. There is no uplifting of a shout in the
night: "Stop! Behold one comes, one comes with the speech
of strangers!" One comes and goes with singing, and there
is no lamentation of mourning people. The towns are settled
again anew; and as for one that ploweth his harvest, he shall
eat of it. Re has turned himself to Egypt; he was born destined to be her protector, even the king Merneptah.' "

> The kings are overthrown, saying, "Salâm!"
> Not one holds up his head among the nine nations of the bow.
> Wasted is Tehenu,
> The Hittite Land is pacified,
> Plundered is the Canaan, with every evil,
> Carried off is Askalon,
> Seized upon is Gezer,
> Yenoam is made as a thing not existing.
> Israel is desolated, her seed is not,
> Palestine has become a [defenseless] widow for Egypt.
> All lands are united, they are pacified;
> Every one that is turbulent is bound by king Merneptah.[1]

[1] III, 616–617.

It is this concluding song, reverting also to Merneptah's triumphs in Asia, which tells us nearly all that we know of his Asiatic war. It is a kind of summary of all his victories, and forms a fitting conclusion of the rejoicing of the people.

Thus the sturdy old Pharaoh, although bowed down with years, had repelled from his empire the first assault, premonitory of the coming storm. He reigned at least five years longer, apparently enjoying profound peace in the north. He strengthened his Asiatic frontier with a fortress bearing his name,[1] and in the south he quelled a rebellion in Nubia.[2] The commonly accepted statement that toward the end of his reign a Syrian at court gained control of Merneptah and became regent is entirely without foundation and due to misunderstanding of the titles of Ben-'Ozen, the Syrian marshal of his court, to whom we have already referred.[3] The long reign of Ramses II, with its prodigality in buildings, left Merneptah little means to gratify his own desires in this respect. Moreover, his days were numbered and there was not time to hew from the quarries and transport the materials for such a temple as it had now become customary for each Pharaoh to erect at Thebes for his own mortuary service. Under these circumstances, Merneptah had no hesitation in resorting to the most brutal destruction of the monuments of his ancestors. To obtain materials for his mortuary temple he made a quarry of the noble sanctuary of Amenhotep III on the western plain, ruthlessly tore down its walls and split up its superb statues to serve as blocks in his own building. Among other things thus appropriated was a magnificent black granite stela over ten feet high (Fig. 171) containing a record of Amenhotep III's buildings.[4] Merneptah erected it in his new building with face to the wall, and his scribes cut upon the back a hymn of victory[5] over the Libyans, of which we have quoted the conclusion above. It has become notable because it contains the earliest known reference to Israel.[6] Mer-

[1] Pap. Anast, VI, pl. 4, l. 13–pl. 5, l. 5.   [2] III, p. 259, note a.
[3] See above, p. 449.   [4] II, 878 ff.   [5] III, 602–617.   [6] See p. 470.

neptah's desecration of the great works of the earlier Pharaohs did not even spare those of his own father who, it
will be remembered, had set him a notorious example in this
respect. Ramses had the audacity, after a life time of such
vandalism, to record in his Abydos temple a long appeal to
his descendants to respect his foundations and his monuments,[1] but not even his own son showed them the respect
which he craved. We find Merneptah's name constantly
on the monuments of his father.

After a reign of at least ten years Merneptah passed away
(1215 B. C.) and was buried at Thebes in the valley with
his ancestors. His body has recently been found there,
quite discomfiting the adherents of the theory that, as the
undoubted Pharaoh of the Hebrew exodus, he must have
been drowned in the Red Sea! However much we may
despise him for his desecration and shameful destruction
of the greatest works of his ancestors, it must be admitted
at the same time that at an advanced age, when such responsibility must have sat heavily, he manfully met a grave
crisis in the history of his country, which might have thrown
it into the hands of a foreign dynasty.

The laxity which had accompanied the long continued rule
of two old men gave ample opportunity for intrigue, conspiracy and the machinations of rival factions. The death
of Merneptah was the beginning of a conflict for the throne
which lasted for many years. Two pretenders were at
first successful: Amenmeses and Merneptah-Siptah.[2] The
former was but an ephemeral usurper, who through some
collateral line of the royal house perhaps possessed a distant claim to the throne. He was hostile to the memory of
Merneptah, while his successor, Merneptah-Siptah, who
quickly supplanted him, took possession of his monuments
in turn and destroyed his tomb in the western valley of
Thebes. We shall now find that Nubia was a fruitful source
of hostility to the royal house. As did the Roman provinces
in the days of that empire, Nubia offered a field, at a safe

[1] III, 486.   [2] III, 641.

distance from the seat of power, where a sentiment against the ruling house and in favour of some pretender might be secretly encouraged without danger of detection. It was perhaps in Nubia that Siptah gained the ascendancy. However this may be, we find him in his first year installing his viceroy there in person, and sending one of his adherents about distributing rewards there.[1] By such methods and by marrying Tewosret, probably a princess of the old Pharaonic line, he succeeded in maintaining himself for at least six years, during which the tribute from Nubia seems to have been regularly delivered,[2] and the customary intercourse with the Syrian provinces maintained.[3] The viceroy whom he appointed in Nubia was one Seti, who was now also, as we have before observed, "governor of the gold country of Amon."[4] This brought him into intimate relations with the powerful priesthood of Amon at Thebes, and it is not impossible that he improved the opportunity of this intercourse and of his influential position to do what Siptah had himself done in Nubia. In any case, as Siptah now disappears a Seti succeeds him as the second of that name. He was later regarded as the sole legitimate king of the three who followed Merneptah. He seems to have ruled with some success, for he built a small temple at Karnak and another at Eshmunen-Hermopolis. He took possession of the tomb of Siptah and his queen, Tewosret, although he was afterward able to excavate one of his own. But his lease of power was brief; the long uncurbed nobility, the hosts of mercenaries in the armies, the powerful priesthoods, the numerous foreigners in positions of rank at court, ambitious pretenders and their adherents,—all these aggressive and conflicting influences demanded for their control a strong hand and unusual qualities of statesmanship in the ruler. These qualities Seti II did not possess, and he fell a victim to conditions which would have mastered many a stronger man than he.

With the disappearance of Seti II those who had over-

[1] III, 643–4.   [2] III, 644.   [3] III, 651.   [4] III, 640.

thrown him were unable to gain the coveted power of which they had deprived him. Complete anarchy ensued. The whole country fell into the hands of the local nobles, chiefs and rulers of towns, and the condition of the common people under such misrule was such as only the orient ever experiences. "Every man was thrown out of his right; they had no chief [literally, 'chief mouth'] for many years formerly until other times. The land of Egypt was in the hands of nobles and rulers of towns; one slew his neighbour, great and small."[1] How long the period of "many years" may have been we cannot now determine, but the nation must have been well on toward dissolution into the petty kingdoms and principalities out of which it was consolidated at the dawn of history. Then came famine, with all the misery which the Arab historians later depict in their annals of similar periods under the Mamluke sultans in Egypt. Indeed the record of this period left us by Ramses III in the great Papyrus Harris,[2] in spite of its brevity, reads like a chapter from the rule of some Mamluke sultan of the fourteenth century. Profiting by the helplessness of the people and the preoccupation of the native rulers, one of those Syrians who had held an official position at the court seized the crown, or at least the power, and ruled in tyranny and violence. "He set the whole land tributary before him together; he united his companions and plundered their possessions. They made the gods like men and no offerings were presented in the temples."[3] Property rights were therefore no longer respected and even the revenues of the temples were diverted.

As might have been expected the Libyans were not long in perceiving the helplessness of Egypt. Immigration across the western frontier of the Delta began again; plundering bands wandered among the towns from the vicinity of Memphis to the Mediterranean, or took possession of the fields and settled on both shores of the Canopic branch.[4] At this juncture, about 1200 B. C., there arose one Setnakht, a strong

<hr />

[1] IV, 398.   [2] Ibid.   [3] Ibid.   [4] IV, 40, ll. 20–22; 405.

man of uncertain origin, but probably a descendant of the old line of Seti I and Ramses II; and although the land was beset with foes within and without, he possessed the qualities of organization and the statesmanship first to make good his claims against the innumerable local aspirants to the crown; and having subdued these, to restore order and reorganize the almost vanished state of the old Pharaohs. His great task was accomplished with brilliant success, but all that we know of it is contained in the brief words left us by his son, Ramses III, who says of him: "But when the gods inclined themselves to peace, to set the land in its right according to its accustomed manner, they established their son, who came forth from their limbs to be ruler of every land, upon their great throne, even king Setnakht. . . . He set in order the entire land, which had been rebellious; he slew the rebels who were in the land of Egypt; he cleansed the great throne of Egypt. . . . Every man knew his brother, who had been walled in [obliged to live behind protecting walls]. He established the temples in possession of the divine offerings to offer to the gods according to their customary stipulations."[1] It will be seen that the Syrian usurper had alienated the priesthoods by violating their endowments, and that Setnakht took advantage of this fact and made head against him by conciliating these the wealthiest and most powerful communities in Egypt.

We shall readily understand that Setnakht's arduous achievement left him little time for monuments which might have perpetuated his memory. Indeed, he could not even find opportunity to excavate for himself a tomb at Thebes; but seized that of Siptah and his queen, Tewosret, which had already been appropriated, but eventually not used by Seti II. His reign must have been brief, for his highest date is his first year, scratched on the back of a leaf of papyrus by a scribe in trying his pen. Before he died (1198 B. C.) he named as his successor his son, Ramses,

[1] IV, 399.

MAP No. 12. EGYPT AND THE ANCIENT WORLD.

(Some modern places and names are inserted for convenience)

the third of the name, who had already been of assistance
to him in the government.

With the Ramessid line, now headed by Ramses III,
Manetho begins a new dynasty, the Twentieth, although the
old line was evidently already interrupted after Merneptah,
and as we have said, probably resumed again in the person
of Setnakht.   Ramses III inherited a situation precisely
like that which confronted Merneptah at his accession; but
being a young and vigourous man, he was better able successfully to cope with it.   He immediately perfected the
organization for military service, dividing all the people
into classes successively liable for such service.   A large
proportion of the standing army, not exactly determinable,
consisted of Sherden mercenaries, as in Ramses II's day,
while a contingent of the Kehek, a Libyan tribe, was also
in the ranks.[1] These mercenaries of course served as long
as they were eligible.   Since the native contingent was constantly shifting, as class after class passed through the army,
the Pharaoh came more and more to depend upon the
mercenaries as the permanent element in his army.   The
affairs of the newly organized government gave Ramses no
opportunity to deal with the chronic situation in the western
Delta until he was rudely awakened to the necessity for
action, as Merneptah had been.   But more serious developments had taken place since the latter's Libyan war.   The
restless and turbulent peoples of the northern Mediterranean,
whom the Egyptians designated the "peoples of the sea,"
were showing themselves in ever increasing numbers in the
south.   Among these, two in particular whom we have not
met before, the Thekel and the Peleset, better known as the
Philistines (Fig. 172) of Hebrew history, were prominently
aggressive.[2] The Peleset were one of the early tribes of
Crete, and the Thekel may have been another branch of the
pre-Greek Sikeli or Sicilians.   Accompanied by contingents
of Denyen (Danaoi), Sherden, Weshesh and Shekelesh, the
first two peoples mentioned had begun an eastward and south-

[1] IV, 402.   [2] IV, 44.

ward movement, doubtless impelled by pressure of other peoples advancing in their rear. Knowing nothing of their language or institutions, and having only a series of Egyptian reliefs, which depict these men, their costumes, weapons, ships and utensils, it is useless for us to speculate as to their racial affinities; but their immigration evidently is one of the earliest instances of that slow but resistless southern shift, which, first observable here, is traceable far down in European history. Moving gradually southward in Syria, some of these immigrants had now advanced perhaps as far as the upper waters of the Orontes and the kingdom of Amor;[1] while the more venturesome of their ships were coasting along the Delta and stealing into the mouths of the river on plundering expeditions.[2] They readily fell in with the plans of the Libyan leaders to invade and plunder the rich and fertile Delta. Meryey, the Libyan king, deposed after his defeat by Merneptah, had been followed by one, Wermer, who in his turn was succeeded by a king Themer, the leader of the present invasion of Egypt. By land and water they advanced into the western Delta where Ramses III promptly met them and gave them battle near a town called "Usermare-Meriamon [Ramses III] is Chastiser of Temeh"[3] [Libya]. Their ships were destroyed or captured and their army beaten back with enormous loss. Over twelve thousand five hundred were slain upon the field and at least a thousand captives were taken. Of the killed a large proportion were from the ranks of the sea-rovers.[4] There was the usual triumph at the royal residence, when the king viewed the captives and the trophies from the balcony of the palace, while his nobles rejoiced below.[5] Amon, who had granted the great victory, did not fail to receive his accustomed sacrifice of living victims,[6] and all Egypt rejoiced in restored security, such that, as Ramses boasted, a woman might walk abroad as far as she wished with her veil raised without fear of molestation.[7] To strengthen his frontier

---

[1] IV, 39.   [2] IV, 44.   [3] IV, 52.   [4] IV, 52–4.
[5] IV, 42, 52–5.   [6] IV, 57–8.   [7] IV, 47, l. 73.

against the Libyans Ramses now built a town and stronghold named after himself upon the western road where it
left the Delta and passed westward into the desert plateau.
It was upon an elevated point known as the "Mount of the
Horns of the Earth," already mentioned by Merneptah in his
war-records.[1]

Meanwhile the rising tide from the north was threatening
gradually to overwhelm the Egyptian Empire; we have seen
its outermost waves breaking on the shores of the Delta.
The advanced galleys and the land forces of the northern
maritime peoples which supported the Libyans against
Ramses III in the year five were but the premonitory skirmish line of a far more serious advance, to which we have
already adverted. It was now in full motion southward
through Syria. Its hosts were approaching both by land,
with their families in curious, heavy, two-wheeled ox-carts,
and by sea in a numerous fleet that skirted the Syrian coast.
Well armed and skilled in warfare as the invaders were,
the Syrian city-states were unable to withstand their onset.
They overran all the Hittite country of northern Syria as
fas as Carchemish on the Euphrates, past Arvad on the
Phœnician coast, and up the Orontes valley to the kingdom
of Amor, which they devastated. The Syrian dominions
of the Hittites must have been lost and the Hittite power in
Syria completely broken. The fleet visited Alasa, or Cyprus;
and nowhere was an effective resistance offered them. "They
came with fire, prepared before them, forward to Egypt.
Their main support was Peleset, Thekel, Shekelesh, Denyen
and Weshesh. These lands were united and they laid their
hands upon the land as far as the circle of the earth."[2]
"The countries, which came from their isles in the midst of
the sea, they advanced to Egypt, their hearts relying upon
their arms."[3] In Amor they established a central camp and
apparently halted for a time.[4]

---

[1] IV, 102, 107; III, 588, 600.
[2] Around which the "Great Circle" (Okeanos) flows (IV, 64).
[3] IV, 77.   [4] IV, 64.

Ramses III threw himself with great energy into the preparations for repelling the attack. He fortified his Syrian frontier and rapidly gathered a fleet, which he distributed in the northern harbours.[1] From his palace balcony he personally superintended the equipment of the infantry,[2] and when all was in readiness he set out for Syria to lead the campaign himself. Where the land-battle took place we are unable to determine, but as the Northerners had advanced to Amor, it was at most not further north than that region. We learn nothing from Ramses III's records concerning it beyond vague and general statements of the defeat of the enemy, although in his reliefs we see his Sherden mercenaries breaking through the scattered lines of the enemy and plundering their ox-carts, bearing the women and children and the belongings of the Northerners. As there were Sherden among the invaders, Ramses III's mercenaries were thus called upon to fight their own countrymen. Ramses was also able to reach the scene of the naval battle, probably in one of the northern harbours on the coast of Phœnicia, early enough to participate in the action from the neighbouring shore. He had manned his fleet with masses of the dreaded Egyptian archers, whose fire was so effective that the ranks of the heavy armed Northerners were completely decimated before they could approach within boarding distance. This fire was augmented and rendered still more effective by bodies of Egyptian archers whom Ramses stationed along the shore, he himself personally drawing his bow against the hostile fleet. As the Egyptians then advanced to board, the enemy's ships were thrown into confusion (Fig. 173). "Capsized and perishing in their places, their hearts are taken, their souls fly away, and their weapons are cast out upon the sea. His arrows pierce whomsoever he will among them, and he who is hit falls into the water."[3] "They were dragged, overturned and laid low upon the beach; slain and made heaps from stern to bow of their galleys, while all their

[1] IV, 6ʊ.   [2] IV, 70–71.   [3] IV, 75.

Fig. 173.—NAVAL VICTORY OF RAMSES III OVER NORTHERN MEDITERRANEAN PEOPLES.

Reliefs on the north wall at Medinet Habu. The Egyptian galleys (at the left), by heavy archery fire, are throwing the enemy (on the right) into confusion. One of the northern galleys has capsized. See p. 480.

things were cast upon the waters, for a remembrance of Egypt."[1] Those who escaped the fleet and swam ashore, were captured by the waiting Egyptians on the beach. In these two engagements the Pharaoh struck his formidable enemy so decisive a blow that his suzerainty, at least as far north as Amor, could not be questioned by the invaders. They continued to arrive in Syria, but Ramses III's double victory made these new settlers and their new settlements vassals of Egypt, paying tribute into the treasury of the Pharaoh. The Egyptian Empire in Asia had again been saved and Ramses returned to his Delta residence to enjoy a well earned triumph.

He was now given a short respite, during which he seems not to have relaxed his vigilance in the least. This was well, for another migration of the peoples in the far west caused an overflow which again threatened the Delta. The Meshwesh, a tribe living behind the Libyans, that is, on the west of them, were the cause of the trouble. The Libyans had undoubtedly received a chastisement in the fifth year of Ramses III such that they had no immediate desire to repeat their attempt upon the Delta; but the Meshwesh invaded the Libyan country and laid it waste,[2] thus forcing the unfortunate Libyans into an alliance against Egypt.[3] Other tribes were involved, but the leader of the movement was Meshesher, son of Keper, king of the Meshwesh, whose firm purpose was to migrate and settle in the Delta. "The hostile foe had taken counsel again to spend their lives in the confines of Egypt, that they might take the hills and plains as their own districts."[4] " 'We will settle in Egypt, so spake they with one accord, and they continuously entered the boundaries of Egypt.' "[5] By the twelfth month in Ramses' eleventh year they had begun the invasion, entering along the western road as in the time of Merneptah and investing the fortress of Hatsho, some eleven miles from the edge of the desert plateau, near the canal called "The Water of Re." Ramses attacked

[1] IV, 66. [2] IV, 87. [3] IV, 86, 95. [4] IV, 95. [5] IV, 88.

31

them under the walls of Hatsho, from the ramparts of which the Egyptian garrison poured a destructive archery fire into the ranks of the Meshwesh, already discomfited by the Pharaoh's onset. The invaders were thus thrown into a tumultuous rout and received the fire of another neighbouring stronghold as they fled.[1] Ramses pressed the pursuit for eleven miles along the western road to the margin of the plateau, thus fairly driving the invaders out of the country.[2] He halted at the fortified town and station, "Town [or House] of Usermare-Meriamon [Ramses III]," which, it will be remembered, he had founded upon some high point at the edge of the plateau, the "Mount of the Horns of the Earth." Meshesher, the chief of the Meshwesh, was slain and his father Keper was captured,[3] two thousand one hundred and seventy five of their followers fell, while two thousand and fifty two, of whom over a fourth were females, were taken captive.[4] Ramses tells of the disposition which he made of these captives: "I settled their leaders in strongholds in my name. I gave to them captains of archers and chief men of the tribes, branded and made into slaves, impressed with my name; their wives and their children likewise."[5] Nearly a thousand of the Meshwesh were assigned to the care of a temple-herd called "Ramses III is the Conqueror of the Meshwesh at the Waters of Re."[6] Similarly he established in celebration of his victory an annual feast which he called in his temple calendar, "Slaying of the Meshwesh";[7] and he assumed in his elaborate titulary after his name the epithets, "Protector of Egypt, Guardian of the Countries, Conqueror of the Meshwesh, Spoiler of the Land of Temeh."[8] The western tribes had thus been hurled back from the borders of the Delta for the third successive time, and Ramses had no occasion to apprehend any further aggressions from that quarter. The expansive power of the Libyan peoples,

[1] IV, 102, 107.   [2] IV, 102.
[3] IV, 90, ll. 11–12; 97; 103, ll. 11–12; 111.   [4] IV, 111.
[5] IV, 405.   [6] IV, 224.   [7] IV, 145.   [8] IV, 84.

although by no means exhausted, now no longer appeared in united national action, but as they had done from prehistoric times they continued to sift gradually into the Delta in scattered and desultory migration, not regarded by the Pharaoh as a source of danger.

The commotion among the northern maritime peoples, although checked by Ramses III upon his Syrian frontier, had evidently greatly disturbed the vassals of Egypt there. Whether as of old in the days of Hittite aggression the king of Amor had made common cause with the invader we cannot now discern; but following closely upon the last Libyan campaign, Ramses found it necessary to appear in Amor with his army. The limits and the course of the campaign are but obscurely hinted at in the meagre records now surviving.[1] He stormed at least five strong cities, one of which was in Amor; another depicted in Ramses' reliefs as surrounded by water was perhaps Kadesh; a third, rising upon a hill, cannot be identified; and both of the remaining two, one of which was called Ereth,[2] were defended by Hittites. He probably did not penetrate far into the Hittite territory, although its cities were rapidly falling away from the Hittite king and much weakened by the attacks of the sea-peoples. It was the last hostile passage between the Pharaoh and the Hittites; both empires were swiftly declining to their fall, and in the annals of Egypt we never again hear of the Hittites in Syria. Ramses places in his lists[3] of conquered regions the cities of northern Syria to the Euphrates, including all that the Empire had ever ruled in its greatest days. These lists, however, are largely copied from those of his great predecessors, and we can place no confidence in them. He now organized the Asiatic possessions of Egypt as stably as possible, the boundary very evidently not being any further north than that of Merneptah, that is, just including the Amorite kingdom on the upper Orontes. To ensure the stability which he desired he built new fortresses wherever

---

[1] IV, 115–135. [2] IV, 120. [3] IV, 131, 135.

necessary in Syria and Palestine;[1] somewhere in Syria he
also erected a temple of Amon, containing a great image of
the state god, before which the Asiatic dynasts were obliged
to declare their fealty to Ramses by depositing their tribute
in its presence every year.[2] Communication with Syria
was facilitated by the excavation of a great well in the desert
of Ayan,[3] east of the Delta, supplementing the watering
stations established there by Seti I. Only a revolt of the
Beduin of Seir interrupted the peaceful government of the
Pharaoh in Asia from this time forth.[4]

The influence of Egyptian commerce and administration
in Syria was evident in one important particular especially,
for it was now that the cumbrous and inconvenient clay tablet
was gradually supplemented in Syria by the handy papyrus
on which the Phœnician rulers began to keep their accounts.
To supply the demand the papyrus factories of the Delta were
exporting their products in exchange for Phœnician commodities.[5] It was of course impracticable, if not impossible, for
the Phœnicians to keep rapid daily records on paper with pen
and ink in the cuneiform hand which was totally unsuited
to such writing materials. With the papyrus paper, therefore, the hand customarily written upon it in Egypt now
made its way into Phœnicia, where before the tenth century B. C. it developed into an alphabet of consonants, which
was quickly transmitted to the Ionian Greeks and thence
to Europe.

The chief function of an oriental despotism, the collection of tribute and taxes, now proceeded with the greatest
regularity. "I taxed them for their impost every year,"
says Ramses, "every town by its name gathered together
bearing their tribute."[6] The suppression of occasional disorders in Nubia[7] caused no disturbance of the profound
peace which now settled down upon the Empire. Ramses
himself depicts it thus: "I made the woman of Egypt to
go with uncovered ears to the place she desired, for no

---

[1] IV, 141.   [2] IV, 219.   [3] IV, 406.   [4] IV, 404.
[5] IV, 576, 58?.   [6] IV, 141.   [7] IV, 136-8.

stranger, nor any one upon the road molested her. I made the infantry and chariotry to dwell at home in my time; the Sherden and the Kehek [mercenaries] were in their towns lying the length of their backs; they had no fear, for there was no enemy from Kush, nor foe from Syria. Their bows and their weapons reposed in their magazines, while they were satisfied and drunk with joy. Their wives were with them, their children at their side; they looked not behind them, but their hearts were confident, for I was with them as the defence and protection of their limbs. I sustained alive the whole land, whether foreigners, common folk, citizens or people male or female. I took a man out of his misfortune and I gave him breath. I rescued him from the oppressor who was of more account that he. I set each man in his security in their towns; I sustained alive others in the hall of petition. I settled the land in the place where it was laid waste. The land was well satisfied in my reign.''[1]

Intercourse and commerce with the outside world were now fostered by the Pharaoh as in the great days of the Empire. The temples of Amon, Re and Ptah had each its own fleet upon the Mediterranean or the Red Sea, transporting to the god's treasury the products of Phœnicia, Syria and Punt.[2] Ramses exploited the copper mines of Atika, a region somewhere in the Peninsula of Sinai, sending a special expedition thither in galleys from some Red Sea port. They returned with great quantities of the metal which the Pharaoh had displayed under the palace balcony that all the people might see it.[3] To the malachite workings of the Peninsula he likewise sent his messengers, who brought back plentiful returns of the costly mineral for the king's splendid gifts to the gods.[4] A more important expedition consisting of a fleet of large ships was sent on the long voyage to Punt. The canal from the Nile through the Wadi Tumilat to the Red Sea, existent long before this age (see p. 188), was now seemingly stopped up and in disuse, for Ramses' ships,

[1] IV, 410.   [2] IV, 211, 270, 328.   [3] IV, 408.   [4] IV, 409.

after a successful voyage, returned to some harbour opposite Coptos, where the entire cargo of the fleet was disembarked, loaded on donkeys and brought overland to Coptos. Here it was reëmbarked upon the river and floated down stream to the royal residence in the eastern Delta.[1] Navigation was now perhaps on a larger and more elaborate scale even than under the great Pharaohs of the Eighteenth Dynasty. Ramses tells of a sacred barge of Amon at Thebes, which was two hundred and twenty four feet long, built in his yards, of enormous timbers of cedar of Lebanon.[2]

The Pharaoh's wealth now enabled him to undertake works of public utility and improvement. Throughout the kingdom, and especially in Thebes and the royal residence, he planted numerous trees, which under a sky so prevailingly cloudless as that of Egypt, offered the people grateful shade, in a land devoid of natural forests.[3] He also resumed building, which had been at a standstill since the death of Ramses II. On the western plain of Thebes, at the point now called Medinet Habu, he built a large and splendid temple (Figs. 174–5) to Amon[4] which he began early in his reign. As the temple was extended and enlarged from rear to front the annals of his campaigns found place on the walls through successive years following the growth of the building until the whole edifice became a vast record of the king's achievements in war which the modern visitor may read, tracing it from year to year as he passes from the earliest halls in the rear to the latest courts and pylon at the front. Here he may see the hordes of the North in battle with Ramses' Sherden mercenaries, who break through and plunder the heavy ox-carts of the invaders, as we have already noticed. The first naval battle on salt water, of which we know anything, is here depicted, and in these reliefs we may study the armour, clothing, weapons, war-ships and equipment of these northern peoples with whose advent Europe for the first time emerges upon the stage of the early world.[5] There was a sacred

[1] IV, 407.   [2] IV, 209.   [3] IV, 213, 215, 410.
[4] IV, 1–20, 189–194.   [5] IV, 69–82.

lake before the temple with an elaborate garden, extensive
out-buildings and magazines, a palace of the king with
massive stone towers in connection with the temple structure, and a wall around the whole forming a great complex which dominated the whole southern end of the western plain of Thebes, whence from the summits of its tall
pylons one might look northward along the stately line of
mortuary temples, built by the emperors. It thus formed,
as it still does, the southern terminus and the last of that
imposing array of buildings, and suggests to the thoughtful
visitor the end of the long line of imperial Pharaohs, of
whom Ramses III was indeed the last. Other buildings of
his have for the most part perished; a small temple of
Amon at Karnak (Fig. 183), which Ramses, quite sensible
of the hopelessness of any attempt to rival the vast Karnak halls, placed across the axis of the main temple there,
still bears witness to his good sense in this respect.[1] Some
small additions to the Karnak temple,[2] besides that of Mut
on the south of the Karnak group,[3] a small sanctuary for
Khonsu only begun by Ramses III;[4] sanctuaries of which
little or no trace has been discovered at Memphis and Heliopolis,[5] and many chapels to various gods throughout the
land [6] have for the most part perished entirely or left but
slight traces. In the residence city he laid out a magnificent
quarter for Amon; "it was furnished with large gardens
and places for walking about, with all sorts of date groves
bearing their fruits, and a sacred avenue brightened with
the flowers of every land."[7] The quarter possessed nearly
eight thousand slaves for its service.[8] He also erected
in the city a temple of Sutekh in the temenos of Ramses
II's temple.[9] The art displayed by these buildings, in so
far as they have survived, is clearly in a decadent stage.
The lines are heavy and indolent, the colonnades have
none of the old time soaring vigour, springing from

[1] IV, 195.   [2] IV, 197–213.   [3] IV, 196.
[4] IV, 214.   [5] IV, 250–265, 311–328.   [6] IV, 355–361.
[7] IV, 215.   [8] IV, 225.   [9] IV, 362, 369.

the pavement and carrying the beholder's eye involuntarily aloft; but they visibly labour under the burden imposed upon them and clearly express the sluggish spirit of the decadent architect who designed them. The work also is careless and slovenly in execution. The reliefs which cover the vast surfaces of the Medinet Habu temple are with few exceptions but weak imitations of the fine sculptures of Seti I at Karnak, badly drawn and executed without feeling. Only here and there do we find a flash of the old-time power, as in the representation of Ramses hunting the wild bull (Fig. 176) on the walls of this same temple, a relief which, in spite of some bad faults in the drawing, is a composition of much strength and feeling, with a notable sense of landscape. A bold and entirely new effort of the time is the representation of the Pharaoh's naval victory on the Syrian coast (Fig. 173), a relief requiring some originality and invention, but too involved for strength and effect.

The imitation so evident in the art of Ramses III's reign is characteristic of the time in all respects. The records of the reign are but weak repetitions of the earlier royal encomiums, embellished with figures so extremely far-fetched as to be often unintelligible. It was with a feeling of depression not easily shaken off that the author emerged from months of application to the vast walls of the Medinet Habu temple covered with hundreds on hundreds of lines of arid verbiage ever reiterating the valour of the king on this or that occasion in conventional terms which dropped from the pen of the fawning scribe, as such words had done for centuries. Taking up any given war, one finds that after working through difficult inscriptions covering several thousand square feet of wall surface, the net result is but a meagre and bald account of a great campaign the facts of which are scattered here and there and buried so deeply beneath scores of meaningless conventional phrases that they can be discovered only with the greatest industry. The inspiring figure of a young and active Pharaoh hurrying his armies from frontier to frontier of his empire and repeatedly hurling back the most formidable invasions Egypt had ever suffered, awoke no response in the conventional soul of the priestly scribe, whose lot it was to write the record of these things for the temple wall. He possessed only the worn and long spent currency of the older dynasties from which he drew whole hymns, songs and lists to be furbished up and made to do service again in perpetuating the glory of a really able and heroic ruler. Perhaps we should not complain of the scribe, for the king himself considered it his highest purpose to restore and reproduce the times of Ramses II. His own name was made up of the first half of Ramses II's throne-name, and the second half of his personal name; he named his children and his horses after those of Ramses II, and like him, he was followed on his campaigns by a tame lion who trotted beside his chariot on the march. The achievements of Ramses III were entirely dictated by the circumstances in which he found himself, rather than by any positive tendencies in his own character. But it must be admitted that he was confronted by a situation against which he could have done little even if he had attempted to make head against it. All immediate danger from without had now apparently disappeared, but the nation was slowly declining as a result of decay from within. While Ramses III had shown himself fully able to cope with the assaults from the outside, he did not possess the qualities of virile independence which in some men would have dictated strenuous opposition to the prevailing tendencies of the time within the state.

This was especially evident in his attitude toward the religious conditions inherited from the Nineteenth Dynasty. We have already pointed out that Setnakht, Ramses III's father, gained the throne by conciliating the priesthoods, as so many of his successful predecessors had done. Ramses III made no effort to shake off the priestly influences with which the crown was thus encumbered. The temples were fast becoming a grave political and economic menace.

In the face of this fact Ramses III continued the policy of his ancestors, and with the most lavish liberality poured the wealth of the royal house into the sacred coffers. He himself says: "I did mighty deeds and benefactions, a numerous multitude, for the gods and goddesses of South and North. I wrought upon their images in the gold-houses, I built that which had fallen to ruin in their temples. I made houses and temples in their courts; I planted for them groves; I dug for them lakes; I founded for them divine offerings of barley and wheat, wine, incense, fruit, cattle and fowl; I built the [chapels called] 'Shadows of Re' for their districts, abiding, with divine offerings for every day."[1] He is here speaking of the smaller temples of the country, while for the three great gods of the land: Amon, Re and Ptah, he did vastly more. The opulent splendour with which the rituals of these gods were daily observed beggars description. "I made for thee," says Ramses to Amon, "a great sacrificial tablet of silver in hammered work, mounted with fine gold, the inlay figures being of Ketem-gold, bearing statues of the king of gold in hammered work, even an offering tablet bearing thy divine offerings, offered before thee. I made for thee a great vase-stand for thy forecourt, mounted with fine gold, with inlay of stone; its vases were of gold, containing wine and beer in order to present them to thee every morning. . . . I made for thee great tablets of gold, in beaten work, engraved with the great name of thy majesty, bearing my prayers. I made for thee other tablets of silver, in beaten work, engraved with the great name of thy majesty, with the decrees of thy house."[2] All that the god used was of the same richness;[3] Ramses says of his sacred barge: "I hewed for thee thy august ship 'Userhet,' of one hundred and thirty cubits [nearly two hundred and twenty four feet length] upon the river, of great cedars of the royal domain, of remarkable size, overlaid with fine gold to the water line, like the barque of the sun, when he comes from the

[1] IV, 363.   [2] IV, 199, 202.   [3] IV, 198–210.

east, and every one lives at the sight of him. A great shrine
was in the midst of it, of fine gold, with inlay of every costly
stone like a palace; rams'-heads of gold from front to rear,
fitted with uræus-serpents wearing crowns.''[1] In making
the great temple balances for weighing the offerings to Re
at Heliopolis nearly two hundred and twelve pounds of
gold and four hundred and sixty one pounds of silver were
consumed.[2] The reader may peruse pages of such descriptions in the great Papyrus Harris,[3] of which we shall later
give some account. Such magnificence, while it might frequently be due to incidental gifts of the king, must nevertheless be supported by an enormous income, derived from
a vast fortune in lands, slaves and revenues. Thus, to
the god Khnum at Elephantine, Ramses III confirmed the
possession of both sides of the river from that city to
Takompso, a strip over seventy miles in length, known to
the Greeks as the Dodekaschoinos or Twelve Schœni.[4] The
records of Ramses III for the first and only time in the
course of Egyptian history, enable us to determine the
total amount of property owned and controlled by the
temples. An inventory in the Papyrus Harris covering
almost all the temples of the country shows that they possessed over one hundred and seven thousand slaves;[5] that
is, one person in every fifty to eighty of the population was
temple property. The first figure is the more probable, so
that in all likelihood one person in every fifty was a slave of
some temple. The temples thus owned two percent of the population. In lands we find the sacred endowments amounting to
nearly three quarters of a million acres, that is, nearly one
seventh, or over fourteen and a half percent of the cultivable
land of the country; and as some of the smaller temples
like that of Khnum just mentioned, are omitted in the inventory it is safe to say that the total holdings of the temples
amounted to fifteen percent of the available land of the
country.[6] These are the only items in the temple estates

---

[1] IV, 209.   [2] IV, 256, 285.   [3] IV, 151–412.
[4] IV, 146–150.   [5] IV, 166.   [6] IV, 16i.

which can be safely compared with the total national wealth and resources; but they by no means complete the list of property held by the temples. They owned nearly a half million head of large and small cattle; their combined fleets numbered eighty eight vessels, some fifty three workshops and ship-yards consumed a portion of the raw materials, which they received as income; while in Syria, Kush and Egypt they owned in all one hundred and sixty nine towns.[1] When we remember that all this vast property in a land of less than ten thousand square miles and some five or six million inhabitants was entirely exempt from taxation[2] it will be seen that the economic equilibrium of the state was endangered.

These extreme conditions were aggravated by the fact that no proper proportion had been observed in the distribution of gifts to the gods. By far too large a share of them had fallen to the lot of Amon, whose insatiable priesthood had so gained the ascendancy that their claims on the royal treasury far exceeded those of all other temples put together. Besides the great group of temples at Thebes, the god possessed numerous other sanctuaries, chapels and statues, with their endowments scattered throughout the land.[3] He had a temple in Syria,[4] as we have already noticed, and a new one in Nubia,[5] besides those built there by Ramses II. In his twelfth year after the victorious conclusion of all his wars, the finally completed temple, which he had erected for Amon at Medinet Habu (Thebes), was inaugurated with a new and elaborate calendar of feasts, the record of which filled all one wall of the temple for almost its entire length.[6] The feast of Opet, the greatest of Amon's feasts, which in the days of Thutmose III was eleven days long, is credited in this calendar with twenty four days; and summarizing the calendar as far as preserved, we find that there was an annual feast day of Amon on an average every three days, not counting the monthly

[1] IV, p. 97. [2] IV, 146. [3] IV, 189–226.
[4] IV, 219. [5] IV, 218. [6] IV, 139–145

Fig. 176.—RAMSES III HUNTING THE WILD BULL.

Relief on the back of the first pylon of the Medinet Habu temple. See p. 488.

Fig. 174.—RAMSES III'S MEDINET HABU TEMPLE.

Looking across first court and second pylon northward from top of first pylon.

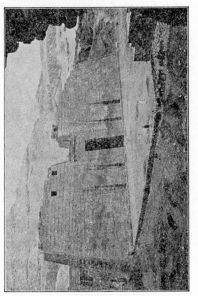

Fig. 175.—RAMSES III'S MEDINET HABU TEMPLE.

View of the first pylon from the wall of the palace gate ("pavilion") which stands before the temple.

feasts.[1] Yet Ramses III later lengthened even the feasts of this calendar, so that the feast of Opet became twenty seven days long and the feast of his own coronation, which lasted but one day as prescribed by the calendar, finally continued for twenty days each year.[2] Little wonder that the records of a band of workmen in the Theban necropolis under one of Ramses III's successors show almost as many holidays as working days.[3] All these lengthened feasts of course mean increased endowment and revenue for the service of Amon. The treasure rooms of this Medinet Habu temple still stand, and their walls bear testimony to the lavish wealth with which they were filled.[4] Ramses himself in another record says: "I filled its treasury with the products of the land of Egypt: gold, silver, every costly stone by the hundred-thousand. Its granary was overflowing with barley and wheat; its lands, its herds, their multitudes were like the sand of the shore. I taxed for it the Southland as well as the Northland; Nubia and Syria came to it, bearing their impost. It was filled with captives, which thou gavest me among the Nine Bows, and with classes [successive enforced levies], which I created by the ten-thousand. . . . I multiplied the divine offerings presented before thee, of bread, wine, beer and fat geese; numerous oxen, bullocks, calves, cows, white oryxes and gazelles offered in his slaughter yard."[5] As in the days of the Eighteenth Dynasty conquerors, the bulk of the spoil from his wars went into the treasury of Amon.[6] The result of this long continued policy was inevitable. Of the nearly three quarters of a million acres of land held by the temples, Amon owned over five hundred and eighty three thousand, over five times as much as his nearest competitor, Re of Heliopolis, who had only one hundred and eight thousand; and over nine times the landed estate of Ptah of Memphis.[7] Of the fifteen percent of the lands of the entire country held by all the temples, Amon thus owned over two thirds. While,

---

[1] IV, 144.   [2] IV, 236–7.   [3] Erman, Life in Ancient Egypt.
[4] IV, 25–34.   [5] IV, 190.   [6] IV, 224, 405.   [7] IV, 167.

as we have stated, the combined temples owned in slaves
not more than two percent of the whole population, Amon
held probably one and a half percent, in number over
eighty six thousand five hundred, which exceeded by seven
times the number owned by Re.[1] In other items of wealth
the same proportion is observable; Amon owned five great
herds, numbering over four hundred and twenty one thousand large and small cattle, of the less than half a million
head held by all the temples; of five hundred and thirteen
temple gardens and groves, Amon owned four hundred and
thirty three; of the fleet of temple ships, numbering eighty
eight, all but five were the property of Amon; and forty
six work shops of the fifty three owned by the temples were
his.[2] He was the only god possessing towns in Syria and
Kush, of which he had nine, but in towns of Egypt he was
surpassed by Re, who owned one hundred and three, as
against only fifty six held by Amon. As we know nothing
of the size and value of these towns, the number is hardly
significant in view of the immense superiority of Amon in
acreage of temple lands. In income Amon received an
annual item of twenty six thousand grains of gold, which
none of the other temples received. This doubtless came
from the "gold country of Amon," of which he had gained
possession toward the end of the Nineteenth Dynasty, as
we have seen. In silver his income exceeded by seventeen
times, in copper by twenty one times, in cattle by seven
times, in wine by nine times, in ships by ten times, the
income of all the other temples combined.[3] His estate and
his revenues, second only to those of the king, now assumed
an important economic role in the state, and the political
power wielded by a community of priests who controlled
such vast wealth was from now on a force which no Pharaoh
could ignore. Without compromising with it and continually conciliating it, no Pharaoh could have ruled long,
although the current conclusion that the gradual usurpation of power and final assumption of the throne by the

[1] IV, 165.   [2] IV, 165.   [3] IV, 170-171.

High Priest of Amon was due solely to the wealth of Amon is not supported by our results. Other forces contributed largely to this result, as we shall see. Among these was the gradual extension of Amon's influence to the other temples and their fortunes. His High Priest had in the Eighteenth Dynasty become head of all the priesthoods of Egypt; in the Nineteenth Dynasty he had gained hereditary hold upon his office; his Theban temple now became the sacerdotal capital, where the records of the other temples were kept; his priesthood was given more or less supervision over their administration,[1] and the furtive power of Amon was thus gradually extended over all the sacred estates in the land.

It is a mistake to suppose, as is commonly done, that Ramses III was solely or even chiefly responsible for these conditions. However lavish his contributions to the sacerdotal wealth, they never could have raised it to the proportions which we have indicated. This is as true of the fortune of Amon in particular as of the temple wealth in general. The gift of over seventy miles of Nubian Nile shores (the Dodekaschoinos) to Khnum by Ramses III was but the confirmation by him of an old title; and the enormous endowments enumerated in the great Papyrus Harris, long supposed to be the gifts of Ramses III, are but inventories of the old sacerdotal estates, in the possession of which the temples are confirmed by him.[2] These long misunderstood inventories are the source of the above statistics, which reveal to us the situation and they show that it was an *inherited* situation, created by the prodigal gifts of the Eighteenth and Nineteenth Dynasties, beginning at least as far back as Thutmose III, who presented three towns in Syria to Amon. By generations of this policy the vast wealth of the temples had gradually been accumulated, and against the insatiable priesthoods long accustomed to the gratification of unlimited exactions, Ramses III was unable, and indeed did not attempt to make a stand. On the con-

[1] IV, 202.   [2] IV, 157–8.

trary, as we have seen, being evidently in need of sacerdotal support to maintain himself, he deliberately continued the traditional policy. Yet his treasury must have sorely felt the draughts upon it, with its income gradually shrinking, while the demands upon it in nowise relaxed. Although we know that payments from the government treasury were as slow in ancient, as they have been until recently in modern Egypt, yet, making all due allowance for this fact, it can hardly be an accident that under the reign of Ramses III we can follow the painful struggles of a band of necropolis workmen in their endeavours to secure the monthly fifty sacks of grain due them. Month after month they are obliged to resort to the extremest measures, climbing the necropolis wall and driven by hunger, threatening to storm the very granary itself if food is not given them. Told by the vizier himself that there is nothing in the treasury or deceived by the glib promises of some intermediate scribe they would return to their daily task only to find starvation forcing them to throw down their work and to gather with cries and tumult at the office of their superior, demanding their monthly rations.[1] Thus while the poor in the employ of the state were starving at the door of an empty treasury, the store-houses of the gods were groaning with plenty, and Amon was yearly receiving over two hundred and five thousand bushels of grain for the offerings at his annual feasts alone.[2]

The only forces which Ramses III and his contemporaries could bring into play against the powerful priestly coteries were the numerous foreigners among the slaves owned by the crown. These, branded with the name of the king, were poured into the ranks of the army in large numbers,[3] augmenting the voluntary service of the mercenaries already there. The armies with which Ramses III beat off the assailants of his empire were, as we have already remarked, largely made up of foreigners, and their numbers constantly increased as the Pharaoh found himself less and less able

---

[1] Erman, Life in Ancient Egypt, 124–126.   [2] IV, 174.   [3] IV, 405.

to maintain the mastery in a situation of ever increasing difficulty and complication. He was soon forced also to surround his person with numbers of these foreign slaves. A class of personal attendants, already known in the Middle Kingdom by a term which we may best translate as "butler," originally rendered service to the table and larder of the nobles or the king. These slaves in Ramses III's service were largely natives of Syria, Asia Minor and Libya, especially Syria, and as the king found them more and more useful, they gradually, although only slaves, gained high office in the state and at the court. It was a situation, as Erman has remarked, precisely like that at the court of the Egyptian sultans of the Middle Ages. Of eleven such "butlers" known to us in the service of Ramses III, five were foreigners in places of power and influence,[1] and we shall soon have occasion to observe the prominent role they played at a fatal crisis in his reign. While all was outwardly splendour and tranquillity and the whole nation was celebrating the king who had saved the Empire, the forces of decay which had for generations been slowly gathering in the state were rapidly reaching the acute stage. An insatiable and insidious priesthood commanding enormous wealth, a foreign army ready to serve the master who paid most liberally, and a personal following of alien slaves whose fidelity likewise depended entirely upon the immediate gain in view,—these were the factors which Ramses III was constantly forced to manipulate and employ, each against the others. Add to these the host of royal relatives and dependents, who were perhaps of all the most dangerous element in the situation, and we shall not wonder at the outcome.

While the whole situation abounded in unhealthy symptoms, the first specific instance of the danger inherent in it, which we are able to discern, is the revolt of Ramses' vizier, who shut himself up in the Delta city of Athribis; but he had miscalculated the power at his command; the

---

[1] IV, 419 ff.

32

place was taken by Ramses and the revolt suppressed.[1]
Peace and outward tranquility were again restored. As
the thirtieth anniversary of the king's appointment as
crown prince approached, elaborate preparations were made
for its commemoration. He sent his new vizier, Ta, southward in the year twenty nine to collect the processional
images of all the gods who participated in a celebration of
the usual splendour at Memphis.[2] Something over a year
after this stately commemoration, as the old king was beginning to feel his years, a more serious crisis developed. The
harem, the source of so many attempts against the throne,
was the origin of the trouble. In the early orient there is
always among the many mothers of the king's children a
princess or queen who feels that her son has a better claim
to the succession than the son of the fortunate rival, who
has succeeded in gaining for him the nomination as the
king's successor. Such a queen in Ramses III's harem,
named Tiy, now began furtive efforts to secure for her
son, Pentewere, the crown, which had been promised to
another prince.[3] A plot against the old king's life was rapidly formed, and Tiy enlisted as her chief coadjutors the
"chief of the chamber," Pebekkamen, and a royal butler
named Mesedsure. With oriental superstition, Pebekkamen
first procured an outfit of magical waxen figures of gods
and men, by which he believed he was empowered to dis-
able or evade the people of the harem guard, who might
otherwise have discovered and intercepted one of their
numerous messages necessary to the development of the
plot. Pebekkamen and Mesedsure then secured the coöperation of ten harem officials of various ranks, four royal
butlers, an overseer of the treasury, a general in the army
named Peyes, three royal scribes in various offices, Pebekkamen's own assistant, and several subordinate officials. As
most of these people were in the personal service of the
Pharaoh, the dangerous character of the complot is evident.
Six wives of the officers of the harem gate were won to

---

[1] IV, 361. [2] IV, 335, 413-15. [3] All the following, from IV, 416-456.

the enterprise, and they proved very useful in securing the transmission of messages from inmates of the harem to their relatives and friends outside. Among these inmates was the sister of the commander of archers in Nubia, who smuggled out a letter to her brother and thus gained his support. All was ripe for a revolt and revolution outside the palace, intended to accompany the murder of the king and enable the conspirators the more easily to seize the government and place their pretender, Pentewere, on the throne. At this juncture the king's party gained full information of the conspiracy, the attempt on the king's life was foiled, the plans for revolt were checkmated, and the people involved in the treason were all seized. The old Pharaoh, sorely shaken by the ordeal, and possibly suffering bodily injury from the attempted assassination, immediately appointed a special court for the trial of the conspirators. The very words of the commission empowering this court indicate his probable consciousness that he would not long survive the shock, while at the same time they lay upon the judges a responsibility for impartial justice on the merits of the case, with a judicial objectivity which is remarkable in one who held the lives of the accused in his unchallenged power and had himself just been the victim of a murderous assault at their hands. The king thus commissioned this special court: "I commission the judges [here follows a list of their names and offices], saying: 'As for the words which the people have spoken, I know them not. Go ye and examine them. When ye go and ye examine them, ye shall cause to die by their own hand those who should die without my knowing it. Ye shall execute punishment upon the others likewise without my knowing it. . . . Give heed and have a care lest ye execute punishment upon [anyone] unjustly. . . . Now I say to you in very truth, as for all that has been done, and those who have done it, let all that they have done fall upon their own heads; while I am protected and defended forever, while I am among the just kings, who are before Amon-Re, king of gods, and before

Osiris, ruler of eternity.'' As Osiris is the god of the dead, the king's closing words possibly indicate that he expected his demise to occur before the conclusion of the trials.[1]

The court thus commissioned consisted of fourteen officials, seven of whom were royal ''butlers,'' and among these were a Libyan, a Lycian, a Syrian named Maharbaal (''Baal hastens''), and another foreigner, probably from Asia Minor. We see how largely the Pharaoh depended in his extremity upon the purchased fidelity of these foreign slaves. The flaccid character of the judges and the dangerous persistence of the accused is shown by a remarkable incident which now followed the appointment of the court. Some of the women conspirators, led by the general, Peyes, gained such influence over the bailiffs in charge of the prisoners that they went with Peyes and the women to the houses of two of the judges, who, with amazing indiscretion, received and caroused with them. The two indiscreet judges, with one of their colleagues, who was really innocent, and the two bailiffs, were immediately put on trial. The innocence of the third judge was made evident and he was acquitted, but the others were found guilty, and were sentenced to have their ears and noses cut off. Immediately following the execution of the sentence, one of the unfortunate judges committed suicide.[2] The trials of the conspirators continued with regularity, and from the records of three different prosecutions[3] we are able to trace the conviction of thirty two officials of all ranks including the unhappy young pretender himself, who was doubtless only an unfortunate tool, and the audacious Peyes, the general who had compromised the two judges. The records of the trial of queen Tiy herself are not preserved, so that we cannot determine her fate, but we have no reason to suppose that it was better than that of all the others, who, as ordered by the king, were allowed to take their own lives. Meantime the thirty second anniversary of the Pharaoh's

[1] IV, 424.   [2] IV, 451-3.   [3] IV, 416-456.

accession was celebrated with the gorgeous twenty days' feast customary since his twenty second year.[1] But the old king survived only twenty days more and before the prosecution of his would-be assassins was ended he passed away (1167 B. C.) having ruled thirty one years and forty days.

[1] IV, 237.

BOOK VII

THE DECADENCE

CHAPTER XXIV

THE FALL OF THE EMPIRE

THE death of Ramses III introduced a long line of nine weaklings all of whom bore the great name Ramses. They were far from bearing it worthily, and under them the waning power of the Pharaohs declined swiftly to its fall in a few decades. We see Ramses IV, the son of Ramses III, struggling feebly with the hopeless situation which he inherited about 1167 B. C. Immediately on his accession the new king prepared in his own behalf and that of his father, one of the most remarkable documents which has reached us from the civilization of ancient Egypt. In order that his father might prosper among the gods and that he himself might gain the benefit of his father's favour among them, the young king compiled for burial with the departed Pharaoh a list of the deceased's good works. It contained an enormous inventory of Ramses III's gifts to the three chief divinities of the nation; Amon of Thebes, Re of Heliopolis and Ptah of Memphis, as well as those also to the minor gods, in so far as the data could be obtained; besides a statement of his achievements in war and of his benefactions toward the people of his empire. All this recorded on papyrus formed a huge roll one hundred and thirty feet long containing one hundred and seventeen columns about twelve inches high. It is now called Papyrus Harris, and is the largest document which has descended to us from the early orient.[1] As the gifts enumerated therein are largely the long inherited estates of the gods merely confirmed by Ramses III at his accession, this unique document enables us to determine the proportion of the wealth of ancient Egypt held by the temples, as the reader

[1] I, IV, 151-412.

has already noticed in the preceding chapter. Accompanied by this extraordinary statement of his benefactions toward gods and men, Ramses III was laid in his tomb, in the lonely Valley of the Kings. In its efficacy in securing him unlimited favour with the gods there could be no doubt; and it contained so many prayers placed in the mouth of Ramses III on behalf of his son and successor that the gods, unable to resist the appeals of the favourite to whom they owed so much, would certainly grant his son a long reign. Indeed it is clear that this motive was powerfully operative in the production of the document. In this decadent age the Pharaoh was more dependent upon such means for the maintenance of his power than upon his own strong arm, and the huge papyrus thus becomes a significant sign of the times. At Abydos Ramses IV has left a unique prayer to Osiris, having the same practical purpose in view,—a prayer which he placed there in his fourth year: "Thou shalt double for me the long life, the prolonged reign of king Ramses II, the great god; for more are the mighty deeds and the benefactions which I do for thy house, in order to supply thy divine offerings, in order to seek every excellent thing, every sort of benefaction, to do them for thy sanctuary daily, during these four years, [more are they] than those things which king Ramses II, the great god, did for thee in his sixty seven years."[1] With fair promises of a long reign the insatiable priesthoods were extorting from the impotent Pharaoh all they demanded, while he was satisfied with the assured favour of the gods. The sources of that virile political life that had sprung up with the expulsion of the Hyksos were now exhausted. The vigourous grasp of affairs which had once enabled the Pharaoh to manipulate with ease the difficult problems of the dominant oriental state had now given way to an excessive devotion to religious works and superstitious belief in their effectiveness, which were rapidly absorbing every function of the state. Indeed, as we have before indicated, the state was

[1] IV. 471.

rapidly moving toward a condition in which its chief function should be religious and sacerdotal, and the assumption of royal power by the High Priest of Amon but a very natural and easy transition.

Naturally the only work of Ramses IV, of which we know, is an enterprise for the benefit of the gods. Early in his second year he went out in person to the quarries of the Wadi Hammamat, five days from the Nile, to look for stone for his temple buildings, and he then followed this journey of inspection by a great expedition of over nine thousand men, which reached the quarries nearly two years later. Although maintained by a long train of pack-bearers and ten carts, each drawn by six yoke of oxen, yet no less than nine hundred of the expedition perished in the heat and exposure, being about ten percent of its people.[1] The destination of the materials secured at so great cost is uncertain; the only surviving building of any extent erected by Ramses IV is the continuation of the rear chambers and the small hypostyle of the Khonsu temple at Thebes already begun by his father.[2] After an inglorious reign of six years he was succeeded in 1161 B. C. by the fifth Ramses, probably his son. The exploitation of the mines of Sinai now ceased, and the last Pharaonic name found there is that of Ramses IV. In quick succession these feeble Ramessids now followed each other; after a few years a collateral line of the family gained the throne in the person of a usurper, probably a grandson of Ramses III, who became Ramses VI, having succeeded in supplanting the son of Ramses V. The seventh and eighth Ramses quickly followed. They all excavated tombs in the Valley of the Kings, but we know nothing of their deeds.[3] Now and again the obscurity lifts, and we catch fleeting glimpses of a great state tottering to its fall. Under Ramses VI, nevertheless, the tomb of Penno, one of his deputies at Ibrim, in Nubia, shows us a picture of peaceful and prosperous administration there under Egyptian officials who have now replaced the native

[1] IV, 457–468. [2] IV, 472. [3] IV, 473 ff.

chief, the ruler of this locality at the close of the Eighteenth
Dynasty. Penno's family and relatives are found holding the important offices of the region, and it is evident
that Egyptian families have now migrated to Nubia and
more fully Egyptianized the country than ever. Penno
himself is sufficiently wealthy to erect a statue of Ramses
VI in the temple at Derr, built by Ramses II, and to endow
it with the income from six parcels of land; whereupon
the Pharaoh honours him with a gift of two vessels of silver,
a distinction which the grateful Penno does not fail to record in his tomb.[1]

From the close of Ramses III's reign to the first years
of Ramses IX, only some twenty five or thirty years elapsed,
and the same High Priest at El Kab who assisted in the
celebration of Ramses III's jubilee was still in office under
Ramses IX.[2] Likewise the High Priest of Amon at Thebes
under Ramses IX, Amenhotep, was the son of the high
priest Ramsesnakht, who held the office under Ramses III
and IV.[3] The high priesthood of Amon which had at least
once descended from father to son in the Nineteenth
Dynasty had thus become permanently hereditary, and
while it was passing from the hands of Ramsesnakht to
his son Amenhotep, with a single uninterrupted transmission of authority, six feeble Ramessids had succeeded
each other, with ever lessening power and prestige, as each
struggled for a brief time to maintain himself upon a
precarious throne. Meanwhile Amenhotep, the High Priest
of Amon, flourished. He sumptuously restored the refectory and kitchen of the priests in the temple of his god at
Karnak[4] built 800 years before by Sesostris I. We see
the crafty priest manipulating the pliant Pharaoh as he
pleases, and obtaining every honour at his hands. In his
tenth year Ramses IX summoned Amenhotep to the great
forecourt of the Amon-temple, where in the presence of the
High Priest's political associates and supporters, the king
presented him with a gorgeous array of gold and silver

vessels, with costly decorations, and precious ointments.
The days when such distinctions were the reward of valour
on the battle fields of Syria are long passed; and skill in
priest-craft is the surest guarantee of preferment. As the
king delivered the rich gifts to the High Priest he accompanied them with words of praise such that one is in doubt
whether they are delivered by the soverign to the subject
or by the subject to his lord. At the same time he informs
Amenhotep that certain revenues formerly paid to the
Pharaoh shall now be rendered to the treasury of Amon,
and although the king's words are not entirely clear it
would seem that all revenues levied by the king's treasury
but later intended for the treasury of the god, shall now be
collected directly by the scribes of the temple, thus putting
the temple to a certain extent in the place of the state. All
these honours were twice recorded by Amenhotep, together
with a record of his buildings on the walls of the Karnak
temple.[1] Both the records of his gifts and honours are accompanied each by a large relief (Fig. 177) showing Amenhotep receiving his gifts from the king, and depicting his
figure in the same heroic stature as that of the king,—an
unprecedented liberty, to which no official had ever before
in the history of Egypt dared to presume. In all such
scenes from time immemorial the official appearing before
the king had been represented as a pigmy before the towering figure of the Pharaoh; but the High Priest of Amon was
now rapidly growing to measure his stature with that of
the Pharaoh himself, both on the temple wall and in the
affairs of government. He had a body of temple troops at
his command, and as he gathered the sinews of the state
into his fingers, gradually gaining control of the treasury,
as we have seen, he did not hesitate to measure his strength
with the Pharaoh. Naturally no records of such struggles,
of the daily friction which must have existed between them,
have survived; but a woman giving testimony in a court
during the reign of Ramses IX dated a theft in her father's

[1] IV, 486–498.

house by telling the court that it happened "when the revolt of the High Priest of Amon took place!"[1]

The state of disorganization and helplessness which was gradually evolving is revealed to us in a chapter from the government of the Theban necropolis, preserved in certain legal archives[2] of Ramses IX's reign. Thebes was now rapidly declining; it had been forsaken as a royal residence by the Pharaohs two hundred years before, but it continued to be the burial place of all the royal dead. There had thus been gathered in its necropolis a great mass of wealth in the form of splendid regalia adorning the royal bodies. In the lonely valley behind the western plain, deep in the heart of the cliffs, slept the great emperors, decked in all the magnificence which the wealth of Asia had brought them; and now again, as at the close of the Eighteenth Dynasty, their degenerate descendants, far from maintaining the empire which they had once won, were not even able to protect their bodies from destruction. In the sixteenth year of Ramses IX's reign the royal tombs of the plain before the western cliffs were found to have been attacked; one of them, that of Sebekemsaf,[3] of the Thirteenth Dynasty, had been robbed of all its mortuary furniture and his royal body and that of his queen violated for the sake of their costly ornaments. Although the authors of this deed were captured and prosecuted, the investigation shows sinister traces that the officials engaged in it were not altogether disinterested. Three years later, when Ramses IX had made his son, Ramses X, coregent with himself, six men were convicted of robbing the tombs of Seti I and Ramses II, showing that the emboldened robbers had now left the plain and entered the cliff tombs of the valley behind. Ramses II, who had himself despoiled the pyramid of Sesostris II at Illahun, was now receiving similar treatment at the hands of his descendants. The tomb of one of Seti I's queens followed next, and then that of the great Amenhotep III. Within a generation, as the work of plunder continued, all

[1] IV, 486.   [2] IV, 499–556.   [3] See Thieves' Confession, above, p. 213.

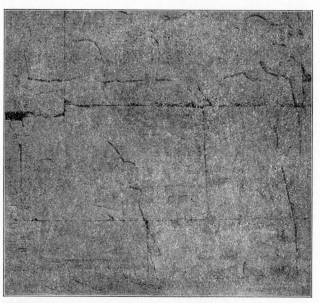

FIG. 177.—THE HIGH PRIEST OF AMON AMENHOTEP DECORATED BY RAMSES IX

Contrary to tradition his figure (on the left) is as tall as that of the king (on the right).

FIG. 178.—SCRIBE'S NOTES ON COFFIN OF
SETI I.

They are records of the removals of the body, till its
final deposit in the Der el-Bahri cache (Fig. 179)
under the priest-kings of the Twenty-first Dynasty.

FIG. 179.—THE DER EL-BAHRI HIDING-
PLACE.

Shaft where royal bodies were concealed is seen as dark
point at top of path leading up beyond the donkeys.
See p. 525.

the bodies of Egypt's kings and emperors buried at Thebes were despoiled, and of the whole line of Pharaohs from the beginning of the Eighteenth to the end of the Twentieth Dynasty, only one body, that of Amenhotep II, has been found still lying in its sarcophagus; although it had by no means escaped spoliation. Thus while the tombs of the Egyptian emperors at Thebes were being ransacked and their bodies rifled and dishonoured, the empire which they conquered was crumbling to ruin.

While we can find nothing of the reign of Ramses X to record, beyond the rifling of the royal tombs, and our knowledge of his successor, the eleventh of the name, is still more meagre, at the accession of Ramses XII we are able to discern the culmination of the tendencies which we have been endeavouring to trace. Before he had been reigning five years a local noble at Tanis named Nesubenebded, the Smendes of the Greeks, had absorbed the entire Delta and made himself king of the North.[1] It was such an enterprise as the unnamed vizier had attempted at Athribis in the time of Ramses III,[2] who was too able and energetic for the audacious noble to succeed. But no longer commanding the undivided resources of Upper Egypt, which he might otherwise have employed against Nesubenebded, there was now nothing for the impotent Pharaoh to do but retire to Thebes,—if this transfer had not indeed already occurred before this,—where he still maintained his precarious throne. Thebes was thus cut off from the sea and the commerce of Asia and Europe by a hostile kingdom in the Delta, and its wealth and power still more rapidly declined. The High Priest of Amon was now virtually at the head of a Theban principality, which we shall see becoming gradually more and more a distinct political unit. Together with this powerful priestly rival, the Pharaoh continued to hold Nubia.

The swift decline of the Ramessids was quickly noticed

[1] IV, 557, 581.   [2] See above, pp. 497–98.

and understood in Syria long before the revolution which resulted in the independence of the Delta. The Thekel and Peleset-Philistines, whose invasion Ramses III had for a time halted, as we have before stated, had continued to arrive in Syria. They had moved gradually southward, pushing before them the Amorites and scattered remnants of the Hittites, who were thus forced to enter Palestine, where they were found later by the Hebrews. Seventy five years after Ramses III had beaten them into submission, the Thekel were already established as an independent king- dom at Dor, just south of the seaward end of Carmel.[1] As we do not find them mentioned in the surviving records of the Hebrews, they must have merged into the larger mass of the Philistines, whose cities gradually extended prob- ably from Beth-Shean in the Jordan valley westward and southward, through the plain of Jezreel or Megiddo to the southern sea-plain, cutting off the northern tribes of Israel from their kinsmen in the south. Their pottery, as found at Lachish and Gezer in southern Palestine, is Cretan, con- firming the Hebrew tradition that the Philistines were strangers who wandered in from Crete (Caphtor).[2] Con- tinually replenished with new arrivals by sea, they threat- ened to crush Israel, as they had done the kingdom of Amor, before the Hebrew tribal leaders should have welded the Pal- estinian Semites into a nation. With their extreme southern frontier at the very gates of Egypt, these hardy and warlike wanderers from the far north could not have paid tribute to the Pharaoh very long after the death of Ramses III (1167 B. C.). In the reign of Ramses IX (1142–1123 B. C.), or about that time, a body of Egyptian envoys were detained at Byblos by the local dynast for seventeen years, and unable to return, they at last died there.[3] The Syrian princes, among whom Ramses III had built a temple to Amon, to which they brought their yearly tribute, were thus indifferent to the power of Egypt within twenty or twenty five years of his death.

[1] IV, 558.　　　　[2] Jer. 47: 4; Amos 9: 7.　　　　[3] IV, 585.

A few years later, under Ramses XII, these same conditions in Syria are vividly portrayed in the report of an Egyptian envoy thither. In response to an oracle, Wenamon, the envoy in question, was dispatched to Byblos, at the foot of Lebanon, to procure cedar for the sacred barge of Amon. Hrihor, the High Priest of Amon, was able to give him only a pitiful sum in gold and silver, and therefore sent with him an image of Amon, called "Amon-of-the-Way," who was able to bestow "life and health," hoping thus to impress the prince of Byblos and compensate for the lack of liberal payment. As Wenamon was obliged to pass through the territory of Nesubenebded, who now ruled the Delta, Hrihor supplied him with letters to the Delta prince, and in this way secured for him passage in a ship commanded by a Syrian captain. Nothing more eloquently portrays the decadent condition of Egypt than the humiliating state of this unhappy envoy, dispatched without ships, with no credentials, with but a beggarly pittance to offer for the timber desired, and only the memory of Egypt's former greatness with which to impress the prince of Byblos. Stopping at Dor on the voyage out, Wenamon was robbed of the little money he had, and was unable to secure any satisfaction from the Thekel prince of that city. After waiting in despair for nine days, he departed for Byblos by way of Tyre, having on the way somehow succeeded in seizing from certain Thekel people a bag of silver as security for his loss at Dor. He finally arrived in safety at Byblos, where Zakar-Baal, the prince of the city, would not even receive him, but ordered him to leave. Such was the state of an Egyptian envoy in Phœnicia, within fifty or sixty years of the death of Ramses III. Finally, as the despairing Wenamon was about to take passage back to Egypt, one of the noble youths in attendance upon Zakar-Baal was seized with a divine frenzy, and in prophetic ecstasy demanded that Wenamon be summoned, honourably treated and dismissed. This earliest known example of Old Testament prophecy in

its earlier form thus secured for Wenamon an interview with
Zakar-Baal, which the envoy himself thus relates:

"When morning came he sent and had me brought up,
when the divine offering occurred in the fortress wherein
he was, on the shore of the sea. I found him sitting in his
upper chamber, leaning his back against a window, while
the waves of the great Syrian sea were beating against the
shore behind him. I said to him, 'Kindness of Amon!'
He said to me: 'How long is it until this day, since thou
camest away from the abode of Amon?' I said, 'Five
months and one day until now.' He said to me, 'Behold
if thou art true, where is the writing of Amon, which is in
thy hand? Where is the letter of the High Priest of Amon,
which is in thy hand?' I said to him, 'I gave them to
Nesubenebded. . . . ' Then he was very wroth, and he
said to me, 'Now behold the writing and the letter are not
in thy hand! Where is the ship of cedar which Nesubenebded gave thee? Where is the Syrian crew? He would
not deliver thy business to this ship-captain, to have thee
killed! That they might cast thee into the sea! From
whom would they have sought the god [Amon-of-the-Way]
then? And thee! From whom would they have sought
thee then?' So spake he to me. I said to him, 'There are
indeed Egyptian ships and Egyptian crews which sail under
Nesubenebded, but he hath no Syrian crews.' He said to
me, 'There are surely twenty ships here in my harbour
which are in connection with Nesubenebded; and at this
Sidon, whither thou also wouldst go, there are indeed 10,000
ships also, which are in connection with Berket-El [probably
a merchant of Tanis], and sail to his house.' Then I was
silent in that great hour. He answered and said to me, 'On
what business hast thou come hither?' I said to him, 'I
have come after the timber for the great and august barge
of Amon-Re, king of gods. Thy father did it, and thou wilt
also do it.' So spake I to him. He said to me, 'They did
it truly. If thou give me something for doing it I will do
it. Indeed my agents transacted the business; the Pharaoh

sent six ships laden with the products of Egypt, and they were unloaded into their store-houses. And thou also shalt bring something for me.' He had the journal of his fathers brought in, and he had them read it before me. They found one thousand deben [about 244 Troy pounds] of every kind of silver, which was in his book. He said to me, 'If the ruler of Egypt were the owner of my property and I were also his servant, he would not send silver and gold, saying, "Do the commandment of Amon." It was not the payment of tribute which they exacted of my father. As for me, I am myself neither thy servant, nor am I the servant of him who sent thee. If I cry out to the Lebanon, the heavens open and the logs lie here upon the shore of the sea. Give me the sails which thou hast certainly brought to propel thy ships which bear thy logs to Egypt! Give me the cordage [which thou hast of course brought to bind], the trees which I fell, in order to make them fast for thee! [What then if a storm comes up] and they break and thou die in the midst of the sea, when Amon thunders in heaven. . . . For [I admit that] Amon equips all lands; he equips them, having first equipped the land of Egypt, whence thou comest. For artisanship came forth from it to reach my place of abode; and teaching came forth from it to reach my place of abode. What then are these miserable journeys which they have had thee make!' I said to him, 'O guilty one! They are no miserable journeys on which I am. There is no ship upon the river which Amon does not own. For his is the sea, and his is Lebanon, of which thou sayest, "It is mine." It grows for the divine barge of Amon, the lord of every ship. Yea, so spake Amon-Re, king of gods, saying to Hrihor, my lord, "Send me," and he made me go, bearing this great god [Amon-of-the-Way]. But behold, thou hast let this great god wait twenty nine days, when he had landed in thy harbour, although thou didst certainly know that he was here. He is indeed still what he once was, while thou standest and bargainest for the Lebanon with Amon, its lord. As for what thou sayest, that the former kings sent silver and gold; if they had given life and health, they would not have sent the valuables; but they sent the valuables to thy fathers instead of life and health. Now as for Amon-Re, king of gods, he is the lord of life and health; and he was the lord of thy fathers, who spent their lives offering to Amon. And thou also art the servant of Amon. If thou sayest to Amon, "I will do it! I will do it!" and thou executest his command, thou shalt live, and thou shalt be prosperous, and thou shalt be healthy, and thou shalt be pleasant to thy whole land and thy people. Wish not for thyself a thing belonging to Amon-Re, king of gods. Yea, the lion loveth his own. Let my scribe be brought to me, that I may send him to Nesubenebded and Tentamon [his wife], the rulers, whom Amon hath given to the North of his land, and they will send all that of which I shall write to them, saying, "Let it be brought," until I return to the South and send to thee all, all thy trifles again [the balance still due].' So spake I to him."

The observing reader will have drawn many conclusions from this remarkable interview. The Phœnician prince quite readily admits the debt of culture which his land owes Egypt as a source of civilization, but emphatically repudiates all political responsibility to the ruler of Egypt, whom he never calls Pharaoh, except in referring to a former sovereign. The situation is clear. A burst of military enthusiasm and a line of able rulers had enabled Egypt to assume for several centuries an imperial position, which her unwarlike people were not by nature adapted to occupy; and their impotent descendants, no longer equal to their imperial role, were now appealing to the days of splendour with an almost pathetic futility. It is characteristic of the time that this appeal should assume a religious or even theological form, as Wenamon boldly proclaims Amon's dominion over Lebanon, where the Phœnician princes had, only two generations before, worshipped and paid tribute at the temple of Amon, erected by Ramses III. With oracles and an image of the god that conferred "life and health" the Egyptian envoy

sought to make his bargain with the contemptuous Phœnician for timber which a Thutmose III or a Seti I had
demanded with his legions behind him.   We can hardly
wonder that the image of "Amon-of-the-Way" failed to
impress Zakar-Baal, as the Pharaoh's armies had impressed
his ancestors; and it was only when Wenamon's messenger
to Egypt returned with a few vessels of silver and gold,
some fine linen, papyrus rolls, ox-hides, coils of cordage, and
the like, that the Phœnician ruler ordered his men to cut
the desired logs; although he had sent some of the heavier
timbers for the hull of the barge in advance, as an evidence
of his good faith.   As Wenamon was about to depart with
his timber, some eight months after he had left Thebes,
Zakar-Baal tells him with grim humour of the fate of the
Egyptian envoys of a former reign who had been detained
seventeen years and had ultimately died in Byblos.   He
even offers to have Wenamon taken and shown their tombs.
This privilege the frightened envoy declines, adding that
the embassy which had been so treated was one of merely
human envoys, while Zakar-Baal was now honoured with
an unparalleled distinction in receiving the god himself!
Promising the prince the payment of the balance due him,
Wenamon proceeded to embark, when he discovered in the
offing a fleet of eleven Thekel ships, coming with instructions to arrest him, doubtless for the seizure of the silver
which he had taken from the Thekel on the voyage from
Tyre to Byblos.   The unhappy Wenamon now lost all hope,
and throwing himself down upon the shore burst into weep-
ing.   Even Zakar-Baal was touched by his misery and sent
to him a reassuring message, with food and wine and an
Egyptian chanteuse.   The next day the prince succeeded
in holding the Thekel of the fleet to an interview, while
Wenamon embarked and escaped.   But a tempest drove him
far out of his course and cast him upon the coast of Cyprus,
where the populace was about to slay him at the palace of
Hatiba, the queen.   Her he fortunately intercepted as she
was passing from one palace to another.   Among her follow-

ing, Wenamon by inquiry found a Cyprian who spoke Egyptian, and he bade this new-found interpreter speak to the queen for him. "Say to my mistress: 'I have heard as far as Thebes, the abode of Amon, that in every city injustice is done; but that justice is done in the land of Alasa [Cyprus]. But, lo, injustice is done every day here.'" She said, "Indeed! What is this that thou sayest?" I said to her, "If the sea raged and the wind drove me to the land where I am, thou wilt not let them take advantage of me to slay me, I being a messenger of Amon. I am one for whom they will seek unceasingly. As for the crew of the prince of Byblos whom they sought to kill, their lord will surely find ten crews of thine, and he will slay them on his part." Wenamon's crew was then summoned, and he himself bidden to lie down and sleep. At this point his report breaks off, and the conclusion is lost; but here again, in Cyprus, whose king, as practically his vassal, the Pharaoh had been wont to call to account for piracy in the old days of splendour, we find the representative of Egypt barely able to save his life. It is to be noticed that his reminder of unpleasant consequences makes no reference to the Pharaoh, while it places fully as much emphasis upon the vengeance of the prince of Byblos as upon that of Egypt; this only two generations after a great war-fleet of Ramses III had destroyed the powerful united navy of his northern enemies in these very waters. This unique and instructive report of Wenamon,[1] therefore, reveals to us the complete collapse of Egyptian prestige abroad and shows with what appalling swiftness the dominant state in the Mediterranean basin had declined under the weak successors of Ramses III. When Tiglath-pileser I appeared in the West about 1100 B. C., a Pharaoh, who was probably Nesubenebded, feeling his exposed position in the Delta, deemed it wise to propitiate the Assyrian with a gift, and sent him a crocodile. Thus all Egyptian influence in Syria had utterly vanished, while in Palestine a fiction of traditional sovereignty, totally without

[1] IV, 557–591.

practical political significance, was maintained at the Pharaoh's court.   In resumption of that sovereignty we shall see
future kings making sporadic campaigns thither after the
establishment of the Hebrew monarchy.

Meanwhile there was but one possible issue for the conditions at Thebes.   The messenger who procured the timber
for the sacred barge of Amon was no longer dispatched by
the Pharaoh, but as we have seen, by the High Priest of
Amon, Hrihor.   The next year he had gained sufficient control of the royal necropolis at Thebes to send his people
thither to rewrap and properly reinter the bodies of Seti I
and Ramses II, which had been violated and robbed in the
first year of Ramses X.[1]   The temple of Khonsu (Fig. 183),
left with only the holy of holies and the rear chambers
finished since the time of Ramses III, was now completed
with a colonnaded hall preceded by a court and pylon.   The
walls of these new additions bear significant evidence of the
transition which was now going on in the Egyptian state.
In the new hall the official dedications on the architraves
are strictly in accordance with the conventional form, customary since the Old Kingdom: "Live king Ramses XII!
He made it as his monument for his father, 'Khonsu in
Thebes, Beautiful Rest,' making for him [the hall called]
'Wearer of Diadems,' for the first time, of fine white limestone, making splendid his temple as a beautiful monument
forever, which the Son of Re, Ramses XII, made for him."[2]
But around the base of the walls are words which have never
been found in a Pharaonic temple before; we read: "High
Priest of Amon-Re, king of gods, commander in chief of the
armies of the South and North, the leader, Hrihor, tri-
umphant; he made it as his monument for 'Khonsu in
Thebes, Beautiful Rest'; making for him a temple for the
first time, in the likeness of the horizon of heaven.[3] . . . "
That the commander in chief of the armies of the South and
North was the real builder of the hall we can hardly doubt.
On either side of the central door which leads out into the

[1] IV, 592-4.   [2] IV, 602.   [3] IV, 609.

court, lying before the hall, is a pair of reliefs, each showing
a festal procession of the god, before whom, in the place for
thousands of years occupied by the Pharaoh, stands the
High Priest Hrihor, offering incense; while strangely
enough, the conventional blessings regularly recorded over
the god, and supposed to be uttered by him to the king, are
still addressed to Ramses XII![1] Like the shadowy caliph,
whom the Egyptian sultans brought from Bagdad to Cairo,
and maintained for a time there, so the unfortunate Ramses
XII had been brought from his Delta residence to Thebes,
that the conventionalities of the old Pharaonic tradition
might still be continued for a brief time. A letter written
to his Nubian viceroy in his seventeenth year shows that he
still retained some voice there up to that time at least;[2] but
the door (Fig. 183), bearing the two reliefs just mentioned,
shows him deprived of his authority there also, for it bears
an inscription of Hrihor, still dated under Ramses XII (the
year is unfortunately broken out), in which the High Priest
appears as "viceroy of Kush."[3] Already at the close of
the Nineteenth Dynasty we recall that Amon had gained
possession of the Nubian gold-country;[4] the High Priest has
now gone a step further and seized the whole of the great
province of the Upper Nile. The same inscription calls him
also "overseer of the double granary," who, as grain was
always Egypt's chief source of wealth, was the most important fiscal officer in the state, next the chief treasurer himself.
There is now nothing left in the way of authority and power
for the High Priest to absorb; he is commander of all the
armies, viceroy of Kush, holds the treasury in his hands, and
executes the buildings of the gods. When the fiction of the
last Ramessid's official existence had been maintained for
at least twenty seven years the final assumption of the High
Priest's supreme position seems to have been confirmed by
an oracle of Khonsu, followed by the approval of Amon.
It is recorded in the above inscription, a document very fragmentary and obscure, engraved on that same fatal door,[5]

[1] IV, 611.   [2] IV, 595–600.   [3] IV, 615.   [4] III, 640.   [5] IV, 614–618.

which in the growth of the Khonsu temple, as in the history of the state, marks the final transition.   For through this door the modern visitor passes from the inner hall bearing the names of both Hrihor and Ramses XII, to the outer court, built by Hrihor, where the shadowy Pharaoh vanishes, and the High Priest's name, preceded by the Pharaonic titles and enclosed in the royal cartouche at last appears alone. Henceforth the name "Ramses" is no longer a personal name, but is worn as a title designating a descendant of the once mighty line.

CHAPTER XXV

PRIESTS AND MERCENARIES: THE SUPREMACY OF
THE LIBYANS

THE result of the development of Thebes into an independent sacerdotal principality was not only the downfall of the empire, but of course also the end of the unity of the kingdom. From now on the sacerdotal princes of Thebes, the High Priests of Amon, will either rule the country themselves or maintain Theban independence. As they rarely succeeded in doing the former the result was constant disunion and division, which continued in more or less pronounced form from the rise of Hrihor and Nesubenebded, in the latter part of the eleventh century, for four hundred and fifty years or more. The complacent Hrihor maintained the fiction of a united "Two Lands," of which he called himself the lord, as if he really ruled them both.[1] With amazing mendacity he filled his titulary with references to his universal power, and affirmed that the Syrian princes bowed down every day to his might.[2] Fortunately we are well informed as to the real attitude of the Syrian dynasts toward Hrihor by the experiences of the redoubtable Wenamon at Dor and Byblos. The High Priest's methods and theory of government were not calculated to compel the respect of the Syrians. The state which he founded was a theocracy, pure and simple. As far back as the days of Thutmose III and Hatshepsut there are remarkable examples of Amon's intervention in the affairs of practical government. Thutmose III himself was crowned by an oracle of the god; Hatshepsut erected her obelisks at his behest and sent her fleet to Punt in response to his special oracular command. But these and other examples of the god's intervention occurred

[1] IV, 620.   [2] IV, 623.

on extraordinary occasions. Under Hrihor's theocracy such
oracles became part of the ordinary machinery of government. Whatever the High Priest wished legally to effect
could be sanctioned by special oracle of the god at any time,
and by prearrangement the cultus image before which the
High Priest made known his desires invariably responded
favourably by violent nodding of the head, or even by
speech. All wills and property conveyances of members of
the High Priest's family were oracles of Amon,[1] and civil
documents thus became divine decrees. Banished political
exiles were recalled by oracle of the god, criminal cases
were tried before him, and by his decision the convicted were
put to death. In the case of a temple official, undoubtedly a
favourite of the High Priest, two documents were placed
before the god, one declaring the accused guilty of embez-
zlement of temple income, and the other declaring him innocent. The god seized the latter document, thus determining
the innocence of the accused.[2] Priestly jugglery, ruling if
necessary in utter disregard of law and justice, thus enabled
the High Priest to cloak with the divine sanction all that he
wished to effect.

Hrihor must have been an old man at his accession (1090
B. C.). He did not long survive Ramses XII, and at his
death his son, Payonekh, also advanced in years, was unable
to maintain the independence of Thebes against Nesubenebded at Tanis, who extended his authority over the whole
country for a brief time. He is called the first king of the
Twenty First Dynasty by Manetho, who knows nothing of
the independence of Thebes.[3] Payonekh's son, Paynozem
I, quickly succeeded him,[4] and while he was ruling at Thebes
in more or less independence, but without royal titles, Nesubenebded was followed at Tanis by Pesibkhenno I, probably
his son. Although unable to regain the royalty of his grandfather, Paynozem I showed considerable energy in his gov-·
ernment of the Theban principality. He continued the
Khonsu temple, restored some of the older temples,[5] and,

[1] IV, 795.   [2] IV, 670-674.   [3] IV, 627. 631.   [4] IV, 631.   [5] IV, 633-5.

unable to protect the royal bodies in the western necropolis
from further molestation, began the policy of transferring
them to a tomb which might be better guarded, selecting for
this purpose the tomb of Seti I.[1] He now achieved a master
stroke of diplomacy and gained in marriage the daughter
of the Tanite, Pesibkhenno I. Thus on the death of the
latter (1067 B. C.), he obtained through his wife the Tanite
crown and the sovereignty over a united Egypt.   He installed his son as High Priest at Thebes, but both he and a
second son whom he appointed to the office died. His third
son, Menkheperre, who now obtained the high priesthood,
appeared at Thebes in the twenty fifth year of his father,[2]
and assumed authority not without suppression of some hostility. The political turmoil of the time is evident in the
fact that he was immediately obliged to appear before Amon
and secure an oracle approving of the return of a body of
political exiles who had been banished to one of the oases.
Exactly who these exiles were does not appear; but we can
surmise that the recall was effected to conciliate the Thebans,
who now began to show themselves as turbulent as they were
in the days of the revolts, which made Thebes notorious
under the Ptolemies.[3]

Paynozem I reigned some forty years at Tanis, and
although his son Menkheperre seems to have gained some
royal titles on his father's death (1026 B. C.)[4] he did not
succeed to the crown, which was obtained by one Amenemopet, whose connection with Paynozem I is entirely prob-
lematical. Of the course of events during his long reign
of half a century we can now discern nothing. These Tanite
kings were not great builders, although Pesibkhenno I raised
a massive enclosure wall eighty feet thick around his temple
at Tanis.[5] As they show little initiative in other directions,
the century and a half during which they maintained themselves was apparently one of steady industrial and economic
decline. We have no data from other periods to aid us by
comparison, but even so it is evident that the price of land

[1] IV, 642.   [2] IV, 650.   [3] IV, 650-658.   [4] IV, 661.   [5] Petrie, Tanis, I, 18.

was very low. Ten "stat" (about six and three quarters acres) of land at Abydos sold for one deben (a little over fourteen hundred grains) of silver at this time.[1] While Nesubenebded did send a large body of men to Thebes to repair the damage done by an unusually high inundation,[2] the Tanites as a whole did nothing for the great capital of the empire, and its decline was steady and rapid. They respected the memory of their royal ancestors and vied with the high priests at Thebes in protecting the bodies of the emperors. During the reign of Siamon, Amenemopet's successor, the bodies of Ramses I, Seti I and Ramses II were taken from the tomb of Seti I and hidden in that of a queen named Inhapi.[3] But such was the insecurity of the times that after a few years, under Pesibkhenno II, the last king of the Tanite Dynasty, they were hurriedly removed to their final hiding place, an old and probably unused tomb of Amenhotep I, near the temple of Der el-Bahri (Fig. 179). Here they were concealed for the last time, and as the officials who superintended the transfer left the place a scribe hurriedly wrote upon the coffins the record[4] of their last removal alongside similar graffiti hastily scrawled there under similar circumstances after earlier transfers beginning as far back as a hundred and fifty years before (Fig. 178). These successive records on the royal coffins and bodies, in which one may trace their transfer from tomb to tomb in the vain effort to find a place of safety, form perhaps the most eloquent testimony of the decadence of the age. The rough passage entering the cliff at the base of a shaft in which they were now deposited was sealed for the last time a few years later, early in the Twenty Second Dynasty, not long after 940 B. C. Here the greatest kings of Egypt slept unmolested for nearly three thousand years, until about 1871 or 1872, when the Theban descendants of those same tomb-robbers whose prosecution under Ramses IX we can still read, discovered the place and the plundering of the royal bodies was begun again. By methods not

[1] IV, 681.   [2] IV, 627 ff.   [3] IV, 664-7.   [4] IV, 691-2.

greatly differing from those employed under Ramses IX the modern authorities forced the thieves to disclose the place. Thus nearly twenty nine centuries after they had been sealed in their hiding place by the ancient scribes, and some three thousand five hundred years after the first interment of the earliest among them, the faces of Egypt's kings and emperors were disclosed to the modern world, and hence the reader of these pages is frequently able to look upon the fleshly features of the monarchs whose deeds of three millenniums ago he has been reading.

Abroad, the Twenty First Dynasty was as feeble as its predecessors at the close of the Twentieth had been. They probably maintained Egyptian power in Nubia, but in Syria they were in no better reputation than in the days of Wenamon's ill-starred mission to the prince of Byblos. A nominal suzerainty over Palestine was probably one of the court fictions in continuance of a century-long tradition. During this period of Egypt's total eclipse the tribes of Israel thus gained the opportunity to consolidate their national organization and under Saul and David they gradually gained the upper hand against the Philistines. Whether the Egyptians had a hand in these events, thus enabling the Israelites to subdue this hardy people of the coast, it is as yet impossible to determine as we have no monuments which throw any light upon Egypt's connection with Asiatic politics in this period. The sea-peoples no longer appear upon the monuments, and from the west the Delta was now the peaceful conquest of the Libyans, who accomplished by gradual immigration what they had failed to gain by hostile invasion. Although there was a native militia, chiefly under command of the High Priest of Amon at Thebes, Libyan mercenaries now filled the ranks of the Egyptian army, and the commanders of the Meshwesh in control of the fortresses and garrisons of the important Delta towns soon gained positions of power and influence. A Tehen-Libyan named Buyuwawa settled at Heracleopolis early in the Twenty First Dynasty; his son Musen was installed as a priest of the Heracleopolitan temple and commander of the mercenaries of the town, and these offices became hereditary in the family.[1] Musen's great grandson, Sheshonk, was a "great chief of the Meshwesh," and a man of wealth and power. He buried his son Namlot at Abydos in great splendour and richly endowed the mortuary service of the tomb with lands, gardens, slaves, attendants and daily oblations. When the administrators of this property proved untrue to their trust Sheshonk was possessed of sufficient influence with one of the Twenty First Dynasty kings, whose name is unfortunately lost, to secure their punishment by oracle of Amon at Thebes.[2] While we cannot follow the fortunes of the other Libyan commanders throughout the Delta in this way, there can be no doubt that they were all enjoying similar prosperity in a greater or less degree, and gradually gathering the reins of authority into their hands. The weak and inglorious Twenty First Dynasty had now been ruling nearly a century and a half and the descendants of the Libyan Buyuwawa at Heracleopolis had been constantly increasing their local authority for an equal length of time, through five generations, when Sheshonk, the grandson of that Sheshonk of whom we have just spoken, succeeded as the representative of the family there. Either this Sheshonk or his immediate ancestors had extended Heracleopolis until it controlled a principality reaching probably as far as Memphis on the north and on the south as far as Siut. Whether the Tanite line died out or its last representative was too feeble to maintain himself we shall probably never know, but such was the power of the Heracleopolitan mercenary commander that he transferred his residence to Bubastis in the eastern Delta, where he seized the royal authority and proclaimed himself Pharaoh about 945 B. C.[3] His line was known to Manetho as the Twenty Second Dynasty. Thus in a little over two centuries after the death of Ramses III, who had smitten them so sorely, the Libyans gained the crown of Egypt without

[1] IV, 785–793.   [2] IV, 669–687.   [3] IV, 785 ff.

so much as drawing the sword. The change which thus placed a soldier and a foreigner upon the venerable throne of the Pharaohs had gone hand in hand with that which had delivered the country to the priests; but the power of the priest had culminated a little more rapidly than that of the soldier, although both were equally rooted in the imperial system of the Eighteenth Dynasty.

Sheshonk immediately gave to the succession of his line a legitimacy which he could not himself possess. He married his son to the daughter of Pesibkhenno II, the last of the Tanite kings of the Twenty First Dynasty, and thus gained for him the right to the throne through his wife, as well as unquestionable legitimacy for his son.[1] A vigourous and an able ruler, it might have been expected that Sheshonk I, as we shall now call him, would be able to weld Egypt anew into a powerful nation; but those elements with which he was obliged to deal in the building up of a new state were not such as could possibly be wrought into any stable fabric. It was essentially a feudal organization which was now effected by Sheshonk I, and the princes who owed him fealty were largely the turbulent Meshwesh chiefs like himself, who would naturally not forget his origin nor fail to see that a successful coup might accomplish for any one of them what he had achieved for himself. Though we cannot demark their geographical power with certainty, it is evident that they ruled the Delta cities, rendering to the Pharaoh their quota of troops, as did the Mamlukes under the Sultans of Moslem Egypt. Upper Egypt was organized into two principalities; that of Heracleopolis embracing, as we have seen, northern Upper Egypt as far south as Siut, where the Theban principality began, which in its turn included all the country to the cataract and perhaps Nubia also. The country thus already fell into three divisions roughly corresponding to those of Ptolemaic and Roman times.[2] Sheshonk by his origin controlled Heracleopolis, and he and his family after him maintained close

1 IV, 738.   2 IV, 745–7.

relations with the High Priests of Ptah at Memphis. Not later than his fifth year[1] he had also acquired Thebes. He attempted to hold its support to his house by appointing his own son as High Priest of Amon there;[2] but it still remained a distinct principality, capable of offering serious opposition to the ruling family in the Delta. The city itself at least was not taxable by the Pharaoh, and was never visited by his fiscal officials.[3] Under these circumstances an outbreak among the Libyan lords of the Delta or in the powerful principalities of the South might be expected as soon as there was no longer over them a strong hand like that of Sheshonk I.

Under the energetic Sheshonk Egypt's foreign policy took on a more aggressive character, and her long merely formal claims upon Palestine were practically pressed. Solomon was evidently an Egyptian vassal who possibly received in marriage a daughter of the Pharaoh and whose territory his Egyptian suzerain extended by the gift of the important city of Gezer.[4] We last heard of it under Merneptah three hundred years before; but never having been subdued by the Israelites, its Canaanite lord had now rebelled. The Pharaoh captured and burned it and presented it to Solomon, who rebuilt it.[5] The Pharaoh with whom Solomon had to deal, a Pharaoh who captured and burned strong cities in Palestine like Gezer, cannot have been one of the degenerate kings at the close of the Twenty First Dynasty, but an aggressive ruler who resumed Egypt's control in Palestine; and we know of no other king at this time who answers this description save Sheshonk I. After the division of the kingdom of the Hebrews under Solomon's successor, Rehoboam, Sheshonk I, who had already harboured the fugitive Jeroboam, Rehoboam's northern enemy, thought it a good opportunity to make his claims in Palestine unquestionable, and in the fifth year of Rehoboam, probably about 926 B. C., he invaded Palestine. His cam-

[1] IV, 700.　　　　　[2] IV, 699.　　　　　[3] IV, 750.
[4] I Kings, 9: 16.　　　[5] I Kings, 9: 15–17.

paign penetrated no further north than the latitude of the
Sea of Galilee and extended eastward probably as far as
Mahanaim on the east of Jordan.[1] Egyptian troops had not
penetrated Asia for over two hundred and seventy years,
and Sheshonk let loose his Libyan mercenaries among the
towns of the plain of Jezreel, which they plundered from
Rehob on the north, through Hapharaim, Megiddo, Taanach
and Shunem, to Beth-shean in the Jordan Valley on the east.
In the South they spoiled Yeraza, Bethhoron, Ajalon,
Gibeon, Socoh, Beth Anoth, Sharuhen and Arad, the last
two places marking their extreme southern activity. According to the Hebrew records[2] they also entered Jerusalem
and despoiled it of the wealth gathered there in Solomon's
day; but it is clear that Sheshonk's campaign was directed
impartially against the two kingdoms and did not affect
Judah alone.[3] He afterward claimed to have pushed as
far north as Mitanni; but this is evidently a mere boast, for
Mitanni had at this time long ceased to exist as a kingdom.[4]
Among other Palestinian towns which Sheshonk records as
taken by him is a place hitherto unnoticed called "Field of
Abram," in which we find the earliest occurrence of the
name of Israel's eponymous hero (Fig. 180). Sheshonk was
able to return with great plunder with which to replenish
the long depleted Pharaonic coffers. He placed a record of
the tribute of Palestine and of Nubia, of which he had now
gained control, beside those of the great conquerors of the
Empire on the walls of the Karnak temple at Thebes.[5] He
installed a new Libyan governor in the Great Oasis, and one
of his Libyan vassal chiefs governed the western Delta and
administered the caravan communication with the oases.[6]
Thus for a time at least the glories of the Empire of the
Nineteenth Dynasty were restored with tribute flowing into
the treasury from a domain extending from northern Palestine to the upper Nile, and from the oases to the Red Sea.

With his treasury thus replenished Sheshonk was able

1 IV, 709 ff., see also my essay, Amer. Jour. of Sem. Lang., XXI, 22–36.
2 I Kings, 14: 25. 3 IV, 709–722. 4 IV, 710. 5 IV, 723–4 A. 6 IV, 782–4.

to revive the customary building enterprises of the Pharaohs which had been discontinued for over two hundred years. He beautified Bubastis, his Delta residence, and at Thebes undertook a vast enlargement of the Karnak temple. His son Yewepet, who was High Priest of Amon there, dispatched an expedition to Silsileh to secure the stone for an enormous court and pylon which were to complete the Karnak temple on the west and give it a magnificent front toward the river. The side walls and colonnades of the court had been planned and erected at some time after the Nineteenth Dynasty, but the pylon was still lacking. It was, and is today, the largest temple court in existence, being over three hundred and fourteen feet wide by two hundred and sixty nine feet deep, fronted by the largest pylon in Egypt, thirty six feet thick, one hundred and fifty feet high and with a front of three hundred and fifty seven feet (Map 11). Sheshonk intended that it should be used at the celebration of his thirty years' jubilee; whether it was ever so used we do not know; but he never lived to see it completed, and the builder's scaffolding and ramps of sun-dried brick still cumber the walls beneath the debris of many centuries. Part of its decoration was however completed, and by the south gate, now known as the Bubastite Portal, the Pharaoh had executed a huge relief in the old style, depicting himself smiting the Asiatics before Amon, who, together with the presiding goddess of Thebes, leads and presents to Sheshonk ten lines of captives, containing one hundred and fifty six Palestinian prisoners, each symbolizing a town or locality captured by Sheshonk and bearing its name.[1] A number of Biblical names may be recognized among them, the chief of which we have already noted.

When Osorkon I, Sheshonk I's son and heir, followed him, probably about 920 B. C., he succeeded by right of inheritance through his wife, the daughter of Pesibkhenno II, the last king of the old line of the Twenty First Dynasty. He inherited a prosperous kingdom and great wealth. During

[1] IV, 709-722.

a little more than the first three years of his reign he gave to the temples of Egypt a total of no less than four hundred and eighty seven thousand pounds Troy of silver, while of gold and silver together he gave over five hundred and sixty thousand pounds Troy, a sum which doubtless includes the above total of silver.[1] These enormous donations form the most striking evidence in our possession for the wealth and prosperity of the Libyan dynasty in its earlier days. In order to control the Heracleopolitan principality, Osorkon I built a stronghold at the mouth of the Fayum,[2] while in the matter of Thebes he followed his father's example and installed one of his sons as High Priest of Amon there. After the death of two of his sons while holding this office, his third son Sheshonk succeeded to the position. This Sheshonk maintained himself at Thebes in great splendour, assumed the titles of royalty and so increased his power that he was able to ensure the succession as sacerdotal prince of Thebes to his son.[3] Thus about 895 B. C., when Takelot I succeeded his father Osorkon I at Bubastis, he had his powerful brother Sheshonk as his rival at Thebes. But after Takelot I's short reign his son Osorkon II was able to regain control of Thebes and executed repairs in the Luxor temple after a great flood there.[4] A prayer of Osorkon II preserved on a statue of his found at Tanis contains a petition which significantly hints at the precarious situation in which the Libyan dynasty now found itself. He prays that his seed may rule over "the High Priests of Amon-Re, king of gods; the great chiefs of the Meshwesh . . .; and the prophets of Harsaphes,"[5] the last being the Libyan dynasts ruling at Heracleopolis, from which the family of the Pharaoh sprang. He adds, "Thou shalt establish my children in the offices which I have given them; let not the heart of brother be exalted [against] his brother."[6] Between the lines of this prayer one can read the story of a dynasty rent asunder by family feuds and constantly threatened by revolt of this or that powerful mer-

[1] IV, 729–737. [2] IV, 853. [3] IV, 738. [4] IV, 742–4. [5] IV, 747. [6] Ibid

cenary commander who feels himself aggrieved or able by force of arms to improve his position.

In all essential particulars these Libyan rulers of Egypt were completely Egyptianized. The grandfather of the first Sheshonk had buried his son in the Egyptian manner at Abydos, and had endowed the tomb in accordance with Egyptian mortuary belief.[1] Although they retained their Libyan names, the Bubastites assumed the full Pharaonic titulary of the form which had been customary for fifteen hundred years in Egypt. Their mercenary vassal commanders still retained their old time native titles, translated into Egyptian as "great chief of the Meshwesh," or as frequently abbreviated on the monuments "great chief of the Me"; but they worshipped the Egyptian gods and presented to the temples endowments of land for the sake of procuring the divine favour as did the Egyptians themselves.[2] While Egyptian culture may have been but a slight veneer and they may have remained Libyan barbarians, yet the process of Egyptianizing was rapidly going on, and in the case of the ruling family was now doubtless practically complete. Thus in his twenty second year we find Osorkon II building an imposing hall at Bubastis for the purpose of celebrating after the old Egyptian manner the thirtieth anniversary of his appointment as crown-prince.[3] But the splendour of this gorgeous jubilee cannot blind us to the decline in which the dangerous forces inherent in the situation were involving the Bubastite family. After a short coregency with his son, Sheshonk II, and the death of this prince,[4] Osorkon II associated with himself another son, who after seven years coregency succeeded as Takelot II, about 860 B. C.

The declining fortunes of the Twenty Second Dynasty from now on can only be traced in the career of the Theban principality, which, however, clearly exhibits the turbulent and restless character of the feudal princes who now make up the state. Here the High Priest Osorkon, who arrived

[1] IV, 669 ff.   [2] IV, 782-4.   [3] IV, 748-51.   [4] IV, 697, No. 13; 772.

at Thebes in the eleventh year of Takelot II, began a series of annals on the walls of the Karnak temple recording his deeds and his gifts to the temples in his own name.[1] These records show that after courting the favour of the Thebans by the inauguration of a new and richly endowed temple calendar he was nevertheless driven from the city by a revolt, which finally spread, involving the North and the South alike in civil war. The High Priest fled and the war lasted for years, until he was finally able to gain the support of his father's followers, when he returned to Thebes amid great rejoicing, as his long fleet of ships on the river drew near the city. He immediately repaired to the temple, from which Amon came forth to meet him in gorgeous procession, and the god thereupon delivered an oracle exempting the Thebans from punishment for revolt. These significant events, preserved in a few meagre and fragmentary lines of the High Priest's annals,[2] are doubtless such as filled the reigns of the last three Bubastites who continued to hold Thebes and ruled for a hundred years; although their city of Bubastis has perished so completely that little or no record of their careers has survived. To revolt must be added hostilities between the two principalities of Thebes and Heracleopolis, of which there are plain traces,[3] and feuds among the mercenary lords of the Delta. The situation will have closely resembled that under the Mamlukes, when the people, groaning under every oppression and especially exorbitant taxation, often successively taxed by two different lords, rose in revolt after revolt, only to be put down by the mercenaries with slaughter and rapine. Under such circumstances the Pharaoh's influence in Palestine must have totally vanished; but, alarmed at the growing power of Nineveh in Syria, one of the Bubastites, probably Takelot II, contributed a quota of a thousand men to the western coalition against the Assyrians, which was defeated by Shalmaneser II at Qarqar on the Orontes in 854 B. C.

[1] IV, 756–770.   [2] IV, 763–9.   [3] IV, 790.

It is impossible to determine with certainty the family connection of the last three Bubastites, who followed Takelot II. Sheshonk III, Pemou and Sheshonk IV may have had no connection with him. They held Memphis and Thebes, and their names occasionally appear here and there on minor monuments. The memorials of Egypt's ancient splendour suffered flagrant destruction at their hands and the vast colossus of Ramses II at Tanis with other earlier monuments were broken up and employed by Sheshonk III in the construction of his Tanis pylon. It is evident that during their rule the local lords and dynasts of the Delta were gradually gaining their independence, and probably many of them had thrown off their allegiance to the Bubastite house long before the death of Sheshonk IV, about 745 B. C., with whom the Twenty Second Dynasty certainly reached its end.

One of these Delta lords, named Pedibast, who had cast off the suzerainty of the Bubastites, gained the dominant position among his rivals at the death of Sheshonk IV, and founded a new house known to Manetho as the Twenty Third Dynasty. Manetho places this dynasty at Tanis, but, as Pedibast's name shows, he was of Bubastite origin, like the family which he unseated, and as we shall later see, his successor ruled at Bubastis. Pedibast gained Thebes and held it until his twenty third year, although from his fourteenth year he was obliged to share its control with king Yewepet, a dynast of the eastern Delta.[1] A late Demotic papyrus in Vienna contains a folk-tale which significantly reveals the unsettled conditions of the time among the turbulent dynasts, whom, like Yewepet, Pedibast was unable to control. It narrates the course of a long and serious feud between Kaamenhotep, the dynast of Mendes in the Delta, and Pemou, the mercenary commander in Heliopolis. The occasion of the quarrel is the seizure of a valuable coat-of-mail by Kaamenhotep, and Pedibast is unable to prevent widespread hostilities among the Delta dynasts, as they pro-

[1] IV, 794, 878, No. 2.

nounce for one or the other of the contending principals.[1]
Under Pedibast's successor, Osorkon III, the power of the
dominant house rapidly waned until there was at last an
independent lord or petty king in every city of the Delta
and up the river as far as Hermopolis. We are acquainted
with the names of eighteen of these dynasts,[2] whose struggles among themselves now led to the total dissolution of
the Egyptian state. The land again resolved itself into
those small and local political units of which it had consisted
in prehistoric days, before there existed any consolidated
and centralized government. Its power was completely
paralyzed and the political sagacity of such statesmen as
the Hebrew prophets was of itself, without the aid of prophetic vision, quite sufficient to perceive how utterly futile
was the policy of the Egyptian party in Israel, which would
have depended upon the support of Egypt against the oppression of Assyria. When the troops of Tiglath-pileser III
devastated the West down to the frontier of Egypt in 734–
732 B. C., the kings of the Delta were too involved in their
own complicated and petty wars to render the wretched
Hebrews any assistance; nor did they foresee that the day
must soon come when the great power on the Tigris would
cross the desert that separated Egypt from Palestine and
absorb the ancient kingdom of the Nile. But before this
inevitable catastrophe should occur, another foreign power
was to possess the throne of the Pharaohs.

[1] Wiener Zeitsch. für die Kunde des Morgenlandes, XVII, sequel to Mitth. aus
der Samml. der Pap. Erzherzog Rainer, VI, 19 ff.

[2] IV, 796 ff.; 830, 878.

FIG. 180.—"THE FIELD OF ABRAM."

Geographical name in the list of Sheshonk I at Karnak containing the earliest
occurrence of the name of Abram. See p. 530.

FIG. 181.—SENJIRLI STELA
OF ESARHADDON.

He leads captive Baal of Tyre
and Taharka, the kneeling
figure, with negroid features.
(Berlin Museum.)

FIG. 182.—SERAPEUM STELA OF
PSAMTIK I.

Recording the death of an Apis in Psamtik I's
twenty-first year which was born twenty-
one years earlier, in the twenty-sixth year
of Taharka.

CHAPTER XXVI

THE ETHIOPIAN SUPREMACY AND THE TRIUMPH OF ASSYRIA

LOWER NUBIA had now been dominated by the Egyptians for over eighteen hundred years, while the country above the second cataract to the region of the fourth cataract had for the most part been under Egyptian control for something like a thousand years. We have seen the country gradually being Egyptianized until there was an imposing Egyptian temple in every larger town of Lower Nubia, and since Ramses II's time the Egyptian gods were everywhere worshipped. While the native language still remained the speech of the people, Egyptian was the language of administration and government and of the Egyptian immigrants who had settled in the country. The fertile and productive lands of Upper Nubia, the rich mines in the mountains east of Lower Nubia, which compensated in some measure for its agricultural poverty, and the active trade from the Sudan which was constantly passing through the country, made it a land of resources and possibilities, which the Egyptianized Nubians, slowly awakening to their birth-right, were now beginning to realize. Nor could the occasional raids of the hostile tribes of the eastern desert, or the negroes of the Sudan, which still continued, essentially interfere with the development of the country.

Sheshonk I had still held Nubia,[1] and the High Priest of Amon at Thebes, in the second half of Takelot II's reign, was able to offer to the god the gold of Nubia,[2] which to be sure may possibly have been obtained in trade. It is probable, however, that the cataract country was still a dependency of Egypt until the middle of the Twenty Second Dynasty,

[1] IV, 724.   [2] IV, 770.

537

about 850 B. C. It will be recalled that Nubia had for some centuries been very closely connected with Thebes and the temple of Amon. There was a "gold country of Amon" there with its own governor as far back as the close of the Nineteenth Dynasty; the High Priest of Amon became viceroy of Nubia at the end of the Twentieth Dynasty; while in the Twenty First Dynasty the sacerdotal princesses of Thebes held the same office.[1] Thus after the Theban hierarchy had been maintaining a strong hold upon Nubia for over a hundred years from the end of the thirteenth century, their control had strengthened into full possession for two hundred and fifty years more. When we recollect that the Tanites of the Twenty First Dynasty had banished to one of the oases the turbulent families of Thebes, who had opposed their suzerainty; and that they were later obliged to recall the exiles; when we remember the long and dangerous revolt of Thebes under Takelot II,[2] and the pardon of the rebellious city by oracle of Amon, it will be evident that under such conditions the priestly families at Thebes may easily have been obliged on some occasion to flee from the vengeance of the northern dynasty and seek safety among the remote Nubian cataracts, which would effectually cut off pursuit. Such a flight would not be likely to find record, and hence we have no direct documentary evidence that it took place; but by the middle of the eighth century B. C. a fully developed Nubian kingdom emerges upon our view, with its seat of government at Napata, just below the fourth cataract. Napata had been an Egyptian frontier station from the days of Amenhotep II, seven hundred years earlier; and long before it was held by Egypt, it had doubtless been an important trading station on the route between Egypt and the Sudan. It was, moreover, the remotest point in Egyptian Nubia, and hence safest from attack from the North.

The state which arose here was, in accordance with our explanation of its origin, a reproduction of the Amonite theocracy at Thebes. The state god was Amon, and he continually intervened directly in the affairs of government by specific oracles. The control of the god was even more absolute than at Thebes, and eventually even the king was obliged to abdicate at the god's demand, who then installed another ruler. This last condition of things was, however, the outcome of a gradual development, and did not obtain at first. In Greek times the priests in Egypt were wont to depict the Ethiopian theocracy as the ideal state, and closely connected with this conception of it was the false notion that Ethiopia was the source of Egyptian civilization, a belief commonly held by the Greeks. The king bore all the Pharaonic titles, calling himself Lord of the Two Lands, as if he governed all Egypt. In the beginning he might be known by an Egyptian name, although this soon disappeared and was replaced by a personal name of pure Nubian origin, the throne-name and other state designations still remaining Egyptian for a long time. He built temples of Egyptian architecture, decorated with Egyptian reliefs and bearing hieroglyphic inscriptions and dedications of the traditional Egyptian form. The ritual depicted on the walls was that in use at Thebes. Of the Egyptian origin of this state there is no doubt; nor can there be any doubt of its Theban character, although there may be some difference of opinion as to how this last fact is to be accounted for.

As we gain our first glimpse of this new kingdom of the upper Nile, just before the middle of the eighth century B. C., it is ruled by a king Kashta.[1] We are unable to trace the extent of his power northward, nor do we know anything of his reign. His son, Piankhi, who succeeded him about 741 B. C. probably began the absorption of Egypt. In any case, by 721 or 722 B. C., he was already in possession of Upper Egypt as far north as Heracleopolis, just south of the Fayum, with Nubian garrisons in the more important towns. At this time the Twenty Third Dynasty, represented by Osorkon III at Bubastis, no longer actually ruling more

[1] IV, 940.

than the district of Bubastis and surrounded by rivals in
every important town of the Delta, was confronted by an
aggressive and powerful opponent in Tefnakhte, the dynast
of Sais, in the western Delta.[1] In Piankhi's twenty first
year his commanders in Upper Egypt reported to him that
Tefnakhte had defeated the dynasts of the entire western
Delta, and of both shores of the Nile above the Delta, almost
as far south as the vicinity of Benihasan. Besides these he
had also gained control of all the eastern and middle Delta
lords, so that he was practically king of all Lower Egypt,
as well as the lower portion of Upper Egypt. Only Heracleopolis, which we have already seen as a powerful principality, was holding out against him, and was suffering a
siege at his hands; while all his vassal lords of the Delta
were lending him aid against it, and personally assisting
in the investment. The wily Piankhi, perceiving that the
balance of power in the North was now destroyed, and
desirous of drawing his enemy further southward, away
from the safety of the impenetrable Delta swamps, quietly
awaited developments. A second appeal from his northern
commanders then informed him that Namlot, king of Hermopolis, had submitted to Tefnakhte. Thereupon Piankhi
sent his commanders in Egypt northward to check Tefnakhte's further southern advance and to besiege Hermopolis. This they did while Piankhi was at the same time
dispatching from Nubia a second army for their support.
Having left Thebes, this second Nubian force met Tefnakhte's fleet coming up and defeated it, capturing many
ships and prisoners. Continuing northward, in all probability down the Bahr Yusuf, they struck Tefnakhte's forces
engaged in the investment of Heracleopolis, and put it to
flight both by land and water. The northerners fled to the
west side of the Bahr Yusuf, whither they were pursued the
next morning by the Nubians, again discomfited and forced
to retreat toward the Delta. Namlot, king of Hermopolis,
who had fought among Tefnakhte's vassals, escaped from

[1] From here on, after the Piankhi Stela (IV, 796–883).

the disaster and returned to protect his own city of Hermopolis against the Nubians.   Hearing of this, the Nubian
commanders returned up the Bahr Yusuf to Hermopolis,
which they then closely beset.

On receiving reports of these operations, Piankhi was
incensed that the northern army had been allowed to escape
into the Delta.   It was now late in the calendar year, and
Piankhi determined, after the celebration of the New Year's
feast at home, to proceed to Thebes to celebrate there the
great feast of Opet in the third month, and then to lead the
campaign against the North in person.   Meanwhile his commanders in Egypt captured the towns below and in the vicinity of Hermopolis, including the important Oxyrhyncus, but
Hermopolis itself still held out against them.   In accordance with his plan, Piankhi then proceeded northward early
in the calendar year, celebrated the feast of Opet at Thebes
as anticipated, in the third month, and went on to assume
charge of the investment of Hermopolis, which had now been
going on for certainly four and probably five months.
Piankhi vigourously pushed the siege; from embankments
and high towers the doomed city was daily showered with arrows and stones; foul odours arose from the masses of dead,
and not long after Piankhi's arrival the place was ripe for
surrender.   Namlot, its king, finding that gifts, even when
his own royal crown was cast down among them, availed
nothing with Piankhi, sent out his queen to plead with the
women of the Nubian that they might intercede with him on
Namlot's behalf.   This device was successful, and assured
at last of his life, Namlot surrendered and turned over the
city and all his wealth to Piankhi, who immediately took
possession of the place.   After an inspection of Namlot's
palace and treasury, Piankhi entered the stables of the Her-
mopolitan: "His majesty proceeded to the stable of the
horses," so say his annals, "and the quarters of the foals.
When he saw that they had suffered hunger, he said: 'I
swear as Re loves me . . . it is more grievous in my heart
that my horses have suffered hunger than any evil deed that

thou hast done in the prosecution of thy desire.' "[1] Namlot's wealth was then assigned to the royal treasury of
Piankhi and the sacred fortune of Amon.

Heracleopolis being already exhausted after its investment at the hands of Tefnakhte, its king, Pefnefdibast,
now came to greet Piankhi and praise him for his deliverance. The advance to the Delta, sailing down the Bahr
Yusuf, was then begun, and all the chief towns of the west
side surrendered one after another on seeing Piankhi's force
except Crocodilopolis in the Fayum, which would have carried him too far from his course past Illahun at the mouth
of the Fayum. On the other hand, he did not touch Aphroditopolis, which lay on the east side of the river, equally
far removed from his route past Medum and Ithtowe to
Memphis. The Nubian king offered sacrifice to the gods
in all the cities which he passed, and took possession of all
the available property for his own treasury and the estate
of Amon.

On reaching Memphis it was found to have been very
strongly fortified by Tefnakhte, who now counted the city
as part of his kingdom. He had long held possession of it
and was priest of Ptah, its great god. Hence in answer
to Piankhi's demand to surrender, the Memphites closed the
gates and made a sortie, which was evidently not very effective. Under cover of night Tefnakhte succeeded in entering
the city and exhorted the garrison to rely on their strong
walls, their plentiful supplies and the high water, which protected the east side from attack, urging them to hold out
while he rode away northward for reinforcements. Having
landed on the north of the city, Piankhi was surprised at
the strength of the place. Some of his people favoured a
siege, others desired to storm the walls upon embankments
and causeways to be raised for the purpose. Piankhi himself decided to assault, but rejecting labourious works, which
besides being too slow would give the enemy exact indication
of the place of attack, he devised a shrewd plan of assault,

[1] IV. 850.

which speaks highly for his skill as a strategist. The high walls on the west of the city had been recently raised still higher, and it was evident that the east side, protected by waters perhaps artificially raised, was being neglected. Here was the harbour, where the ships now floated so high that their bow ropes were fastened among the houses of the city. Piankhi sent his fleet against the harbour and quickly captured all the shipping. Then taking command in person, he rapidly ranged the captured craft together with his own fleet along the eastern walls, thus furnishing footing for his assaulting lines, which he immediately sent over the ramparts and captured the city before its eastern defenses could be strengthened against him. A great slaughter now ensued, but all sanctuaries were respected and protected, and Ptah of course repudiated Tefnakhte and recognized Piankhi as king.

The entire region of Memphis then submitted, whereupon the Delta dynasts also appeared in numbers with gifts for Piankhi and signified their submission. After dividing the wealth of Memphis between the treasuries of Amon and Ptah, Piankhi crossed the river, worshipped in the ancient sanctuary of Khereha-Babylon, and followed the old sacred road thence to Heliopolis, where he camped by the harbour. His annals narrate at length how he entered the holy of holies of the sun-god here, that he might be recognized as his son and heir to the throne of Egypt, according to custom usual since the remote days of the Fifth Dynasty. Here king Osorkon III of the Twenty Third Dynasty at Bubastis, now but a petty dynast like the rest, visited Piankhi and recognized the Nubian's suzerainty. Having then moved his camp to a point just east of Athribis, by a town called Keheni, Piankhi there received the submission of the Delta lords. Of these there were fifteen: being two kings, the said Osorkon III, who was still with him, and king Yewepet of Tentremu in the eastern Delta, who had once shared Thebes with Pedibast, Osorkon III's predecessor; nine princes, who governed Mendes, Sebennytos, Saft el-Henneh, Busiris,

Hesebka (the eleventh nome), Phagroriopolis, Khereha-Babylon, and other towns of the Delta and vicinity which cannot be identified with certainty; and finally a mercenary commander in Hermopolis Parva, son of the prince of Mendes, besides a priest of Horus who had founded a sacerdotal principality at Letopolis, like that of the priests at Heracleopolis, from whom the Twenty Second Dynasty sprang. Among all these, Pediese, prince of Athribis, showed himself especially loyal to Piankhi and invited him thither, placing all his wealth at the Nubian's disposal. Thereupon Piankhi proceeded to Athribis, received the gifts of Pediese, and that he might choose for himself the best steeds, even entered Pediese's stables, which the shrewd Athribite, observing his love for horses, had particularly invited him to do. The fifteen Delta lords, except of course Pediese, were here dismissed at their own request, that they might go back to their cities and return to Piankhi with further gifts, in emulation of Pediese.

Meantime the desperate Tefnakhte had garrisoned Mesed, a town of uncertain location, but probably somewhere on his Saite frontier. Rather than have them captured by Piankhi he burned the ships and supplies which he could not save. Piankhi then sent a body of troops against Mesed, and they slew the garrison. Tefnakhte had meanwhile taken refuge on one of the remote islands in the western mouths of the Nile. Many miles of vast Delta morass and a network of irrigation canals separated Piankhi from the fugitive. It would have been a hazardous undertaking to dispatch an army into such a region. When, therefore, Tefnakhte sent gifts and an humble message of submission requesting that Piankhi send to him a messenger with whom he might go to a neighbouring temple and take the oath of allegiance to his Nubian suzerain, Piankhi was very glad to accept the proposal. In this less humiliating, not to say much less dangerous manner, Tefnakhte then accepted the suzerainty of Piankhi. When, therefore, the two kings of the Fayum and Aphroditopolis whom, as we have seen, he had not molested on his way northward, appeared with their gifts a Nubian Pharaoh had obtained complete recognition, had supplanted the Libyans and was lord of all Egypt.

When his Delta vassals had paid Piankhi a last visit he loaded his ships with the wealth of the North and sailed away for his southern capital amid the acclamations of the people. If we have devoted an apparently disproportionate amount of space to the campaign which was now concluded it is because it displays to us more clearly than ever before or after, the conditions which always arose in Egypt whenever any weakening of the central power betrayed to the local dynasts that they might without danger assume their independence or even gradually usurp the crown of the Pharaoh. Arrived at Napata, Piankhi erected in the temple of Amon a magnificent granite stela,[1] inscribed on all four sides, recording in detail the entire campaign, in which he, the son of Amon, had humiliated the rivals of that god in the North. With the possible exception of the Annals of Thutmose III and the documents of Ramses II on the battle of Kadesh, this remarkable literary monument is the clearest and most rational account of a military expedition which has survived from ancient Egypt. It displays literary skill and an appreciation of dramatic situations which is notable, while the vivacious touches found here and there quite relieve it of the arid tone usual in such hieroglyphic documents. The imagination endues the personages appearing here more easily with life than those of any other similar historical narrative of Egypt; and the humane Piankhi especially, the lover of horses, remains a *man* far removed from the conventional companion and equal of the gods who inevitably occupies the exalted throne of the Pharaohs in all other such records. It is this document of course which has enabled us to follow Piankhi in his conquest of the North.

Tefnakhte, while he had nominally submitted to Piankhi, only awaited the withdrawal of the Ethiopian to resume his

[1] IV, 796–883.

35

designs. He eventually succeeded in establishing a kingdom of Lower Egypt, assumed the Pharaonic titles and
ruled at least eight years over a feudal state like that of
the Twenty Second Dynasty. His reign is parallel with the
last years of the Twenty Third Dynasty, which seems to
have struggled on at Bubastis as vassal princes under him.
It is evident that Tefnakhte was of a type far superior to
the ordinary Delta dynast; he must have greatly increased
the power and prestige of Sais, for his son Bocchoris, on
succeeding to his father's throne, was later regarded as
the founder of the Twenty Fourth Dynasty. In Upper
Egypt Piankhi's rule continued for a brief period. He controlled Thebes long enough to do some slight building in
the temple of Mut, where he left a relief representing a
festal voyage of his ships, perhaps his return from the
North; for among the vessels appears the state barge of
Sais, captured from Tefnakhte's fleet in the northern war.
Piankhi was then still in control as far north as Heracleopolis, whose commandant appears in the relief as admiral
of the Nubian fleet.[1] In order to gain control of the fortune
of Amon with an appearance of legitimacy, Piankhi caused
his sister-wife, Amenardis, to be adopted by Shepnupet, the
daughter of Osorkon III, who was sacerdotal princess of
Thebes.[2] The device was probably not new. But as Piankhi
withdrew the decadent Twenty Third Dynasty put forth
its last expiring effort and established an ephemeral authority in Thebes, where Osorkon III seems to have ruled
for a short time as coregent with an otherwise unknown
Takelot, the third of the name. Piankhi's invasion of Egypt
and entire reign there seem therefore to have fallen within
the reign of Osorkon III. But the rising power of Sais soon
overwhelmed the failing Bubastites, and, as we have noted,
Bocchoris, son of Tefnakhte of Sais, gained the throne of
Lower Egypt probably about 718 B. C. to be later known
as the founder, and in so far as we know, the sole king of
the Twenty Fourth Dynasty. We know nothing from the

[1] IV, 811.　　　　　　　　　　　　　　　　[2] IV, 940.

Egyptian monuments regarding his brief reign; the only contemporary monument bearing his name is an inscription dating the burial of an Apis bull in the Memphite Serapeum in his sixth year.[1] A doubtless reliable tradition of Greek times makes him a wise lawgiver who revised the laws of the land and himself rendered the legal decisions of the most remarkable shrewdness. We may easily believe that the agitated times through which the country had passed made such new legislation necessary. A remarkable Demotic papyrus dated in the thirty fourth year of the Roman Emperor Augustus narrates the prophecies of a lamb uttered in the sixth year of Bocchoris, in which the imminent invasion of Egypt and its conquest by the Assyrians are foretold seemingly accompanied by the assurance that the misfortunes of the unhappy country should continue nine hundred years.[2] It is the last example of that school of prophetic literature of which Ipuwer of the Middle Kingdom was the earliest representative known to us.[2] Manetho characteristically narrates this marvellous tale as an important occurrence of Bocchoris's reign.

Egypt had now been under the divided authority of numerous local dynasts for probably over a century and a half. The total disintegration of centralized power had unavoidably involved the sacrifice of economic prosperity. Egypt's foreign commerce inevitably dwindled to the vanishing point; agriculture and industry were at the lowest ebb and the resources of the country, at the mercy of irresponsible lords and princes, were necessarily being rapidly drained. With its vast works of irrigation slowly going to ruin, its roads unprotected, intercourse between cities unsafe and the larger communities suffering from constant turmoil and agitation, the productive capacity of the country was steadily waning. While these conclusions are not based upon contemporary documents,—for such conditions in such an age are rarely even indirectly the subject of record,— yet they may be safely inferred from the known results of

[1] IV, 884.　　　[2] Krall, in Festgaben für Büdinger, Innsbruck, 1898.
[2] See above, pp. 204-05.

similar political conditions in later times. The hopeless state of the country was clearly understood by the sagacious Isaiah, who declared to his people: "Behold the Lord rideth upon a swift cloud and cometh unto Egypt; and the idols of Egypt shall be moved at his presence, and the heart of Egypt shall melt in the midst of it. And I will stir up the Egyptians against the Egyptians; and they shall fight every one against his brother, and every one against his neighbour; city against city and kingdom against king- dom. . . . And I will give over the Egyptians into the hand of a cruel lord; and a fierce king shall rule over them, saith the Lord, the Lord of Hosts. . . . The princes of Zoan are utterly foolish; the counsel of the wisest counsellors of Pharaoh is become brutish. . . . The princes of Zoan [Tanis] are become fools, the princes of Noph [Napata?] are deceived; they have caused Egypt to go astray that are the corner stone of her tribes. The Lord hath mingled a spirit of perverseness in the midst of her; they have caused Egypt to go astray in every work thereof, as a drunken man staggering in his vomit. Neither shall there be for Egypt any work which head or tail, palm-branch or rush, may do."[1] No truer picture could possibly be portrayed.

In spite of these unfavourable conditions, one important element of culture in Egypt was inspired with new life. As in the turbulent age of the Medicis, Italy, and especially Florence, enjoyed an artistic transformation, in which works of the highest genius were produced with an amazing fecun- dity; as in Cairo under the constant revolutions, assassina- tions, usurpations and incessant oppression of the Mam- lukes, while the land was economically going to ruin, the mosque form was developed, perfected and the noblest monu- ments of Saracen architecture were erected; so now under similar seemingly adverse influences the sculptors of Egypt were slowly ushering in a new era in the history of art and feeling impulses which we shall find attaining their highest fruition in the Restoration which was to follow after an- other half century of foreign aggression and political decay.

[1] Isaiah, 19.

Naturally little of such work has survived, but a modest chapel, erected under Osorkon III at Thebes, contains reliefs showing clearly the new capacity which needed only social, political and economic opportunity to produce the greatest works of oriental art.

Meantime those profound political changes, fraught with the greatest danger to Egypt, which the reader has foreseen, were taking place in Asia. The powerful military state on the Tigris had for centuries been seeking to establish itself as the dominant power in western Asia. As far back as 1100 B. C. Nesubenebded, the first of the Tanites, had sent a gift to Tiglath Pileser I on his appearance in the west; and two hundred and fifty years later the Pharaoh had contributed a quota to the western alliance which had hoped to break the power of Shalmaneser II at Qarqar in 854 B. C. Rousing Assyria from a period of temporary decadence, Tiglath-pileser III had brought her full power to bear upon the West, and in 734 to 732 B. C. had ravaged Syria-Palestine to the very borders of Egypt. The Aramæan kingdom of Damascus fell and the whole west was organized as dependencies of Assyria. In the short reign of Shalmaneser V, who followed Tiglath Pileser III, Israel with others was encouraged to revolt by Sewa or So,[1] who was either an otherwise unknown Delta dynast or ruler of Musri, a kingdom of North Arabia, the name of which is so like that of Egypt as to cause confusion in our understanding of the documents of the time, a confusion which perhaps already existed in the minds of the cuneiform scribes. Before the Assyrian invasion which resulted, Samaria held out for some years; but under Shalmaneser V's great successor, Sargon II, it fell in 722 B. C. The chief families of Israel were deported and the nation as such was annihilated. Unable to oppose the formidable armies of Assyria, the petty kinglets of Egypt constantly fomented discontent and revolt among the Syro-Palestinian states in order if possible to create a fringe of buffer states

[1] II Kings, 17: 4.

between them and the Assyrian. In 720 B. C. Sargon again appeared in the west to suppress a revolt in which Egypt doubtless had a hand. Completely victorious in the north, he marched southward to Raphia, where he totally defeated the allies of the south, among whom Egypt had a levy of troops under a commander named Sib'i.[1] The Assyrian hosts had now twice swept down to the very borders of Egypt and the dynasts must by this time have been fully aware of their danger. Probably nothing but the traditional reputation of Egypt, the memory of the old days when she had been supreme in Asia, and Ninevite kings had sought her friendship with gifts, kept Tiglath Pileser III and Sargon from invading her frontier and discovering how lamentably weak she was. The situation was now reversed; in 715 B. C. Sargon's records report the reception of gifts from Pir'u (Pharaoh) of Egypt,[2] who will probably have been Bocchoris.

Such was the threatening situation of Egypt when, probably about 711 B. C., after an interval of some ten years since the retirement of Piankhi, the Nubian kings again appeared in the North. Piankhi had now been succeeded by his brother, Shabaka, with whom the uninterrupted series of pure Ethiopian royal names begins. He had married Piankhi's daughter[3] and of course based his claim to the throne, as in Egypt, not only upon his own birth, but also upon this alliance. We possess no native records of his conquest of the country, but Manetho states that he burned Bocchoris alive. Lower Egypt was completely subdued, Ethiopian supremacy acknowledged and Shabaka entrenched himself so firmly that he became the founder of the Twenty Fifth or Ethiopian Dynasty, as reported by Manetho. Appreciating the serious danger of the presence of so formidable a state as Assyria on his very borders, Shabaka immediately sent his agents among the Syro-Palestinian states to excite them to revolt. In Philistia,

---

[1] Winckler, Unters. zur Altoriental. Geschichte, p. 93.

[2] Winckler, Ibid., p. 94.

[3] IV 920.

Judah, Moab and Edom[1] he promised the vassals of Assyria support in rebellion against their Ninevite suzerain. Remembering the ancient supremacy of Egypt, failing to understand the state of decadent impotence into which she had fallen, and anxious to shake off the oppressive Assyrian yoke, they lent a ready ear to the emissaries of Shabaka. Only in Judah did the prophet-statesman Isaiah foresee the futility of depending upon Egypt, and the final catastrophe which should overtake her at the hands of Assyria.[2] The vigilant Assyrian, however, hearing of the projected alliance, acted so quickly that the conspirators were glad to drop their designs and protest fidelity. In spite of difficulties in Babylon and rebellions in the north, the able and aggressive Sargon pushed the consolidation of his power with brilliant success and left to his son Sennacherib in 705 B. C. the first stable and firmly compacted empire ever founded by a Semitic power.

Sennacherib was embarrassed in his earlier years with the usual complications in Babylon. Mardukbaliddin, an able and active claimant of the Babylonian throne, who had already caused Sennacherib's father much trouble, now sent his emissaries to stir up defection and create a diversion in his favour in the west. As a result Luli, the energetic king of Tyre, Hezekiah of Judah, the dynasts of Edom, Moab and Ammon, with the chiefs of their Beduin neighbours, in fact, all the southern half of the Assyrian conquests in the west besides Egypt were finally organized in a great alliance against Ninevah. Before the allies could act in concert, Sennacherib suddenly appeared in the west, marched down the Phœnician coast, capturing all its strongholds save Tyre; and pressed on southward to the revolting Philistine cities. Here having punished Askalon, he advanced to Altaqu, where he came upon the motley army gathered by the tardy Shabaka among his northern vassals, whom Sennacherib calls "the kings of Musri" (Egypt). We know nothing of the strength of this force, although

---

[1] Winckler, Ibid.   [2] Isaiah 20.

Sennacherib claims that they were "without number"; but it is safe to conclude that it was not a formidable army. With the dissolution of the central government in Egypt the standing army, even made up chiefly of mercenaries as it was, had disappeared and the illy organized aggregation of levies from the domains of the local Delta princes was little fitted to meet the compact and finely organized armies which the Assyrian kings had gradually developed, till they had become the dread and terror of the west. Although small Egyptian contingents had before served as auxiliaries against the Assyrians, the armies of the two empires on the Nile and the Tigris had never before faced each other. Sennacherib led his own power in person while the Egyptian army was entrusted by Shabaka to his nephew, a son of Piankhi, named Taharka,[1] who some thirteen or fourteen years afterward became king of Ethiopia, a fact which led the Hebrew annalist to give him that title already at the time of this campaign.[2] There was but one possible issue for the battle; Sennacherib disposed of Taharka's army without difficulty, having meanwhile beleaguered Jerusalem and devastated Judah far and wide. He had effectually stamped out the disaffection in the west and completely discomfited the allies, but before he could take Jerusalem the plague-infected winds from the malarial shores of the eastern Delta had scattered death among his troops. This overwhelming catastrophe, together with disquieting news from Babylon, forced him hastily to retire to Nineveh, thus bringing to Jerusalem the deliverance promised by Isaiah, an event in which pious tradition afterward saw the destroying angel of the Lord. This deliverance was perhaps as fortunate for Egypt as for Jerusalem. For the third time the invincible Assyrian army had stood on the very threshold of Egypt, while favouring circumstances had each time caused its withdrawal and saved the decrepit nation on the Nile for a little time from the inevitable humiliation which was now so near. The Syro-Palestinian princes, however, were so thor-

---

[1] IV, 892.   [2] II Kings, 19: 9.

ɔughly cowed that the inglorious Ethiopians were thenceforth unable to seduce them to rebellion. Like the Hebrews, they at last recognized the truth, as mockingly stated by the officers of Sennacherib to the unhappy ambassadors of Jerusalem: "Now behold, thou trustest upon the staff of this bruised reed, even upon Egypt; whereon if a man lean it will go into his hand and pierce it; so is Pharaoh king of Egypt unto all that trust on him."[1]

Shabaka apparently ruled his vassal Egyptian states for the remainder of his reign in peace. The fragments of a clay tablet bearing the seal of Shabaka and a king of Assyria, found at Kuyunjik, may indicate some agreement between the two nations. Shabaka showed great partiality to the priesthoods and favoured the temples. His restoration of an ancient religious text of great importance in the temple of Ptah rescued and enabled us to employ in this work one of the most remarkable documents surviving from ancient Egypt.[2] At Thebes he reinstated Amenardis, his sister, who must have been temporarily expelled by Osorkon III. Together with her, he built a chapel at Karnak, and his building operations necessitated an expedition to the distant quarries of Hammamat. We also find records of his temple restorations at Thebes,[3] and it is evident that he governed Egypt at least in his relations with the temples, precisely as a native Pharaoh would have done. His sister, Amenardis, seems to have actually ruled Thebes with a large degree of independence, and in spite of his partiality to the priests, it was probably Shabaka who broke the power of the High Priest of Amon, of whose impotence we shall see further evidence as we proceed.

About 700 B. C., having reigned probably twelve years in Egypt, although he may have ruled over Nubia for some years before his advent in Egypt, Shabaka was succeeded by Shabataka, another Ethiopian, whose connection with the reigning Ethiopian or Nubian family is a little uncertain, although Manetho, who calls him Sebichos, makes him a son

[1] II Kings, 18: 21.   [2] See p. 357.   [3] IV, 886, 889

of Shabaka. As the western vassals remained quiet and Sennacherib was now absorbed in his operations at the other extremity of his empire, Shabataka was unmolested by the Assyrian. His name is rare in Egypt, but it is evident from the conditions which survived him that he was entirely unable to exterminate the local dynasts and consolidate the power of Egypt for the supreme struggle which was before her. It was indeed now patent that the Ethiopians were quite unfitted for the imperial task before them. The southern strain with which their blood was tinctured began to appear as the reign of Shabataka drew to a close about 688 B. C.

It is at this juncture that we can trace the rising fortunes of prince Taharka, a son of Piankhi, who had gone north from Napata as a youth of only twenty years with a king whose name is unfortunately lost, who nevertheless must have been Shabaka.[1] He was the son of a Nubian woman and his features, as preserved in contemporary sculptures, show unmistakable negroid characteristics. A son of the great Piankhi, he played a prominent role, and as we have seen, he was entrusted with the command of the army in the campaign against Sennacherib. We know nothing of the circumstances which brought about his advent to the throne, but Manetho states, that leading an army from Ethiopia he slew Sebichos, who must be Shabataka, and seized the crown. Having thus disposed of the usurper, the contemporary monuments without intimation of these events, abruptly picture him in Tanis as king, summoning his mother, whom he has not seen for many years, from Napata to Tanis, that she may assume her proper station as queen-mother there.[2] In view of this fact and the trouble to be anticipated from Assyria, it is not improbable that the Ethiopians at this time maintained Tanis as their Egyptian residence.

For some thirteen years Taharka ruled his kingdom without molestation from Asia. Meantime he was able to execute buildings of minor importance in Tanis and Memphis,

---

[1] IV, 892. 895.

[2] IV, 892–6.

and more considerable monuments in Thebes. But he evidently foresaw the coming struggle and duly made his preparations to meet it. The west had for twenty years seen nothing of Sennacherib, who was now assassinated by his sons, in 681 B. C. As soon as his son, Esarhaddon, could arrange the affairs of the great empire to which he had succeeded, he determined to resort to the only possible remedy for the constant interference of Egypt with the authority of Assyria in Palestine, viz., the conquest of the Nile country and humiliation of the Pharaoh. With farseeing thoroughness, he laid his plans for the execution of this purpose, and his army was knocking at the frontier fortresses of the eastern Delta in 674 B. C.[1] But Taharka, who was a man of far greater ability than his two predecessors on the throne, must have made a supreme effort to meet the crisis. The outcome of the battle (673 B. C.) was unfavourable for the Assyrian if, as the documents perhaps indicate, he did not suffer positive defeat. But Esarhaddon nevertheless quietly continued his preparations for the conquest of Egypt. Baal, king of Tyre, perhaps encouraged by the undecisive result of the first Assyrian invasion, then rebelled, making common cause with Taharka. In 670 B. C. Esarhaddon was again in the West at the head of his forces. Having invested Tyre, he was aided in his march across the desert to the Delta by the native Beduin, whose camel-caravans furnished him with water. Taharka was now no longer equal to the persistent struggle maintained against him by the obdurate Esarhaddon, and the Egyptian army was defeated and scattered. As the Ethiopian fell back upon Memphis, Esarhaddon pressed him closely, and besieged and captured the city, which fell a rich prey to the cruel and rapacious Ninevite army. Taharka fled southward, abandoning Lower Egypt, which was immediately organized by Esarhaddon into dependencies of Assyria. He records the names of twenty lords of the Delta, formerly

[1] See the sources for the following campaigns of Esarhaddon in Winckler, Ibid., pp. 97–106.

Ethiopian vassals, who now took the oath of fealty to him.
Among these names, written in cuneiform, a number may be
recognized as those of the same men, or at least the same
families, with whom Piankhi had to deal in the same region.
Necho, doubtless a descendant of Tefnakhte, occupies the
most prominent place among them as prince of Sais and
Memphis. The list also includes a prince of Thebes, but
Esarhaddon certainly possessed no more than a merely
nominal authority in Upper Egypt at this time. As he returned to Ninevah, northward along the coast road, he hewed
in the rocks at the Nahr el-Kelb, beside the triumphant stelæ
of Ramses II, a record of his great achievement (Fig. 158);
while in Samal (Senjirli), in north Syria, he erected a
similar monument representing himself of heroic stature,
leading two captives, of whom one is probably Baal of Tyre,
and the other, as his negroid features indicate, is the unfortunate Taharka (Fig. 181).

After the domination of Libyan and Nubian in turn,
Egypt was now a prey to a third foreign conqueror, whose
supremacy was however totally different from that of the
aliens who had preceded. Both Libyan and Nubian were
largely Egyptianized and, as we have seen, ruled as Egyptian Pharaohs; whereas the Delta was now subject to an
overlord, who was the head of a great Asiatic empire, having
not the slightest sympathy with Egyptian institutions or
customs. The result was that the Delta kinglets, who had
sworn allegiance to the Ninevite, immediately plotted with
Taharka for the resumption of his rule in Lower Egypt,
which he thereupon assumed without much delay on the
withdrawal of the Assyrian army. Esarhaddon was thus
forced to begin his work over again; but in 668 B. C., while
on the march to resume operations in Egypt, he died. With
but slight delay the campaign was continued by his son,
Ashurbanipal, who placed one of his commanders in charge
of the expedition. Between Memphis and the frontier of
the eastern Delta, Taharka was again routed. Not attempting to hold Memphis, he fled southward, this time pursued

by the enemy, and took refuge in Thebes; but the Assyrians, reinforced by native levies among their Delta vassals, made the forty days' march thither, determined to expel him from Egypt. They did force him to abandon Thebes, but he entrenched himself further up the river and the Assyrians did not push the pursuit against him. Whether the enemy actually captured Thebes at this time is somewhat doubtful. In any case, Ashurbanipal was still unable to extend his authority to Upper Egypt. He had hardly restored his supremacy in the Delta when his vassals there again began communicating with Taharka, purposing his restoration as before. The ringleaders were Necho, whom Esarhaddon had established as king of Sais, Sharuludari of Tanis and Pakruru of Persepet (Saft el-Henneh); but their correspondence with Taharka was discovered by the Assyrian officials in Egypt, and they were sent to Nineveh in chains. There the wily Necho was able to win the confidence of Ashurbanipal, who pardoned him, loaded him with honours and restored him to his kingdom in Sais, while his son was appointed to rule Athribis. At the same time Ashurbanipal accompanied him with Assyrian officials, intended of course to be a check upon his conduct. This plan worked well and Taharka was unable to gain any further foothold among the Assyrian vassals in the Delta, although the priesthood of the Ptah temple secretly dated in his name the record of an Apis burial in one of the subterranean passages of the Serapeum at Memphis in his twenty fourth year [1] (664 B. C.).

Several years passed in this way; Upper Egypt continued under the actual authority of Taharka. At Thebes the High Priest of Amon was now a mere figure-head. The real authority was in the hands of one Mentemhet, who, as "prince of Thebes" and "governor of the South," also held the sacerdotal primacy of Egypt. His rank in the Theban priesthood, however, was only that of "fourth prophet." The Theban hierarchy as a political power had thus been dissolved; while the power and wealth of this prince of

[1] IV, 917 ff.

Thebes, who completed costly restorations in the temples, perhaps after destruction by the Assyrians, were considerable, even in these days of Egypt's poverty and disorganization.[1] Taharka held the fortune of Amon at his disposal by causing his sister, Shepnupet, to be adopted by Amenardis the "Divine Votress," or sacerdotal princess of Thebes, who had been appointed by Piankhi in the same way.[2] At Napata Taharka either built or enlarged two considerable temples, and the Ethiopian capital evidently became a worthy royal residence in his time.[3]

Taharka had now been ruling twenty five years and he was growing old, when in 663 B. C. he accepted as coregent, perhaps not voluntarily, a son of Shabaka, named Tanutamon, whom he appointed over Upper Egypt. Tanutamon probably resided at Thebes, where Mentemhet, the prince of the Theban principality, was still in control, while Taharka himself, worn out with the unequal struggle against Assyria, had long before retired to Napata. There he survived the appointment of Tanutamon less than a year, dying in 663 B. C., whereupon the latter hastened to Napata to assume the sole kingship.[4] Before these events, Tanutamon had been informed in a dream[5] that he was to gain the sovereignty of both the North and the South, and in response to this vision, he now immediately invaded Lower Egypt (663 B. C.). All was repeated as in the days of Taharka. Upper Egypt of course received him with acclamation, and it was not until he arrived in the vicinity of Memphis that he met hostile opposition. The Assyrian garrison and doubtless some of the Delta lords, who now stood in great fear of their Ninevite suzerain, gave him battle; but he defeated them and succeeded in taking Memphis.[6] Necho of Sais probably fell in the action, and according to Herodotus, his son Psamtik fled to Syria. Elated with his triumph, Tanutamon sent some of the spoil immediately to Napata with orders to erect new temple buildings there.[7]

[1] IV, 901 ff.	[2] IV, 940.	[3] IV, 897 ff.	[4] IV, 923 ff.
[5] IV, 922.	[6] IV, 925-8.	[7] IV, 929.	

Meanwhile the Delta vassals of Assyria dared not yield to the Ethiopian, in view of the inevitable consequences, and he therefore advanced against them, but was unable to draw them into battle or capture their towns.[1] On his return to Memphis after this fruitless attempt a number of the Delta lords finally came to do him homage, but undoubtedly in such a form as to save their standing with their Assyrian over-lord.[2]

Content with the appearance of unchallenged supremacy in Lower Egypt, Tanutamon settled himself in Memphis as Pharaoh of all Egypt, in fulfillment of his divine vision. Meanwhile, on the first news of his departure from Napata, the Assyrian officers in the Delta had sent with all haste to Nineveh to notify Ashurbanipal, and in 661 B. C. the great king's army drove the Ethiopian for the last time from Lower Egypt. The Assyrians pursued him to Thebes, and as he ingloriously withdrew southward, they sacked and plundered the magnificent capital of Egypt's days of splendour. The rich cultus images, the gorgeous ritual furniture and implements, with which the pious Theban prince, Mentemhet, had equipped the temples, fell a prey to the fierce Assyrian soldiery, while "two enormous obelisks, wrought of bright silver, whose weight was 2,500 talents, the adornment of a temple-door," which they carried off to Nineveh, indicate the wealth still remaining in the temples of the long devastated nation.[3] The story of the ruin of Thebes spread to all the peoples around. When the prophet Nahum was denouncing the coming destruction of Nineveh, fifty years later, the desolation of Thebes was still fresh in his mind as he addressed the doomed city: "Art thou better than No-Amon [Thebes], that was situate among the rivers, that had the waters round about her; whose rampart was the sea, and her wall was of the sea? Ethiopia and Egypt were her strength and it was infinite; Put and Lubim were thy helpers. Yet was she carried away, she went into captivity: her young children also were dashed to pieces at the top of all the

[1] IV, 930.   [2] IV, 931.   [3] Winckler, op. cit.

streets: and they cast lots for her honourable men, and all her great men were bound in chains.''[1] From this time the fortunes of the venerable city steadily declined and its splendours, such as no city of the early orient had ever displayed, gradually faded. It entered upon the long centuries of lingering decay which have left it at the present day still the mightiest ruin surviving from the ancient world (Fig. 183).

The retirement of Tanutamon to Napata was the termination of Ethiopian supremacy in Egypt. His whole career was characteristic of the feeble and inglorious line from which he sprang. Emerging from the remote reaches of the upper Nile, the Ethiopians had attempted an imperial role and aspired to intervene in the international politics of western Asia. At a time when Assyria was dominating the East, without a worthy rival elsewhere to stay her hand, it was to be expected that the historic people of the Nile should confront her and dispute her progress on even terms. To this great task the Ethiopians were appointed; but there was never a line of kings so ill suited to their high destiny. Unable to weld together the nation they had conquered into any effective weapon against the Assyrians, every attempt to stay the advance of their formidable enemy furnished only another example of feebleness and futility. Only once does Taharka seem to cope successfully with the internal difficulties of his situation and to check for a brief moment the triumphant progress of Esarhaddon; but the indomitable Assyrian quickly breaks the resistance of the Ethiopian, and Taharka seeks ignoble security on the upper Nile. In a word, Assyria was never dealing with a first class power in her conquest of Egypt, when the unhappy Nile-dwellers were without a strong ruler; and for such a ruler they looked in vain during the supremacy of the inglorious Ethiopians.

Withdrawing to Napata, the Ethiopians never made another attempt to subdue the kingdom of the lower river, but gave their attention to the development of Nubia. As the Egyptians resident in the country died out and were not replaced by others, the Egyptian gloss which the people had

[1] Nahum, 3: 8–10.

FIG. 183.—GENERAL VIEW OF KARNAK FROM THE SOUTH.

From the pylon of the Khonsu temple begun by Ramses III. Rear halls of the latter in the foreground; the light in the deep shadow is seen through the door referred to on pp. 520—21.

received began rapidly to disappear, and the land relapsed into a semi-barbaric condition. The theocratic character of the government became more and more pronounced until the king was but a puppet in the hands of the priests, at whose behest he was obliged even to take his own life and make way for another weakling whom the priests might choose. While the earlier kings had built up and beautified Napata, their successors were obliged to move the royal residence up the river. The first impulse toward this change was doubtless due to the campaign of Psamtik II against lower Nubia early in the sixth century. In any case at this time the kingdom began to expand southward. The rich lands on the Blue Nile of which the most important district was known to the Arab geographers as Aloa, were added to the kingdom. Napata was separated from all this by the upper cataracts. As trade connections with the south were established and new acquisitions there developed more fully the royal residence was transferred above the cataracts, and by 560 B. C. the Nubian kings were occupying their new capital, known to the Greeks as Meroe. Apart from other considerations, the wisdom of thus placing the difficult cataract region between the capital and invaders from the north was shown by the discomfiture of Cambyses' expedition against Nubia at the hands of its king Nastesen in 525 B. C. As the nation shifted southward it was completely withdrawn from contact with the northern world; and Ethiopia gradually lost behind a mist of legend, became the wonderland celebrated in Greek story as the source of civilization. The Egyptian language and hieroglyphics, which the kings had hitherto used for their records, now slowly disappeared, and by the beginning of our era the native language was finally written in a script which as yet is undeciphered. When a century or two after the Roman conquest the Ethiopian kingdom slowly collapsed and fell to pieces, its northern districts were absorbed by wild hordes of the Blemmyes who pushed in from the east; while in the south it was succeeded by the Christian kingdom of Abyssinia, which rose at the sources of the Blue Nile in the fourth century A. D. and assumed the name of its ancient predecessor.

36

BOOK VIII

THE RESTORATION AND THE END

CHAPTER XXVII

THE RESTORATION

On the death of Necho of Sais, probably at the hands of Tanutamon, Psamtik his son, as we have seen, had fled to the Assyrians. Having thus shown his fidelity, he was installed over his father's kingdom of Sais and Memphis by Ashurbanipal. Egypt now seemed more hopelessly in the grasp of the Assyrians than ever. Deportations of foreigners were brought in and the vassal organization was strengthened. The Delta thus continued under the mercenary lords in control there with some interruptions since the Twenty First Dynasty. The condition of Upper Egypt is uncertain, but Mentemhet still maintained himself as prince there. Outwardly there was little indication of the brilliant day which was now dawning upon the long afflicted nation. As the years passed Psamtik was gradually reaching out for the control of those resources which should enable him to realize the ambitious designs always cherished by his house. He was a descendant of the aggressive Tefnakhte, the head of the Saitic family in Piankhi's day, and all his line, as far as known to us, had been men of marked power and political sagacity. He soon shook off the restraint and supervision of the resident Assyrian officials. He can hardly have been unaware that Ashurbanipal was ere long to be engaged in a deadly struggle with his brother, the king of Babylon, involving dangerous complications with Elam. As this war came on (652 B. C.) an attempt of the Arabian tribes to send aid to Babylon demanded an Assyrian expedition thither; while disturbances among the peoples on the northern borders of the Ninevite empire and the necessity of meeting the Cimmerians in Cilicia required liberal assignments of Ashurbanipal's available military forces to these regions. It was over twelve years before these difficulties were all adjusted, and when in 640 B. C. peace at last settled upon the Assyrian empire, Psamtik's movement had gone too far and Ashurbanipal evidently did not care to risk opposing it.

With Psamtik, the Greek traditions regarding Egypt begin to be fairly trustworthy, if the folk-tales which the Greeks so readily credited be properly sifted. Herodotus tells the familiar story of how Psamtik was one of twelve kings who had amicably divided all Egypt between them and ruled in the greatest harmony. There came an oracle, however, which declared that whosoever of them should offer a libation in the temple of Vulcan from a brazen bowl should be king of all Egypt. Some time afterward, as they were all offering libations in the temple, the officiating priest failed to supply them with enough golden bowls, and Psamtik, taking off his brazen helmet, used it in lieu of the lacking bowl. He was thereupon banished to the Delta swamps by his companions, and being warned by another oracle that he should be revenged upon them when brazen men from the sea should appear, he awaited his opportunity. Certain Carian and Ionian mercenaries, having been diverted to the coast of the Delta by a tempest, now suddenly appeared in brazen armour, plundering the rich Delta plains. Psamtik secured their services and subduing his rivals, made himself king of all Egypt. Divested of the folk-lore, with which the tale is distorted, it contains the essential facts of Psamtik's early operations. The twelve kings are of course the mercenary lords of the Delta with whom we are so familiar; while the Ionians and Carians, as Meyer has seen, are the levies of mercenaries dispatched from Asia Minor by Gyges, king of Lydia, who at this juncture, after courting the Assyrians to save himself from the Cimmerian hordes, is anxious to combine with Egypt in common opposition to Ninevite aggression. The Assyrian annals state that he sent assistance to Egypt. It is not to be doubted that Psamtik took advantage of these favouring circumstances in the creation of which he had of course had a hand, and by such means gained permanent ascendency over the local dynasts.

His progress was rapid. By 654 B. C., just as Ashurbanipal was advancing on Babylon, he had gained Thebes, where Mentemhet, Taharka's favourite, acknowledged him.[1] The political power of the Theban hierarchy, as we have seen, had been completely shattered under the Ethiopians, so that Psamtik was not called upon to meet that perplexing problem. In order to obtain legitimate control of the fortune of Amon, now of course much depleted, he decreed that his daughter Nitocris should be adopted by the Divine Votress at Thebes, Shepnupet, the sister of the deceased Taharka. The decree of adoption, which has survived, is the only considerable hieroglyphic document of the reign of Psamtik I known to us; it contains the transfer of all Shepnupet's property and revenues to Nitocris.[2] The collapse of the high priesthood of Amon was now so complete that within sixty years the once powerful office was actually held by these sacerdotal princesses. The High Priest of Amon was a woman![3] In the suppression of the mercenary lords and local dynasts, Psamtik made an end of the intolerable conditions of semi-anarchy which had so long blighted an unhappy land. The nation was at last rescued from the unstable rule of a body of feudal lords and their turbulent military adherents, under whose irresponsible tyranny it had suffered, with but brief respites, for some four hundred years. This remarkable achievement of Psamtik I places him among the ablest rulers who ever sat on the throne of the Pharaohs. Indeed the conditions by which he was confronted were so adverse, and the evils with which he was obliged to cope were so old, persistent and deeply rooted that his success should perhaps rank him higher than either Amenemhet I, the founder of the Twelfth Dynasty, or Ahmose I, the conqueror of the Hyksos. He was not, however, able completely to exterminate the dynasts, as is commonly stated. Some

---

[1] IV, 937, 949.   [2] IV, 935-958.   [3] IV, 988 D.

of them would of course espouse his cause and thus gain immunity, and of such we find clear traces. At Thebes Mentemhet remained as prince and "governor of the South";[1] and in Heracleopolis, the other principality of Upper Egypt, we find prince Hor, with the rank of a general, building a temple in his own name at least a generation after Psamtik I's time.[2] Such an enormous tomb as that of Pediamenemopet at Thebes could only have been excavated by a noble of immense wealth and extensive power. It is to be noticed, however, that at Thebes Mentemhet is called upon to make liberal contributions to the revenues of Nitocris, Psamtik's daughter;[3] and what is still more important, he was not succeeded by his eldest son Nesuptah, but by one Pedihor, who gained the titles, "prince of Thebes and governor of the South."[4] It was perhaps Psamtik I's policy to withdraw from the feudal lords their rights of inheritance and thus to rid himself of them as an hereditary class. Enjoying certain privileges, some of the old dynasts therefore still survived, but the strong and skilful hand of Psamtik held them firmly in check, as in the days of the early Middle Kingdom under Amenemhet I. They no longer endangered the unity of the nation.

A not less troublesome problem was the organization of the military class. The now completely Egyptianized Libyans who had lived in Egypt for centuries had finally developed into a warrior-class of no great effectiveness, whose numbers at this time, absurdly exaggerated by Herodotus, we cannot determine. In two classes, the Hermotybies and Calasiries, enigmatical designations employed by Herodotus, they inhabited chiefly the Delta cities and contributed nothing to the economic life of the nation. Besides that of the feudal lords, it was also the opposition of this class which Psamtik had been obliged to face; and he had no recourse but to pit against them his northern mercenaries, the Greeks and Carians. Thus Egypt, having suffered the inevitable fate of a military kingdom in the ancient world,

[1] IV, 949.   [2] IV, 967–973.   [3] IV, 949.   [4] IV, 902 end.

was passing into the control of one foreign warrior-class
after another. The army which Psamtik I now put together
was made up of Greeks, Carians and Syrians on the one
hand, and on the other of Libyans and their Egyptianized
kindred. The Ionians and Carians were stationed on the
northeastern frontier near Daphnæ, with a branch of the
Nile running through their camp; while the border of the
western Delta was secured by a body of the warrior-class
in a stronghold at Marea, not far from the site of later
Alexandria. At Elephantine a similar garrison was maintained against any invasion from the south. Herodotus relates that two hundred and forty thousand of the warrior-
class, having been kept at one station for three years without
being relieved, thereupon deserted and departed in a body
southward to offer their services to the king of Ethiopia
at Meroe. While his numbers are incredibly exaggerated,
as usual, the story must contain a germ of fact as it accords
with all that we know of the conditions in Psamtik's time.
As a concession to this class his body-guard contained a
thousand men from each of the two classes, the Hermotybies
and Calasyries; but he will have had many more of his
hardy Greeks and Carians at his hand on all occasions.

The prosperous and powerful Egypt which was now
emerging from the long Decadence was totally different
from the Egypt of any earlier renascence. It was impossible again to rouse the nation to arms as in the days when
the Hyksos were expelled; it was therefore inevitably the
deliberate policy of Psamtik I, while expending every effort
to put the nation on a sound economic basis, at the same
time to depend upon foreign soldiery for the military power
indispensable to an oriental ruler. His necessarily constant care was to transmute the economic prosperity of the
land into military power. In a word, the wealth of the land
must nourish and maintain a formidable army, even though
the effective portion of this army might be aliens. This was
an evil which Psamtik was powerless to alter. In such a
state the conservation of the productive capacities of the

nation is as important as, or we may better say, indispensable to, the maintenance of the army. Neither can live without the other. In this respect Psamtik I was confronted by the same problem which faced Omar and the early Caliphs. A revival under such conditions as these is due almost solely to the personal initiative of the sovereign who manipulates the available forces: those of power and those of industry; so employing them all in harmonious interaction that prosperity and effective power result. Psamtik was himself the motive and creative power, while the people were but given the opportunity to fulfil their proper functions and to move freely in their wonted channels. There was no longer any great relative vitality in the nation (and here Psamtik's task differed strikingly from that of the early Caliphs), and the return of ordered government and consequent prosperity enabled them to indulge the tendency to retrospect already observable in the Twenty Third Dynasty. Instead of an exuberant energy expressing itself in the spontaneous development of new forms, as at the beginning of the Empire, the nation fell back upon the past and consciously endeavoured to restore and rehabilitate the vanished state of the old days before the changes and innovations introduced by the Empire. Seen through the mist of over a thousand years, what was to *them* ancient Egypt was endowed with the ideal perfection of the divine regime which had preceded it. The worship of the kings who had ruled at Memphis in those remote days was revived and the ritual of their mortuary service maintained and endowed. Their pyramids were even extensively restored and repaired. The archaic titles and the long array of dignities worn by the lords at the court and in the government of the pyramid-builders were again brought into requisition, and in the externals of government everything possible was done to clothe it with the appearance of remote antiquity. The writing of the time was also given an archaic colour on formal and official monuments, and its antique forms must have cost the Saite scribes long and weary study. In religion every effort was made to purify the pantheon of all modern interlopers and to rid the ritual of every innovation. Everything foreign in religion was banished, and Set, the god of the waste and the desert, was everywhere exterminated. An inexorable exclusiveness like that which was soon to take possession of the new-born Jewish community was also now universally enforced. The ancient mortuary texts of the pyramids were revived, and although frequently not understood were engraved upon the massive stone sarcophagi. The Book of the Dead, which now received its last redaction, becoming a roll sixty feet long, shows plain traces of the revival of this ancient mortuary literature. In the tomb-chapels we find again the fresh and pleasing pictures from the life of the people in marsh and meadow, in workshop and ship-yard. They are perfect reproductions of the relief scenes in the mastabas of the Old Kingdom, so perfect indeed that at the first glance one is not infrequently in doubt as to the age of the monument. Indeed, a man named Aba at Thebes sent his artists to an Old Kingdom tomb near Siut to copy the reliefs thence for use in his own Theban tomb, because the owner of the ancient tomb was also named Aba.

In this endeavour to reconstitute modern religion, society and government upon ancient lines, the archaizers must consciously or unconsciously have been constantly thwarted by the inevitable mutability of the social, political and economic conditions of a race. The two thousand years which had elapsed since the Old Kingdom could not be annihilated. Through the deceptive mantle of antiquity with which they cloaked contemporary conditions, the inexorable realities of the present were discernible. The solution of this difficulty, when perceived, was the same as that attempted by the Hebrews in a similar dilemma: it was but to attribute to the modern elements also a hoary antiquity, as the whole body of Hebrew legislation was attributed to Moses. The theoretical revival was thus rescued. This was especially easy for the Egyptian of the Saitic restoration; for, long

before his time it had been customary to attribute to the
Old Kingdom especially sacred mortuary texts, favourite
medical prescriptions and collections of proverbial wisdom.
While in some cases such attribution may have been correct in the days of the Empire, this was no longer generally
true in the Twenty Sixth Dynasty. In one particular especially, it was impossible to force the present into the
ancient mould; I refer to the artistic capacity of the people.
This always fruitful element of their culture was now a
marked exception to the lifeless lack of initiative displayed
in all other functions of life. Here their creative vitality,
already revived in the Ethiopian period, was still unblighted
and their artistic sense was keenly alive to the new possibilities open to them under the new order. We have seen
that the Restoration in religion demanded the revival of
the old subjects in the tomb-chapel reliefs, and in spite of
the likeness of these copies to their ancient models, more
than a superficial examination invariably discloses a distinct character and manner peculiarly their own. There is
just that touch of freedom which the art of the Old Kingdom lacked, and a soft beauty in their sinuous and sweeping
lines which adds an indescribable grace to the reliefs of the
Saitic school. If this tendency be sometimes extreme to
the point of effeminacy, it is compensated for by the qualities which the new freedom brought with it. While the old
canons and conventionalities still prevailed in general, there
was now and then an artist who could shake them off and
place the human body in relief with the shoulders drawn
in proper relations and freed from the distortion of the Old
Kingdom. It was this freedom and ability to see things as
they are which led to a school of portraiture far surpassing
the best work of the Old Kingdom. Among the Saitic mortuary reliefs the conventional heads prescribed by the Old
Kingdom canons are still almost invariable; but the artist
could now and then insert a portrait of such marked individuality as to stand out in sharp contrast with the uni-
formity of the neighbouring heads. Portraits of the same

character appear also in the round (Fig. 186), displaying a study of the bony conformation of the skull, the folds and wrinkies of the skin, in fine a mastery of the entire anatomical development and a grasp of individual character such as no early art had yet achieved. Such works can only be compared with the portraits of the Greek sculptors at the height of their skill, and they do not suffer by the comparison. The artist in bronze was now supreme, *hollow* casts of considerable size were made and animal forms are especially fine (Fig. 185). Superb bronze statues elaborately inlaid with rich designs in gold, silver and electrum display surprising refinements in technique. Works in bronze are now very numerous and most of those which fill the modern museums were produced in this age. Industrial art flourished as never before and the Egyptian craftsman was rarely rivalled. In fayence the manufactories of the time were especially successful and prolific, and the museum collections are filled with works of this period. The architecture of the time has, alas, perished, and if we may judge from the achievements of the Saitic sculptor, we have in this respect suffered irreparable loss; for it is probable that we owe the origin of the rich and beautiful columns of Ptolemaic temples to the Saite architect.

While the material products of art offered visual evidence of marked divergence from the ancient prototype which it was supposed to follow, such incongruities in the organization of the government, while not less real, were probably not so evident. From the few surviving monuments of the period the real character of the state is not clearly determinable. Geographically the Delta had forever become the dominant region. The development of commerce with the northern world and related political reasons had made this northward shift inevitable and permanent. Psamtik and his descendants lived in their native Sais, which now became a great and splendid city, adorned with temples and palaces. Thebes no longer possessed either political or religious significance. The valley of the Nile was but an appendage upon the Delta. We have already referred to the survival of certain of the feudal lords. They may have retained their lands, but judging from the case of Mentemhet of Thebes, they could not bequeath them to their sons. With these exceptions all the land belonged to the crown and was worked by the peasant serfs, who rendered twenty percent of the yield to the Pharaoh. Priests and soldiers were exempt from taxation. The administration must have been conducted as under the Empire by local officials of the central government, who collected the taxes and possessed judicial powers. The archaic titles which they bear, as far as I have been able to trace them, usually correspond to no real functions in government. In education and training these men are fundamentally different from the scribal officials of the Empire, in that they are not of necessity possessed of a knowledge of the old hieroglyphic. Since the Ethiopian Dynasty there has grown up a very cursive form of hieratic, the ancient running hand. This new and more rapid form, an unconscious development, is better suited to the needs of practical business and administration, and being in common and everyday use, was therefore known to the Greeks as "demotic" writing, a term now usually applied to it at the present day. It represented the language then spoken, while the hieroglyphic of the time, which continued to lead an artificial existence, employed the archaic form of the language which had prevailed centuries before. That this fundamental change was but one among many modifications and alterations in the government, must of necessity have resulted from the changed conditions. Socially, the influence of revived industry had divided the people into more or less sharply defined classes or guilds, determined by their occupations; but "caste" in the proper significance of the term, was as unknown as at any time in Egyptian history.

The priests succeeded little better than the officials in their revival of the good old times. It is, indeed, to the priesthoods in general that the attempted restoration must be largely attributed. The religious, like the political, centre, had completely shifted; Thebes, as we have stated, no longer possessed any religious significance. In the Delta cities of Sais, Athribis and Buto were the wealthiest temples. Quite in contrast with conditions in the Old Kingdom, the priests now constituted a more exclusive and distinct class than ever before, and the office had become inalienably hereditary. Venerated by the people, it was a political necessity that their maintenance should be provided for by liberal revenues. While they no longer possessed any political influence to be compared with that which they exercised under the Empire, yet we find the old count of Thinis deprived of his ancient revenues from the oases and the local ferry, that they may be transferred to Osiris.[1] The reverse was, however, the rule, as we shall see. The old gods could not be resuscitated; among them only Osiris still maintained himself. His consort, Isis, contrary to the ancient customs, acquired an elaborate cultus, and the wide celebrity which afterward brought her such general favour in the classic world. Imhotep, the wise man of Zoser's court twenty five hundred years earlier, now gained a place among the gods, as son of Ptah, an innovation of which the priests were unconscious. The religion which the priests represented was the inevitable result of the tendencies observable at the close of the Empire. It consisted as far as daily life and conduct were concerned, like the Rabbinical faith born under very similar conditions, in innumerable external usages, and the most painful observance of the laws of ceremonial purity. We find nobles and officials everywhere erecting sanctuaries to the gods.[2] While formerly only one of a class of animals was sacred, now in many cases every representative of that class was inviolable. The increased reverence for these manifestations of the gods is especially illustrated in the elaborate worship of the Apis-bull, a form of Ptah, and the vast sepulchre, where they now received their gorgeous burial, the Serapeum of Memphis became famous among the Greeks. While a slight inclination

[1] IV, 1016, 1024.   IV, 967 ff., 989 ff., 1015 ff.

toward this tendency was observable already in the Old
Kingdom, it now took on the crass form, which finally led
to the fanatical excesses of the Alexandrians in Roman times.
It is probable that the priests read into all these outward
manifestations, as into their mythological tales, a higher
meaning, which they never originally possessed. Of this procedure we have already seen an example in the Empire,[1]
but we are unable to determine whether they actually
taught all that the Greeks attribute to them of this character. While their education in the Empire had kept them
in contact with the living times, they were now obliged to
learn a language and a method of writing, and to acquaint
themselves with a mass of inherited literature, with which
the busy world around them had long parted company. It
was by this process that the ancient writing, already early
regarded as of divine origin, became a sacred accomplishment, the especial characteristic of sacred learning, and was
therefore called by the Greeks "hieroglyphs" or sacred
glyphs. Such an education necessarily projected the priests
far into a long forgotten world, whose inherited wisdom, as
among the Chinese or the Mohammedans, was the final word.
The writings and sacred rolls of the past were now eagerly
sought out, and with the dust of ages upon them, they were
collected, sorted and arranged. Thus the past was supreme;
the priest who cherished it lived in a realm of shadows, and
for the contemporary world he had no vital meaning. Likewise in Babylon the same retrospective spirit was now the
dominant characteristic of the reviving empire of Nebuchadrezzar. The world was already growing old, and everywhere men were fondly dwelling on her faraway youth.

While the internal aspects of the Saitic period are so
largely retrospective that it has been well called the Restoration, yet its foreign policy shows little consideration for
the past. In sharp contrast with the attempted restoration
and especially with the national exclusiveness, now more
intense than ever, was the foreign policy of Psamtik I. The

[1] See above, pp. 356–58.

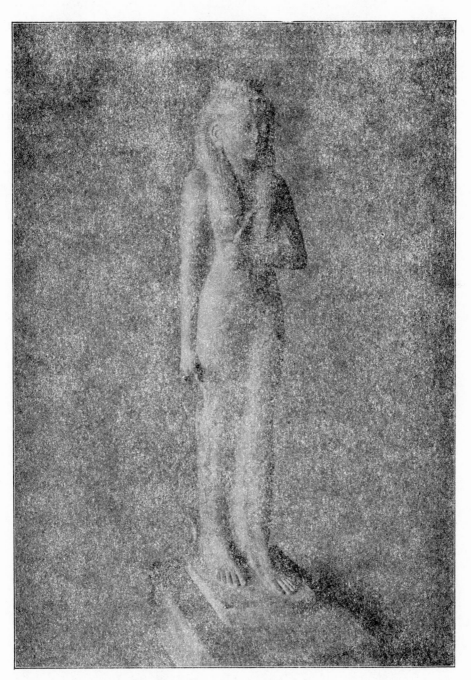

Fig. 184.—ALABASTER STATUE OF AMENARDIS, SISTER OF PIANKHI. CAIRO MUSEUM.

reorganization of ordered and centralized government, and
the restoration of the elaborate irrigation system, were quite
sufficient to ensure the internal prosperity of the country
along traditional lines. But Psamtik's early life and training led him to do more than this. He had personally seen
the great arteries of trade throbbing from one end to the
other of the vast Assyrian Empire; he comprehended the
great economic value of foreign traffic to the nation he was
building up; nor did he fail to perceive that such traffic might
be variously taxed and made to yield very considerable revenues for his own treasury. He therefore revived the old
connections with Syria; Phœnician galleys filled the Nile
mouths, and Semitic merchants, forerunners of the Aramæans so numerous in Persian times, thronged the Delta.
If Psamtik was able to employ the Greeks in his army he
found them not less useful in the furtherance of his commercial projects. From the eighth century B. C. those
southern movements of the northerners, of which the incursions of the "sea-peoples" over five hundred years earlier[1]
were the premonitory symptom, had now become daily
occurrences. The Greeks, pushing in from the far North,
and emerging clearly for the first time into history, had
long since gained possession of the Greek peninsula and its
adjacent archipelago, with their centres of Mycænean civilization, and they now appeared as prosperous communities
and rapidly growing maritime states, whose fleets, penetrating throughout the Mediterranean, offered the Phœnicians sharp and incessant competition. Their colonies and
industrial settlements, with active manufactories, rapidly
fringed the Mediterranean and penetrated the Black Sea.
Psamtik was probably the first of the Egyptian rulers who
favoured such colonies in Egypt. Ere long the country
was filled with Greek merchants, and their manufacturing
settlements were permitted, especially in the western Delta,
near the royal residence at Sais. There was a Greek and
also a Carian quarter in Memphis, and not unlikely other

[1] See pp. 477–83.
37

large cities were similarly apportioned to accommodate foreigners, especially Greeks.

Lines of communication between the Greek states and
Egypt soon established direct, continuous and in some respects intimate relations between them. Greek recruits for
the army of course followed constantly upon those whom
Psamtik had employed in his conquest, and these, with the
active intercourse of the indefatigable Greek merchants, carried back to the mother-country an ever increasing fund of
folk-tales, telling of the wondrous Egyptian world, which
was so new and strange to them. The marvels of Thebes
were celebrated in the Homeric songs, now assuming their
final form, and Egyptian gods appeared in their myths.

Ultimately the Greeks became very familiar with the
externals of Egyptian civilization, but they never learned to
read its curious writing sufficiently well to understand its
surviving records, or to learn the truth as to its ancient history. As time passed a body of interpreters arose, who
became so numerous as to form a recognized class. By
these such questioners as Herodotus were often grossly imposed upon. The impenetrable reserve of the Egyptians,
and again their unlimited claims, profoundly impressed the
imaginative Greek. This impression could only be deep-
ened by the marvels with which the land was filled: the
enormous buildings and temples, whose construction was
often a mystery to him; the mystic writing which covered
their walls; the strange river, unlike any he had ever seen;
the remarkable religion, whose mysterious ritual seemed to
him the cloak for the most profound truths; the unquestionably vast antiquity of countless impressive monuments all
about him; all this, where an unprejudiced, objective study
of the people and their history was impossible, inevitably
blinded even the Greek of the highest intelligence and culture, who now visited the country. Thus the real character of the Egyptian and his civilization was never cor-
rectly understood by the Greeks, and their writings regarding the Nile country, even though often ridiculing its strange

customs, have transmitted to us a false impression as to the value especially of its intellectual achievements. The Greek, with his insatiable thirst for the truth, and his constant attitude of healthy inquiry, was vastly superior, I need hardly say, to the Egyptian, whose reputed wisdom he so venerated. Under these circumstances it was only the later political history of the country, the course of which came under their own immediate observation, with which the Greeks were familiar. From the time of Psamtik I we possess a fund of popular Greek tradition regarding the Twenty Sixth Dynasty, which, if properly used, throws an invaluable light upon a time when native records and monuments, located as they were in the exposed Delta, have almost entirely perished.

Before the impact of the foreign life, which thus flowed in upon Egypt, the Egyptian showed himself entirely unmoved, and held himself aloof, fortified behind his ceremonial purity and his inviolable reserve. If he could have had his way he would have banished the foreigners one and all from his shores; under the circumstances, like the modern Chinese, he trafficked with them and was reconciled to their presence by the gain they brought him. Thus while the Saitic Pharaohs, as we shall further see, were profoundly influenced by the character of the Greeks, the mass of the Egyptians were unscathed by it. On the other hand, the Greeks must have profited much by the intercourse with Nile valley civilization, although it will have been chiefly material profit which they gained. They found there, perfected and ready at hand, the technical processes, which their unique genius was so singularly able to apply to the realization of higher ends than those governing the older civilizations. They certainly borrowed artistic forms in plenty, and the artistic influences from the Nile, which had been felt in the Mycenæan centres of civilizations as far back at least as the Twelfth Dynasty (2000 B. C.), were still a power in the same regions of the North. It can be no accident, in spite of the wide spread 'law of frontality,'

that the archaic (so-called) Apollos reproduce the standing
posture prevalent in Egypt in every detail, including
the characteristic thrusting forward of the left foot. Of
the Saitic portrait sculptor, the Greeks might have learned
much, even far down toward the days of their highest
artistic achievements. Evidence of intellectual influence is
more elusive, but there is a grain of truth in the Greek tradition that they received their philosophy from Egypt. The
philosophizing theology of the Egyptian priests contained
suggestive germs, which may easily have found their way
into the early Ionian systems. The notion of the primeval
intelligence and the creative "word," already conceived as
far back as the Eighteenth Dynasty,[1] could hardly fail to
influence the educated Greeks who very early visited Egypt,
long before such a conception had arisen in Greece. The
insistent belief of the Egyptian in the life hereafter and his
elaborate mortuary usages, unquestionably exerted a strong
influence upon Greek and Roman alike; and the wide dis-
semination of Egyptian religion in the classic world, dem-
onstrates the deep impression which it now made. To this
day its symbols are turned up by the spade throughout
the Mediterranean basin. It was under Psamtik I that these
influences from Egypt began to be felt by the states, which
were then laying the foundations of later European civilization; and it is significant as an indication of the great restorer's personal prestige in the Greek world that the powerful
Periander of Corinth named his nephew and successor
Psammetichos.

By 640 B. C. Psamtik felt himself strong enough to resume
the old projects of conquest in Asia, to revive Egypt's traditional claims upon Syria-Palestine, and to dispute their possession with Assyria. He invaded Philistia and for many
years besieged Ashdod; but his ambitions there were rudely
dashed by the influx of Scythian peoples from the far north,
who overran Assyria and penetrated southward to the frontier of Egypt. According to Herodotus they were bought

[1] See above, pp. 356–58.

off by Psamtik, who by liberal gifts succeeded thus in ransoming his kingdom. It was more probably his own strong arm that delivered his land. He had already saved it from centuries of weakness and decay, and when he died after a reign of fifty four years, he left Egypt enjoying such peaceable prosperity as had not been hers since the death of Ramses III, five hundred years before.

CHAPTER XXVIII

THE FINAL STRUGGLES: BABYLON AND PERSIA

WHEN Necho succeeded his father Psamtik I on the throne of Egypt in 609 B. C., there seemed to be nothing to prevent his reëstablishment of the Egyptian Empire in Asia. As Psamtik's kingdom had prospered, that of the once powerful Ninevites had rapidly declined. From the fearful visitation of the Scythian hordes in the reign of Psamtik I, it never recovered, and when Babylon made common cause with Cyaxares, king of the rising Median states, Nineveh was unable to withstand their united assaults. Its inevitable fall was anticipated by the western peoples, and being clearly foreseen by the Hebrew, Nahum, he exultingly predicted its destruction. At the accession of Necho it was in such a state of collapse that he immediately began the realization of his father's imperial designs in Asia. He built a war-fleet both in the Mediterranean and the Red Sea, and in his first year invaded Philistia. Gaza and Askalon, which offered resistance, were taken and punished,[1] and with a great army Necho then pushed northward. In Judah, now freed from the Assyrians, the prophetic party was in the ascendancy. As they had been delivered from Sennacherib nearly a century before, so they fondly believed they might now face Egypt with the same assurance of deliverance. On the historic plain of Megiddo, where Egypt had first won the supremacy of Asia nearly nine hundred years before, the young Josiah recklessly threw himself upon Necho's great army. His pitiful force was quickly routed and he himself, fatally wounded, retired to die at Jerusalem. Expecting to meet at least some attempt on the part of Assyria to save her western dominions, Necho pressed on to the Euphrates

[1] Jer. 47. 1 and 5.

without delay. But Assyria was now too near her end to make even the feeblest effort to stay his progress; he found no army there to meet him, and not feeling himself strong enough to advance against Nineveh, he returned southward, having gained all Syria, and at one stroke recovered the whole of the old Egyptian conquests of the Empire. Arriving at Ribleh on the Orontes, three months after the battle of Megiddo, he sent for Josiah's son, Jehoahaz, whom the Judeans had placed upon his father's throne, and threw him into chains. He then installed Eliakim, another son of Josiah, as king of Judah under the name Jehoiakim, and imposed upon him a tribute of one hundred talents of silver and one of gold. The unfortunate Jehoahaz was carried to Egypt by the Pharaoh and died there. It is characteristic of the altered spirit of the times that Necho dedicated to the Milesian Branchidæ the corselet which he had worn on this victorious campaign,—of course in recognition of the Greek mercenaries, to whom he owed his successes. How different all this from the days of Amon's supremacy, when victory came from him alone! Fragments of a stela dating from Necho's supremacy in Syria and bearing his name in hieroglyphic, have been found at Sidon.[1]

Necho's new Asiatic empire was not of long duration. In less than two years the combined forces of Nabopolassar, the king of Babylon, and of the Medes under Cyaxares, had accomplished the overthrow of Nineveh. The city was destroyed and the nation utterly annihilated as a political force. The two conquerors divided the territory made available by their conquest, the Mede taking the north and northeast and the Babylonian the south and southwest. Thus Syria fell by inheritance t, Nabopolassar. He was now old and unable to undertake its recovery; but he quickly dispatched his son, Nebuchadrezzar, to oppose Necho. Hearing of his coming, Necho was wise enough to collect his forces and hasten to meet him at the northern frontier on the Euphrates in 605 B. C. At Carchemish the motley army of

---

[1] Proceedings Soc. of Biblical Arch., XVI (1894), pp. 91 f.

the Pharaoh was completely routed by the Babylonians. The victory was so decisive that Necho did not attempt to make another stand or to save Palestine, but retreated in haste to the Delta followed by Nebuchadrezzar. The ignominious retreat of Necho's proud army, as it hurried through Palestine, created a profound impression among the Hebrews of Judah, and Jeremiah, who was interpreting to his people in Jerusalem the movements of the nations, hurled after the discomfited Egyptians his burden of sarcasm and derision.[1] Had not the young Kaldean prince now been summoned to Babylon by the death of his father, the conquest of Egypt, or at least its further humiliation, must inevitably have followed. Unwilling to prolong his absence from the capital under these circumstances, Nebuchadrezzar came to an understanding with Necho, and returned home to assume the crown of Babylon. Thus Syria-Palestine became Babylonian dominion.

Necho's agreement with Babylon involved the relinquishment of his ambitious designs in Asia. He held to the compact, and made no further attempt to maintain Egyptian sovereignty there, as the Hebrew annals record: "And the king of Egypt came not again any more out of his land: for the king of Babylon had taken from the brook of Egypt unto the river Euphrates, all that pertained to the king of Egypt."[2] He even made no effort to intervene when Nebuchadrezzar besieged and captured Jerusalem and deported the chief families of Judah in 596 B. C. The Pharaoh's energies were now employed in the furtherance of his father's commercial enterprises. He attempted to reëxcavate the ancient canal from the Delta, connecting the eastern arm of the Nile with the Red Sea. Herodotus claims that one hundred and twenty thousand men perished in this enterprise, from which the Pharaoh at last desisted, in response to an oracle; while Diodorus avers that the king's engineers warned him of the danger of flooding Egypt, demonstrating that the Red Sea was higher than the Delta. This was prob-

[1] Jer. 46: 1–12.　　　　　　　　[2] II Kings 24: 7.

ably the real motive for discontinuing so important a work; maritime connection between the Red Sea and the Mediterranean by way of the Nile would have been of incalculable commercial benefit to Egypt at this time, and would also have involved valuable strategic advantages in case of war. Necho's interest in maritime progress is further evidenced by his famous exploring expedition. He dispatched a crew of Phœnician mariners with instructions to sail around Africa, or as Herodotus calls it, Libya. As the Egyptians had from the earliest time supposed their land to be surrounded by sea, the Oceanos of the Greeks, with which the Nile had connection in the south, the feat of the Phœnicians, which they actually accomplished in three years, excited no surprise.

Psamtik II, who followed his father Necho about 593 B. C., either regarded Egypt's prospects in Asia as hopeless or continued the compact of his father with Babylon. Unable to accomplish anything in the North, he turned his attention southward and attempted the recovery of Nubia, lost to Egypt since the foundation of the Ethiopian kingdom. He invaded lower Nubia, and an advanced body of his troops pushed up almost to the second cataract, where they left a record of their visit at Abu Simbel, in a Greek inscription on one of the colossi of Ramses II, before his great temple there. Although, as we have before remarked, this invasion doubtless furnished the Ethiopians a further reason for transferring their capital above the cataracts to Meroe, yet the results of the expedition were probably not lasting, and Lower Nubia never became an integral part of the Saite kingdom. Relations with the Greeks continued on the old friendly basis and Herodotus relates how the Eleans sent a delegation to Psamtik II to obtain his judgment on the fairness of their management of the Olympian games. At home he continued the Saitic control of Thebes by arranging for the adoption of his daughter, Enekhnes-nefribre, by his aged aunt, the daughter of Psamtik I, Nitocris, who still survived as Divine Votress or sacerdotal princess of Thebes. Psamtik II conferred upon his daughter the title "High Priest of Amon," and she received the fortune of Nitocris, who died nine years afterward. She continued in control of Thebes until the advent of the Persians nearly seventy years later.[1]

Meanwhile the Saites were still casting longing eyes upon the ancient dominions of Egypt in Asia, and when Apries (the Ha'abre' of the Egyptians, or Hophra' of the Hebrews) succeeded his father Psamtik II early in 588 B. C., he immediately resumed the old designs of his house to recover them. Already under Necho, in 597 B. C., as we have seen, Nebuchadrezzar had been obliged to advance on Jerusalem in consequence of the rebellion of Jehoiachin, an event in which Necho may have secretly had a hand. The next year the unhappy city capitulated, and some nine or ten thousand of the better class were deported to Babylonia, leaving only "the poorest sort of the people of the land."[2] Jehoichin's uncle, Zedekiah, was appointed by Nebuchadrezzar as king over the afflicted land. When he had been ruling nine years we find him in revolt against Babylon. The reasons for this foolish policy are quite evident. The date of his rebellion coincides with the accession of Apries. Tyre and Sidon, Moab and Ammon had also sent their emissaries to the Judean king, and when the weighty influence of Apries also fell into the scales the vacillating Zedekiah was no longer able to withstand, and he half-heartedly joined the rest in casting off the sovereignty of Babylon. The events formerly following similar revolts from Assyrian authority were now reënacted under the Babylonians; the allies were unable to act quickly in concert. Indeed Apries made it impossible that they should do so by attacking Tyre and Sidon. He dispatched an expedition to attempt the conquest of the north by sea, perhaps hoping to meet Nebuchadrezzar on the Euphrates as his grandfather Necho had done. He fought a victorious naval engagement with the Tyrians and Cyprians and landed enough troops to take Sidon, whereupon the other Phœnician cities yielded.[3] It is possible

[1] IV, 988 A-988 J.   [2] II Kings 24: 15.   [3] Diodorus, I, 68.

also that he hoped thus to divert Nebuchadrezzar from the south where a portion of his army had appeared early in 587, or to cut off this southern army now operating against Jerusalem; and if so, the movement was brilliantly conceived. But it was never pushed far enough to accomplish anything inland; and Nebuchadrezzar wisely fixed his base of operations well northward, at Ribleh on the Orontes, where he was able to contemplate the Egyptian operations without concern. His enemies were exhausting themselves against each other, and had Apries advanced inland Nebuchadrezzar could have quickly confronted him with a force from Ribleh. It is perhaps during this brief supremacy of the Pharaoh in Phœnicia that we should place the fragmentary Egyptian monuments, pieces of stone statues, altars and bits of inscribed stone from the Saite age, found by Renan at Arvad, Tyre and Sidon.[1] Now also the Pharaoh apparently controlled for a time a domain in Lebanon.[2]

When in the spring of 586 B. C. the troops of Apries at last appeared in the south to threaten the Babylonian besiegers of Jerusalem, they brought the beleagured city a brief moment's respite only; for the Egyptian forces again showed themselves unable to cope with the armies of Asia. Indeed, it is possible that Apries relinquished his claims in Palestine without a blow. Thus the predictions of Jeremiah, who had constantly proclaimed the folly of depending upon assistance from Egypt, were brilliantly confirmed; but the unhappy prophet paid dearly for the sanity of his statesmanlike views and barely escaped with his life. In the summer of 586 B. C. Jerusalem fell; it was razed to the ground and the inglorious Zedekiah, having been taken to Nebuchadrezzar's camp at Ribleh, was blinded, after witnessing the slaughter of his sons. The Judean nation was annihilated, but no decisive blow had been struck which might cripple the power of Egypt, the instigator of the trouble. It was not for many years that Nebuchadrezzar was able to attempt anything in this direction; his first obligation being the pun-

[1] Rougé, letter to Renan, Revue arch. n. s., VII, 1863[1], pp. 194–8.
[2] IV, 970.

ishment of Tyre, which maintained itself for thirteen years, finally yielding in 573 B. C.

In spite of ill success in Asia, Apries enjoyed unbounded prosperity in the internal administration of his realm, and the kingdom flourished as only under his great grandfather, its founder. From the west also he received the revenues of the Oasis region and in the Northern Oasis his official Wah-ibrenofer built a temple.[1]   But in the full enjoyment of his wealth and splendour a tragic end was awaiting him from an unexpected quarter. He found great difficulty in bridling his troops, of whatever nationality. On one occasion the Libyans, Greeks and Syrians attempted to desert and mi-grate to Nubia, as in the days of Psamtik I a body of the warrior-class had done. How many were involved in this revolt under Apries it is impossible to establish, but they were sufficiently numerous to render the king very appre-hensive, and the record of the event distinctly states that "his majesty feared." As the deserters approached the first cataract Nesuhor, the governor of Assuan, an astute official, succeeded in dissuading them from their purpose and delivering them to the king who then punished them.[2] Another misunderstanding with the *native* warrior-class did not end so happily. The new Greek settlement at Cyrene was growing into a flourishing state and encroaching upon the Libyans who lay between Cyrene and Egypt.   Apries deemed it wise to check the development of the Greek colony and sent to the aid of the Libyans a body of Egyptian troops naturally not including among them any of his Greek mer-cenaries. Despising their adversaries, the Egyptians ad-vanced in careless confidence, but were totally defeated and almost annihilated by the Cyrenian Greeks. Smarting un-der their discomfiture they were so filled with resentment toward Apries that they concluded he had dispatched them against Cyrene with the purpose of ridding himself of them. A revolt of the warrior-class followed, which swelled to dangerous proportions. Apries thereupon commissioned

[1] Steindorff, Berichte der phil.-hist. Classe der Königl. Sächs, Gesellschaft der Wissenschaften zu Leipzig, 1900, p. 226.   [2] IV, 989.

one Ahmose, or Amasis, as Herodotus calls him, a relative
of the royal house, to conciliate the revolters and curb them
into submission. Amasis was a chamberlain or marshal of
the palace, and besides this office at court he held an important judicial position. Being a person of unusual shrewdness and insight, his selection at this time might equally
well have been the salvation or the ruin of Apries. So
skilfully did Amasis manipulate the situation that the disaffected soldiery soon proclaimed him king, and a messenger
of Apries, sent to recall the traitor, was dismissed with in-
sult and contumely. The enraged Pharaoh was now so
foolish as to expend his wrath on the luckless messenger
who, although he was a man of rank, immediately suffered
the loss of nose and ears. Seeing one of their colleagues so
unjustly punished, many of Apries' nobles and adherents
forsook him and espoused the cause of Amasis. Herodotus
narrates that a battle now ensued in which the Greek mercenaries of Apries, heavily outnumbered by the native
troops of Amasis, were beaten and Apries taken prisoner.
It is possible that he is here confusing the situation with the
later battle which, as we know from a contemporary document, occurred between the forces of the two rivals. However this may be, Amasis, while treating Apries with kindness and not yet dethroning him, laid a vigourous hand upon
the sceptre. A coregency ensued in which Apries doubtless
played but a feeble part; and a monument or two showing
the two rulers together has survived. Alongside the cartouche, which he now assumed, Amasis continued to bear
the old titles belonging to his former less exalted offices.[1]
In the third year of the coregency, however, a struggle
between the two regents arose. Apries, as Herodotus knew,
gained the adherence of the Greeks, and with an army of
these mercenaries, supported by a fleet, advanced upon Sais
from the North. Amasis quickly collected his forces and attacked, putting Apries and his army to flight and scattering
them far and wide. As they continued for some months to

[1] IV, 999 f.

rove the North, infesting the roads, and of course living by plunder, Amasis dispatched a force against tnem. It would seem that Apries had meantime been a fugitive. In any case, he was slain during this pursuit, while taking his ease on one of the surviving vessels of his fleet. Amasis gave him honourable burial, befitting a king, among his ancestors in Sais, and established for him mortuary offerings endowed with a liberal revenue.[1]

It might have been supposed that Amasis, who owed his crown to an ebullition of national feeling, as opposed to the partiality shown the Greeks, would now have evinced his appreciation of this indebtedness in a marked reaction against foreign influence; but for this he was too sagacious a statesman. While seeming to curtail the privileges of the Greeks, he really gave to them all they wanted. The Greek merchants, who had hitherto enjoyed unlimited latitude in their selection of a field for their merchandizing, were now not allowed to land anywhere in the Delta, save at a city appointed for them by Amasis. On the Canopic mouth of the Nile in the western Delta, at a place where there was probably an older settlement of but slight importance, Amasis founded the new city of Naucratis as a home and market for the Greeks, which they speedily made the most important commercial centre of Egypt, if not of the whole Mediterranean. It was in all essentials a Greek city, and the wares which were manufactured within its walls were, with but slight exceptions, in no sense Egyptian. The busy life which throbbed in its thronging markets and factories, the constitution of the city and its daily administration, were just such as prevailed in any industrial and commercial Greek community of the mother country. All the Greeks were concerned more or less in its success and prosperity. Hence when the chief temple of Naucratis was to be erected, the Ionian cities of Chios, Teos, Phocæa and Clazomenæ, with Rhodes, Cnidus, Halicarnassus and Phaselis of the Dorians, and the Æolian Mitylene, together contributed a

[1] IV, 996 ff.

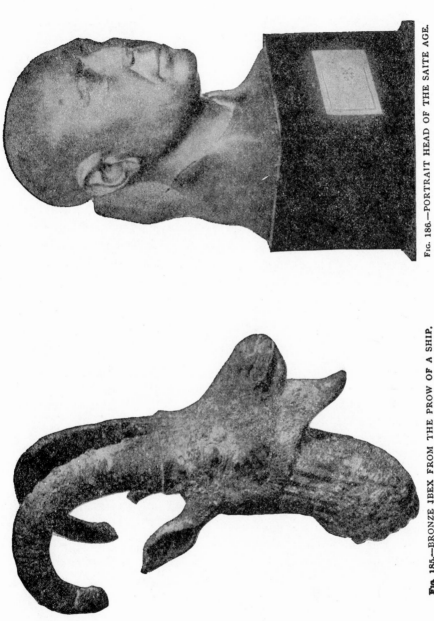

Fig. 186.—PORTRAIT HEAD OF THE SAITE AGE.

Green basaltic stone. See pp. 572-73. (Berlin Museum.)

Fig. 185.—BRONZE IBEX FROM THE PROW OF A SHIP.

Saite age. See p. 573. (Berlin Museum.)

common fund to erect the Hellenium, a large and stately sanctuary, with a spacious enclosure, protected by a massive wall. The powerful states of Ægina, Miletus and Samos, however, were able to possess each a temple of their own. Thus while apparently restricted, the Greeks were still enjoying the greatest privileges in Egypt, nor did the regulations of Amasis ever impress them as hostile to their welfare in his land. When an embassy of the Delphians approached him for a contribution toward the erection of their temple, which had been burned (548 B. C.), he responded liberally. He sent gifts likewise to the temples of Lindos, Samos and Cyrene, and presented a magnificent corselet to the Spartans. He thus maintained close relations with the Greek world in Europe and Asia, and with the wealthy and powerful Polycrates of Samos he sustained a friendship which amounted to an alliance. He was always very popular with the Greeks, both at home and abroad, and many tales of his career and personal character circulated among them.

Unfortunately it is almost solely in his dealings with the Greeks that we know anything of the achievements of Amasis. He did not neglect his interests among the Egyptians, as in view of the catastrophe which had overtaken Apries, he was not likely to do. He built splendid additions to the temples of Sais and Memphis, and a vast monolithic chapel from the quarries of the first cataract, which he set up in Sais, excited the admiration of Herodotus. The people enjoyed the greatest prosperity, and Herodotus avers that the land "contained at that time twenty thousand cities." He again revised the system of laws, one of which, demanding that every inhabitant "should annually declare to the governor of his district by what means he maintained himself," was adopted by Solon on his visit to Egypt, and enforced at Athens. But eventually his evident liking for the Greeks could not escape the notice of the Egyptian party. He had two frontier forts in the northeastern Delta,[1] and from Daphnæ, one of these two, he was obliged to transfer

[1] IV, 1014.

the Greek garrison stationed there to Memphis, and thus
ensure the safety of the latter strong and populous city, so
near his residence at Sais. He was finally compelled to
throw off the mask, and for the support of his mercenary
army and fleet to draw upon the fortunes and revenues of
the temples.[1] It was no longer compatible with modern
statesmanship that the priesthoods should be permitted to
absorb so large a proportion of the resources of the land. A
navy such as Egypt now possessed, and the large body of
mercenaries in his army, drew heavily upon the treasury
of Amasis; and his curtailment of the temple incomes was
inevitable. It was the beginning of still more serious inroads
upon the temple-estates in the Persian period, resulting
under the Ptolemies in great reduction of the priestly revenues and the taxation of the temple-property. Politically
impotent, the priesthoods could only swallow their discontent, which, however, gradually permeated all the upper
classes. But Amasis, with a cleverness which became
proverbial, was always able so to manipulate the forces at
his command that the Egyptian party found itself helpless
and obliged to accede to his wishes.

The good understanding which Amasis constantly maintained with the Greeks made him secure upon the Mediterranean. In the west he controlled the oases and erected a
temple in the Northern Oasis;[2] but he was not so fortunate
in his relations with the east. His usurpation of the crown
had furnished Nebuchadrezzar with the coveted opportunity of humiliating Egypt, which the Kaldean naturally
supposed would have been weakened by the internal dissensions incident to such a revolution. Already before the
death of Apries in 568 B. C., the army of the Kaldeans
appeared on the Delta frontier, but the course of the subsequent operations is unknown. It is not probable that Nebuchadrezzar purposed the conquest of Egypt, which was
now in a condition very different from the state of impotent

[1] Revillout, Revue égyptologique, I, 59 ff., III, 105.

[2] Steindorff, Berichte der phil.-hist. Classe der Königl. Sächs, Gesellschaft
der Wissenschaften zu Leipzig, 1900, p. 226.

anarchy in which the Assyrians had found it under the
Ethiopians. In any case, he did not achieve the conquest
of the country; and Jeremiah[1] and Ezekiel,[2] who were
awaiting with feverish longing the complete overthrow of
the hated Pharaoh's kingdom, must have been sorely disap-
pointed that the catastrophe which they had confidently predicted to their countrymen failed to occur. As a result of
the campaign, however, Amasis was obliged to renounce any
ambitions which he may have cherished for the conquest of
Syria-Palestine. His strong navy, nevertheless, enabled him
completely to subdue Cyprus, which he organized as an
Egyptian dependency, paying tribute to him. His naval
strength, which now became formidable, was the foundation
of the sea-power, which, under the Ptolemies, made Egypt
the dominant state on the Mediterranean.

Meanwhile Nebuchadrezzar had died (562 B. C.), and the
disappearance of his powerful personality distinctly dimin-
ished the prestige of the Babylonian Empire. As internal
dissensions arose, the alliance with the Medes was no longer
possible, and when finally Cyrus of Anshan, a Persian, succeeded in supplanting the Median dynasty by the overthrow
of the Median king, Astyages (550 B. C.), the position of
Babylon was critical in the extreme. The extraordinary
career of Cyrus was now a spectacle upon which all eyes in
the west were fastened with wonder and alarm. Amasis
was fully alive to the new danger which threatened his kingdom in common with all the other powers of the West. He
therefore in 547 B. C. made common cause with them, forming a league with Crœsus of Lydia, and the Spartans in the
west; and in the east with Nabuna'id of Babylon. Before
the allies could move together, Crœsus was defeated and
dethroned (546-5 B. C.); and the overflowing energies of
the new conqueror and his people, fresh and unspent for
centuries among their native hills, were then directed upon
Babylon, which fell in 539 B. C. Amasis was powerless to
check their progress, while the vast Persian Empire was

[1] Jer. 43: 8-13.   [2] Ezek. 40: 10-18.

being raised upon the ruins of the Semitic states in the valley of the two rivers and the kingdoms of Asia Minor. It was inevitable that the new world power should now look toward Egypt, and the last years of Amasis must have been darkened with anxious forebodings as he contemplated the undisputed supremacy of Cyrus. But he was spared the fate of Crœsus, for when he died, late in 526 or early in 525 B. C., the impending catastrophe had not yet overtaken his kingdom.

Amasis had ample opportunity during his long reign of forty four years to display his qualities as a statesman. With his fertility of resource and never-failing cleverness, he belonged to and was largely the product of the Greek world. His nature was fundamentally opposed to the conventional and sacerdotal conception of the Pharaoh, which so dominated the ancient kingship that its monuments, largely of priestly origin, force all the Pharaohs into the same mould, and depict them as rigid and colourless forms, each like all the others, with the same monotonous catalogue of divine attributes. These formal and priestly traditions of what constituted a Pharaoh were treated with scant consideration by Amasis. When he had devoted the morning hours to the transaction of public business, he loved to throw aside the pomp and formalities of state, and gathering at his table a few choice friends, he gave himself without reserve to the enjoyment of conviviality, in which wine played no small part. A thorough man of the world of his day, not too refined, open to every influence and to every pleasure which did not endanger his position, he showed himself nevertheless a statesman of the first rank. Of his wit and humour the Greeks told many a tale, while the light and skilful touch with which he manipulated men and affairs won their constant admiration. But the character and policies of Amasis clearly disclose the fact that the old Egyptian world, whose career we have been following, has already ceased to be. Its vitality, which flickered again into a flame, in the art of the Saitic age, is now quenched forever. The

Saitic state is but an artificial structure, skilfully built up and sustained by sagacious rulers, but that national career, the characteristics of which were determined by the initiative and vital force of the nation itself had long ago ended. The fall of Egypt and the close of her characteristic history, were already an irrevocable fact long before the relentless Cambyses knocked at the doors of Pelusium. The Saitic state was a creation of rulers who looked into the future, who belonged to it, and had little or no connection with the past. They were as essentially non-Egyptian as the Ptolemies who followed the Persians. The Persian conquest in 525 B. C., which deprived Psamtik III, the son of Amasis of his throne and kingdom, was but a change of rulers, a purely external fact. And if a feeble burst of national feeling enabled this or that Egyptian to thrust off the Persian yoke for a brief period, the movement may be likened to the convulsive contractions which sometimes lend momentary motion to limbs from which conscious life has long departed. With the fall of Psamtik III, Egypt belonged to a new world, toward the development of which she had contributed much, but in which she could no longer play an active part. Her great work was done, and unable, like Nineveh and Babylon, to disappear from the scene, she lived on her artificial life for a time under the Persians and the Ptolemies, ever sinking, till she became merely the granary of Rome, to be visited as a land of ancient marvels by wealthy Greeks and Romans, who have left their names scratched here and there upon her hoary monuments, just as the modern tourists, admiring the same marvels, still continue to do. But her unwarlike people, still making Egypt a garden of the world, show no signs of an awakening and the words of the Hebrew seer, "There shall be no more a prince out of the land of Egypt,"[1] have been literally fulfilled.

[1] Ezek. 30: 13.

CHRONOLOGICAL TABLE OF KINGS.

(See Ancient Records of Egypt, I, 38–75.)

NOTE: All dates with asterisk are astronomically fixed.

Introduction of calendar .... 4241 B. C.
Accession of Menes and Beginning of Dynasties 3400 B. C.

FIRST AND SECOND DYNASTIES, 3400–2980 B. C.

Eighteen Kings, 420 years.

THIRD DYNASTY, 2980–2900 B. C.

Zoser to Snefru, 80 years.

FOURTH DYNASTY, 2900–2750 B. C.

Khufu..............	23	years.
Dedefre............	8	"
Khafre	x	"
Menkure..........	x	"
——————	x	"
——————	18	"
Shepseskaf	4	"
——————	2	"
Total	55	" Known minimum 150 years.

FIFTH DYNASTY, 2750–2625 B. C.

Userkaf	7	years.
Sahure	12	"
Neferirkere......	x	"
Shepseskere	7	"
Khaneferre	x	"
Nuserre...........	30 (+ x)	years.
Menkuhor........	8	years.
Dedkere-Isesi ...	28	"
Unis	30	"
Total	122 (+ 3x)	years. Minimum 125 years.

SIXTH DYNASTY, 2625–2475 B. C.

Teti II	x	years.
Userkere	x	"

Pepi I..............   21 years
Mernere I........   4   "
Pepi II............   90 (+ x) years.
Mernere II.......   1 year.
     Total........ 116 (+ 3x) years.   Known length 150 years.

SEVENTH AND EIGHTH DYNASTIES, 2475–2445 B. C.
Known total 30 years.

NINTH AND TENTH DYNASTIES, 2445–2160 B. C.
Eighteen Heracleopolitans, estimated 285 years.

ELEVENTH DYNASTY.

Horus Wahenekh-Intef I..............   50 (+ **x**) **years.**
Horus Nakhtneb-Tepnefer-Intef II   x years.
Horus Senekhibtowe-Mentuhotep I   x   "
Nibhapetre-Mentuhotep II   x   "
Nibtowere-Mentuhotep III...........   2 (+ x) years.
Nibhepetre-Mentuhotep IV ....   46 (+ x)   "
Senekhkere-Mentuhotep V...........   8 (+ x)   "
     Total.................. 106 (+ x)   "   Known total 160 years.

TWELFTH DYNASTY, 2000–1788 B. C.

COREGENCIES.

Amenemhet I..	30 years 2000*–1970* B. C.	2000–1980 B. C., alone. 1980–1970 " with his son.	
Sesostris I......	45 years 1980*–1935* B. C.	1980–1970 B. C., with his father. 1970–1938 B. C., alone. 1938–1935 " with his son.	
Amenemhet II.	35 years 1938*–1903* B. C.	1938–1935 B. C., with his father. 1935–1906 B. C., alone. 1906–1903 " with his son.	
Sesostris II......	19 years 1906*–1887* B. C.	1906–1903 B. C., with his father. 1903–1887 B. C., alone.	
Sesostris III....	38 years 1887*–1849* B. C.	Uncertain period with his son.	

Amenemhet III   48 years 1849*–1801* B. C. { Uncertain period with his father.
Uncertain period with his son.

Amenemhet IV   9 years 1801*–1792* B. C. { Uncertain period with his father.

Sebeknefrure...   4 years 1792*–1788* B. C.
Total...........   228 years.
Allowance for coregencies...   15 years.
Actual total 213 years.

THIRTEENTH TO SEVENTEENTH DYNASTIES, 1788*–1580 B. C.
Including the Hyksos, 208 years.

EIGHTEENTH DYNASTY, 1580–1350, B. C.

Ahmose I...........................22(+ x) years, 1580–1557* B. C.
Amenhotep I..10(+ x) years } 56   "   1557*–1501*   "
Thutmose I....30(+ x)   "
Thutmose III ....54 years, May 3, 1501*, to Mar. 17, 1447* B.C
(Including Thutmose II and Hatshepsut.)
Amenhotep II.......................26(+ x) years, 1448*–1420 B. C.
Thutmose IV........................ 8(+ x)   "   1420–1411   "
Amenhotep III......................36   "   1411–1375   "
Amenhotep IV..17(+ x) years
(or Ikhnaton 1375–1358 B. C.)
Sakere x   years   } 25   "   1375–1350   "
Tutenkhamon...x   "
Eye.................3(+ x)   "

Total.........227(+ 4x)   "   Minimum, 230 years.

NINETEENTH DYNASTY, 1350–1205 B. C.

Harmhab................. 34(+ x) years, 1350–1315 B. C.
Ramses I................. 2   "   1315–1314   "
Seti I..................... 21(+ x)   "   1313–1292   "
Ramses II.............. 67   "   1292–1225   "
Merneptah .... 10(+ x)   "   1225–1215   "
Amenmeses.... x   "   1215   "
Siptah .... 6(+ x)   "   1215–1209   "
Seti II................... 2(+ x)   "   1209–1205   "

Total.........142(+ 6x)   "   Minimum 145 years.

INTERIM.

Anarchy and reign of Syrian usurper, 5(+ x) years, 1205–1200 B. C.

TWENTIETH DYNASTY, 1200–1090 B. C.

Setnakht	1(+ x) years,	1200–1198	B. C.
Ramses III	31	"	1198–1167	"
Ramses IV	6	"	1167–1161	"
Ramses V	4(+ x)	"	1161–1157	"
Ramses VI..... x years ⎫				
Ramses VII... x " ⎬	15	"	1157–1142	"
Ramses VIII.. x " ⎭				
Ramses IX	19	"	1142–1123	"
Ramses X	1(+ x)	"	1123–1121	"
Ramses XI	x	"	1121–1118	"
Ramses XII	27(+ x)	"	1118–1090	"
Total	104(+ 5x)	"	Minimum 110 years.

TWENTY-FIRST DYNASTY, 1090–945 B. C.

Nesubenebded ⎫ Hrihor .... ⎭	x	years,	1090–1085	"
Pesibkhenno I...	17(+ x)	"	1085–1067	"
Paynozem I	40(+ x)	"	1067–1026	"
Amenemopet	49(+ x)	"	1026–976	"
Siamon	16(+ x)	"	976–958	"
Pesibkhenno II.	12(+ x)	"	958–945	"
Total	134(+ 6x)	"	Minimum 145 years.

TWENTY-SECOND DYNASTY, 945–745 B. C.

Sheshonk I	21(+ x) years,	945–924 B. C.
Osorkon I	36(+ x)	"	924–895	"
Takelot I	23(+ x)	"	895–874	"
Osorkon II	30(+ x)	"	874–853	"
Sheshonk II	00	"	(died c. 877 B. C. during coregency with Osorkon II.)
Takelot II	25(+ x)	"	860–834 B. C.

(7 years coregent with Osorkon II.)

Sheshonk III	52	years,	834–784 B. C.
Pemou	6(+ x)	"	784–782	"
Sheshonk IV	37(+ x)	"	782–745	"
Total	230(+ x)	"	
Allowance for possible coregencies	30		
Grand total	200(+ x)	"	Minimum 200 years.

TWENTY THIRD DYNASTY, 745-718 B. C.

Pedibast............................ 23 (+ x) years, 745-721 B. C.
Osorkon III .... 14 (+ x)   "
Takelot III...................... x   "
    Total .... 37 (+ 3x) "
Allowance for coregencies... 10   "
    Final total.................. 27 (+ x)   "   Minimum 27 years.

TWENTY FOURTH DYNASTY, 718-712 B. C.

Bekneranef (Bocchoris) 6 (+ x) years, 718-712 B. C.
          Minimum 6 years.

TWENTY FIFTH DYNASTY, 712-663 B. C.

Shabaka......... 12 years, 712-700 B. C.
Shabataka 12   "   700*-688   "
Taharka 26   "   688-663   "
    Total....... 50   "   Minimum 50 years.

TWENTY SIXTH DYNASTY, 663-525 B. C.

Psamtik I............................ 54 years, 663-609 B. C.
Necho 16   "   609-593   "
Psamtik II.......................... 5   "   593-588   "
Apries (Hophra).................. 19   "   588-569   "
Ahmose II 44   "   569-525   "
Psamtik III......A few months   525   "
    Total..... 138   "

CONQUEST BY THE PERSIANS (TWENTY SEVENTH DYNASTY), 525 B. C.
Egypt a Persian province with short interruptions by ephemeral native
  dynasties (Twenty Eight to Thirty) 525-332, B. C.

ALEXANDER THE GREAT SEIZED EGYPT 332 B. C.
Egypt under Alexander and his successors, the Ptolemies, 332 to 30 B. C.
EGYPT BECAME A ROMAN PROVINCE 30 B. C.

INDEX

Note: Names of Pharaohs and queens who served as such are in small capitals.

A.

Aba, 571

Ababdeh, 6

Abbasids, 214

Abdashirta, 352, 382

Abdkhiba, 387, 388

Abimilki, 336, 383

Abram, earliest mention of, 530, Fig. 180

Abram, field of, 530

Absha, 188

Abshai, 188

Aburoâsh, 120

Abu Simbel, 451; begun by Seti I, 415; visit of Khetasar depicted at, 439; Psamtik's II's expedition reaches, 585

Abusir, pyramids of, 129

Abydos, 37, 44, 132, 168; reputed home of Osiris, 60; northern boundary of Theban Kingdom, 150, 151; sanctity of burial at, 172; memorial tablets at, 172, 182, 185-86, 187, 212; as abode of the dead, 174; access to oases from, 182; new Twelfth Dynasty temple at, 196; Seti I's temple at, 415, 416, 417, 420-21; Ramses II completes Seti I's temple at, 420-21; Ramses II's temple at, 443, 445-46

Abyssinia, 4, 8; Christian kingdom of, 561

Achæans, 467

Acre, 294

Administration, Local, in Old Kingdom, 79, 80; in Middle Kingdom, see Nomarch; in Empire, 236-37

Adultery, 173

Ægean, 260, 261, 262; ware in Egypt in first two dynasties, 49; commerce with, in Old Kingdom, 142-43; commerce with, in Middle Kingdom, 188-89; influence of Thutmose III in, 305; commerce with Egypt in Empire, 337-38; races plunder Delta, 462

Ægina, 591

Æolians, 590

Africa, 3; inner, 6, 138; earliest exploration of inner, 138-42; pigmies of inner, 139-40; northern Mediterranean peoples migrating to, 467; circumnavigated by Necho's expedition, 585

Africans (see also Nubians and Negroes), kinship with Egyptians and imigration into Egypt, 7, 25-26

Africans, 14

Agriculture, 9, 28-29, 92

Ahmose I, reign of, 225-33, 233-35, 252, 253; rebellions against, 226, 228; buildings of, 252; mother of, 252; age of, 252; tomb of, 252; body of, 252, Fig. 252; compared with Psamtik I, 567

Ahmose II, see Amasis

Ahmose (wife of Thutmose I), 255; death of, 266; children of, 266; mother of Hatshepsut by Amon, 273

Ahmose-Pen-Nekhbet, under Ahmose I, 227; under Amenhotep I, 253; under Thutmose I, 256, 263-64; under Thutmose II, 270; under Hatshepsut, 272

Ahmose Son of Ebana, under Ahmose I, 225, 226-27, 228, 234; under Amenhotep I, 253, 254; under Thutmose I, 256, 263-64

Ajalon, 387, 530

Akhetaton, founding of, 364-66; landmarks (stelas) of, 365, Fig. 140; decay of, 392-93; destruction of temples of, 402; destruction of tombs of, 402

Akhthoes, 148

Akizzi, 335-36, 352

Akko, 389

Alabaster, source of, 6, 93; vessels of, 39; floors of, 120

Alabastronopolis, 399, 400, 402

Alasa (see Cyprus), 518

Aleppo, 303, 314, 427; as ally of Hittites, 424; rescue of king of, 433-34

Alexander, 320
Alexandria, 5, 569
Alexandrians, 576
Algebra, 100
Ali Baba, tale of, 312, 453
Allah, 248
Aloa, 561
Alphabet, earliest appearance of, 45;
introduced into Syria from Egypt,
484; transmitted to Greeks, 484
Altaqu, scene of first battle between
Assyria and Egypt, 551–52
Altar, 62
Amâda, 317, 414, Amenhotep II's tablet at, 326
AMASIS (AHMOSE II), rise of, 589;
defeats Apries, 589, 589–90; coregency with Apries, 589; treatment of the Greeks, 590–91; buildings of, 591; prosperity under, 591;
draws upon temple wealth, 592;
thwarted in Asia by Nebuchadrezzar, 592–93; acquires Cyprus, 593;
alliances against Persia, 593–94;
character of, 594–95
Amenardis, adopted by Shepnupet I,
546; reinstated by Shabaka, 553;
adopts Shepnupet II, 558
Amenemhab, 301, 302, 303, 304, 311,
313, 314, 315, 316
AMENEMHET I, rise of, 155; treatment of nomarchs, 155–56, 161–62;
prosperity under, 177; conspiracy
against, 177–78; campaign in Nubia,
178; instruction of, 178–79, 204;
pyramid of, 198, 201; portrait-
statues of, 201; compared with
Psamtik I, 567
AMENEMHET II, 201, as crown prince
in Nubia, 181; reign of, 182–83;
pyramid of, 198, 201; portrait-
statues of, 201
AMENEMHET III, reign of, 189–95,
208; equipment of stations in
Sanai, 190–91, 208; irrigation works
of, 191–95; prosperity under, 195;
buildings of, 196; pyramid of, 198;
St. Petersburg portrait of, 202, Fig.
90
AMENEMHET IV, reign of, 208; pyramid of, 198
Amenemhet (vizier of Mentuhotep
IV), 153–55; possible identity with
Amenemhet I, 154–55
AMENEMOPET, 524–25
AMENHOTEP I, 252, 296; reign of,
253–55; Nubian campaign, 253–54;
Libyan campaign, 254; Asiatic cam-
paign, 254, 257, 263; in Phœnicia
(?), 298; death of, 255; tomb of,

278, 525; becomes local god of
Thebes, 459; royal mummies concealed in old tomb of, 525
AMENHOTEP II, coregency of, 318;
Asiatic war, 323–25; Nubian campaign of, 325–26; buildings of, 326;
jubilee of, 326–27; body of, 327,
Fig. 121, 511
AMENHOTEP III, 242; parentage of,
328; accession of, 329; marriage to
Tiy, 329–30; Nubian campaign,
330–31; supremacy in Asia, 332;
letter to Kallimmasin of Babylon, 332; royal marriage betweeen
Babylon and house of, 333; marriage to Gilukhipa, 333; at Sidon,
337, 352; luxury of, 339; development of architecture by, 343–46;
monumental development of Thebes
by, 344–46; buildings of, 343–46,
348, 351; obelisks of, 344, 345;
mortuary temple of, 345–46, 348,
471; splendour of, 348–52; month
named after, 350; as hunter, 350–
51; modern tendency of, 351; worship of, 351; jubilees of, 351–52;
Hittites invade dependencies of,
352–53; death of, 353–54; Ikhnaton
erases name of, 363–64; Merneptah
destroys mortuary temple of, 471;
robbery of tomb of, 510
AMENHOTEP IV, see IKHNATON
Amenhotep, son of Hapi, 341, 344
Amenhotep (High Priest of Amon),
508–10
Ameni, 160–61, 162, 180, 181, 182
AMENMESES, 472
Amki, 382
Ammon, 551, 586
Amon (see also High Priest of Amon,
Priests and Karnak), rise of, 170–
71; estate of, 239; organization of
priests under high priest of, 247;
supremacy of, 248, 362; father of
Hatshepsut, 273; oracle of, 274, 277,
400, 520–21, 522–23, 524, 527, 534;
royal mortuary temples of, 279;
Thutmose III's gifts to, 294; reorganization of temple of, 310;
hymn to Thutmose III, 319; love
of truth, 320; claims to be universal god, 359; hostility toward Aton,
361–62, 390–91; victory of Aton
over, 362–63; persecution of, 363–
64; restoration of worship of, 393;
triumph of, 403; reinsertion of
name of, 393, 402; barge of, 410,
486, 513–19; Seti I's restoration of
inscriptions to, 414; growth in
power of, 456–57; disproportionate

wealth of, 492–96; gains gold-country in Nubia, 457, 494; hymn to, 458; personal faith in, 458; temple of, in Syria, 298, 484; Ramses III's temple of, in Delta residence, 487; Ramses III's splendid gifts to, 490–91, 492–96; feasts of, 492–93; gains enlarged control over revenues, 509; bestower of civilization, 515, 516; god of the Nubian kingdom, 538; wealth controlled by Nubians, 546, 558; wealth controlled by Saites, 567, 585; decay of, 583

Amon-of-the-Way, 513, 515, 517

Amon, high priest of, 239, 272, 362, 508, 513, 514; also chief treasurer, 362; also vizier, 272, 362; power of, 302; growth in power of, 456–57, 494–95, 507, 508–10, 511, 519, 520; gains hereditary control of office, 456–57, 508; gains throne, 494–95, 507, 520–21; becomes commander-in-chief of the army, 519; becomes viceroy of Nubia, 520; theocratic rule introduced by, 522–23; in Twenty First Dynasty, 520–28; commands native militia, 526; in the Twenty Second Dynasty, 529–31, 532, 533–34; declining power of, 553; final fall of, 557, 567; woman becomes, 567, 586

Amon-Re, see Amon

Amor, 382, 383, 412; Egyptian trade with, 447–48; city of Merneptah in, 465; occupied by Northern peoples, 478, 479; Ramses III in, 483; included in empire of Ramses III, 483

Amorite, see Amor

Amusements, in Old Kingdom, 89–91

Anath, in Egypt, 449, 460

Anath-herte, 449

Animals, extinct, 30

Animals, sacred, 60; worship of, 460; Saite excesses, 575–76

Annals, earliest, 45, 109; of Thutmose III, 312–13

Anshan, 593

Anubis, 46; as embalmer, 58

Aphroditopolis, nomarch of, surviving under Empire, 228, 542, 544

Apion, Josephus against, 215

Apis, 46, 557; Saite popularity of, 575

Apollos, archaic, 580

Apophis, in Avaris, 216, 223; altar of, 217; wide rule of, 218; three kings named, 221; mathematical papyrus of, 221, 222; relations with

Thebes, 223–24; tale of, 215–16, 223–24, 453–54

Apries, 586; resumes attempt to recover Syria-Palestine, 586; Asiatic war, 586–87; attacks Tyre and Sidon, 586; repelled by Nebuchadrezzar, 587; prosperity of, 588; trouble with mercenaries, 588–89; Cyrenian expedition, 588; forsaken by the Egyptians, 589; defeated by Amasis, 589, 589–90; coregent with Amasis, 589; slain, 590; buried by Amasis, 590

Arabia, 258, 259, 549, 565

Arabians, 217, 219

Arad, 530

Araina, 314

Aramæans, 259, 577

Arch, 101

Archery, 234

Architect, earliest, 42; chief, in Old Kingdom, 83; Imhotep, 112; in Empire, 254–55, 265, 266, 271–72, 278–79, 295, 306, 340–41, 366

Architecture (see also Dwelling, Temple, Tomb), earliest, 27–28; early dynasties, 41–42; earliest stone, 42, Fig. 25; in Old Kingdom, 106–07; of temple, 106–07; Babylonian, 107; progress of, under Imhotep, 113; in Twelfth Dynasty, 200–01; in Empire, 340–46, 417, 450, 486–88; Egyptian origin of cathedral of architecture, 343–44; in Twenty Second Dynasty, 531; in Saite period, 573 and frontispiece

Archives of State, 82, 240; vizier in charge of state, 240–41; legal, 510–11

Arko, Sebekhotep the Great at, 212, 257; Thutmose I at, 256

Armour, Syrian, 292

Army (see also Troops, and Mercenaries), in Old Kingdom, 84, 134–35; provisioning of, 153; in Middle Kingdom, 167–68; in Empire, 233–35, 243, 285, 404; weapons of, 234; of Thutmose III, 285; lack of discipline in, 299; mercenaries in, see Mercenaries; size of, 424, 425; decline of, 441, 464; reorganized by Ramses III, 477; in Nubian period, 552; in Saite period, 568–69, 569–70

Arrapakhitis, 315

Arsinoe, 194

Art, of early dynasties, 39–40; of Old Kingdom, 102–07, 129; of Middle Kingdom, 201–02; impersonal characters of, 207; of Empire, 341–49, 378, 417, 448, 487–88; interpretation of life in, 346–47; of Amarna period, 378; decadence of, 487–88; of the Libyan-Nubian period, 548–49; of the Saite period, 571, 572–73, 579–80

Artatama, 333; Thutmose IV marries daughter of, 328

Aruna, 286 (map), 287, 288

Arvad, 260, 479; Thutmose III captures, 298; revolt of, 301; as ally of Hittites, 424; monuments of Necho at, 587

Ashdod, 580

Ashurbanipal, 556–66; defeats Taharka, 556–57; retakes Memphis and possibly captures Thebes, 556–57; drives out Tanutamon, 559; captures Thebes, 559–60; relinquishes hold on the West, 565–66

Asia (see also Syria, Palestine and Syria-Palestine), 136, 180, 203, 280; desert of, 3; invasion from, 7, 25–26, 214–19; intimate intercourse with, 322; Egyptian boundary in, 264, 303, 324; supremacy of Egypt in, 332–37; loss of Egyptian Empire in, 389; Egyptian trade with, 447–48; gods of, in Egypt, 460

Asia Minor, 3, 188, 260, 566; Egyptian notion of, 261; peoples of, 262–63, 424; high position in Egypt gained by natives of, 497, 500

Asiatics, 178, 239, 263, 319; in Egypt, 215; Hyksos called, 217; as captives in Egypt, 308–09

Askalon, 387; taken by Ramses II, 435–36; revolts against Merneptah, 465; captured by Merneptah, 470; captured by Sennacherib, 551; captured by Necho, 582

Assuan, 7; tombs of, 138

Assyria, 259, 322; beginnings of Assyria, 263; kings of, 292; sends gifts to Thutmose III, 296; seeks Egyptian alliance, 332; Amenhotep III sends gold to king of, 334–35; some Tanite sends crocodile to Tiglath-Pileser I of, 518; Takelot II sends a thousand men against Shalmaneser II of, 534; Western supremacy of, 549–60; fall of, 582, 583

Assyrians, 216, 217, 534

Astarte, in Egypt, 448, 460; temple in Memphis, 448

Astronomy, 100

Astyages, 593

Atbara, 4, 127

Athens, 591

Athribis, 497, 543, 544; under the

Assyrians, 557; great religious centre in Saite period, 575

Atika, 485

Atlantic, 3

Aton, rise of, 360; identity of Re and, 360; nature of, 360–61; symbol of, 361; temples of, 361, 364, 366–67, 389, 393, 402; hostility toward Amon, 362; becomes sole god, 362–64; city of, see Akhetaton; inauguration of temple of, 366–67; high priest of, 360, 367; hymns to, 371–76; name changed, 390; decline of, 393, 402; fall of, 402–03; temples of, destroyed, 402

" Attendants," 167

Atum, 59

Augustus, 166, 547

Avaris, 217; Asiatics in, 215; siege of, 215, 226; length of siege of, 226–27; Apophis in, 216; Sutekh, god of, 217; disappearance of, 218; canal of, 226; capture of, 226

Ayan, 252, 484; quarries at, 93

Aziru, 352, 382, 383, 386; Egyptian deputy slain by, 385

B.

Baal, 22, 259; in Egypt, 448, 460; temple in Memphis, 448

Baal (King of Tyre), 555

Baba, 225

Baboons, 276

Babylon, 259, 595; Middle Kingdom commerce with, 188; decline of, 263; sends gifts to Thutmose III, 304; loses commercial leadership, 263, 322; struggle with Assyria, 565, 567; retrospective character of revival in, 576

Babylon (in Egypt), 543, 544

Babyionia, 28, 447; life after death, 173; influence of, in the West, 262; loss of influence in the West, 322; Thutmose IV in alliance with, 328; Amenhotep III in alliance with, 332; royal marriages between Egypt and, 333, 379; Egyptian trade with, 388–89, 447–48; decline and fall of Second Empire of, 593

Bagdad, 520

Bahr Yusuf, 5, 6; used by Piankhi, 540, 542

Balances, 277, 491

Ba'lat, 259

Banishment, 404, 524

Barge, temple, 410

Barley, 92

Barque of the sun-god, see Sun-god

Barter, 97
Basilica, 344
Bast, 59
"Beautiful are the Ways of Khekure," 183
Beduin, in Sanai, 48, 134–35, 190, 191; in Palestine, 135, 270, 315, 386, 409–10, 484; on west shore of Red Sea, 142; as mercenaries, 386, 387; absorb Palestine, 387–89, 409–10; defeated by Seti I, 410; admitted to Egypt, 187–88, 447
Bega, 25
Beket, 162
Bek, 366, 378
Beketaton, 366
Bekhten, 440
Belgium, 6
Ben-Anath, 449
Beni-Hasan, 160, 170, 187; birthplace of Khufu, 116; tombs of, 156, 160; inscription of Hatshepsut at, 215, 280
Ben-'Ozen, 449, 471
Berber, 466
Berût, during Hittite invasion, 386; stelæ near, 423, 439, Fig. 159
Beth-Anoth, 530
Bethhoron, 530
Beth-Shean, 512, 530
Bet Khallâf, 114; great mastaba of, 113, Fig. 62
Bikhuru, 386, 388
Bint-Anath, 449, 450
Biography, 109, 134; earliest, 133
Birds, as souls, 64
Birket el-Kurun, 192–93
Bitter Lakes, 115
Black Sea, 577
Blasphemy, 173
Blemmyes, 561
Boat (see also Ships), earliest dynastic; Fig. 27; earliest hunting, 30; earliest cargo, 30; earliest sail, 30; as shrine, 62; of ferryman of the dead, 65, 176; building in Old Kingdom, 95, 136, 137; kinds of, 95; Nile traffic in, 97, 114, 136, 164; model, 176; Sesostris III's mortuary, 176, Fig. 82; heavy transportation in, 266, 281, 282
BOCCHORIS, reign of, 546–47; sends gifts to Sargon, 550; death of, 550
Body-guard, of Pharaoh, 235, 243, Fig. 163
Book of the Dead, 250; rise of, 175; growth of, 249; Saite recension of, 571
"Book of the Portals," 250
"Book of the Two Ways," 175

"Book of What is in the Netherworld," 250
Bow and arrows, earliest use of, 30
"Bow-Land," 178
Branchidæ, Milesian, 583
Brick, earliest, 27–28; making as an industry, 94–95; pyramids of, 198–200, 224
Briefs, legal, Old Kingdom, 81–82
Bronze, 93, 263, 274; Saite plastic in, 573
Bubastis, 59, 119, 216, 414; Twelfth Dynasty in, 197, 201; Twenty Second Dynasty makes residence at, 527; Twenty Second Dynasty buildings in, 531, 533
Building (see also Architecture), captives employed in, 309, 414
Burded, 128, 140
Burial, archaic, 34–35; at Abydos, 172, 196
Burraburyash, 379, 389
Business, 97–98, 195; records, 98
Busiris, 60, 543
Butlers of Pharaoh, 497, 498, 500
Buto (city), 34, 44; religious importance in Saite times, 575
Buto (goddess), 34, 38
Buyuwawa, 526, 527
Byblos, 259, 260, 352; Egyptian temples at, 323; during Hittite invasion, 382, 383, 385, 386; Egyptian envoys detained at, 512; mission of Wenamon at, 513–18

C.

Cairo, 520, 548; museum, 224; citadel of, 309
Calasiries, 568, 569
Calendar, introduction of, 32; character of, 32–33; dating, 44; year, 44; control of, 244
Caliph, 520, 570
Cambyses, 326, 595; expedition to Nubia, 561
Canaan, 410; Merneptah wastes, 470
Canaanites, 259
Canal, through First Cataract, 136, 183, 184, 256, 257, 318; into Fayum, 193; canal out of Fayum, 5; of Avaris, 226; connecting Nile with Red Sea, 142, 276, 277, 411, 485–86, 584; at Tharu, 411
Canopic Branch, 474, 590
Caphtor, 512
Cappadocia, 188, 380
Captives, foreign, arrival of, 308–09, 325, 411, 412; disposal of, 309, 328, 329, 339, 414, 482; sacrifice of, 325, 411; labour of, 309, 414, 446

Caravan-conductor, 138
Carchemish, 303; as ally of Hittites, 424; battle of, 583–84
Carians, 566; as mercenaries, 566, 568, 569; Memphite quarter for, 577
Carmel, 188, 258, 287, 288, 387
Carthaginian colonies of Phœnicia, 261
Caste, unknown in Egypt, 574
Cataracts, 4, 6; commerce through, 7; canal through first, 136, 183, 184, 256; as a barrier, 136; region of, 136–37; tribes of, 136–37
Cattle (see also Herds), 237; yards as Department of White House, 237–38; due from officials, 238; wild, 350; owned by temples, 492
Cavalry, 234
Cedar, 252, 328, 410; source of, 95, 168, 265, 513–17
Cemeteries, archaic, 34; Old Kingdom, 116
Census, 44, 165–66, 211
Chapel, mortuary, see Temple, Mortuary
"Chapters of Going Forth by Day," 175
Chariot, 226, 264, 289, 290, 292, 319, 381, 447; making, 235, 260
Chariotry, 234, 381; at battle of Kadesh, 428–32
Charms, protecting the dead, 69
Chiaroscuro, earliest, 378
"Chief of All Works of the King," 83
China, 351
Chinese, 576, 579
Chios, 590
Christian, 64
Chronology, 21–23, 597–601
Cilicians, 565; as allies of Hittites, 424
Cimmerians, 565, 566
Cinnamon, 276
Circle, Great, 56, 261, 319
Citizen, 167, 168
"Citizens of the Army," Middle Kingdom, 246; in Empire, 246, 404
Civilization, earliest, 26–31
Clazomenæ, 590
Clear-Story, Egyptian origin of, 344
Climate, 7–8, 9–10
Cnidus, 590
Cnossos, Hyksos remains in, 218; monuments of Khian in, 218; Egyptian commerce with, 337
Coffin, 69
Colonnade, 274, Fig. 113, Egypt the source of the, 107, Fig. 61, 198; at Luxor, 343, Fig. 128

Colossi, see Statue
Column, 107, Figs. 60 and 61; Saite origin of Ptolemaic, 573
Commerce, 260, 485; with the North, 337–39, 381, 447; regulation of, 338–39; Saite revival of, 577
Commodus, 214
"Divine Consort," 248, 546, 558, 567, 585
Conspiracy, 134, 177–78, 241, 242, 498–500
Constantinople, obelisk, 306
Contracts, 70–71, 165, 240
Copper, earliest use of, 28; protodynastic vessels of, 39; tools of, 39, 93; Sinaitic mines of, 48; smith, 93, 169; vessels of, 94; as money, 97, 195; life-size statue of, 104; mines of Cyprus, 260, 313; from Syria, 325; weapons of, 469; mines of Atika, 485
Coptos, 212; route to Red Sea, 128, 159, 182; nomarch of, 159; organization of gold-country of, 310
Corinth, 580
Cornelius Gallus, 166
Cosmetic, 187–88, 276
Costume, primitive, 27; royal, see Pharaoh; in Old Kingdom, 88–89; in Empire, 340
"Council," 241
Count, in the Middle Kingdom, 157–58, 161; in the Empire, 237; becomes administrative title, 237
Court of Pharaoh, 74–75, 243
Courts of Justice, see Justice
Cow of the sky, 54, Fig. 30, 56
Craftsmen, see also Industries, 169, 170, 202–03, 346, 573
Crete, 261; Egyptian influence in, 338; Philistines migrating from, 512
Criminals, trial of, 240; punishment of, 404, 500, 523, 527
Crocodile, 91, 319; as foe of the dead, 175, 194
Crocodilopolis, 194, 542
Crœsus, 593
Crowns, 32, 38
Crystal, rock, 39
Cultus, earliest, 62
Cuneiform, use in the West, 262; used by Hittites, 380
Currency, see Money
Custodian, under-, 134; superior, 134
Custom houses, 338
Cyaxares, 582, 583
Cyprus, 260, 319, 338, 381, 479, 517; vassal of Egypt, 305; tribute of, 313, 315, 411; Egyptian commerce

with, 337, 447; defeated by Necho, 586

Cyrene, 588, 591

Cyrus, 593

D.

Dahabiyeh, 95

Dalailama, 351

Damascus, 352, 353; taken by Tiglath-pileser III, 549

Damiette, 5

Danaoi, 477

Daphnae, 569, 591

Dardanians, as allies of Hittites, 424

Dashur, stone pyramids of, 114; double slope pyramid of, 115; Middle Kingdom pyramids of, 198

Dating, method of, 44

David, 205

Daughter, inheritance through eldest, 161

Dead, equipment of, 63, 67–73, 176, Fig. 81, 251–52; equipment of royal, 41, 71–73, 176, 251; abode of, 64–65, 174, 175; food and clothing for, 65, 69, 70; endowment of, 70, 71, 265; ferryman of, 65; voyage of, 65, 176; earliest ethical test awaiting, 65, 67; dwelling in tomb, 67–68; burial of, 69; charms for protecting, 69 (see also Book of the Dead); cultus statue of, 69–70; Osirian judgment of, 173–74, 175; destiny of, 64–65, 174; dangers and foes of, 174–75; intercede with gods for the living, 421, 506; afflict the living, 460–61

Dead Sea, 258

Deben, 195

Decadence, history of, 505–64; nine Ramessids, 505–21; final loss of Asiatic empire in, 511–19; triumph of priests of Amon in, 508–10, 519–26; Tanitic supremacy in, 523–28; Libyan supremacy in, 528–36; Nubian supremacy in, 537–61; Assyrian conquest in, 555–67; rise of Saites in, 540–46, 556, 565

Dedefre, 119–20, 123

Dedu, home of Osiris, 60

Dedwen, 184

Deeds and transfers, 567

Delphians, 591

Delta (see also Delta), Kingdom of the, 31–32; symbols of, 32, 38; capitals, 33–34; patron divinities, 34; history of, 35–36; union with Upper Egypt, 36, 42–44, 47; rebellions against Upper Egypt, 47; door of, in the palace, 78; administra-

tion of, 79–80; reëstablished by Nesubenebded, 511

Delta (see also Kingdom of), 5, 214; marshals of, 5; coast of, 6; immigration through, 7; rains in, 7, 10; eastern frontier fortresses of, 115, 178, 188, 447, 569, 591; buildings and prosperity under the Twelfth Dynasty, 188, 197; in Thirteenth Dynasty, 211; Hyksos rule in eastern, 215, 216; Libyan invasion of western, 47, 49, 179, 254, 411, 462, 466–71, 474, 477–79, 481–83, 526–27; Thutmose III restores, 309; center of commerce, 322; becomes seat of power, 442; Nineteenth Dynasty develops eastern, 442–43; frontier fortresses of western, 469, 478–79, 481, 482, 569; royal residence in, 442–43, 486; absorbed by Nesubenebded, 511, 515; Libyan absorption of, 526–27; Libyan lords of, 528–29, 532–33, 534, 535–36, 555–56, 568; conquered by Piankhi, 543–44; conquered by Esarhaddon, 555–56; plots with Taharka against Esarhaddon, 556; against Ashurbanipal, 557; finally lost to Assyria, 565; plundered by Greeks and Carians, 566; Psamtik I suppresses dynasts of, 567; final supremacy of, 573

Demotic, rise and introduction of, 574

Dendera, temple, 35, 59; goddess of, 59; temple built by Khufu, 119

Denyen, 477, 479

Deper, 436

Der el-Bahri, Hatshepsut's temple at, begun, 269; Thutmose II's reliefs in, 270–71; birth reliefs in, 272–73; building resumed, 273; character of, 274, 277–78; Punt reliefs, 277–78; reliefs of obelisk-transport, 282; concealment of royal mummies at, 525

Dêr el-Bahri, Mentuhotep II's temple at, 152; royal mummies discovered at, 224; Hatshepsut's temple at, 269, 270–71

Desert, of northern Africa continued in Asia, 3; limestone plateau of, 5; Libyan, 6, 192; Arabian, 6; earliest man in Libyan, 25

Destruction of man, 56

Desuk, 119

Diodorus, 242, 584

Diorite, 28, 39, 93

Districts, administrative, in Old Kingdom, 79; in Middle Kingdom, 165; in Empire, 236–37

Dodekaschoinos, gift of, by Zoser, 112, by Ramses III, 491, 495
Dogs, 276
Dog River (Nahr el-Kelb), 423; stela of Esarhaddon at, 556
Door, false, 68
" Door of the North," Abydos as, 151
"Door of the South," 135; keeper of the, 135, 150, 152–53, 154
Dor, Thekel kingdom at, 512, 513
Dorians, 590
Drama, earliest known, 171, 207
Dream, 468, 558
Dushratta, 33, 381; letter to Amenhotep III from, 333; repels Hittites, 352; writes to Tiy, 379; writes to Ikhnaton, 379
Dwarf, 41, 139–40
Dwelling, earliest, 27–28; of lower classes, 86–87; Map 1; of the nobles, 88, 89, 90; architecture of, 106, 200
Dynasties, 13–14
—— First and Second, 127; civilization of, 37–40; history of, 36–37, 40–50; tombs of, 40–42, 49; fate of tombs of, 49–50, 420; prosperity of, 48; public works of, 48; commerce with Ægean, 49; later reverence for, 415; Seti I's list of, 415; Abydos chapel to, 415
—— Third, 40; neglect of Horus-worship by, 46; war with Delta, 47; history of, 112–16
—— Fourth, 127; history of, 116–23; inner circle of related officials of, 77; origin of, 116; folk-tale of fall of, 122–23
—— Fifth, 156; folk-tale of rise of, 122–23, 203; history of, 123–30
—— Sixth, history of, 131–44
—— Seventh and Eighth, 147; state of country during, 148–49
—— Ninth and Tenth (see also Heracleopolis), 148; supported by Siut, 149
—— Eleventh, 160; history of, 149–55
—— Twelfth, origin of, 154–55; residence of, 157, 194; history of, 177–208; Nubian conquest of, 180–87; relations with Asia, 187–91; irrigation enterprises of, 191–94; development of eastern Delta by, 188; exploitation of Sinai, 163, 164, 182, 190–91; buildings of, 195–200; art of, 201–02; literature of, 203–08; fall of, 208
—— Thirteenth, reign of, 211–13; at Thebes, 212–13

Dynasty, Fourteenth, 214
—— Fifteenth to Seventeenth, 221
—— Seventeenth, 225
—— Eighteenth (see also Empire, First Period), rise of, 225–29; history of, 253–365
—— Nineteenth (see also Empire, Second Period), vandalism of, 195; history of, 399–474; anarchy at close of, 473–74
—— Twentieth (see also Empire, Second Period and Decadence), accession of, 474–77; history of, 477–521; power of priests and fall of Empire in, 489–521
—— Twenty First, accession of, 511, 513, 514, 515; history of, 522–27; decline under, 524–25; weakness abroad, 526; rise of Israel during, 526
—— Twenty Second (see also Libyans), rise and accession of, 526–27; history of, 527–35; transfers to Bubastis, 527; Egyptianized character of, 533; civil war during, 532, 534; vandalism of, 535
—— Twenty Third (Nubian Period), 535–36, 543, 546; decline of Egypt under, 547–48; conquest by Nubians in, 539–50
—— Twenty Fourth (Nubian Period), 546–47
—— Twenty Fifth (Nubian Dynasty), history of, 550–60
—— Twenty Sixth, see Restoration

E.

Earth-god, 54, 55
Eavesdropping, 173
Ebgig, 194
Ebony, 39, 127, 136, 276, 277
Ecstacy, 513–14
Edfu, 4, 37, 113, 178, 196
Edom, plots with Egypt against Assyria, 550–51, 551
Edomite, 447
Education, in Old Kingdom, 98–100
Egypt, extent of, 4; area of, 5–6; natural boundaries of, 7; shape of, 7; local differences produced by shape of, 7; climate, 7–8; aspect of land, 10–11; isolation of, 6, 10; influence of land on people, 10–11, 53, 61; influence of, abroad, 11–12; anciently regarded as source of civilization, 515, 516
—— Lower, kingdom of, see Delta
—— Upper, kingdom of, 33; capitals of, 33; symbols of, 33, 38; divini-

ties of, 34; history of, 35–36; union with Delta, 36, 42–44, 47; door of, in the palace, 78; administration of, 79–80; governing Delta, 132; becomes two principalities (see Heracleopolis and Thebes), 528–29, 532; conquered by Piankhi, 539–42; conquered by Esarhaddon, 556

Egyptians, ethnic affinities, 25; physical characteristics, 26–27; civilization of, earliest, 26–31; love of nature, 91; love of beauty, 102; unwarlike spirit of, 135

Ekereth, see Ugarit

Ekwesh, 467

El Bersheh, 163, 168

Eleans, 585

Electrum, Fig. 27, 127, 187; by the bushel, 281; by the ton, 308

Elephant, 30, 181; in Syria, 271, 304

Elephantine, 4, 30, 112, 132, Fig. 74, 138, 141; Old Kingdom nobles of, 135, 137–38, 139–42, 168; expeditions of nobles of, 137–42; Middle Kingdom nobles of, 181; Amenhotep II's tablet at, 326; Saite garrison at, 569

Eleutheros, 259, 299

Eliakim, 583

El Kab, 33, 38, 44, 226, 228; early Nubian frontier at, 186, 253–54, 255; great wall built by Amenemhet III, 196, 208; as ally of Thebes, 225–29; survival of nomarchs of, 229; nomarch's rule south of Thebes, 229; country south of, transferred to vizier, 236; northern Nubia governed by mayor of, 253–54

El Khargeh, first intercourse with, 182

Elam, 565

Eloquent Peasant, tale of the, 204

Embalmers, 141, 251

Empire, rise of, 225–33; State in, 233–45; society in, 245–47; army in, 233–35, 243, 285
   First Period:
      History of, 266–395; internal feuds, 266–83; conquest of Syria-Palestine, 284–354; religious revolution, 355–78; loss of Asiatic empire, 379–89; fall of, 389–95; religion in, 247–52, 355–78; literature in, 350; art in, 341–49, 378; luxury in, 339–40, 348–51; changes in life in, 340
   Second Period:
      Restoration, 399–422; partial recovery of Asiatic empire, 423–41; cosmopolitan character of, 447–50; limits of empire, 450; army in, 404, 424–25, 448–49, Fig. 163, 485; art of, 417, 448, 450–53, 487–88; literature of, 453–55; religion of, 401–03, 455–60; sacerdotalization of State in, 456–57

Emu, 276

Enekhnes-Merire, 134, 139

Enekhnesneferibre, adopted by Nitocris, 585; becomes High Priest of Amon, 586

Enenkhet, 142

Enkhosnepaaton, 392

Enkhu, 221

Enneads, 56

Ensigns, on early boats, 30

Eratosthenes, 143

Ereth, 483

Erkatu, 316

Ernen, 437

Erwenet, 424

Esarhaddon, 555–56; conquest of Delta by, 555–56; takes Memphis, 555; controls Upper Egypt, 556; Dog River (Nahr el-Kelb) stela of, 556, Fig. 158; Senjirli stela of, 556, Fig. 181; death of, 556

Esdraelon, plain of (see also Jezreel), 258, 287, 288, 291; harvest of, 292

Eshmunen, 473

Esneh, 160; El Kab nomarchs hold, 229

Ethics, earliest, 65–66, 67; influence from Osiris myth, 173–74, 250

Ethiopia, see Nubia

Ethiopian Dynasty, see Twenty Fifth Dynasty

Ethiopians, see Nubians

Etruscans, 467

Euphrates, 3, 259, 284; Egyptian designation of, 11; Middle Kingdom commerce on, 188; first campaign to (?), 254; northern boundary of conquest, 257; valley of, 258; sources of, 261; Mitannians on, 262–63; Thutmose I's boundary tablet at, 264, 303; Thutmose III crosses, 303, 306; Thutmose III's boundary tablet at, 303; Amenhotep II's boundary tablet at, 324; reached by Necho, 582, 583

Europe (see also Ægean, Greek, Ionians, Mycenæan, etc.), earliest traces of, in Egypt, 189

Eusebius, 14

Ewibre, 202, Fig. 88, 208
Extradition, treaty of, 438
Eye, as a noble, 355, 369; as king, 394; tomb at Akhetaton, 394; tomb at Thebes, 394
Ezekiel, 593

F.

Family, 85
Famine, 160, 161
"Favourite Place of Re," 124
Fayence, 95, 573
Fayum, 5; 544; origin of, 6; irrigation works of Twelfth Dynasty in, 191–95, 198; submits to Piankhi, 544–45
Feasts, religious, 62, 401; of victory, 294, 482; of Opet, 294, 309, 393, 400, 420, 492, 541
Fenkhu, 287
Feudal, age, 151–229; lords disappear, 229; organization of Sheshonk I, 528; lords under Psamtik I, 567–68; lords in Saite period, 567–68, 575
Fief, 161
"First of the Westerners," 66
Fish, 93
Fishing, 90–91
Flax, 96
Flint, early wrought, 28
Florence, 548
Fly, Order of the, 301
"Followers of His Majesty," 167
Food, 88
Furniture, earliest, 28; of royal palace, 39, 88; in royal tomb, 41; of nobles, 88; of leather, 96; Syrian, 292

G.

Galilee, taken by Ramses II, 436
Galla, 25
Gaza, 285, 409; captured by Necho, 582
Gebelen, 160; Hyksos monuments at, 221
Gebel Zebâra, 416
Gem-Aton, 361, 364, 393
Geometry, 100–01
Gezer, 387; Sixth Dynasty scarab at, 135; Middle Kingdom monuments at, 187; Hittite pottery at, 262; Philistine pottery at, 512; Thutmose IV at, 328; revolts against Merneptah, 465; captured by Merneptah, 466, 470; presented by Sheshonk I to Solomon, 529
Gibeon, 530
Gilia, 334
Ginti-Kirmil, 387

Giraffe, 30
Gizeh, pyramids of, 101, 117–19, 120, 121, 122, Map 2; museum of, 139
Glaze, earliest, 28, 39; Old Kingdom, 96
God, rise of idea of universal, 359, 376–77; Ikhnaton expunges plural of, 363; beneficence of, 376–77
Gods, chief, 53–60; expungement of names of, 363–64; Ikhnaton expunges the word, 363; triumph and restoration of, 401–02; reinsertion of names of, 402; Semitic, in Egypt, 448, 460; of Asia in Egypt, 448, 460
"God's-Land," 127, 274, 276, 280, 319
Gold, sources of, 6, 94, 136, 181, 310, 314, 317, 331, 490, 491, 494; earliest use of, 28; as money, 97; royal income from Nubian, 163; royal income from Coptos, 163, 181; of Wadi Alâki, 181, 416, 421–22; of Punt, 276; of Syria, 292, 293, 325; relative value of silver and, 98, 185, 338; due from officials, 238; images of, 245; commercial rings of, 277, 307; king of Mitanni asks for, 334; mines of Gebel Zebâra, 416; country of Amon, 457, 494; Osorkon I gives vast weight of, 531–32
"Gold of Praise," 141, 367, Fig. 139, 399, Fig. 148, 509, Fig. 177
"Gold of Valor," 226, 227
"Gold-house," 104, 245; double, 164
Goldsmith, earliest, 39; in Old Kingdom, 94, 104; in Middle Kingdom, 169, 201–02
"Good God," 74, 324
Governor (of a town), 237
"Governor of Foreign Countries," 141
Governor of Gold Country of Amon, 457, 473
"Governor of the North," office not found, 132
Governor of the north countries, 312, 322, 323
"Governor of the (Residence) City," 139, 154, 162; vizier appointed as, 133, 139
"Governor of the South," 132, 133, 134, 135, 138; as honourary title, 138; disappearance of, 165; reappearance in Nubian and Saite times, 557, 568
"Governor of the South Countries" (see also Nubia, viceroy of), first appointment of, 255
Governor, local, 79, 84; hereditary succession, 126, 131; becomes hered-

itary noble, 131–32; disappearance of, 131
Graffiti, archaic, 30
Grain, 92, 237; due from officials, 238
Granary, royal, 164, 237–38; of nomarch, 158, Fig. 79; as department of White House, 237–38
Granite, 4, 6, 42, 49, 61, 104, 201, 266, 442; quarries, 93, 135, 136, 281; Khafre's portal of, 120
"Great Chief," 131
"Great Chief of Artificers," 63
"Great Circle," 56, 261, 319
Great Council, 241
"Great House," centralization of local administration in, 80
"Great Houses," six, 164, 166, 240
"Great Lord," local governor becomes, 131; appointment by Pharaoh, 131–32; solicitude for domain by, 132; of Hare-nome, 133, 134; of Middle Egypt, 150
"Great Men of the Town," 241
"Great Seer," 63, 360, 367
Greece (see also Greek), 260; Egyptian commerce with, 337
Greek, traditions of Egypt, 215, 566, 578–79; mercenaries, 566, 568, 569, 578, 588, 589; portraiture, 573; states arise, 577–78; colonies in Egypt, 577–78, 590; quarter in Memphis, 577; acquaintance with Egypt, 578–79; debt to Egypt, 579–80; philosophy derives ideas from Egypt, 580
Gryphon, 91
Gyges, 566

H.

HA'ABRE', 586
Hadadnirari, 352
Halicarnassus, 590
Hamath, southern limit of Hittite monuments, 380
Hammamat, quarries at, 93, 159; Isesi in, 128; Pepi I in, 133; Iti in, 143; Imhotep in, 143; gap in records during Seventh and Eighth Dynasties at, 147; Mentuhotep III (Henu) in, 153; Mentuhotep IV in, 153–54; largest expedition to, 153–54; Middle Kingdom revenue from, 163, 164; Amenemhet I in, 178; Ramses IV in, 507
Hands (cut off as trophies), 264, 290
Hapharaim, 530
Hapuseneb, 272, 279, 362; fall of, 283
Harem, 75, 85, 134, 179, 498–500

Hare-nome, 133, 134, 159, 162, 163, 201
Harkhuf, career of, 138–39, 139–40
HARMHAB, 154, 242; as a noble, 391, 399; reign of, 400–08; rise of, 399–400; restoration of, 401–06; reforms of, 403–06; foreign policy of, 406–07; tomb of, 408, Fig. 119, Fig. 147, Fig. 148, Fig. 150
Harp, 349
Harris, Papyrus, 491; origin of, 505–06
Harsaphes, 196
Harûn er-Rashîd, 349
Harzozef, 123, 206
Hathor, 46; as a destroyer of men, 56; of Dendera, 59; of Sanai, 115, 190
Hatiba, 517
Hatnub, 93; opened by Khufu, 119; Pepi I at, 133; records of nomarchs of Hare-nome during Seventh and Eighth Dynasties at, 148; colossus cut from, 159
HATSHEPSUT, 215, 222, 228; parentage of, 266; rise of party of, 266–67; reign of, 267, 269–70, 271–83; rise of, 269; deposition of, 271; co-regency of, 271; triumph of party of, 271; leaders of the party of, 272, 283; their fall, 283; court fiction of birth of, 272–73; coronation by the gods, 273; tomb of, 279; extent of empire of, 279–80; restoration of temples by, 280; jubilee of, 280–82; obelisks of, 280–82, Fig. 114; Sinai expeditions, 282; death of, 282; Thutmose III's treatment of deceased, 282–83
Hatshepsut-Meretre, 318
Hatsho, 481, 482
Haunebu, 188–89
Hauran, stela of Seti I in, 410; stela of Ramses II in, 436
Hawara, pyramid of, 198–200
Hawk (sacred animal), 38, 40, n. 2, 319; as sun-god, 54; bearing dead, 65; golden, of Hieraconpolis, 104–05
Heart, as mind, 357–58
Hebrews (see also Israel), Egyptian origin of Messianic prophecy of, 205; in Egypt, 220, 447; tradition of Joseph, 229; tradition of, 238; strategic situation of, 262; settle in Palestine, 409–10; Ramses II probable oppressor of, 446–47; exodus of, 447; Egyptian larded with language of, 448–49; prophets of the, 536; retrospection of, 571; rejoice at Necho's defeat, 584
Heh, 184

Heliopolis, 44, 121, 268; High Priest of, 62–63, 126; Middle Kingdom temple at, 196–97; residence of northern vizier, 236, 240, 405, 443; judicial court of, 241; sacerdotally inferior to Thebes, 247; origin of Aton theology at, 360; temple of Seti I at, 415; Ramses II's buildings at, 443

Hellenium, 591

Hemset, 103

Henu, 153

Heracleopolis, 44, 150; supremacy of, 148–51; supported by Siut nomarchs, 149–51; war with Thebes, 149–51, 534; fall of, 152; temple at, 196; Ramses II's temple at, 445; absorbed by Libyan family, 526–27; Post-Empire principality of, 527, 528, 532, 534, 540–42, 569

Herald, royal, 226; duties of, 311

Herds, 92–93

Hereditary succession in office, rise of, 126–27, 131

Herenkeru, 293

Hermes, = Thoth, 59

Hermonthis, 149–50

Hermopolis, 59, 473, 540–42; captured by Piankhi, 541

Hermopolis Parva, 544

Hermotybies, 568, 569

Herodotus, in Egypt, 578

Hesebka, 544

Hesire, wooden panels of, 105, Fig. 59

Hezekiah, 551

Hieraconpolis, 33, 40, 44, 46, 47, 49, 119

Hieratic, 99–100; displaced by demotic, 574

Hieroglyphic (see also Writing), Saite revival of archaic, 574, 576

"High Place," at Gezer, 187

High Priest (see also Amon), 62; in Empire, 248

Hippopotamus, 30, 91; slain by Pharaoh, 39; noise of, 223

Hittites, 447; earliest industries of, 188; civilization of, 379–81; use of cuneiform by, 262; send gifts to Thutmose III, 304, 315; invade Mitanni, 352; invade Syria, 352–53; absorb Syria, 379–87, 413; writing of, 380; early relations of Egypt and, 381; embassy to Ikhnaton, 381; and Harmhab, 407; treaty with Seti I, 412, 423; war with Ramses II, 423–41; allies of, 424, 465; temporarily dislodged from southern Syria, 436; Ramses

II concludes treaty of peace with, 437–39; gods of, 438; Ramses II marries princess of, 439–40; Egyptian trade with, 447–48; Merneptah at peace with, 465; Merneptah's war with, 465–66, 470; lose Syria, 479; Ramses III fighting, 483; last hostilities between Egypt and, 483; sift into Palestine, 512

Ḥk', 217

Holy of Holies, 61

Hophra', 586

Hor, 568

"Horizon of Horus," 162

Horse, introduced by Hyksos, 222, 234; as tribute, 271; in Syria, 289, 290, 292, 316; from Babylon, 296; kindness to, 541

Horus, 38, 40, n. 2, 46; temple of, 40, 46; Thinite worship of, 46; as son of Osiris and Isis, 58; feud with Set, 58; popularity of, 59; four sons of, 65; of Heracleopolis, 148; Pool of, 331; of Alabastronpolis, 400, 402

"Horus" (royal title), 38, 122, 124; applied to a queen!, 269

"Horus, Worshippers of," 36, 46

"Worship of Horus" (feast called), 46

Hotep-Sesostris, 87, 194, 198

"House of the North," 47

"House of Thirty," 164, 166

Hrihor, 513, 515, 519, 520; usurpation of, 520–21; reign of, 522–23

Hua, 331

Hunting, in first two dynasties, 39; in Old Kingdom, 89–90; in Empire, 350–51

Huy, 394

"Hyk," 217

Hyksos, 214–27; origin of, 216, 217, 218, 219–20; origin of name of, 217; in Memphis, 216; called Asiatics, 217; Upper and Lower Egypt tributary to, 216, 221; Josephus on the, 216–17; monuments of, in Crete, 218; in Bagdad, 218; in Palestine, 218; wide empire of, 218–19; Kadesh, seat of empire of, 219–20, 317; reign of, 220–22; date of rise of, 221; length of rule of, 221; barbarities of, 221–22, 264; benefits from rule of, 22; expulsion of, 223–27

Hypostyle, 343

I.

Iannas, 221

Ibhet, 330

Ibis, bearing dead, 65
Ibrim, 256, 330, 331, 507
Ikathi, 323, 324
Ikhernofret, 166, 185
IKHNATON, parentage of, 355; accession of, 355; advisers of, 355–56; idealistic character of, 355–56, 376–77; religious revolution of, 359–78; changes his name, 363–64; as high priest of Aton, 360; abandons Thebes, 364; conciliation of officials by, 367–69; composes hymns to Aton, 371–76; naturalism of, 377–78; influence on art, 378; Asiatic rule of, 379–89; leniency, 385–86; loss of Asiatic empire by, 382–89; consequences of religious revolution of, 390–91; failure of, 390–91; foes of, 390–91, 402; destruction of tomb of, 402; later designation of, 402
Ikudidi, 182
Illahun, 87, 198
Image, cultus, 61–62
Imhotep (king), 143
Imhotep, 83, 107, 206; career of, 112–13; popularity in Saite period, 575
Immorality, 86
Immortality, 66; conferred by Osiris, 66
Incense, 276
Industries, in Old Kingdom, 92–98; in the nomes, 160
Ineni, 265; under Thutmose I, 265, 266, 278–79; under Hatshepsut, 271–72
Inheritance, line of, 86; of avocation, 169
Instruction, literature of, see Literature
INTEFS, of the Eleventh Dynasty, 150–56; of the Thirteenth Dynasty, 212; pyramids of Thirteenth Dynasty, 212
Intef (nomarch), 150
INTEF I, reign of, 151
INTEF II, 151
INTEF III, 152
Intef (Thutmose III's herald), 310–11; governor of the oases, 305
Interpreters, in Greek times, 578
Inundation, 7–9; influence on mechanical skill, 9; government observation of, 191, 211, 239
Ionians, 566, 590; as mercenaries, 566, 568, 569
Ipuwer, 204, 546
Irem, 313
Iri, 138
Iron, source (?) of, 136

Irrigation, 8–9, 160; by Twelfth Dynasty, 191–94; controlled by vizier, 244
Irthet, 137; location of, 137; expedition to, 139, 141
Isaiah, 548, 551, 552
ISESI, expedition to Hammamat, 128; expedition to Punt, 128, 140
Ishtar, 334; sent to Egypt, 353–54
Isis, 66; parentage of, 56; myth of Isis, 58, 59; flourishes in Saite times, 575; popularity of, 59–60
Isis (wife of Thutmose I), 267
"Isles of the Sea," 261, 424; controlled by Egypt, 305; Syria invaded by peoples of, 479
Israel (see also Hebrews and Palestine), life hereafter in, 173; Hyksos king, a chief of Israel, 220; entrance into Egypt, 220; revolts against Merneptah, 465; punished by Merneptah, 466; earliest reference to, 466, 470; stela, 471–72; rise of the nation, 526; Egyptian party in, 536; revolts against Shalmaneser IV, 549; fall of, 549
Itakama, 382, 387
Ithtowe, 157, 179, 196; founding of, 157; seat of six courts of justice, 164
Iti, 142
Ivory, 28, 39, 136, 141, 276, 277; from Libya, 280

J.

Jackal, 319
Jackal-nome, 162
Jacob, 220
Jacob-El, 220
Jacob-Her, 220, 221
Jehoahaz, 583
Jehoiachin, 586
Jehoiakim, 583
Jeremiah, 584, 587, 593
Jeroboam, 529
Jerusalem, earliest mention of, 387; plundered by Sheshonk I, 530; delivered from Sennacherib, 552; captured by Nebuchadrezzar (first time), 584; (second time), 586–587; destruction of, 587
Jewelry, earliest, 39–40; Thinite, 50; in Old Kingdom, 94; in Middle Kingdom, 202–03. Figs. 97–98, 213; in Empire, 252, Fig. 103
Jezreel (see also Esdraelon), 287, 410, 512, 530
Joppa, 312; tale of capture of, 312, 454

Jordan, 258, 530

Joseph, 229, 238, 244, 443, 447; official position of, 244; Egyptian origin of tale of temptation of, 455

Josephus, 14, 214, 215, 216

Josiah, 582

Jubilee, royal, 39

Judah (see also Palestine), 227, 258, 530; plots with Egypt against Assyria, 550–51; devastated by Sennacherib, 552; resists Necho, 582; rejoices at Necho's defeat, 584; Nebuchadrezzar deports chief families of, 584; carried captive by Nebuchadrezzar, 586–87

Judea, 284

Judge, 7, 134, 165; in Old Kingdom, 79, 80–82, 126; vizier as chief, 82, 119, 139; chief, son of Khufu, 119; chief, in Middle Kingdom, 154; in Empire, 239–42, 405–06, 499–500; Harmhab remits tax on office of, 405

Judgment of dead, earliest, 65, 67; Osirian, 173–74, 175, 249–50; evasion of, 249–50

Justice, administration of, in First and Second Dynasties, 42; in Old Kingdom, 80–82, 134; in nome, 158; in Middle Kingdom, 164–65, 166; in Empire, 239–42, 405–06, 499–500, 510–11; corruption in, 241–42, 405–06, 500, 510–11

K.

Ka, 63–64

Kaamenhotep, 535

Kabyles, 26

Kadesh, 219, 259, 263, 483; map of vicinity of, 426; seat of Hyksos power, 219–20, 259; commanding location of, 259, 299–300; leadership against Thutmose III, 284–85, 315–16; king of, 290, 291, 293, his family, 292; spoil of, 292; strength of, 299–300; first siege of, 301; first capture of, 301; second siege and capture of, 316; final suppression of, 317; seized by Itakama, 382; held by Hittites, 413, 423; as ally of Hittites, 424, battle of, 427–35; report of battle of, 433–34; Ramses II takes, 436; poem on battle of, 434, 453; reliefs of battle of, 433–34, 451–53

Kadesh (in Galilee), 412

Fafr, 119

KAKAI, birth of, 123

Kalabsheh, 317

Kallimmasin (Kadashman-Bel), letters of, to Amenhotep, III, 332–33

Karnak, 252; plan of, 444; Ahmose I in, 252; gate of Amenhotep I in, 254, 296; building of Thutmose I in, 263–66; halls of Thutmose III, 294–95, 296–297; Hatshepsut in, 280–82; royal list of, 297; building of Amenhotep II, 326; building of Amenhotep III at, 344; garden, 344; building of Seti I, 414–15; great hall of, 408, 414–15, 417, 443, 450–51; Ramses II at, 443; temple of Ramses III at, 487; Khonsu temple of, 487, Fig. 183, 507, 519–21, 523–24; Twenty Second Dynasty buildings, 531; first pylon, 531; Shabaka's buildings at, 553

Karoy, 325; southern boundary at, 330; gold of, 331

Kash, 387

Kashta, 539

Kasr-Sayyâd, 132

Katna, 302, 335–36, 352, 353

Keb, 54, 55, 56; parentage of, 56

Kebehu-Hor, 331

Kedesh, 460

Keftyew, 261, 319; character and home of, 261; in Egypt, 338

Kegemne, instruction of, 83, 107, 204

Kehek, 477, 485

Keheni, 543

KEMOSE, reign of, 224, 225

Keper, 481, 482

Ketne, same as Katna, q. v.

Kezweden, 424

Khabiri, 353; absorb Palestine, 387–89

KHAFRE, reign of, 120, 121

Khai, 385

Khamwese, 461, 462

Khani, 385

Khartum, 4

KHASEKHEM, statues of, 40, 47, Figs. 20, 21; war with Delta, 47; Hieraconpolis vase of, 47 (Figs. 20, 21).

KHASEKHEMUI, 111; tomb of, 42, Fig. 25; last king of Second Dynasty, 111

Khayu, 36

KHENZER, 221

Khepri, 59

Khereha, 543, 544

Kheta, see Hittites

Kheta, Great, 381

Khetasar, accession of, 437; makes treaty of peace with Ramses II, 437–39; gives daughter to Ramses II, 439–40; visits Egypt, 439;

gives second daughter to Ramses II, 440
Kheti I (nomarch of Siut), 149
Kheti II (nomarch of Siut), 150–51
Kheti (treasurer of Mentuhotep II), 152
Kheti (daughter of nomarch), 162
KHIAN, 217, 221, wide range of monuments of, 218; in Crete, 218; in Bagdad, 218; same as Iannas, 221
Khnum, receives Dodekaschoinos, 112, 491, 495
Khnumhotep I, 156, 161–62
Khnumhotep II, 162; Asiatics in tomb of, 187
KHNUM-KHUFU, 116
Khonsu, Ramses III's temple of, 487, Fig. 183; continued by Ramses IV, 507; continued by Ramses XII and Hrihor, 519–21; continued by Paynozem I, 523–24
KHUFU, parentage of, 116; reign of, 116–20, 121; folk-tale of, 122–23
Kina, 288, 289
Kinanat, 353
Kingship, origin of, 74
" King's-Son of Kush," first appointment of, 255
Kode, as ally of Hittites, 424, 439
Korusko, 178
Kosêr, 142, 183
Kubbân, 255, 330, 416; stela, 422
Kumidi, 385, 388
Kummeh, 181, 317; fortress of, 184, 185
Kurigalzu, fidelity toward Amenhotep III, 332
Kurna, 415
Kush (see also Nubia), location of, 136–37; first mention of, 137, 141; first campaign in, 180; campaigns of Sesostris I in, 180–81; campaigns of Sesostris III in, 184–87; King's-son of, see Nubia; limits of, 255; government of, 255, 256, 317; viceroy of, see Nubia.
Kuyunjik, 553

L.

Labour (= Taxes), 238
Labourers, treatment of, 414, 496
Labyrinth, 194, 200; Cretan, 194
Lachish, 387; Hittite pottery at, 262; Philistine pottery at, 512
Lake, artificial, 349
LAMARES, 193
Lamb, prophesying, 547
Land, ownership of, in first two dynasties, 44; registration of, in Old Kingdom, 82; owned by Pharaoh, 84, 229, 237; held by nobles, 84–85, 237; held by middle class, 85, 169, 237; held by nomarch, 161; office, 165; of El Kab nomarchs not confiscated, 229; of feudal lords confiscated, 229; cases (legal), 240; held by temples, 491, 493; price of, 524–25; in Saite period, 574
Language, Egyptian, Semitic structure of, 25; African tincture, 25
Lapis-lazuli, 296, 304, 344
Law, in Old Kingdom, 81; in Middle Kingdom, 165, 242; in Empire, 242, 404–06; public access to code of, 242; Pharaoh subject to, 242; Pharaoh source of, 242, 404–06; against corrupt officials, 405–06; Bocchoris giver of, 547; Amasis revises system of, 591
Lead, earliest use of, 28
Learning, 98–100
Leather, 96, 404; manuscript rolls of, 197, 313
Lebanon, 259, 260, 515; intercourse with, in Old Kingdom, 115–42; in Middle Kingdom, 168; conformation of, 258; anti-, 258, 259; Tripolis in, 293; Thutmose III's fortress in, 293; revolt against Amenhotep II, 324; Thutmose IV in, 328; Seti I in, 410; city of Ramses II in, 425; controlled by Necho, 587
Lebu, 466
Lector (or Ritual Priest), 171
Letopolis, 544
Letters, 98, 455, 514, 516; of Pharaoh, 77, 140, 141, 166, 185, 520; model, 203, 455
Leucos Limên, 142, 183
Libya, 585
Libyans, 319; immigration into Egypt, 7, 31, 32, 47, 49, 179, 254, 411, 462, 466–71, 474, 477–78, 481–83, 526–27; kinship with Egyptians, 25–26, 31–32; earliest wars of Egypt with, 47, 49; Amenemhet I's war with, 179; Amenhotep I's war with, 254; Seti's war with, 411–12; peoples of the, 466–67; origin of, 467; Merneptah's war with, 468–71; northern allies of, 467–68, 477–78; first defeat by Ramses III, 478; invaded by Meshwesh, 481; second defeat by Ramses III, 481–83; gain high official position at court, 497, 500; absorb the Delta, 526–27; gain the throne, 527–28; lords of, in Twenty Second Dynasty, see Meshwesh; decline of Egypt under, 547–48; become a military class in Egypt, 568;

as mercenaries, 449, 477, 485, 526, 528–29, 532–33, 534, 568, 588; Cyrene encroaches upon, 588
Libyan Dynasty, see Twenty Second and Twenty Third Dynasties; see Libyans
Limestone, 5
Linen, 96; fineness of, 96; due from officials, 238
Lion, 30, 319, 372; order of the, 301; hunting, 350–51; king's tame, 489
Lisht, 157, 198
Litâny, 425
Literature, of the Old Kingdom, 107–08; of the Middle Kingdom, 203–08; earliest, of entertainment, 203; artificial style in, 204; of instruction, 204, 458–59; impersonal character of, 207; form and content of, 207–08; of the Empire, 318–19, 453–55; of the Nubian period, 545
Logos, 358
London obelisk of Thutmose III at, 306
" Look behind," 65
Louis XV, 349
Lubim, 559
Luli, 551
Lute, 349
Luther, 250
Luxor, building of Ahmose I in, 252; temple of Amenhotep III in, 343–44; building of Ramses II in, 451
Lycians, 338; as allies of Hittites, 424, 467; plunder the Delta, 462; as allies of Libyans, 467; gain high official position at Egyptian court, 500
Lydia, 566, 593
Lying, 173
Lyre, 349

M.

Mace, pear-shaped, 28, 40
Magic, 123; influence on medicine, 101–02; mortuary (see also Book of the Dead), 175, 249–50; Ikhnaton suppresses mortuary, 369–70, 390; evil influence on religion of, 249–50, 459; in harem conspiracy, 498
Magician, 123
Magnate of the Southern Ten, 79–80, 165
Mahanaim, 530
Maharbaal, 500
Mai, 369
Makere, see Hatshepsut
Malachite, 344, 485
Mamlukes, 214, 229, 548

Manakhbiria, 317, 383
Manetho, 13–14, 36
Mani, 334
Mardukbaliddin, forms coalition in west, 551
Marea, 569
Mariette, 252
Marriage, 85, 86
Maryland, 6
Masonry, earliest, 27–28; brick, 41, 42; stone, 42, Fig. 25; of great pyramid, 118; temple, 343
Mastaba, 68–69, Fig. 34, Fig. 57; of Zoser, 113; disappearance of, 176, 198; Saite revival of sculptures of Old Kingdom, 571
Mathematics, 100–101
Matnefrure, 439
Matoi, 137
Matuga, 186
Maxyes, 466
Mayor, 237
Mazoi, location of, 137; as mercenaries, 137, 424; prisoners, 178
Mechanics, 101
Medes, 582, 583, 593
Medicine, earliest books on, 45, 76; knowledge of, 101; transition to Europe, 101; cultivated by Imhotep, 112
Medicis, 548
Medinet Habu, temple records in, 486–87; dedication of, 492; treasury of, 493
Mediterranean, 259; culture significance of eastern, 3, 4; commerce on, 447
Medum, ducks, 106, Fig. 55; pyramid of, 115
Megiddo, 287, 387, 530; map of, 286; occupation by King of Kadesh, 287; pass of, 288; Thutmose III's march to, 287–89; battle of, 289–90; siege of, 290–91; fall of, 291; spoil of, 292
Meketaton, 392
Mekhu, 141
Memphis, 5, 37, 44, 132, 141, 196; supremacy of, 111; origin of name of, 132–33; fall of, 148; Hyksos in, 216; sacerdotal inferiority to Thebes, 247; temple of Ahmose I in, 252; building of Amenhotep I in, 326; theology of, 356–58; under Nubians, 542–43, 554–56, 558–59; temple of Seti I at, 415; temple of Ramses II at, 443; under the Assyrians, 555–57, 559, 565; under Saites, 577–78, 591, 592; buildings of Amasis in, 591

Menes, 74; reign of, 36–37; tomb of, 37; regalia of, 37, and Fig. 13; tablet of, Fig. 27
Mendes, 535, 543, 544
Menet-Khufu, 116, 162, 187
MENKHEPERRE (High Priest of Amon), 524
Menkheperre-seneb, 295, 317
MENKURE, 127; reign of, 121
Mentemhet, 557–58, 559, 565, 567, 568
MENTUHOTEPS, 150–156
MENTUHOTEP I, 151
MENTUHOTEP II, 152
MENTUHOTEP III, 152–53
MENTUHOTEP IV, 153–54
Mentuhotep (commander in Nubia), 166, 181
Mentuhotep (vizier), 164
Merasar, 412, 437
Mercenaries, Nubian, 134, 137, 330, 336, 424, 449; Beduin, 386; Sherden, 336, 386, 424–25, 448, Fig. 163, 449, 477, 485; sources of, 449–50; Libyan, 449, 477, 526, 528–29, 532–33, 534, 568, 588; Kehek, 477, 485; Meshwesh, 526; Carian, 566, 568, 569; Greek, 566, 568, 569, 578, 588; Syrian, 569, 588; desertion of, 569, 588; dependence of Saites upon, 569–70; attempt flight to Nubia, 588; desert Apries, 588
Merchants, in Old Kingdom, 85; in Middle Kingdom, 168, 170; in Empire, 246, 448; Phœnician, 260–61, 448, 577; Saite, 577, 590; Greek, 577, 590
MERIKERE, 150
Merire, 367
Meritaton, 391
MERMESHU, 212
Mermose, 330
MERNEPTAH, 456; reign of, 464–72; Asiatic war of, 447, 465–66; sends grain to Hittites, 465; resubdues Palestine, 465–66; punishes Israel, 466; Libyan war of, 468–71; buildings of, 471; vandalism of, 471–72; destroys mortuary temple of Amenhotep III, 471; body of, 472; strife after death of, 472–73
MERNEPTAH-SIPTAH, 472–73
MERNERE, parentage of, 134; reign of, 135–39; relief at first cataract, 137; visit to Nubia, 137; burial of, 139; body of, 139, Fig. 77
Meroe, 561, 585
Meryey, 467, 468, 478; dethronement of, 469
Mesed, 544

Mesedsure, 498–500
Meshesher, 481, 482
Meshwesh, home of, 466; invade Libyan country, 481; invade Egypt, 481; defeat of, 481–82; commanders absorb the Delta, 526–27; appropriate Heracleopolis, 526–27; commanders during Twenty Second and Twenty Third Dynasties, 528–29, 532–33, 534, 535–36
Messiah, 205
Metella, 413; treaty with Seti I, 413, 423; allies and mercenaries of, 424; at the battle of Kadesh, 427, 452; death of, 437
Methen, 88
Middle Class, in Old Kingdom, 85; in Middle Kingdom, 164, 165, 168–70; in the army, 167, 234–35; tombs of, 251
Middle Kingdom, rise of, 149–56; state in, 157–68; Nubian conquest in, 152, 180–87; relations with Asia, 187–91; irrigation enterprises of, 191–94; development of Delta by, 188, 197; development of Sanai by, 163, 164, 182, 190–91; art of, 201–02; literature of, 203–08; fall of, 208–11; anarchy following, 211–14
MIEBIS, 47; campaign of, in Sinai, 48
"Mighty is Khekure," 184
Miletus, 591
"Military Commander of Middle Egypt," 149
"Military Commander of the Whole Land," 150
Mind, 357–58
Mining, 190–91
Min, 46, archaic statues of, 28; power in Hammamat, 153; relation to Amon, 248
MISPHRAGMOUTHOSIS, 220
Mitanni, 262, 319; origin of people of, 262–63; hostility to Thutmose III, 285; Thutmose III in, 303; revolt against Amenhotep II, 323–25; alliance of Thutmose IV with, 328; Thutmose IV marries daughter of king of, 328; seeks alliance with Egypt, 332; alliance of Amenhotep III with, 333, 353–54; royal marriages betweeen Egypt and, 333; invaded by Hittites, 352; seeks alliance with Ikhnaton, 379; latest reference to, 530
Mitylene, 590
Moab, 258; plots with Egypt against Assyria, 550–51, 551; against Babylon, 586
Moeris, Lake, 193

Mohammed Ali, 229
Mohammedans, 576
Money, earliest, 97–98
Monkeys, 276
Monuments, vast number surviving, 11
Moon-god, see Thoth
Moslem, 248; viceroys, 214; Egypt, 214
Mother, inheritance through, 86, 149, 161; duty toward, 86
"Mount of the Horns of the Earth," 468, 482; fortified by Ramses III, 479
Mummies, royal, concealment at Der el-Bahri, 525; discovery of, 525–26
Mummy, burial of, 69
Murder, 173
Musen, 526–27
Music, in Old Kingdom, 109; in Empire, 248, 349
Musical instruments, in Old Kingdom, 109–10
Musri, 549, 551
Mut, Karnak temple of, 344; banishment of, by Ikhnaton, 370
Mutemuya, 328
Mutnezmet, 401
Mutnofret, 267
Mycenæ, 338
Mycenæan, Age, 188, 261; civilization and Egypt, 261; settlements in, commerce with Egypt, 337–38; art influenced by Egypt, 338
Myrrh, 276, 277, 305; source of, 127; terraces, 274; traffic in, 274
Mysians, as allies of Hittites, 424
Myth, 54–60; of Re, 54, 58–59; of Osiris, 58, 59–60, 171–72, 174, 207, 250; philosophical interpretation of, 356–58; dramatized, 171–72, 207

N.

Nabopolassar, 583
Nabuna'id, 593
Naharin, Thutmose I in, 263–64; first revolt against Thutmose III, 283–84; Thutmose III in, 302–03; second revolt against Thutmose III in, 314; third revolt against Thutmose III, 315–16; remembrance of Thutmose III in, 317; revolt against Amenhotep II, 323–25; Thutmose IV in, 328; northern frontier in, 330; loyalty to Amenhotep III, 353; Hittite invasion of, 353; as ally of Hittites, 424; temporarily recovered by Ramses II, 436, 438–39; Egyptian trade with, 447; tale of daughter of king of, 454

Nahr el-Kebîr, 315–16
Nahr el-Kelb, see Dog River
Nahum, 559–60, 582
Nakht, 162
Namlot (king of Hermopolis), 540–42
Namlot (son of Meshwesh chief Sheshonk), 527
Napata, 331; southern limit of Nubian viceroy's jurisdiction, 255; southern frontier established at, 325, 450; first capital of Nubian kingdom, 538; Taharka's buildings at, 558; Tanutamon's buildings at, 558; forsaken as capital of Nubian kingdom, 561
Napoleon, 291, 294, 311, 320
Narmer, war with Delta, 47; Libyan war of, 49
Nastesen, 561
Naucratis, founding of, 590; Greek character of, 590
Navy (see also Ships), 243, 480; Saite, 582, 593
Nebesheh, 188
Nebuchadrezzar, 576; defeats Necho, 583–84; conquers Syria-Palestine, 583–84; captures Jerusalem (first time), 584, (second time), 586, 587; attempts punishment of Egypt, 592–93; death of, 593
Necho (dynast of Sais), 556, 557; death of, 558, 565
Necho, recovers Syria-Palestine, 582–83; defeated at Carchemish, 583–84; relinquishes Syria-Palestine, 584; reëxcavates the Nile-Red Sea canal, 584; sends expedition to circumnavigate Africa, 585
Neferhotep, 221; reign of, 212; stelæ of, 212; vizier of, 221
Neferhotep (priest), 403
Neferkheprure-Intef, 212; decree of, 212
Neferkhere-Sebekhotep (the Great), 212
Nefernefruaton, 371, 376
Nefretiri (Eighteenth Dynasty queen), becomes local goddess at Thebes, 459
Nefretiri (Queen of Ramses II), 446
Nefrure, 272
Negadeh, 37
Negeb, 315, 410
Negro, mercenaries, 134, 137, 330, 424, 449; as Pharaoh, 212
Nehi, 317
Nehri, 162
Nehsi (Pharaoh), 212
Nehsi (chief treasurer), 272, 277; Punt expedition dispatched by, 276; fall of, 283

Neit, 30, 32, 46, 59
Nekhbet, 34, 38
Nekheb (see also El Kab), 33
Nekhen (see also El Kab), 33, 42, 44, 186; "Judge Attached to," 81; northern Nubian frontier at, 186, 253-54, 255
Nekure, 70
Nemathap, 111
Nephthys, 66; parentage of, 56
NESUBENEBDED, 511, 513, 514, 515, 525; sends crocodile to Tiglath-Pileser I, 518; reign of, 522-23; gains whole country, 523
Nesuhor, 588
Nesuptah, 568
NETERIMU, war against Delta, 47
New Towns, 126
New York obelisk of Thutmose III at, 306
Nile, 3; course and valley of the, 4-6; White, 4; Blue, 4, 8, 127, 561; cataracts of, 4, 6; cañon of, 5; alluvium of, 5, 8; width and velocity, 5; delta of, 5; mouths of, 5; cliffs of cañon, 6; isolation of valley, 6; gateway to Sudan, 7; influence of navigation of, 7; inundation, 7-8; of the nether world, 54; mythical sources of, 56, 374, 375; nearest point to Red Sea, 128; in Nubia, 136; kingdom of the Blue, 561
Nilometer, earliest, 191, 211
Nimmuria, 333
Nineveh, 263, 595; fall of, 582, 583
Nitocris, in Sixth Dynasty, 143
Nitocris, 568; adopted by Shepnupet (II), 567; adopts Enekhnesneferibre, 585-86
Niy, 270, 353; Thutmose III captures, 304; Amenhotep II captures, 324; taken by Aziru, 382, 383
No-Amon, 559
Nobles, 84-85; Old Kingdom tombs of, 116; political rise of, 128-29, 131, 143; independence of Sixth Dynasty, 143; of the Empire, 246-47
Nomarch (see also Great Lord), 157; rise of, 131-32; relations of Pharaoh with, 134, 161-63; of Thinis, 134; of Siut, 148-51, 160; character of rule of, 148-49; 159-61, 202; curbed by Amenemhet I, 155-56; of Oryx-nome, 156, 159, 161, 162, 180, 181, 182; in Middle Kingdom, 157-62; of Coptos, 159; militia of, 167; buildings of, 159, 197; of Hare-nome, 133, 134, 159, 162, 163, 201; wars of, 211 ff., 224, 226, 228; south of El Kab, 225; of El Kab, 225-26;

surviving under the Empire, 228; royal titles granted to, 228; disappearance of, 228-29; of Alabastronpolis, 399
Nome, 31, 79; early administration of, 80; militia of, 84; independence of, in Old Kingdom, 143; in Middle Kingdom, 157-62; archives of, 240
North, kingdom of the, see Delta
North, canal called, 5
Notre Dame, cathedral of, 450
Nubia, tableland of, 4; earliest Egyptian campaign in, 37; gold of, 94 (see also Gold); control by Zoser, 112; campaign of Snefru in, 115; Userkaf in, 127; Sahure in, 127-28; Pepi I in, 134; nobles of Elephantine in, 135-39; character and resources of, 136-39, 537; tribes and people of, 136-39; imports from, 136; first visit of Pharaoh to, 137; Mernere in, 138-39; Pepi II begins conquest of, 139-42; relations of Elephantine nobles with, 135-42; Mentuhotep II in, 152; Middle Kingdom income from, 163, 183, 185; conquest of, 178, 180-87; Amenemhet I's campaign in, 178; Sesostris I's campaigns in, 180-81; fortresses in, 183, 184, Fig. 83, 211; Sesostris III's campaigns in, 183-87; Neferkere-Sebekhotep in, 212; Ahmose I resumes control of, 227-28; Amenhotep I's campaign in, 253-54; mayor of Nekhen governs northern, 253-54, 255; northern frontier of, 178, 186, 253-54, 255; southern frontier of, 325-26; first viceroy of, 255-56; campaign of Thutmose I in, 256-57; campaign of Thutmose II in, 270; impost of, 277, 302, 308, 314, 317, 331, 394, 473, 530; Thutmose III in, 302, 313, 317-18; Thutmose III's lists of towns of, 318; Amenhotep II in, 325-26; Thutmose IV in, 328-29; Amenhotep III in, 330-31; last great Pharaonic invasion of, 331; Egyptianization of, 330-31, 508, 537; administration of, 253-54, 255-56, 331-32, 394, 446, 507-08; viceroy of, 317, 330, 331, 394, 421, 422, 456, 473, 520; viceroy of, becomes governor of gold country of Amon, 457; Aton temple in, 364, 393; Harmhab in, 407; Ramses I in, 408; Seti I in, 408-09; Ramses II's campaign in, 440; Ramses II's temples in, 446; gold country of Amon in, 457; Merneptah in, 471;

source of usurpers, 472–73, 499; Siptah in, 473; Ramses VI in, 507–08; Twenty First Dynasty in, 525; Sheshonk I holds, 530, 537; under post-Empire principality of Thebes, 528; rise of kingdom of, 537–38; character of kingdom of, 538–39, 561; Egypt ruled by, 539–60; later history of kingdom of, 560–61; writing of, 561; end of kingdom of, 561; Psamtik II attempts recovery of, 585; mercenaries desert to, 569; mercenaries attempt desertion to, 588

Nubian, 239; as Pharaoh, 212, 550–60; in Egyptian army, 134, 137, 330

Nubian Dynasty, see Twenty Fifth Dynasty; see Nubians

Nubkhas, 213

Nuges, 293, 313, 315; as ally of Hittites, 424

Nukhashshi, 352, 353; Hittite advance into, 382, 385

"Numberings," fiscal, 44

Nut, 54, Fig. 31, 56, 59

O.

Oases, 6; 192; earliest control of northern (?), 115; earliest intercourse with southern, 182; controlled by Thutmose III, 305; Libyan invasion of northern, 467; banishment to, 524; Twenty Second Dynasty control of, 530; under Saites, 588, 592

Obelisks, of Re, 124–25; transport of, 266, 280–81; of Thutmose I, 266; of Hatshepsut, 280–82; of Thutmose III (Lateran), 306, 329; of Amenhotep II, 327; of Thutmose IV, 329; place of, 343; of Amenhotep III, 352; of Seti I, 418; captured by Assyrians, 559

Obsidian, 105

Ocean, 56, 261, 319

Œdipus, 455

"Offering," the, 226

Officials, corruption of, 200, 403–06, 523, 527; taxes due from, 238–39; demission of same, 405; as judges, 240; Harmhab reorganizes, 403–06; liberality of Harmhab to, 406

Official class, first records of, 128–29, 133–34; in Middle Kingdom, 169; in Empire, 245–46

Oil, 237

Okapi, 30

Okeanos, 56

Old Kingdom, government and society,

74–92; industry and art, 92–110; history of the, 111–44; meagre sources for history of, 111–12; beginning of Nubian conquest by, 112, 115, 127, 127–28, 134, 135–39, 139–42; wide foreign connections of, 142; fall of, 143; later reverence for, 144; destruction of monuments of, 147; Saitic revival of, 570–76

Omar, 570

On (Heliopolis), 59

Opet, feast of, 294, 309, 393, 400, 541; length of, 492, 493

Orchomenos, 338

Orontes, 219, 258, 259; valley of, 258, 426–27

Orthography, introduction of consistent, 203

Oryx-nome, 156, 159, 161, 162, 180, 181, 182; hereditary succession of nomarchs of, 161–62

Osiris, 46, 59; reconciler of the Two Kingdoms, 47; parentage of, 56; temple of, 196, 265; as King of the Dead, 58; myth of, 58, 59, 60, 171–72, 174; ethical elements in myth of, 67, 173, 250; popularity of, 59–60; home of, 60; outward form of, 60; rise as supreme mortuary god, 66–67; mortuary customs from myth of, 171; popular triumph of, 171; drama of myth of, 171–72, 207; tomb of at Abydos, 172; memorial tablets to, 172, 182, 185–86, 187; image of, 185–86; suppressed by Ikhnaton, 390; Seti I's Abydos temple of, 415; in Saite period, 575

Osorkon I, 531–32

Osorkon II, 532–33; jubilee hall of, 532

Osorkon III, 536, 539–40, 553; submits to Piankhi, 543; art under, 548–49

Osorkon (High Priest of Amon), annals of, 533–34

Ostrich, 136

Othu, 411

Ox, wild, 30, 91

P.

Painting, in Old Kingdom, 105–06; in Middle Kingdom, 202; in Empire, 308, 348, 378, 417

Pakhons, 285

Pakht, 280

Pakruru, 557

Palace, 39, 78; its double character, 78; construction of, 88; of Amenhotep III, 348–49

Paleolithic man, 25
Palermo Stone, 45 (Fig. 28)
Palestine (see also Syria-Palestine), 26; earliest expedition into, 135; pre-Israelitish civilization of, 188; pursuit of Hyksos into, 215; poverty of, 258; first tributary to Egypt, 264; campaign of Thutmose II in, 270; involved in revolt against Thutmose III, 284; Beduin of, 315; absorbed by Khabiri, 387–89; inhabitants flee to Egypt before Khabiri, 388; road from Egypt to, 409; at beginning of Nineteenth Dynasty, 409; Hebrew settlement of, 409–10; recovered by Seti I, 411; revolts against Ramses II, 435–36; recovered by Ramses II, 436; Egyptian garrisons in, 322, 387–88, 447; Egyptian trade with, 447–48; dialects of, in Egypt, 448–49; revolts against Merneptah, 465; wasted by Merneptah, 466, 470; final loss of, 512–19; survival of fiction of Pharaoh's sovereignty over, 518–19, 526; Twenty Second Dynasty (Sheshonk I) attempts recovery of, 529–30, 531; tribute of, 530; list of towns of, 531; absorbed by Assyria, 549; Psamtik I attempts recovery of, 580; Necho's conquest of, 582–83; Babylonian conquest of, 583–84; Apries' war in, 586–87; Amasis' designs on, 592–93
Palettes, slate, 40, 47 (Fig. 19)
Panther, 136, 276, 277; five cubits long, 280
Paper, see Papyrus
Papyrus, 85; uses of, 97; paper introduced into Syria, 484, 517
Paris, obelisk of Ramses II at, 445
Patonemhab, 403
Paynozem I, 523–24; marries daughter of Pesibkhenno I, 524
Payonekh, 523
Pazedku, 226
Pe, 34, 42, 44
Pebekkamen, 498–500
Pedes, 424
Pediamenemopet, tomb of, 568
PEDIBAST, 535–36
Pediese, 544
Pedihor, 568
Pefnefdibast, 542
Peleset, 477, 479; settlement in Palestine, 512
Pelusium, 595
PEMOU, 535
Pemou (mercenary commander), 535

Penno, 507–08
Pentaur, poem of, 434, 453
Pentewere, poem of, 434, 453
Pentewere (son of Ramses III), 498–500
PEPI I, 35; reign of, 133–35
PEPI II, parentage of, 134, 139; reign of, 139–43
Pepinakht, 141, 142
Perehu, 276
Periander, 580
Perire, 468
Per-Ramses, 442–43
Perrot, 106
Persepet, see Saft el-Henneh
Persian Empire, rise of, 593
Persian Gulf, 259
Personality, 63–64
PESIBKHENNO I, 523–24
PESIBKHENNO II, 525; daughter marries son of Sheshonk I, 528
Petition, 240–41
Peyes, 498–500
Phagroriopolis, 544
Pharaoh, origin of title, 74; symbols of, 38. 39, 40 and n. 2; titles of, 38, 74, 124; regalia of, 38, 39; public appearances, 38–39; costume of, 38–39, 340; toilet of, 75; diversions of, 39, 122, 204; estate of, 39; as high priest, 62, 456; mortuary service of, 71, 265; reverence for, 74; court of, 74–75; women of, 75; relations with nobles, 76–77, 166–67; limitation of power of, 77; education and character of, 77, 457–58; duties of, 77–78, 235–36; residence of, 78; judicial prerogatives of, 81, 499–500; legal appeal to, 81–82; as owner of all lands, 84, 574; as son of Re, 122–23, 272–73, 400–01, 543; decline of his power in Old Kingdom, 129, 131–32; letters of, 77, 140, 141, 166, 185, 520; benefits of office of, 143–44; first accompanying campaign in foreign country, 181; hymn to, 206–07; body guard of, 235, 243, Fig. 163; power of, 235; offices of, 79–80, 236, 243; lease of property of, 237; subject to law, 242; source of law, 242, 404–06; tomb of (see also Pyramid), 250–52; theological aspects of, 358–59, 456; sacerdotalization of, 457, 506–07; justice of, 134, 499–500
Phaselis, 590
Philistia, Psamtik I invades, 580; Necho invades, 582
Philistines, 477, Fig. 172, 479; set-

tlement in Palestine, 512; suppression by Israel, 526

Philosophy, 204, 356–61; myths interpreted as, 356; origin of Greek, 358, 580; Greek, 361

Phocæa, 590

Phœnicia, 215; commerce with under Snefru, 115; Thutmose III in, 298, 302; temple of Amon in, 298; harbours of, employed and equipped by Pharaoh, 302, 304, 313, 315, 317, 424; galleys of, in Egypt, 307; papyrus and Egyptian alphabet introduced into, 484

Phœnicians, 217, 219; rise of, 260–61; disseminators of oriental civilization, 262

Physician, of court, 75, 101

PIANKHI, reign of, 539–46; conquers Upper Egypt, 539–42; captures Memphis, 542–43; is recognized as Pharaoh by Re, 543; conquers the Delta, 543–45; stela of, 545

Pillar, 107

Pipes, double, 349

Pir'u (Pharaoh), 550

Pithom, 442, Fig. 162; Beduin dwelling by, 447

Poetry, earliest, 109; in Middle Kingdom, 205–07; in Empire, 318–19, 371–76, 434, 453, 455, 458

Police, marine, 338

Polycrates, 591

Population, 9

Porphyry, 28

Pottery, earliest, 28; protodynastic, 39; Old Kingdom, 95–96; Ægean, 189

Prayer, 458–59, 506; mortuary, in king's name, 71; of Ramses IV, 458, 506

Priests, in first two dynasties, 46; in State, 62, 63; in Old Kingdom, 62–63; mortuary, 70, 134; in Middle Kingdom, 171; laymen as, 171; sale of rolls for gain by, 175, 176, 249–50; as judges, 241; in Empire, 241, 247, 249–50, 272, 362, 401–03, 475, 489–90; rise of political power of, 241, 247, 272; universal organization of, 247, 272, 362; as social class, 247; reorganization by Harmhab, 401–03; conciliated by Setnakht, 475; by Ramses III, 489–96; become a political and economic menace, 489–96, 497, 506–07; triumph of, 520–23; rule of, 520–28; in Saite period, 574–76; exempt from taxation, 574; become an hereditary class,

575; Amasis appropriates wealth of, 592

Priestesses, 63

Princes, royal, in Old Kingdom, 75, 126; revenues of royal, 75; in government office, 119; in the army, 234, 461; feuds between, 418; as high priest of Ptah, 461

Prophecy, 547; literature of, 204–05; messianic, 204–05; origin of messianic, 205; ecstatic, 513–14

Prostitution, 86

Proverbs, 107–08

Psammetichos, 580

PSAMTIK I, flees to Syria, 558; reinstated by Ashurbanipal, 565; rise of, 565–67; organization of, 567–70; foreign policy of, 576–77; Asiatic war of, 580; repels Scythians, 580–81; death of, 581

PSAMTIK II, 561, 585–86; attempts recovery of Nubia, 585

PSAMTIK III, 595

Ptah, 46, 60, 196, 439; high priest of, 63, 126; Karnak temple of, 295; philosophical interpretation of, 356–58; splendour of Ramses III's gifts to, 490; relations of Twenty Second Dynasty with high priests of, 528–29, in Saite period, 575

Ptah-hotep, five viziers, 126; Instruction of, 83, 107, 204

PTOLEMY I, 14

PTOLEMIES, 183, 593, 595

Puemre, 306

Punt, earliest voyage to, 127, 140; Sahure in, 127; Isesi in, 127, 140; route to, 128, 142; imports from, 136; Pepi II in, 142; relations of Elephantine nobles with, 142; development of intercourse with, 142; Mentuhotep III in, 153; traffic, a royal prerogative, 163; Middle Kingdom expeditions to, 153, 182–83; in popular tale, 183, 203; in Der el-Bahri temple, 274, 277; Hatshepsut's expedition to, 274–78; Thutmose III's expedition to, 305; Ramses III's expedition to, 485–86

Puntites, 276; affinity with Egyptians, 26; in Egypt, 127, 277

Put, 559

Putukhipa, 437

Pylon, 343, Fig. 126

Pyramid, temple of, 71–73; causeway leading to, 72, Fig. 35; enclosure, 71–73; location of, 78; origin of, 114, 115, 116; of Snefru, 115–16; of Khufu, see Pyramid, Great; of Khafre, 120; of Menkure, 121; of

Shepseskaf, 121; decline of Fifth Dynasty, 129; of Mernere, 135; in Eleventh Dynasty, 155; in Middle Kingdom, 176, 198–200; of Hawara, 198–200; discontinuance of, 200, 250, 278; of Thirteenth Dynasty, 212, 213; of Seventeenth Dynasty, 224

Pyramid, Great, 101, 117–19; significance of, 119

Pyramid texts, 67, 69, 109, 175; earliest, 130; Saite revival of, 171

Pyramidion, 197

Q.

Qarqar, battle of, 534

Queen, position of, 75; prominence at close of Eighteenth Dynasty, 329–30, 367; conspiracy of, 134, 241, 242, 498–500

R.

RADEDEF, 120

Rain (see also Climate), 153

Ramesseum, 443, 451; colossus of, 445

Ramose, 362

Ramessids, 212, 224; of the Twentieth Dynasty (after Ramses III), 505–21; tombs of, 507; chronology of late, 508; disorganization under late, 510–11; decline of, 518

RAMSES I, reign of, 408–09; body concealed in tomb of Inhapi, 525; final concealment of body at Der el-Bahri, 525

RAMSES II, not Sesostris, 189; vandalism of, 195, 443–45; displaces elder brother, 418–19, Fig. 419; accession of, 418–20; completes Seti I's Abydos temple, 420–21; exploits Nubian gold country, 421–22; Hittite war of, 423–41; route of march against, 425–26; founds city in Lebanon, 425; at battle of Kadesh, 427–35, 452; Palestine war, 435–36; partially recovers Syria, 436–37; concludes treaty of peace with the Hittites, 437–39; marries Hittite princesses, 439–40; Nubian campaigns, 440; Libyan campaign, 440–41; buildings of, 442–46; obelisks of, 445; jubilees of, 414, 461; prodigality in endowing temples, 446; the oppressor of Hebrew tradition, 446–47; daughter marries a Syrian, 449; character and personality of, 460–61; family of, 461; splendour of, 450, 461–62; senility of, 462; western Delta lost

by, 462; death of, 462; influence of memory of, 462–63; robbery of tomb of, 519; restoration of body of, 519; body concealed in tomb of Inhapi, 525; final concealment of body at Der el-Bahri, 525

RAMSES III, accession of, 476–77; reign of, 477–501; first Libyan war, 477–78; war with northern sea peoples, 480–81; second Libyan war, 481–83; Syrian war, 483; storms Hittite cities, 483; Asiatic boundary of, 483; peace under, 484–86; buildings of, 486–88; Medinet Habu annals of, 486–87, 488–89; imitative character of reign of, 488–89; conciliation of priesthood by, 489–96; not solely responsible for temple wealth, 495–96; embarrassment of treasury of, 496; revolt of vizier, 497–98; jubilee of, 498; conspiracy against, 498–500; death of, 501

RAMSES IV, reign of, 505–07; prayer of, 458, 506; builds Khonsu-temple, 507; exploitation of Sinai ceases after, 507

RAMSES V, 507

RAMSES VI, 507–08

RAMSES VII, 507

RAMSES VIII, 507

RAMSES IX, 508–11, 512

RAMSES X, 510–11

RAMSES XI, 511

RAMSES XII, reign of, 511–521

Ramses, the land of, 443

Ramsesnakht, 508

Ranofer, 103

Re, 46, 59, 76, 133; as king, 56; high priest of, 63; dead accompanying, 64, 174; king prays to, 76; political rise of, 120, 121–26; as king and father of Pharaoh, 122–24, 126, 272–73, 400–01; in royal name, 123–24; Fifth Dynasty temples of, 124–26; Middle Kingdom temple of, 196–97; Temple barques of, 125; political triumph of, 170; Hyksos disregard of, 215; claims to be universal god, 359; origin of Aton theology in, 360, 366, 371; of Ernen, 437; splendour of Ramses III's gifts to, 490

Rebu, 466

Red, as color of Delta kingdom, 32

Redesiyeh, 416

Red House, 32, 42

Red Sea, 3, 6; harbours of, 6, 183, 486; routes to, 6, 128, 142, 153, 164, 182–83, 486; connection with Nile, 142, 276, 277, 411, 485–86, 584

Re-Harakhte, see Re
Rehob, 530
Rehoboam, 529
Rekhmire, 238, 239, 307, 320
Relief, see Sculpture
Religion, earliest, 35; literature of earliest, 44, 45; of first two dynasties, 45; early, 53-73; symbols of, 60; local differences in, 61; spread of local beliefs, resulting inconsistency, 61; political, accompanying religious supremacy, 61; state, 121-26, 129; literature of, 129-30; of Middle Kingdom, 170-76; of Empire, 247-52, 355-78, 401-03, 455-60, 505-06; restoration of the gods by Harmhab, 401-03; personal, 458-59; of the masses, 459-60; Asiatic influences in, 460; of Saite period, 570-72, 574-76; of Egypt influences Europe, 580
"Repulse of the Troglodytes," 186
Reshep, 460
Restoration, history of, 565-95; organization of the State in, 567-70, 573-74; society in, 574; religion in, 570-72, 574-76; art in, 571, 572-73, 579-80; industries in, 573; retrospective character of, 570-76; writing in, 570; exclusiveness of, 570, 579; intimate intercourse with Greece in, 578; artificial character of, 595
Retenu, Middle Kingdom campaign in, 187; in Empire, 289, 294, 319
Reviling, 173
Rhodes, 260, 590; Egyptian commerce with, 337
Rib-Addi, 352, 353, 383, 385, 386, 387, 393
Ribleh, 427; Necho at, 583; Nebuchadrezzar's base at, 587
Ritual (see also Cultus), 248
Rome, obelisk of Thutmose III at, 306; obelisks of Ramses II at, 445
Rosetta, mouth, 5
Royenet, 225
Rudder, introduction of, 142
"Ruler of Countries" (or "Hill-Countries"), 217, 218
"Ruler of the Hill-Country," 188

S.

Sacrifice, human, 325, 411, 478
Saft el-Henneh, 543, 547
Sag, 91
Sahara, 4, 5, 6
SAHURE, birth of, 123; reign of, 127; expedition to Punt, 127, 128

Sais, 30, 31-32, 44, 59; political rise of, 540-46, 556, 565, splendour of in Twenty Sixth Dynasty, 573-74; religious importance in restoration, 575; buildings of Amasis in, 591
Saite Nome, 216
Saite Period, see Restoration
SAKERE, as coregent, 391; as king, 392
Sakkara, pyramids of, 129
Saladin, 309
SALATIS, 216
Samal, 556
Samaria, Assyrians take, 549
Samos, 591
Sandals, 27, 97, 188, 340
Sandstone, 4; quarries, 93, 361
"Sand-dwellers," 178, 319
Sarbut el-Khadem, equipped by Amenemhet III, 190-91, 208
Sarcophagus, 135
Sardinians, see Sherden
Sargon II takes Samaria, 549; defeats western coalition at Raphia, 550
"Satisfaction of Re," 124
Scarabæus (or scarab), mortuary heart, 249; of marriage with Tiy, 329-30; of marriage with Gilukhipa, 333; of opening of sacred lake, 349-50; of wild cattle hunt, 350; of lion hunting, 350-51
Schoinoi, 491
Schools, in Old Kingdom, 98-100
Scorpion, 36
Scribe, 98-100, 169
Sculpture, earliest, 28; early dynastic, 40; in tomb, 69-70; in the Old Kingdom, 102-05, 129; methods of, 103; character of Old Kingdom, 106; in Middle Kingdom, 201-02; tradition in, 201-02; gods determine canons of, 201-02; in Empire, 346-48, 378, 417, 450-53, 488; decline in, 488; in Libyan-Nubian period, 548-49; in Saite period, 571, 572-73; relief sculpture, in Old Kingdom, 105, 125; in Middle Kingdom, 202; in Empire, 273, 343, 346-47, 414-15, 417, 433-34, 451-53, 488; of temple, 343, 414-15, 417, 451-53, 488; battle of Kadesh series, 433-34, 451-53; decline in, 488; in Saite period, 571, 572
Scythians, 580, 582
Sea, of the sky, 54; peop.. s of the, 477, 526; earliest known battle on, 480-81
SEBEKEMSAF, robbery of tomb of, 213, 510
SEBEKHOTEP, 212, 221

Sebek-khu, 187
Sebennytos, 543
SEBK-NEFRU-RE, 195, 208
Sebni, Nubian expedition of, 140–41
Sed, feast of, see Jubilee Royal
Sedeinga, 351
Sehel, 257
Sehetepibre, 167
Seir, 387, 484
Seka, 36
SEKENENRE, ruler of Thebes, 215, 221, 223–24; three kings named, 224, 225; mummy of, 224, Fig. 100; tale of, 215–16, 223–24, 453–54
SEKENENRE III, 225
Sekmem, 187
SEKHEMRE-KHUTOWE, reign of, 211
SEMERKHET, Sinai tablet of, 43 (Fig. 2ᵃ); Sinai campaign of, 48
Semites, 188; immigration into Egypt, 7, 25–26; trading in Egypt, 187; invading Egypt, 7, 25–26, 214–19; immigration into Syria, 219, 259, 260; captive in Egypt, 339, 448; flee to Egypt before Khabiri, 388; gain official power in Egypt, 449, 474
Semneh, 317; stelæ, 184, 186; fortress of, 184, Fig. 83; records of Nile-levels at, 191
Senmen, 272, fall of, 283
Senmut, 272, 277, 282, as architect at Der el-Bahri, 274; in reliefs at Der el-Bahri, 277, 278; fall of, 283
Sennacherib, 551–55; destruction of army of, 552
Senzar, 302, 353
Seplel, 412, 437; congratulates Ikhnaton at accession, 381
Serapeum, 557, 575
Serdab, 70
Serfs, in Old Kingdom, 84, 85; life of, 86; in Middle Kingdom, 169, 170; in Empire, 246, 247, 491; held by the temples, 491, 493–94; slow payment of royal, 496; in Saite period, 574
Serpent, as goddess, see Uræus; as foe of the dead, 175
SESOSTRIS I, 17, 166, as coregent, 178; dispatched against Nubia, 178; dispatched against Libyans, 179; reign of, 179–82; Nubian wars of, 181; obelisk of, 194; buildings of, 196, 508; pyramid of, 198
SESOSTRIS II, reign of, 182–83; town of, 87, 194, 198; pyramid of, 198, 200–01, 445; Ramses II plunders pyramid of, 445
SESOSTRIS III, reign of, 183–90; campaigns in Nubia, 183–87; as god of Nubia, 186, 269, 317; invasion of Syria by, 187; buildings of, 196–97; pyramid of, 198; portrait-statues of, 201, 202; hymn to, 206–07
" Sesostris is Contented," 194
Sesostris of Greek tradition, 189
Set, 38, 46; parentage of, 56; in Pharaonic title, 38, 124; Sutekh original form of name of, 222, 460; banished in Saite times, 571
Sethroite, Nome, 216
Sethu, 137; location of, 137; expedition to, 139
SETI I, reign of, 408–18; Asiatic wars of, 409–14; received at Tharu, 411; Libyan war of, 412; treaty with Hittites, 412, 423; Hittite war of, 412–13; Asiatic policy of, 413; peaceful enterprises of, 414–18; restores monuments of Amon, 414; buildings of, 414–15; exploitation of gold mines, 416; tomb of, 417–18, Fig. 109; obelisks of, 418; jubilee of, 418; succession after, 418; body of, 418, Fig. 158, 519; robbery of tomb of, 510; body concealed in tomb of Inhapi, 525; final concealment of body at Der el-Bahri, 525
SETI II, 473
SETNAKHT, 474–75
Sewa, 549
Sexual impurity, 173
SHABAKA, reign of, 550–53, 554; forms coalition against Assyria, 550–51; possible treaty between Assyria and, 553; building at Thebes, 553
SHABATAKA, 553–54
Shabtuna, 427
Shadûf, 8
Shalmaneser II, 534
Shalmaneser IV, 549
Sharon, 286
Sharuhen, 530; siege of, 227; faithfulness of, 284
Sharuludari, 557
Shasu, 410
Shekelesh, 467, 479; as allies of Libyans, 467, 477
Shekh-Sa'îd, 132
Shemesh-Edom, 324
Shemre, 47
Sheol, 173
Shephelah, 286
Shepherd Kings, 217
Shepnupet (I, daughter of Osorkon III), 546

Shepnupet (II, sister of Taharka), adopted by Amenardis, 558; adopts Nitocris, 567

SHEPSESKAF, 121, 123

Sherden, 440, 462, 480; as mercenaries, 336, 386, 448, Fig. 163, 477, 480, 485; as allies of Libyans, 467, 477

SHESHONK I, usurpation of, 527-28; organization by, 528; campaign in Palestine, 529-30; records tribute of Palestine and Nubia, 530; buildings of, 530; jubilee of, 531

SHESHONK II, 533

SHESHONK III, 535

SHESHONK IV, 535

Sheshonk (" Great Chief of the Meshwesh "), 527

Sheshonk (High Priest of Amon, son of Osorkon I), 532

Shet, 181

" Shining in Memphis," 226

Ships (see also Boats), 421, 490, 517; earliest sea-going, 115, 127; war, 135, 150, 151, 226, 298, 308, 479, 480, 540, 582; building of, 136, 142, 153, 160; improvement of, 142; Keftyew, 261; of Hatshepsut, 276-77; to Syria, 448; enlargement of, 486, 490

Shiri, 387

Shos, see Shasu

Shmûn, 59 (see Eshmunen)

Shrine, portable, 62

Shu, 55; birth of, 56

Shunem, 530

Shuttarna, 333

SIAMON, 525

Sib'i, 550

Sibylline literature, 204-05

Sicily, 467, 477

Sidon, 260; stela of Necho at, 583; in Saite period, 583, 586; monuments of Necho at, 587

Siege, of Sharuhen, 227; of Avaris, 226-27; of Megiddo, 290-91; methods of, 290-91, 541

SINATHOR (Pharaoh), 212

Sihathor, 201

Sikeli, 467, 477

Silsileh, quarries at, 93, 361, 531

Silver, 292, 293, 302, 304, 490, 491, 494, 515, 559; earliest use of, 28; source of, 94; relative value of gold and, 98, 185, 338; due from officials, 238; in commercial rings, 304, 307; Osorkon I gives vast weight of, 531-32

Silver-house, double, 164

Simyra, 260, 302, 411; during Hittite invasion, 382, 383, 385, 386

Sin, sense of, 65, 67, 173-74, 175, 458

Sinai, 6; first Egyptian expedition in, 48; copper mines in, 93; Zoser's expedition to, 112; Snefru in, 114-15; Khufu in, 119; Sahure in, 127; Pepi I in, 133-34, 135-36; protection of, 136; gap in records during Seventh and Eighth Dynasties at, 147; Middle Kingdom revenue from, 163, 164, 182, 190-91; Amenemhet III in, 190-91, 208; hardships of mining in, 190-91; water-route to, 190; Egyptians buried in, 191; desert of, 258; Ramses III, 485; close of Pharaonic exploitation of, 507

Sindebad, the Sailor, 203

Sinuhe, flight of, 179-80, 188; story of, 203

Sirius, 33, 244

Siut, 5, 168, 237; nomarchs of, 148-51, 160; tomb-inscriptions of, 151; boundary between jurisdiction of two viziers, 236

SKEMIOPHRIS, 208

Sky, as a cow, 54; as a sea, 54; as a woman, 54; goddess of, 59

Slander, 173

Slaves (see also Serfs), foreign, 308-09, 339, 496-97; rise to official power of royal, 496-97

SMENDES, 511

SNEFRU, reign of, 114-16

So, 549

Sobk, 170; temple of, 194; rise of in Twelfth Dynasty, 195

Sobk-Re, 170

Society, in first two dynasties, 44; in Old Kingdom, 84-87; in Middle Kingdom, 168-70; in the Empire, 245

Socoh, 530

Sokar, 46

Soldier, professional, 233-34; earliest, 167; as a class, 246-47; rise of the, 246-47; lawlessness of, 404; triumph of the, 527-28; exempt from taxation in Saite time, 574

Soleb, 318, 347, 393

Solomon, 529

Solon, 591

Somali, 25, 26

Son, eldest, builds father's tomb, 76

Song, folk-, 92 (legend of Fig. 39), 109, 205-06, 455; of the harper, 205-06; love-, 455

Soped, 115

Sophocles, 455

"Sos," 217

Soul, 64, 204

Sources, character and extent of documentary, 23–24

South, Kingdom of the, see Upper Egypt

Southern city, 215, 216, 223, 224

Southern Ten, 79–80; Southern Tens, 165, 239–40

Spanish, colonies of Phœnicia, 261

Spartans, 591, 593

Sphinx, origin of great, 120; stela, 120, 327; Thutmose IV clears great, 327

Spinner, 96

Spirits, local, 53

Stars, as dead, 64

Stat, 228

State, earliest, 30, 31; fusion of earliest states, 31; in First and Second Dynasties, 42–45; in the Old Kingdom, 74–84, 126–27; twofold character of, 78–79, 82; weakness of in Old Kingdom, 83–84; in Middle Kingdom, 157-68; in Empire, 233–45; centralization of, in Empire, 243; sacerdotallizing of, 456–57, 506–07; in Saite period, 567–70, 573–74

"Station of the King," 268, 345, 348

Statue (see also Sculpture, mortuary), 70, 102, 176; of Khafre, 103; of Hemset, 103; of Ranofer, 103; of Shekh el-Beled, 104; of Louvre scribe, 104; life-size, in copper, 104; of Pepi I, in copper, 104; seven of Khafre, 120; of Mentuhotep III, 153; colossal, 159, 194, 201–02, 343, 344, 345, 346, 348, Fig. 131, 442, 445, 450; of honour to noblemen, 176; of Sesostris III on southern frontier, 186; of Amenemhet III in Fayum, 194, 201; in Middle Kingdom, 201–02; Syrian, 292; in temple of Karnak, 297; in Empire, 346, 450; of Ramses II in Turin, 450, Fig. 168; of gold, 490; endowment of royal, 508

Stealing, 173

Stone, working of hard, 93; vessels of, 95; beginning of building in, 113; transportation of, 117, 159, 266, 281, 282; heavy blocks of, 118, 199-200, 281-82, 343, 450, 451, 591

Strabo, 193

Strategy, military, 297–98, 410–11, 423; at battle of Kadesh, 426–34

Strophe, earliest example of, 206

Suan (Egyptian for Assuan, q. v.), 7, 188; on east of Delta, 188

Sudan, 7; route to, 185; trade with, 185

Suez, Isthmus of, 115, fortifications on, 447

Suez, Gulf of, 190

Sun-god, daily birth of, 54; celestial barque of, 54, 55, Fig. 32, 59, 125; origin of, 56; supremacy of, 58–59; voyage of, 59, 64, 250; dead transported by, 65; dominance in empire, 248; recognition of newly-crowned Pharaoh by, 268, 543; becomes god of the Empire, 360–61

Survey, preliminary, 13–21

Sutekh, 437, 460; god of Hyksos, 216, 222; temple of, 216; lord of Avaris, 217; Ramses III's temple of, 487

Syria (see also Syria-Palestine), first invasion of, 187; Sesostris III's campaign in, 187; Middle Kingdom intercourse with, 187–88; pursuit of Hyksos into, 215; campaign of Amenhotep I in, 254, 257; campaign of Thutmose I in, 257–65; campaigns of Thutmose III in, see Thutmose III; campaign of Amenhotep II in, 323–25; campaign of Thutmose IV in, 327–28; first invaded by Hittites, 352–53; Aton temple in, 364; Hittite absorption of, 379–87; loss of, by Ikhnaton, 388; water-route to, 302, 304, 313, 315, 317, 411; campaign of Seti I in, 409–14; temporarily recovered by Ramses II, 436; campaign of Merneptah in, 465–66; campaigns of Ramses III in, 480–81, 483; Egyptian trade with 447–48, gods of, in Egypt, 460; invaded by "peoples of the sea" and northerners, 477–78, 479, 481; temple of Amon in, 298, 484; papyrus and Egyptian alphabet introduced into, 484; final loss of southern, 512–19; absorbed by Assyria, 549; absorbed by Babylonia, 583–84

Syrians, in Egypt, 449; throne seized by one of the, 474; gain high official position at court, 497, 500; as mercenaries, 569, 588

Syria-Palestine (see also Syria; see also Palestine), Middle Kingdom raids in, 163–64; Middle Kingdom intercourse with, 187–88; earliest Egyptians dwelling in, 187, 188; civilization of, 188, 259–63; conditions in, at beginning of Empire, 257–58; geography and topography of, 258–59; influence of Egypt in, 261–62; influence of early Babylonia in, 262; leadership of Kadesh in, 219–20, 259, 284–85; Egyptian conquest of, 284–354; Amenhotep I's possible campaign in, 254, 257, 263, 298; Thutmose I's campaign in, 257–64, 298; Thutmose II's campaign in, 270–71; campaigns of Thutmose III in, (see also Thutmose III), 284–316; campaign of Amenhotep II in, 323–25; campaign of Thutmose IV in, 327–28; Ikhnaton loses, 388; Seti I's wars in, 409–14; Ramses II's campaigns in, 423–41; Merneptah's war in, 465–66; Ramses III's wars in, 480–81, 483; Egyptian administration of, 293, 322–23, 335–36, 483–84; fidelity of princes of, 335–37; Nineteenth Dynasty intercourse with, 447; final loss of, 512–19; Sheshonk I's campaign in, 529–30; absorbed by Assyria, 549; Psamtik I attempts recovery of, 580; Necho's conquest of, 582–83; Babylonian conquest of, 583–84; Apries' campaigns in, 586–87; Amasis' designs on, 592–93

T.

Ta, 498
Taanach, 288, 530
Tabor, 436
Tactics, military, 234; in battle of Megiddo, 288–90
Tadukhipa, 333
TAHARKA, in command at Altaqu before accession, 552; rise of, 554; buildings of, 554–55, 558; repulses Esarhaddon, 555; defeated by Esarhaddon, 555; plots with Delta dynasts against Esarhaddon, 556; defeated by Ashurbanipal, 556–57; controls fortune of Amon, 558; makes Tanutamon coregent, 558; retires to Napata, 558; death of, 558
TAKELOT I, 532
TAKELOT II, 533–35; sends a thousand men against Shalmaneser II, 534
TAKELOT III, 546
Takompso, 112, 491
Tale, folk, of Khufu, 122–23; of Punt, 183; in Middle Kingdom, 203–04; of expulsion of Hyksos, 215–16, 223–24, 453–54; of Thutmose III's gen-

erals, 311–12; of the princess of Bekhten, 440; of Thutiy, 311–12, 454; of the doomed prince, 454–55; of the two brothers, 455; in Greek traditions of Egypt, 455, 566; of Pedibast, 535–36
Tangur, 256, 257
Tanis, Twelfth Dynasty in, 188, 197, 201; developed by Nineteenth Dynasty, 442; Dynasty of, see Twenty First Dynasty; Twenty First Dynasty wall of, 524; probable Egyptian residence of Nubian Dynasty, 554; under Assyria, 557
Tanner, 96
TANUTAMON, 558–60; conquers Upper Egypt, 558; captures Memphis, 558; buildings at Napata, 558; compromises with the Delta, 559; expelled by Assyrians from Egypt, 559
Tapedet, 178
Tapestry, 349
Taxes, 161, 165, 237–38; lists for, 211; called labour, 238; amount of, 238; collection of, 238, 403–05; due from officials, 238–39; corruption in collection of, 403–05; temples pay no, 492; Amon gains partial control of collection of, 509; priests and soldiers in Saitic age pay no, 574
Tefibi, 150–51
TEFNAKHTE, 539–46, 565; submits to Piankhi, 544–45
Tefnut, 56; parentage of, 56
Tehenu, 280, 466, 467, 470, 526
Tell el-Amarna, 365, 393; destruction of tombs of, 402
Tell el-Amarna Letters, 332–37, 382–89; discovery of, 393
Tell el-Yehudîyeh, 442
Temeh (or Temehu), in the south, 138
Temple, earliest, 35; first two dynasties, Fig. 27, 45–46; earliest stone, 46; early development of, 61; endowment of, 62, 63, 129, 416, 421, 445–46; of pyramid, 71, 120; of sphinx, 120; of Re, in Fifth Dynasty, 124–26; built by nomarch, 159, 197; in Middle Kingdom, 171, 200; overseer of the, 171; foundation ceremonies of, 196; dedicatory inscription of, 196–97; lake of, 197, 486–87; mortuary, 71, 120, 197, 198, 202, 251, 278–79; property controlled by vizier, 239; vizier's control of, 243; wealth of, in Empire, 247–48, 416, 489–96; wealth of, under Bubastites, 531–32; of Der el-Bahri, 273, 277–78; in Empire, 248,

251, 273, 277–78, 341–46, 416, 489–96; peripteral, 341–42; Pylon temple, 342–43; violation of endowment of, 420, 523; fleet, 421, 485, 492, 494; cliff, 451; name of, 456; economic danger of disproportionate wealth of, 489–96; lands, 491–92, 493; slaves, 491, 494; cattle, 491, 494; workshops and shipyards, 492, 494; towns, 492, 494; income in gold and silver, 457, 494; income exempt from taxation, 492; troops, 63, 509; theocratic rule of, 522–23; Amasis appropriates wealth of, 592

Tentamon, 515

Tentremu, 543

Teos, 590

Teresh, 467

TETI II, 134

Teti-en, 228

Tewosret, 473

Textiles, 96, 237

Thaneni, 312–13

Tharu, 285, 425; banishment to, 404; road to Palestine from, 409, 447; reception of Seti I at, 411

Thebes, 170, 240; first rise of, 149–52; second rise of, 212, 223–29; defeat of, by Tefibi, 150–51; war with Heracleopolis, 149–51; oldest (Eleventh Dynasty) building in, 152; nome of, 160; buildings of Twelfth Dynasty at, 196; under the Hyksos, 215–16, 221, 223–24; under Sekenenre, 215–16, 223–24; residence of southern vizier, 236, 240, 405; judicial court of, 241; quarter for mortuary industries at, 251; building of Ahmose I in, 252; building of Amenhotep I at, 254; building of Thutmose I at, 263–66; buildings of Thutmose III at, 294–95, 296–97; foreign life and products in Thebes, 307–08; buildings of Amenhotep II in, 326; buildings of Amenhotep III at, 340–46, 347–48; given architectural unity by Amenhotep III, 344–46; Amenhotep III's quarter in, 349–50; splendour of, in the Empire, 339–50; Aton temple in, 361; abandoned by Ikhnaton, 362–64; becomes royal residence again, 392; Thebes in anarchy, 394; forsaken as royal residence by Nineteenth Dynasty, 442; Ramses II's buildings at, 443; Ramses III's buildings at, 486–487; decline of, 510, 511, 525; Necropolis of, 250–52, Fig. 131, Fig. 166, Fig. 108, Fig. 109, Fig. 110, 278–79, 510–11; post-

Empire principality of, 511, 522, 528–29, 532, 533–34, 557, 559, 567; return of Ramses XII to, 511, 520; under the priests of Amon, 522–28, 529, 531, 532, 533–34, 553; exempt from taxation, 529; under the Twenty Second Dynasty, 528–29, 532, 533–34; buildings of Twenty Second Dynasty at, 530; under Twenty Third Dynasty, 535; buildings of the Nubians in, 553, 555; under the Assyrians, 556, 557, 559; possibly taken by Ashurbanipal, 557; captured and plundered by Assyrians, 559–60; destruction of, 559–60; under Saites, 567, 573

Thekel, 477, 479, 517; immigration into Palestine, 512

Themer, 478

Theodosius, 390

Thesh, 36

Thibet, 351

Thinis, 37, 44; nomarch of, 134, 139; nomarch of, made vizier, 139; nomarch of, surviving under Empire, 228, 305

Thinites, overthrow of, 111

Thoth, 46, 57, 320; as vizier, 57; defender of Horus, 58; personal prayer to, 459

Throw-sticks, 277

Thure, 256, 257

Thuthotep, 163, 201

Thutiy (architect of Hatshepsut), 272, 274, 281; fall of, 283, 295

Thutiy (general of Thutmose III), 305, 312, 322, 323; tale of, 312

THUTMOSE I, parentage of, 255; coronation proclamation of, 255; Nubian campaign of, 256–57; Asiatic campaign, 257–64; in Phœnicia (?), 298; buildings of, 264–65; obelisks of, 266; jubilee of, 266; successors of, 266–68; children of, 266–67; deposition of, 267–68; return to power, 270; death of, 271; acknowledgment of Hatshepsut's succession by, 273; tomb of, 278–79

THUTMOSE II, parentage of, 267; reign of, 267, 269–71; Nubian war of, 270; Asiatic war of, 270–71; coregency with Thutmose I, 270, 271; coregency with Thutmose III, 271; death of, 271

THUTMOSE III, 219–20, 254, 267, 405; parentage of, 267; early career of, 267–68; overthrower of Hyksos, 219–20; accession, 267–69; reign of, 267–70, 271–321; Nubian buildings of, 269; deposition of, 270; return

to power, 271; Asiatic wars of, 284–
317; first campaign, 284–94; second campaign, 295–96; third campaign, 297; fourth campaign, 297;
fifth campaign, 298–99; sixth campaign, 299–301; seventh campaign,
301–02; eighth campaign, 302–05;
ninth campaign, 313; tenth campaign, 314; eleventh campaign, 315;
twelfth campaign, 315; thirteenth
campaign, 315; fourteenth campaign, 315; fifteenth campaign, 315;
sixteenth campaign, 315; seventeenth campaign, 315–16; remembrance of, in Syria, 383; strategy
of, 297–98; fleet of, 298; hunts
Syrian elephant, 304; in possession
of the oases, 305; obelisks of, 306,
329; jubilees of, 306; monuments in
Thebes, 294–95, 296–97, 306; victorious records in Thebes, 306–07;
lists of, 306–07; annals of, 306–07;
triumphs in Thebes, 307–08; occupations at home, 309–10; buildings of, 294–95, 296–97, 306, 309,
310; designs temple vessels, 310; organization of campaigns of, 310–11;
generals of, 311–12, 454; annals of,
312–13; Nubian campaigns and
buildings, 317–18; death of, 318;
hymn of victory, 318–19; characterization of, 319–20
Thutmose IV, and Sphinx Stela, 120,
327; tale of accession, 327; Asiatic
war of, 327–28; obelisk of Thutmose III erected by, 329
Thutmosids, feud of, 266–82
Tiglath-pileser I, 518
Tiglath-pileser III, 536, 549
Tigro-Euphrates valley, 3
Tikhsi, 314, 324, 325
Timaios, 216
Timsah, Lake, 447
Tishub, 334
Titles, loss of significance of, 134
Tiy (Queen), 329–30, 355, 366, 379;
worship of, in Nubia, 351
Tiy (nurse of Ikhnaton), 394
Tiy (queen of Ramses III), 498–500
Tomb (see also Pyramid, Burial),
earliest, 34–35; early dynastic, 40–
42; endowment of, 41, 70, 71, 527;
in Old Kingdom, 57, Fig. 33, 116,
117–19; equipment of, 63, 67, 69,
176, Fig. 81, 251–52; immense size
of, 68, 568; chapel of, 69 (see also
Temple), 571; royal assistance in
building and endowment of, 71, 369–
70; of common people, 73; development of, 113; location in Sixth Dy-

nasty, 132; in Middle Kingdom,
197–200; cliff-, 198, 250–52, Fig.
131, Fig. 166, Fig. 108, Fig. 109,
Fig. 110, 278–79; robbery, 212–13,
327, 510–11, 525–26; in Empire,
250–52, 278–79; of middle class,
251; of poor, 251–52; origin of
royal cliff-, 278–79, Fig. 109, Fig.
110; of Tell el-Amarna, 369–71; of
Pediamenemopet, 568
Tombos, fortress of Thutmose I on,
257; stela, 257
Tomeri, 470
Tosorthros, 113
Towns, earliest, 31; in first two dynasties, 44; in Old Kingdom, 86,
87; in Middle Kingdom, 87; held by
royal princes, 75; rulers of, 237;
held by temples, 492, 494
Treasurer, chief, in Old Kingdom, 80;
of the God, 80, 119, 128, 133, 164,
191; chief, in Middle Kingdom, 153,
164, 185, 188; in nome, 158, 160,
169; assistant, 201; chief, in Empire, 235–36; 238, 243, 272, 276,
277, 325, 328, 362
Treasury, 190; in first and second
dynasties, 42; in Old Kingdom, 80,
132; centralization of local administration in, 80; in Middle Kingdom, 162–64; boats, 164; in Empire, 236, 237–39, 272, 352, 403–04;
gold and silver, 272, 317; corruption in the, 403–04
Treaty, between Egypt and Hittites,
437–39
Trees, of Egypt, 95; planted by Ramses III, 486
Triads, divine, 56
Tribute, 277, 307–08, 315, 328, 331,
389, 530; under charge of vizier,
239, 307–08; Syrian, 264, 484;
Thutmose II's record of, 271; of
Libya, 280; state reception of, 307–
08, 450; amount of, 308, Asiatic,
323, 336, 389, 530
Tripolis, in Lebanon, taken by Thutmose III, 293; presented to Amon,
294
"Triumphant," 174
Troglodytes, of Sinai, 48; northern,
178; of Nubia, 253
Troia, 252; quarries at, 93
Troops, of temple, 63
"True of Speech," 174
Truth, 173; symbol of, 173; recognized
by Ikhnaton, 377–78
Tunip, 298, 302, 315, 317, 427; Mitan-
nian influence in, 263; during Hit-
tite invasion, 382, 385; begs Ikhna-

ton for assistance, 382–83; temporarily held by Ramses II, 436
Tuphium, 160
Turin, royal papyrus of, 211, 213, 221
"Turn-face," 65
TUTENKHAMON, 392, 393; changes his name, 393–94; relations with Asia, 394
TUTENKHATON, or TUTENKHAMON, q. v.
Tutu, 385
Tuya, 418
Tyre, 260, 411; special privileges of, 298; during Hittite invasion, 383; in Assyrian period, 551, 555; in Saite period, 586, 587, 588; monuments of Necho in, 587; sustains thirteen years' siege against Nebuchadrezzar, 587–88
Tyrsenians, 467

U.

Ubi, 352, 353
Ugarit, 382; as ally of Hittites, 424
Ullaza, 302, 411
Uneshek, 331
Uni, career of, 134, 135, 136
Unis, 131; in Nubia, 128; pyramid of, 130
Uræus, 38
Uronarti, 186
USEPHAIS, tomb of, 42, 47; Sinai expedition of, 48; ivory tablet of, 48 (Fig. 26); expedition to northern Nubia, 49
Userhet, 490
USERKAF, 126; birth of, 123; reign of, 127
USERMARE-MERIAMON, 478; town of, 482
USERMARE-SETEPNERE, same as Ramses II, q. v.
Ushebti, 249, Fig. 106
Utentyew, 319

V.

Valley of the Kings' Tombs, 250–51, 278–79
Vegetable culture, 92
Vessels, of stone, 28, 39
Vienna, Demotic papyrus of, 535
Vineyards, 92
Vizier, 57, 154, 162, 164, 166, 182, 191, 221, 248, 429, 458, 498; tomb of, 68; functions of, in Old Kingdom, 82–83; power and popularity of, 83, 244; son of Khufu, 119; no longer son of king, 126; hereditary succession as, 126; becomes governor of royal residence, 133; becoming chief treasurer, 166; bringing back gold, 182; appointment of two, 236; chief treasurer under authority of, 238; functions of, in Empire, 238–45; as finance minister, 239; universal power of, 243–44; appointment of, 244; royal instructions to, 244–45; as High Priest of Amon, 272, 362; in charge of foreign tribute, 239, 307–08, 328; Harmhab's selection of, 405; revolt of Ramses III's, 497–98
Votress, Divine, see Consort Divine
Vulcan, 566
Vulture (as goddess), 38

W.

Wadi Alâki, 181; Seti I in, 416; Ramses II in, 421–22
Wadi Foakhir, 94
Wadi Gasûs, 183
Wadi Halfa, 181, 255, 317, 408; earliest record at, 181; fortress at, 186
Wadi Hammamat, earliest expedition to, 128
Wadi Maghara, 48, Pepi I in, 133–34; Hatshepsut in, 282
Wadi Tumilat, 178, 442; canal through, 276, 442, 485–86; fortress in, 447
Wahibrenofer, 588
Wan, height of, 302
War, in Old Kingdom, 135; in Middle Kingdom, 168; minister of, 243; in Empire, see Tactics, Strategy
Water of Re, the, 481
Wawat, 256; location of, 136; expedition to, 139, 141, 152, 178; fortresses in, 183; government of, 256; gold of, 317
Wealth, agriculture chief source of, 9; general sources of, 92–98
Weapons, Syrian manufacture of, 260, 303
Weaver, 96
Wenamon, report of, 513–18
Wermer, 478
Weshesh, 477, 479
Westcar, Papyrus, 122–23, 203
Wheat, 92
White, as colour of southern kingdom, 33, 37
White House, 33, 42, 44, 164; registers in, 237; sub-departments in, 237–38
White Wall, 37, 44, 111, 132
Wife, 226; position of, 85
Wills, in Old Kingdom, 82; in Empire, 237, 240; under priests of Amon, 523

Wine, 237
Wisdom, see Literature of Instruction
Witness, false, 173
Woman, position of, 85
Wood, industries in, 95
Wool, Syrian industry in, 260
Word, see Logos
World, of Egyptian people, 11, 56; of the dead, 64–65; conquest modifying idea of, 358–59
Writing, earliest, 35, 43 (Fig. 27); in first two dynasties, 45; spread to Phœnicia and Europe, 97, 484; methods of, taught in school, 99–100; influence of introduction of, 99; orthography of, 203; Nubian, 561; archaic character of Saitic, 570; Demotic, 574

X.

Xois, 214

Y.

Yam, 137; location of, 137; expeditions to, 138–39, 139

Yaru, field of, 64, 174, 249
Year, see Calendar
Yehem, 286, 287, 288
Yenoam, 293, 410; revolts against Merneptah, 465; captured by Merneptah, 470
Yeraza, 284, 530
YEWEPET (rival of Pedibast), 535, 543
Yewepet (son of Sheshonk I), 531
YUFNI, 211

Z.

Zahi, 290, 313, 318; Ahmose I in, 227; in revolt against Thutmose III, 285
Zakar-Baal, 513–17
Zau, 139
Zâwiyet el-Metîn, 132
Zedekiah, 586, 587
Zefti, 286 (map), 287
ZER, tomb of, 49, 172; jewelry of queen of, 50
Zimrida, 383
ZOSER, parentage of, 111, reign of, 112–14; tomb of, 113–14

INDEX TO OLD TESTAMENT PASSAGES.

Gen. 47: 19–20, 229; 47: 23–27, 238; 47: 21, 246
Josh. 19: 6, 227
II Sam. 10: 10, 188
I Kings 9: 15–17, 529; I Kings 9: 16, 529; I Kings 14: 25, 530; I Kings 15: 23, 291; I Kings 17: 4, 549
II Kings 18: 21, 553; II Kings 19: 9, 552; II Kings 24: 7, 584; II Kings 24: 15, 586

Psalm, 104, 371–74
Isaiah 19, 548; Isaiah 20, 551
Jer. 43: 8–13, 593; Jer. 46: 1–12, 584; Jer. 47: 4, 512; Jer. 47: 1 and 5, 582
Ezek. 30: 13, 595; Ezek. 40: 10–18, 593
Amos 9: 7, 512
Nahum 3: 8–10, 559–60; Nahum 2–4, 582

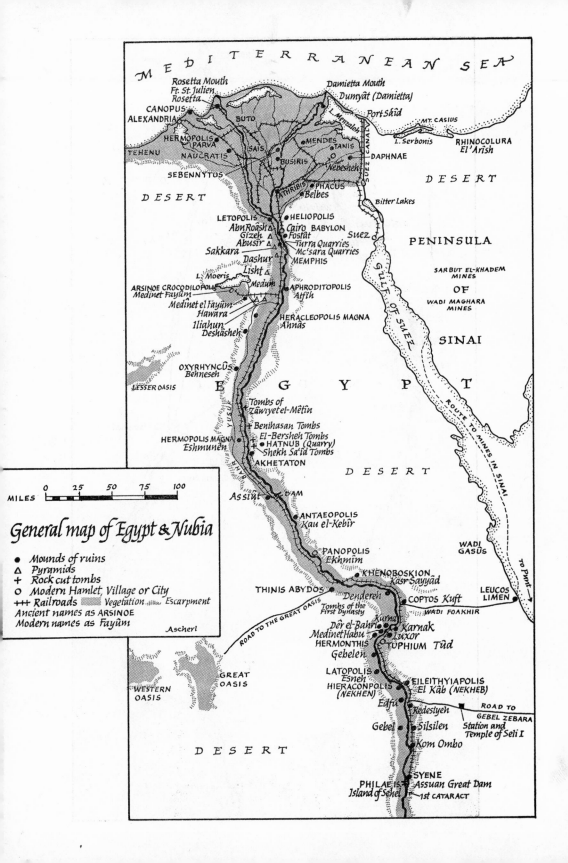

MEDITERRANEAN SEA

Rosetta Mouth
Ft. St. Julien
Rosetta
CANOPUS
ALEXANDRIA

Damietta Mouth
Dumyât (Damietta)
Port Sâid

MT. CASIUS
L. Menzaleh
L. Serbonis
RHINOCOLURA
El 'Arish

BUTO
HERMOPOLIS
PARVA
NAUCRATIS
TEHENU
SAIS
MENDES
TANIS
Nebesheh

DESERT

SEBENNYTUS
BUSIRIS
ATHRIBIS
PHACUS
Belbes

DAPHNAE

DESERT

LETOPOLIS
Abu Roash
Gizeh
Abusir
Sakkara
Dashur
Lisht
Medum

HELIOPOLIS
Cairo BABYLON
Fostât
Turra Quarries
Mc'sara Quarries
MEMPHIS

Suez

Bitter Lakes

PENINSULA

SARBUT EL-KHADEM
MINES

OF

WADI MAGHARA
MINES

ARSINOE CROCODILOPOLIS
Medinet Fayûm
Medinet el Fayûm
Hawara
Iliahun
Deshâsheh

L. Moeris

APHRODITOPOLIS
Atfîh

HERACLEOPOLIS MAGNA
Ahnas

SINAI

OXYRHYNCUS
Behneseh

LESSER OASIS

E G Y P T

Tombs of
Zâwiyet el-Mêtin

Benihasan Tombs
El-Bersheh Tombs
HATNUB (Quarry)
Shekh Sa'îd Tombs

HERMOPOLIS MAGNA
Eshmunên

AKHETATON

DESERT

Assiût
DAM

ANTAEOPOLIS
Kau el-Kebîr

WADI
GASÛS

PANOPOLIS
Ekhmîm

KHENOBOSKION
Kasr Sayyâd

LEUCOS
LIMEN

THINIS ABYDOS

Denderen
Tombs of the
First Dynasty

COPTOS Kuft

WADI FOAKHIR

ROAD TO THE GREAT OASIS

Kurna
Dêr el-Bahri
Medinet Habu
HERMONTHIS
Gebelen

Karnak
Luxor
TUPHIUM Tûd

GREAT
OASIS

WESTERN
OASIS

LATOPOLIS
Esneh
HIERACONPOLIS
(NEKHEN)

Edfû

Gebel

EILEITHYIAPOLIS
El Kâb (NEKHEB)

ROAD TO
GEBEL ZEBARA
Station and
Temple of Seti I

Redesiyeh
Silsilen

Kom Ombo

SYENE
Assuan Great Dam
1st CATARACT

PHILAE IS.
Island of Sehel

DESERT

ROUTE TO MINES IN SINAI

To Punt

GULF OF SUEZ

SUEZ CANAL

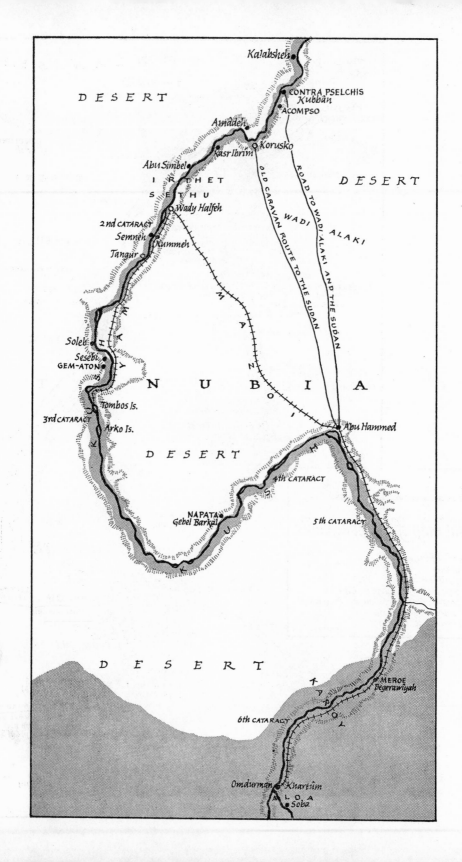

A history of Egypt from the earliest
time to the Persian conquest.